Harry S. Truman

Missouri Biography Series

William E. Foley, Editor

Other Books on Truman by
ROBERT H. FERRELL

Off the Record: The Private Papers of Harry S. Truman

The Autobiography of Harry S. Truman

Dear Bess: The Letters from Harry to Bess Truman, 1910–1959

Harry S. Truman and the Modern American Presidency

Truman: A Centenary Remembrance

Truman in the White House: The Diary of Eben A. Ayers

Harry S. Truman: His Life on the Family Farms

Choosing Truman: The Democratic Convention of 1944

Harry S. Truman

A Life

ROBERT H. FERRELL

University of Missouri Press
Columbia and London

Copyright © 1994 by
The Curators of the University of Missouri
University of Missouri Press, Columbia, Missouri 65201
Printed and bound in the United States of America
All rights reserved
5 4 3 2 1   98 97 96 95 94

Library of Congress Cataloging-in-Publication Data

Ferrell, Robert H.
    Harry S. Truman : a life / Robert H. Ferrell.
        p. cm. — (Missouri biography series)
    Includes bibliographical references (p.) and index.
    ISBN 0-8262-0953-X
    1. Truman, Harry S., 1884–1972. 2. Presidents—United States—
Biography. I. Title. II. Series.
E814.F46 1994
973.918'092—dc20
[B]   94-21919
                                                                    CIP

∞™ This paper meets the requirements of the American National
Standard for Permanence of Paper for Printed Library Materials, Z39.48, 1984.

Designer: Rhonda Miller
Typesetter: Connell-Zeko Type & Graphics
Printer and Binder: Thomson-Shore, Inc.
Typefaces: Palatino and Shelley Volante Script

All illustrations are reproduced through the courtesy of
the Harry S. Truman Library, Independence, Missouri.

For Samuel Flagg Bemis (1891–1973),
Richard Brandon Morris (1904–1989),
and Henry Steele Commager (1902–).
Exemplary historians, unforgettable friends.

Contents

Preface

*H*arry S. Truman of Independence, Missouri, aged sixty when he took up the duties of president of the United States, was the right man for his time, an awkward era in domestic politics and a downright dangerous period in foreign relations. With much experience in domestic affairs, none in foreign, he took the measure of his responsibilities and made few errors. He was not the complete leader; he was capable of errors. He tended to believe that anyone who opposed him did so on political grounds, and he sometimes believed the worst of people who happened to differ from him. He trusted his friends—they could do no wrong, and he would back them beyond the usual limits of politics. He was hypersensitive to criticism of his family, and anyone who erred in that regard was in instant trouble. He was almost demonic in his habits of work and could labor to the point of being near the end of his nervous energy. Especially in the second term of his presidency he began to tire more than he realized, and this could lead to poor judgment. Withal, he possessed many positive qualities. He would make up his mind in what he described as a "jump" decision, after which he submitted the tentative conclusion to every test that time and energy allowed; when he decided he was ready he could snap off a decision in what looked like carelessness but was not, after which he put indecision out of mind, knowing it would do no further good. He listened to people, and not in a pro-forma way; he knew he could learn from them and was anxious for instruction. He liked people, liked to think good of them until they displayed nasty tendencies. Contrary to the behavior of his predecessor, he never tried to be a manipulator. He was an inveterate idealist, unashamed, occasionally tearful, and one may be permitted to observe that in the latter half of a century not noted for idealism such people were nice to have around.

Harry Truman was not dedicated to himself; he had no feelings of self-importance. This was a precious attribute. He always distinguished between himself and the office he happened to occupy. Only a few presidents have done this; 1600 Pennsylvania Avenue is a palace, not a house, and it touches almost all occupants. One untouchable, it is interesting to relate, looking back a long time, was Calvin Coolidge, he of the dour countenance and thin-lipped smile: he knew that as president of the United States he deserved respect but hoped that when people came to see him they understood the difference between the presidency and the citizen who occupied the office. When people asked to shake his hand he would present the appendage, hanging limply from the wrist, and they could shake it if they wished. Truman shook hands more gracefully, and always squeezed a citizen's hand before it was fully within his, thereby preventing a bone-twisting greeting, but he felt the same way. He knew that if he lost the distinction between the office and the man, becoming the office, he would lose his ability to make fair judgments. He often spoke of a disease afflicting only officeholders in the vicinity of the nation's capital, a dangerous malady called Potomac fever, incurable in its advanced stages, and he was accustomed to inquire of his personal physician, Wallace Graham, a fellow Missourian whom he saw daily, whether so-and-so might possibly, just possibly, be suffering from the disease.

Through the long years of politics—ten as a county commissioner in Jackson County, Missouri; ten in the Senate; eight in the vice presidency and presidency—Truman took pride that he was a *politician*, a word that in his estimate required explanation. He believed a political leader should be no different from people in other professions, such as physicians or clergymen; he was not pursuing politics for money and in a real sense was, like members of other professions, a servant of the people, and not of the people who elected him but of all the people in his bailiwick, Jackson County or the state of Missouri or, ultimately, the United States.

The country's thirty-third president was a very special chief executive, assuredly not a simple American who suddenly found himself in a high place. He liked to say he was just an average American and there were a million others who could have done what he did, but there was no truth in the claim. For he had attained a rare balance of qualities that made him, despite some debits on his balance sheet, one of the best choices fate could have provided when, in April 1945, Franklin D. Roosevelt passed on.

Acknowledgments

My thanks first of all to three individuals who read the book's chapters: Robert F. Byrnes, my friend and colleague at Indiana University; William E. Foley, editor of the Missouri Biography Series; and Francis H. Heller, of the School of Law, University of Kansas—especially Francis Heller, who forty years ago found himself on what one might describe as the other end of manuscript reading: he was drafting chapters of the memoirs of Harry S. Truman, and each night the author of that book took them home to read.

And then there are the friends who helped with parts of the book: Terry H. Anderson, Cecil K. Byrd, J. Garry Clifford, Eugene Davidson, Charles M. Dobbs, Edward J. Drea, Andrew J. Dunar, James F. Goode, Daniel F. Harrington, Brenda L. Heaster, David Herschler, Howard Jones, Lawrence S. Kaplan, John L. Kelley, David Lowenthal, John Lukacs, Robert J. Maddox, Richard Lawrence Miller, Arnold A. Offner, Monte M. Poen, Steven L. Rearden, Bernard Sternsher, Stephen L. Vaughn, John Edward Wilz.

As for friends who remembered Mr. Truman, my heartfelt appreciation goes to the late Charles F. Brannan, the last surviving (and along with Dean Acheson the most effective, said the president) member of the cabinet; Donald S. Dawson, presidential assistant, now president of the Harry S. Truman Library Institute; George M. Elsey, likewise an assistant, who occasionally recalls that he lives in the nation's capital on MacArthur Boulevard; the late Alonzo Fields, White House maître d'hôtel; Sue Gentry, longtime (since 1929) reporter for the *Independence Examiner*; Wallace and Velma Graham, two of the nicest people, for their friendship over the years; William P. Hannegan, son of Robert E. Hannegan, former chairman of the Democratic national committee and postmaster general; the late Ardis Haukenberry, Mr. Truman's cousin, resident of 216 North Delaware Street, across from the Truman house; Ken Hechler, White House staffer, who studied political science and then studied it again; John K. Hulston, Ozarks lawyer, who as a youth sixty years ago drove his father and a friend to the Forty-fifth Everton Annual Picnic; the Reverend and Mrs. Thomas Melton, the Trumans' next-door neighbors, across Truman Road; Reathel Odum, who worked in the senator's office in the 1930s and continued through the White House years; David H. Stowe, presidential assistant, whose stories of "the boss" are affectionately hilarious; and McKinley Wooden, aet. ninety-nine, last survivor of Battery D, 129th Field Artillery, AEF.

Again thanks to Benedict K. Zobrist, director of the Harry S. Truman Library, and his predecessor, the late Philip C. Brooks; George Curtis, assistant director; Elizabeth Safly, librarian, who makes the library so pleasant for all researchers; and the staff members over the years: Vicky Alexander, Dennis E. Bilger, Lenore Bradley, Carol Briley, Mildred L. Carol, Donna Clark, Harry Clark, John Curry, Pat Dorsey, J. R. Fuchs, Raymond Geselbracht, Niel M. Johnson, Philip D. Lagerquist, Mary Jo Minter, Erwin J. Mueller, Warren Ohrvall, Doris Pesek, Sam Rushay, Randy Sowell, Pauline Testerman.

So much kind assistance came from the staff of the University of Missouri Press. Upon inquiry to Beverly Jarrett, director and editor-in-chief, as to the possibility of publishing a biography of Truman, the response was that "he was the most famous person ever to come out of Missouri" and why would she not be interested? Tim Fox, now of the Missouri Historical Society in St. Louis, watched every word and phrase. Jane Lago, managing editor, put it all together.

Once more a thank you to Lila and Carolyn.

Harry S. Truman

Chapter One

Early Years

*H*arry S. Truman was born on May 8, 1884, in the farm village of Lamar, Missouri, 120 miles south of Kansas City. The time was four o'clock in the afternoon, the place the small white frame house of his parents. His father and mother had married two and a half years before, and Harry was the second child—the first, also a boy, had been stillborn.

Such were the vital statistics, and behind their barrenness lay still other aridities. The scene that spring day in Missouri more than a century ago comes easily to mind: Lamar was a village of seven hundred people, made up of retired farmers and merchants who catered to farmers; the streets were arranged in regular fashion, lined by rows of houses with alleys and horse barns behind; at the center of the village stood the courthouse, on a square, around which the stores arranged themselves, facing each other, a motley assemblage, with their false fronts vying for attention. And away in all directions stretched the landscape of Missouri, which, like so much of the American Middle West, does not make the heart leap up: uninspiring countryside, most of it rolling fields, as far as the eye can see. When the child Harry Truman lived in Lamar the land raised wheat and corn, oats for horses and mules, and clover to rest the ground and, like oats, feed work animals. Dirt roads ran north and south, east and west, laid out to mark the square miles so readily discernible from an airplane window today; the Ordinance of 1785 had organized the Northwest Territory that way, and Missouri followed the pattern. Houses and barns fronted the roads, and every half-dozen miles was a village that looked like the preceding one. Near the center of each county a traveler encountered another village like Lamar, with a square, within which rose another courthouse. Missouri had, and still has, 114 counties.

The picture is deceptive. Missouri scenery may be beautiful only to the native beholder, but this does not mean Missourians lack imagination to do important things, as Truman proved in his lifetime. Indeed, nondescription is an advantage: if the commonplaces of Missouri offer no feasts to the eye, they serve to concentrate the mind. And Missouri has another advantage. Kansas City, near which Harry Truman spent the first fifty years of his life, lies almost in the geographical center of the United States. In that sense, the perspective is perfect.

1

The roster of Truman's forebears reached back into the eighteenth century, beyond which the lineage, like that of most Americans, was suspect. None of his known ancestors offered any evidence that the child of 1884 would become a national and international figure, his name a household word. Among the later president's more remote relatives, several possessed personalities that stood out, although not remarkably so; most families can discover such relatives on their family trees. Truman's great-grandmother on his father's side, Nancy Drusilla Tyler Holmes, born in Kentucky in 1780, married Jesse Holmes in 1803 and went out to Missouri with her husband, who died in 1840. Thereafter she moved from house to house of her children. Wherever she went she carried her husband's tall beaver hat, in its original box. Nancy Holmes's father had been a soldier in the Revolutionary War, and his absences left her mother with a household of children and slaves, whom the mother sometimes had to defend against the Indians. Once she drove the Indians from the door, only to have them try to come down the chimney; she smoked them out by stuffing a featherbed in the fireplace. Reportedly Nancy one time was scalped, and survived by lying still. A photograph taken in old age showing her with lace bonnet wrapped tightly around her head seems to offer credence to the story, though in actual fact there was no truth to it; the Truman family genealogist, Cousin Ethel Noland, eventual owner of the bonnet photograph, inquired of her mother, Aunt Ella, who lived to the age of ninety-nine. Ella said that as a young girl she had combed the long beautiful hair of Nancy, who died in 1874.[1]

The later president liked to say that Nancy Holmes's maiden name of Tyler related the family to President John Tyler. "One of Tyler's father's brothers moved to Kentucky," he wrote, "and my great-grandmother was his daughter. We never bragged about the fact though because none of the family thought much of old man Tyler as a President."[2] Truman found Tyler unimpressive because in 1861, living in Virginia, he had thrown in his lot with the Confederacy; the twentieth-century president had no fondness for the lost cause. But as for Tyler's being a relative, this was a figment of Harry Truman's imagination. Perhaps he espied the relationship because the nineteenth-century president established the precedent of making the vice president, when he assumed the presidency, the president and not acting president.

On his father's side, Nancy Tyler Holmes was the only remarkable ancestor. Truman did, however, remember well his Grandfather Anderson Shipp

Truman, a pleasant, slight old man who died in 1887. Grandfather Truman was one of those people who pass through life without leaving much of an impression. A photograph shows the broad Truman forehead but a weak chin, almost hidden by a scraggly beard. After marrying Nancy Tyler Holmes's daughter Mary Jane while resident in Kentucky, Anderson Truman worried about what he had done—Mary Jane had been visiting in Kentucky and her mother was out in Missouri. Anderson had not asked permission to marry. To relieve his mind he saddled a horse, rode to Missouri, found his mother-in-law, begged forgiveness, received it, and, retracing his steps, collected Mary Jane and moved to Missouri. Grandfather Truman's politics were "the Union as it was"; that is, he was a Whig. He was also a slaveholder, having inherited his human chattels from the Holmes family. All his slaves were women, and he never bought one or sold one. Mary Jane died in 1878 and Anderson spent his remaining years with his son. When Harry Truman's parents bought the house in Lamar, they provided a room with a stove for the arthritic grandfather. After the birth of his grandson he said many times that Harry Truman would be president of the United States, but Harry's parents never believed such nonsense, nor did the grandfather.

One of the grandson's earliest memories was of being in the room when the old man died. Harry Truman heard an aunt say sadly, "He's gone," and ran to the bedside to pull at his grandfather's beard to awaken him.

On the maternal side of the family stood a formidable set of grandparents, whom young Harry knew far better than his paternal grandfather. Like the Anderson Trumans, Solomon and Harriet Louisa Young came from Kentucky. In 1841 they had taken a steamboat named the *Fanny Wheeling* from Louisville to St. Louis, and another to Westport Landing in present-day Kansas City. One can almost see the steamers, primitive craft in the 1840s, only a generation removed from Robert Fulton's *Clermont*—and dangerous craft, too, for they had an annoying habit of blowing up. Their tall funnels gave out wood smoke as paddle wheels noisily made the rounds. Half-floating, half-winding downriver, and then fighting slowly up the wide Missouri, the boats plied their way. On all sides stood forests, with hardly a cabin in sight until their arrival at the primitive landings, when the squat, ugly boats took on more wood and the passengers went ashore for whatever amenities the natives offered.

Upon reaching the City of Kansas, the Youngs clambered up the cliffs to find lodging and purchase a team and wagon. They thereafter acquired large amounts of land, thousands of acres. Solomon and Louisa always worked together. After halting their prairie schooner at the first portion of what would become their great holdings, Grandfather Young built a rail pen and threw brush over it, and grandmother stayed there—the rule of homesteading was that one had to remain on the land so many nights and cook so many meals—while grandfather rode to Clinton and entered the tract.

In addition to farming, Solomon Young drove wagon trains to Salt Lake

City and San Francisco. For twenty-five years, he was gone on trips that lasted months at a time. On one trip he reached Salt Lake City to discover that goods he believed on consignment for the U.S. Army were not really sold. He discussed his predicament with the Mormon leader Brigham Young (no relation), who advised him to rent space on the main street and place his goods on display, saying that he would guarantee Solomon lost no money; this proved the case. During one of his trips Grandfather Young was said to have purchased a tract in the vicinity of present-day Sacramento, and if he had retained it would have become a rich man. An associate went bankrupt, however, according to the story, and Solomon lost the holding after paying the associate's debts.[3]

During Solomon's absences Grandmother Young kept house in Missouri, and the work was not merely strenuous but dangerous. One day in 1861 a Union irregular, James H. "Jim" Lane, arrived with his men and forced Harriet Young to bake biscuits until her fingers blistered. The raiders killed all four hundred hogs, hacked off the hams and slung them across their saddles, set the barns on fire, and rode off. Ever afterward Grandmother Young and her daughter Martha Ellen hated Northerners. During this visitation the family silver disappeared, and once when her son came home from a trip to Kansas, Mrs. John Truman inquired if he had seen his grandmother's silver.[4]

Grandfather Young died in 1892. His wife survived until 1909, when she passed on at the age of ninety-one. She had seen a great deal during her long life. Red-haired in youth, she had lived in the house in Kentucky where Stephen Foster composed his songs, and she knew him. Coming out to Missouri shortly after its founding, she watched the frontier give way to settlement; having witnessed both the great flood of 1844 and another flood of 1903, she said the more recent flood was no larger, but there was so much more to destroy. A few years later, wrinkled and gray, her mind confused and perhaps almost gone (a visitor said that she was accustomed to sit in her room, hour after hour, staring silently), she posed for her photograph, sitting in a rocker outside her farmhouse, with Harry Truman and his mother standing behind her. She represented the wealth and adventure and patience and, it could be said, grit of older times.

Harry Truman's father, John Anderson Truman, born in 1851, was an animal trader and farmer all his life except for two years when he was a night watchman in a Kansas City grain elevator. No one would have considered him the likely father of a president of the United States, least of all John Truman himself: one Sunday afternoon in the late summer of 1914, propped on his deathbed in a downstairs room of his bleak farmhouse, he told a neighboring couple, come to call, who were trying to cheer him, that his life had been a failure.

John Truman was no striking figure; he would have fit into any crowd. His nose was prominent and his eyes seemed quiet, though it might be said they peered rather than looked. Unlike many of his contemporaries, he did not favor the fashion of beards and mustaches that came in with the Civil War (the soldiers of 1861–1865 supposedly were too busy to shave); his was an unadorned face that in summers must have sunburned and then tanned with the sun and wind. He was a small man; as a child he had been disturbingly small, even tiny, and in manhood he stood five feet four, two inches shorter than his wife. His granddaughter Margaret would remark how photographs of Mr. and Mrs. John Truman showed the wife sitting, husband standing, and thought it because of her grandfather's height.[5] But that, one suspects, was simply the way Victorian photographers posed husbands and wives.

For some reason—perhaps he was trying to make up for his size—the elder Truman was highly tempered. Because he was a dealer in horses, mules, cows, goats, and sheep, John Truman often carried a stub of a buggy whip, and one day a man appeared in an Independence livery stable to get his horse and buggy, face bleeding, almost in tears; he had gotten into an argument with John, who struck him with the whip. Another story related to a court trial in Independence. An unfriendly attorney, a big, bluff man, was interrogating John. After asking a question and receiving an answer he said, in an effort to change the witness's testimony, "Now, John, you know that's just a damn lie." John Truman jumped out of the witness chair and chased the big attorney out of the courthouse. Still another story related to farm years after the turn of the present century, when the Trumans were on the big farm of Mrs. Truman's mother near the village of Grandview. Neighbors allegedly saw Harry Truman's brother, Vivian, riding a horse down a road at great speed, with the boys' father seated behind, holding a hatchet. Father and son were on their way to a neighbor's to settle an argument about a fence.

John Truman's irritabilities seldom spilled over into family life. He never laid hands on the children; words sufficed. In fact, he could show a gentler side at home: he loved to sing when the family spent time around the piano in the evenings. Harry and his sister, Mary Jane, remembered their father singing hymns in a light, pleasant voice. The only time the later president remembered his father showing choler at home was once when Harry was a child on the farm accustomed to riding behind his father's horse on a Shetland pony. One day he fell off, and his father forced him to walk a half-mile, on the theory that if he could not stay on a pony he deserved to walk. This may not have been evidence of temper, rather just an effort to teach a youngster how to stay in a saddle, although Martha Ellen Truman, John's wife, was not happy over the affair.

The father of the president sometimes exhibited another notable quality: willingness to take a chance. Where this trait came from is difficult to say. In livestock dealings he naturally took chances, as people were bound to deceive him. Such experiences probably had nothing to do with larger chance-taking. Perhaps it derived from a vein of restlessness. He never stayed in one place.

When the family moved about, it often was because he was trying a new farm. He once acquired a farm that ran right up the side of a hill, impossible ground except for scrub trees and groundhogs, but he hoped it might be worthwhile. One summer he took his elder son through a dozen creek crossings and forty miles to look it over. He was an amateur inventor, and patented a staple-puller and a wire-stretcher for barbed-wire fences; it is unclear whether he made any money on them. He seems to have invented an automatic railroad switch, and the Missouri Pacific offered two thousand dollars a year in royalties, a dollar a switch for two thousand of the devices. The Chicago and Alton offered twenty-five hundred. Ever the chance-taker, John set a price of two dollars a switch, for twenty-five hundred: that meant five thousand dollars a year. Both lines rejected his price. Later the Missouri Pacific used an improved version of the invention, and John was unable to establish further claim to it.

In 1901 John Truman put everything he had, and everything his wife had inherited, into grain futures. He had become acquainted with a high roller in Kansas City, William T. Kemper, the founder of one of the great fortunes in the United States. Kemper possessed an instinct for investments and always multiplied his money. John Truman did not have the touch—nor, for that matter, enough money to have a touch—and lost everything. He was forced to move his family to Kansas City and become a watchman. His disastrous speculation prevented Harry Truman from going to college, something the son wanted to do.

Harry Truman's mother lived much longer than John Truman and hence was of more importance in her son's life. Martha Ellen Truman was a darkly pretty young woman upon her marriage in 1881, and a bent, gnarled old lady with a prominent, hawklike nose when she passed on in 1947 during her son's presidency. Her famous son was immensely fond of her.

The most notable trait of Harry Truman's mother was her outspokenness. Martha Ellen Truman held opinions and did not mind relating them. Her son was frank on occasion, sometimes when diplomacy dictated otherwise, and doubtless obtained the habit from his mother. Truman, however, was never as outspoken as she, or he could not have risen in politics. He was capable of outbursts, but he never showed feelings to the extent his mother did. One time when he was presiding judge—that is, principal county commissioner—of Jackson County, he spent a few days on the farm, tired out, trying to get away from office seekers, and heard his mother raking everyone she could think of. It got on his nerves, though he did not tell her.

Martha Ellen Truman always did what she wanted. She had attended the Baptist Female College in Lexington, Missouri, where she studied music and art, and it is possible that exposure to these finer things of life made her a prima donna when she married a livestock trader. She hated to cook, and seldom did, save for her single specialty, fried chicken. When her elder son and his wife and daughter went to her house, they invariably ate fried chicken; otherwise, they were not well fed. Threshers never saw Mrs. Truman help in the dining room or kitchen—her daughter, Mary Jane, together with Harry, served the meals. The elder Mrs. Truman accomplished this near miracle of farm life by refusing to do what she did not want. In her first years of married life she cooked, but she quit as soon as she could get kitchen help. She never learned to milk a cow, explaining: "Papa told me that if I never learned, I'd never have to do it." As she grew older, and infirm, her daughter, who never married, remained with her, and she must have been a considerable burden. Some of Mary Jane's later crotchets—taking the family car when her sister-in-law, Bess Truman, wanted it, or burning the letters her famous brother sent her—may have come from years of frustration caring for the prima donna, her mother.[6]

There was no question about Mrs. John Truman's taking care of her children. If she disdained some chores of rural life, she drew the line at neglecting children. "If you get married, you ought to stay home and take care of your babies," she once said. She made the remark in great old age, after World War II, when American mothers were deserting the home. The awkwardness of the remark did not bother Mamma Truman a bit.

Of the child Harry Truman we do not know a great deal, for almost no records have survived—quite different from the childhood of Franklin D. Roosevelt. Born two years before Truman, Roosevelt had a mother who was so sure that her Franklin would become president of the United States that she made a record for posterity, including his earliest childhood compositions and all other signs of this child's brilliant political future. For the childhood of Truman there are only a few memories, mostly those of the later president. His life in Lamar is a blank. A letter has come down from Grandfather Truman, stained and almost illegible, offering a few testimonies to the six churches in Lamar, the largest belonging to the Baptists, who rejoiced in having a young minister. During this period John Truman may never have written a letter. One or two of his wife's are in the Harry S. Truman Library in Independence; she said little about what her family was doing. The little clapboard house, we do know, for it has survived, was twenty feet by twenty-eight, with three rooms downstairs and two bedrooms up, no closets or attic or basement, and a well, smokehouse, and toilet outside. John and Martha Ellen had it built for $685, a novel procedure for newlyweds in those days. In Lamar the elder Truman conducted his animal business from a lot across the street. The summer of his son's birth an advertisement appeared in the *Lamar Democrat:* "Wanted, a few good mules and horses. Will pay highest cash prices for same. J. A. Truman, White barn near Missouri Pacific depot."[7] He bought locally and sold horses and mules to farmers; the other animals went to stockyards and slaughterhouses.

When the Trumans moved away the next year they sold the house for sixteen hundred dollars. Lamar then passed from their minds. When Harry Truman ran for U.S. senator in 1934 he returned; there is no evidence he had visited earlier. Nominated for the vice presidency in 1944, he chose Lamar for the notification ceremony, but until that year his wife and daughter had not seen the place. In the late 1950s the United Automobile Workers bought the house for six thousand dollars from Everett M. Earp, distantly related to Wyatt Earp, who had been the first constable of Lamar, and restored it to what people thought it had been in 1884, removing a picket fence and porch and summer kitchen and opening it as a national shrine.

We know nothing of the next place to which the Truman family moved, a farm north of Lamar near Harrisonville, other than the fact that John Truman reestablished his animal business there.

On the seventy-one-acre Dye farm, four and one half miles southeast of Belton, near Peculiar, the Missouri town known for its name, Truman's father took to raising corn. Harry Truman's first memory was of chasing a frog around a puddle in the backyard of that farm in 1885 or 1886; as he chased it he jumped up and down, laughing, and remembered Grandmother Young watching and laughing too. Nearby Belton must not have meant much more to the Trumans than a place to sell corn, and the family probably did not know that Carry Nation, the crusader against the Demon Rum, who for a while changed life across the United States, once lived nearby. Nation was a hell-raiser whose husband, an unsuccessful preacher, finally sued for divorce: "David was too slow for me," she said. Mrs. Nation was buried in the town cemetery. Belton became the burial place of another famous American, Dale Carnegie, who taught millions how to win friends and influence people.

After a year on the Dye farm the Trumans moved again, for seventy-one acres were barely enough for survival in the Middle West of that time.[8] This move in 1887 brought them to the Young farm, where they spent three years helping with the six hundred acres and another nearby farm of nine hundred or a thousand, also owned by Grandfather and Grandmother Young.

On the Young farm Harry Truman's memories were more clear; he was four years old when the family moved there. Some memories were of tasks performed—there always was something to do on the farm. He recalled the work of his mother together with Grandmother Young and Aunt Mary Martha (Aunt Mat), a spinster schoolteacher who spent much time with the family. In autumn they dried peaches and buried apples. They rendered lard and worked over sausage, using a recipe for the lard that caused it to be "just as white as snow and to keep forever. They stored it in large tin cans and fixed some of the sausage." So Harry wrote a correspondent: "[A]s you fixed it, in two jars you sent me, and then they would put the rest of it in sacks and smoke it with the hams and bacon. When I went back to the farm in 1906 we carried on the hog killing time just as our grandparents had done it but it is a lost art now."[9] During these years he became acquainted with farm animals.

He watched the daily field work—plowing, sowing, harvesting, and threshing of wheat and oats; planting, cutting, and shocking corn; mowing, raking, and stacking hay. Each evening at suppertime he heard his father tell a dozen farmhands what to do and how to do it.

One memory was of a joint venture with Grandfather Young that involved putting Vivian—born in 1886—in a high chair and cutting off his long curls, an act that irritated his mother, although she said nothing to her father. Not long afterward, perhaps evidence of divine retribution, Harry Truman was sitting on the edge of a chair in front of the mirror to comb his hair and fell off backward and broke his collarbone. In the same room a few months later he was eating a peach and swallowed the seed, which lodged halfway down his throat. He almost choked to death before his mother pushed the seed down with her finger.

But then there was fun; the years on the Young farm seemed filled with it. One of the future president's favorite memories was of attending the Cass County Fair in 1889. Grandfather Young took him in a cart pulled by a strawberry roan. He drove the six miles to the fair at Belton, and for all six days the two went to the fair and sat gravely in the judges' stand when races were called. Another was of games taught him by Uncle Harrison Young, who worked on Grandfather Young's farm. He had been named for Uncle Harrison—given the diminutive of Harry. Harrison was a character: hardly dedicated to farming, he was more interested in expeditions to Kansas City, where, as the nephew later described his chief and favorite activity, he could get three fingers around a small glass. Harry loved to play games with the uncle, who was a genius at checkers, chess, and poker (Truman learned the game from Harrison under the watchful eyes of his mother). He also learned seven-up, from which the soft drink took its name, pitch, and cooncan. This last game, which takes its name from the Spanish *con quien,* or "with whom," is a game of strategy. Perhaps the world's oldest rummy game, it requires a regular deck stripped of eights, nines, and tens; it is the only form of rummy played before the turn of the century that is still popular.

Some memories related to pets. Harry had an old Maltese gray cat named Bob, so named because an inch of its tail was burned off. It had been asleep in front of the big fireplace in the dining room when a coal popped out and lit the end of its tail. The child never forgot the yowls as the cat ran up the corner of the room all the way to the ceiling. He also had a little dog, named Tandy because it was black and tan. One day the boy was in the yard poking at toads with a stick. After a while he wandered away, following the dog down a corn row. Eventually he was discovered half a mile away, watching Bob and Tandy catch field mice. Someone told Harry's mother he had wandered off and gotten lost, but she was unconcerned; she said that when the dog came back it would lead them to Harry.

For the most part Harry Truman remembered the Young farm as a place to play. The two Truman boys used to play in the south pasture of the farm, a lovely meadow sown in bluegrass. It was the sort of place that a mother could send her children to and forget about them, knowing they could hardly get in harm's way. It was so far removed from the dangers of the town or city, where children could get into trouble. On only one occasion did Harry disappoint his mother. At the end of the pasture, he ruefully recalled, was a mudhole. The Truman boys had a little red wagon that they took on their adventures in the pasture, and one day they wound up at the mudhole with a neighbor boy about their age, John Chancellor; Harry loaded Vivian and John into the wagon, hauled them into the mudhole, and upset the wagon. "What a spanking I received. I can feel it yet! Every stitch of clothes on all three of us had to be changed, scrubbed and dried, and so did we!"[10]

It was during the years on the Young farm that Harry Truman found he had a problem with his eyes. The family went to Grandview in 1889 to celebrate the Fourth of July, and the climax of the occasion was a series of rockets that exploded clusters of stars into the sky. Harry jumped when each rocket blew up, but ignored the showers of fizzing stars. He did not know they were there. Before this Mamma Truman had worried, as mothers do, for when she pointed out distant objects, such as a buggy coming down the road or a cow or horse at the end of the pasture, her son did not see them. Suddenly she knew the reason. She probably imagined the most dire of possibilities: Harry was going blind. In that period many families had blind children, and word spread of how life had passed them by. A resolute individual, Mrs. Truman did not tarry in finding out what was wrong. The family physician, Dr. Charlie Lester, advised her to take Harry to an ophthalmologist, Dr. Thompson, Lester's brother-in-law in Kansas City. In those days children rarely went to ophthalmologists, who typically treated old people. Harry's mother was alone because her husband was away on a trip. She hitched two horses to the farm wagon, put her boy up on the seat beside her, and drove into Kansas City. There she learned all was not lost, even though the boy did have a problem. Dr. Thompson diagnosed "flat eyeballs," nearsightedness of an unusual sort, and prescribed a pair of expensive, thick glasses. The doctor warned Harry not to engage in sports such as baseball or participate in roughhousing, because he might break his glasses. The prescription was essentially correct and remained almost unchanged through the many times Harry Truman was "fineprinted," as he described measurement of his eyes.

The Truman children never forgot the Young farm, which became known as the Truman farm when the family moved back after the turn of the century. They of course remembered it well from being there as grownups, but their fondest memories were of childhood. They usually had played by themselves, and Harry, the oldest, took care of Vivian and Mary Jane, who was born there in 1889. She remembered how he combed her hair when she was a baby and sang as he rocked her to sleep.

2

The idyll of farm life (one uses the word advisedly, as nineteenth-century farming was idyllic only for children) came to an end in 1890, when the family moved to Independence. The reason was the town's school system. According to a brochure of 1902, Independence possessed "[a]bsolutely the finest system of public schools in the state. We do not bar Kansas City. It costs $230,000 a year to maintain this system."[11]

Independence's history reached back to Missouri's early times. Founded in 1827, just before Andrew Jackson's election to the presidency, the town received its name from the general's national program. It was the seat of a county named for the Tennessee statesman. To the north lay a town named Liberty, seat of a county named after Henry Clay.

Independence was—and is—a place of importance in the history of American religion. In 1831, when still a village, it attracted a small sect led by Joseph Smith, Jr. Not long afterward talk of "gentiles" antagonized the inhabitants, who destroyed the sect's newspaper and told its members to leave. The group repaired to Nauvoo in Illinois, near which a few years later a mob murdered Smith. The group divided, one part joining Brigham Young in a migration to the Great Salt Lake in 1846. The remnant took the name of Reorganized Church of Jesus Christ of Latter Day Saints (RLDS); its adherents returned to Independence in 1867, and others followed. Independence became world headquarters for the RLDS, with eventual construction of a seven-thousand-seat auditorium and, in 1990–1993, a sixteen-story temple that now dominates the skyline. Members of the RLDS and the followers of Brigham Young, the Mormons, both believe the Last Judgment will take place in Independence, near the auditorium, on a small plot of land inconveniently in possession of a splinter sect known as the Hedrickites.

Independence also was a jumping-off place for the Western trails to Santa Fe and Oregon and California. Settlers came down the Ohio River, took steamboats up the Missouri, got off at Wayne City Landing, and journeyed four miles on the first chartered railroad west of the Mississippi, the Independence Special, a mule-drawn conveyance on wooden rails that sometimes made it to Independence without falling off the tracks. In the town they bought oxen, wagons, and stores, and set out on the trails. Many visitors passed through Independence. In 1832 the writer Washington Irving saw Independence and wrote of it to his sister:

> We arrived at this place the day before yesterday. . . . Yesterday I was out on a deer hunt in the vicinity of this place, which led me through some scenery that only wanted a castle, or a gentleman's seat here and there interspersed to have equalled some of the most celebrated park scenery of England. . . . The soil is like that of a garden and the luxuriance and the beauty of the forests exceed any that I have seen.

In 1846, Francis Parkman was preparing for a trip to the Far West:

> Being at leisure one day I rode over to Independence. The town was crowded. A multitude of shops had sprung up to furnish the emigrants and Santa Fe traders with necessities for their journey; and there was an incessant hammering and banging from a dozen blacksmiths' sheds, where the heavy wagons were being repaired, and the horses and oxen shod. The streets were thronged with men, horses, and mules.[12]

In 1850 the first stage to Salt Lake City started from Independence. Fare was $150 in winter, $125 in summer, with food, arms, and ammunition furnished by the proprietors.

Frontier conditions continued until well after the Civil War, which brought fighting to the vicinity. There were two short occupations of the town by the Confederates, for Missouri was a border state and, like Kentucky, gave trouble to the Union—Confederates tried to push both states into secession. Perhaps because of the turmoil, desperadoes were on the loose for years afterward, with brawls and shoot-outs. Notable were the activities of the James boys, Jesse and Frank, prominent in "sticking up" trains between Kansas City and Independence.

By the time the Trumans came to Independence, things had settled down. The rising metropolis of Kansas City lay to the west. No longer a scraggly collection of huts and hovels along the river, it boasted tall buildings and department stores and theaters. It acted as a civilizing agent for Independence. Connection was easy. Residents of Independence took passage on Willard Winner's Dummy Line of horse-drawn and later electric-powered cars to the eastern edge of the city, whence they rode cable cars downtown. To the north lay the Air Line, a freight line. Independence in 1890 had grown to six thousand inhabitants, and the population had doubled to twelve thousand by 1902. An Empire-style courthouse went up on the square in the 1870s, and by the turn of the century it had become a sort of railroad-station edifice with a tower at one end. (During the early 1930s, when Harry Truman was the county's presiding judge, he changed the railroad station into a replica of Independence Hall in Philadelphia.)

In the 1890s the Trumans first lived in a house on Crysler Street, between Ruby and Haywood, across the Missouri Pacific tracks from courthouse square. It was not on the wrong side of the tracks; nearby were several expensive houses. They bought their house from a Jewish couple, Sam and Clara Blitz, putting down one thousand dollars and giving a mortgage for three thousand. The property included six lots, and in 1892 John Truman for six hundred dollars bought two more on Railroad Avenue. Space was necessary so that he could resume the animal business conducted in Lamar and on the farm near Harrisonville. The son long remembered the horses and cattle and sheep and goats. John Truman went around town in a spring wagon with a seat, the horse-drawn version of a pickup truck. He used it to take lambs and calves to the stockyards in Kansas City. Occasionally he drove stock to the yards.

The Crysler Street house attracted neighborhood children, and Harry recalled how everyone congregated—how much fun it was. In addition to animals in transit, the Truman children had pets: "We always had dogs and cats, pigeons and pet pigs." And pet goats: "Vivian had a team of red goats and a wagon. . . . My goat was bald with a black face." Harry remembered the town harness-maker, "old man Rummell," who made a harness for Vivian's goat team.[13] Rummell ran for county judge against Truman in 1924 and, because of a factional fight within the Democratic party, won the election.

The Crysler house held another attraction: it was lighted by gas. At a time when gas was available only in cities, electricity likewise, the Trumans had their own private supply of natural gas. The reason was a well John Truman had drilled to obtain water for the stock. Drillers first brought up sulfur water, and farther down struck gas. He asked them to case the well, which for several years produced gas for the house and that of a neighbor.

Trader that he was, in 1895 the elder Truman exchanged the Crysler house for another on West Waldo and River Boulevard. It was a good, even brilliant, trade—the two adjacent lots had brought his investment in the Crysler property to $4,600, and he swapped for the Waldo house and received in addition $5,400 in cash and good notes. Waldo was a half-dozen blocks north of Crysler and two blocks west of Delaware Street, the latter Independence's elite avenue featuring the best houses, with the exception of the town's three mansions—the house of Colonel E. T. Vaile, a red-brick monstrosity; the lovely Bingham-Waggoner house near Crysler Street, once owned by the painter George Caleb Bingham; and the house of Colonel Thomas H. Swope, scene of a bizarre series of murders in 1909. Waldo Street ran at a right angle to Delaware. River Boulevard paralleled Delaware, extending far to the north, crossing the Air Line, continuing until it reached the Missouri River (thence its name). It once had been the road for the Independence Special.

The Crysler and Waldo Street houses still stand, but new owners remodeled them, and new houses surround them. The present-day visitor walks along the streets, or drives along, and someone points out where Harry Truman once lived. Because of changes, it is difficult to imagine his living there a hundred years ago.

Close to Waldo Street, on Delaware, was the Gates house, later the Wallace house, now the Truman house—currently surrounded by an iron fence and sidewalks filled with tourists taking pictures and dropping Kleenexes. The grandfather of the later Bess Truman built the big Victorian house at 219 North Delaware in stages after the Civil War. Apart from size—it has seventeen rooms—its principal characteristics are a rounded porch, what appear to be stained-glass windows (but in fact are mostly flashed glass), and eaves decorated by fancy woodwork. In the 1890s, George Porterfield Gates was one of the leading men of Independence, co-proprietor of a mill that produced Queen of the Pantry Flour, "the best biscuit and cake flour in the world."

Gates, incidentally, must have been not merely a successful miller but also a man who enjoyed a hearty laugh now and then, for he created a poster-sized advertisement for his flour that should have inspired laughter all over the Middle West. The poster shows a man of middle age standing next to a fair young lady clad in starched uniform and apron, obviously the maid, engaged in the manufacture of some confection requiring Queen of the Pantry Flour, a sack of which is in plain view. To the right stands the man of the house's wife, who seems to have come upon the scene with undue suddenness and for some reason is horror-struck. Upon the back of the jacket of the man are the flour-imprinted marks of the maid's arms and hands.

Down Delaware at 610 lived the daughter of Mr. and Mrs. Gates, Madge Gates Wallace, prettiest of the three Gates daughters—Margaret (Madge), Maud, and Myra. Their adoring father contrived a decorative picture for his flour sacks: beaded curtain, palm, and young lady with a bustle, supposedly a composite of the daughters but looking mostly like Madge. Madge's husband, David W. Wallace—a handsome man, with sideburns—was county recorder and later held an appointment in the customs office in Kansas City. The Wallace family eventually included four children, of whom Bessie was the oldest.

It would be possible to describe life in the Independence of the 1890s as drawn by two daughters of the lawyer John Paxton, who lived next to the Wallace family, one member of which, Mary, was Bessie Wallace's best friend. Both left attractive descriptions—Mary wrote two books about her memories. The Paxtons wrote of Bessie riding her tricycle up the hexagon-flagstoned sidewalk from 610 North Delaware to 219, and of porches and lawns in front, and behind the vegetable and flower gardens, the latter filled with lilacs. In summers, as the children grew older, the young people contrived parties, with Japanese lanterns strung across the backyards. It was a charming life to be young and to grow up on Delaware Street. An early photograph of Bessie Wallace shows her and friends sitting under a large tree eating slices of watermelon and holding them up for the photographer. Sometimes the young people forsook their backyards to go on long walks to such places as the neighboring town of Lee's Summit, and then, being happily tired, took the train back. Mary Paxton wrote of one such expedition with Bessie, each girl accompanied by a beau (in Bessie's case, not Harry Truman). Mary took along deviled eggs, but, unbeknownst to her, one of her younger brothers had filled them with red pepper. The couples decided to eat while sitting on a bridge, Mary and beau on the down part of the stream, Bess and friend on the upper.

Mary noticed eggs floating past her and said, "What's the matter with the eggs?" They said, "Taste them."[14]

The temptation of biographers of Harry Truman has been to turn to such accounts. While it is true that some experiences of Delaware Street children may have touched the early years of the later president, they mostly marked those of the more privileged boys and girls of the town. The difficulty, then, with the stories of Mary Paxton Keeley and Elizabeth Paxton Forsling is that they relate experiences in which Harry Truman did not share. Living round the corner on Waldo, he and his family were not members of the town's society, for several reasons. For one thing, they lacked the money. Perhaps of equal importance, they did not belong to the proper churches. Mary Paxton remembered that in the hierarchy of church membership the Presbyterians were at the top, followed by the Campbellites (the Disciples of Christ); below them were the Methodists and Lutherans. Farther down yet were the Baptists, Catholics, and RLDS members. At first, upon arriving in Independence, Harry and his brother and sister attended Presbyterian Sunday school, but their attendance seems to have lapsed and, anyway, they assuredly were not members.[15] Another of the reasons Harry Truman stood apart from the Paxton girls and Bessie Wallace was that he wore glasses and therefore could not play with neighborhood children. In the parlance of generations of youngsters, he was "four eyes." After he became famous, friends recalled growing up with him, and there were brave descriptions of how Harry did not play baseball or catch or whatever, but sometimes he would come out and hit the ball for a home run, or explain to a confused group who the James brothers were. These were good efforts at covering up the fact that a youth in a family of modest means who had to wear glasses was forced to protect them; young Harry Truman could not simply go out to play in the streets or roughhouse in the backyards.

Too, he was taking piano lessons. Many years afterward he liked to say he arose early and practiced two hours before school. This may have happened. For several years, apparently from age fourteen onward, he took lessons on a regular basis, once or twice a week. The family bought an upright piano in 1898 from the Kimball Piano Company of Chicago, paying the first installment of fifty dollars that August, the next, eighty-four dollars, the following April. How many installments were made is difficult to say, but they continued for several years—Truman mentioned later that the piano was paid off in 1906. He began instruction with his mother, and then went to the next-door neighbor, Miss Florence Burrus, sister of John Truman's lawyer, Olney Burrus. Miss Burrus taught a special method of reading music that involved figures rather than notes, and Harry thrived on it; an advertising flyer, dated 1901, from Muncie, Indiana, cited young "Harry Trueman" as a testimonial to the method: "He will play at sight on the piano any piece set before him, seemingly as well as if he had been drilled for the occasion. . . . He will instantly improvise any style of music desired and change off to other styles as fast as they are suggested."[16] He thereafter studied with Mrs. E. C. White in Kansas City. She lived in a large old-fashioned brick house and possessed a Steinway grand. An unusual teacher, she had studied in Vienna with Theodor Leschetizky, teacher of Anton Rubinstein, Ignacy Paderewski, and Josef Lhévinne.

For five years, apparently until early 1905 (by which time the Trumans were in Kansas City), Harry Truman studied with Mrs. White and was her best pupil. A recital program of Mrs. White's students in 1904 has survived, saved by Mary Jane, in which he played Mendelssohn's "Song without Words." At one point he was learning Paderewski's "Minuet in G," and having trouble with the thematic turn at the beginning. Mrs. White took him to a concert by Paderewski and afterward escorted him backstage, introduced the boy to the pianist, and related the trouble. According to what Truman told Paul Hume, the music critic of the *Washington Post* (some years after the set-to in which Hume criticized the singing of Truman's daughter, Margaret, and the president penned a famous letter), Paderewski sat down at a piano and spent fifteen minutes demonstrating the turn.[17]

Truman always gave the impression he was not very serious about playing, and sometimes he passed it off with a joke. On occasion he related that while in high school he began to fear playing was a sissy occupation, and so quit.[18] The truth is he enjoyed playing—he took it seriously, and quit only when he had to, when the family, after moving to Kansas City, moved again, to Clinton, where Truman's father once more took up farming. The move to Clinton separated Harry from the piano, as he stayed behind to work in the city and the piano moved with the family. Harry moved into an aunt's house and thence into a rooming house.

Still another reason Harry Truman did not participate in the social life of Delaware Street was that he had work to do at home. Decades later, in 1948, he remarked to students at the Girard College chapel in Philadelphia that a half-century earlier his life had not been as easy as theirs: "Now when I was a young man—a boy your age—I had to milk a cow night and morning," he began, and one suspects the students' eyes glazed as he described how he had to

carry the milk to the house, and put it in a cooler so I could have milk for breakfast. You just go out on the back porch and pick up a bottle, you don't know where it comes from. When I was a boy, we didn't have any mechanical dishwashers. I had to wash the dishes, and wash the lamp chimneys, so that we could have clean dishes for the next meal, and for light. If we didn't have clean lamps, we didn't have any light. I had to split wood and carry it and put it in the woodbox behind the stove, so I could get up in the morning and start a fire so that we could have breakfast. Now all you do is turn on a gadget.[19]

When old enough to get a job outside the house, he worked in Clinton's Drugstore. Mary Paxton remembered riding around the square in a surrey pulled by an old gray horse, with Bessie Wallace and a girl named Nellie alongside. The girls were singing and carrying on until they spotted Harry Truman sweeping out the drugstore. Bessie's face sobered as she caught sight of him. She stopped singing.

"What's the matter?" Mary asked.

Bessie caught his eye; he grinned and waved, and stood leaning on his broom until they turned the corner of the square.

"Poor Harry!" Bess said. "It's not fair. He has to work all the time and never has any fun like we do."

"Oh well, we can't help it if he is poor and a Baptist," said Nellie.

"No, but I wish I could," Bess responded.[20]

Clinton's Drugstore reminded the adult Harry Truman of what a job could turn into. The store sounded attractive in the Independence brochure of 1902:

> J. H. Clinton, druggist, is located in the Clinton block on the North side of the square. He handles all druggist's supplies, medicines, paints, oils, toilet articles, etc. All his clerks are efficient pharmacists and you may rest assured that you will get what you ordered. His drug store is probably the nicest arrangement in town with tile floor, mirrors, etc. He also handles Ice-cream soda and fine candies. Mr. Clinton manufactures a number of articles in the drug line. An invitation is extended to all to give him a trial.

But the hours of work were hardly attractive. Truman worked for Clinton from seven o'clock until schooltime and from four to ten. Nor were the tasks attractive. He had to turn the ice cream freezer for each day's output, dispense ice cream behind the soda fountain, carry out the trash, and sweep up. And then there were the bottles: he remembered hundreds of them. He had to dust and wipe them—not all of them each day, for that would have been impossible, but each morning he had to start on the row where he had left off the day before. Some bore cryptic Latin abbreviations, and one Harry never forgot was "Ici. Toed. Foet." Although he never knew what it meant, he never forgot it either: the proprietor, Mr. Jim Clinton, had told him to take care with the bottle containing Icy Toed Feet because if he broke that bottle there were no more. Admittedly, the contents of some of the other bottles were easier to understand. "Clinton's Magical Oil for all Pains and Aches" cost fifty cents a bottle. "Clinton's Rose Cream for all Roughness on Hands and Face" cost two bits. "Clinton's One Hour Cough Cure" was "for All Coughs and Colds," and "Clinton's Golden Eye Water" was "for Inflamed and Sore Eyes." "Clinton's Hair Renewer" softened the scalp, and Clinton said it "renewed Growth of Hair."

The job produced two other memories. One was unpleasant, of the way in which town church members and Anti-Saloon Leaguers came in each morning, looked around, entered a little area behind the prescription case, and took early morning drinks of whiskey at ten cents an ounce. They would wipe their mouths, peep through the observation hole in front of the case, and depart furtively. The other memory, a happier one, was of his first week's pay: three silver dollars. The money looked like three million, and it meant even more. He bought a present for his mother, and tried to give the rest to his father, who would not take it.[21]

All the while young Harry Truman was attending school. He entered what was called the Noland School (no connection with Aunt Ella Noland, who lived in Independence) in the autumn of 1892 when he was eight and a half. Just why his parents waited until then—after all, they had come to Independence because of the schools—is impossible to know.

He entered in a presidential election year, and this fact led to an incident that he often remembered. His father favored Grover Cleveland, who had lost to Benjamin Harrison four years earlier by failing to obtain enough electoral votes, although he had received a majority of the popular vote. This failure had to be redeemed, and Harry took part in the redemption, appearing one day at school wearing a white hat that said "Cleveland and Stevenson," the latter referring to Adlai Stevenson, grandfather of the candidate of 1952 and 1956. As Truman related it, some big Republican boys took his hat and tore it up, "and the Republican boys have been trying to do that to me ever since!"[22]

When the Democrats won, John Truman climbed the cupola of the Crysler Street house and nailed a flag to the weather vane, atop which was a rooster, and said the flag would remain during the second Cleveland administration.

Harry Truman entered second grade in 1893, but in January 1894 came an interruption when he contracted diphtheria. In those days people possessed little understanding of the disease, and when both he and Vivian came down with it their parents sent Mary Jane to Grandmother Young's farm. "Old Letch" Simpson, husband of the Trumans' cook, Aunt Caroline, drove her in the wagon, and the family did not know of her safe arrival until his return two days later. Vivian gradually recovered, and Harry seemed to, but while sitting at the dinner table one evening drinking a glass of milk, he suddenly realized that he could not swallow—his mother, father, and brother saw milk coming out of his mouth, his tongue paralyzed. Indeed, he suffered general paralysis. Slowly he improved, although upon her return from Grandmother Young's Mary Jane had to wheel him around in a baby buggy.

After tutoring he was able to go back to school that autumn, and he not merely kept up but skipped third grade—a not uncommon practice in those relaxed days. As a fourth grader he entered the Columbian School, so named because of construction in 1892–1893. Altogether he went through six grades and three years of high school. In his senior year he again changed buildings, to a new school town children would use until it burned in 1939.

Instruction in his grade and high schools seems to have been of high quality. His grade-school teachers were women—Mira Ewin was first, at the Noland School. Several high school teachers were men. Some, such as George S. Bryant, were known as "professor," an honorific term, although Bryant had some right to it: he had managed Woodland College, a small institution two blocks from the Truman house on Waldo Street; when Woodland went under, Bryant became principal of the Independence High School. Another of Truman's teachers was Professor Patrick, superintendent of the entire Independence school system.

Truman was fond of his teachers, and some were still active when he became president. Ardelia Hardin, who married Professor W. L. C. Palmer and thus had to retire (a married woman could not teach), spoke with pride of his ability in Latin—pharmaceutical abbreviations aside—in which she had instructed him. She noticed how some problem or other had prompted Chief Justice Fred M. Vinson to remark in President Truman's presence, "Well, like old Cato said in the Roman senate, 'It ought to be destroyed, Carthage ought to be destroyed, *Carthago delenda est.*'" Harry had replied, "You didn't say that right. You should have said, '*Delenda est Carthago.*'" She recalled how pleased she had been half a century before when Harry, Dr. Twyman's son Elmer, and the class valedictorian, Charles Ross, devoted several afternoons to building a bridge on the model of one they had read about in Caesar's *Commentaries*.[23]

Truman appreciated the serious manner in which teachers dealt with students, believing that was the way in which students learned. Even if teachers "told off" students, that was all right. After he returned to Independence in 1953, he used part of his retirement to talk to groups, and on one occasion addressed the teachers of the Independence schools. He told them of "a woman named Montessori," who believed children needed to do as they pleased because it developed character. She was an authority, he said, on backward and mentally defective youngsters, but "in my opinion the application of her methods to normal children spoils those children and ruins character." He recalled Professor Patrick, who permitted no student nonsense. One day Patrick had ventured into a class, an awesome visitor with a head as bald as an onion—he kept it covered with a skullcap. Charlie Ross was discussing the mistakes of Generals Lee and Meade at Gettysburg, excoriating the generals, and after Charlie sat down the professor looked him over and said, "Young man, don't you know that any schoolboy's afterthought is worth more than the greatest general's forethought?"[24]

After school young Truman was often in the Independence public library, which was in the high school building, reading books or taking them out; this fact has led to speculation about how he spent his time during his school years. He liked to say that by the time he was twelve he had read the Bible two or three times, all the way through, and claimed to have read every book in the Independence library, including the encyclopedias. He later became known as a student of history. He did not deny it, and in fact was inclined to prove it, sometimes to doubting newspapermen who tried to trap him. But the president's assertions about all the books he read when he was a student deserve no great amount of attention, because he grossly exaggerated. He read Charles F. Horne's *Great Men and Famous Women,* a massive four-volume compendium of biographical sketches, brown books trimmed in gold, published in 1894, which began with Nebuchadrezzar and ended with Sarah Bernhardt.[25] His mother bought the volumes from a door-to-door salesman for Harry's twelfth birthday. The sketches were by illustrious writers of the time, including the Honorable Theodore Roosevelt, "late of the U.S. Civil Service Commission." The rest of the reading seems impossible. The library filled two rooms and contained seventeen hundred books, not the four thousand he remembered; if he had read every book in the library, it would have meant an enormous list, a book a day or more, for five or six years, not counting the encyclopedias.[26] And during all this time he was practicing the piano, doing home chores, and working in Clinton's. A friendly biographer, Jonathan Daniels, who saw a good deal of the president and had known his predecessor in the White House, said Truman's understanding of history when compared to that of Roosevelt was superficial: "Truman imagined himself a great historian but actually Truman knew the kind of history that McGuffey would have put in his readers, and he liked the historical anecdote that expressed a moral. Whereas Roosevelt was a pretty rangy fellow with a lot of juicy information."[27]

As the school years passed, the future president did not think a great deal about politics, national or international, for he was busy with other things. He served as a page during the Democratic national convention in Kansas City in 1900; his father's friend, Kemper, arranged the job. Long afterward Truman remembered the speakers, especially the party's nominee, William Jennings Bryan, whose voice filled the auditorium, soaring to the rafters in those days without the amplification of so-called loudspeakers. "I was up on the roof garden, looking down at him, and he didn't appear to be more than six inches high, and I could hear him just as well up there in that roof garden as the front row."[28] The Independence schoolboy showed almost no other sign of interest in what became his occupation years later. Nor did the international politics of the time engage him. The nations of Europe were vying for empire amid the rivalries that brought World War I. The Spanish-American War did produce a little interest, however, for he and a dozen friends aged fourteen or thereabouts organized a rifle company so as to be prepared in event the country needed them; they armed themselves with .22 rifles, engaged in drills, and hid out in the woods north of town where they shot and cooked stray chickens. Every other day they elected a captain and lieutenant, for a day or two was as long, Truman recalled, as any one boy could remain popular. The war—that is, the war in Cuba—lasted only three months, and the nation did not call upon Captain (or was it Lieutenant?) Truman and his brave men.

If there was a single concern larger than school and the tasks out of school, it was the unabashed idealism of those years at the turn of the century. Youths naturally turn to the future, which usually seems so bright; the world of ideals beckons. Such was the case in 1901. In an effort to grasp what lay before them, the class at Independence High that year decided to publish an annual entitled *The Gleam,* after Tennyson's poem:

> Not of the sunlight,
> Not of the moonlight;
> Not of the starlight!
> O young Mariner,
> Down to the haven,
> Call your companions,
> Launch your vessel
> And crowd your canvas,
> And, ere it vanishes
> Over the margin,
> After it, follow it,
> Follow the Gleam.

The class artist sketched a ship setting out under full sail. To each side stretched the cliffs of certainty.

Tennyson truly attracted Truman, and one day during that last school year the young man copied off for himself another poem, another piece of idealism, that looked more closely to what he would attempt during his time of national and international prominence. The first lines read: "For I dipt into the future, far as human eye could see, / Saw the Vision of the world, and all the wonder that would be." One part promised a dire confrontation: "Heard the heavens fill with shouting, and there rain'd a ghastly dew / From the nations' airy navies grappling in the central blue." At a dinner for members of Congress in 1952 the president remarked how this passage foretold nuclear weapons.[29] But he then recited the best-known lines: "Till the war-drum throbb'd no longer, and the battle-flags were furled / In the Parliament of Man, the Federation of the World."

During Truman's presidency the writer John Hersey, doing an article for the *New Yorker,* told him how someone had said that for many years the nation's chief executive carried some poetry in his wallet, and asked if he still did. "Yes," the president said, "I still carry it." It was, of course, *Locksley Hall.*[30]

Chapter Two

The Bank

*A*fter graduating from high school, Harry Truman followed a remarkably indirect course in choosing a career, until he ran for public office in the early 1920s and finally discovered what he wanted to do. The youngster, setting out on life's journey in 1901 at the age of seventeen, was led by one thing after another. At the outset each job came along by chance, and he seized upon it for the moment, with nothing larger in mind. He was possessed of a good deal of the desire to "get ahead" that is evident in most youngsters—that is, he wanted to do well. But at least into the farm years, which began in 1906, he had none of the driving ambition that is evident in some young people and marks them off as very special. No one would have seen Harry Truman as ambitious, and years later, when he became famous, some people had a difficult time remembering that they had seen Harry Truman at all, even though he had been in close proximity.

He was a slight youngster in 1901, thin and sharp-faced, with a shock of hair flopped across his forehead and the large Truman nose protruding, his eyes watching interestedly but languidly. He seems to have been addicted to bow ties and hats of a rakish sort; he was photographed in such. But that did not prove anything, for such was the dress of the day, together with the inevitable dark suits—dark because they did not show the dirt of the streets and thus did not have to be washed in those days before dry cleaning.

The scene of his endeavors, Kansas City, was as nondescript as was Truman. Community leaders were making efforts to beautify the city, but they had not gotten far; at least, their efforts had not advanced to the places where Truman lived. The houses were boxlike affairs with porches across their fronts, not far from the street, perhaps so that sewer lines would not have to run far; a tree or two might stand out in front. They were new, put up in the nineties perhaps, but were drably alike; as the youth walked along he probably had trouble knowing where he was going. And then there were the sights of Kansas City's downtown, which in Truman's time—this long before the mall movement depopulated the centers of American cities—was filled with people and noise and must have been exciting to a young man, especially a young man just out of high school, who had spent his few years in semirural Independence or on farms to the south between Independence and Lamar. Still, it too, like the city's residential areas, was hardly memorable. Kansas City was no Chicago, Boston, Philadelphia, or New York. The downtown area was perched on a series of rounded hills, some of which had been scooped out and the others not. The buildings had been erected without the slightest consideration of neighboring structures and usually without the slightest architectural merit, in whatever was the style of the time. One of them was as high as eleven stories, with arrays of windows all looking down with boredom, maybe, on the people who thronged the sidewalks.

And yet there was a logic in Harry Truman's life over the years until he found himself—even though he did not see the logic until long afterward. He later said that if someone wanted to go into politics he needed preparation in three fields. One of them was finance, and in his first years after high school he learned finance of a sort: he worked in two large banks in Kansas City. The second was farming, and when he went out to the Grandview farm to help his father—his parents had moved back the preceding year—he remained eleven years, and, after his father's death in 1914, he managed the farm himself. The third requirement, he said, was experience in the U.S. Army: in 1905–1911 he served two three-year enlistments in the National Guard. In 1917 he enlisted again, and after the war remained in the army as a reserve officer.

The preparation gained from these three experiences was general and often only vaguely pertinent; it had little to do with later requisites for a career in politics, especially when compared to attending a prestigious law school or a modern-day institution such as the Kennedy School of Government at Harvard University. Truman never believed in such formalities, and their cost would have been impossible because of his meager finances. But beyond question the pursuits into which he wandered helped him, sometimes mightily, when the time of responsibility came.

1

Finding an occupation after high school was not so much a task as an exercise in doing what came along. The only evidence that the young Truman gave any thought at all to the problem was his effort, for a few months, to gain admission to the United States Military Academy at West Point. Reading *Great Men and Famous Women* had aroused his interest in military affairs, and of course during the Spanish-American War he and the neighborhood youths had drilled for a week or two, dreamed of entering the army, and settled for killing chickens. In his senior year he talked over the possibilities with his friend Fielding Houchens, and the two sought out their history teacher, Miss

Maggie Phelps, who tutored them two nights a week in history and geography. They were serious about applying to West Point and Annapolis—in those days, it was necessary to apply to both academies, to place one's name on a common list, and then the appointing senator received places for presentable candidates.

The desire to attend West Point derived from several purposes, confused in the way young people dream from several inspirations. For one, he aspired to get a free college education. For another, he hoped to be a great general; he later confessed that when he was supposed to be working in Clinton's Drugstore he only pretended to work:

> I ate ice cream and candy and usually failed to show up when windows were to be washed. . . . I spent most of my odd moments and many that belonged to my employer reading the Life of Napoleon, always hoping that in the end he'd win the Battle of Waterloo. Hannibal was another one of my heroes along with Alexander, Caesar, and Robert E. Lee. I hoped for a chance to go to West Point or Annapolis and perhaps imitate one of 'em when I was old enough.[1]

And beyond the hope of being a second Napoleon, there was hope of impressing Bessie Wallace. Years afterward, in France and in the army, Captain Truman of Battery D of the 129th Field Artillery Regiment wrote the young woman, who by then was known as Bess, that she would laugh if he told her he had wanted to go to West Point so he could be a famous general and she could be a famous general's lady, "so you could be the leading lady of the palace or empire or whatever it was I wanted to build."[2]

Houchens eventually went to Annapolis but failed after a year. Harry did not get that far. When he visited a recruiting station, probably in Kansas City, he learned that his eyesight was not good enough.

What might have happened had Truman attended West Point, and if shortly thereafter a youngster born in 1890 who lived one hundred and fifty miles due west, in Abilene, Kansas, had pursued his own bent and gone (as the class seer of Abilene High predicted) to Yale and become a professor of history there? The twentieth century might have been a different place.

After graduation, with no hope of a professional military career, Truman, like many young people in a state of confusion, took a vacation. He visited his mother's youngest sister, Ada, Mrs. Joseph Van Cloostere, in Murphysboro in southern Illinois. It was his first trip away from home. He spent a month there and enjoyed it, as his Aunt Sallie Chiles's older married daughter, Suda Wells, lived with Ada and had four children, two about his age. On the way home he stopped in St. Louis to see his mother's aunt, Hettie Powell, half-sister of Solomon Young, who had visited on the farm when he, Harry, was a child. Her son John took him and three other boys to the races, Harry's first real horse race. In his memoirs he wrote guardedly that he "had a fine time," but it was a bit more than that. The boys each put in a dollar for a five-dollar bet on a horse named Claude, who paid off twenty-five to one. Twenty-five dollars improved his finances considerably, as he had gone to St. Louis with eighteen silver dollars. The whole thing was luck; before the race it had rained, and Claude was the best mud horse in the United States. Truman said afterward it was his first and last bet on a horse. Years later he occasionally went to the tracks to see the political leader of Kansas City, Boss Thomas J. Pendergast, who loved the horses, but these were business trips and involved no betting.

That summer Truman went to Texas with his cousin Ralph, who had been in the Spanish-American War and served in the Philippines, and visited Ralph's father on a farm near Lone Oak. They were there in September when President William McKinley was shot in Buffalo. Afterward they went to Wilmer, Texas, to visit Ralph's sister Grace, who had stayed with the Truman family when they lived in Lamar; Grace had since married. Ralph remained in Texas for a while, and Harry came home by himself. It is possible that during this trip Harry and Ralph "rode the rails." Many years later Ralph told a friend they had done it, taking Missouri Pacific freights, so-called side-door Pullmans. Harry Truman never said anything about such behavior. For Ralph, a hardened young man, who in 1898 had enlisted in a company that had no officers and got all the way to Cuba by the will and ingenuity of its elected "foreman," it would have been nothing unusual to travel to Texas in a side-door Pullman.[3]

Between these two trips, to Illinois and to Texas, Harry Truman had entered Spalding's Commercial College in Kansas City, a considerable institution. Its years in operation were "a guarantee of honest methods, and a record unequaled by any other Western Business College," the ads said. "Practical Course of Study . . . esteem and confidence of the Business Public in this City and throughout the West. . . . Over 17,000 Graduates and former students. . . . Free Employment Bureau." In the *Encyclopedia of the History of Missouri*, a six-volume work published in 1901, Spalding's appeared as large as in the ads:

> A school founded in Kansas City in 1865 by James Franklin Spalding, and chartered in 1867 at the urgent request of leading business men. It is located in the east wing of the New York Life building, where it occupies twenty suitable rooms, employing sixteen teachers. It affords four courses of study, namely: Commercial course, shorthand course, telegraphy course and an English course. It has both day and evening classes. The school deserves the high reputation it enjoys and its students are now among the high business men of the city. It has had a long and successful career, and is one of the best known institutions of that city.[4]

Here Truman seems to have taken a year of instruction in debit and credit bookkeeping, Isaac Pitman shorthand, and typewriting. The first he used in later years, and in one instance almost immediately after leaving the college in 1902. The shorthand never had any utility, nor did the typing, although the earliest letter in the Truman Library, dated July 1, 1901, is a little half-sheet of typing, containing a few typewritten errors: writing to Grandmother Young, Uncle Harrison, and Aunt Laura Everhart (apparently visiting at the farm), the typist related that he would like to come out for the Fourth of July and might bring a friend, a young man he had met.[5] Apart from the letter, which survived probably because Harry's country relatives thought it interesting, being written on a typewriter and by a Truman, there is almost no evidence of what he did at Spalding's. It must have been a straitened experience, back and forth to the city each day on the Dummy Line and the city streetcars. His parents customarily gave him carfare and a quarter to eat lunch, and he ate at Herman's at 809 Main Street. Sometimes he went into the ice cream parlor managed by Jesse James, Jr. On one such occasion he purchased an ice cream soda, only to discover he lacked the nickel to pay for it. He possessed only a streetcar ticket to get home. He explained his predicament to Mr. James, who said, "Oh that's all right, pay when you come in again." Next day, he paid.

During the year at Spalding's it became clear that Harry Truman was not going to go to a real college, a four-year institution—his father had gotten into the speculation in grain futures. According to the son, "He got the notion he could get rich."[6] He lost the 160-acre farm his wife inherited from her father, and thirty or forty thousand dollars in cash and other personal property, much of it similarly obtained. The Trumans had to give up the house on Waldo Street; they had bought it for four thousand dollars, and sold it in 1902 for thirty-five hundred. Moving to a little house at 902 North Liberty Street, they moved again in 1903 to a house in Kansas City at 2108 Park Avenue.

In August 1902 Truman went to work in the mail room of the *Kansas City Star*, "wrapping singles" at $7.00 the first week, $5.40 the second. One wonders if Spalding's employment bureau secured the job. However he got it, it meant stuffing one section of the paper into another, as fast as possible, and lifting and stacking the papers and tying bundles. All probably in a room heavy with noise and the vibrations of machinery, with printer's ink griming the hands of the stuffers.

He quit to become timekeeper for the L. J. Smith Construction Company, which was doubletracking the Santa Fe line from Sheffield, between Independence and Kansas City, to Courtney, four or five miles northeast, at the tip of a bend in the Missouri River. Truman's father suggested the job because one of the members of Harry's graduating class, Tasker P. Taylor, had been timekeeper, but he went swimming in the treacherous river and drowned. Taylor's demise, one should add, was not quite the end of the story, for one day after Harry went to work he and the daughter of L. J. Smith were sitting on the riverbank and the body of Taylor suddenly came to the surface. The daughter fainted. Harry "didn't know what to do."[7]

He rode each day from Independence to Courtney on a handcar he pumped, and the job lasted six months, until February 1903. It was rough work. Lucius Junius Smith paid thirty-five cents an hour to workers with wagons and teams, and laborers received $1.50 for ten-hour days with subtraction of fifty cents for board. Blacksmiths, cooks, and other specialists received $1.75. "That," Truman said many years later, "is where I learned about minimum wages." If men drew money under two weeks, Smith discounted checks 10 percent. Twice daily the future president traveled between three construction camps five miles apart and checked the hours of four hundred men. He paid off the men every other Saturday night, in saloons, such as John Schmidt's in Sheffield, where the workers invariably drank up their money over the weekend; this was part of Smith's plan, for they were back on the job, sober and broke, the following Monday morning. Their drinking during payday weekends produced a story Truman often told, albeit in two versions. One was that he heard a hobo asking Schmidt, the saloonkeeper, what a man did to keep from getting drunk when he took rounds of drinks with friends. The saloonkeeper said, "Damned if I know. I always want the most of my money." The other version was that Schmidt "stroked his beard and said he didn't know but if the man found out he shouldn't tell him as 'I likes to get the worst of my liquor.'"[8] For all this the timekeeper received fifty dollars a month, fifteen taken out for board. Overpayments to the men came out of the timekeeper's pay. If he underpaid, Smith kept the difference.

The railroad job came to an end with nothing in sight, but opportunity beckoned again. Truman had become acquainted with a young man named Edwin H. Green, who was rooming in the Kansas City house of his widowed Aunt Emma Colgan. One day Ed asked if Harry would like to work in a bank. The response was, "I can't tell about that until I've done it. But I certainly would like to have a chance to try it. I'd like to have an opportunity to use my brains again, and what little education I have. I did all right as a timekeeper."[9] Harry filled out the bank's application form, which contained questions that years later would have provoked a lawsuit. He answered plausibly. The form inquired if he used tobacco or liquor, gambled, or was in debt. These traits apparently were all considered equal. The form also asked whether he had "tastes or habits extravagant in proportion to your means." The answers were all "no." As to how he spent evenings and Sundays: "at home."[10]

He did not obtain his bank job without recommendations. To the National Bank of Commerce in Kansas City he submitted names of three individuals who would recommend him. One was the cashier of the Bank of Independence, M. G. Wood, who gave a good reference. So did Dr. G. T. Twyman: "I have known Harry Truman since his infancy. He is a model young man and worthy all confidence being strictly truthful, sober and industrious. The only employment I know of his having was as timekeeper in R.R. construction work where he gave eminent satisfaction." R. E. Booth, bookkeeper of Sparks Brothers Mule and Horse Company (address: Kansas City stockyards), doubtless a friend of John Truman, wrote: "I have known him for long time; I know his parents—he comes of a good family. He is an honest straightforward steady boy and unquestionably would make a good clerk. I don't think he has had a great deal of experience."[11]

He thereupon entered the employ of the Commerce Bank, taking the oath of allegiance: "obedience to my superiors, and cheerful compliance with all established rules and regulations. I also promise to devote my entire time, energy and ability to the exclusive service of the Bank."

It was an impressive place, tellers' cages fronted with wainscoting and brasswork, cage openings carefully barred. The room's ornamental pillars bore Corinthian capitals, and globe lights hung from the ceiling. In front of each cage stood a spittoon. Truman worked in the basement in a caged section affectionately known as the zoo, together with a hundred other utility clerks. He listed and distributed checks drawn on twelve hundred country banks in Missouri, Kansas, and Oklahoma, a clearinghouse operation that large banks performed before the days of the Federal Reserve System.

He did well, engaging the attention of the bank's vice president, Charles H. Moore, a much feared personage whose job was

> to do the official bawling out. He was an artist at it. He could have humiliated the nerviest man in the world. Anyway, all the boys in the Commerce Zoo were afraid of him, as were all the tellers and bookkeepers. He was never so happy as when he could call some poor inoffensive little clerk up before him in the grand lobby of the biggest bank west of the Mississippi and tell him how dumb and inefficient he was because he'd sent a check belonging in the remittance of the State Bank of Oakland, Kansas, to Ogden, Utah. He would always remember that trivial mistake when that clerk asked for a raise.[12]

Moore checked upon Truman in a note of October 13, 1903, asking the chief clerk, who bore the Dickensian name of A. D. Flintom: "Report to me on H. S. Truman. What he is doing, how he is doing it and all about him." Fortunately, Flintom espied

> [a]n exceptionally bright young man [who] is keeping the work up in the vault better than it has ever been kept. He is a willing worker, almost always here and tries hard to please everybody. We never had a boy in the vault like him before. He watches everything very closely and by his watchfulness, detects many errors which a careless boy would let slip through. His appearance is good and his habits and character are of the best.[13]

Moore made him the personal filing clerk to the cashier and to the bank's owner and president, Dr. William S. Woods. The latter was a formidable character: he had been a country doctor in Fulton, Missouri, but discovered a truth later known to many physicians, that the distance between medicine and banking is not far. He owned several banks, among them the Clay County State Bank at Excelsior Springs and the Woods and Ruby Bank at Golden, Colorado, and he managed many other enterprises. He gave his name ("against his protest") to William Woods College in Fulton, an institution for young women, suitably adjacent to Westminster College for young men in the same town. All this he did for reasons best known to himself. According to a contemporary biographical sketch, which he almost certainly saw in advance and probably paid for, he was "imbued with the spirit which is becoming more and more prevalent," the spirit that "recognizes individual obligations and responsibilities proportionate to one's powers and opportunities."[14] Woods used his powers to seize opportunities.

After nearly a year, by September 28, 1904, Moore and Woods were quite pleased with their assistant. According to Flintom,

> Trueman [*sic*] has charge of the filing vault and handles the work of filing the bank's correspondence and cancelled checks in a much better manner than it has ever been handled. He is a young man of excellent character and good habits and always at his post of duty and his work is always up. He is very accurate in the filing of letters and the boy is very ambitious and tries hard to please everybody he comes in contact with. I do not know of a better young man in the bank than Trueman.[15]

Harry's brother worked in the same bank, but Vivian turned out poorly as a banker—he did not have the stuff. Flintom reported him of a peculiar disposition and without ambition. On October 19, 1903, he refused to go to work unless the bank raised his salary, and when officials refused he left, although two days later he asked for and received reinstatement. He seemed all right as a collector, but Flintom informed Moore on July 27, 1904, that he was ill a good deal of the time and wrote a poor hand: "He is a willing worker but possessed of very little ability and will never amount to much as a bank clerk. He is a very different boy from his brother who runs our filing vault." Sometime after this appraisal Vivian quit; he presumably went with his parents to Clinton. He came back to work on March 1, 1907, but soon said he would quit April 15 because he was going out of town; he did not say where (it must have been the Grandview farm, to which by that time his parents and Harry had gone).[16]

Long before Vivian quit the second time, Truman had left for a rival bank, the Union National. When he became Woods's assistant he had received a raise from thirty-five to forty dollars a month, but raises were "hard to get and if a man got an additional five dollars on his monthly pay he was a go-getter, because he'd outtalked the bawler-out and taken something from the tightest-wad bank president on record."[17] The Union National had offered sixty dollars a month, an increase Moore refused to meet. Before long the Union was paying a hundred, an impressive sum. At the Union he no longer associated with a bank vice president and president, an honor, to be sure, that he considered hardly worth five dollars a month—but then he did not have to go downstairs to a zoo, either. He became a blotter clerk, a teller's assistant: while the teller waited on customers, the blotter clerk recorded the give-and-take. He and his partner handled as much as a million dollars a day. He did this work for a year or so until he gave it up, to return to the farm.

2

The years in Kansas City marked a sort of financial education, in that Truman learned to keep accounts—much more so than he had learned from L. J. Smith—but, in another sense, they served as a more general education in the ways of city life. While a child on the farm and during the years in Independence beginning in 1890, he had known so little about the city. His mother took him there on occasion, and he went by himself while studying at Spalding's, but these experiences were transitory, for he returned to Independence every evening. Working for the banks, making his own money, he could concentrate on his instruction in city ways.

In Kansas City everything was becoming bigger. In times not long distant, "K.C." had been a small locality: just a few houses, warehouses, and merchandise stores, alongside the welcoming Gilliss House, all on a bluff. People tended to poke fun at it as a jumping-off place for the Western trails, like Independence. But a statesman like Senator Thomas Hart Benton knew better: "There, gentlemen," he said, "where the rocky bluff meets and turns aside the sweeping current of this mighty river: here, where the Missouri, after pursuing her southward course for nearly 2,000 miles, turns eastward to meet the Mississippi, a large commercial and manufacturing community will congregate, and less than a generation will see a great city on these hills." As the statesman predicted, after the Civil War the city grew tremendously, reaching 32,260 inhabitants in 1870. In 1906 it boasted 165,000, and its population doubled in a generation. Given its location at the confluence of the Kansas and Missouri rivers, also that it was the largest city between St. Louis and San Francisco, it was an obvious place for railroads, which came out to the city from the East and departed in all directions into an area "greater than all of Europe outside of Russia, containing 60 per cent of the area of the United States, but only 14.7 per cent of its population." Kansas City was the second largest railway center of America. Of 57,000 miles of track laid in the United States in 1903, 30 percent was laid in Oklahoma, Indian Territory, Texas, and Missouri, and all this new land paid tribute to Kansas City merchants and manufacturers. Thirty-nine lines ran into Kansas City, covering a total of 55,000 miles, nearly one-fourth of the United States, and traversing thirty-one states and territories. It was possible to reach the capitals of sixteen states and three territories from Kansas City without a change of cars. In Truman's time a new railroad enterprise "rapidly reaching consummation" was the Kansas City, Mexico and Orient. This project, 1,629 miles long, was the most important railroad venture undertaken in the United States for years.[18]

All this says nothing of the buildings then under construction within the great city. During Truman's last year there, 1906, three skyscrapers were rising, one as high as seventeen stories ("fifteen being above street level").[19] Compared to the new buildings, the eleven-story New York Life Building—a Romanesque concoction with a gaudy central tower completed in 1890, home to Spalding's Commercial College—looked like a hand-me-down. The skyscrapers were completed in 1907 at a combined cost of $4 million and boasted the latest in everything: elevators without peer, fireproofing perfectly safe, cleaning equipment fully automatic—this last item featured electrically driven vacuum tubes that, according to advertisement, pulled dust and germs out of every corner.

In such a metropolis the conveniences of city life were much in evidence. A myriad of wires reached from building to building, some on poles, most strung to the masonry, as if giant spiders had been at work; some of the wires carried electricity, and many carried the spoken word, as Kansas City was served by two telephone systems, the Bell and the Home, the latter the result of an antitrust ruling. By Truman's time each telephone system enrolled twenty thousand subscribers, and to the confusion of everyone neither cooperated with the other: this meant two kinds of pay phones, two telephone books, two phones in some houses. The city's streets were well paved, with asphalt surfacing totaling 165.32 miles by 1907 and paving of every sort equaling 240.65 miles. A few horseless carriages traversed the pavement, but traffic was composed mostly of horses and delivery wagons and buggies. In the middle of streets in the business district passed the cars of the Kansas City Metropolitan Street Railway, which operated six hundred streetcars over 223 miles of single track. In the twelve months ending May 31, 1907, the Metropolitan's streetcars carried 136 million people. Downtown Ninth Street was doubletracked, Main northbound, Delaware southbound. Ninth Street cars were red, Independence Avenue cars green. Ninth Street cars made connection with the Dummy Line. For country people new to the city, it was very confusing. A crossing watchman once pulled Truman's mother back to the curb at a dangerous place, probably on Ninth Street, and when she turned on him to tell him off said, "Only saving your life, madam, only saving your life." He had pulled her back in time to miss a westbound car, when she and her son wanted to go east.[20]

People crowded the sidewalks night and day, and for their enlightenment merchants filled the space overhead with a canopy of signboards and other advertisements, including the new electric signs and clocks on pedestals near the curbs announcing jewelers' businesses. Calling, shouting, and the general hubbub of humanity made the city a babel, although linguistically it was hardly that, for Kansas City was only 10 percent foreign-born. A similar percentage of Kansas Citians were blacks.

What to do in the city? The question had many answers. It was always possible to exchange money, probably losing it. An advertisement related "DERBY TURF EXCHANGE. No. 8 and 10 Ewing Street, Kansas City, Kansas. Book-betting on all racing throughout the country. Take 'L' cars to state line and walk one block west. Telephone 436 Hickory."[21] This sort of betting probably was illegal on the Missouri side. Vice of other sorts was available in a city that later, in the 1920s and 1930s, was next to New Orleans the most wide-open metropolis in the country. Truman did not go for either of the above money-losing ventures, but he took pleasure in the theater. In an era when motion pictures were in their infancy and vaudeville reigned, he seems to have seen every stage show that came to Kansas City. The business district offered several theaters; his favorites were the Orpheum on West Ninth and the Grand at Seventh and Walnut—Saturday afternoons he ushered at the Grand.[22] There he saw a galaxy of stars, such as the minstrels Primrose and Dockstader, together with Williams and Walker, Chauncey Alcott, Eddie Foy, Chick Sale, and "The Four Cohans," including George M.

Until the Shubert opened in 1906, the principal legitimate theater was the Willis Wood, with its ornate columns and arches topped by what might have been a wedding cake, out of which sprang a circular tower. The theater's founder is not to be confused with Dr. Woods of the Commerce Bank; Colonel Wood had been a wholesale dry-goods magnate in St. Joseph. At the Willis Wood, Truman saw Richard Mansfield in *Dr. Jekyll and Mr. Hyde*—it was so scary that he was afraid to go home afterward. He also saw Walker Whiteside in *Richard III* and Henry Irving and Ellen Terry in *The Merchant of Venice, Julius Caesar,* and *Hamlet.*

At Convention Hall, the cavernous structure erected in 1900 for the Democratic national convention, he heard piano recitals. It was the city's principal concert hall until the opening of the Shubert. The hall had a history known to everyone in Kansas City. An earlier hall had opened in 1899, suitably with a concert by John Philip Sousa and band, but a fire broke out on April 4 of the next year and destroyed it. The city fathers had lured the Democratic national convention of that year on a promise of availability of a great hall, and Kansas Citians took the fire as a challenge and raised a new hall within weeks, in time for the convention, which opened July 4. The "pep and sense" with which people did things in Kansas City was known as "the Kansas City spirit."[23] It was in the new building that Truman served as a page and heard William Jennings Bryan speak. The new hall accommodated fifteen thousand people, and during the convention it was said it managed thirty thousand. Through ingenious rearrangement it could reduce seating to as few as eighteen hundred. The acoustics were excellent, and Paderewski played to six thousand there, his largest audience ever. Here Truman heard all the great romantic pianists, including Moriz Rosenthal, Augusta Kotlow, and "the greatest of them all," Lhévinne, who played the Chopin he so admired.[24] When he became president he met Lhévinne's widow, Rosa, herself a great pianist (and teacher of Van Cliburn and John Browning), and afterward wrote her that he considered her husband the best of all the pianists who passed through Kansas City.

The Metropolitan Opera came to Kansas City, but it did not touch the young Truman, who professed to be unmoved, although he said he tried to find out why music lovers admired opera. To make up his mind he heard *Parsifal*, which was enough to overwhelm anyone's patience, and also *Lohengrin, Pagliacci, Les Huguenots*, and *Cavalleria Rusticana*. A few years later he would write Bess:

> I have some cousins in Kansas City who affect intellect. They once persuaded me to go to a season of Grand Opera with them. . . . Well I haven't recovered from the siege of Grand Opera yet. Perhaps if they had given me small doses I might have been trained, because I do love music. I can even appreciate Chopin when he is played on the piano. But when it comes to a lot of would-be actors and actresses running around over the stage and spouting song and hugging and killing each other promiscuously, why I had rather go to the Orpheum.[25]

The only opera he liked was light opera. He admired *Pinafore*, the parodies of which were not far out of date when he sat in Kansas City audiences.

In 1904, Truman's father traded the Park Avenue house for an eighty-acre farm in Henry County, his parents and Mary Jane moved to Clinton (they lived in town and John Truman commuted to "the eighty"), and Harry roomed for a while at Aunt Emma's house, at 2650 East Twenty-ninth. While there he seems to have played an elaborate trick on his roommate, the same Ed Green who had gotten him the job at the Commerce; he perhaps did it to get even with someone who had introduced him to Flintom, Moore, and Dr. Woods. He included his cousin Fred Colgan in the trick for some good if now forgotten reason. Ed and Fred had gone fishing in the Big Blue River, and were foolish enough to admit they had placed a message in a pop bottle addressed to a nameless girl, telling her all about what promising young men they were—handsome young businessmen, fairly perishing for love—and asking if she wouldn't write back. The bottle floated lazily down the Blue toward the Missouri, and the boys speculated that it might reach the Mississippi, maybe the Gulf, perhaps Brazil. Ten days later a letter arrived postmarked Greenville, Mississippi, sent by an eighteen-year-old girl who lived on a big plantation in a house with tall, white pillars. Her mother, she told them, would have fits if she knew she was writing a couple of boys she had never been introduced to, but they sounded so attractive and would they please write and tell her about Kansas City and much, much more about themselves? Answering at once, the boys told her plenty, and the correspondence went on and on. At last she wrote and said she planned to come to Independence. The boys received another note: she had arrived, unpacked, pressed her summer things, and was about to leave her aunt's household to meet her correspondents when a plague of scarlet fever descended and quarantined her; she hoped the paper she wrote on would not carry the disease, and asked for more letters to comfort her. For Ed and Fred the denouement then was disconcerting: one evening at the Colgan house Harry's cousin Mary led a crowd of young people into the dining room, where on the table lay a pile of letters sent by Ed and Fred to the Greenville princess; to the delight of the crowd, Mary began to read them. Harry Truman was the princess, and he had dictated the letters to Mary, who sent them to a Greenville friend to remail.[26]

Harry also lived in a rooming house on 1314 Troost kept by a Mrs. Trow, with roomers two to a room and two meals a day, room and board costing five dollars a week. He usually bought a ten-cent box lunch at a place on East Eighth Street and spent the noon hour eating it in a five-cent picture show. At Mrs. Trow's lived a young bank messenger named Arthur Eisenhower, older brother of Dwight D. The lad from Abilene knew nothing of city life and "didn't know how to turn on a gas jet when he came to Kansas City—asked old Mrs. Trow our boarding housekeeper for a coal oil lamp." Writing of Arthur to his daughter, Margaret, in 1944, when Arthur Eisenhower's brother had become famous, Senator Truman explained, "But that's not to his discredit."[27]

In the Kansas City years Truman does not appear to have read books or in any way continued his high school interest in learning about great figures, military and political, of the past. Yet another question on the Commerce Bank application of 1903 inquired, "In what forms of recreation or amusement do you find pleasure?" Answer: "theaters and reading." But he seems to have had little time for the latter. In 1949, nearly half a century later, he told Jonathan Daniels that when he first lived in the city with his family they collected dimes and placed them in the tray of an old trunk, that it was surprising how fast the dimes accumulated, and this allowed the family to buy the Book Lover's Edition of Shakespeare, published in 1901. At the time of the Daniels interview, Truman had the Shakespeare books in their red bindings in Blair House, where he was living while the White House was undergoing renovation. The interviewer furtively looked at the set and observed to himself, "They don't look like they have been much used."[28]

In the bank years the future president revealed almost no interest in politics. His only description of a political event was an occasion in 1903 when Theodore Roosevelt came to Kansas City. Having become president after McKinley's assassination, "T. R." was about to seek election in his own right and was showing himself around the country. Truman was working at the Commerce, and together with "half a dozen of us little clerks in the zoo" ran the block from Tenth and Walnut to the corner of Tenth and Main. He was so winded that he could hardly breathe, all to see what a president of the United States looked like. Roosevelt, he reported, made a good speech; he had a high tenor voice and it carried well. But "nobody went down there to hear him speak; they wanted to see him grin and show his teeth, which he did." And Truman was disappointed to discover not a tall, impressive-looking man, only a short, middle-aged man, who appeared to be about five feet, six inches tall. He spoke from the back of a car, and he had a cushion in the bottom so he could stand on it and look taller.[29]

The youthful Truman showed continuing interest in the military, and in 1905 when he was twenty-one years old he enlisted in the Missouri National Guard. A Kansas City acquaintance, George R. Collins, organized a company of light artillery that year, Battery B (Battery A was in St. Louis, Battery C would be organized in Independence), and the youth signed up for three years on Flag Day, June 14; upon expiration of his term in 1908, he signed for another three years. In joining he acted against the wishes of his mother and father. In those days the legal date for coming of age was twenty-one, and his parents refused their consent before that time. The refusal doubtless derived from their southern sympathies, which on Truman's mother's side came from Grandmother Young. Right after he joined he dressed in his new uniform— blue, with red stripes down the trouser legs, red piping on the cuffs, and a red fourragère near the shoulder—and had his photograph taken. The photographer took a standing portrait with hat and a sitting one without. Afterward, Harry went to the farm to show himself to Uncle Harrison and his grandmother, which was a mistake—the grandmother took one look at him and, as he remembered, he knew he "was going to catch it." She said, "Harry, this is the first time since 1863 that a blue uniform has been in this house. Don't bring it here again."[30]

The Guard had several advantages, of which he was doubtless aware. For one, it was a way to meet people; the battery was full of bank clerks and salesmen and lawyers. Too, it was an outlet for the patriotism of the time, not long after the Spanish-American War and the Filipino insurrection, the taking of the Panama Canal Zone, and amid all the talk about protecting the Caribbean nations or those in Central America, perhaps South America (fortunately, the American nation never undertook this last task). One opportunity that does not seem to have entered his consciousness was the chance for leadership, although a year after signing up he was advanced to the rank of corporal, a rank he later said he appreciated more than all the promotions he received thereafter, even the presidency of the United States.

Every summer the battery spent a week in camp, and that was fun: in 1906 it was held at Camp DeArmond near Cape Girardeau, another year at St. Joseph, another at Fort Riley in central Kansas, another at Sparta, Wisconsin. The DeArmond trip involved a long train ride to St. Louis and a steamboat cruise down to camp. Harry remembered that some boys were inside the boat when it left St. Louis and first headed upstream and never did know it turned, so that "One of our good fellows shut his eyes when the boat went into Cape Girardeau and when it docked he had his directions straight."[31] At St. Joseph the weather was bad—it rained all the time, and lightning struck the brigade headquarters tent and killed a sergeant and private. But the principal diversion that year was for the men to dig holes in front of their tents, where the water was three feet deep (Truman claimed), and lure sergeants and second lieutenants into them. At Fort Riley the battery fired the army's three-inch artillery piece, and an inexperienced soldier left one of his fingers in the breechblock.

After only a year in the Guard, in 1906, the Kansas City experience came to an end. In the previous year the Grand River near Clinton had flooded and washed out his parents' corn crop. Grandmother Young asked them to go back to her place, for John Truman needed a farm and she was about to lose her farmer, Harrison, who wanted to move to Kansas City. Harry took his grandmother's proposition to Clinton and urged his parents to accept it, and a year later he too returned to the Grandview farm.

One might ask what Harry Truman's years in the metropolis added to, other than providing some of the training he later considered important for a career in politics. They did not last, and only part of the time was he on his own. The bank work, we may be certain, did not fascinate him, for during his leisure hours in evenings and on weekends he never did anything that related to banking. He could have returned to Spalding's and studied more accounting, but the thought never entered his mind, or if it did he never told anyone. The minute he walked out the doors of the banks, it was not a question of how to be a better banker but how to have a good time. Probably there was some maturing involved, being away from the family, although it is difficult to know—when the opportunity appeared to return to the farm, to be again with the family, he took it without question. The Kansas City chapter, one can only say, began and ended in an accidental way, and anything more one attempts to draw out of it can only be imagination. This particular chapter in Harry S. Truman's life is there—it happened, it took place—but it disappeared without a great deal of meaning, contrary to what most of us think chapters in our lives ought to do.

Chapter Three

The Farm

The Young farm, as it was known in Grandmother Young's lifetime, afterward the Truman farm, was an impressive place. The entrance showed the size of the establishment. The farm lay along a county road next to a little cemetery, which Truman often described to visitors so they might identify the farm ("that is where you get off").[1] A visitor turned at right angles from the road and up a long lane lined with four rows of big maples. Grandfather Young and Harry's mother had planted those trees after the Civil War. At the end of the lane stood the house. A couple of hundred feet behind was the barn, a sloped-roof affair, inside of which were stalls for the horses, mules, and cows. Other buildings lay behind, including a smaller hay barn. The farm looked like a big farm ought to look. The son of a neighbor liked to sit out on the back porch of his house during evenings and look at the Young farm and pastureland, which to him was a beautiful sight. Recently, two photographs have turned up of the Young farm in its heyday, when the Trumans were there before World War I. They show rural beauty of a sort one rarely sees now, a family farm that stretched out in accord with the size of surrounding fields, a place to contemplate. The photograph taken in summer has the dull, cloudless sky of turn-of-the-century pictures, but displays the farm's sweeping proportions. The winter photo reveals the loneliness, the isolation, and the independence of the farm.

During Grandfather Young's time the farmhouse at the end of the lane was a virtual mansion, built in 1867 or 1868. This was the house in which the Trumans had lived, along with the grandparents, before going to Independence in 1890. It burned a year after the grandfather's death, in 1893. Grandmother Young replaced it with a much smaller place, intending it as a tenant house. She never built another big house. Erected on the same foundation as its predecessor, this smaller house was the place that became so familiar to Harry Truman when the family returned to help the grandmother. Like the former house, albeit on a much smaller scale, the new one had two rooms in front, living room and parlor, in accord with custom of the time. In back of them was a small dining room, and in back of it a narrow kitchen. The latter had an outside screened porch, quite small compared to the extended porches of the burned house. Separating parlor and living room was a stairway that took residents to bedrooms over each. Harry Truman's mother and sister had the bedrooms. Behind was a small room with a sloped ceiling—Harry's bedroom. Like the little house in Lamar, the Grandview farmhouse was not "modern"; there was no running water. Outside the porch, convenient to the kitchen, was a well with a wooden frame over it, wheel at the top, around which stretched the rope on which one pulled to raise the bucket below.

But what a comedown it must have been for Harry Truman to go back to the farm after having lived in Kansas City, to reduce his circumstances to a farm, even one like the Young farm! He had been happy in the city, not with the bank work but with the wonderful opportunities for entertainment and fun in evenings and on weekends. It was exhilarating to live in the midst of the fast-moving metropolis, at the very time it was growing in an almost astonishing manner—population increasing, skyscrapers rising, new theaters opening.

Whatever the young man's feelings he kept them to himself. He did say years later that when he went to the farm his friends thought he would stay a week, a month, no more than a year. For whatever their surprise was worth, he fooled them. He stayed eleven years. His father and mother and Mary Jane moved from Clinton in 1905; Harry quit the bank and went out late the next year; Vivian meanwhile came from Kansas City. Vivian married in 1911 and left for a farm of his own. Harry Truman farmed with his father for a while, until the elder Truman died in 1914 after lifting a huge boulder in his role as township road overseer; the exertion aggravated a hernia, and an operation failed. Harry was sitting up with him one evening, and nodded off, and when he awoke his father was dead. Thereafter he did the farming himself, together with one or two hired men, with more helpers at busy times, until he went into military service in 1917.

1

It is possible that when Harry Truman went to the farm he decided he would do the work as well as he could, since he had to be there. He may have thought that if he tried to do it well he would enjoy it more. His father was present for eight of his eleven years on the farm, and John Truman was a perfectionist, intolerant of sloppy work from anyone, especially one of his sons. There also was something about Harry that became thoroughly evident in later years, something that prompted him to do his best: he too was a perfectionist.

Whatever the reason, he tried to do things on the farm as well as he could. He was unsatisfied with ordinary procedures if they produced ordinary results. His farm contemporaries noticed this. George Arington, who lived on an adjoining place and whose sons were about Truman's age, said, "He spent every spare moment either readin' or figurin'." He built the first derrick and swing in his section of the country for stacking hay. After he stacked the first cutting, he sometimes covered it with boards for protection against the weather, and when the second cutting was ready, he removed the covering and put the hay on top of the first cutting. The veterinarian Ed Young, who did Truman's animal work from 1912 to 1917, said, "Harry was always bustling around getting things done. I remember once when the Trumans were putting out a big corn crop, of seeing three corn planters running. A few days later I went by and was surprised to see the same three teams cultivating the corn before it was up. That was something new to me but it worked, as it gave Harry a head start on the weeds."[2]

It was said of him that he was one of the "weed-fightin'-est" farmers around; when he came into town and bought additional hoes, that meant he had rounded up some extra help to cut cockleburs and thistles. Twice a year he moved his fencerows, so he could rid them of weeds and waste.

He practiced careful rotation of crops. In a speech many years later he related that he had studied soil improvement and farm management. After sowing wheat on a field in September, he planted clover on the same field the next spring. When the wheat was ready in July, it was cut and shocked. In the fall he would cut a crop of stubble and clover. The next year he would have a fine crop of hay and also harvest a crop of clover seed. He broke up the clover field in the fall and planted corn the next spring. When he had cut corn he used the stalk field as pasture all winter and then cut up the stalks and sowed oats; after a fall plowing, he would sow wheat again. It took five years to make the complete rotation—wheat, clover, corn, oats, wheat.[3]

Soon after moving to the farm, Truman and his father bought a manure spreader from a company in Waterloo, Iowa, and used it on the clover fields. Nearly every family in Grandview, a town of three hundred people, kept a cow or two and a horse, and the Trumans picked up manure from village barns and stables to spread on the clover.

The result of rotation and manure was a marked increase in crop yield. The proud farmer wrote that wheat went from thirteen to nineteen bushels per acre, oats from eight to fifty, corn from thirty-five to seventy. In addition, the clover fields produced two excellent hay crops and at least one seed crop.

On American farms at the turn of the century, as in farm eras before and since, everything began with the plowing. The Trumans first used a walking plow but eventually resorted to a gang plow made by the Emerson Plow Company: two twelve-inch moldboards on a three-wheeled frame. Pulled by four horses or mules, or two of each, it turned over a two-foot furrow. If a farmer could get an early start, he could break up five or six acres in a day— not an eight-hour day, Harry liked to add, but a ten- or twelve-hour day. In spring when the weather was cool and he could keep teams moving longer without resting them, he needed less time. The new plow was far more efficient than a walking plow. Moreover, riding a plow all day, day after day, gave opportunity to think: "I've settled all the ills of mankind in one way and another while riding along," he said.[4]

Once ground was ready he "put in" wheat, oats, and corn. For the first two he used a twelve-disk drill that covered eight feet and had a marker so no places would be skipped. Once in a while the wind blew, and in a letter to Bess (he commenced an active courtship of his future wife in 1910, and his letters from the farm to Bess in Independence are highly descriptive of what he was doing) he used a little farm exaggeration. He told her that one day when putting in oats he had to tie himself to the drill to keep from being blown into the Missouri River; every time an oat came out of the drill it went five miles before touching the ground. Corn planting took equal attention. In those days farmers planted in hills and checkrowed each hill an exact number of inches from the next, so they could cultivate horizontally and vertically. Harry Truman's mother was proud of the way her son could lay out a corn row. She was supposed to have said he could plow as straight a furrow as any man in Jackson County, but she was speaking of his corn rows.

Harvesting presented different problems. For wheat and oats, the unreliability of binders was one. The binders were an enormous improvement over cradles—no farmer wanted to return to cradles, as they meant backbreaking, slow work—but the machines were frequently cantankerous. "I have been working over an old binder," Truman wrote Bess in July 1912. "My hands and face and my clothes are as black as the ace of spades—blacker, because the ace has a white background. . . . I hate the job I have before me. If the machine goes well, it is well; if not, it is a word rhyming with well (?) literally."[5]

Once when in trouble with a binder Truman went to a friendly old blacksmith named George Plummer, who came out to the farm and followed the machine around a wheat field, a walk of a mile and a half, trying to get the tying mechanism to work. The later president never forgot the result, although for the blacksmith it was a rueful experience. The day was hot, "102 degrees in the shade and no shade," and when Plummer came to the starting corner he was, of course, thirsty. "He rushed to the corner shock of wheat and grabbed the first jug he came to. It contained lubricating oil instead of water. He took a long gulp and then he lost his lunch, dinner, breakfast, and the supper of the night before."[6]

Threshing in the old days was not at all like what it became after the invention of combines. In the village of Grandview a man named Leslie C. Hall owned two or three steam threshing machines, and during threshing time he took them from farm to farm. For each machine local farmers organized rings, working for each other, prorating work if acreage varied. The system operated rather well, but it had its problems, and Truman almost hated to see the great lumbering machine arrive at the farm. One time when the thresher came up the lane, his first thought was that, thank goodness, it was arriving after supper. Otherwise the Trumans (Harry and Mary, not their mother) would have had to feed all the ravenous visitors. They did have to put the threshers up for the night. As Harry described it, "We will have men and boys roosting from cellar to roof (we have no attic) and over the front yard too." The next day would come the threshing and the inevitable accidents:

> Just as we get to going and the thing begins to behave, why some pinhead with a young team will run into the belt and throw it or dislocate some of the innards of the thresher itself by backing into it. Both happened today. I didn't happen to be the pinhead either time. If that doesn't happen, some gink who is tired will throw a half-dozen bundles in the seemingly insatiable maw and choke her down. Then it's time for the owner to cuss and the engine to buck and snort. Any blockhead can choke a machine, but it takes a smart man to feed it all it'll eat and still go at a very rapid gait. I am not one of them.[7]

Harvesting corn was an almost equally complex task. Before getting the mechanical cutter into the field, it was necessary to cut two rows by hand to make room for the horse and machine. Writing one evening, Harry told Bess he had scratched his face badly during the chore. He then tied skeleton shocks for the hired hands to fill, and a corn blade got in his eye; it did not hurt at first but soon began to smart. A blade, he wrote, was like a razor—men who shocked corn wore gloves and scarves.[8]

After this he shelled the corn, a dirty job. One Saturday he worked all day and "got my eyes so full of dust that I could almost scoop it out." The next day his eyes looked like those of a drunk. "It is a job invented by Satan himself. Dante sure left something from the tenth circle when he failed to say that the inhabitants of that dire place shucked shock corn."[9]

Hay, a crop that was not nearly as profitable as wheat, oats, and corn, was necessary to feed animals in winter and to rest the land. Hay, like other crops, had its special difficulties. It required concentration and very hard work. To rake it Truman hitched his team behind the rake, not in front—an awkward arrangement. "If you desire to go to the right, it is necessary to make the left-hand horse move and the right one stand still. It works like the tiller on a boat—wrong end to. Sometimes you aim for a pile of hay and get one some distance away. I have arrived at the stage where I can generally go where I'm looking." Afterward came stacking, a devilish job. "You've no idea what a job it is to put up a stack unless you do it once."[10] The first day his father permitted him to do it, the son calculated he walked thirty-five or forty miles around a stack thirty feet in diameter. It was necessary to keep tramping because if one did not, the stack would settle in an irregular manner and the hay spoil when water got inside. Nor was that all: after the first stack there were ten or twelve more, day after hot day.

The worst task with hay was loading bales into a railroad car. He believed it the hottest job of any on the farm or anywhere else, save that of shoveling coal for His Majesty—that is, the devil. He and one of the hired hands finally got 289 bales, he said, each weighing eighty-five pounds, into a car at 7:30 P.M.

So much for the tasks. One turns, secondly, to the subject of farm animals—in Truman's case, the most important were the teams of horses and mules that pulled the wagons and machinery. In 1919, two years after he left the farm, Missouri farms boasted more than one million horses and mules. The state's farmers were running only seventy-two hundred light tractors, the sort the Trumans could have used; light tractors had not appeared until 1911, and for a while dealers sold only a few.

In the era of horse and mule power, driving teams of either variety was about the same; the only difference was that horses were not as smart as mules—one had to watch horses to see that they did not eat while hot or drink too much water. Harry Truman remembered with affection the farm's mules—sixteen hands high, weighing fifteen or sixteen hundred pounds. They understood the rules about eating and drinking: "[T]urn them loose in the lots where the corn is in full sight and the water's plenty and they won't drink too much and won't eat too much. They have really about, or maybe more, sense than a man who's trying to take care of them."[11] Mules, indeed, had many useful virtues. A joke seems to have circulated when Missouri was being settled for farming that Missourians had a choice between employing mules or Swedes, and they chose mules because they were smarter than Swedes.

The principal problem with animal power was dealing with the different personalities of animals on a team. Truman was much bothered by the four horses he had to drive, for they were no team at all. He considered himself a horse psychologist, and yet it was all he could do to handle William, Samuel, Jane, and X (a bronco). William, known in the field as Bill, was an ex-buggy horse who hated work. His master found himself shouting at Bill in his sleep, holloing, "Bill, Bill, go on!" Sometimes he was shouting the same message to Sam, a large ex-dray horse who never hurried unless poked with a stick or inspired by a baling-wire whip. Jane, the lady, always behaved. Then there was the bronco, X, who always sought to arrive at the other end of the field in the shortest time.

It was necessary to feed the horses and mules, morning and night, a chore Truman's father left to Harry; John Truman usually did the milking. To do the feeding Harry had to get up every morning at five o'clock. He did not mind after he went outside, as for the most part—he wrote to Bess in November 1911—it was not too cold; but he found it "awful" to start.[12]

Cows were attractive to farmers in western Missouri because they brought good prices in Kansas City. The metropolis had doubled in population from 1900 to 1920, reaching 235,000 in the latter year, and such a population could consume a great deal of beef. Moreover, railroads had linked the city to the East Coast, where big steel refrigerator ships could carry Missouri beef overseas. Cattle, together with pigs, were an economical way of disposing of the corn crop. In the Middle West of that time, less than one-fifth of the crop was shipped out of the county of origin. According to *Wallaces' Farmer*, in 1913, 90 percent of the corn crop should never leave the farm on which it was grown. A farmer was able to "condense" his freight charges by feeding cattle. Every steer could carry one hundred bushels.

But apart from their ability to bring good prices and to carry corn, cows (so far as Truman was concerned) had a drawback—they were uninteresting animals, not at all like horses or mules. Cows, he wrote to Bess, lacked attractive personalities. And sometimes they were just plain malevolent. When it was possible to get them fodder without any trouble, they would not look at it. When it was hard to get, in winter, they developed insatiable appetites. "I guess I'll have to stay home tomorrow," Truman wrote, "and dig out a load of fodder for the benefit of a lot of beastly old cows." Their perversity appeared when one tried to milk them. One cow let Harry Truman milk her without any trouble: "She is the old standby and the old rip gives about a bushel at a milking." Her name was Nellie Bly, and he called her Purple after the poem by Gelett Burgess:

> I never saw a Purple Cow
> I never hope to see one;
> But I can tell you, anyhow,
> I'd rather see than be one.

The others had to be milked after their calves had obtained a share, and one had to be approached in a gentle and smiling mood: "Whoa, you nice cow. That's a nice cow." After the rope landed it was, "Now get away you blankety-blank speckled rip. Let's see you chase around the lot now."[13]

Cows almost became the bane of Harry Truman's existence. One day a man came to the house and wanted to buy a Truman cow for $42.50 and have the animal delivered to Grandview. Father and son spent a half hour chasing the cow and then decided to weigh it to see if the price was right. They attached it to the rear of a wagon and dragged it on the scales; it weighed 930 pounds and would bring $54.00 in Kansas City. To the son's disgust, John Truman decided that ten dollars was too much of a present for the buyer and turned the cow loose. It reminded Harry of Uncle Harrison's description of two yoke of cattle. Of the first yoke, one was named Episcopalian because it wouldn't eat at the proper time and tried to prevent the others from eating; its partner was named Catholic because it wanted all the food. Of the second yoke, one was Methodist, always battling; the other was Baptist, because it wanted to run and jump into every hole of water. Harry said the cow his father turned loose was of the Catholic persuasion.

Truman told Bess he was no gentleman farmer, and that if any of his cows got funny they would get a board instead of seeing his hat come off. But that was easier said than done. In the spring of 1913 he was setting fence posts when a big malevolent calf, under direct order from His Majesty, broke Harry's leg. He had not been too diplomatic with this calf, had seized the tail of the three-hundred-pound beast, "and made a wild grab for his ear in order to guide him around properly when he stuck his head between my legs, backed me into the center of the lot, and when I went to get off threw me over his head with a buck and a bawl and went off seemingly satisfied, I guess, for I didn't look." For weeks Harry's leg was in a cast, and he had to remain in bed or hobble around. During that time he contemplated the calf "gracing a platter," and John Truman did put a chain on the animal.[14]

After Harry's accident one of the hired men said the Truman place was hoodooed because people kept breaking their legs there. John Truman had been bridling a mule, and the mule jerked a timber loose and broke his leg. A neighbor woman, Mrs. Hagney, was driving a buggy along the county road; when she came in front of the Truman farm, her horse turned the buggy over, breaking *her* leg.

The Trumans raised Shorthorns and registered some of them. At the time John Truman died in 1914, they had begun to stock the farm with Black Angus. Mary Jane believed her brother sold them to pay the expenses connected with their father's death. One suspects he sold them just to get rid of them.

The farm's pigs were certainly not Harry Truman's favorites either. There was always something to do with or to them, such as putting rings in their noses:

> I have been to the lot and put about a hundred rings in half as many hogs' noses. You really haven't any idea what a soul-stirring job it is, especially on a day when the mud is knee deep and about the consistency of cake dough. Every hog's voice is pitched in a different key and about time you get used to a squeal pitched in G minor that hog has to be loosed and the next one is in A flat. This makes a violent discord and is very hard on the nerves of a high-strung person. It is very much harder on the hogs' nerves. We have a patent shoot (chute maybe) which takes Mr. Hog right behind the ears and he has to stand and let his nose be bejeweled to any extent the ringer sees fit. I don't like to do it, but when a nice bluegrass pasture is at stake I'd carve the whole hog tribe to small bits rather than see it ruined. Besides it only hurts them for about an hour and about one in every three loses his rings inside of a week and has to endure the agony over again.[15]

Like cows, pigs were perverse animals. A pig's head was always turned the wrong way; this was a hard and fast rule. One time Truman had to load twenty-nine pigs and managed to get fifteen into the barn. He then put corn in the barn to attract the others. All the rest went in except an "extra smart one," which grabbed an ear and ran out between Truman's legs before he could shut the door. He fell down, and all the pigs ran out. When, however, the barn door was open and he did not want them in there, every pig would go right in.[16]

Frequently hogs became ill from cholera, a dread disease that decimated— and in epidemic form could wipe out—the animals. For many years it ran rampant through the Middle West. As late as 1913, 10 percent of American hogs died from cholera; prior to about 1915 heavy losses from epidemics made it exceedingly speculative to raise hogs in large numbers. An epidemic struck Truman's hogs in 1912, and they began to die. He wrote Bess that his hogs had a perfect right to "kick the bucket," but ought to allow some packinghouse to do the honors. Of ninety hogs he managed to send thirteen to market; the rest took ill and died one after the other, until twelve remained. In accord with the law he had to burn or bury the carcasses within a given radius of the place of death. When the dozen had departed, he wrote, and he had performed "the last sad rites" over their burial, he hoped that as a result of his "dumping the whole works into one hole and one ceremony" the hog population would be zero.[17] This experience, he believed, beat Mark Twain's prescription for the quickest way to pass from affluence to poverty: Twain had thought politics was the quickest, but Truman said it was hogs.

For a quarter of a century veterinarians searched for the causative agent of hog cholera, but they did not find it until 1906; U.S. Bureau of Animal Husbandry researchers at Ames, Iowa, came upon an effective serum the same year. Truman had helped vaccinate a neighbor's hogs in 1912, shortly before Truman's were struck. Vaccinating pigs was hard work. Some pigs weighed two hundred pounds and were as strong as mules:

> It was necessary to sneak up and grab a hind leg, then hold on until someone else got another hold wherever he could, and then proceed to throw Mr. Hog and sit on him while he got what the Mo University says is good for him. A two-hundred-pound hog can almost jerk the ribs loose from your backbone when you get him by the hind leg. It is far and away the best exercise in the list. It beats Jack Johnson's whole training camp as a muscle toughener.[18]

For fifty years the vets and farmers thus vaccinated pigs until they tabulated the last case of hog cholera in August 1976. On January 3, 1978, they announced the United States "hog cholera free."

In Harry Truman's days on the farm, hogs were worth the trouble, if—as Harry said—Mr. Hog could survive hog diseases and turn into sausage. Harry alone had the task of stuffing the sausage. Mamma Truman always wanted to do it, but when she did it made her sick. Mary Jane and John Truman would not. Harry's hands blistered, and toward the end he put blisters into the sacks, which he did not believe injured the flavor of the sausage. He got sausage in his hair, on his clothes and shoes, all over the kitchen floor; but it was worth it when the time came to eat sausage.

The Trumans and their neighbors the Aringtons argued over who raised better hogs. Harry had Hampshires, the Aringtons a heavier breed. Once Harry smiled and said, "All right, George, you raise the lard and I'll raise the meat."[19]

In the roster of farm animals, chickens hardly counted. Their only advantage on the Truman farm was that they were the principal ingredient in Mrs. Truman's culinary specialty. Problems with the Truman chickens seem never to have concerned Harry Truman, perhaps because there was essentially only one—lice—and Mamma Truman had the difficulty in hand. The lice problem came up in a letter from Bess, who kept chickens in back of her house in Independence. Her chickens were dying. This news brought a quick response: Harry gave Bess his mother's recipe for chicken dip. The recipe must have been effective, for the lice would not have liked it. According to her son, Mrs. Truman took twist tobacco and steeped it in hot water as if she were making tea, with four twists to one bucket. She put in enough cold water to cover the hen and make the dip the right temperature. She added a tablespoonful of melted grease. Then she put her hand over the chicken's bill and eyes and "soused him good." Proclaiming the recipe, her son said, "Young and old alike can go through this process without harm." Harry advised Bess to pick a warm day. He also remarked that he would not fancy the job of dipping them and suggested (one could have expected as much in rural, negrophobic Missouri), "Maybe you can force that negro you have working for you to do it."[20]

2

In his years on the farm, Truman spent most of his daytime hours in the fields or around the barns, save for some slackness during the winter season, and yet found time in the evenings and on Sundays, much as he had done in Kansas City, to do other things. For a while he continued with the National Guard, although that was only an evening every other week, except for summer camp of a week or so. He gave that up in 1911. Meanwhile he took interest in the Masonic Order, and never gave that up; he was a dedicated Mason for the rest of his life. He spent little time in reading, or with music. Politics still did not attract him. Then, commencing late in 1910, he turned to a pursuit that for several years kept him far busier than anything else.

Let it be said in passing that Truman, like many other farmers, was not nearly as isolated on the farm as people said at the time and later. It is not just that all the talk and a good deal of the historical literature about the perils of farm life—how terribly remote it was, how distant farmers were from people other than their neighbors, how twisted and almost grotesquely malformed farmers' outlooks became as a result—did not apply to Harry Truman during his farm years, but also that such dire views did not measure the experiences of many farmers throughout the Middle West. It is possible that farmers in the East during the years after the Civil War, the Ethan Fromes of that section of the country, turned inward. It was alleged that Calvin Coolidge, for example, growing up in Plymouth Notch, Vermont, therefore acquired some of the pinched aspects of life, the narrowness of view, that he—so it was said (this in fact was not true)—took into the presidency. That may have been true for some New England farmers, because the soil there was so rock-bound, so inhospitable. In the Far West, and surely for farms along the Canadian border, there was real isolation, the sort of thing that the novelist Ole Rölvaag described as the hardness, the decades-long experiences of dreariness, of farmers in South Dakota. Aroused by the clamor of Eastern and Western "progressives," President Theodore Roosevelt in 1908 created the Country Life Commission to look into the remote, deprived lives of country people. The commission duly reported, early in 1909, with suitable literary exaggeration: "The underlying problem is to develop and maintain on our farms a civilization in full harmony with the best American ideals." But Truman did not have to worry about what he would have described as "hogwash," the commission's activities and report, for already the conveniences of civilization had opened social and intellectual possibilities for farmers, and he immediately, upon entrance into farm life, undertook to make the most of them. If anyone would have told him he was culturally deprived, he would have laughed in his or her face. In one of his letters to Bess Wallace he made fun of the Country Life Commission, intimating that President Roosevelt did not understand the American people, at least that large group of American people who made their livelihoods on farms and were hardly as backward as the president, that effete Easterner, believed.

Consider, then, all the nonfarming activities in which Harry Truman participated. There were his activities, every other week, in the National Guard. And there were the Masons. He was first attracted to the Masons when a cousin came into the barnyard in 1908 and talked him into attending a lodge meeting in Belton; he eventually joined the Belton lodge. The Masons so intrigued him that he organized a lodge in Grandview and became its first Master. He learned the ritual so well—he later said he taught it to the plow horses—that he was much in demand in nearby villages and towns, where he participated in induction of new members and the taking of degrees. Placed in the Grand Lodge line years afterward, he eventually became Grand Master of the Grand Lodge of the Masons of Missouri, a high honor. During his presidency he received the thirty-third degree.

As for reading books during the years on the farm, Harry Truman did do some, but not a great deal. In the first letter he wrote Bess, at the beginning of their courtship, he mentioned reading: "I am very glad you liked the book," he related (we do not know what it was). "I liked it so well myself I nearly kept it. I saw it advertised in *Life* and remembered that you were fond of Scott when we went to school."[21] But on the farm his reading quite clearly did not amount to much. It was mainly of magazines, in which he read light stories. He admired *Everybody's,* which printed illustrated short stories and serials, gay and sad. He liked the blood and thunder of *Adventure,* none too adventurous by later standards, but full of enough derring-do to keep tired farmers awake. Beyond these journalistic entertainments he read a few novels of the sort that today fill shelves of secondhand bookstores—stories of love and remorse and death, of happiness and bliss alongside ineffable tragedy, assisted by tipped-in illustrations of young men in elegant suits and willowy young ladies in long, lacy dresses.

Of serious literature there is very little evidence in the letters to Bess. He admired Mark Twain, the celebrated humorist who died in 1910, for his droll stories, gusto, and admiration of American virtues. Bess took pleasure in Dickens and Stevenson and tried vainly to get Harry to read their longer novels. His mother admired Alexander Pope, and Harry gave her a copy of Pope's poems for her birthday; but there is no indication he ever read them. Nor in the correspondence is there evidence that Harry, during this very considerable period of his life, eleven years, read anything about history, his principal interest when in high school. One searches in vain through the several hundred letters he wrote to Bess from the farm for references to serious literature, nonfiction or fiction, apart from Mark Twain.

The young man's other intellectual interest during the years in Independence and Kansas City, music, similarly withered during his time on the farm. While in Kansas City working in the banks he had not merely taken piano lessons but also attended the concerts of the great pianists, but there is little commentary in the letters about such concerts. About all one can say concerning his musical tastes during these eleven years is that he enjoyed operettas and musicals such as *Florodora,* a popular hit of the time. His playing of the piano notably languished while on the farm, and he mentioned it only in passing and with such expressions of regret as to make it have seemed unimportant—he would tell Bess he had hoped, in younger days, to have been an ivory tickler. Many years later a neighboring youth, Gaylon Babcock, recalled the threshing days and perhaps caught unknowingly a certain wistfulness in the harried life of Harry Truman. He remembered how the threshers would come to the Truman farm and sit around in the house after work, mostly on the porch, waiting for supper. Harry had duties in its preparation, but if he had a little time before serving the meal, instead of coming out and "associating with us men," he would play the piano.[22] It must have been one of the few times he had to enjoy the music that once had fascinated him.

He displayed only a slight interest in politics. His father had been road overseer, an appointed job, until his death, at which time Harry received the appointment; he kept it for a few months until he got into an argument with the county engineer. For several months in 1915 he was postmaster of Grand-view, an office he solicited because, he wrote Bess, there was an effort to put the post office in a so-called drugstore that was nought but a "booze emporium."[23] He gave the work and money to Ella Hall, daughter of the operator of the threshing machine that served the farm. She was a Republican. He ran for township committeeman in the 1916 primary and lost. He did take more interest in national politics, and once he and Bess went to hear the perennial Democratic presidential contender, William Jennings Bryan. A wonderful, quick-witted orator, Bryan at this country gathering had no platform to stand on, so someone wheeled out a manure spreader; climbing up on it, he announced that this was the first time he had ever spoken from a Republican platform. In the summer of 1912, the race for the Democratic presidential nomination between Champ Clark, a Missourian and Speaker of the House of Representatives, and Governor Woodrow Wilson of New Jersey took his attention. His father was for Clark, he for Wilson. On July 2 he was driving a binder in a wheat field of one hundred and sixty acres, two miles around. Every time he went around he would tie the horses and mules—he was driving a four-animal team, two of each—and rest them while he ran over to the telegraph station along the railroad to see how the convention in Baltimore was going. Wilson won on the thirty-eighth ballot.

Courtship of Bess was by far Harry Truman's most important outside interest while on the farm, taking much more time than the Guard and Masonry. It was indeed his consuming interest, though it had begun almost by accident, apparently in early December 1910. Before that date the Grandview farmer seems not to have seen, let alone communicated with, Bess since their graduation from high school. During the first years, 1901–1903, the Trumans were still in Independence, but Bess moved in a different social circle, belonging to the town's upper crust, being a Presbyterian (until she and her mother joined the Episcopal church). After high school, perhaps even before, Harry Truman returned to the Baptists. When he moved to Kansas City in 1903 he was baptized in the Little Blue River and joined a city church. That same year Bess's family suffered an irreparable tragedy; Bess's father went into the bathroom of their house on Delaware Street early one morning and took his life with a pistol. He was an alcoholic, had difficulty holding a job, and was in debt to his wealthy father-in-law. For a year after his death the Wallace family, including Bess's three younger brothers, lived with an uncle in Colorado Springs. Upon returning to Independence, they moved into the house of Grandfather and Grandmother Gates.

When Harry Truman was working in the banks in Kansas City he was only ten miles from Independence, and after he went to the farm he was just fifteen as a crow might fly, but there was one technical problem: Bess had never really reciprocated his feelings for her, feelings that arose from their first meeting in Sunday school and continued through high school. He may never have mentioned them. She certainly never said anything to him. And he needed to discover an occasion when he might, as people said in those days, call upon her.

The occasion by which Bess and Harry met was typical of the time. Bess's mother, Mrs. Wallace, had sent over a cake to the Noland family across the street—their house was at 216 North Delaware, opposite the Gates house at 219. By chance Harry Truman was visiting the Nolands, Aunt Ella and her daughters, Ethel and Nellie. He had spent the night in their parlor, and the next morning he came out into the kitchen, saw the plate from the cake, and heard his aunt explain that it had come from the Wallaces and needed to be returned. What then happened would be much remarked in the Truman family. Margaret Truman often heard the story, and she has related that her father, according to the Nolands, seized the plate "with something approaching the speed of light," announced that he, himself, would return it, and disappeared out the front door. When he rang the bell at the Wallace house, Bess opened the door. She had just divested herself of a boyfriend, and looked at him closely as he explained what he had come for. "Come in," she said.[24]

Thereupon commenced the courtship in which Truman went to Independence for Sunday evening dinners or to pick up Bess for a Saturday night in Kansas City. On other occasions they met in the city to go to lunch or dinner and thence some sort of entertainment, frequently a vaudeville show.

The courtship moved very rapidly, and soon he was proposing marriage in a letter that glanced into the subject and then, having found it, seized it: "From all appearances I am not such a very pious person am I? The elements evidently mistook one of my wishes for dry instead of wet. I guess we'll all have to go to drinking whiskey if it doesn't rain very soon. Water and potatoes will soon be as much of a luxury as pineapples and diamonds. Speaking of diamonds, would you wear a solitaire on your left hand should I get it?"[25]

Bess carefully and graciously, judging from Harry's description, turned him down:

> You know that you turned me down so easy that I am almost happy anyway. I never was fool enough to think that a girl like you could ever care for a fellow like me but I couldn't help telling you how I felt. I have always wanted you to have some fine, rich, good-looking man, but I knew that if ever I got the chance I'd tell you how I felt even if I didn't even get to say another word to you. What makes me feel real good is that you were good enough to answer me seriously and not make fun of me anyway.[26]

Thereafter they took things gradually. Not too long after the turndown they "promised" themselves to each other, without formality. By the time Harry entered the army in 1917, they were engaged.

The reason for the delay was essentially Bess's mother, who desired her future son-in-law to be a man of means. In later years critics would write of how she opposed the marriage of Bess to a farmer. But it was more than likely not his occupation she objected to: from all accounts of the time, she enjoyed the farmer's frequent presence at meals in the Gates house. She and her four children, however, were living with Grandfather and Grandmother Gates; everything they received came from them. Before that, her husband had accepted money from her father. She therefore must have been extremely sensitive of her dependence, and did not want Bess ever to have such an experience. The result was a series of efforts to impress Bess's mother that he, a Jackson County farmer, possessed enough money to marry her daughter. These efforts consumed almost as much time as Farmer Harry spent in courting Bess.

To secure the money he needed to marry Bess, the man from Grandview took part in two farm raffles—awards by lot of homesteads—sponsored by the federal government to promote settlement of virgin land in South Dakota and Montana. In October 1911, Harry went up for the first of them, as required, accompanied by one of his Kansas City cousins, Murray Colgan. They took a sleeper to Omaha and there boarded a special train for Gregory, a town just over the Montana border. There they registered at a wooden shack, the Cow Palace, where they encountered twenty notaries inside a hollow square. Harry also registered for a Spanish-American War veteran, so he had a chance not merely to obtain a quarter section, one hundred and sixty acres, but half of another if the veteran won. The government had arranged the lottery so that there were many prizes of different value, ranging from, at the top, claims worth between eight thousand and twelve thousand dollars, down to several thousand claims of value from four thousand to forty, depending on location.

When Harry's name was not drawn for South Dakota, nor, for that matter, the name of his veteran friend, he tried the lottery at Glasgow, Montana. Word came that he was in luck, having drawn claim 6,199. Then he heard about the climate. In May 1914, it snowed seven inches in South Dakota, and he reasoned that no such snow would have the "impudence" to "miss the great state of Montana." Over the winter the temperature, he learned, had gone down to 47° below. The wind, someone said, blew sixty miles an hour right out of Alaska. "I guess I can get me a cowskin cloak and a beaver cap and manage to keep warm."[27] Coal was two dollars a ton in Montana, but each resident, he guessed, burned seventy tons a week. He decided not to accept his claim.

In these years of attempting to produce enough money to marry Bess, Harry Truman sought to persuade Uncle Harrison to "let loose" of money so the two of them could undertake a speculation of one sort or another. In a small way Harrison was a chance taker, and he seems to have shown signs of letting loose, although his usual recourse was to change his mind, probably in the thought that even small sums were useful in Kansas City. At one point he and Harry looked over the proposal of an inventor of an ice machine. At another the two went to Texas to look over land for sale. Owners who had bought land two or three years before said Texas was a virtual Eden. But then Harrison began to tell jokes about Texas. He told the nephew that if he would stick to Texas when it was dry, Texas would stick to him when it was wet. Harrison put off his decision, and for him putting off meant refusal.

By this time Harry was crazy, he wrote Bess, to marry. Together with a young salesman named Jerry Culbertson and a neighboring farmer, Thomas R. Hughes, he went into business as the T-C-H Mining Company; they operated a lead and zinc mine near the little locality of Commerce, Oklahoma, on the Missouri border near Joplin in the far southwestern part of the state. Harry was secretary-treasurer, which, as matters turned out, meant the money-raiser and money-dispenser, which proved the most important activity. Culbertson never spent much time at the mine nor took interest in its finances. Hughes was more interested, but lightning struck his barn soon after the mine opened, and he rushed back home. That was virtually the end of him as a partner.

Truman sought to get the mine, already dug and known as the Eureka Mine, in running order, and for a while his hopes rose. But the mine quickly became a major problem. His first sign of trouble was the mine boss, who was something of a braggart; he fired him and engaged another. Then, each new employee, boss or worker, seems to have told the partner the mine was almost ready to produce marvelous ore: they had discovered the vein and were about to bring its ore to the surface. From somewhere the miners would dig out a half ton or ton and bring it up and promise more. The partner eagerly added the promises and multiplied successful days and calculated how the ore would pay back the investment within a month or six weeks and there would be only "clover." Meanwhile he repaired to the local bank to obtain loans to meet payrolls. When the ore was slow, he kited the payrolls.

After many weeks, and hopes that rose and fell, Truman finally had to give up. It became obvious that the mine did not contain enough ore to be profitable. At that moment of truth, he was aghast. If more work on his part would have saved the mine, he would have done it. The fact was that he and Hughes had bought a mine that someone else had worked out. Nothing could avail against this hard truth. Truman took his lumps, which he told Bess were $7,500 worth, and returned to the farm, which he had left in charge of Mary and the hired men.

In the last months of 1916 and early in 1917, just before the United States entered the World War and Truman himself went to war, he engaged in one more effort to make money. Not long after returning from Commerce he became acquainted, actually through Culbertson, with an oil wildcatter, David H. Morgan, and went in with him in a venture that involved buying leases in

Kansas, Oklahoma, Texas, and Louisiana. In the Kansas City directory for 1916, under "Oil," appeared the advertisement of "Morgan & Company, Oil Investments, Suite 703, New Ridge Arcade." At the top of the ad appeared the officers: D. H. Morgan, president; Harry S. Truman, treasurer; Jerry Culbertson, secretary; S. J. Hatch, consulting geologist. The ad said, with sly exaggeration, "All Phones Main 2832." Below was the statement of occupation: "The only exclusive OIL INVESTMENT Firm in Kansas City." Truman's principal duty was to inhabit the office in Kansas City during the slack winter months on the farm, welcome any investors Culbertson could entice, and take care of correspondence. For his portion of the partnership he signed five thousand-dollar notes endorsed by his mother, which his associates Morgan and Culbertson could use as collateral for a bank loan. He jocularly told Bess the investment belonged to her.

At the beginning the enterprise went well, and excited the treasurer:

> It is now 8:30 p.m. and I haven't been to supper yet. We sold 636 shares and collected $1,592.50 today. I have just finished getting out yesterday's receipts. We got about $800 yesterday. The refinery is bought and so is another 200-acre lease adjoining it with some nine producing wells. Your shares now have 1,500 acres of deeded land and 1,300 acres of leases at Chanute, besides a 200-acre lease in Allen County and a contract for 5,000 acres in Sumner County, Kansas, and 5,000 acres in Garfield County, Oklahoma. The money is coming in by the basketful and it looks as if the Atlas-Okla Lands Syndicate should be in the [moving] pictures before many days.[28]

The Atlas-Okla Oil Lands Syndicate was the operating end of Morgan and Company.

Unlike the lead and zinc mine, Morgan and Company did hold promise. At least one associate, Morgan, knew the business. The company put a well down in Kansas to a depth of nine hundred feet. A photograph of Truman has survived from late in 1916 that shows him standing next to a derrick, grinning at the camera, natty suit and tie almost shining in the winter sun. It was the closest he ever came to wealth. He probably was standing on top of one of the Morgan & Company properties, what later proved to be the famous Teter Pool, to which no one ever sank a dry hole.

But he lost again. When the United States entered the World War, the company had not yet gotten its well down far enough. The manpower shortage forced the company's officers to dispose of the leases and go out of business. Not long afterward one of the major national oil companies tapped the pool. Had Truman done it, he would have become a millionaire.

And what, in sum, did the farm experience do for the later president of the United States? We know what the extracurricular experiences, so to speak, did or did not do, but what of the farm work, the long years of effort to cultivate the land? Truman thought the farm one of his three requisites for success in politics, but the farmer never explained why the farm was so important, and it is necessary to guess. The present writer's guess is that from the farm he learned, first of all, a kind of formula that he applied to politics. The formula was that hard work plus patience would amount to the best he could do, after which he had to let nature take its course. The farm taught him that in whatever he undertook he himself could only do so much, after which the weather would make all the difference.

Another lesson from the farm took the form of a trait—a stoicism that Truman very much possessed. After much consideration, he could make a decision and, while not forgetting about it, to be sure, get it over with; once a decision was made, the moment for worry had passed. Every day on the farm, for the first time in his life, he had to think about or make decisions. The experience of growing up in Independence and then of working at different jobs, including the bank jobs, required little decisiveness. The farm did, especially after his father died, when the decisions were his alone. Some of them he made each year, but even those routine decisions contained variations, due to weather perhaps, and he had to consider them anew.

Third, while the farm had little to do with leadership, which he experienced beginning in 1917, his life on the farm properly increased the solitude that must be a part of everyone's makeup if that person is to do large things. Despite the opportunities to get off the farm on evenings and on weekends—for Guard meetings or lodge meetings or the many pleasures of seeing his Bess in Independence and Kansas City—the solitude was undeniable. The Grandview farm was large enough to get away from road traffic, what little of it there was in 1906–1917, and hear only the sound of work animals, their breathing and measured plodding; after a while, the farmer heard no more and found himself alone. If he went out armed only with a hoe or a sickle, it was absolute, total silence, save for the wind, if there was any. During that time he occupied himself with thoughts, as Truman wrote, an experience denied to city folks, who became a part of the noise that surrounded their days and consumed any thoughts.

Perhaps as important as the solitude, the farm also probably afforded the perspective needed to dream of bigger things. Physically speaking, it was slightly undulating, but for the most part it offered views off in all directions, lying on the ridge between two rivers, the Big and Little Blue, not quite reaching either. The ridge, known as Blue Ridge, extended down to Arkansas—a sort of little divide, as Ethel Noland described it, like the Great Divide in the Rocky Mountains.[29] To the north the ridge shortly came to an end. The fall in the land from Grandview to Kansas City was so considerable that in Truman's youth the Kansas City Southern Railroad, which ran through the farm, kept a helper engine in Grandview; whenever a large train came out of the city on its way to southern places, the helper engine backed down to the metropolis and hooked the train. From the farm, so well placed, Farmer

Truman could not see to Lawrence, Kansas, but it was possible to know that it lay off in the distance as he stood on his eminence (that was why the nearby village was named Grandview). He could gain much perspective as he looked into the far distance, beyond the interminable forty-acre fields, the "forties," into which the farms had been divided according to the Ordinance of 1785. As he looked out, he must have felt he was on a huge saucer between the earth and the canopy of the sky: overhead, clouds floated in slow, lazy ways, or scudded as if by some strange but clear purpose, often making gigantic shadow pictures across the fields. From this vantage, he could dream of what lay beyond—perhaps to the West, with Lawrence and its bucolic little university, lonely on a little hill; or to the north, with Kansas City in its haze of smoke; or to the east, with its tens of thousands of Missouri farm forties, the great river, and, beyond it, more farms, his ancestral Kentucky, and finally the industrial East and the cities he had never seen. He undoubtedly never dreamed of the presidency in faraway Washington. But he must have decided, even while he walked along or bumped along on the planter or cultivator behind the work animals, or while he hoed the corn, fighting the weeds, in early summer, that he was good enough, able enough, to undertake larger tasks if they somehow, in some yet unknown way, presented themselves.

Chapter Four

The Army

*T*he decision to go into the army during World War I was the crucial event of Harry Truman's life, and he made that decision, let it be added, because he was a patriotic citizen of the United States, and not because of what the army might do for him. To be sure, he was no student of the great issues that divided Europe, and if he read about the carnage on the front—the killing by machine guns, artillery, and poison gas—he never mentioned it in letters to Bess. Nor did he understand the submarine issue that divided the United States and Imperial Germany. The sinking of great liners with frightful loss of life does not seem to have crossed his mind; again, he never mentioned it. Like millions of other Americans, he had felt as remote from Europe as if Jackson County were somewhere in China surrounded by the Great Wall. Then, of a sudden, the country was at war. President Wilson established its purpose:

> But the right is more precious than peace, and we shall fight for the things which we have always carried nearest our hearts—for democracy, for the right of those who submit to authority to have a voice in their own governments, for the rights and liberties of small nations, for a universal dominion of right by such a concert of free peoples as shall bring peace and safety to all nations and make the world itself at last free.

It was Wilson's supreme oratorical effort, the greatest speech of the twentieth century. To such a task, the soon-to-be war president said, Americans could dedicate life and fortune, spend blood and might for the principles that gave the nation birth and happiness and peace. "God helping her, she can do no other!"

The farmer near Grandview was an unlikely candidate for the draft; he would not have to go—he was thirty-three years old—but he had belonged to the Guard and thought he should volunteer. "I believe that the great majority of the country was stirred by the same flame that stirred me in those great days. I felt that I was a Galahad after the Grail."[1]

The decision meant much for the direction of his life, far beyond anything he imagined. From it followed a whole series of experiences over two years, in the United States and abroad, that stretched his mind beyond anything he had known in Kansas City and on the farm. The army itself was instructive, and years later he wrote his nephew Fred, Vivian's son, who was in the army in another war, of the wisdom the army had taught him. The ways of the army were peculiar, he told Fred, and then recited the well-known three ways to do things—the right way, the wrong way, and the army way. But out of that experience came understanding of the varieties of human conduct when under pressure from a system: "I went through a lot of it in the last war and it is rather difficult to fool me on facts and conditions."[2]

Much more important, the army also showed him that he could be a leader of men. Never before had he undergone such an experience. The Guard was a casual organization, really just a lot of fun. But when he became commander of Battery D, he found himself with 193 men of diverse backgrounds, far different from the bank clerks and salesmen and lawyers in the Guard. He had to control them, else they would control him. His success made him understand he could do the same on a much larger scale.

And, as matters turned out, when he came back to Kansas City after the war he had a political base. At that time Guard units across the country were raised locally, inducted en masse, and kept together. In World War II this practice had to be abandoned, because local units sent to dangerous assignments could be wiped out en masse as well, causing the morale of people back home to suffer dramatically. In World War I, Truman found he possessed the friendship not merely of his battery but of hundreds of other men in his field artillery regiment, which had enlisted from Kansas City or nearby. If he ran for public office in Jackson County, they would vote for him. Service in the army made it possible. "My whole political career," he once said, "is based upon my war service and war associates."[3]

1

When the president of the United States on April 6, 1917, signed a declaration of war against Germany, Missouri Guard officers reorganized the three light artillery batteries—A in St. Louis, B in Kansas City, and C in Independence—into two regiments. From Guard headquarters in Convention Hall, Harry Truman and many of his old Guard friends helped reorganize B and C, doing office work and soliciting enlistments on the streets. He worked so hard, he said afterward, that he told his associates they should make him a sergeant. Instead, they made him a first lieutenant.

It is now almost forgotten that as late as World War I the men of Guard units elected their company officers, and the company officers then elected the field-grade officers. Such had been the practice of militia units going back to the Revolution. After his own election, Truman entered the field-grade hustings with vigor, not for himself, for he was too junior, but for a Kansas City man, Karl D. Klemm, a 1907 graduate of West Point and a Guard major who aspired to the regiment's colonelcy. The Independence officers championed a local man, Edward M. Stayton, also a Guard major. In a burst of enthusiasm during a Guard dinner, Truman made a speech favoring Klemm; although it may not have turned any tide, Klemm did receive the colonelcy. Truman, however, came to dislike him, seeing him not only as a social climber who had married a wealthy woman, but also as a martinet. At the end of the war, the colonel infuriated his men by finding an excuse to return to the United States earlier than the rest of the regiment. When the men came back in the early summer of 1919, the by-then Captain Truman wrote Bess angrily that Klemm had better not show his face in the Kansas City parade before demobilization. In the 1920s Truman would employ Klemm's disappointed rival, Stayton, in construction of Jackson County roads, and the two became close friends, for Stayton was a thorough engineer. Klemm became involved in business ventures that did not prosper, and eventually committed suicide.

The regiment's choice of Klemm caused many troubles, and curiously one of them occurred almost at the beginning. While the regiment was being organized, most of the officers and men lived at home. Officers from outside the city stayed in hotels—Truman wrote Bess occasionally from the Densmore. Some enlisted men lived in Convention Hall. One day drivers from the Shaw Taxicab Company beat up two enlisted men, and that night fifty or sixty men started out to clean up on the drivers. The men were found out by a lieutenant, who turned them in to Klemm. The latter lined them up, stood there holding his swagger stick, and called for anyone involved to step forward. The whole group stepped forward. Klemm was furious.

After army authorities in Washington arranged for construction of cantonments throughout the country—tent camps in the South, wooden barracks in the North—they mustered Guard units into federal service, and the Second Missouri Field Artillery Regiment became the 129th Field Artillery Regiment attached to the 35th Division. In September the 129th entrained for Camp Doniphan, Oklahoma, a tent camp erected on the reservation of the artillery school at Fort Sill.

For Truman the departure from Kansas City must have been painful. As early as July he was writing Bess from the Densmore that he was "dead crazy to ask you to marry me before I leave," but explained he did not believe he had the right to ask because after the war she might find he was a cripple. The last time he saw her, he confessed, he had come close to tears, and would have been embarrassed if she had discovered it—"a weeping man is an abomination unto the Lord." He had seen two big tears come into his mother's eyes the night before when he started off to lodge meeting in his uniform: "You are the two people in the world that I would rather see smile and that I like to cause to smile, and here I've gone done the opposite to both of you."[4]

The regiment arrived at Doniphan to find the new post not altogether attractive. For one thing it was so new the engineers had not cleaned the pipes that brought water to the camp; for the next two weeks until they remedied the situation the men drank the polluted water, which nauseated them. For another, they arrived in camp at the end of September, almost the beginning of winter in that part of the country, the American West. Officers and troops huddled in their tents. There was no supply of underwear or winter clothes until December, and they depended on the Red Cross. The little Sibley stoves, invented after the Mexican War, seemed useless: "We have an oil stove and the cussed thing smokes like Vesuvius. It smells like a refinery and tastes like quinine in here now."[5] Men kept them red hot.

In addition to the bad water, cold autumn weather, and summer uniforms, the wind soon was blowing. Sand blew everywhere, through tent walls, into the food. A mess sergeant gave Truman a piece of apple dumpling, and his teeth grated as he ate the sand frosting. It was impossible to see a tent at fifty yards. Men who could find goggles wore them. Mornings might appear beautiful, with a clear sky and no breeze. Truman and his friends discovered the hill known as Medicine Hat, the origin for local winds; he rode out to it to get exercise. But by noon the wind was howling.

And as autumn turned into winter, the snow was driving. On January 10, 1918, he wrote Bess of "a terrific blizzard going here. It began raining this morning from the east. It turned to snow and the wind got around in Hiawatha's corner and ice balls began blowing in straight lines like bullets right from Medicine Hat's worst mixture. You can't see ten feet from you now and the wind is blowing about sixty miles an hour." He thought of storms years before: "This must be one of the kind I've heard my grandfather speak of when he crossed the plains." Fort Sill, he declared, was designed for disagreeableness, high enough to catch every misting air current passing from the Arctic to the Gulf of Mexico. Sill was getting surplus snow from the Klondike.[6]

At Doniphan the regiment went to school, which kept everyone occupied and helped take their minds off the living conditions. From his military background Klemm instructed the officers, who instructed the troops. How helpful this tuition was for fighting the war in France is difficult to say. One suspects it was theoretical instruction that had kept generations of West Point cadets out of mischief and might have applied to the Mexican and Civil Wars, possibly that of 1898. A typical problem concerned a scout who measured the angle found by two trees on the opposite bank of a river as 150 mils ($\frac{1}{6400}$ of a circle). The scout walked back fifty yards and the angle between the same trees was 120. How wide was the river? (The answer, and Truman arrived at it, was two hundred yards.) This problem, incidentally, was one of five in an examination: "We'll sure be wise birds," Lieutenant Truman opined, "when the war's over."[7]

At last artillery pieces arrived—not the sort the men would use in France, French seventy-fives, but the army's standard three-inch piece, which Truman had fired at camp during Guard days. He now was adjutant of Battery A, and he soon discovered that training with a battery was far more difficult than summer frolics with the Guard. Senior officers—the brigade commander and regimental colonels—were present as batteries went out to shoot; some of these viewers were expert, and willing to point out elementary errors made not merely by the batteries' men but by their officers as well. Truman told Bess there were seven separate things the soldiers had to do, otherwise the colonel would blow his whistle. If the seven occurred without a bobble, the battery would shoot bing, bing, bing, bing, at two-second intervals. Then came the agony, for all four shots stayed in the air for what seemed like an hour, and when they burst they often had crossed, number-one being where number-four should have been. It took seven and a half seconds for shots to go three thousand yards. The men looked at the targets and licked their lips. When the colonel would have to blow his whistle, "the general [would summon] the whole world around to pick you to pieces and perhaps ask if you have any brains." Fortunately, the general was not present when Truman fired, "so I got away better than some."[8]

To take tenseness out of firing exercises, perhaps, certainly to put "pep" into the training, a British colonel came to Doniphan about this time and gave a talk that, according to Truman, made everyone want to brace up and go to it and get to the front, otherwise they would be left out of the greatest history-making epoch the world had ever seen. The colonel related the horrors of German rule in event of Allied defeat: there would be nothing for Allied troops to live for. Truman told Bess the alternative was victory, which would allow the regiment to come home with heads up to "the greatest old country on earth."[9]

The months at Doniphan passed in a variety of such experiences. Truman described them in detailed letters. Among them he related his assignment as regimental canteen officer. Klemm delegated him to set up a small store, staffed by men designated by regimental order, in which soldiers could purchase items the army did not issue and which, if available locally, would have required a trip to the nearby town of Lawton.

The canteen proved an instant success. Truman displayed judgment by bringing in Sergeant Edward Jacobson, whom he had known when working in the National Bank of Commerce. Jacobson then was a clerk in a men's furnishings store at Eighth and Walnut. Born in New York City in 1891, son of a shoemaker, he had moved to Leavenworth, Kansas, with his parents, and later entered the clothing business in Kansas City, in which, by 1917, he had

had ten years of experience. Truman rightly was proud of his canteen manager: "I have a Jew in charge of the canteen by the name of Jacobson and he is a crackerjack." One of the first things Eddie did was, metaphorically speaking, "sew up the pockets" of men in the canteen by installing cash registers. Each day he and Truman counted the money, and they knew immediately when they were short. Once in a while assistants' hands went into the register. Truman caught a man with ten dollars in one pocket, two in another, three in another, three in another: "They say the poor fellow is a good soldier but so much money in sight all at once was too much for him. There has been someone stealing constantly from the till for the last two days. I suppose he was the guy." The lieutenant put him up for court-martial and estimated the sentence at two years, although the soldier (only "one of my thieves") seems to have received three months: "Pretty expensive eighteen dollars."[10]

Truman and Jacobson gained a reputation throughout the division for the variety of items they sold, a result of ingenuity in going out after goods. They drove not only to Lawton but also to Oklahoma City, even to Guthrie in the north. They purchased apples, candy, cakes, and huge quantities of a soft drink called Puritan—this after attempting to stock Coca-Cola, only to discover that local dealers would not let them have more than fifty cases; they needed much more, for one evening the canteen sold six hundred bottles of Puritan in two hours. They bought goggles and writing paper and pencils and pens. Truman became known as Lieutenant Graballsky. In his purchasing, the automobile he bought in 1913, a 1911 Stafford car, played a stellar role. Truman appears to have brought it to Doniphan by train, after which he turned it into a pickup.[11] Truman brought in a Kansas City barber, Morris Stearns, and a tailor to rework army uniforms, sew buttons, and make other repairs. The canteen soon was taking in from five hundred to six hundred dollars a day. After six months the lieutenant and Jacobson paid back the twenty-two hundred dollars the regiment's men had contributed, plus fifteen thousand dollars in dividends.

At Doniphan the future president met several officers whom he long remembered, if for different reasons. One was Second Lieutenant Harry H. Vaughan, who would become his military aide and a major general. The meeting was memorable because Brigadier General Lucien G. Berry was holding an officers call, with Truman "on the carpet" because Berry had discovered something amiss with the canteen, perhaps trash on the floor. Unaware of the proceedings, Vaughan came in late, and Berry turned on him.

"What is your name, Mister?" asked the general.

"Vaughan, sir," was the answer.

"How long have you been an officer in the United States Army?"

"Three days, sir."

Berry told Vaughan he could not be an officer if he lived to be a hundred; the message took three minutes, during which Truman carefully stepped back into the ranks. At the end Berry forgot whom he had been talking to and departed in brassy disgust. Truman took Vaughan by the arm. "Much obliged, Mister," he said. "You got me off the hook nicely."[12]

Among the ranking officers at Doniphan, Berry became the nemesis of the first lieutenant from near Kansas City. Truman went up before a promotion board, and Berry again turned on him. This time the general did not want to find out what the lieutenant and two other officers knew, but how much they did not know. When they could answer it displeased him; when they could not, he rattled his false teeth, pulled his handlebar mustache, and stalked up and down the room shouting, "Ah, you don't know, do you? I thought you were just ignorant rookies! Now, you aspire to be officers and generals, sure enough, by becoming captains in the United States Army. It will be a disaster to the country to let you command men."[13] Truman and friends had to await these proceedings by standing out in the cold, with the temperature near zero, for more than an hour, and afterward took terrible colds. Truman could not get up for reveille the next morning. They all felt they had failed. In the event—Truman did not discover the result until he was in France—they all passed.

It was during the Doniphan months that Truman met Colonel Robert M. Danford, later commandant of cadets at West Point and major general for all army artillery. Unlike Berry, Danford was a gentleman who treated everyone, not least Missouri farmers, with respect. He was the author of a treatise on artillery, and he taught the men everything he could. When he was summoned to Washington for promotion, his departure almost brought tears. Captain Thomas S. McGee told his first sergeant about it as they were walking to the stable, and the sergeant stopped and said, "The Hell!" Danford offered his horse to Truman, a Kentucky-bred saddle animal, "pretty as a picture and gentle as a dog," a dark sorrel with dark mane and tail and "a pretty, little intelligent head like Rosa Bonheur puts on her horses." The price was one hundred dollars, a ridiculously low figure, with the proviso that after the war Truman would sell the animal back if Danford wanted it. Truman sent it to the farm. Klemm was much peeved: "You lucky Jew you get all the plums that fall, don't you?" said he, in the parlance of the time. Truman told him he took plums when someone threw them at him.[14]

Finally, the time came to go overseas. Truman anticipated it, and the winter's correspondence was replete with warnings to Bess, in hopes she would come to visit. His mother and Mary visited, but Bess seems not to have. Truman was in the advance party of a hundred men and ten officers: "We are rolling along through Iowa . . . now," he wrote. He then explained why, passing through Kansas City, he had called her at 5:00 A.M. Mrs. Wallace had come to the phone and seems to have been irritated, although Bess was pleased. He had been in a place named Armourdale, in the Rock Island yards, and there was a single Bell phone in the yardmaster's office. He asked if he could use it—he had spent fifteen minutes hunting a phone and had only five more. "Call her," the man said. "The phone's yours. But if she doesn't break the engagement at five o'clock in the morning, she really loves you."[15]

The detachment stayed a few days at Camp Merritt in New Jersey. When everyone went into New York, Harry wrote from the Hotel McAlpin. He related how the subway began aboveground but went down and then up. Broadway, he said, was dingy, part of it torn up, no better than Twelfth Street in Kansas City. Fifth Avenue was all right. He and several friends went up in the Woolworth Building, 792 feet and one inch—the inch amused him—and for fifty cents saw the city together with Brooklyn, Jersey City, Hoboken, and Weehawken (he said). He found an optician, a member of the Scottish Rite, who sent him to an oculist who made a thorough examination, and charged $5; Dr. Leonard in Kansas City charged ten. He returned to the oculist, who charged $17.50, less 10 percent, for two pairs of regulation aluminum frames and glasses, with an extra lens he had chipped on the edge in grinding, this when "Watts stung me for $22.00 for two pairs." The store was on Madison Avenue just off Forty-second Street, "and I know he pays more rent for a week than Watts does for a month."[16] The oculist, by name of Haustetter, said the name cost him business.

The group then boarded the USS *George Washington*, a former German liner, the same ship President Wilson later took to the Paris Peace Conference.

2

Like most of the two million men in the Allied Expeditionary Forces, Harry Truman spent a year out of the United States: a few months in the war, the rest waiting to go home.

The trip across proved uneventful, and perhaps for that reason tedious, broken for Truman only by a short bout, one day, with seasickness. Everyone, he wrote, had a remedy, and none worked but Christian Science, and sometimes it failed in a rough sea. He enjoyed a stateroom, albeit with five other lieutenants, a room that in peacetime would have accommodated two people at most. He and the others played cards or "hunted submarines" or ate. There was no scenery save water—blue when the sun shone, lead-colored when it did not, copper at sunrise and sunset: "The sunsets on the sea aren't half as good to see as those on our prairies at home. You see just as far as the rim, which they tell me is twenty miles away. The funny part of it is we never catch up with that rim."[17]

After landing "somewhere in France," actually Brest, April 13, 10:00 A.M., after a fourteen-day passage, the lieutenant and friends spent a few days in the Hotel des Voyageurs. They had a nice room, decorated with etchings of Henry IV and his children and of Henry VIII of England at a state function; the fireplace featured a white marble mantel, on which stood a Dutch clock under a glass case. The chairs were upholstered in red plush. Truman decided it was perhaps a count's bedroom, but it was cold as an icicle.

Thereafter, the advance contingent of the 129th, officers and men, went to school—which, despite the emergency on the front, was General John J. Pershing's procedure for men new to the AEF (American Expeditionary Forces). At the time Truman went over to France, the war on the western front was in its climactic stage: the fighting was more fierce than ever before, and crucial. The removal of Russia from the war after the Bolshevik Revolution of November 1917, and the Treaty of Brest-Litovsk between Germany and Russia, had given the Germans a chance to bring their troops from the eastern to the western front and overwhelm the Allies before American troops could come into the line. But the American commanding general refused to commit his troops until properly trained. He had decided, so he said at the time and wrote afterward, that Allied tactics were defensive, rather than offensive, as they properly should be, and this Allied failure required separate schooling for American troops. Moreover, he did not like the training they received in the United States, and his schools trained them again. Truman's assignment, naturally, was to artillery school, despite training under Danford. He felt odd about the schooling ("I am still somewhere in France going to school like a darned kid"[18]), but it probably reinforced the work he had done; later he liked to relate that he had studied with a nephew of President Wilson's postmaster general, Dick "By God" Burleson, who knew artillery.

Truman failed to shine as a student, and he described the result as "just sneaking through." He encountered men who were college graduates. The best students, however, remained at the school as instructors, and this made him feel better, for he yearned for action. Too, he kidded the college graduates, telling them he was a graduate of Moler's Barber College and that he and his friends belonged to QTF, the Quinine Tonic Fraternity.

After school he became a teacher, and he said he gave the rest of the regimental officers "bunk" and made them like it. He was teaching trigonometry, logarithms, surveying, engineering, "and a lot of other highbrow stuff that nearly cracks my head open to learn just before class and then if some inquisitive nut asks me a question, I'm up a creek and usually answer him by telling him he's ahead of the schedule and I'll tell him tomorrow."[19]

During what time remained he attempted to adjust himself to France, to understand the strangely beautiful country in which he found himself. Accustomed to the fields of Missouri, he found the new landscape more interesting. In an inverse way he almost admitted the fact: "I wouldn't trade any of U.S. for an equal part of France but if I had to give up being a Missourian I'd be a citizen of France by second choice." The only thing that bothered him were the boundary lines, which unlike Missouri's square miles and square forties ran "every which direction, and I don't see how they ever describe a piece of property when they want to transfer it." And yet the diversity made for beauty. The fields formed an irregular patchwork of landscape, "and if I were a painter I'd surely want to go to work on the scenery right away."[20] Any exploration, too, was likely to turn up something interesting, as when he and a fellow officer happened upon a private road, marked Chemin Particulier; the sign did not mean much to them, so they walked along, only to discover a beautiful château. A man at the gate invited them in and showed them a park with a little stream and a swan and green and white ducks. The park contained an old flour mill, and the château had its own ice plant, electric dynamo, six kinds of horse vehicles (no horses, which had gone to war), and three automobiles. A six-foot wall surrounded everything. On another investigation, another day, he and Major Marvin H. Gates attended mass in a cold church and watched the display of vestments and the quaint swinging of censers, the smell of incense filling the pews. They listened to the sermon, neither one of them understanding much, Truman less than Major Gates, who said the priest told the congregation that girls should not flirt with the exuberant Americans.

The introduction to France, and simultaneously the incessant schooling, was preparatory to assignment on July 11, 1918, at reveille, as commander of Battery D.

At the beginning, the men of the battery resisted their new commander. They appear to have had difficulties with the three preceding commanders, although it was not true that, as was later said, they had broken those commanders. The first may have gotten involved with a redheaded woman, and the mess fund seems to have disappeared; he had been football coach at Rockhurst College in Kansas City, a Jesuit high school, whence many of the men had come. The next was ignorant of artillery commands and had to be relieved after a routine drill nearly killed a man. The third received promotion to battalion adjutant. The battery, however, was unruly, many of the men Irish-Americans or German-Americans, good Catholics but not about to listen to their fourth commander, a Protestant farmer who wore thick glasses. The battery also had acquired a group of draftees from New York City, who were tough and streetwise. And so they gave Truman a hard time. As Vere C. "Pup" Leigh, one of the Kansas Citians, recalled, when Captain Truman took command

> he stood there and he was kind of a rather short fellow, compact, serious face, wearing glasses; and we'd had all kinds of officers and this was just another one you know. And he announced to the Battery that he was going to be in charge and when he gave orders he wanted them carried out. He made it pretty plain; and then he turned the Battery over to the First Sergeant and the First Sergeant told us to fall out, and then we gave Captain Truman the Bronx cheer, that's a fact.

That evening "the boys" entertained the captain by letting the horses loose and stampeding them. According to Pup Leigh, he just sat on his horse, watched the horses run, smiled, and told the men to bring them back when the entertainment was over.

The next morning, the personality of the new commander began to register. On the bulletin board, Leigh recalled, "about half the noncoms and most of the first-class privates were busted. And then we knew that we had a different 'cat' to do business with than we had up to that time. He didn't hesitate at all."[21]

In good military fashion, and according to common sense, Truman told the remaining sergeants and corporals that he was in charge, leaving discipline up to them with the understanding that any delinquencies were their fault. In short order, he was in control. The battery's members would do anything he asked; his hold on them was uncanny. Time upon time they showed their desire to follow him—in breaking camp and loading guns and horses on trains (no easy task when enemy and friendly guns alike were booming, the horses were frightened, and the men were not altogether sure of the situation); in moving down muddy roads at night, men and equipment stretching back hundreds of yards; in keeping the tired, thin French horses in as good condition as possible; in watching the readiness of the guns; and in getting the guns into position, wheeling them out, taking coordinates, converting them to ranges, and firing fast as possible: bing, bing, bing, bing, just like at Doniphan.

Truman liked to say that infantrymen were the heroes of World War I and artillerymen had "soft jobs" ("Join the artillery and ride"). This was true for some artillery units, but Truman's battery saw more than its share of action, first in a quiet sector in the Vosges Mountains, then at St.-Mihiel, the Meuse-Argonne, and Verdun. Indeed, the action in the quiet sector produced what battery members described as the Battle of Who Run, which was no easy affair and showed coolness on the part of the battery commander. American troops were known for stirring things in quiet sectors, and Truman's regiment sent over several hundred rounds of gas. German troops had been on the sector for a long time and knew the positions of their adversaries; the captain told his first sergeant to bring up the horses quickly after the battery fired the gas shells, so the men could get the guns out of there fast. The sergeant was twenty-five minutes late, and arrived to find shrapnel raining on the battery. He shouted, "Run boys, they got a bracket on us!" Truman thereupon turned the situation around, shouting for the men to return, using words they had not heard before. The regimental chaplain, Father L. Curtis Tiernan, was on the scene, and said the captain was extraordinarily effective—he took the skin off their ears: "It turned those boys right around." The words may have been harsher than usual, because just before the bombardment his horse slipped into a shell hole, threw him, and fell on him, nearly suffocating him before his lieutenant pulled him out. Among other things, he seems to have made some reflections on the ancestry of the Irish members of the battery.

The battery left two guns in the mud that night; the men returned the next night and took them out. No one was lost in this action. Truman broke and transferred the first sergeant.

St.-Mihiel was mainly a huge bombardment, in which Truman's battery was on hand but took no part. German troops were evacuating the salient on September 12 when the AEF struck. The battle became a race to push the Germans out, accomplished in four days.

The Meuse-Argonne was something else, a terrifically hard battle that began on September 26, lasted until the end of the war, and cost the lives of twenty-six thousand Americans, nearly the equivalent of a big World War I square division. It was the most costly battle in the nation's history. In preparation, several hundred thousand troops marched from St.-Mihiel, to the east of Verdun, across to the west, waiting in forests in daytime and moving at night. Captain Truman marched his men for twenty-two nights, and on one stretch believed he did not sleep for sixty hours. Horses died by the thousands. Men weakened with the strain—Truman's weight dropped from 175 pounds to 135. After the battle opened, the 129th got into several actions. According to Truman's chief mechanic, McKinley Wooden, "They'd fire those guns, then they'd pour a bucket of water down the muzzle and it'd come out the breech just a-steaming, you know." At one point the battery was coming along a road and two engineers told them that if they didn't get the guns up on the hill the Germans would kill all the men in an American regiment: "We pulled up around the hill, and we put a gun under an old apple tree, each gun, and we commenced shooting at machine guns. There was a valley down there and then a slope up, and this slope was lined with machine guns in pillboxes. The old boys would just look down the barrel and give a yank. If they didn't get him with the first shot, on the next shot you'd see him go up in the air." A little before sundown one day, a German plane came right over the battery's position; Truman moved the guns back a hundred yards and to the right two hundred, and not fifteen minutes later "they just shot that orchard all to hell. If he hadn't done that there might not have been a one of us left."[22]

Once the captain received the opportunity all battery commanders hope for: he happened to see an enemy battery coming into range and setting up its guns. He waited until the commander sent back the horses, and then gave his own battery the order to fire as fast as possible. The men sent up forty-nine rounds in two minutes, smothering the enemy battery. For this act Klemm called Truman on the field telephone and threatened a court-martial, for he had fired into another division's sector: "Go ahead!" was the response. "I'll never pass up a chance like that. We plastered 'em." Nothing happened.[23]

The 35th Division was two weeks in the line at the Meuse-Argonne, and after resting went back for three more in front of Verdun, a grisly place. Every time a German shell came over, it dug up bodies left from the battle of 1916. Wooden spread his blankets in a place on Dead Man's Hill, woke up the next morning, and "I looked over on this shelf, and there was a skull there, a bullet hole right through there. Then, over here on this shelf, there was another skull, a bullet hole right through here. I looked outside and saw a blown-off man's leg sticking up out of the ground."[24] The battery remained there until the armistice ending the war.

After such experiences the armistice was a great relief. At breakfast on November 11, Sergeant Edward Meisburger reported to Captain Truman's dugout to find the captain with a wide grin on his face, stretched out on the ground eating blueberry pie. He gave the sergeant a piece and said, between bites, handing Meisburger a sheet of paper: "Sergeant, you will take this back and read it to the members of the battery."[25] The men thus learned the war would end at 11:00 A.M. Fifteen minutes before the end, the battery fired its last shell. The men had sent ten thousand rounds into the German lines. A battery of French 155s behind Truman's battery shot off its surplus ammunition until just before 11:00, and for the rest of the day the Frenchmen held a celebration, then caroused through the night. At one point they insisted upon saluting their next-door neighbor, the local American commander, one man at a time, which kept Truman awake as they marched past: *"Vive Président Wilson! Vive le capitaine d'artillerie américaine!"*[26]

3

Not long afterward the letters to Bess began to anticipate return home. Truman had two pockets in his blouse: Bess's picture was in the left-hand one, Mary's and Mamma's in the other. Bess had sent her photograph to Doniphan, and on the back of a card for "Miss Bessie Wallace" had written: "I'm depending on this to take you to France and back—All Safe and Sound." For Christmas 1918, her friend sent her two shell cases turned into vases; as he explained, they were the only presents he could find.

Christmas dinner at Battery D was a feast made possible by a gift of five hundred dollars from a group of young Kansas City women headed by Miss Mary Jane Tierney, which raised the money by selling a quilt. Battery members bought an enormous five-hundred-pound pig for $235, and the cook roasted and served it with all the trimmings, including new potatoes, canned corn, chicken dumplings, apple cobbler, jelly, and coffee. At the dinner, Corporal Eugene P. Donnelly presided as toastmaster, officers made talks, and a musical program followed, with festivities ended by the battery quartet leading singing, after which the boys gave three cheers for the girls.

For a while, before and after Christmas, officers and soldiers managed leaves, and Captain Truman obtained his share. He was in Paris in late November, where he saw Notre Dame, Napoleon's tomb, the Madeleine, and the Folies Bergères. He and fellow officers engaged a taxi and drove down the "Champ Ellesee" (he gave up on the spelling, he said), the rue Rivoli, across the Alexander III Bridge, and down the boulevard de l'Opéra and many side streets. Traveling to Marseilles, the Truman group attended a performance by the dancer Gaby, who threw a bunch of violets, caught by the future president of the United States. In Nice they took rooms at the Hotel de la Méditerranée, "a dandy place overlooking the sea." Truman and Major Gates "bought an interest in an auto" and drove across the border into Italy at Menton, back by way of the Grande Corniche, Napoleon's road running on top of the foothills of the Alps: "It is a very crooked road and around every turn is a more beautiful view than the last one."[27] The group visited Monte Carlo and went inside the casino, but could not gamble because they were in uniform.

But as months passed, and a lack of ships kept the AEF from returning home ("Lafayette, we are still here"), discipline began to slip. General Pershing pushed his generals, who pushed the colonels, and officers found themselves having to enforce a discipline they disliked because, they believed, it was unnecessary. Truman hated to be mean to men who had followed him into battle. A young man named Bobby—there were three Bobbys in the battery and he liked them all—got into trouble, and he had to dress him down. Bobby's punishment was to clean the stables on weekends and to wash dirty wagons. The regiment's lieutenant colonel, Arthur J. Elliott, caught Battery D men shooting dice and referred this serious matter to Truman: "Well," the captain said, "as many places as there are here to hide to shoot dice in this little town, if you don't know any better than to get out there where the colonel can find you, you can just peel potatoes three days."[28] But it was the inspectors from headquarters who caused the most trouble. According to Truman one of them advised him to feed horses oatmeal, another that he sift chaff from hay, salt it, and feed it. He claimed to believe that after the war such officers could have only two occupations. One was to run "thirst emporiums," that is, bars, for they all were drinkers; the other, he wrote, was to be waiters, and that, he opined, was unlikely because so many people were beginning to patronize the new places for dining out known as cafeterias.

During all this time the larger political and diplomatic scenery passed Truman by. The letters show no interest in the proceedings of the Paris Peace Conference. He wrote two or three to Bess and the Noland sisters referring facetiously to "Woodie"—President Wilson—and relating his contempt for subjects that aroused the American president: "For my part, and every A.E.F. man feels the same way, I don't give a whoop (to put it mildly) whether there's a League of Nations or whether Russia has a Red government or a Purple one, and if the President of the Czecho-Slovaks wants to pry the throne from under the King of Bohemia, let him pry but send us home."[29] On one occasion Captain Truman saw President Wilson. He and a group of soldiers stood across the street from the Hotel Crillon while Wilson walked down the steps to a waiting automobile.

After remaining near Verdun the battery shifted to Rosières, near Bar-le-

Duc. This may have been the place remembered by Captain Roger Sermon, afterward mayor of Independence, where, to keep from going crazy, so Sermon told Jonathan Daniels, the officers held an almost continuous poker game. One night they repaired to the quarters of Captain Spencer Salisbury, who was billeted in a house occupied downstairs by two old maids. To get to Salisbury's quarters it was necessary to climb a high, narrow stairway, which was equally difficult to go down. When nature called for Sermon, he decided to relieve himself out a window rather than navigate the stairs. Truman and the others joined. The colonel received a protest from the ladies, and ordered Sermon, as regimental adjutant, to reprimand Salisbury, sponsor of this event, before the entire officers' mess, which he did.[30]

After Rosières they entrained for Le Mans, a staging area for the voyage back. The members of Battery D boarded the new fourteen-thousand-ton German steamer *Zeppelin,* which after a rough passage (stevedores overloaded the ship at the front, and the bow would plunge underwater, followed by wallowing from one side to the other) landed at New York on Easter morning, April 20, 1919. During the voyage the men whiled away their time playing poker, taking a percentage from each game to buy a sixteen-inch-high loving cup inscribed to "Captain Harry S. Truman. Presented by the members of Battery D in appreciation of his justice, ability and leadership."

The rest was anticlimax. In New York the mayor's welcome boat came out and the band played "Home, Sweet Home," and almost everyone wept— even the most hardened member of the battery sniffed, Truman said. Welfare organizations overwhelmed the men with gifts. "The Jews gave us handkerchiefs, the Y.M.C.A. chocolate, the Knights of Columbus, cigarettes; the Red Cross, real homemade cake; and the Salvation Army, God bless 'em, sent telegrams free and gave us Easter eggs made of chocolate." The unit crossed from Hoboken to Camp Mills on Long Island, and there everyone ate mountains of ice cream. Captain Truman went into the city and visited the house of the sister of his battery barber, Frank Spina, where he ate spaghetti and "nearly foundered."[31] Thereafter came the train ride out to Camp Funston, Kansas, with a stop for the parade in Kansas City, and mustering out on May 6.

The experience was unforgettable, its importance for the future national and international leader crucial. Not at once, to be sure, did the army service work its spell, for first it was necessary to try the haberdashery. Four years after the armistice, however, Harry Truman was elected county judge for Jackson County, which included Independence and Kansas City, and was on his way, albeit slowly, to high office.

The memories of the battery never dimmed, neither those of the commander nor those of his men. In Truman's twenty-one-line article in *Who's Who,* he devoted five lines to military service in World War I, including the Guard and Reserves, and only two to the presidency. The files of the Truman Library contain hundreds of letters to the president of the United States from former members of the battery, and every time a letter arrived for "Captain Harry" it received a personally dictated answer, usually with a handwritten postscript. Each year the division held a reunion; at one of them, in Kansas City in the late 1940s, the battery assembled in a large room, and President Truman brought in General Eisenhower, then army chief of staff, and Fleet Admiral William D. Leahy, the president's personal chief of staff. He went around and introduced each member of the battery: "By God," Wooden remembered, "he called pretty near all of us by our first names."[32] At the inaugural in 1949, the president invited the battery to Washington. That morning everyone had breakfast together. Someone called him "Mr. President," and he put up his hand. "We'll have none of that here," he said. "I'm Captain Harry."[33] Battery D marched in the inaugural parade in single file on each side of the president's automobile, each man carrying a cane and wearing a red armband with a gold-colored *D*.

After Truman's retirement to Independence, the correspondence continued, and if anything letters became more numerous, although the correspondents were diminishing. When Truman died in 1972, one of his members of Battery D, Abe Gladstone, said: "Captain Harry had a few favorites but I wasn't one of them. But he was my favorite and always will be."[34] When Bess passed on, ten years later, five veterans of the battery attended her funeral, four of them in wheelchairs.

Chapter Five

Boom and Bust

*D*uring the years from 1919 to 1922, Harry Truman ran a haberdashery in Kansas City with his army friend Eddie Jacobson. At the outset, everything seemed fine. He and Bess married, and that change in the organization of his life brought an end to the doubt that had plagued him for years. No longer would he have to keep persuading Bess of his love, or worry that something would happen and she would be unwilling to marry him. He had done everything he could to bring her to consent to marry, and her private consent had given way to a formal engagement, but he could not be certain until marriage itself, which now took place. And with the store in the center of Kansas City, he was back in the life of the metropolis he so enjoyed. He became a member of the Kansas City Club, paying $225 for the privilege. The club afforded a dining room where he could take friends for lunch. The haberdashery also was much more than a store; it became a headquarters to promote activities for the city, and indeed the entire country, as when the American Legion held its first annual convention in Kansas City in 1921— Truman was a member of the decorations committee, which required him to solicit businessmen and organizations to put out as much bunting and as many flags as possible. The store, too, was a sort of club, to which his army buddies came to spend time. Prominently displayed was the Battery D loving cup. Whenever people entered the store they found several former comrades in attendance, talking about army experiences, reliving Camp Doniphan or France.

But then another business failure befell him, and it was a bitter one, involving a much larger financial loss than anything he had experienced before. The nationwide economic recession of 1921–1922 drastically lowered prices of farm produce and manufactured goods. Farmers lost out badly. So did businessmen, whose inventories dropped in value while orders went down dramatically. The recession closed the haberdashery and plunged Truman into a financial morass that took him to the verge of bankruptcy—he would be a dozen years getting out of. It was a tragic experience. He never forgot it; he could not forget it.

1

Marriage was, to be sure, the most important event of Harry Truman's life. He had courted Bess for eight and a half years, far beyond what he had expected. His letters had set out how keenly he looked forward to a life together. And to his great good fortune the venture proved extraordinarily successful.

After his discharge from the army it was clear that marriage would come quickly. The captain had bought a wedding ring in Paris on the rue de la Paix.[1] As for where the wedding might take place, his first suggestion did not work out—he had suggested that Bess meet him in New York and that they marry in the Little-Church-around-the-Corner near Broadway. An Episcopal church, it enjoyed a reputation among theatrical folk as a good place for marriages, and he may have liked its casual name. But Bess opted for another little church around the corner, a few blocks from Delaware Street, where relatives and friends might attend the ceremony. They thereupon chose the day, June 28, 1919—by chance the same day that another ceremony took place in faraway Versailles, with President Wilson and a galaxy of European statesmen signing the peace treaty with Germany that officially ended the state of war that still existed, after the armistice, with Germany.

It was a typical small-town wedding. An observer might have described it as a bit prosaic, for tens of thousands of weddings in 1919 must have been almost the same. The day before, Harry and his sister picked daisies in a field near the farm, and the daisies became part of the church decorations. The day of the wedding Mary and her mother were terribly busy, for the threshers came for the wheat—"my mother and I cooked dinner for twelve threshers and then we had to clean up and hurry." She long remembered the excitement of her brother as she saw him come out of the vestry room.[2] Bess did not wear a veil, and two bridesmaids, cousins, accompanied her. The Reverend John W. Plunkett read the service. An account appeared in the *Independence Examiner,* written by the wife of the editor, Mrs. William Southern, Jr., whose daughter had married Bess's brother George:

A wedding of unusual beauty and interest, was that of Miss Bess Wallace and Capt. Harry Truman, on Saturday afternoon at four o'clock, at Trinity Episcopal church. Miss Wallace has lived in Independence all her life and has a large circle of friends. Independence also claims Capt. Truman although he has spent much time away. It was in this setting of love and devoted friendship that the marriage was solemnized. The church was beautifully decorated with garden flowers in pastel shades. The altar was a mass of daisies, pink hollyhocks and pale blue larkspur against a soft green background, lighted with tall cathedral candles.[3]

A reception followed in the backyard of 219 North Delaware. It was a very hot day, and guests must have appreciated the location under the trees. The couple left for a trip to Chicago, Detroit, and finally Port Huron, where they visited Harry's cousin Mary Colgan, by then Mary Romine, with whom fifteen years before he had played the joke on Mary's brother, Fred, and Harry's roommate, Ed Green. Harry and Mary undoubtedly discussed that extended prank.

The newlyweds moved into 219 North Delaware. The physical circumstances, living in the house in which Bess already had spent fifteen years and had known since a child as her grandparents' house, were certainly familiar to the new wife, and that must have made marriage easier. The husband knew the house too; he had been there many times over the years since 1910. It was a large house, its many rooms offering a privacy that the Grandview farmhouse never could have boasted. To be sure, it was Mrs. Wallace's house, not that of the bride and groom, but that was a nominal matter: Mrs. Wallace was not wealthy, and from the beginning it is probable that Truman was in fact the head of the household, paying the bills through his wife. Writers looking at the way in which the former captain of the AEF, the erstwhile farmer from Grandview, moved into his mother-in-law's house have sometimes offered an almost cramped view of the circumstances, which in fact must have seemed quite spacious.

As it happened, Delaware Street—in which Truman and his wife were to live for sixteen years without interruption—became the familial home base from which they departed only for temporary reasons. In 1935 when Truman became a U.S. senator they began a life of back-and-forth, moving to Washington for half years at first, and then during World War II closing the house while Mrs. Wallace came to Washington to stay with them in their Connecticut Avenue apartment. After the war, even with residence in the White House, Bess and Mrs. Wallace again alternated from one "big house" to the other, never quite settling down in the capital city.

Within the household there was a clear-cut division of labor, which despite some confusions worked out well.[4] There certainly was no question of two careers jangling against each other. In what is now an old-fashioned way Bess kept to the household tasks and Harry to his career tasks. Bess was not really domestic and does not seem to have kept house very well. She had a cook who did the kitchen tasks, and as for the dusting and cleaning, she and the cook appear to have done some of it together. The house was not very orderly. Many years later when the National Park Service took over the house in 1982 it was in a surprisingly primitive condition. The general sloppiness of Bess's housekeeping prevented the couple, perhaps, from having houseguests, save on extraordinary occasions. They surely did not use the house for entertainment, except once in a long while. Many of Truman's close friends were never in the house. Mr. and Mrs. Eddie Jacobson were never invited to the

house, albeit that failure may have been because (as Bluma Jacobson believed)
the Trumans did not invite Jews to their house. But then the obverse of Bess's
failures at housekeeping, if such they were, was the fact that from the very
beginning of her correspondence with her husband she secreted his letters in
various convenient places in the large house—sometimes in drawers, sometimes under sofas—and this wonderful correspondence, the most detailed
and intimate and complete of any correspondence by any president of the
United States, managed to survive until the late 1970s when Margaret Truman
allowed staff members of the Truman Library to enter the house surrep-
titiously (Bess, an invalid, was still living there) and gather it up from its
many depositories.

Bess was not much interested in politics, and this virtual disinterest—she
liked political news and political gossip—did not help her husband when he
turned to politics. One suspects there were plenty of times when she could
have been out on the hustings shaking hands, or could otherwise have done
him good turns, and she simply did not, preferring to stay home. His letters
show no protests over such lapses. Because almost none of Bess's letters to her
husband survive, we do not know how she justified her failure to play a
public role, if she bothered to explain it.

Bess sometimes was given to sharpness. Whenever instances arose, her
husband failed to see them. He let them go, without criticism. Only once in
the extraordinarily detailed written record of the marriage—the "Dear Bess
letters," as his sixteen hundred surviving letters to his wife now are known—
was there any hint that he was unhappy with her. In the autumn of 1945 she
had gone back to Independence. He continued in the White House and worked
incessantly. He was new to the job, World War II had just ended, demobilization was in course, and as president he was attempting to direct reconversion
from a wartime to peacetime economy, an extremely difficult task. By Christ-
mastime he was tired out. He flew to Kansas City to spend the holidays with
the family. Weather was terrible, and the plane trip was close to dangerous.
When he walked into the living room at 219 North Delaware, Bess was in a
mood and, instead of welcoming her husband, snapped that he must have
come home because he could not find any reason to stay away. She hurt him
badly. After return to Washington he penned a letter in which he remarked,
"I feel like a last year's bird's nest which is on its second year":

> You can never appreciate what it means to come home as I did the other
> evening after doing at least one hundred things I didn't want to do and have the
> only person in the world whose approval and good opinion I value look at me
> like I'm something the cat dragged in. . . . This head of mine should have been
> bigger and better proportioned. There ought to have been more brain and a
> larger bump of ego or something . . . you, Margie, and everyone else who may
> have any influence on my actions must give me help and assistance, because no
> one ever needed help and assistance as I do now. If I can get the use of the best

brains in the country and a little bit of help from those I have on a pedestal at home, the job will be done.[5]

The president thought better of sending this letter, and put it in his desk, where it was found after he died.

Beyond question what held the marriage together was the intense affection each had for the other. This they had demonstrated during the long years of courtship; a chemistry was at work there that sufficed for an enduring marriage. Bess's Harry was a broad-shouldered farmer when she saw him standing at the door of the Delaware Street house in 1910. She surely liked the looks of him. On his side there was equal attraction. About the time the courtship started she had a snapshot taken standing alongside a tree in the backyard of the Delaware Street house, and she looked girlishly beautiful. In later years she seldom took a good picture. She was short, and as the years passed she put on weight that made her less attractive. But it did not matter, for long before they had fallen in love, and the chemistry that had brought them together never left.

It was said by biographers and other observers that marriage brought not merely Bess but her mother, that he found himself with a domineering mother-in-law, with whom he never got along and whose presence created trouble during the rest of Mrs. Wallace's life, until her death in 1952. There is some evidence to that effect. In 1948, when giving a speech before one hundred thousand farmers in Dexter, Iowa—one of the principal occasions of that campaign, which may have done more than any speech elsewhere to elect him president in his own right—he told a mother-in-law joke. According to the joke, a man was attending the funeral service of his wife. After the church service, the undertaker inquired if the man would ride down to the cemetery in the same car with his mother-in-law. The man said, "Well, I can do it, but it's just going to spoil the whole day for me."[6] Was he talking about Mrs. Wallace? She may have told a reporter that year that she would vote for Governor Thomas E. Dewey. The president's sister-in-law, May Wallace, related years later that when Harry Truman came back from the army he wanted to return to the farm, but Bess hated it there and conspired with her mother, who wanted her at 219 North Delaware. According to May, Mrs. Wallace feigned illness, and Bess undertook to care for her, forcing her husband to take up residence in his mother-in-law's house. Mrs. Wallace appears to have kept her eye on everyone. May said that her sister-in-law, Natalie Wallace, who lived next to May's house (the two lived in bungalows directly behind 219), greatly disliked the fact that Mrs. Wallace wanted to supervise her every move. One day May noticed Natalie passing her house. Asked where she was going, Natalie answered: "To Kansas City. But I'm not going to get the streetcar at the corner because if I do, Mother Wallace is going to come out of the house and ask me where I'm going. I'm not planning to do anything wrong. I just want to go someplace without telling her about it!"[7]

Margaret Truman, who should have been able to divine this situation, has related that Mrs. Wallace did not get along with her son-in-law, and that although there was no public dissension, disagreement in private was frequent.[8]

When Mrs. Wallace's father died during World War I, he had left his wife an annuity that lasted until her death a few years later, and divided the rest of his estate among his five children, giving Mrs. Wallace $23,247.39. It was no tremendous amount of money, and it would have to last for the rest of her life, which proved a long time. Margaret believes that she had no financial sense whatsoever and gradually spent the money on what pleased her, including the education of her son Fred at the University of Missouri. When the haberdashery was closing its doors in April 1922, she made no effort to help, and was planning a trip with Fred to the East Coast as soon as he finished the school year.[9] But then this sounds as if she was thoughtless rather than thoughtful, unthinking about, rather than actively disliking, her son-in-law.

Mrs. Wallace owned the house on North Delaware, which she purchased from the trustees of her father's estate. (This means she did not retain for long the $23,247.39 she inherited, spending $10,000 or $15,000 buying the house.) When she died in 1952 her will bequeathed it to her four children and forced the then president of the United States, who by that time had lived in the house thirty-three years, to buy out the brothers so he could retire; the house should have been his long since, for Mrs. Wallace's inheritance would have run out years before, and he had been supporting her. Again, one suspects she did not think much about all this.

Truman never spoke openly against his mother-in-law, nor wrote critically about her privately. On one occasion he took pains to set down his disgust with mother-in-law jokes, the Dexter, Iowa, incident notwithstanding. Early one morning in 1952, as she lay dying just across the hall from him in the White House, he sat at his desk and wrote how she was slipping away, and how she had been a good mother-in-law.

Perhaps the best explanation of Mrs. Wallace's relations with Harry Truman over the years came from Ardis Haukenberry, niece of Ethel and Nellie Noland, daughter of their sister Ruth, who had married and moved away. After the aunts and her mother passed on, she went back to Independence and spent her last years in the Noland house at 216 North Delaware. Ardis told the present writer that Mrs. Wallace felt her son-in-law was not good enough for Bess.[10] She liked him, seldom disagreed with him, enjoyed his presence when he was courting Bess, and welcomed him as a returning veteran, but for years believed Bess could have done better.

Here must be the truth. She saw him as a man who could not succeed at anything. According to Ardis, Mrs. Wallace never anticipated her son-in-law would become president of the United States. In this regard one recalls the remark of a newspaperman and television reporter in Kansas City, Randall Jessee, who was close to Truman during the years of retirement and became the family spokesman at the time of the president's death. He may have talked to Truman about Mrs. Wallace. Jessee's remark was another mother-in-law joke: "Behind every great man there's a loyal wife and a surprised mother-in-law."[11]

After marriage, Harry Truman did not make any change in relationships on his side of the family. To his mother, with whom he had been so close, he remained as dutiful as before. The best man at the wedding, Ted Marks, formerly captain in the 129th and a tailor in Kansas City—he had made the groom's suit, a gray-striped affair that cost seventy dollars, and made a similar suit for himself—took Harry's mother down to the railroad station in Kansas City to see the couple off. Mrs. Truman had Ted by the arm, and he said to her, "Well, now, Mrs. Truman, you've lost Harry." A small woman, she looked up at him and said, "Indeed I haven't."[12] Her son was to prove dutiful for the rest of her life: he visited when possible, called on the telephone, and wrote letters that became known in his memoirs, when they began to consider matters of national and international importance, as the Dear Mamma and Mary letters.

The marriage proved long-lasting. Although marriage came when Bess was thirty-four and Harry thirty-five, the couple celebrated their golden wedding anniversary in 1969 and went on together for three more years.

2

The origin of the haberdashery was the successful canteen at Camp Doniphan in 1917–1918. A good deal of calculation went into it. Eddie Jacobson's wife, Bluma, said years later that soon after Harry and Bess's marriage, Truman happened on her husband on a street in Kansas City, and the two talked about a store. But Eddie and Harry had signed a lease for the store on May 27, 1919, a month before the wedding, and the two must have talked about a store before they came home from France. For Eddie, who had been in the men's furnishings business, it was a congenial arrangement. It recommended itself to Truman as a similarly easy solution to several of his concerns.

First among the haberdashery's advantages to Harry was that it would allow him to leave the farm. He could not live in Independence and run the farm: he could have driven back and forth, but because of the farm's livestock he would have become dependent on a hired man or hired men, and it would have been difficult to find people who would live in, or nearby, and watch the stock. Moreover, in winter months, lacking work with the crops, hired men were prohibitively expensive. He also believed that year in, year out, the farm could not bring in the living Bess desired. The wartime years had been profitable, but there was no certainty grain prices would continue once European farmland returned to productivity. The Grandview farm also was divided in ownership: his mother owned one half exclusively, and the other half was owned by his mother, Vivian, Mary, and himself. They had inherited the latter half from Uncle Harrison, who died in 1916. This division required a fivefold distribution of yearly profits. All in all, the farm no longer attracted him, despite his wartime commentaries about desiring to follow a mule down a corn row all the rest of his days.[13]

As if this were not recommendation enough, Bess did not want to live on the farm. May Wallace's story of a conspiracy between her and her mother may not have been true, but Margaret Truman has stated flatly that her mother hated the farm.

Some time was necessary to arrange a sale of the livestock and implements, but when it happened it proved a great success. The 16 pigs Truman had left to the care of Mary and the hired men, for which he paid ninety-six dollars, had increased to 234 and brought four thousand dollars. Cows, horses, and implements brought eleven thousand more. How he divided this we do not know. As the responsible farmer he may have received the entire amount, not sharing it with Mary or his mother, nor Vivian, who had left the farm years before.[14]

He divested himself of his interest in the farm, the share from Uncle Harrison's will, seventy-five acres. In what form he took this payment is unknown. He had lost seventy-five hundred dollars in the lead and zinc mine, and presumably owed his mother for that. She had co-signed the five thousand-dollar notes he put into Morgan and Company, as collateral for a loan; his associates may have called the notes, his mother paying them, for when he got out of Morgan and Company after the war he received a house at 3404 Karnes Boulevard in Kansas City owned by Morgan, and, after trading it for another at 3932 Bell, he made yet another trade, this for a farm of one hundred and sixty acres in nearby Johnson County, Kansas.

Truman put down most of the money necessary to establish the haberdashery, close to five thousand dollars, which was obtained through sale of the pigs, horses, cows, and machinery or of his seventy-five acres, less what he owed his mother for the lead and zinc mine and the oil investment. It is possible he put in a considerably larger sum. His finances at this time are difficult to know, and he later seems to have been uncertain what he had in the store.

Eddie Jacobson invested nine hundred or a thousand dollars. Some of the partners' money went for the store's lease. When they signed it with a real estate operator named Louis Oppenstein, they paid an advance. Presumably, they had money for other start-up costs. They established a line of credit with the Security State Bank, where Harry Jobes, former captain of the 129th's supply company, worked. They dealt also with the Twelfth Street Bank. Initial consignments of stock were on credit, payable after one to three months.

The store opened late in November 1919, and the partners were full of confidence. Truman wrote his first lieutenant in Battery D, Victor H. Housholder: "Eddie Jacobson and I have opened a successor to the 129th Field Artillery canteen over on 12th Street opposite the Muehlebach Hotel. We have notified all the boys about what we have done and they have been coming in in droves. Of course, we are not handling any booze or candy or apples or things of that kind, but our shirt line and the rest of it are as good as money can buy."[15] They gave away blotters on which they advertised in large letters an eye-catcher credited to Dr. A. Gloom Chaser: "It takes 65 muscles of the face to make a frown and 12 to make a smile—why work overtime?" Underneath they offered an explanation: "Buy your men's furnishings from us at new prices. You will smile at the great reductions. We will smile at the increased business. Then none of us will be overworked."

The store was well stocked. "Truman and Jacobson" did not sell suits—only shirts, ties, underwear, and men's jewelry. Panels above the two front showcase windows advertised the other items: hosiery, gloves, belts, and hats.

The hours were 8:00 A.M. to 9:00 P.M., six days a week. Both partners waited on customers and had reverse shifts. They kept a clerk all the time. In their spare time, Truman was the bookkeeper and Jacobson the buyer.

All business was nominally for cash, no credit. Eddie remembered that Harry lent money to veterans for hospital expenses—an operation, or the birth of a child—"and once he gave away our entire stock of pajamas to the wounded soldiers in the Kansas City vets' hospital." Eddie said he got so he could always tell when a man came in to touch his partner: if he addressed the partner as "Captain Truman," he was a cash customer; if he said "Captain Harry," that meant credit. But Eddie quickly added that his partner's generosity was not the cause of the haberdashery's eventual troubles. Creditors paid back practically all the loans.[16]

The store was in a five-story brick building listed in 1895 as the Navarro Block. In 1919, it was bought by the Oppenstein brothers. The building had space for five stores on the ground floor. The rest was a hotel—the Glennon, as it was called—for which E. F. Geraughty took a ten-year lease at twenty-five thousand dollars per year. It had a first-floor lobby and offices and ninety-eight guest rooms with rates from two to five dollars. It operated from 1920 until 1930, when it was razed to make way for the twenty-story Phillips Hotel, the tallest hotel in Kansas City when finished in 1931.

The location was first-rate, on the northwest corner of Twelfth and Baltimore, across from the city's largest and newest hotel, the Muehlebach. Twelfth Street was busy day and night, always full of people, which justified the store's late closing hours. The area admittedly had its raffish side. When the U.S. Navy closed the red-light district of New Orleans during World War I, prostitutes migrated north to Kansas City, among other places, and promenaded nightly on Twelfth Street; some of the "shoppers" were hardly looking for men's furnishings. Jazz bands accompanied the emigrants, and one of the results was a notable composition, "Twelfth Street Rag." Gambling flourished. Two houses operated in the Dixon Hotel, near the Truman and Jacobson establishment: one in the basement and the other upstairs, the principal game being craps. According to a reliable account of Kansas City at this time, substantial citizens in the vicinity of Twelfth Street included a wire handler for a national syndicate for horse bookings, Hard Luck Charley Hampton; a blind bookie, who earned a fortune by never making a mistake with his mathematics, Harry Brewer; a gambler, who was nice to people who lost and always respected his obligations, Jake Feinberg; and an ethical crapshooter named Gold Tooth Maxie.[17] Still, Kansas City had always been this sort of metropolis, and so were many other American cities of the time—to describe the lowlife is to overlook the legitimate shoppers and respectable downtown businesses. With these latter elements, the foundation of the city's prosperity, the firm of Truman and Jacobson fitted nicely.

The partners had an uneasy experience with their first clerk, Oliver M. Solinger. Perhaps such episodes are a likely happening for any new retail business, even when the owners should be able to anticipate trouble—it was Truman and Jacobson, after all, who had "sewn up the pockets" in the Doniphan canteen. In any event, they came to suspect that their clerk was cheating at the cash register and hired a private detective to loiter in the store and watch him work. The detective saw the clerk ring up a $4.04 sale as $3.04 and pocket the difference, and turn an $8.80 sale into a $3.80 sale, this within a half-hour: "Sol" was acquiring a full day's wages in thirty minutes. He must have been responsible for several hundred dollars in losses. The partners confronted him and he confessed, in tears, on his knees. Truman relented and eventually brought Jacobson around, on a promise that Sol would move to another city and make restitution as soon as he could. He did not keep his word. Eddie wrote him:

> Sol, your obligation to us is a deep one. The mere payment of the money is about the least thing you could do. If you have any manhood left in you come clean. This is a small world, and Harry Truman and I are getting a little bigger each day. Don't be an ungrateful pup like you have almost made me believe you are; you need us. God only knows how much more than we need you. There is only one answer. COME CLEAN.

To no avail, and Eddie wrote again:

> You have no more manhood about you than the dirty gutter rats that infest 12th and live off the earnings of the women on the street. . . . Must hear from you with a remittance by the 25th day of January or else—I will mail a copy of this

letter and copy of your confession to your mother. I will swear out a warrant for your arrest and bring you back to face the music. This is my final letter to you.[18]

Sol never paid.

The store offered moments of humor, which took the sting out of the losses caused by Solinger. All kinds of people passed through. Truman recalled a big Swede who came in one day and asked for heavy underwear; Jacobson got out the heaviest in stock, but the Swede said it was not heavy enough. Jacobson climbed up and dug around on the shelves until he came out with a box containing underwear of a different color, otherwise the same. It was what the Swede wanted. "These will cost you a couple of dollars more," Jacobson replied. "I didn't know you wanted to pay that much." Truman was unable to keep a straight face and walked to the back of the store, out of sight.[19]

The first full year of operations, January through December 1920, grossed seventy thousand dollars. The partners sold expensive merchandise, silk shirts at sixteen dollars. Flush times after the war encouraged such sales.

It was a good life while it lasted. Both Truman and Jacobson must have enjoyed walking along the city's busiest street to discover a store bearing their names, Truman and Jacobson, on black tiles across the white-tiled entrance-way. And as they looked up, almost in wonder, they could see the two large plate-glass windows, smaller windows on each side of the entrance, which they had "dressed" in the ways of the time, meaning that the dresser had stuffed an extraordinary amount of merchandise in the windows. Hanging down like lattices were detachable, ever-clean, celluloid "Hoover" collars. Everything else the store sold was there, as many examples as possible. Across the top of the plate-glass windows was an advertisement for "Ide" shirts and collars, the store brand. No men's furnishings store in the city looked better. It was the culmination of their experience with the canteen at Doniphan—but with such an increase in arrangements! No boarded, make-shift shed with rough-hewn tables in front, no tired and dusty "doughboys" lounging at the tables drinking Puritan. The Twelfth Street store sold elegant goods to elegant people.

During the years of the store's operation Truman naturally was active in veterans' affairs. Battery D held annual reunions on St. Patrick's Day, and almost all the men and officers attended. Photographs show everyone at round banquet tables, sitting solemnly for the cameraman. But this must have been before the fun started. One of "the boys" wrote in advance of the 1920 reunion that there should be "No Wild Wimmen," as he was under contract.[20] That year they sang songs, including "As the caissons go rolling along" and "Keep your head down, Fritzie boy" (or they'd open rapid-fire). The latter song had a variant:

> Keep your shades down, Mary Ann.
> Keep your shades down, Mary Ann.

Last night by the pale moonlight.
We saw you, we saw you.
You were combing your auburn hair.
It was hanging upon a chair.
If you want to keep your secrets
From your future man,
Keep your shades down, Mary Ann.

What happened after that song, what others were sung, or what they led to, is not difficult to imagine.

The 1921 reunion turned into an "uproarious" time when the dinner was served. A letter from the head of the dining room of the Benevolent and Protective Order of Elks, E. J. Becker, to Truman, dated March 12, used exactly that word and explained that "three members of your company went into our kitchen and threw dishes and glassware at the colored help working therein." The restaurant owner presented a bill of $17.80 for breakage and cleanup and apparently "Captain Harry" paid it, out of his own pocket.[21] One of the boys, Eddie McKim, remembered other details, possibly from another reunion. He, Eddie, was toastmaster at the time, and everything went all right until someone asked someone to pass the soup "and he airlined it." Eddie went under the table, where he found Colonel Klemm. Someone skipped a sugar bowl down the tile floor. Eddie ducked it. Two policemen turned up, one of them George Brice, who had been in the battery: "They proceeded to practically undress him."[22]

Nor was that all, according to Eddie McKim. After the dinner Eddie took one fellow home and leaned him against the doorjamb while he rang the bell. No one answered, so he dragged him in and laid him out on the divan. At that moment his mother and sister came in and the mother screamed, "Oh, you got my boy drunk!" Eddie was wearing a derby hat, and she crowned him, put that hat right down beyond his ears.

It was during the haberdashery era, in 1920, that Truman helped organize the first Reserve Officers Association in the country, comprising officers from all services—army, navy, and marines. Seventy-five men met at a restaurant, Morton's, on Baltimore Avenue. From the meeting came associations around the United States.

When the first national convention of the American Legion was held in Kansas City in 1921, a galaxy of Allied generals and admirals attended, including General Pershing, Marshal Ferdinand Foch, and Admiral Sir David Beatty. Truman was vice chairman of the committee on decorations, and he undertook to make businessmen sensitive to the occasion. He shrewdly allowed one company to become the Official Decorators. He let everyone else work, however, and two months before the convention he began a propaganda campaign through the newspapers. Speakers appeared before business organizations, asking for flags on every house in the city, Allied flags where possible. Truman's budget was four thousand dollars. The Terminal Railway alone spent fifteen hundred dollars on Union Station. The local Catholic bishop told priests to tell their congregations to decorate. So did the Ministers Alliance. Decorations were everywhere. "When Convention week came we had so much rivalry between the merchants large and small that the town was a riot of color."[23]

The convention itself was a huge success. In the course of festivities the dignitaries dedicated what would become the Liberty Memorial, a vast monument to Kansas City's participation in the first World War. The memorial consists of a plaza of stone built on a bluff, with two large exhibition halls on the east and west ends and a tower in the center that looks north over Union Station to the city's business district. Finished in 1926 at a cost of two million dollars, it was opened by President Calvin Coolidge.

The convention had its lighter side. Some of the boys went down to the stockyards, obtained a steer, brought it to the Baltimore Hotel, put it on an elevator, and took it to the fifth or sixth floor. From the windows of the Muehlebach, ladies' negligees floated down and lodged on trolley wires. Battery D, out in force, was in charge of transportation for wounded soldiers. The battery was supposed to march, but they may have been too drunk to do so: according to Eddie McKim, half of them decided they were wounded soldiers.

3

For a while everything worked with the store, but then the bottom fell out of the nation's economy and out of the partnership of Truman and Jacobson. Across the country inventories piled up; frantic postwar production of industrial and consumer goods came to an end. After the war farm prices stopped going up; for a while they held because of government loans to the Allies and even to enemy nations, all in need of American wheat. But as soon as farms abroad went back into production, exports collapsed, and wheat dropped from $2.40 a bushel in 1920 to $.87 in 1921. Boom times were over, as was the haberdashery.

A good Democrat, Truman liked to say it was all the fault of President Warren G. Harding's secretary of the treasury, Andrew W. Mellon, who not merely allowed but encouraged prices to fall. The fault, if it was a matter for politicians, was with Truman's president, Wilson, who had done nothing to protect manufacturers and farmers. Wilson's secretary of the treasury, his son-in-law, William G. McAdoo, financed the war by a rough arrangement of one-third taxes, two-thirds bonds. He had to do it that way, for at the beginning of the war the country was not prepared for sacrifice. Businessmen would have resisted, and Congress, anyway, would have moved slowly with taxes. The result was horrendous inflation, nearly 100 percent. After the war and peace conference, Wilson became ill and gave the economy no attention. He would not have understood it anyway, as economics were not his forte. Besides, there was no precedent for the government to intervene in a peacetime economy. Every American war had produced boom and bust. Moreover, the government did not possess enough statistical information to enable the treasury's experts to do anything. Too, economists could not have used the information if they had it, for they possessed almost no understanding of business cycles. Economics was a new science, and the nation's few economists had fascinated themselves with the country's money supply and such recent subtleties as the Federal Reserve System, which was supposed to regulate banking but, as they later discovered, did nothing of the sort.

Prices broke in 1921 in a free fall: everything went down. Bankers rushed to get out from under, never thinking that if they bore no responsibility for the inflation they at least bore some for the loosening of credit that trapped many of them as well as their debtors. The index of wholesale commodity prices plunged from 227.9 in 1920 (the standard, set in 1913, was 100) to 150.6 in 1921, throwing 4.7 million people out of work.

The price deflation collapsed the value of the inventory of the partnership of Truman and Jacobson. Neither of the partners had understood anything about the national economy, and they were blindly unaware of the danger. Because they had been financing the store with credit from suppliers and banks, they were caught with an inventory initially valued at thirty thousand dollars that they now might sell, if they could find a buyer, at less than cost.

Nothing could save them. Truman—not Jacobson, who was no student— might have ruefully remembered the Latin phrase *caveat emptor* when thinking about how they had signed their way into business. They held a closing-out sale in April 1922. "We are quitting business," the top of the ad read. "Save your money." Below stood lists of items at bargain prices. New fall hats were $2.95, any cap in the store $1.45, Wilson Bros. gloves $.89, French cape gloves $1.85, wool-lined gloves for a similar price, French folded silk ties $.39, heavy silk ties $.85, Wilson Bros. silk hose $.59, any belt in the store $.69, heavy cotton-ribbed union suits $1.29, Wilson and Arrow shirts $1.30. The ad listed "Shelving for sale—light fixtures for sale. Show cases for sale—hat case for sale."

The partners consulted a lawyer, Phineas Rosenberg, who advised a division of their obligations. He recommended negotiating with the suppliers who had profited from doing business with the partnership to reach a percentage settlement. With two exceptions—a cloak and suit company and a shirt company—the suppliers agreed. The shirt company, Cluett, Peabody, seized a small Truman account in the City Bank of Kansas City. The partners promised that eventually, when they could, they would pay everyone in full.

In addition to the suppliers' loans, they had signed a five-year lease on the store, held by Louis Oppenstein, and its fine print said the lessor had to approve any assigning or subletting; this gave the wily building owner opportunity to refuse any settlement save full payment. In January 1924, he took a judgment for thirty-two hundred dollars. Fortunately he did nothing to collect it. A later writer perhaps has guessed why: throughout the later 1920s, the city government of Kansas City was in the hands of a Democratic machine that supported Truman, and if Oppenstein got out of line the organization could be hard on him—"[H]e knew what the . . . city government could do to a large Republican downtown real estate operator such as himself."[24] In 1933 he settled for what Truman remembered as fifty cents on the dollar.

An obligation of sorts consisted of stock in a corporation Truman and Jacobson formed in February 1921, a scheme that had been a simple effort to raise money. The corporation had not displaced the partnership, but it produced money that passed into the partnership. There was not much to do about it; the partners had no money to pay the shareholders, and if the shareholders had any claim on assets of the partnership it obviously was last claim. Who was involved in this loss is not clear. Harry Jobes invested a thousand dollars, or received a certificate to that effect. Truman's brother-in-law, Frank Wallace, put money into the store, probably into the corporation. How much was lost is also hard to say; the later president of the United States said the corporation raised twelve thousand dollars, a considerable sum.

Of all the debts owed by Truman and Jacobson, a bank loan proved the most troublesome.[25] There were in fact two bank loans. The smaller, from the Twelfth Street Bank, which in a reorganization became the Baltimore Bank, was for $2,800, and the partners paid it off over two years, by 1924, in sums as small as $25. The loan from the Security State Bank was much more of a problem because of its size, $6,800. In January 1923, Truman paid $1,000, thereafter a little more, bringing it down to $5,592.78. By April 30, 1929, when the bank took a judgment, accumulated interest had increased the note to $8,944.78.

The Security State note pushed the partners hard, forcing Jacobson into bankruptcy in 1925 (he listed debts of $10,676.50, mostly the note, and assets of $507, including $28 cash on hand), and Truman managed to avoid bankruptcy only because of a special reason—namely, that he was a public official and the bank could not garnishee his salary. Years later, during his presidency, he explained the situation to a correspondent, at the bottom of whose letter he wrote: "Was a partnership. Jacobson was forced into bankruptcy. Holding public office I could not be forced."[26] He similarly put the case to the writer William Hillman: "Our creditors drove Eddie into bankruptcy, but I became a public official and they couldn't do that to me."[27] The judgment of 1929 permitted seizure of real estate and bank accounts, but he appeared to have possessed neither. His mother-in-law owned the Independence house, and he may not have had bank accounts except in unknown places. In 1930 the bank's attorney, Omar E. Robinson, discovered a $110.87 account in the Manufacturers and Mechanics Bank and took it. In the summer of 1934, Robinson tried again, and attachment orders went to three Independence and Kansas City banks suspected of having Truman accounts, but nothing turned up.[28]

One should add that over the years Truman talked himself into believing he had no real reason to pay the Security State loan, and in light of the circumstances his reasoning made some sense. People who lived through the troubles of 1921–1922 and especially the Great Depression of 1929–1941 easily understood what happened. He and Jacobson contracted the loan in boom times, and the bank asked payment in bust times—when a dollar was worth much more. Truman put up the Johnson County farm as collateral, in which his equity was $5,000, about the same amount as the loan; when he bought the farm it had two mortgages totaling $8,800, and he believed it worth at least his equity plus the mortgages, a total of $13,800. After the wring-out, it was worth no more than the mortgages; the bank took the farm, and after the mortgages nothing was left.[29] It might have been worth less than the mortgages—it had sold mortgage-free in 1909 for $2,250. In any event, in the way of debtors, he made an even exchange: he lost $5,000 or more, and so did the bank.

As it happened, the Security State note passed into the hands of a successor bank, the Continental National Bank, which failed in 1933; when Continental National's assets went up at a sheriff's sale in 1935, Truman obtained the note for a thousand dollars.

Truman's willingness to pay the note if he could get it cheaply shows that behind his contention that he already had paid it he was not, perhaps, so sure. Too, the way in which the later president bought back the note involved some use of friendships, which proves again—and it is hardly necessary to do so— that the law offers more to people with influence than to those without. Eddie Jacobson went into bankruptcy in 1925, but Truman, after staving it off for ten years, got back the note after paying a good deal less than ten cents on the dollar (the note accumulated interest even after judgment in 1929).

The opportunity to buy the note began on December 15, 1934, when the receiver of the Continental National decided to put the bank's assets up for sale. The bank's attorney advertised it, grouping it anonymously in one of several parcels of assets for sale. Truman or his lawyer, Fred A. Boxley, saw the advertisement, and the question immediately became how to get hold of the note. The canny lawyer for Continental (and former lawyer for Security State), Robinson, several of whose private clients had notes in the parcels coming up for sale, apparently was playing both sides, preparing to assist both the bank and his clients. As for anyone outside his practice he was willing to offer their notes, in advance, at perhaps higher prices. Robinson may have intimated to the federal judge in charge of the Continental, Albert L. Reeves, a Republican, that a price of a thousand dollars for Truman's note was reasonable. In any event Reeves so priced it. Robinson told Truman's brother, Vivian, who was working with Boxley, that a thousand dollars would resolve the problem. Vivian was prepared to pay.

On the day of the sale, January 17, 1935, Robinson balked at selling the Truman note. Perhaps he had talked with his brother-in-law, J. F. Meade, president of Continental, about the possibility of a higher price, or the possibility of embarrassing a Democratic politician—in faraway Washington, just two weeks before, Truman had taken the oath as junior senator from Missouri. After conferring with Boxley, Vivian rushed to the owner of the Commerce Trust of Kansas City, William T. Kemper, the same who had arranged for young Harry Truman to be a page at the Democratic national convention in 1900 and had brought Truman's father into the grain speculation that nearly ruined John Truman in 1901–1902. Kemper telephoned an attorney, H. Gavin Leedy, who had been one of Truman's teachers at the Kansas City School of Law when the then county judge spent two years trying vainly—he had to give it up—to obtain a law degree. The banker offered to lend Leedy the money to buy all of Continental's assets; Leedy could act as an intermediary in a delicate situation. Leedy's brother-in-law, Clifton B. Liter, bought the assets that same day, and Boxley arranged for Vivian to buy the note from Leedy.

Why did Kemper get involved? There are several possibilities. As a long-time Democrat, he may only have been trying to protect Truman from Republican adversaries. After the sale there was a little legal scuffling in Kansas City, Robinson trying to get Leedy to pay court costs and Leedy refusing; more to the point, Meade was angling to keep the note. Leedy, Boxley told Truman, was "watching carefully to see that Meade gets no control over it."[30] Another reason Kemper had Leedy buy the Truman note could be that it was simply good business. Leedy bought the parcel containing the Truman note for $1,075, in knowledge that Vivian would repurchase his brother's note for $1,000, leaving Kemper with $90,926 worth of judgments for the price of $75. Any good lawyer could have worked over that pile of judgments and obtained far more than $75, through salary garnisheeing or confiscation of real estate or bank accounts. The most likely possibility for Kemper's intervention, however, is that he wanted to do a favor for a U.S. senator. This sort of thing must have occurred to Kemper. Taking a presumption a step further, it must have occurred to Truman, too.

W. T. Kemper was one of two major donors to Truman's senatorial primary campaign in the summer of 1934, contributing $1,000. This, to be sure, was the cost of the note when it came up for sale.

In the event, nothing untoward happened, so far as anyone knows; Kemper never seems to have gone to Senator Truman for assistance on a matter of bank business. The banker died in 1938, leaving an estate of $30 million, a large sum for the time. He had done well. His sons and grandsons did even better, going on to establish one of the great family banking, investment, and insurance fortunes in the country. But Senator and later President Truman never showed any special friendship for the Kempers. The only question over the sale of the note and its possible relation to W. T. Kemper's business might have arisen from a remark in a letter Boxley wrote Truman as everything was being lined up, the same letter in which he told about the machinations of Meade: "I am writing you a little separate letter," he added, "in regard to a favor that Leedy asked me for, and I told him that I would write you today and sent him copy of the letter." Unfortunately, Boxley's papers have disappeared, Truman's too for the first senatorial term, and it is impossible to know what Leedy was asking. Perhaps it was only a favor for himself.[31]

What did the haberdashery's failure teach Harry Truman? Never again would he be so naive about money as when he put what few eggs he possessed into the small basket known as Truman and Jacobson. Ignorance and enthusiasm had trapped him, and he never forgot it. At the beginning the enterprise had been so simple, for he merely signed his name on pieces of paper. It was enjoyable to stand behind the big, shining cash register in a menswear store across from the Muehlebach and ring up sales—the machine's bell ringing as the cash drawer slid open—all day long and into the evening, while Twelfth Street jumped and the customers sauntered into the store and went out with sacks and parcels. The men of the 129th Field Artillery, and for that matter the entire 35th Division, would buy the store's merchandise. It was impossible to lose. Meanwhile, with membership in the city's most prestigious club, he could take people to lunch. Evenings after the store closed he would drive home or take the streetcar, secure in knowledge that he was providing Bess with a decent income, that he no longer was on the farm but in Independence where she wanted him to be. The future was bright, a shimmering mirage of ever more sales, more ringing of the cash register, more lunches at the Kansas City Club. Then in 1920–1921 sales vanished, everything dissolved, and the pieces of paper, especially the one to Security State, came back to haunt the partnership of Truman and Jacobson.

From that time on, Truman was a fiscal conservative. When he went into politics the critics railed because, they said, he was a failed haberdasher and knew nothing about money. They could not have been more wrong; the haberdashery should have been his best recommendation. When he was in county politics he watched over nickels and even pennies, trying to do everything with the least money. In the Senate he voted for New Deal measures in belief the times required them, but when he had the opportunity in 1941 he organized a "watchdog" committee over war expenditures. During his presidency the record was remarkable: eight years of Truman budgets showed four in deficit, four in surplus, with a small net surplus, this despite the huge expenditures of the Korean War and rearmament against the Soviet Union.

He was to make only a single additional personal error with money, this beginning in 1941 when he was in the Senate, and continuing into the vice presidency. But his second miscalculation was more a matter of judgment, perhaps morality, than of economics. Temptation led him into it, as it can do to anyone, and for a brief and not very shining moment in the summer of 1944 he thought it would foreclose the largest opportunity of his political life. Then, unlike the haberdashery note, this other awkwardness dropped from sight, forgotten by others if not himself, and overlooked in almost all the contemporary and later appraisals of the many events of his presidency.

Chapter Six

County Judge

*I*n the 1920s and early 1930s, Harry S. Truman was a slightly jowly man with a straight mouth and friendly eyes. His hands had lost the horned touch of the farmer; they were fleshy, almost soft—this was no farmer, so a handshaker might have thought, but a businessman, and if not that at least a city dweller or, since he lived in Independence, a town man. And how to appraise him otherwise? It was the era of George F. Babbitt, and Truman was a good deal like Babbitt. He was full of his American Legion activities and his Masonic initiations; he took friends and acquaintances to the Kansas City Club, dressed with care, and sported the flashy neckties of the time. He looked like a thousand other middle-aged denizens of downtown Kansas City, maybe several thousands of them.

But there was something different about him. Inside this no-longer-young-but-not-quite-old man (he turned forty in 1924) was a burning something or other, a desire to succeed that differed from that of other people. Everyone wanted to succeed, but in Truman's case there was an intricately balanced combination of the ideal and real, a kind of poise, that was almost bursting, if one can put it that way, seeking to emerge. The haberdashery could not hold it. The prosaic—as one easily can see—business of being a booster had limits, despite his susceptibilities. This was a man who, when he met the right opportunity, could do marvelous things.

In the past he had not known what he wanted to do. He engaged in pursuits or enterprises he had begun by requirement or happenstance, and either they did not fascinate him or he did not succeed at them or both. In Independence in the 1890s he had enjoyed school but did not do exceedingly well: in the list of five honors graduates of Independence High School in 1901, among forty-one class members, his name did not appear. Nor did he like working in banks in Kansas City. He did what was necessary, and considerably more, and his supervisors believed him a valuable employee, but beyond that he spent no time thinking about banks, and instead of returning to

Spalding's Commercial College he attended the theater. The farm had been a familial necessity—his father needed him. He was a good farmer; John Truman demanded it, and the son enjoyed farming anyway and tried to excel. But the farm never brought in a great deal of money, certainly not enough to support Bess in the way he or she wished, and in any event Bess would not have stayed on the farm. The lead and zinc mine held promise, but it required a great deal of work, and then he lost out. The oil business did no more than break even; he and Morgan had not gotten the pipe down deeply enough to tap the Teter Pool. The army took two years, and he enjoyed them, but essentially he was a civilian soldier. The haberdashery, which he entered with such bright prospects, was a financial disaster.

His two early avocations he may have been forced into, and in any event he failed to take them very far. As a youth he displayed a bent for books about history, and he read far more than most youngsters, but the reason he did it may have been the inability to play childhood games because of his expensive glasses. Eventually he stopped reading history books. His interest in the piano, so much remarked, perhaps also arose because of the glasses. He found the piano interesting but gave it up. When he moved into Mrs. Wallace's house at 219 North Delaware, there was no piano in the house for thirteen years.

All this was preliminary to a day in July or August 1921, when the haberdashery was failing. As he stood behind the cash register gazing at the empty store, he happened to look out the front door and see the Locomobile of Michael J. Pendergast, political boss of eastern Jackson County and brother of Thomas J. Pendergast, "big boss" of Kansas City. Mike was accompanied by his son Jim, who had been an officer in the 129th Field Artillery. Father and son came in and proposed that Captain Harry run for eastern judge of the county. Harry Truman had little else to do and agreed.

It was another decision he did not take so much as he was seized by it. But in this way he discovered what he would describe later, with great pride, as his profession—the profession of politics. Properly undertaken, he maintained, it was a noble career, every bit as important as the work of any doctor, lawyer, or teacher. He threw all his enormous energies into it, every waking hour. He brought to the enterprise all the attention he had denied earlier pursuits. This did not mean that beginning in 1921–1922 he was in full control of his destiny, that thereafter he could point himself toward whatever office he desired and obtain it. As is true of almost anyone pursuing a large and idealistic purpose, he discovered he was not master of his fate; adversity could buffet him, and did so on many occasions. Still, from this point onward in his life, he did everything possible to control the forces surrounding him. He knew what he wanted, hoped for fortune, and was willing to seize all opportunities. Every higher political office that came over the horizon served as his immediate goal. And considering his extraordinary talents, the result was something to watch.

1

The name *Pendergast* is essential to understanding Truman's campaign in 1922 for eastern judge of Jackson County, that is, county commissioner for the eastern or rural portion including Independence. Had it not been for a special need of the Pendergast machine, Truman might never have gone into politics. From participation in county politics, to be sure, he would learn a great deal about how to run for office and hold it once elected. From Pendergast machine politics, moreover, he acquired a reputation of having approved of illegality because he profited from it. An aura of connivance attached itself to his political career, and long afterward many of his fellow Americans would be critical of his background and, they believed, his susceptibilities.

To set out the nature of the Pendergast machine is not difficult. A one-time reporter for the *New York Times* and biographer of the president, Cabell Phillips, wrote an appropriate description years ago. "A political organization," he averred, "is not an uplift society; it is a blunt instrument for seizing and using power."[1] As for the way things work with a machine, a reporter once asked Thomas J. Pendergast about that: "We want to know something about you, about your philosophy, if not of life, of politics. You are a realist, are you not?"

"What do you mean?" asked the boss.

"You take a practical view of things?"

"That's me," was the answer.

Politics, said Tom Pendergast, required organization:

> There are no alibis in politics. The delivery of the votes is what counts. And it is efficient organization in every little ward and precinct that determines national as well as local elections. . . . All the ballyhoo and showmanship such as they have at the national conventions is all right, it's a great show. It gives folks a run for their money. It makes everybody feel good. But the man who makes the organization possible is the man who delivers the votes, and he doesn't deliver them by oratory. Politics is a business, just like anything else.[2]

One day a British woman, a member of Parliament no less, Marjorie Graves, came to see the boss of Kansas City. She had been curious to see a boss, and an interview was laid on. Pendergast received her with as much decorum as he could muster, and she found herself in a brisk conversation.

"Tell me something of the system of your organization," said Graves. "Is it by the bloc or how?"

"Yes," replied Tom, with no attempt at humor. "The block system. We're organized in every block in the city."[3]

The founder of the machine was James Pendergast, known as Alderman Jim, brother of Mike and Tom. The alderman had come to Kansas City from St. Joseph in the 1880s, when the city's politics were young and unformed. As befitted an impecunious Irishman, he settled in the poorest district, known as the West Bottoms, and after a few preliminaries opened a saloon. He loved to eat, and his sizable frame—he was a stocky youth with thick neck and big chest and hamlike hands—began to fill out, his weight increasing to somewhere beyond two hundred pounds. In the custom of the time he sported a Bismarck mustache, but he was easily distinguishable in Kansas City's First Ward by his size and especially his hallmark, a small bow tie.

From the vantage point of the Climax Saloon, Alderman Jim soon beheld local needs that the city fathers were hardly catering to. He began taking care of the needy, an action that enlisted voters, and he financed his good works from the saloon and the Jefferson Hotel, which he also owned. The Jefferson was a third-class hostelry that housed dice games and a bevy of prostitutes.

It is an interesting fact that Alderman Jim seems never to have cheated in politics; that is, he did not vote dead people or buy votes or otherwise stuff ballot boxes. He liked to say he had no need for such unseemly behavior. "I never needed a crooked vote," he said. "All I want is a chance for my friends to get to the polls."[4] He certainly had many friends. Elected to the city council in 1892, he held his seat until he retired because of ill health in 1910. He died of Bright's disease the next year. Long afterward his memory was green in the West Bottoms and in the adjoining Second Ward, which he dominated through the same procedures as in the First, in this instance establishing a saloon across from city hall.

Meanwhile three younger brothers had come from St. Joe, and one proved a far more able organizer than Alderman Jim. This was Tom, one of the most successful bosses in American history, comparable to Frank Hague of Jersey City, Edward J. Flynn of the Bronx, and, later, Richard J. Daley of Chicago. Tom was not of prepossessing appearance. To hostile observers he was "a thick-skulled, heavy-jowled oaf."[5] He had some of the features of his older brother—stocky frame, round face, thick neck, for a while a massive mustache. His hair was lighter, and there was (for a while) more of it. Whereas Jim spoke in a mild baritone, Tom's voice was deep and demanding. As a young man, Tom was remarkably strong. It is possible to contend he was the equal of the fightingest man of his generation, Jack Dempsey: Fireman Jim Flynn, the only man who ever knocked out Dempsey, got into a barroom fight with Tom Pendergast and lost. (Admittedly Jim was drunk, or at least not sober.)[6]

Young Tom began his rise in Kansas City politics just after the turn of the century, and before long he was doing extraordinarily well. In 1902 his brother Jim arranged an appointment as superintendent of streets through the complaisant mayor, James A. Reed.[7] At this task Tom was an instant success. An account of Kansas City that year related of Superintendent Pendergast: "He has given his entire time and attention to the work, and his figure is a familiar one on the streets, standing in a snowstorm in winter, or in the broiling sun of summer, superintending the work of his men."[8] He took over his brother's two ward organizations shortly before his brother died, and soon he was doing even better with them. He sensed far easier ways of participation in politics than saloon-keeping, gambling, and prostitution: he renewed a franchise for the local street railway and sold tax abatements.

Boss Tom cut a far wider swathe in Kansas City politics than his brother ever managed. He justified tax deals because they enlarged his brother's charitable projects. And as the money poured in, he used some of it personally. His standard of living rose, and in the 1920s he took to traveling in Europe, staying in the best hotels. In 1931 he purchased a house on the city's most fashionable avenue, Ward Parkway, at a cost of $150,000. A French Regency mansion, it boasted a spacious hall, wrought-iron stairs, and paneled walls: "The combination of rosehued bricks, laid in white mortar, with softshaded slate, makes the few exterior decorations stand out prominently. The massive wrought-iron door with its vertical panes of glass, the cut stone cornucopia placed above the stone frame that encloses it, and the three sturdy chimneys attract the eye of the beholder."[9] The design came from the desk of Edward W. Tanner, architect for the city's largest real estate developer, J. C. Nichols. The Nichols Company had constructed the first shopping mall in the United States some blocks to the south of central Kansas City and east of the Pendergast mansion, a Spanish colonial extravaganza replete with fountains, statues, and a tower. In an act of helpfulness to Nichols, Pendergast arranged for his cement firm, the Ready-Mixed Concrete Company, to pave nearby Brush Creek, providing one of the few paved creeks in the nation. It ran for several miles and was seventy feet wide. Reportedly, it was six feet thick. Actually, he made it only eight inches thick.[10]

Withal, Tom Pendergast was an irreproachably moral man in his family life. He married only once and lived with his wife and daughter. Almost every morning, in addition to Sundays, he attended mass.

Boss Tom arranged for his older brother Mike to handle the Tenth Ward, which he brought into his political domain. Mike also represented Tom in the eastern part of the county. The eastern portion, Independence and its rural environs, did not attract Tom culturally, although he was pleased to have its votes on issues that concerned him.

It was in regard to an exigency in the eastern portion of Jackson County that Mike Pendergast visited Truman at the haberdashery in 1921.[11] The exigency was complicated and dated back some years, to 1914. The government of Jackson County, which was apart from Kansas City's government (the latter, of course, was in Boss Tom's pocket), provided nine hundred jobs; control of the jobs rested in the three members of the county court, not a judicial body but equivalent to a county commission, with an eastern judge representing Independence and its hinterland, a western judge representing Kansas City, and a presiding judge elected at large. In 1914 Pendergast controlled the western judge, and to get control of the court he sponsored a friendly collaborator in Kansas City's Second Ward, Miles J. Bulger, as presiding judge. Bulger was a small man, known in his ward as the Little Czar. A critic once described him as a bantam who ran with the large roosters.[12] Unfortunately, as presiding judge he acquired visions of grandeur, espied an opportunity to acquire independence from Pendergast, and used the county payroll to create a machine of his own.

Pendergast smashed Bulger's machine in the primary election in 1920, but only by a heroic measure: he allied with a hated rival, Joseph B. Shannon, proprietor of the largest voting district in Kansas City, the Ninth Ward. To secure Shannon's allegiance he was forced to divide the nine hundred county jobs on a fifty-fifty basis. This was a considerable concession, for Shannon was not nearly as important a figure in Kansas City's politics as was Pendergast, but it was necessary in order to discourage Shannon from allying with the Republicans, something he was inclined to do when thwarted. The Ninth Ward's leader, people said, looked like President Harding. But he was smarter than Harding, and Pendergast did not underestimate him.

Pendergast was restive under the arrangement with Shannon, and there were signs that the Ninth Ward's leader was restive too. In the 1922 primary Shannon put up a candidate for eastern judge; Bulger sponsored a candidate that year as well. There were two more candidates, without organizational backing, known to organization men as "snowflakes." Pendergast needed a candidate strong enough not merely to defeat both Shannon and Bulger but especially to discourage the former from going over to the Republicans in the November election. The machine hence chose Truman: he could give the appearance of being an independent; he was a Baptist and Mason and former farmer who had spent almost all his life in the county and had relatives there and was well known; and he was a veteran, which meant far more after World War I than after World War II. Veterans had supported him when he established the haberdashery, and they would support him in politics. When he declared his candidacy at a meeting in Lee's Summit near Independence in March 1922, the Robert M. Clure Post of the American Legion arranged the meeting and held it in the auditorium of the Memorial Building. Major Stayton of the 129th presented him to a group of three hundred cheering ex-servicemen from all parts of the county.

In running for eastern judge the candidate distanced himself from Pendergast by seeking support from the editor of the *Independence Examiner,* Colonel Southern, father of his sister-in-law. Southern was anti-Pendergast. He was a power not only politically through his newspaper, which he founded in 1898, but also religiously through the weekly Sunday school lessons he delivered to the many churchgoers in the rural part of Jackson County. After Southern came out in favor, the Pendergast organization officially endorsed Truman, who allowed as how he appreciated support of organization Democrats.

Truman flirted with the Ku Klux Klan, a rising organization at the time, and gave ten dollars to a friend to give to an organizer. However, when the friend demanded a pledge not to appoint Catholics to county jobs, the candidate indignantly refused, for many of the men in Battery D had been Catholics. The organizer gave back the money. Years later, in 1944, when he was running for the vice presidency, someone said he had joined the Klan. A friendly newspaperman talked to the one-time state Kleagle, who lived in a fashionable section of Kansas City and had the state membership rolls in his attic. Truman's name was not on them.[13]

For the primary campaign, which was what counted in Missouri politics, the law allowed an expenditure of $800, and Truman spent $524.80. The money went for fifteen thousand Jackson County maps. The candidate spoke to audiences around the eastern part of the county. To raise a crowd he enlisted the chief bugler of the Boy Scout Drum and Bugle Corps, John Woodhouse, who received a call from scout headquarters asking if he would like to work three nights a week for the next two weeks, at two dollars a night. Truman picked him up each night and brought him home; he also picked up another scout, and the three drove to such places as Oak Grove, Grandview, Grain Valley, and Buckner. The scouts would start at one end of the town and walk to the other, the bugler playing First Call, Reveille, Mess Call, Assembly, and To the Colors on the way. The second scout carried a sandwich board that said where the meeting would be, usually a schoolhouse or Methodist church. Truman, it said, was speaking. He met them afterward at an agreed-upon place. Both scouts wore their uniforms.[14]

From all testimony the candidate's first speeches were not models of oratory: Harry Truman was no W. J. Bryan. Years later someone asked Eddie McKim of the 129th Field Artillery about Truman's speaking ability, and Eddie did not think he had any.[15] He read from a text, and his custom was to finish as quickly as possible, which often made his speeches unintelligible. He had a dull voice, worsened by his natural Missouri twang. Consider his speech at Lee's Summit following his nomination. His military supporters may have known about his speaking abilities, or lack thereof, for the meeting began with an adult wrestling match, followed by a child match, then another adult match. Mrs. Ethel Lee Buxton sang "Can't You Hear Me Calling Caroline?," "When Irish Eyes Are Smiling," and a parody on "Smiles" written by soldiers who heard her in France. Two men then offered a comedy sketch, volunteers did buck-and-wing dancing, and Mrs. Buxton reappeared for "Mother Machree." O. V. Slaughter, the candidate's onetime farm neighbor and a friend of his parents, related what fine neighbors the Trumans were.[16] After these preliminaries Truman rose, but he was so tongue-tied he could only stammer thanks. He admitted later that he had been "a complete failure."

At an outdoor meeting veterans listened as they sat on the side of a small hill. As the speech droned on, some of them began sliding, and slid all the way to the bottom—so they said afterward. At another meeting, a picnic, the candidate went up in a World War "Jenny" that circled the audience while he threw out handbills. The pilot, a Kansas City garage owner, Clarence England, brought the plane down in a field, missing a barbed-wire fence by three feet. Truman, airsick, emerged from the plane and—in full sight of his audience—leaned over the fence and threw up.

On election night a tense situation developed because the vote among the five Democratic candidates was close. Out of 12,000 ballots cast, Truman ran slightly ahead of the Shannon candidate, a banker from Blue Springs named Emmett Montgomery. The count was 4,230 to 3,951. It occurred to Shannon that if someone stuffed a single precinct ballot box Truman would lose. He tried it personally at Mt. Washington, between Independence and Kansas City, then a timbered area and ideal for the purpose. A Shannon lieutenant in Independence, however, tipped off the Pendergast forces, who went to Marshal John Miles, a Republican but former major of the 129th, who sent his brother and another former member of the 129th, John W. Gibson, out to guard the box. The polling place had a little porch, and when two Truman friends arrived with the guards they found Shannon there: one of his "toughs," Pete Kelley, could be seen running away, for dear life, to warn the waiting three carloads of Shannon supporters not to do what they were about to do. The Truman friends departed, and within minutes, probably because Kelley could not find them, the supporters surged out of the woods and up to the porch where one of them put a gun in the stomach of Marshal Miles's brother. Gibson turned and put one in Shannon's stomach. "Mr. Shannon," he said, "your gang may get Miles, but I will get you." Shannon threw up his hands in terror and shouted to his friends, "Go away, boys, go away; everything is all right here."

Unsatisfied with this attempt, Shannon tried again on the following Thursday, when Truman's friend Brown Harris and two other men were in the election commissioner's office making an informal canvass of the election, with all the pollbooks and tally sheets out. Harris happened to look up and saw six or seven of Shannon's men from Kansas City standing in front of the counter. He grabbed an armful of sheets and books and threw them into the vault. In perhaps five minutes Shannon's friend Kelley arrived and said the Truman group was not a canvassing board, only a registration board, and that Shannon had instructed him to seize the sheets and books and turn them over to the county clerk. Harris told him, of course, as pleasantly as he could, that everything was in the safe.[17]

The November election was perfunctory. Again each candidate received an allowance of $800, and Truman spent $125; Colonel Southern printed a flyer with Truman's photograph and program: "My Platform: Good Roads, A Budgeted Road Fund, Economy, A Day's Work for a Day's Pay, Fewer Automobiles and More Work for County Employees. Harry S. Truman." He received 9,062 votes, his Republican opponent, 6,314.

2

The term as eastern judge on the Jackson County court, from January 1, 1923, until January 1, 1925, was a learning experience. Harry Truman discovered how politics worked in a big Missouri county with half a million people, and he learned to deal with the problem of power. When he went back on the court in 1927 as presiding judge, an office he held until 1935, he was adept in politics and accumulated a record that became the envy of other politicians.

One particular lesson he learned from his early political experiences, especially in retrospect, was the necessity of starting on the local level. Years later he recalled the case of his friend President Herbert Hoover, whom he admired greatly but whose political education had been deficient: "[O]ne of the difficulties was that he, in a political way, started at the top instead of at the bottom and it would be just like my starting into his engineering career without knowing anything about engineering."[18] Similarly President Franklin D. Roosevelt's secretary of agriculture, Henry A. Wallace, "didn't know the political setup from the ground up."[19] In Truman's writings are many testimonies to the need to begin at the beginning. "I was raised a politician," he said with exaggeration, considering that except for his unsuccessful run for township committeeman in the 1916 primary, he had hardly thought of the subject until 1921. But he added, correctly, that he "went from precinct to president."[20] He once wrote Margaret that "Politics is a great game. . . . [I]t is a game of people and how they will act under certain conditions. You never can tell, but you can sometimes guess and I've been a good guesser."[21] This was what he learned after some failures during his first term on the county court.

At the outset everything seemed easy enough. The task was to move in alliance with the other Pendergast judge, Henry F. McElroy, who represented Kansas City, against the presiding judge, Elihu W. Hayes, a Shannon man. The Pendergast machine suspected Hayes not merely because he was Shannon's representative but because of the possibility that at Shannon's behest he might attempt to ally with the remnants of the Bulger-ites (Bulger, elected presiding judge in 1914, had served two four-year terms, and just passed the office to Hayes).

The first move was against a Bulger man, also a Republican, the county engineer, Leo Koehler. Koehler controlled the court's road program, which was most of the court's business; the two new judges were not about to let him continue with that sort of power. They therefore sold his automobiles: "You must also remember that our present $8,000 highway engineer seems to have but one ambition," Truman wrote a friend, "and that is to spend the county's money for high-powered automobiles that his henchmen may joyride at the county's expense. This county will have to have a new highway engineer before any real constructive road work can really be done."[22] Selling the cars was a nominal blow at Koehler, but it indicated more to come, and the engineer could not let it pass. He went to a circuit court judge and obtained an injunction, which a deputy served on McElroy and Hayes; he was unable, however, to find Truman, who appeared at the county garage, picked up the cars, and delivered them to their purchasers.

Having humiliated Koehler, Truman and McElroy did the same thing to Judge Hayes. They voted to take his personal automobile and dismiss his driver, a Bulger man named Fred Snyder.

Relations with Hayes descended to a low point when the judges moved against the county purchasing agent, Eugene Jarboe. Like Hayes, Jarboe was a Shannon man, and he told McElroy in full court, "Politically I don't care a damn for you and personally I think you could stand flatfooted and kiss a gnat." Versions differ, and one has it that he described a part of the gnat's anatomy. Jarboe walked out, leaving the place in an uproar. Hayes said, "The young man was mad and did not mean what he said." The sheriff brought him back, and he apologized to the court. Asked to apologize to McElroy, he said, "I'll go to jail first"; he did, for two days, and then lost his job. Hayes was close to tears, not so much because of what Jarboe said or what happened to him but because of the job: "This man was my only appointee," he declared. "He was the only one I was permitted to name. He should not have been discharged."[23]

Meanwhile, Bulger was entering the equation. When Koehler lost the automobiles pertaining to his office the county engineer took his case to Bulger, now a state legislator in Jefferson City, and Bulger introduced a bill forbidding county judges to appoint road overseers, which would bring roads under state authority. It would be a body blow to Truman and McElroy, who had appointed all the overseers in Jackson County. The bill passed and went before the governor, Arthur M. Hyde, a Republican and future cabinet member in the Hoover administration. Hyde may not have understood what Bulger was up to. Mercifully, he vetoed the bill.

Bulger's hand appeared in another matter. After Judge Hayes lost his own automobile, McElroy, who was a physically slight man, was walking along a street in Kansas City when two men appeared and attacked him. Passersby called the police, who apprehended the men. They turned out to be Hayes's dismissed driver, Snyder, and Bulger.

Bulger now became the center of a considerable attention from the two Pendergast judges. When he had been presiding judge he had established the Miles Bulger Industrial Home for Negro Boys. Truman and McElroy did what they could to correct the most egregious error with this new home. Bulger, after naming the institution for himself, had placed a bronze tablet a yard square at its entrance, costing $1,100, and the home itself came to $165,000, an outrageous sum for a building to house sixty youths. The judges passed the matter to a grand jury, which reported the expenditure disgraceful. Truman and McElroy appeared before a businessmen's organization in Kansas City, the Triangle Club, and called the home to the attention of community leaders. McElroy asked them to investigate. They did, and found wainscoting of polished marble, radiators encased in marble with brass gratings, a main hall of polished marble and mahoganized wood, a gorgeous drinking fountain, marble settees, and stairways of marble or terrazzo. The club's committee found that the building compared with Kansas City's most exclusive clubs and "may more properly be designated as a monument such as a grateful people might erect or dedicate to the memory of a Lincoln." It was the wrong edifice for juveniles, especially, as the thinking of the day went, black juveniles.[24]

In regard to the personal attack by Snyder and Bulger, McElroy chose not to prefer charges; instead, he and Truman took revenge by engaging Arthur Young and Company to audit county finances, knowing Bulger was vulnerable. Though Bulger had been out of office long enough to come under the statute of limitations, the audit showed that he had entered office with a deficit of $117 and left with the county owing $1.2 million. He had been notorious for "piecrust" roads, most of which his henchmen built during his last year.

The judges thereupon prepared for reelection. With assistance from the Arthur Young firm, they engaged in creative finance to show a large county surplus, a quarter of a million dollars, based on a fourteen-month year for 1923, extending it to March 7, 1924. They delayed the payment of debts and juggled accounts at the county homes.

Over the course of his term Truman had grown more comfortable with public speaking, and he gave a rousing speech pointing out how the court had done its best despite the behavior of Hayes. He pointed out that he and McElroy had brought business methods to the court. The court, he said, did not discontinue the Widows Pension List; it cut the charity payroll, which someone had attached to the list: "We put a man to investigating that list and found that there were property owners, California residents and people out in the State, drawing Jackson County's pauper money." He and McElroy cut it by $500, bringing it down to $1,800. The court had been paying for ineligible people to stay at the county poor farm, and they also stopped that. A deputy clerk with a monthly salary of $150 had his father at the poor farm, costing $25 a month: "We thought he ought to take care of his father and not send the old man to the poorhouse, and when we got after him the old man went home and he's been there since." People were sending relatives to insane asylums at St. Joseph, Nevada, and Fulton; forty-seven of these individuals were perfectly capable of caring for themselves, or their people were capable of caring for them. This last situation, cleared up, saved the county $900 a month. "[I]f you want the scoop shovel gang back in the County treasury, if you want your road fund dissipated," then support the friends of Judge Hayes, Truman said.[25]

But a combination of difficulties brought defeat for the brave judges who fought Hayes and Bulger. The opposition circulated a brochure showing that Truman did not pay any real estate tax—true enough, because Mrs. Wallace owned the house. It also said he declared his possessions as one horse worth $30, one automobile worth $50, and household goods at $150. His taxes were 98 cents. His salary was $5,000. "Compare these figures to your own and see if you are getting a square deal from the man who wants your vote August 5th. . . . If any Goat [Pendergast supporter] denies this take them to the records."[26]

The Klan turned on Truman in memory of his uncooperativeness two years before, and it was much stronger in 1924. Truman and two friends drove out into the country one night, and there in the darkness they met the former marshal of Jackson County, Harry Hoffman, who was helping organize the county for the Klan and appeared ready to cut a deal with Truman, promising five thousand votes. Perhaps in memory of his earlier defiance of the Klan, surely also in conviction that he and the Klan had little in common, the judge laughed at the former county official, and the Klan's votes went into opposition. Klan members were mostly Republicans, but there were enough Democrats to make Klan opposition serious.

Truman had another disadvantage—his reputation for being straitlaced. He had acted against the "chicken dinner farms" in the rural part of the county, having his friend Miles, the marshal, close them. Newspapers related "Gloom at Chicken Farms." Kansas City formerly had housed such establishments, which were none other than drinking establishments and bawdy houses; the increasing numbers of automobiles had inspired them to move into the country. One suspects that the Pendergast machine was skimming such places in Kansas City, and country places paid no tolls—which may explain why McElroy joined with Truman against the chicken farms.[27]

The National Association for the Advancement of Colored People refused support to Truman and McElroy as well, because they had not equipped the Bulger Home, not yet opened. This may not have been a large factor in Truman's calculations, because the county black vote was insignificant and in Kansas City it was only 10 percent, but in a close election every vote counted.

Truman and McElroy also had tried to take the county homes from control of the circuit court judges, and this did their cause no good. Not least in their calculations was the fact that with Bulger at Jefferson City there was a chance that, beginning with the road overseers, and working with the circuit judges to get the patronage of the homes, he would arrange legislation taking all the remaining power of the county court and that this time Governor Hyde would sign the bill. Appearances were on the side of the county court. Circuit court control looked like bad government, for the circuit court allocated money to the homes and the county court had to find the money. Indeed, the county board of education had a hand in the homes as well, creating a three-headed monster. Eventually the state supreme court ruled in favor of Truman and

McElroy on the homes, against Bulger, but too late to save the county judges in the election.

The Pendergast judges decided to redeem many of the county's outstanding warrants—short-term county certificates of indebtedness—and this proved a fiasco. Prior to that time warrants had floated, redeemed according to numbers handed out politically: a friend of the court might receive a low number, an average citizen an intermediate number, an enemy a high one. Banks purchasing warrants discounted them by number. Individuals accepting warrants for work done for the county probably padded their bills to cover discounts. Truman and McElroy's purpose in attempting to redeem most of the warrants may have been to appeal to the business community in Kansas City, already aroused by the excesses of the Miles Bulger Industrial Home for Negro Boys. The judges went ahead, but word got out, and speculators bought up discounted warrants.

A final miscalculation occurred when the judges decided not to raise taxes to redeem the warrants, but rather to dismiss county employees—Shannon employees. Shannon would thus finance warrant redemption. This displeased him; it clearly violated the fifty-fifty agreement, still nominally in effect. Shannon gave the November county court election to the Republicans.

Truman met defeat from a candidate who at first was no candidate at all—Henry W. Rummell, the harness maker who once had made a harness for the goats that pulled Vivian's little wagon. The vote was Truman, 7,932, Rummell, 8,791. In a little pamphlet biography of Truman published in 1949, Henry A. Bundschu, owner of Bundschu's Department Store on the square in Independence and a later Republican supporter of Truman, explained what happened.[28] Truman's army friend Miles had telephoned Bundschu and said no one had filed for eastern judge on the Republican ticket; Bundschu suggested that one of Miles's deputies, Rummell, file, with the understanding he would withdraw in favor of a more likely candidate. Bundschu filed Rummell without his permission. Afterward, Miles went to Rummell and asked him to drop out, but he refused, for Shannon—seeking revenge—had offered support. Rummell was the second Republican elected to the court from the eastern district since the Civil War. It was the second and last time (the first had been for township committeeman in the 1916 primary) Harry Truman lost an election.

3

The years 1925 and 1926 marked a hiatus in Truman's political career, which he filled in various ways. His first move was to quit law school. During his initial year as eastern judge he had enrolled in the Kansas City School of Law, now part of the University of Missouri at Kansas City. He completed two years of the four-year course. The school had no full-time faculty, attracting prominent community lawyers as teachers. Classes were at night, and graduates included many successful men, even an associate justice of the U.S. Supreme Court, Charles Whitaker. Truman's grades were fairly good, all A's or B's, except a C minus in "Sales." He was chosen as one of two speakers at a Washington's Birthday banquet, an occasion when his co-speaker told jokes and Truman spoke on "Honor and the Government." But he could not go on. Remembering the situation later, he explained that he was driven out by the importuning of people for jobs; he remembered being accosted on the stairs and in the doorways of the court of appeals law library. The truth was, however, that out of office, he had to earn a living.

He sold memberships in the Kansas City Automobile Club. The club was a symbol of the times, an indication that automobiles were increasing and their owners needed assistance no previous organization had offered. The Kansas City club did not enjoy affiliation with the state club, a difficulty in any membership drive, but Truman went ahead. His former fellow battery captain, Spencer Salisbury, who worked for the Internal Revenue Bureau, gave access to the bureau's records; this allowed Harry to discover names of Kansas Citians who could afford club memberships. He did not sell memberships himself but employed salesmen, trying out sixty men, from whom he chose five. They obtained a thousand new members. Memberships cost fifteen dollars, so he paid ten thousand dollars in commissions and kept five thousand for himself. He did this work until mid-1926.

Another activity was soliciting accounts for the Farm and Home Savings and Loan Association, an opportunity arranged through former lieutenant colonel Arthur Elliott of the 129th Field Artillery, once captain of Kansas City's Battery B. A fellow worker was Newell T. Paterson, a major in the 129th. Years later Paterson related that "almost any night you could find him calling on those he could not contact during the day."[29]

A third source of income was the Community Savings and Loan of Independence. He was again helped by his army friend Salisbury, who got him into Community. Truman had known Salisbury long before the two were in the 129th; Salisbury's sister Agnes was a close friend of Bess's. The institution had its origins in the South Central Savings and Loan Association of Kansas City, organized after Truman became eastern judge. Truman started with Community in September 1925 as manager of stock sales. At that time it had $6,613.13 in assets and the same in liabilities; the assets included $168.46 in the bank in cash and $149.50 for furniture and fixtures. For a while sales of Community stock went well. Stock, one should perhaps explain, was in effect deposits. Money obtained from stock sales went out in loans, and this was how savings and loans made money. Community's ads, written by Truman, were attractive:

We Pay you 6% to Save Your Own Money.
Community Savings and Loan Association
Harry S. Truman, General Manager

Let me tell you how to make small monthly savings pay you a competence for your old age. We pay you 6% to save your own money with safety, security, and profit to you.

Prepare for your Child's Education
Start a Savings Account Now
$10.00 per Month Consistently Saved
Will send him to College.[30]

For the work of soliciting stock Truman organized a partnership of himself, Salisbury, Arthur Metzger (a Kansas City leader of DeMolay, the young men's organization for Masonry), and H. H. Halvorson (a Kansas City business-man). He brought in his automobile club salesmen to do double duty, for a 2 percent commission. They sold stock on the installment plan, by the month. Commissions presumably were up front. The law of that time also allowed Community to establish its capital as the total amount of stock sold, regardless of what purchasers paid in at the moment; future installments of stockholders became immediate assets. By August 1927, the partners had collected $110,000 but assets were $925,000.

The connection with Community proved unprofitable, and after several years Truman got out. The problem essentially was Salisbury; it would have been better if Truman had been more careful in associating with him. During the war he and his battery had been known as the "forty thieves" because of stealing from other batteries. Truman's biographer Jonathan Daniels described Salisbury as "a gentleman by birth, and a scamp by choice." Eddie McKim said he was an eighteen-karat crook.[31] In 1927, an audit showed a $1,200 deficit. In 1930, another showed $6,440. Losses were credited variously to the partners, and they could not agree on how to pay them. To be on the safe side in case of future losses, they reorganized the partnership into the Community Investment Company, a corporation, which could hold the bag. They created another corporation, Rural Investment Company, as a holding company for Community Savings and Loan. Halvorson, who was siding with Truman against Metzger and Salisbury, insisted that Truman come into the Rural Investment Company. Salisbury never got around to giving Truman his one-fourth share of the holding company's stock. Halvorson then dropped out. By that time Truman was back on the county court as presiding judge and busy with county affairs, and he announced, "So far as Metzger and Salisbury are concerned I am through with them in a business way, and they can take the Community and run it into the ground or any place else they care to." Salisbury did what Truman advised. After gaining control, he looted Community, and went to jail.

For a few weeks early in 1926, Truman got involved with a fourth money-making activity, the Citizens Security Bank of Englewood. He and two associates, Salisbury and Lou E. Holland, the latter the head of Holland Engraving Company and a leader in the Kansas City Chamber of Commerce, acquired Citizens only to discover that the cashier, Paul E. Cole, had emptied the bank in a scheme that involved the cashier's brother-in-law and Charles Becker, then Missouri's secretary of state. Prior to the takeover and immediately afterward, Truman's group had audited the books, but before they came in, Becker arranged a deposit of $25,000 in state automobile license fees. The cashier made several bad loans, purchased worthless bonds, lent himself two thousand dollars, and presided over the simple disappearance of three thousand in cash. Some quick actions, including confiscation of a deposit belonging to one of the miscreants, brought a semblance of order. Truman and his associates then backed out, selling the bank to B. Manly Houchens and his brother-in-law, Novus Reed, a minister. The sale did Truman's reputation no good, although he was not at fault for what happened thereafter. Houchens and Reed had the bad judgment to allow the former cashier, Cole, back in, and this time the cashier took everything. The state demanded its $25,000, and Houchens covered it by selling all his personal assets and borrowing from his father-in-law, after which he put an automobile hose to his mouth.[32]

On the personal side during these years when Truman was trying to make money any way he could, and indeed for the entire 1920s and the first years of the 1930s, his life was, in many ways, a happy one. The most important event was the birth of Mary Margaret Truman (*Mary* for Judge Truman's sister, *Margaret* for Mrs. Wallace) in 1924. Her mother was thirty-nine, and, having endured two miscarriages, she was so uncertain she could bear a child she refused to make any preparation; when the baby arrived there were no clothes and not even a bassinet. The infant came during a February snowstorm, and it was all the doctor could do to get to the house. As for clothes, they were improvised. So was the bassinet; Margaret was placed in a bureau drawer, which served until Judge Truman could get to a store.

From an infant the child grew into a spindly little girl who rode a tricycle around the house on Delaware Street. When old enough to ride the tricycle up and down sidewalks, she rode on the same hexagon-shaped flagstones her mother had used. If Margaret tired of activities in the "big house," she could pedal around the corner to the bungalows of two of her aunts and uncles behind the Delaware Street house on Van Horn Road. As she grew older she wrote letters to her father, sometimes away from Independence, relating what she was doing and how she liked it. The family was close-knit, and with pride the judge and his wife watched everything Margaret did.

On election day, 1930, the Trumans had a scare. With the depression just beginning, Kansas City was out of joint, and for some reason there was talk that someone was going to kidnap two high-level Democratic politicians. In fact the Republican chairman of the Jackson County election board was kidnapped that morning and, after a beating, released in the evening. But that morning in Independence, at Bryant School—a big, gloomy Victorian edifice named for one of Harry Truman's high school teachers and built on the site of the defunct Woodland College and an adjoining and beautiful pond—a strange man came to the door of Margaret's first-grade classroom and told her teacher, Madeline Etzenhauser, that he had come to pick up Mary Truman. He used the child's first name. He kept his hat on. The teacher reported the request to the principal, who called Mrs. Truman, who called the judge, and by the time he and the sheriff got there the man had disappeared. Margaret later reported, "The episode wreaked havoc on Mother's nerves. Thereafter she never let me go to school alone, a rule she enforced until I was well into my teens."[33]

In 1932 Truman bought a Steinway grand piano for his daughter. It was something he long had wanted, and perhaps he translated that desire into her Christmas present. Sooner or later all parents make such mistakes: on Christmas morning the child came downstairs expectantly, saw the piano, and burst into tears. She had wanted an electric train.

Other than such episodes as the above, it is difficult to know much of the Trumans' family life in this period, apart from the clear evidence that it was happy and usually quiet. In the early part of the county judge era the judge's wife occupied herself with the imminence and then the presence of Margaret. Because her husband was home so much—when he was not in his Independence courthouse office a few blocks away he was at the downtown Kansas City courthouse or, at most, spending a day or so in Jeff City—he wrote hardly any Dear Bess letters. A few came during summer camp with the army reserves or when he was on trips for the National Old Trails Road Association. In 1923, Bess had a tooth pulled that took the local dentist an inordinate time to extract. From summer camp her husband said he felt like "busting" the dentist. Two years later the topic was getting her hair bobbed, with the judge in reluctant agreement; he wrote, "You usually do as you like about things and that's what I want you to do." As for participation in her husband's "great game," politics, she tolerated it.[34]

The family all lived together with Grandmother Wallace and her youngest son, Fred, in the big house at 219. Margaret has drawn an attractive picture of them there each evening, month after month, year after year. For dinner they all ate in the dining room, with her father at one end of the table, Grandmother Wallace at the other. During daytime the grandmother wore her iron-gray hair in a bun at the back of her neck, but for dinner she put her hair up on top of her head and changed her dress. "Whenever I was seated next to her at the dinner table I was the best-behaved little girl in Independence," Margaret wrote. Afterward everyone adjourned to the living room.

There, in the far-right-hand corner, the grandmother sat in a rocking chair, straight as a ramrod, shawl around her shoulders, doing needlework. Margaret's father and mother read—her father was never without a book. She herself did homework. The grandmother indulged Margaret and Uncle Fred by allowing a tiny mouse, which came out of its hole at night, to caper back and forth on the rocker of her chair while the Atwater Kent radio played music from station WLW in Cincinnati.[35]

Throughout the 1920s and 1930s, Truman remained in the army reserves, and each year he attended camp, partly because it removed him from job seekers and contractors, and partly because he liked it—the routine, so different from politics, allowed him to rest. He wrote home frequently, sometimes describing amusing scenes. In 1925 at Fort Riley—by this time he was a lieutenant colonel—he called on the local general and the general's lady, passing through the receiving line on the general's front porch, on at one end, off the other. Each year the general kidded Truman about his political interests, and that year Truman told the general that without politicians to run the government he, the general, would not be a general. "That usually stops the conversation—at least it did last evening."[36] Another time it was another of his "finger stories," this when a man stuck his finger in the breech mechanism, amputating a piece of it: someone looked at the gun trail, noticed the piece lying there, and asked who lost it. While everyone looked to see who the guilty party was, the man to whom it belonged was running across the field toward the hospital. One of the fellows picked up the piece and started after him—but, in the excitement, he lost it.[37]

In 1926 at Riley he took a photograph of a horse-drawn battery passing along a ridge road lined with willowy trees, so reminiscent of northern France a few years before. By that time he was a full colonel.

4

For eight years in the later 1920s and early 1930s, January 1, 1927, until January 1, 1935, Harry Truman served as presiding judge of Jackson County. Typically, he came into the county's number-one office in a roundabout way. At first he had proposed to run for county collector, a job fairly well down the hierarchy of offices, but it paid remarkably well because of being based on fees collected. The job would have paid all of Truman's haberdashery debts. But that year the Pendergast organization gave in to a suggestion of the banker W. T. Kemper, who himself had a candidate for collector.[38] The result was an offer of the presiding judgeship, which Truman quickly accepted. This time there was no question of his nomination and election, for Pendergast and Shannon had buried the hatchet. The two men met accidentally on the street in Kansas City and, to the fascination of onlookers, got into a shouting match; sensing they were behaving like fools, they met in private a day or two later and patched their differences.

During his two four-year terms as presiding judge Truman revealed a remarkable grasp of the county's politics. One of his court colleagues, Eugene I. Purcell, said in 1931 that "if a man can't stand the heat he ought to stay out of the kitchen." Truman stood the heat; he was a natural politician. He carefully controlled the judges with whom he sat. There was a kaleidoscopic succession of them, as their terms were for two years, and each, he discovered, had his price. One was a ladies' man, and Truman had to protect him in this role—in part because he was a big man in Kansas City and needed protection that way. Another was a West Point graduate who was not averse to graft; to control him Truman had to let him have some of the county payroll. Another, Thomas B. Bash, was essentially honest, and certainly brave: later, when he was sheriff, he encountered a gang execution while driving through Kansas City. After pulling a riot gun out of his car, he killed two of the gangsters and captured a third when the latter's ammunition ran out just as he was charging the sheriff. Bash, unfortunately, had no political instincts. Another of the county judges was plain incompetent. Another was a devotee of Civil War history, and Truman distracted him with Civil War stories while passing measures in the name of the court. "Now, Judge, you sign this," he would say, and keep talking about the war. A friend relating this story about Judge Battle McCardle said, "He didn't know whether he was signing the Declaration of Independence or what."[39] Two of the judges loved to gamble below their desks on the floor of the courtroom, hidden from the view of the public in front; Truman encouraged this pastime, and took decisions in their names while they were so occupied.

During these years he managed to get the best of the "big boss," Pendergast, whose heavy hand otherwise might have made him the organization's servant. He did not meet Boss Tom until 1926. Up until that time he had been the protégé of Tom's brother Mike. Thereafter the two worked closely. On Truman's part, however, the relationship displayed a considerable independence. Early in his first term as presiding judge, he asked the boss for permission to propose a large bond issue for road construction, and Pendergast told him it would never pass; Truman insisted that by promising to handle the construction honestly he could persuade the voters. With reluctance the boss told him to go ahead. The proposal passed. Truman thereupon awarded contracts on the basis of secret bids, always choosing the lowest. When he gave a $400,000 contract to the American Road Building Company of South Dakota, a group of local contractors assembled in Pendergast's office, and the boss summoned the presiding judge to explain. Truman refused to give in. Furious, Pendergast told the contractors that Truman was the "contrariest cuss in Missouri."

What Truman did with Pendergast was to establish himself as an obviously honest man who could control eleven thousand votes in eastern Jackson County. In this respect the boss still found him useful. It was a very interesting alliance, and Truman could have taken, and perhaps did take, much satisfaction in what he had done. He saw to it that Pendergast men obtained county jobs. For the boss it was convenient to point to Judge Truman's sterling honesty, as the judge's credentials deflected attention from his own infelicities. When Mike Pendergast died in 1929, Truman became Tom's representative in the eastern part of the county.

By that time Pendergast had so improved his position in Kansas City that he probably felt no special need to discipline Truman. In 1925 the voters of the city decided to eliminate corruption by combining the city's political divisions, the wards, into nine districts, with the resultant nine-member city council appointing a city manager. Pendergast could not say enough in favor of the proposed reorganization, came out for good government, and elected five councilmen. Truman's former colleague on the county court, McElroy, thereupon became city manager and ran the city for the benefit of Pendergast. If Truman refused to give money to the organization, Pendergast could get it from McElroy.

In relating Truman's modus operandi as presiding judge, one must add that his achievement in making himself independent was not quite as substantial as it appeared: he had to make some compromises. On several occasions in the early 1930s, while staying overnight in the Hotel Pickwick in downtown Kansas City, he wrote out his thoughts about political accommodations. These memoranda to himself, interestingly, have survived, and in one of them he admitted that ten thousand dollars disappeared in a contract to a friend of Boss Tom, whom he knew to be "a former saloonkeeper and murderer," because one of the county judges insisted on it; he could not handle the situation any other way. "Was I right or did I compound a felony? I don't know. . . . The boss tells me that in Kansas City they doctor every bid so that the inside gentlemen get the contract." Over the several years of road construction, he estimated, he had to give away "about a million in general revenue to satisfy the politicians. But if I hadn't done that the crooks would have had half the seven million." (The latter figure was the amount of a bond issue.) The arrangement bothered him: "I wonder if I did right to put a lot of no account sons of bitches on the payroll and pay other sons of bitches more money for supplies than they were worth in order to satisfy the political powers and save $3,500,000.00. I believe I did do right. Anyway, I'm not a partner of any of them and I'll go out poorer in every way than when I came into office."[40]

Whatever the afterthoughts, he went ahead with a remarkable program for improvement of Jackson County. He realized that the automobile, together with the nation's rapid industrialization, required a vast new system of roads, and that roadbuilding would have to begin on the county level. He had helped Pendergast defeat Bulger partly because of Bulger's piecrusts. As he said on one occasion:

> Jackson County's roads were built before autos became so cheap and so numerous. Those roads were built for two-ton traffic going three miles per hour and for horse-drawn pleasure vehicles weighing five hundred pounds moving about five miles per hour. Now you have five to fifteen tons moving from twelve to twenty-five miles per hour and 2,000- to 5,000-pound pleasure cars moving from twenty-five to sixty miles per hour.[41]

He dedicated himself to getting two county bond issues in 1928 and 1931 that made $10 million available for roads.

His preparation for the first and crucial bond issue was thorough. The county had 1,100 miles of roads: 350 paved, 670 graded and oiled, 70 unimproved. They cost $900,000 a year to maintain. The issue required a three-fourths vote, which seemed impossible. Pendergast's domination of the city government was raising questions about bond issues, and most of the people in the county lived in Kansas City. Truman decided to bring in two engineers—his army friend Major Stayton, an Independence Democrat, and a Kansas City Republican, N. T. Veatch, Jr. They reported on May 14, 1927, that it would be cheaper to build new roads than maintain the old ones. County judges had known little about engineering, and many roads were of water-bound macadam, improperly arranged at curves and turns, undrained, and repaired by piling a little surface material on worn places. With support from the two engineers, Truman proposed 336 miles of new roads, placed so that no farm resident in the county would be farther than two and a half miles from a paved road.

The first bond issue passed on May 8, 1928, Truman's birthday; at the same time voters refused a city bond issue proposed by McElroy. The county issue was the more remarkable, because Kansas City taxpayers would foot almost all the bill for building roads outside the city. The county court constructed the first group of roads, 244 miles, without the slightest evidence of fraud. Boss Tom's cement company received only a half-mile of the contracts. Pendergast may have gotten more work through subcontracts, but at least Truman was not responsible.

Construction was done so honestly, with contracts to the lowest bidders, that $75,000 was left over. Part of that sum Truman used for a statue of the man for whom Jackson County was named. The rest he dedicated to a mammoth barbecue at Sni-a-Bar Farms, to which he invited everyone in the county. A great success, the barbecue produced the worst traffic jam in Jackson County history.

Judge Truman completed the road program after the second bond issue passed in 1931. The literal meaning of *Missouri* is "big muddy," and one of his high school teachers, Mrs. W. L. C. Palmer, the former Ardelia Hardin, told a reporter years later: "[B]y the time Harry got through with that program . . . he pulled Jackson County out of the mud."[42] Only two counties in the entire United States were ahead of Jackson County in road systems: Wayne County (Detroit), Michigan, and Westchester County, New York.

During his eighth year on the court, 1932, Truman sponsored a large illustrated booklet entitled "Jackson County: Results of County Planning," which described the roads. A local photographer took pictures of the winding cement roads: there were beautiful scenes of rolling Missouri farmland, with barns and houses fronting the new roads; the ribbonlike highway stretching toward Lee's Summit; the road wending its way past wheat and oats fields in early summer near Independence; the road curling up to and over the railroad tracks in the center of a village named Levasy. Such scenes testified to the accomplishment. He sent copies to every county in the state.

The presiding judge had hoped to plant thousands of elms and poplars along the new highways, with the idea that when the maples died the elms would have gotten growth; this was in memory of the roads in France. He managed seven thousand trees, but farmers found them a nuisance, preventing cultivation close to the road, and ran their mowing machines through them.

He arranged for a remodeling of the courthouse in Independence, and for a skyscraper replacement of the Victorian firetrap courthouse in Kansas City (in an unusual departure, Jackson County had two courthouses). Remodeling the Independence courthouse changed a building remodeled several times from the four-chimneyed courtroom constructed in 1836. Under Truman's guidance it became a Georgian building that looked like Independence Hall in Philadelphia. Ready for occupancy in 1933, it was an ornament to the town. But the new Kansas City courthouse was an even more remarkable construction. Truman drove halfway around the country to find a style of architecture he liked, and a likable architect, and found both in the Caddo Parish courthouse in Louisiana and its architect, Edward T. Neild. The twenty-eight-story, three-hundred-foot-high, $4 million art deco masterpiece in Kansas City set a new architectural standard for downtown office buildings and would offer relief from the city's flash cubes and boxes of later years. Inside, its stylized celebration of the 1920s and early 1930s was almost overwhelming. On top of the building Judge Truman planned to put the statue of General Andrew Jackson paid for with money saved on the roads; Jackson would survey Kansas City, the place on the bluffs that was virtually uninhabited when Old Hickory was president. By the time of the building's completion in the depths of the depression, it seemed absurd to put Jackson up there where only a bird could see him, and the presiding judge settled for the general astride a horse in front of the building. He dedicated the skyscraper courthouse in his last month in office, December 1934.

The judge's desire to change the face of Jackson County was evident in another project he found impossible to carry out, the Greater Kansas City Regional Plan. This plan sought cooperation among the governments of five counties around Kansas City, including three Kansas counties. For one thing it seemed ridiculous that a city at the western end of the state that spilled over into Kansas should have two governments, one for the much smaller Kansas City, Kansas. For another, nearby Clay County, Missouri, was becoming a suburb and needed to be included in the metropolis. Highway engineers lacked a plan to coordinate roads. The regional plan died when Truman went to Washington.

He hoped to reorganize Missouri's state government by combining its 114 counties into 30. He wanted to abolish the townships. He sought to consolidate local school boards into county boards, to streamline (a word tossed around a lot in the 1930s) the state legislature into two houses of sixty to seventy-five representatives and thirty senators, to authorize the governor to appoint cabinet members to head departments rather than continue the popular election of unknowns. He called for a gasoline tax in place of property levies, reduction of property tax exemptions, and taxation of intangibles. These reforms would await later generations.

The Missouri State Planning Association, formed in 1930, chose him as its chairman. That same year he received election to the board of directors of the National Conference on City Planning, a group founded at the turn of the century when New York and Washington and Chicago were setting the pace for organizing attractive combinations of parks, roads, and public buildings.

Beginning in 1926 he served as president of the National Old Trails Road Association, by then a fourteen-year-old organization based in Kansas City. It sought to correct the haphazard numbering of the nation's highways and to encourage states west of Missouri to hard-surface the historic trails, making them accessible to year-round automobile traffic. The Trails Road Association had several divisions: Cumberland, Mississippi Valley, Santa Fe, and Grand Canyon, each with its officers. Every time a community or county or state did its duty and paved part of a trail, the association marked the result. On Highway 24 through Independence it set out markers in red, white, and blue, with a portrait of George Washington and thirteen stars across the top. The metal markers bore the legend "National Old Trails, Dedicated to the Pioneers." All this was in accord with the times, which the association's officers realized required advertising. The reverse side of one of the association's brochures related: "The old adage that the public will wear a beaten track to the home of the maker of the best mousetrap is not applicable to our modern age; for the man who makes a good mousetrap and thoroughly advertises its advantages gets the business."

Truman was proud of his work with the National Old Trails Road Association. He told audiences that American history provided wonderful narratives associated with the trails, and "All these would make the *Iliad* and the

Odyssey tame stories."[43] He loved to relate how Senator Benton had led the effort to extend the Cumberland Road, making it a national highway, from Independence to Santa Fe, which was then a part of Mexico. (Actually, the Santa Fe Trail, begun in 1822, started not in Independence but at Old Franklin, Missouri, where two sons of Daniel Boone, Nathan and Daniel, Jr., evaporated salt. Steamboats then made it possible to take settlers up the Missouri to Independence or Westport Landing.) Like the Santa Fe Trail, Independence's other trail, that to Oregon, likewise needed paving as a national highway. Over a quarter-million people had set out on the Oregon Trail, sometimes described as the nation's longest cemetery. The trip to Oregon took six months, and to survivors it was the most important event of their lives. At Guernsey, Wyoming, one could see the wagon ruts etched deeply in the sandstone.

In the early 1930s a special assignment came Truman's way that lay outside his work with the court, with planning for the county and state, and with activities pertaining to the National Old Trails Road Association. He accepted it reluctantly, and yet he was the natural nominee because of his position on the court and his reputation in the County Judges Association, of which he was president. He became national reemployment director for Missouri.

Before 1929 he had been uncertain of the obligation of government to care for the indigent. Jackson County maintained homes for orphaned or otherwise unsupported children. The court maintained a home for the white aged or infirm, another for blacks. It gave pensions to widowed mothers. It paid for the keep of insane persons committed to state or private institutions. Even in good times, the cost was high. All this "charity," Truman complained in 1929, cost the county a million dollars a year. But as times changed, he changed his mind about who should handle relief: "I think charity is a public matter," he began to say, "and should be handled by the government by a tax levy and not by charity drives where the burden falls on a few."[44] Inspired by the National Industrial Recovery Act of 1933, the National Reemployment Service functioned under the labor department in Washington as a go-between for unemployed workers and federal public works contractors. In 1933–1934 it helped connect individual need with government projects through the Civil Works Administration, until it was replaced by more thoroughgoing solutions such as the Works Progress Administration and Civilian Conservation Corps.

Such were Truman's activities when his second term as presiding judge began to run out, and he commenced to wonder what he was going to do next. In county politics it was customary to take only two terms as presiding judge; after that custom dictated the job should be passed around. He was not quite fifty years old, too young to retire. If he retired from politics—it was the middle of the depression—he did not know if he could get a job elsewhere. The only thing that lay open was return to the farm, and for Bess that was unacceptable. He could hardly exist on the charity of his mother-in-law, Mrs. Wallace, for by this time she had spent her father's inheritance—all she owned was the house, a big barn of a place that was run-down and could not have been sold in the depression.

At first the judge had hoped to be governor. The *Clinton (Mo.) Eye* in 1929 was boosting him, and the next year the *Odessa Democrat* followed suit. In 1931 the judge's cousin, Ralph E. "Snapper" Truman, the same who had accompanied him to Texas in 1901, began to stir a movement in the country counties around Springfield. Truman was available; he said he was no candidate, but if a situation would develop Missourians "might find me ready at their command to enter the lists." At the end of the year, however, Pendergast, who had not committed himself, threw his support to another man, and Truman's friends at once gave up.[45]

His next hope was to become a congressman. In 1932 the state's politicians organized a redistricting convention, and he put together several city districts of Kansas City and the eastern part of Jackson County as a congressional district for himself. He prepared to ask Boss Tom for the nomination. His relations with the boss were good. Judging from the ease with which he could telephone Pendergast or see him in his office at 1908 Main Street in Kansas City, everything was all right. In April 1933 he was having a little trouble with city manager McElroy, whose usual fine Italian hand, the judge said, was maneuvering with a recent action of the state board of assessments. He felt he would triumph against McElroy: "As long as the Big Boss believes in me I don't care what the others do, and McElroy will be kissing me before the month is out."[46]

When he asked Pendergast for the congressional seat the boss seemed agreeable and even offered an alternative, the attractive county collectorship, which paid ten thousand dollars a year as opposed to seventy-five hundred for a congressman. Truman put the case in a letter to Bess, who together with Margaret was then in Biloxi, Mississippi—Margaret was suffering from rheumatic fever and her parents believed the Gulf climate would help her. He wanted Bess to think of the alternatives: "Congressman pays $7,500 and has to live in Washington six months a year, collector will pay $10,000 and stay at home; a political sky-high career ends with eight years collector. I have an opportunity to be a power in the nation as Congressman. I don't have to make a decision until next year. Think about it." A little later he elaborated: "[M]aybe I can retire as collector and you and the young lady can take some European and South American tours when they'll do you most good; or maybe go to live in Washington and see all the greats and near greats in action."[47]

By January 1934, he had arrived at his decision, to run in the new Fourth District. He met with Pendergast, but the meeting was most unsatisfactory. To his astonishment he heard the boss say the district would go to a special Pendergast friend, C. Jasper Bell, a circuit court judge, whose conduct earlier, in 1925, had commended him to the boss; as a new city councilman under the charter just passed he had cast the decisive vote for McElroy as city manager: "I wanted to be Congressman from the new fourth Missouri district," Truman wrote afterward, "but a circuit judge wanted it also and the dignity of the court had to be upheld."[48] Boss Tom sensed Truman's disappointment and proposed that Truman might be senator. The presiding judge was annoyed, although careful not to show his feelings; the usual progress to senator was via not a county judgeship but a term as governor. Pendergast, he thought, was engaging in a pleasantry.

Shortly afterward came a second blow. William T. Kemper, now Kansas City's principal banker, again asked the boss for the collectorship for a friend. Pendergast gave it to him.

Truman had the sure feeling Pendergast was going to turn him loose, after long and faithful service, and that there was no alternative to retirement. In her biography of her father, Margaret Truman has written that never had his almost perennial optimism, his belief that things would work out, come so close to disappearing as during that spring of 1934. Then, of a sudden, Pendergast offered the nomination for senator.

Martha Ellen and John Anderson Truman on their wedding day, December 28, 1881. (Deane photo)

Harry as a baby, 1884, and with his brother, Vivian, in 1888. (D.P. Thompson photo [as a baby])

Harry Truman at age thirteen, in 1897.

Bess Wallace at the time of her high school graduation, 1901.

Grandview, Missouri, in 1911.

The Truman farm in winter.

First Lieutenant Truman, wearing the insignia of Missouri, before the enlarged Kansas City battery was taken into federal service.

The Harry Truman and Eddie Jacobson haberdashery.

*Judge Truman with
Bess and Margaret,
1928.*

The "Truman for Senator" campaign, 1934.

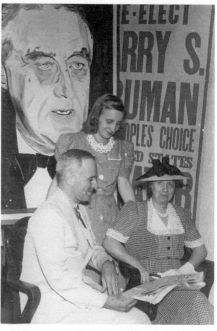

The Truman family campaigning. Bess once said that a woman's job during a campaign was to keep quiet in public and be sure her hat was on straight.

Senator Truman and Thomas J. Pendergast at the Democratic national convention in Philadelphia, 1936.

Campaigning for reelection to the Senate, 1940.

The Truman committee conducting its investigations into the national defense program, 1943.

Truman in his senatorial office before becoming president, talking with Colonel Harry H. Vaughan, 1944–1945. (Office of War Information)

Chapter Seven

Senator from Pendergast

When Truman ran for and received election as a United States senator from Missouri in the mid-1930s, he found himself an object of derision. People described him as the senator from Pendergast. Boss Tom himself may have inspired the remark; in an expansive moment Pendergast seems to have said that some senators represented oil and steel, others utilities and railroads, and he, the boss, had decided to send his own man. There were other gibes, such as the comment of the veteran head of the Missouri Farmers Association, William Hirth, who described the state's junior senator as a bellhop. The remark perhaps derived from the description of one of Truman's rivals in the primary, who had said that as senator the Jackson County judge would get "calluses on his ears listening on the long-distance telephone to the orders of his boss." And there was the episode early in 1938, when Truman passed through St. Louis and attended a gridiron dinner of the St. Louis Advertising Club; at the dinner, he watched a skit in which a character inquired of another, who looked like the ventriloquist Edgar Bergen's dummy, Charlie McCarthy, "What is Senator Truman's relationship to Tom Pendergast?" The would-be Charlie replied, "You know my relationship to Edgar Bergen— weell—" The audience roared with laughter.[1]

Truman could not do much about such ribbing, and for years he struggled to remove the stigma of Pendergast. Politicians and observers alike took the supposed relationship for granted. At the beginning of his first term the boss was such a fixture in Missouri politics that whatever independence Truman might have claimed, no one would have believed it. The connection became downright embarrassing a few years later, when it was discovered that Pendergast had accepted a massive bribe from fourteen fire insurance companies for arranging a favorable division of $9 million in premiums impounded by a federal court; after throwing himself on the mercy of the court, he went to jail.

1

When Truman took the oath as senator on January 3, 1935, Tom Pendergast controlled the entire state of Missouri. It was not quite the apogee of his power: that came later in the year with appointment of his henchman, Matthew S. Murray, as state director of the Works Progress Administration, giving Pendergast control over tens of thousands of federal jobs. But by 1935 he controlled the state's entire delegation to the U.S. House of Representatives, both senators, together with the governor, Guy B. Park, and Park's principal assistants.[2] During Pendergast's heyday the Missouri artist Thomas Hart Benton undertook a large mural for the statehouse in Jefferson City and asked Boss Tom to pose for one of the figures, which the boss willingly did. The figure was of a burly man eating dinner. When the mural was unveiled, there was a considerable fuss. Unperturbed, Benton said he had included Pendergast because he was part of Missouri. It looked like the boss was running the state? Well, he was.

The way in which Boss Tom came to control the Commonwealth of Missouri was thoroughly understandable in its particulars, even if the result was almost unbelievable. The principal moves had come in 1932, two years before Truman was elected to the Senate. At the outset of that presidential year the boss had announced for the former Missouri senator (and erstwhile mayor of Kansas City), James "Jim" Reed. The boss knew that Reed's presidential candidacy was impossible, for too many Missourians disliked him, and he had no national support. Nonetheless, the old man insisted on running, and Boss Tom obliged him. Pendergast cagily planned his strategy— indeed, so cagily that years later, when he went to jail, people said it was because he had come out for Reed, and that Roosevelt had not forgotten it and hence encouraged the treasury department to investigate Pendergast's income taxes. Privately, however, he was behind Roosevelt from the beginning, and let the leading Democratic aspirant know that. He arranged for Missouri's delegates to desert Reed after the first ballot. He carefully failed to instruct the delegation to vote according to unit rule; this had the advantage of bringing in the state's support gradually, giving the appearance of reluctance. At that time the son of Champ Clark, Bennett C. Clark of St. Louis, was running for the Senate on an anti-Pendergast platform and did not understand what was going on. After Roosevelt received the nomination, Clark angrily criticized Pendergast to the Democratic national chairman, James A. Farley. "Oh, Pendergast was all right," was the reply. "Was with us all the time. Reed had him hog-tied but I saw him every day and he was with us from the start."[3] As payment, Boss Tom received the WPA jobs.

It was also in 1932 that Pendergast turned another situation to his advantage. In the decennial census of 1930, Missouri showed a marked loss of population, forcing a reduction of the state's congressional representation from sixteen seats to thirteen and making redistricting necessary. The state legislature produced such a collection of gerrymanders that Governor Henry Caulfield vetoed the bill in disgust. This meant that all candidates for the House of Representatives in 1932 had to run at large on a statewide basis, and that each and every one of them, if he wanted the ghost vote in Kansas City, had to go to Pendergast hat in hand.

At this time the governorship came under his control. At the beginning it was not a sure thing, but luck, or perhaps one should say fate, made it possible. Pendergast had sponsored a great Missouri statesman type for governor, Francis M. Wilson—a poetical, oratorical fellow, dignified yet humorous, he was possessed of red hair and freckles and known as the "Red Headed Peckerwood of the Platte." Wilson was well aware of the need for the boss's support, but as an independent he might have given trouble to Pendergast had he been elected. He won the primary with no difficulty, and the November election would have been a formality, but a few weeks before it the candidate suffered a heart attack and died. Pendergast had to find another candidate in a hurry. He chose a friend of Wilson, a circuit judge from Platte City, Guy Park. A little-known country lawyer, Park was almost a cipher compared to the departed candidate, but he was an ideal replacement: he did not consider himself a machine candidate; he was an innocent man rather than a nefarious one.[4] He was so grateful for his elevation that he allowed Boss Tom to name all important appointive state officials. For this reason it was said that after Park's inauguration in 1933, Pendergast's office at 1908 Main Street in Kansas City was the state capitol, and the capitol in Jeff City was Uncle Tom's cabin.

Truman's place in this scheme of things—*scheme* is hardly the right word, for Boss Tom was only seizing his opportunities—was at first unclear, even to Pendergast. Pendergast's calculations only gradually led him to Truman as a candidate for senator in 1934. The boss's problem was to find a candidate to defeat the machinations of Bennett Clark, who had been elected to the Senate in 1932. The custom was that each of the state's metropolises, Kansas City and St. Louis, should have a senator, and Clark thoughtfully put up Jacob L. "Tuck" Milligan of Richmond, a town north of Kansas City; if elected, Milligan would be Clark's man. Boss Tom tried at least three, perhaps four, possible candidates. He offered the nomination to Reed, who refused, for he was getting on in years, into his seventies. He offered it to Joe Shannon, whom Pendergast meanwhile had called to the U.S. House of Representatives. Shannon backed away. He may have seen a plot; he had a safe House district, and it looked like Pendergast was trying to get him into a losing race. Moreover, any winning candidate almost certainly would have to be in favor of President Roosevelt, and Shannon considered FDR a fraud; a reporter heard him say that Roosevelt was no more a Jeffersonian Democrat than was a jackrabbit. The Jackson County Democratic chairman, James P. Aylward, refused the nomination too. As he later explained, "I had a family to raise and a law practice; I made up my mind I didn't want a political job. If I went to Washington and then got beat I wouldn't have had a law practice to come back to."[5] In near desperation, Pendergast may have also offered the nomination to the defeated (by Clark) machine candidate in 1932, Charles M. Howell, but Howell, according to rumor, espied a more difficult race against Milligan than the one he had lost against Clark, and so refused.

Pendergast, the boss's nephew Jim, and Aylward then got together. Aylward said he had some suggestions and gave the two Pendergasts the names of ten persons, business and professional, all qualified, he said, for the Senate.

"I don't know any of them," growled the boss.

"Well," was the response, "what kind of a senator do you want?"

"I'd like to have someone I can talk to—close enough to talk to."

"That's reasonable," said the chairman, who made another suggestion: "Well, why don't you run Harry S. Truman for the United States Senate? He's a former soldier. He soldiered with Jim here, your nephew. He's a member of the Masonic Order; he's a Baptist; he's been active in affairs around here."

"Nobody knows him," was the response. "He's an ordinary county judge and not known outside Jackson County. Do you mean seriously to tell me that you actually believe that Truman can be nominated and elected to the United States Senate?"

Aylward had the answer: "Yes, at this time. We're in a position to do it because we have all the contacts. We know all of the politicians in this state—everybody who's interested in state, county, and town politics. They're all our friends and they're willing to go along but they're becoming committed . . . and unless you do something about it there'll be an exodus from our crowd into the other crowd and we'll be in bad shape."[6] Truman perhaps was, counting Aylward's ten names, Pendergast's fifteenth choice.

When the telephone call came that would change his life, May 13, 1934, he was making a small speaking tour, thirty-five speeches in thirty-five counties, for a state bond issue to help with unemployment. He was staying at the Osage Hotel in Warsaw, a modest hostelry, which offered rooms at two dollars a night. Until a plumber made an arrangement just the year before, the building had lacked indoor facilities. Meals were fifty cents, and the proprietors, Mr. and Mrs. Elbert Edwards, served family style, telling guests to "Pitch until you win." The dining room was in the basement and seated seventy-five people, and the menu featured chicken three times a week and always on Sunday.

Judge Truman took the call on the hotel's only telephone, which hung on the wall in the lobby. He was advised to drive to nearby Sedalia and meet Aylward and Jim Pendergast at the Terry Hotel. There the two men offered the boss's endorsement for the Senate race.

Pendergast's offer was not an unalloyed advantage, and Truman may have wondered how valuable it was. After all, he had to win the primary, in which he would face not merely Bennett Clark's candidate, Milligan, but also Congressman John J. Cochran of St. Louis, who was the *St. Louis Post-Dispatch*'s candidate. Cochran, indeed, would become Truman's principal rival. Too, Pendergast may have been trying to get rid of Truman; Colonel Southern believed such was the case. The boss may have resented his unwillingness to cooperate in awarding road contracts. Truman's friend Edgar G. Hinde, later postmaster of Independence, said, "We always thought that they thought maybe he was getting a little too big for the organization, and they were getting a little afraid of him."[7]

Truman knew his best course was to seize the moment and not get analytical. He was coming to the end of his second, and by custom last, term as presiding judge, and had no other political possibility in mind—both the House seat and the collectorship were gone. After all, too, this was the U.S. Senate. He accepted at once.

After establishing a one-person secretarial staff (Mildred Latimer, later a member of his senatorial office staff) across the street from the Independence courthouse, in a little place called Puckett's Vegetable Stand, the judge went about organizing his campaign. A month later he opened headquarters in Kansas City at Twelfth and Oak streets.[8]

By mid-June he was on the road. He opened in Moberly on June 19, condemning Republican misrule, praising the New Deal and Roosevelt, and declaring that he backed the president to the limit. He said he knew his opponents, Milligan and Cochran, personally, and if either obtained the nomination he would get out and support him: "I'm just that kind of a Democrat." He said Missouri had not received its share of federal relief money: "We would get our share if our men were on the job. . . . Why shouldn't we have brains in government as well as business?" He did not want to quibble about any issues and invited anyone to come forward and meet him and ask questions on both state issues and national issues. Many persons reportedly went forward.[9]

The primary that year was a matter of endurance, and Truman possessed a great deal of that. He always had been able to produce whatever stamina a situation required, and he was undaunted by the heat in Missouri that summer, the hottest summer on record (over one hundred degrees on twenty-one days, surpassing the previous record of sixteen days set in 1901). Sometimes he drove by himself, which was dangerous, for he was a terrible driver. After he got into an accident, bruising his forehead and breaking two ribs, he had his friend Fred A. Canfil drive. He and Fred made it their business to come into a town promptly, where the candidate gave a speech, and then they left. Afterward they stopped by the side of a road and slept, or Truman studied notes for the next speech. He made two to ten appearances a day and covered sixty county seats. "I went from town to town and from county to county and from daylight until midnight made speeches and shook hands with about a hundred thousand people."[10]

He visited one county seat after another and took any other opportunity to talk he could get. Typical must have been the speeches in Everton and Springfield. John K. Hulston, veteran Ozarks lawyer, then a teenager, remembers those speeches of sixty years ago, how on the morning of July 28, 1934, he drove his father and a friend eight miles from Ash Grove to the Forty-fifth Everton Annual Picnic, on the south side of Sinking Creek in a Dade County park. The passenger said he believed that by campaigning hard he—the passsenger was Truman—could beat out the two other candidates seeking the Democratic senatorial nomination. Upon arrival at the picnic, Hulston's father introduced Judge Truman to the noontime crowd of mostly farmers. "You folks won't get a chance very often," he said, "to vote for a farmer for United States senator. You'd better make the most of it and be for this man, Harry Truman. He's our kind of people. Why, his hands fit cultivator handles just like owl's claws fit a limb." As for the speech, the judge told the group that Tuck Milligan would be a stooge for Bennett Clark and that Jack Cochran of St. Louis would work for his hometown only. Truman promised to represent all the people of the state, just like he had represented all the people of Jackson County on their county court. That night Truman spoke in Springfield at Grant Beach Park. Sam H. Wear, state committeeman, introduced him to four hundred of the party faithful, who came out to hear him say the same thing.[11]

The differences among the candidates were not numerous. Milligan and Cochran opposed immediate payment of the World War veterans' bonus, a national issue at the time; Truman favored payment. All three supported Roosevelt. Milligan and Cochran accused Truman of being Pendergast's candidate. Truman pointed out that both had sought Pendergast's support in the 1932 at-large election for the House of Representatives.

In the course of the campaign Senator Clark, moving around the state, attacked Truman personally for "conducting a campaign of mendacity and imbecility unparalleled in the history of Missouri."[12] In the state's annals this might have been an exaggeration.

Beyond the speechmaking Truman enlisted his friends, among them Governor Park, whom he asked to shake up the state employees. Writing from Joplin, Truman said: "In talking to some of my young Democratic friends down here, they tell me that some of the State employees are saying that I am a *nice* fellow and that they are for me but they think Cochran will win. I'd rather be called any sort of ———— than to be damned with faint praise. Thought perhaps you might be able to get them to say they think I can win and that I'll do the job when I do." Park presumably did as he was asked, then went a bit further: he heard from C. M. Buford of Wellington that he, Buford, did not know how Colonel Petros stood on the Senate race but "[i]f he is for Truman, and can control the Soldiers home vote, it will mean at least 400 votes at the St. James precinct."[13]

The candidate enlisted D. R. Spalding of Spalding's Commercial College, who appealed to graduates from Missouri during the past ten years: "Recalling your attendance at this College and our personal acquaintance during that time, I am taking the liberty of asking as a personal favor that you VOTE for Judge Harry S. Truman. . . . Enclosed please find circulars and cards, which I sincerely believe will convince you." Spalding enclosed a card with Truman's name and the Senate race emblazoned on the front, along with the future senator's picture in an oval frame; on the other side it came to the point, quoting the *Independence Examiner* of May 31, 1934: "Missouri this year has an opportunity to get away from the two large cities and elect a country boy to the Senate. Judge Harry S. Truman of Independence is distinctively a product of the country. He was born and reared between the plow handles on a Jackson County farm."[14]

It gradually became clear that Truman possessed a base in the "outstate" or country counties that his opponents had not counted on. The *Post-Dispatch* said Missouri, like Gaul, was divided into three parts: the two cities and the outstate. Rural Missourians liked him. He had been attending Masonic grand lodge meetings for twenty-five years, had attended every American Legion meeting ever held in the state, was an active participant in—and had headed— the county judges association (he knew 342 judges, not to mention former judges and would-be judges), and, because of the prominence of Jackson County, was acquainted with all the legislators and state senators in Jeff City. It was true that the state's two major newspapers, the *Post-Dispatch* and the *Kansas City Star*, opposed him, but they had been doing that for years. He afterward concluded that during the primary the papers told so many lies that if only for that reason outstate people voted for him.

The contest seemed close, and it may have been a blunder by the St. Louis Democrats that allowed Truman to win. They bragged that their city would give Cochran 125,000 votes, and this forced Boss Tom to add to the vote he intended to bring in for Truman in Kansas City. Out of 148,000 votes cast in Kansas City on August 7, 1934, 137,000 were for Truman. The work of the Kansas City machine was heroic. The *Post-Dispatch* sarcastically pointed out that Pendergast obtained those votes for Truman from Kansas City's population of 399,000, while Cochran received 104,000 votes (less than Pendergast expected) from St. Louis's population of 822,000. Truman carried Kansas City's First District by 17,485 to 49 for his St. Louis opponent, the Second District by 15,145 to 24, and the Third by 8,182 to 34. The three alone gave him 40,000 votes, his statewide margin.[15]

In passing something should be said about the sadly deteriorating scene in Kansas City that existed about the time Truman received the nomination for U.S. senator, courtesy of the Pendergast organization. It is impossible not to wonder what he was thinking about such support. In 1933, Kansas City had been treated to a gangland shoot-out in front of the downtown railroad station, in which Charles "Pretty Boy" Floyd and two friends killed four police officers and a criminal the officers were escorting; Floyd was attempting to free the criminal. The person who got Floyd and friends out of town afterward was a Pendergast lieutenant, John Lazia, controller of the city's North Side section known as Little Italy. In June 1934, Lazia was machine-gunned. In March of that year occurred the most disorderly primary election in the city's history. A group of college youths known as the National Youth Movement was trying to elect decent, nonmachine candidates through a Citizens-Fusion ticket that combined antimachine Democrats and Republicans; the machine's enforcers shot four people and severely injured eleven, all while the machine-dominated police looked on. Why this happened is difficult to understand. It could be that Lazia's power was beginning to overshadow that of Pendergast. Perhaps the boss's resorts to lawlessness over the years encouraged excess. Or perhaps his triumphs in 1932—because of Roosevelt's victory, the at-large election of all the state's congressmen, and Judge Park's victory—had gone to his head.

Conditions in Kansas City were so bad that they should have deeply embarrassed Truman. Whether it was right to wash his hands of Kansas City while profiting from the place is a nice question. He decided in the affirmative. A few years later he wrote his Guard friend from the farm years, George Collins: "Any man would have been very foolish to turn down the support of the organization which at that time controlled 100,000 votes, and I acted just as every other candidate would have done."[16]

In the general election in November, the machine's Senate candidate easily defeated his Republican opponent, Roscoe C. Patterson. A staunch conservative, named after the Republican leader of the post–Civil War era, Roscoe Conkling, Patterson also was a prohibitionist and had almost no Senate record—only one enactment, the Lindbergh or Federal Kidnaping Act. His issues were totalitarian dictatorship, loss of the free enterprise system, and communism. Truman won by more than a quarter-million votes.

In what few weeks remained until his swearing-in, the senator-elect and his family had barely time to receive the plaudits of his supporters and to pack for the move to Washington. On December 17 a farewell took place at the Christian Church in Independence. The toastmaster, Colonel Southern, set the theme by protesting the "farewell" part of it. Martha Ellen Truman was present, as well as the winning candidate's other relatives, and "Mamma" Truman received a standing tribute. A speaker said she had kept the senator-elect's feet on the ground; his sister Mary Jane, it was explained, performed the sisterly duty of taking the conceit out of him; Vivian had convinced him years ago that he could not lick the world single-handed. Ardelia Hardin Palmer recalled the two guests of honor as simply Harry and Bess. When Bess entered the high school's assembly hall, the teacher said, she put her books on her desk rather like saying, "Well, there they are, and that's that." Bess, she said, had backed the senator in an equally workmanlike manner. The Masonic Order was represented. Major Stayton spoke for the veterans. Mrs. Henry Chiles represented the National Old Trails Road Association; she had been a classmate at Independence High. Judge Purcell reviewed the achievements of the county court: highway building and other public improvements, including the new courthouse in Kansas City. He spoke of the regional plan for counties surrounding Kansas City, lost in the depression. Judge McCardle pointed out how in 1932 he had taken the oath of office in the county's first courthouse, a log cabin a block south of Independence Square, in use during remodeling of the courthouse, and would finish in the new skyscraper in Kansas City, a change like successive scenes in the Arabian Nights. Judge Bell, about to be Congressman Bell, spoke, and Truman's change of fortune may have astonished him more than McCardle's astonishment over courthouse buildings. Truman's response was brief. Nothing he could say would "anywhere near tell you how much we appreciate this. You're expecting too much. All I can say is that I will do my best."[17]

Among speakers that evening was the postmistress at Marceline, Anne Watson, who told Truman, "Someday you will be elected President and I will be there to see you inaugurated." Reportedly he laughed louder than the entire crowd put together.[18]

2

For the Trumans the transition to Washington was not too difficult. They rented the first of what proved a series of apartments. Mrs. Wallace remained in the house on North Delaware, for Fred Wallace and wife were there. Bess, Margaret, and the senator actually were together only each spring. In summer the Truman women returned to Independence, and in the fall Margaret enrolled in school there. They went back to Washington when Congress convened, and Margaret enrolled each spring in a private school, Gunston Hall.

For Bess and Margaret, life in the capital seems to have been enjoyable. Margaret liked the school. Her mother came to feel at home among Washington's senatorial wives, discovering many were from small towns, some from the farm. They were easy to meet and know, and amounted to a new circle of friends.

The senator found Washington a cold place, beginning with President Roosevelt and administration officialdom, but surprisingly including the Senate itself. The "greatest of the greats," as he once described the president, had little time for him. The senator always admired Roosevelt. He had reservations about FDR's self-centeredness and his family that became pronounced over the years, but as one politician to another he knew he was looking at a "pro." He admired him partly for the way in which FDR looked like a president, partly for what he accomplished. "I always thought Franklin Roosevelt came nearer being the ideal President than anyone we'd had during my lifetime," he once said, "and I can remember back to the second term of Grover Cleveland, in 1892."[19] Roosevelt brought the monetary system of the country to Washington, taking it away from New York bankers; he rescued the banks; he organized the WPA and CCC. The prospect of visiting him in the White House was exhilarating, an event for a "country boy," as Truman described himself. The actuality was considerably less impressive. After arrival in Washington the senator asked his administrative assistant, Victor Messall, to obtain an appointment so he might pay his respects. The president's calendar was full, an appointment difficult. After five months the president fitted him in. He and Messall went to the west wing to the reception room outside the oval office, and noticed cabinet members and other important officials waiting there. At last the president's appointments secretary, Edwin M. "Pa" Watson, told Truman he could go in. Roosevelt was "as cordial and nice to me as he could be." The appointment was for fifteen minutes, and the senator came out after seven.[20]

Nor were the high officials interested in the junior senator from Missouri. Before he entered the Senate he and Bennett Clark had gone around to see Secretary of the Treasury Henry Morgenthau, Jr., and Morgenthau was not in—intentionally, Truman always believed. When he and Messall went for the appointment with Roosevelt they had seen Secretary of the Interior Harold L. Ickes and Secretary of Agriculture Henry A. Wallace, among other individuals. No one spoke to them. Truman always liked Harry Hopkins, whom he had met when national reemployment director for Missouri, and recalled he was "one of the few people who were kind to me when I first came to Washington." In 1949 he explained to Jonathan Daniels that he was "under a cloud," by which he meant his connection with Pendergast.[21]

In the Senate he was similarly ignored. He received a desk in the last row on the Democratic side. In the office building his suite consisted of three rooms on the second floor looking out on the grass-covered inner court. Only a few senators showed any consideration, among them Burton K. Wheeler of Montana, with whom he became close.[22] Another was Sherman H. Minton of Indiana, whom years later he elevated to the Supreme Court. Another was the Senate dandy, Hamilton Lewis of Illinois, who beneath his dignity was a warmhearted human being.

He bided his time. One of his county judge friends had given advice he now received from Ham Lewis: "Harry, don't you go to the Senate with an inferiority complex. You sit there about six months, and you wonder how you got there. And after that you wonder how the rest of them got there."[23] He may have recalled the quotation from Josh Billings, of which he was fond, concerning poor relatives—"Dont dispize yure poor relashuns, they may bekum suddenly ritch, and then it will be awkward to explain things to them."[24]

Senator Truman kept his own counsel based on beliefs he had acquired many years before. One of the best sources of his outlook in this difficult time is his letters to young Margaret when she was home in Independence. It is fairly clear he was not merely instructing his daughter, but stating what he himself believed. In one of them he told her it was necessary to believe in something; he was talking about religion, but setting out a point of view:

It doesn't matter whether you are a Methodist, L.D.S. [member of the Reorganized Church of Jesus Christ of Latter Day Saints], Catholic, Mormon, Jew, or what you believe—if you believe it and live it. They all hope to get to the same place sometime. Judge men and women by what they are and how they act, not by their religious label. Personally I'd like 'em all to be Baptists, but I'm not barring any of them from heaven because they're not.

It was necessary to try to achieve: "There are some who can win and make others happy by doing it and some who make enemies. You can be one who wins and makes friends and it is so much happier that way." It was essential to work: "Lazy people never get anywhere in anything." Here he touched the core of his behavior in the Senate during the 1930s:

It just takes work and more work to accomplish anything—and your dad knows it better than anyone. It's been my policy to do every job assigned to me just a little better than anyone else has done it. It takes work to do anything well. Most people expect everything and do nothing to get it. That is why some people are leaders in society, in politics, in religion, on the stage and elsewhere, and some just stand and cry that they haven't been treated fairly.[25]

Observing his fellow senators, Truman soon noticed they were not paying attention to business. He beheld their peculiarities, as he put it, and "what happens in the Senate is usually due to what has happened to Senators the evening before or what they have heard in conversation, by mail or have read in the papers." Senator Robert Wagner of New York one day was trying to work out a set of amendments to his "rather slovenly drawn housing bill," when Senator Tom Connally of Texas rushed into the chamber at 4:00 P.M., not having been there all day, and made a point of order against Wagner's holding the floor while senators were voting on the amendments. The president pro tem sustained the point, and Connally "succeeded in relieving his system of a speech on a totally extraneous subject," the right of President Roosevelt to appoint a justice of the Supreme Court when the Senate was not in session.[26]

He observed the dignity with which senators comported themselves. One day he was talking to a stenographer, who reported a young man bouncing around a meeting of the banking and currency committee; the stenographer thought it was a new reporter for some big daily paper. It turned out to be Senator Henry Cabot Lodge, Jr., of Massachusetts. The stenographer said Lodge had not yet "acquired the senatorial movement in his walk."[27]

Following the advice of Senator Carl Hayden of Arizona, Truman decided to be a workhorse rather than a show horse. He did not make a speech until 1937. Nor was he much at introducing bills: in 1935–1936 he introduced thirty-one; in 1937–1938, forty-two; and in 1939–1941, forty-four. In his abbreviated second term ending January 1945, there were fewer: in 1941–1942, twenty-six; in 1943–1944, twenty-one; and in 1945, two. Most were worthy projects he felt impelled to pursue even though he knew they would be assigned to committee and die. Typically, he sponsored a bill for agricultural insurance; the Senate passed similar bills, but not Truman's. Only in one instance did he sponsor a bill peculiarly his own, a bill that showed remarkable foresight and should have passed: it proposed state drivers' tests, according to federal standards, for all drivers who crossed state lines.

On New Deal issues he went down the line for Roosevelt. Sometimes he was glad to see the administration lose in the Supreme Court, as when the court declared the National Industrial Recovery Act unconstitutional. "The N.R.A. decision was all right. It upheld the Constitution. Emergency measures should be made to fit the Constitution and not the Constitution to fit the emergency measures."[28] But he supported the president when the court ruled against the Agricultural Adjustment Act; the farm problem was a national issue and the court was sending it back to the states. On FDR's effort to enlarge the court, he took a public position in favor; it had been done before, and there was nothing sacrosanct about a court of nine justices:

> The cry is that the President wants to pack the court. Well, if that were possible, the court is packed now, and has been for 50 years, against progressive legislation. If you don't believe it, read some of the dissenting opinions of Justices Clark, Harlan, Holmes, and Stone, and even Chief Justice Hughes, in whose beard certain people . . . believe reposes more wisdom than Daniel Webster had in his head.[29]

When court-packing attracted opposition, his mail running twenty-to-one against, he changed his mind. He talked it over with his close Kansas City friend, the drugstore magnate Tom L. Evans, and expressed himself against packing, but out of loyalty to the president he avoided public statements.[30]

Incidentally, voting a New Deal line may not have been a totally good idea, for Truman's colleague Clark obtained attention from the White House by voting unpredictably. Clark received virtually all the federal patronage. Drunk much of the time, he gave little attention to his Senate duties, nor to the needs of constituents, who took their troubles, including correspondence, to Truman. Clark finally became so impossible that the president took the patronage away. The assumption would have been that he gave it to Truman. Such was not the case.

On a single non–New Deal issue the senator opposed Roosevelt—this was early payment of a veterans' bonus. The president vetoed the Bonus bill, and Truman voted to override. His position was logical enough: when the initial bill authorizing a bonus but delaying payment passed in the early 1920s, when he was in county politics, he had been against it; a veteran and active Legionnaire, he was at variance with his friends. Once the measure passed, and after the depression began, he voted for early payment because veterans needed it. This had been his position during the campaign.

But during his first Senate term the need for national transportation legislation caught his attention. He had first hoped to obtain a seat on the military affairs committee, but he lacked seniority and had to satisfy himself with the interstate commerce committee. The assignment was not too bad, considering the work he had done with roads in Jackson County and his longtime interest in a national highway system. It offered a chance to study the nation's economy. He also needed something to do: "I keep wanting to do something—there's a driving force inside me that makes me get into things. I can't sit still and do nothing. I've read the interstate commerce law in the last two days and will start on the court decisions unless something interferes. I'm going to be better informed on the transportation problem than anyone here."[31] Interstate commerce involved not merely automobiles and trucks; it looked to railroads, water transport, pipelines, and planes as well. Congress had created a patchwork of rules affecting single modes of transport, and the need was a statute for everything. During the 1930s the need grew acute because of excess facilities, the competition hurting all carriers.

As matters turned out, a subcommittee of Truman and Warren Austin of Vermont dealt with aeronautics, the newest, smallest, and for that reason easiest of the carriers to regulate. The Missouri senator preferred regulation under the Interstate Commerce Commission (ICC). He urged the case with Roosevelt, in writing, but the president took no interest, and it proved necessary to sponsor a Civil Aeronautics Board. The senators arranged for the new body to proceed under the same rules as the ICC: everything could go according to practices evolved since creation of the ICC a half-century before, practices the courts had tested many times.

In debate over the Civil Aeronautics bill, Truman proposed that President Roosevelt control the board. The president would appoint its chairman with consent of the Senate. To advocate Roosevelt's authority was awkward in the midst of the court-packing fight, but he again demonstrated loyalty.

The bill created trouble of a sort the freshman senator had not anticipated. Senator Pat McCarran of Nevada, chairman of the interstate commerce committee, removed it from the calendar and reintroduced it as his own bill, with a proviso to keep regulation under Congress. When it passed and went to conference, no one thought to make Truman a member of the conference committee. Senator Clark made a scene with Vice President John N. Garner, going so far as to say—which he never for a moment meant, and Garner knew it—he would resign his seat if Truman were not on the committee. Garner made the change, and over McCarran's protest Truman gradually revived his bill.

The Civil Aeronautics Act, signed by Roosevelt in 1938, provided a legal foundation for the aviation industry for forty years, until deregulation in 1978. During his work on the bill Truman had spoken in terms that must have seemed hyperbole, and yet displayed a large prescience. The potential of commercial aviation, he said, was unlimited: "Air transport will make Europe, Asia, South America, and Polynesia our next-door neighbors. Shanghai is not as far from San Francisco by air as New York is by rail. Rio de Janeiro is closer to Miami by air than Chicago is by rail."[32]

All this was prelude to the Transportation Act of 1940. The need for a transportation statute was obvious, if only from a listing of laws enacted by Congress during the 1930s: the Emergency Railroad Transportation Act (1933), the Intercoastal Shipping Act (1933), the Motor Carrier Act (1935), the Merchant Marine Act (1936), the Civil Aeronautics Act (1938). Truman labored over it during the latter part of his first term, in partnership with Wheeler. Indeed, the act of 1940 became known as the Truman-Wheeler Act.

In drawing up the Transportation Act, Truman and Wheeler found themselves considering whether to support water transportation against rail.[33] The problem encompassed a mixture of interests: the conflict between farmers and railroaders, the U.S. Army's desire to keep the engineer corps busy, the need of such depression programs as the Public Works Administration for construction projects, and the propriety of government support of one sort of transportation (water) at a time of declining traffic carried by another, privately financed sort (railroad).

The strain between farmers and railroaders went back to the 1870s and was based on a perception of the former that price gouging by railroads was responsible in large part for their woes. There were other factors as well, of course. As a group, farmers had come on bad times after the war, when prices collapsed because of return of world competition. Also, hybrid seeds and better ways of cultivation had increased production. The result of all this was that farmers had an inordinate amount of debt. While farmers were powerless in the face of such developments, the railroads were one institution they felt they could affect; thus, they went after the railroad companies, championing the dredging of rivers and the enlargement of the Mississippi carrying system. The government put close to $2 billion into water transport, and annual operating costs were running at $700 million. The system served Pittsburgh, Chicago and the Great Lakes, Sioux City, Kansas City, and Omaha, reaching two thousand miles north and south, and another two thousand east and west, into the agricultural heart of the nation, putting water ports within an average of 155 miles of all inland shipping points. Increased earnings to farmers amounted to six cents and more per bushel for corn and wheat. All the while the railroads' business was diminishing. In 1926 they handled three-fourths of the nation's traffic, and in 1938 they were down to two-thirds; shipments of livestock, easily measurable, dropped by half.

What made so difficult the simple establishment, by law, of fair competition was the extraordinary chicanery of railroads' financing in the 1920s and early 1930s. Truman and Wheeler came from rural backgrounds, railroad-dominated states. Wheeler instinctively knew that all railroads were guilty of something, and he suspected each was guiltier than the others. As a boy, Truman had sat on the roof of the Crysler Street house and watched Missouri Pacific trains passing through the Independence station. Both were prepared to believe in the perfidy of the Eastern bankers and lawyers. But as they dug into details of railroad finance, they were shocked. The 1920s, it turned out, had opened opportunities for gross overcapitalization. Because the investing public had wearied of the watering of railroad stock, and refused to put money into such paper evidences of value, the roads resorted to bond issues. As long as prosperity held, they could pay interest, but it did not take much of a jolt to throw them into receivership. Reorganization gave huge fees to lawyers and bankers, who worked together to profit from the companies' distress.

The crusading senators caught public attention by hearings that forced representatives of the great New York and Chicago law firms, together with their collaborators, railroad presidents and vice presidents, to defend themselves. Through exacting staff work in records of railroad corporations, and from borrowing dozens of books from the Library of Congress, Truman mastered the intricacies of railroad financing. One time he had the library send over fifty books. In 1937, 1938, and 1939 he and Wheeler brought out what had happened, especially the use of holding companies. Wheeler had sponsored the Public Utilities Holding Company Act, and instructed Truman in details of that special device for chicanery.

The facts were startling. The senator wrote Margaret describing the Missouri Pacific hearings as "really a dogfight from start to finish. It is like pulling teeth to get a straight answer. These people are trying to steal a great railroad and of course they don't want to get caught." He described the pages accumulated in a few days as "a pile a foot and a half high" and added, "I have to read them all."[34] Toward the end of May 1937, he heard testimony from seven railroad executives and a week later made his first speech on the floor, demonstrating the difference between operating companies—Missouri Pacific, Great Western, Frisco—and holding companies. The former sought money from moving traffic, the latter from manipulating stock prices. The senators focused on the Alleghany Corporation, a Cleveland holding company formed by the two Van Sweringen brothers, O. P. and M. J., with assistance of J. P. Morgan, Jr. Under their supervision, beginning in 1930, the

Missouri Pacific became a cash cow, giving dividends unjustified by earnings, with no income going into surplus—all done by juggling accounts, cutting payroll, skimping maintenance, postponing improvements. The Morgan firm hired Price, Waterhouse to make everything look good. When the Van Sweringens went broke during the depression, Robert R. Young seized the Alleghany Corporation, gaining control of $3 billion worth of assets for $255,000, equal to spending $2.55 to acquire a $30,000 business (Truman was sensitive to the latter comparison). Despite Young's takeover, Morgan continued to profit. His partners sold Alleghany shares to friends at $15 under market price. The senator concluded: "The Money boys control the country, and there's no use trying to keep 'em from it. All we can do is to make the yoke as easy as possible."[35]

Dealing with the Missouri Pacific endangered Truman's chances for re-election in 1940. His principal investigator, Max Lowenthal, later said Truman told him, "You treat this as you would any other hearing." He refused to go easy with the hearing. "If I quit this thing now," he said, "they'll say Kemper and the Boss pulled me off."[36]

The Missouri Pacific hearings, like the others, were revelations, and at one point Truman had to recess them while he gathered his temper. "I wanted to punch the witnesses rather than question them," he wrote Bess, "because they'd robbed and abused a great property and a lot of 'widows and orphans' you hear so much about. I really had to verbally pulverize the ringleader yesterday." There also were satisfactions: "New York papers had my picture on the financial page and really gave me a nice write-up. Even Mr. Hearst gave me the best of it. So I'm calming down somewhat."[37]

Another investigation revealed how the Bremo holding company took control of the Chicago, Great Western by buying stock on margin, obtaining some margin on margin. Owners were traffic managers from packinghouses (Swift, Cudahy, Wilson), automobile companies (Dodge), oil companies (Shell, Standard of Indiana), or grocers (Libby, Kroger) and took their companies' business to their own railroad. J. P. Morgan, Jr., helped them. The railroad's former chairman described the new owners as a "lot of pirates."[38]

Bitter controversy surrounded hearings over the Chicago, Milwaukee, St. Paul, and Pacific. Because the Milwaukee ran through Montana, Wheeler let Truman take over. Roswell L. Gilpatric, later an illustrious public servant, member of the Truman, John F. Kennedy, and Lyndon B. Johnson administrations, was a youthful member of the New York firm of Cravath, de Gersdorff, Swaine and Wood, which was involved financially with the Milwaukee. He watched the senator and his assistant, Lowenthal, grill Robert T. Swaine and thought Truman very fair "in spite of the tribulations we had to endure at Max Lowenthal's hands."[39] In December 1934, the St. Paul had applied for and secured a loan of $4 million from the Reconstruction Finance Corporation, after the Interstate Commerce Commission certified that the St. Paul was not in need of reorganization "at present"; this allowed bankers to unload St. Paul securities before the road went under two months later. Kuhn, Loeb and the National City Bank made application to a federal judge in charge of the receivership, and Truman charged collusion in the judge's quick acceptance of a plan of reorganization.

Security holders had put $5 billion in railroads, and the question was where it went. In a Senate speech Truman likened railroad financiers to his own Missouri character, Jesse James:

> Speaking of the Rock Island reminds me that the first railroad robbery was committed on the Rock Island back in 1873 just east of Council Bluffs, Iowa. The man who committed that robbery used a gun and a horse and got up early in the morning. He and his gang took a chance of being killed and eventually most were. That railroad robber's name was Jesse James. The same Jesse James held up the Missouri Pacific in 1876 and took the paltry sum of seventeen thousand dollars from the express car. About thirty years after the Council Bluffs holdup, the Rock Island went through a looting by some gentlemen known as the "Tin Plate Millionaires." They used no guns but they ruined the railroad and got away with seventy million dollars or more. They did it by means of holding companies. Senators can see what "pikers" Mr. James and his crowd were alongside of some real artists.[40]

Hearings focused on the need for regulation. It was hard work, especially for Truman, because his colleague Wheeler became involved in the fight over the Supreme Court, and the Missouri senator found himself with most of the load. The danger was that water carriers—not old enough to need to reorganize, and with farmer, army, and PWA support—would gain more than they deserved. To keep things balanced, Truman and Wheeler had to defend the railroads. Secretary of Agriculture Wallace entered the fray, together with Secretary of the Interior Ickes. The Roosevelt administration was accustomed to internecine warfare, and the president watched benignly. But the result at long last was passage of a bill for fair competition among the nation's carriers under the ICC (with the exception of aeronautics under the Civil Aeronautics Board). The president, who had done little to help, signed the bill into law.

3

Meanwhile, Senator Truman was engaged in the political fight of his life, for reelection. In 1940, in a field of three candidates in the primary and out of 665,000 votes cast, he squeaked through with a plurality of a little less than 8,000; that is, 1 percent of the popular vote.

The calamity that nearly finished him off was the fall of Pendergast, a totally unexpected event. Even now, after half a century, the collapse of the machine seems an impossibility. From its grandeur in 1935, it tumbled into oblivion. The machine was like a huge building that had stood on its foundations for years, but when someone decided to tear it down, experts arranged a massive demolition, so that at the moment of explosion it stood still for a second or two, as if nothing had happened, and then mortar, bricks, windows, roof, the entire structure fell in on itself with a rumble and roar, dust rising to the heavens.

The most obvious of Pendergast's troubles was ill health; when it afflicted him in the summer of 1936, it came with a vengeance. He had returned from a trip to Europe and was staying in New York on the twenty-ninth floor of the Waldorf Astoria, enjoying the hostelry's marble corridors and palm-lined dining rooms, the suites with thick carpets and expensive furniture, filled with bric-a-brac to make inhabitants feel they were getting their money's worth. He took a parlor car down to Philadelphia to attend the Democratic national convention. There he met leaders of the party, as he had been accustomed to for many years. He shook hands with them all, keeping his hat on so as to hide his bald head. Smoking a cigarette through its natty holder, he posed with his friend Senator Truman, the national chairman, Farley, and several other politicos, all looking at him, with the tall Farley dwarfing the others. Everyone was smiling, including Pendergast, the picture of health. But that first evening he suffered a digestive upset and was desperately ill the next day; it developed that he had had a heart attack. He was also diagnosed as suffering from cancer of the bowel, requiring a colostomy. Never again was he the robust human being whose face and bulk reminded people of earlier days, when he could punch anyone who got in his way. After weeks of uncertain convalescence he took the train to Kansas City and reappeared at the Main Street office, sallow-faced and shrunken.

But by this time he had contracted another disease that was not so immediately recognizable. This was a mania, difficult to understand because it was so self-destructive. Each morning until noon he continued to see suppliants at the office, after which observers might have thought he rested or retired to 5650 Ward Parkway. Nothing of the sort: he closeted himself in the office and opened three direct lines to racetracks around the nation, with his secretary at hand to record his bets. He bet with cash, leaving no record of where the money came from or went.

He was betting large amounts. Truman's friend Tom Evans managed to get into the Main Street office one afternoon after business hours and found Pendergast betting 10/-20/-30, place-show-win. Tom told Pendergast's receptionist, a tall, retired steamboat pilot named Elijah "Cap" Matheus, to put him down for the same. When he came out he said, "Cap, call me when you pick up this winning and I'll come over and get it."

"What do you mean—winning?" said Cap in his gruff way.

"Well," said Tom, "you made those bets for me."

"Did you want those bets made?"

"Why certainly I wanted them made; why wouldn't I?"

"You know what the old man was betting, don't you?" said Cap. "He was betting ten thousand, twenty thousand and thirty thousand dollars; did you want that bet?"[41]

Pendergast had gone crazy, scattering bets everywhere. Once he won nearly $250,000. He tried to beat that, wagering $2 million in 1935. As government figures showed, he lost $600,000 that year alone.

It was said that Pendergast gave his kingdom for a horse. The betting mania brought him to his downfall: his losses mounted, his need for money became insatiable, and he was willing to pick up money from sources that were dangerous to him.

The boss's solution to his money problems was sadly understandable. Years earlier, when he was just beginning in politics, he had turned to graft as a way to provide for his welfare organization, which dispensed food and fuel, money for lodging, turkeys on Thanksgiving, chickens on Christmas. He took money from the Kansas City traction company in return for friendly renewal of its franchise, and acquired money from companies in need of tax abatements. He established his own companies, the cement company and a wholesale liquor company, which were highly profitable. His upward mobility had some part in the eventual collapse; he moved out of the West Bottoms to Ward Parkway, and otherwise spent a great deal of money on his family. His political successes in the early 1930s probably emboldened him, making him think he could get away with anything. His connection with Lazia encouraged him to wink at lawlessness. Then the horses beckoned, with enormous losses, hundreds of thousands a year after 1933. The special needs of Missouri's fire insurance companies offered a partial way out of his betting losses. In 1929 they had raised their rates 16⅔ percent, and the state insurance superintendent refused the increase; the companies obtained a federal injunction, and the judge impounded the extra premiums pending a settlement. By 1935 the companies wanted their money—$9 million, with an additional $2 million impounded by state courts. At the request of Pendergast, Governor Park had appointed R. Emmet O'Malley as insurance superintendent, and O'Malley proposed a settlement of 80 percent to the companies, the balance to policyholders, with a bribe to Pendergast of $750,000. After a meeting in Chicago between the boss and the vice president of the Great American Insurance Company, Charles R. Street, the companies paid off not only Pendergast but also O'Malley and the president of the Missouri Association of Insurance Agents, A. L. McCormack. Too many people were involved, not merely the four principals but fourteen insurance companies.

An unrelated event, overenthusiastic behavior by the Kansas City machine in 1936, worsened Pendergast's predicament. In the county, state, and national election of 1936, the machine brought out the ghost vote in eccentric numbers compared to the local adult population. In past years large fraudulent majorities in Kansas City had been necessary to offset either St. Louis cheating or the outstate vote. This time it was silly, for there was no opposition. The national election was a shoo-in for Roosevelt; Governor Alf Landon of Kansas did not have a chance. The state gubernatorial election was no problem; state law limited Governor Park to a single four-year term, but Pendergast had lined up Lloyd C. Stark, an apparently estimable candidate who had long aspired to the governor's chair. Stark was a World War veteran, having been a major of field artillery. He was proprietor of the largest nursery in the United States, in Louisiana, Missouri; his nursery's specialty was the famed Stark Delicious apple. But to demonstrate its efficiency, the machine brought out the vote, and took no precautions in doing so. It registered voters without the slightest effort to spread out addresses: a house at 912 Tracy Street contained 141 registered voters; at 700 Main Street, 112 voters lived in a vacant lot. On the day of the primary, spooks, sleepers, and riders were everywhere. The dead were the easiest to vote; "Now is the time," someone said, "for all good cemeteries to come to the aid of the party." Sleepers once had resided in their precincts but moved, yet their names remained on the lists. Riders rode the range of precincts, leaving their brands on ballots in every corral. In addition, Republican votes were changed. In one precinct a ballotsmith erased 113 Republican ballots. It was hard work. He complained, "I am all in. Some of these damned Republicans marked their ballots so hard it was all I could do to rub them out."[42] By such arrangements Kansas City's Second District, with a population of 18,478, brought in 19,202 votes for Pendergast's candidate for governor, with 12 for his opponent. The entire Kansas City vote would have been possible statistically only if the city contained 200,000 more adults.

The open cheating, like Pendergast's arrangement with the fire insurance companies, was dangerous. Too many people knew what had happened. Any prominent public figure in Missouri who turned against Pendergast would have a good chance to bring the machine down. This is exactly what the apple grower from Louisiana, Missouri, the machine candidate for the governorship, "a severe, humorless man with the eyes of a zealot and the mouth of a Puritan," undertook to do.[43]

Stark was, of course, an ingrate. When O'Malley and McElroy later described him as a polecat, they were not off the mark; McElroy told someone who offered him a Stark Delicious apple that he would take it home and give it to a dog. In 1935, seeking the governorship, Stark solicited Pendergast's help, and Truman worked hard to get it. During the beginning or end of one of the boss's trips abroad, when Pendergast was in New York, Truman and Bennett Clark and Stark went up from Washington to see him. After Stark displayed himself, the boss met privately with the senators. He was not in favor: "I don't like the . . . ," Tom said. "He's a no-good . . ." Truman talked him into supporting Stark. On the train back to Washington, Stark was jubilant, and according to Truman, "I almost had to leave the drawing room to prevent his hugging and kissing me."[44] During 1936, with Stark running for governor, Truman and Stark continued their good relations, and the senator wrote Stark: "Whenever I can be of any service in any way whatever, all you need to do is to indicate it, and I will be right there." Stark sent word to Fred Canfil: "Of course, you know that Harry is one of the best friends I have in the world."[45] But after taking office he turned on his benefactors. In July 1937, Boss Tom Pendergast went to Colorado Springs for a much-needed vacation and sent a virtual summons to the governor, who was returning from a vacation in Alaska, to stop and see him on the way home. The meeting took place and amounted to a showdown, with reporters well informed by both of the participants. Pendergast, as was his way, came right to the point with Stark. First, he wanted suitable appointments to a new state election board that otherwise could cause trouble in Kansas City. Second, he wanted O'Malley appointed for a second four-year term. Stark refused the initial request, and added insult to injury by letting Pendergast know that O'Malley's days as insurance commissioner were coming to an end.

In the autumn the governor fired O'Malley; it was not a bad idea, but he could not have known the details of O'Malley's malfeasance and did the good deed out of spite. He must have noticed that Pendergast was sensitive to O'Malley's remaining in office, and strangely so, because during the election O'Malley had accused the benevolent and protective orders in the state, such as the Moose and Elks, which had insurance programs, of malfeasance. It was well known that O'Malley had cost the machine tens of thousands of votes, as many Missourians belonged to the orders. Machine Democrats wanted O'Malley out of office, and Pendergast, oddly, did not. This encouraged Stark to get him out.

Stark and Pendergast thereafter headed into another showdown, this over a Stark appointee to fill a vacancy on the state supreme court, a young lawyer named James M. Douglas. Late in 1937 the court, in a four-to-three decision, rejected the O'Malley insurance compromise, so far as it applied to the $2 million state-impounded fund, and Douglas voted with the majority. He was up for nomination in the 1938 primary, and Pendergast sponsored a circuit judge against him. Stark marshaled St. Louis and the outstate areas, and Douglas won the nomination by 120,000 votes, although he lost by 87,000 in Jackson County. Stark meanwhile encouraged the federal attorney in Kansas City, Maurice M. Milligan, younger brother of Tuck, to move against the machine for vote fraud in the 1936 primary.

The fight between Stark and Pendergast naturally affected Senator Truman, and as one thing led to another the senator could easily understand that he, as well as the boss, was in deep trouble. The first indication coincided so exactly with a downturn in Stark-Pendergast relations that it seemed almost to have been timed. On the same day as the conversation between Stark and Pendergast in Colorado Springs, July 19, 1937, Pendergast received a telephone call from Postmaster General Farley in Washington, where the fight over the Supreme Court had taken an unexpected turn. The Senate majority leader, Joseph T. Robinson of Arkansas, had died of a heart attack, and his friends and enemies united in saying that the job of protecting the president in the fight over the court had caused his death. Passions rose high, and went higher when President Roosevelt addressed a letter to Senator Alben W. Barkley of Kentucky as "acting" majority leader, which seemed to say Roosevelt was trying to dictate Robinson's successor. The popular Senator Pat Harrison of Mississippi was opposing Barkley for majority leader. Truman promised Harrison his vote. In the call to Pendergast, Farley asked the boss to ask Truman to change his vote.

The administration had made a careful check of votes in the Barkley-Harrison contest for leader and decided they were even, and that was where Truman came in. Actually, the president sought to move two senators, the other being William H. Dieterich of Illinois, whom he did move by threatening through his emissary, either WPA administrator Hopkins or the New Deal lawyer Thomas G. Corcoran (Farley refused to call Dieterich directly), to take WPA funds away from Chicago's Mayor Edward J. Kelly. Receiving Farley's call, Pendergast called Truman, but ended by saying the issue did not make a great deal of difference to him. Truman refused to change, and showed his ballot, marked for Harrison, to Senator Clyde L. Herring of Iowa just before he cast it.[46]

The incident was disquieting. The Missouri senator had the feeling that the president had treated him shabbily, not talking to him but trying to put on pressure through Pendergast. Why take the great circle route of Washington–Colorado Springs–Washington when a simple phone call would have availed? The timing also, when Stark was pressing Pendergast about O'Malley, seemed more than a coincidence. It was possible the president arranged it with Stark.

Months later, on February 15, 1938, perhaps in memory of this Rooseveltian maneuver, and with a full sensation of how Stark and Milligan were cooperating against the Pendergast machine, Truman made a large miscalculation, in fact a blunder: he lost control of himself on the Senate floor, resorting to an emotionalism of which he was seldom guilty. He long since had discovered politics to be a careful affair in which one had to calculate forces and not become emotional. In the case of Stark's apostasy he did just the latter, and he turned it on the wrong person, Maurice Milligan.

Milligan was no fit subject for the senator's wrath, but Truman tried to get at him. The district attorney was up for reappointment. Roosevelt telephoned the senator and asked him not to declare Milligan "personally obnoxious," which would have ensured his defeat. In a speech on the floor Truman opposed him without using the fatal phrase. He pointed out that he was a poor lawyer, which was true, and accepted large fees from bankruptcy proceedings in the two Kansas City federal district courts, also true:[47]

I have never thought, and I do not now think, that Mr. Milligan is qualified for the position of district attorney for the western district of Missouri. He is not professionally qualified, nor is he morally qualified. My opposition to Mr. Milligan began long before vote frauds were brought to light in Kansas City. . . . Mr. Milligan . . . has received more money in fees in one case than his salary has been from the Federal Treasury for a whole year.[48]

Milligan, he said, was in debt to two of the most partisan jurists in the country:

The Federal court at Kansas City is presided over by two as violently partisan judges as have ever sat on a Federal bench since the Federalist judges of Jefferson's administration. They are Merrill E. Otis and Albert L. Reeves. Mr. Reeves was appointed by that great advocate of clean nonpartisan government, Warren G. Harding, and Mr. Otis was appointed by that other great progressive nonpartisan, Calvin Coolidge. . . . These two judges have made it perfectly plain to Mr. Milligan—and he has been able to see eye to eye with them, due to the bankruptcy emoluments—that convictions of Democrats is what they want. . . . I say to the Senate, Mr. President, that a Jackson County, Mo., Democrat has as much chance of a fair trial in the Federal District Court of Western Missouri as a Jew would have in a Hitler court or a Trotsky follower before Stalin.[49]

All the senator did was make himself look foolish. Milligan was obtaining indictments against machine workers who had engaged in the outlandish vote frauds in 1936. Upon becoming district attorney in 1934 he had done nothing against Pendergast until Stark egged him on—until the governor saw a chance to bring down the boss, whereupon Milligan discovered sin in Kansas City. In his speech in the Senate, Truman proposed to continue Milligan as special prosecutor until settlement of the indictments. He argued that he was not trying to obstruct justice, but it was to no avail, for the Senate reconfirmed Milligan unanimously, save for Truman's negative vote. His Democratic colleagues as well as the Republicans all voted against Truman and for Milligan.

One wonders why his colleagues could not have prevented this outburst, interrupted his tirade, persuaded him to "amend his remarks" and keep the whole thing out of the *Record*. They let him make a fool of himself.

Truman realized he had gone too far. A few days later he wrote Joseph H. Leib: "Replying to your inquiry, I will not be a candidate for reelection to the Senate, in view of my speech on the Senate floor on Tuesday." He followed with the comment: "This is a personal and confidential letter to you and I request that you do not publish it whatsoever." When two years later he decided to run he asked Leib to give back the letter. According to Leib, "He said he wouldn't run as long as I had that original." Leib sent it. "But he always sent you a copy of his letters and I held on to the copy. He forgot he gave one to me." Leib thoughtfully did not release the copy for publication until half a dozen years after Truman's death.[50]

In March 1939, a little more than a year after the speech against Milligan, a year and a half after the Barkley-Harrison vote, Truman again was at odds with the administration. He had begun to see that the president was willing to push him around. Full of good humor, a warm human being in his personal relations, in politics Roosevelt was cold and calculating. His daughter, Anna, who knew him better than any member of his family—a good deal better than his wife, from whom he had been estranged for years—once so described him.[51] With exception of the Bonus bill, Truman had voted a straight party line. Against his own judgment, he had supported Roosevelt on the court issue. He should have been able to expect a little gratitude.

The president needed help with the administration's bill to reorganize the executive offices, and he took Truman for granted. The bill was a worthy undertaking. The president had enlisted the help of several eminent political scientists, but because of the court-packing bill, relations with Congress were at an all-time low and reorganization was in trouble. On March 21 Truman was in Jeff City speaking on good government to a joint session of the legislature. Governor Stark did not manage to attend the address; he was present at a luncheon afterward but did not talk to the senator. On that busy day, Farley telephoned to ask Truman to return and cast his vote the next day for the administration. The president's press secretary, Stephen T. Early, called with the same message. Truman decided to play the game and return, taking a risky night flight back to Washington in a terrible snowstorm. Back safely on the ground, he lost his temper and called the White House. Unable to get Roosevelt, he spoke to Early. "Well," he snapped, "I'm here, at your request, and I damn near got killed getting here by plane in time to vote. . . . I don't think the bill amounts to a tinker's damn, and I expect to be kicked in the . . . just as I always have in the past in return for my services."

"Well, Senator," said Early, "what is it you want?"

"I don't want a . . . thing," was the response. "My vote is not for sale. I vote my convictions, just as I always have, but I think the President ought to have the decency and respect to treat me like the Senator from Missouri and not like a . . . office boy, and you can tell him what I said. If he wants me to, I'll come down and tell him myself."

"All right, Senator," replied Early, "I'll tell the President."[52]

The next day Roosevelt invited Truman for a friendly conversation, but it was hardly a reassuring one. The senator found himself blackmailed. Roosevelt warmly thanked him for the trip to save the bill, and then turned to Missouri politics. He inquired after Pendergast's health, which Truman said was excellent. The senator said the state would go Democratic in 1940 and that he, Truman, would be reelected. Roosevelt said he wanted Missouri politics cleaned up, and he revealed intimate knowledge of the Kansas City situation, from the indictment of the Jackson County attorney, W. W. Graves, Jr., down to attempts by the machine's police chief, Otto P. Higgins, to get Washington to intervene against Stark and Milligan.

Two weeks later came the machine's fall. The intermediary with the insurance companies, McCormack, confessed, and this raised an immediate problem with Pendergast's income tax returns. On April 7, 1939, Good Friday, a grand jury indicted the boss, who said he was being treated like Jesus Christ. Arraigned on May Day, he pleaded innocent, but three weeks later he threw himself on the mercy of the court; Judge Otis fined him $350,000 and sent him to Leavenworth. A marshal served O'Malley as he came out of church, and the insurance commissioner joined Pendergast. City Manager McElroy resigned; Kansas Citians discovered the fact when the siren and red light disappeared from his automobile. Investigators found millions in city funds—estimates ran as high as $20 million—squandered in obscure ways. McElroy, aged perceptibly, took to a wheelchair, and just before proceedings commenced against him suffered a fatal heart attack. WPA boss Matt Murray went to jail, and so did Police Chief Higgins. All the while the 1936 election frauds brought in the heelers. Milligan arraigned 278 members of the machine and obtained 259 convictions.

Senator Truman was dumbstruck. He had no idea Pendergast had gone to the lengths that were now becoming visible. Governor Stark described all this activity in Kansas City as "the final blow in the destruction of the Pendergast organization's death grip on that city and of its insidious influence in state and national affairs."[53]

The Missouri senator asked his friend Burt Wheeler if he should resign, for he said he owed his election to Pendergast. Wheeler, honest to the core, perhaps made honest by the innocence of politics in Montana, where there were no large cities, looked Truman in the eye and asked if the scandal involved him. Truman said it did not; his friend saw no reason to resign.[54]

The next question, initially, was how to deal with Stark, who in September 1939 declared for Truman's Senate seat. The question, however, quickly became one of how to deal with the president, who had shamelessly allied with the governor. Missouri law prevented Stark from holding more than one four-year term. The apple man went to Roosevelt, and together they hatched a plan to get Truman out by offering him an attractive federal appointment. The following notes of a meeting with Roosevelt on November 9, scribbled on a tiny pad, are in Stark's papers:

> Pr: . . . Tru friends say Roos for T. vs Stark for Sen. Pr. give him job & tell can't get elected.
> LCS: Want keep in race easiest beat. Wait after Pri.
> Pr: Tell short time before Pri he'll get job & he won't work so hard.[55]

Truman had anticipated this sort of thing, and in 1937 he extracted from Farley a pledge that the administration would not interfere in his reelection. But to his horror he soon discovered that the national chairman was on his way out. Farley had taken Roosevelt's third-term denials seriously and was lining up a ticket of Secretary of State Cordell Hull for president and himself for vice president; Roosevelt encouraged the scheme and then dumped Farley (offering Hull only the vice presidency, which the secretary turned down).

The junior senator from Missouri knew what he had to do. He was in the Statler Hotel in St. Louis at the end of January 1940 when the telephone call came from the president's hatchet man, Early. Roosevelt was offering a lifetime appointment on the Interstate Commerce Commission, which paid more than the salary of a U.S. senator. Vic Messall took the call. Truman told Vic to tell Early to tell the president to go to hell.[56]

Tom Evans remembered a meeting shortly afterward in the Hotel President in Kansas City with himself, Truman, Messall, and a young assistant from the senator's Washington staff, Kenneth Miller. The deadline for filing for the senatorial race was the next day. The group discussed the situation and Truman said, "I've decided one thing. Vic, you and Ken go down and file at Jefferson City. Go down today, and be sure and be there and file, because there's one moral cinch, if I don't get anybody's vote, I'll get the boss's [Bess's] and my own."

"I can get you two more, my wife's and mine," said Tom. "I don't think Vic is eligible to vote, so you'll only be assured of four. Ken can't vote because he lives in Washington where they don't allow them to vote."[57]

That day, according to Evans, something else happened that was a necessary preliminary to winning the primary for the man of Independence. It was the sort of thing Tom Evans would do. He had grown up with politics, for his parents' house in Kansas City stood next to Mike Pendergast's Tenth Ward Democratic Club, and Tom had attended meetings by climbing into the hall via an upstairs window. Tall for his age, he began voting at the age of fourteen. Once, Mike Pendergast gave him a baseball pass good for two for an entire summer. His brother-in-law, Ernest Webster, drove Mike Pendergast's Locomobile. The day Truman sent Messall and Miller down to file, Evans went over to see Tuck Milligan. He knew that Tuck's brother, Maurice, was seething over the way the governor was taking credit for destroying the Pendergast machine.

"Tuck," said the irrepressible Tom, "I think it would be a good idea—I think if your brother is nominated, he can be elected and would make a good senator; and I want to tell you that I will be glad to help you out with a financial contribution when your committee for his election is set up, I'll give you $500."

"Give it to me now," Tuck said, "because the committee is already set up."

Evans went back and told Senator Truman that for once he, Tom, was supporting the candidate who was opposing him, "and he looked at me kind of funny and said, 'What do you mean? When did you quit me?' I said, 'Well, I just think Maurice Milligan will make a pretty good senator. I went over and contributed to his campaign.' He said, 'I don't want to know anything about that. I wish a lot of my friends were off of me as much as you are. I might be elected.'"[58] Milligan's entrance vastly confused the contest between Truman and Stark, for "good government" voters now had a choice.

The senator kept his campaign suitably low-key. Doubling as campaign manager, Messall advised a cautious stance: cars decorated with American flags, red-and-white streamers, and signs reading "Make Government Human with Men like Truman," "Boone Country Trumanized," "Keep a True Man on the Job—Senator Harry S. Truman," "Tried and True, That's Truman," "Senator Truman loyal to his Country, loyal to the People," and "Safe with Truman." A card the senator and his friends handed out related: "The people of Missouri should not be deprived of his six years' experience in the United States Senate." And: "HIS POLITICAL PROMISES HAVE BEEN FULFILLED."[59] The senator visited the county seats, to talk to whatever crowds he could assemble. Alben Barkley, Sherman Minton, Lewis B. Schwellenbach of Washington, and Carl Hatch of New Mexico spoke for Truman. In St. Louis—where Truman needed help of any sort—a volunteer assistant, David Berenstein, produced the idea of having senators send messages, and two dozen did so. Railroad unions came out in favor; one of them published a weekly newspaper in Washington entitled *Labor* and printed a special edition for Missouri, telling what a friend Truman was. Half a million copies were put out for distribution by Missouri's fifty thousand railroadmen, including a copy to every RFD mailbox. This helped a lot, because among the state's newspapers Truman had support only of the *Kansas City Journal*, the *Jefferson City Daily Capitol News*, the *Dade County Advocate*, and the weekly paper in Harrisonville.[60] The president of the Brotherhood of Railroad Trainmen, Alexander F. Whitney, with whom Truman was to have words in 1946, sent a personal check for $200, serious money in a campaign that cost $21,000 (of which the candidate contributed $3,700). At this time the senator was chosen grand master of the Grand Lodge of Missouri, and that helped.

Ever the Machiavel, Roosevelt added and subtracted from Stark's chances. The governor was doing everything possible to keep the president fascinated by the Missouri political scene, and he was constantly in touch with the White House. A note of December 29, 1939, from Pa Watson to the president related that Governor Stark had called and said that for the forthcoming convention he was weaning the Missouri delegation from Senator Clark so it would come out four-square for the president's third term. "He does, however," wrote Watson, "want you to know that at any time you consider his method faulty, to please advise him and he will change immediately, as your wishes are his wishes." Roosevelt appreciated such wishes, and a few months later, on April 6, 1940, he gave Stark a boost. A note in the president's hand, which found its way into Watson's papers, instructed a White House staff member to "Tell Col. Casteel to go ahead and clean house of old Pendergast crowd. Not use W.P.A. against Gov. Stark in either convention or Aug. primary."[61] But the president took as well as gave, and the "taking" took the form of apparent "giving": he dangled other offices in front of the governor; he talked about a cabinet post, secretary of the navy, to replace Charles Edison, who had resigned, as well as the vice presidency. In regard to the vice presidency, Stark went to the national convention in Chicago and gave away bushels of apples; the delegates ate them, and then voted for Roosevelt's choice, Secretary of Agriculture Wallace. Back in Missouri, the governor had to explain his tactic of running for three offices at once.

Stark did himself no good by exhibiting his egoism—he forced his chauffeur to salute him and appeared at meetings surrounded by uniformed Missouri colonels. He "put the lug on" state employees, forcing them to contribute 5 percent of their annual salaries to his campaign if they earned over sixty dollars a month.

In a close election any bloc of votes makes the difference. Three days before the primary the young county chairman of St. Louis, Robert E. Hannegan, who controlled eight or nine "delivery wards" and could produce votes in a hurry, told his heelers to get out and bring them in for the senator. His inspiration came from at least two groups of fellow Democrats. It is likely that in combination they convinced him; Hannegan could marshal a lot of votes, and he needed a sizable number in trade. One of his persuaders was the mayor of Independence, Roger T. Sermon, former adjutant of the 129th Field Artillery. He called the St. Louis candidate for governor, Lawrence McDaniel, and said that if he and Hannegan and the latter's ally, Mayor Bernard L. Dickmann, did not support Truman they, the Jackson County Democrats (with the collapse of the machine no one knew who could speak for it, and Sermon claimed to be doing so), would kill McDaniel's chances in the fall election.[62] The other convincer was Roy W. Harper, later a federal judge, then a young lawyer in Caruthersville in the southeast "bootheel" region of the state. Harper, along with J. V. Conran, the prosecuting attorney of New Madrid County, controlled a group of voters there, and they also wanted Hannegan's delivery wards for Truman in exchange for McDaniel. Harper, years later, said that he and Conran already had a deal with Hannegan, and there never was any switch on Hannegan's part, only some last-minute evidence that the St. Louis Democrats thought Truman was going to lose and might back out on their agreement so they could vote for a winner. It was, one should add, a delicate situation; it is possible that Hannegan, by seeming to wobble, was only showing a certain extra friendship for Stark. However, it was not really friendship that Hannegan was showing—Harper and Conran mistook it: Hannegan was urging Stark for the vice presidency, perhaps in hope of getting him out of Missouri ("I would like to have a Missourian on the national ticket because it would be a great help to the party in the November election").[63] Whatever, Harper and Conran took alarm. Harper was close to Bennett Clark, who was beginning to realize that Truman was a better friend than Stark possibly could be. The senior senator was willing to do something for Truman. It may be that Harper pushed him a little, for Clark needed pushing to do anything. Late in July, Clark came out for Truman.[64] Harper then used him as a messenger to deliver a warning to Hannegan and Dickmann: "[W]hen we make a bargain we keep it. We're going to deliver, and they damn well better deliver because if they don't deliver and their man is nominated, we'll cut his goddamn throat in the fall." These testimonies were Missouri politics at their most understandable. With such words (the Hannegan people were "hot as hell" about it, Harper remembered) the 7,976 votes by which Truman won came from St. Louis.[65]

Truman returned to Washington in triumph. "Never saw so many letters to sign in my life," the senator protested to Margaret. "We've used $35.00 for stamps on congratulation acknowledgments—and piles yet unanswered."[66] When he walked onto the Senate floor all business stopped and his colleagues crowded around him.

Chapter Eight

Wartime Washington

*T*hat Truman's second term as senator would lead straight into the presidency was hardly a foregone conclusion in the autumn of 1940, even after he had won the primary against Governor Stark and, as he liked to put it, sent Stark back to the nursery. Indeed, the very possibility of becoming president seems never to have entered his mind. Nor would it have occurred to anyone of that era, which was dominated politically by the grand figure of Franklin D. Roosevelt. To Roosevelt himself, to be sure, the absurdity of a Missouri successor would have brought a great presidential laugh—FDR would have thrown his head back and laughed until tears came to his eyes. From Independence, Missouri, to the White House was an impossible distance.[1]

The junior senator from Missouri contemplated another course about this time, and although nothing came of it his willingness to try it displayed his total ignorance of the future. After passage of the Draft Act on September 16, 1940, he decided to go on active duty. Dressed in the uniform of a colonel of field artillery, he presented himself at the headquarters of General George C. Marshall, army chief of staff. Years later he described what happened. He said to Marshall, "General, I would like very much to have a chance to work in this war as a field artillery colonel."

The general pulled his spectacles down on his nose and looked at Truman as if the colonel were on inspection. "Senator," he inquired, "how old are you?"

"Well, I'm fifty-six years old," was the answer.

"You're too damned old," was the response. "You'd better stay home and work in the Senate."[2]

The prospect was for the routine of the past to continue. His days he would spend in the Senate office building. Long afterward, one of his four office secretaries, Reathel Odum, recalled how everything there was businesslike. The senator was an easy taskmaster, but a distant personage, seldom joking or kidding. Almost his sole effort at humor, which to the staff became an annoyance, was a comment each morning that he would fire everyone that evening if he did not receive a letter from Independence.[3]

Most of the office work consisted of letters. Truman had double his share because Senator Clark paid no attention to constituent mail. Routine answers he handled in the way of busy people—he let the staff do them. Some he embellished with postscripts, to remove coldness or soften brevity. But many demanded personal attention and received it. Looking over the flow of mail, such as has survived in the library in Independence, flimsies attached to yellowing letters of inquiry, one wonders how he kept everything in mind for those more important letters.

The schedule was usually frantic. The senator set it out one day for Margaret:

> ... letters to dictate as usual, a man who had the aluminum problem solved, so he said, who had to be interviewed; a meeting of a subcommittee in my office on the oil pipeline situation; an interview at the same time with the chief counsel of the American Association of Railroads; a conference with two feature writers from *Fortune* magazine; some people from Independence, Frank Monroe from Sedalia; a look-in on a Military Committee presided over by the Hon. Bob Reynolds of North Carolina, and attendance on a subcommittee of Military Appropriations of the Appropriations Committee, before which Mr. Knudson was testifying and then the Senate session, considering the Labor Appropriations Bill and the W.P.A. Appropriations Bill, an interview with Ass't Counsel of my Committee on Aluminum—a couple of hundred letters to sign— in between times running over to the Senate to vote on various amendments and then going to the Mayflower to meet Neil Helm, Cong. Zimmerman, Cong. Frank Boykin and Vic on some cotton legislation and then back here to finish signing mail and to write to my sweet daughter.[4]

The office suite was convenient to the Senate chamber, whenever the bell rang. In the rear was a room known as the "doghouse," where the senator placed his signed photographs and other mementos, in the way of Washington politicos, and met colleagues and studied reports and memos and drafted speeches.

Evenings he spent in the apartment. After moving every year, the Trumans in 1941 took an apartment in a building at 4701 Connecticut Avenue, Northwest, and became full-time residents of Washington until 1945. The five-story brick structure built in the 1920s, with a Moorish motif of the sort fashionable at the time, boasted a small foyer and elevators run by real elevator operators—people who said "Good morning" and "Good evening" and "Watch your step, please, senator." Tiles lined the foyer and hallways. The floors in the apartments were of oak, and number 209, the Trumans' two-bedroom (living room, dining room, kitchen, single bath), was quiet enough for the Baldwin spinet, on which the senator and Margaret played duets.

When the family returned to Independence for the summers, Truman remained in the apartment, and went out to Missouri when he could.

1

Soon after his second term began—in the November 1940 election the senator fairly easily (by 44,000 votes, somewhat less than Roosevelt's majority in Missouri over Wendell L. Willkie) defeated his Republican opponent, Manvel Davis—Truman became involved in the "committee for the investigation of the national defense program." Apart from regular Senate duties, it consumed every minute of his time until the summer of 1944 and his nomination for the vice presidency.[5]

In the beginning he was simply curious about how the Roosevelt program for national defense, for rearmament, was going. He was not concerned that his own state should receive more contracts, for the administration had taken care of Missouri: in November 1940 the army shifted the Seventh Corps area training center from Iowa to Fort Leonard Wood, near Rolla, Missouri; ordnance and ammunition plants and airports and depots were throughout Missouri, with the ordnance department picking a site just outside Independence for an ammunition plant; and the army air corps put an airfield near Grandview. By mid-1941 the senator would be writing constituents that their state had received more than half of all defense expenditures between the Mississippi and the Rocky Mountains. But he remembered what had happened before and during American participation in World War I: the Wilson administration, trumpeting preparedness in 1915–1916, did little about it, and much of the country's war production in 1917–1918 was a failure. The nation was not in the war long enough to get production going; when in France he had noticed that the AEF used French seventy-fives, for no American-made artillery was available. He wondered whether President Roosevelt was following in Wilson's footsteps. There was also the question of how much it was costing. He knew the administration was spending a great deal, and that the U.S. Army had charge of much of it. The West Point Protective Association, he believed, always threw money at any problem.

When word came from constituents in the vicinity of Fort Leonard Wood that all sorts of scandals were in the making, he decided to see for himself. One day his secretary, who was no longer Messall but his World War I friend Harry Vaughan, went into his office with a batch of correspondence on construction of barracks for draftees—it was Vaughan's habit to wait until he had a group of letters before going to the senator and getting ideas on answers. To his surprise, Truman responded: "Don't answer that until next week. The Senate is going to be in recess for two or three days next week and I'll—if this is happening in Missouri, it's happening out here too, so I'm going to take my car and drive around." He went to cantonments near Washington, to Camps

Lee and Pickett, and to Forts Eustis and Meade. The result was an eye-opener: "Boy, they are really wasting manpower and materiel and everything else. I think something ought to be done."[6] He then took his car and drove in a great arc around half the country, three thousand miles (he remembered it as thirty thousand), through Maryland to Florida, across to Texas, north through Oklahoma to Nebraska, back through Wisconsin and Michigan.

While on this trip to see what was happening, he came to two conclusions. The first involved the arrangement with contractors and suppliers known as "cost plus." The principal formula for construction of camps, and for that matter anything the army was ordering from industry, the cost-plus arrangement provided for payment at cost plus a fixed percentage of profit. This, Truman saw, was an invitation to padding. His other conclusion was that small businesses were not getting a chance at the contracts. The railroad investigation had demonstrated the rapid consolidation of corporate enterprise, and he found that in the last seven months of 1940 the army and navy let contracts for more than $11 billion, with twenty companies receiving most of them: in metals, for example, forty-five thousand companies were eligible, but only ten thousand had contracts, while the National Association of Manufacturers reported that half the country's machine tool capacity was standing idle.

He did not know what to do about the cost-plus problem. He took the small-business problem to the president, without result. He wrote Lou Holland—a small-businessman—in Kansas City: "I don't know whether I made any impression or not, because the President is always courteous and cordial when any one calls on him, and when you come out you think you are getting what you wanted when nine times out of ten you are just getting cordial treatment."[7]

The solution to the two problems arose when *Kansas City Journal-Post* reporter William P. Helm came into the senator's office one day and said, "Why don't you call for a committee to investigate this rotten situation? That would be doing something besides just making a speech, wouldn't it?"

"It surely would," Truman said eagerly.

"You, of course, would head that committee; you'd be its chairman. You'd have the power of the United States behind you. You could go anywhere, examine anything. You could turn such a live-wire current of publicity on these bastards that they'd be running for cover when they saw you coming."

Senator Truman, Helm wrote, slapped Helm's knee, got up from his seat, and pounded his arm. "You're right, Bill!" he exclaimed. "You're absolutely right. I *will* do something about it. I'm going to do just what you've suggested!"[8]

At the beginning no one in the Senate paid much attention. Sixteen senators were on the floor when Truman's resolution received approval, without objection, on March 1, 1941. Senator James F. Byrnes of South Carolina, who was to figure so large during the Truman administration, was in charge of committee budgets, and when Truman asked for $25,000, the diminutive, hyperactive, calculating South Carolinian gave him $15,000; this was not a good beginning, for Byrnes may have called the White House and been advised by the president to starve the committee.[9] Ignoring this development, Truman went ahead. To obtain people to do the work he resorted to an arrangement often made; that is, he borrowed them from government agencies. At the beginning his staff comprised little more than the chief counsel, the lawyer Hugh Fulton. His chief investigator, Matthew J. Connelly, went on the justice department's payroll. At the end of three months he had ten investigators and as many clerks and stenographers. He had difficulty finding colleagues to serve on the committee, for in those days each senator belonged to several standing committees and service on special committees was likely to be perfunctory, but he filled out his group as best he could, with "workhorses" from both parties and strategic geographical spread.

Throughout the committee's existence (it lasted into 1948) the chairman and members had trouble with the House military affairs committee, with which relations were consistently unhappy; the House group followed virtually every Truman committee report with one of its own, and in every instance it was in opposition. The U.S. military, usually under criticism from the Senate, could point out its innocence as announced by the House committee.

The Truman committee started its investigations with a fairly simple problem: construction of training camps. In nine camps, costs were twice estimates. Camp construction costs estimated at $515 million rose to $828 million. During World War I, housing per man averaged $216; in World War II, $697. Part of the cost was poor sites; agents seeking to sell sites received a percentage of prices, and they loaded commissions into the figures. Contractors used cost plus; Truman wanted them to take a percentage of savings if they finished contracts with less material and labor, or pay a percentage of increases in material and labor. All this said nothing of unions, which charged excessive initiation fees and arranged excessive use of time-and-a-half for overtime. Truman blamed the high costs on the army's quartermaster, Lieutenant General Brehon B. Somervell, a tall, proud officer who "cared absolutely nothing about money." The army followed Truman's suggestion and transferred construction from the quartermaster corps to the engineer corps.[10]

The committee probed production of strategic metals, especially aluminum and magnesium, and became increasingly critical of the Aluminum Corporation of America (Alcoa), which was not expanding production rapidly enough. Aware of the need for electrical power to produce aluminum, the corporation had acquired practically all available power sites. But Truman sensed its vulnerability. In the 1920s the German firm of I. G. Farben had demanded that Alcoa limit production of magnesium, which it did, and the subsequent higher prices deterred aircraft manufacturers from using it. At the start of World War II, Germany had four times the magnesium production of the United States. The Truman committee brought out this arrangement, and the result was the organization of the Reynolds Metals Company and the breaking of a bottleneck.

The committee looked into rubber production, where Farben had prevented construction of synthetic-rubber factories; Standard Oil went along with Farben because of an arrangement to get his oil patents. The committee also investigated the army's Canol project, a plan to provide a local supply of oil products for construction of an Alaskan highway. Undertaken on Somervell's initiative, the project was supposed to come to an end in October 1942, at a cost of $134 million. It was still going a year later and needed $34 million more. The committee tried to force abandonment, but Somervell claimed national security. This was one of the few times the committee did not prevail over the military.[11] Then there was a close look at the Wright Aeronautical Corporation, an Ohio subsidiary of Curtiss-Wright, which delivered defective engines. Truman also tangled with the navy, which collaborated with U.S. Steel to accept inferior plate for ships. The committee took issue with the navy's publicity organization, which complacently announced figures of ship production not good enough to counter losses from German submarines; Secretary of the Navy Frank Knox claimed Truman released false figures of sinkings but under pressure recanted, admitting Truman's figures were correct.

A minor investigation that caught more attention than anything else was a look into the army's motion-picture division, in which Hollywood executives and stars enrolled. Lieutenant Colonel Darryl F. Zanuck of Twentieth Century Fox remained on his company's payroll at five thousand dollars a week while he arranged for army contracts. Warner Brothers managed a draft deferment for the youthful matinee idol Ronald Reagan until he could finish a picture; the studios were desperate to hold their male box-office stars. The attention people gave to such studio capers annoyed Truman, who could do little more than point them out and try to shame the principals.

The committee reluctantly stayed away from one subject—the dollar-a-year men, who, as in World War I, again entered government employ. Truman wanted all such appointees on salary, so they would feel some kind of allegiance to the government; it seemed impossible that the chairman of the board of General Electric, Philip D. Reed, working for a dollar a year, plus $120,000 from GE, could take a pro-government position in case of a conflict of interest involving GE. But the head of the War Production Board, a fellow Missourian, Donald M. Nelson, said it was impossible to get along without these dollar-a-year men.

In two other concerns, strikes and racial discrimination, the chairman similarly held off, leaving these matters to the administration, which for the most part did little or nothing. People said that by not taking positions he showed himself as a politician, but here it was necessary to decide whether during the war, with all the rancor when he attacked individuals or corporations seeking federal money, it was wise to move into social issues. Not that he did not have personal opinions about strikes in wartime: in the case of one strike in a defense plant he told the Senate that refusal to work was disgusting. In hearings on this strike, which he arranged, he was short-tempered, failing to understand the larger issue in a Bethlehem Steel Corporation shipyard in San Francisco, where inflation and the cost of housing produced a strike. The committee also stayed away from instances of racial discrimination, which were not difficult to find. The Roosevelt administration was not about to bring trouble in the South.

A prime problem, confronted unsuccessfully in the war's last year, was reconversion back to a peacetime economy. The production of war materials, long delayed, neared completion in late 1943. Requirements no longer were outrunning capacity. The requirement for a major indicator, aluminum, went down drastically. Surplus facilities and materials appeared. At this juncture a decision was necessary; it was foolish to produce what the military could not use: it was time to reconvert factories to civilian production. Anyone who measured the situation knew that after the war a huge demand for civilian goods would arise; if the nation's economy was unprepared, all kinds of trouble could ensue. What was at stake was nothing less than postwar stability. The committee and especially its chairman contended with both military and civil leaders of the army and navy. But the generals, the admirals, and the secretaries of war and of the navy feared the effect of reconversion on the country's morale and the potential for harm to the war's principal campaigns that would come in 1944 and 1945. And the president sided with the military. Roosevelt was tired, did not want an argument, and (as Truman said privately) "passed the buck." The senator had no idea that FDR was passing the buck to him, that as president he, Truman, would receive criticism for postwar scarcities, inflation, and labor trouble.

By 1944 it nonetheless was clear that the Missouri senator had taken on a delicate task and carried it through with aplomb. The principal achievement of the committee was that its chairman forced the president to organize war production during a great national emergency. Roosevelt's long suit was hardly organization—he was an abominable administrator. First had come the Office of Production Management. Truman properly "went for" this agency, presenting a report on January 15, 1942, little more than a month after the attack on Pearl Harbor. The next day, January 16, Roosevelt created a new agency, the War Production Board. But its administrator, Nelson, never realized the power he possessed, and he allowed the military to continue issuing contracts and setting priorities for raw materials. When shortages threatened, the president created "czars," who operated outside the WPB. Early in 1943 a rumor arose that Roosevelt was about to create an overall czar in the person of the World War I head of economic mobilization, Bernard M. Baruch, a big, tall man who had accumulated a reputation as "adviser to presidents." It is difficult to know what he could have done to improve matters. With unaccustomed vigor Nelson announced a reorganization of the WPB. After a short while the WPB gave way to a third agency, the Office of War Mobilization. In May 1943 the president asked former senator Byrnes, who had resigned as associate justice of the Supreme Court to become his principal White House assistant, to be "assistant president" in charge of the OWM. A year later, the loser, Nelson, accepted a Rooseveltian way out: he took a mission to organize the war effort of China, a hopeless enterprise.

During all this Truman managed good relations with the president, avoiding antagonism such as had arisen over a similar committee during the Civil War. Turned into an enemy, Roosevelt could have hurt Truman's committee. No president of the twentieth century was so sensitive to criticism. Only once did the senator come close to losing his position as the principal nonadministration figure in managing war production. In October 1942, with committee battles yet to win and preoccupied by the pressures of running the staff, he allowed a writer for *American* magazine to put together an account of the committee that appeared under his name. In a preface, the magazine's editor described Truman as "probably closer to the facts about the prosecution of the war in Washington than any other man in Congress," which may have been true, but was likely to come to presidential attention. The editor announced the piece as a "shocking article." Beyond doubt, he expressed Truman's point of view when he had the senator saying the nation needed a single leader of war production "who can stand up to the generals and admirals and tell them where to head in." Truman foolishly underlined all this by going on the *March of Time* newsreel and describing the civil-military battle over production as "the most important question of the day." He said the military should keep to their business, that "any attempt on the part of these ambitious generals and admirals to take complete control over the nation's economy" would threaten not merely wartime production but "our postwar political and economic structure" as well. Fortunately, the editor suppressed the last part of his writer's article, which was a jeremiad; the editor, it turned out, needed to save space. And the North African invasion, then under way, took attention from both the article and the newsreel. Truman emerged from this crisis with a sigh—he knew how close he had come—and thereafter measured his relations with the White House carefully.[12]

More than three years thus passed, largely in overseeing the committee. Its members met every two weeks in full session, but it was more effective to use subcommittees for investigations and the drawing up of reports. Truman insisted that reports have unanimous approval. Before printing a report he sent a typewritten copy to the agency under investigation and asked for comment. The agency was to comment only on facts, not opinions, and the committee made all necessary corrections. This had much to do with the acceptability of reports, for no agency could say, "You don't know what you're talking about."[13] The committee carried on from five to fifteen investigations at one time. Each could last a month or more. They eventually produced thirty-two reports.

The days fell into a routine: the senator arrived early at the office to read mail and dictate, signed answers in spare moments, and attended meeting after meeting. He made inspection trips about the country with other committee members, seldom by himself—train trips aboard sleepers appended to coaches full of war workers changing jobs and servicemen going home or back to camp; these were nerve-wrackingly slow trips, beyond the imagination of latter-day Americans accustomed to air travel. Once in a while he and his colleagues flew in DC-3s, the air buses of their time, which went up and down because of their limited range, the engines droning, the unpressurized cabins either too hot or too cold and always drafty.

Meanwhile he handled his ordinary senatorial tasks. When Congress was in session this meant chamber entrances and exits for votes and roll calls; senators do not often listen to speeches, for they can read them in the *Record*. Like the work of the committee, Truman did his ordinary Senate business in meetings with fellow senators or staff members.

Private life, like the public, went on routinely. During summers, when his wife and daughter were in Independence, he sent long handwritten letters, in which he told of the lonely apartment and anything else he could think of, such as papers he took home, restaurant meals, or conversations on the Hill. A cleaning woman came in to keep the apartment in order, but sometimes the senator did the cleaning. Before each trip to Missouri he ran the vacuum sweeper and dusted, so that he could tell Bess and Margaret and Mrs. Wallace, who lived with them beginning in 1943, that things were in order.

It was not much of a life, even if he was getting his name ever more into the newspapers. Editors now knew who he was, unlike one earlier story to which an editor attached the wrong picture.

During the war he looked all right physically but was not in the best of shape. He seems not to have had any more of the stomach upsets that had bothered him during his first term and previously as presiding judge. But the pressure showed. He looked thin, his cheekbones protruding from his angular face. Tiredness showed around his eyes, in the crow's-feet that seemed to be spreading and the dark circles that betrayed too much night reading. His tightly trimmed hair was turning gray, almost white around the sides.

If asked, Truman would have ascribed his appearance to age, for in 1944 he turned sixty; that many years before he had been born in the farm village of Lamar, 120 miles south of Kansas City. He must have thought, if he had time for it, that he would manage one or two more terms, until 1953 or 1959, and retire back to Delaware Street.

2

What followed, instead, was nomination for the vice presidency in 1944. Here was the most extraordinary political arrangement of the present century.[14]

The foundational problem was that Roosevelt—who was running for an unprecedented fourth term—was coming apart physically. The leaders of the Democratic party knew this; indeed, anyone who saw the president closely knew this. The leaders saw how his hands shook; they noticed how he allowed his mouth to gape open, giving the impression he had suffered a small stroke and could not control his facial muscles; they noticed that his weight was dropping. They were not reassured by the advice of his personal physician, Vice Admiral Ross T. McIntire. A genial man, who looked like a family doctor, McIntire described the president's trouble as bronchitis and was accustomed to say he was reasonably healthy, as good as one might expect for a man of his age. What they did not know was that on March 27, 1944, Roosevelt was seen in consultation by a young cardiologist at Bethesda Naval Hospital, Lieutenant Commander Howard G. Bruenn, who discovered that McIntire had been misdiagnosing the president: Roosevelt was in heart failure. Bruenn later described the president's condition as "God-awful." The doctor prescribed rest and digitalis, which could help for a while. But the president's cardiovascular disease was so far advanced, with systolic and diastolic readings at alarming heights, that any such prescription in an era before the availability of blood pressure pills was bound to be very temporary in effect.[15]

Having discerned the president's fatal illness, even if not understanding it, the party leaders wanted Roosevelt to choose a running mate other than Vice President Henry A. Wallace. The latter was a study in contrasts. Tall, angular, with an unruly shock of graying hair that made him look like a college youth, he seemed friendly enough, open to advice or suggestions; in reality, however, he was almost an ethereal sort, difficult to know, hard to talk to. The leaders did not like much of anything about him, especially not his liberal politics or his talk about "the century of the common man." They themselves had been common men, at some time or other, and still considered themselves such, but they considered the notion fuzzy. Wallace, they believed, possessed no real political judgment, and he certainly had little political experience—appointed secretary of agriculture in 1933, he had run only once for office, for the vice presidency in 1940. He had little support in the South, a politically conservative part of the country with much anti-Roosevelt feeling, especially in Texas. He had failed as presiding officer of the Senate, where he managed to antagonize the entire membership, not so much by anything he had done but by ignoring the senators. After the forthcoming peace conference, President Roosevelt would need a persuasive vice president to keep the senators in favor of the peace treaties. The same held for the United Nations Charter. Moreover, rumor was circulating, as in 1940, that Wallace had consulted a clairvoyant, writing dozens of letters to a woman in New York who professed to read the future in the stars. In fact, he had written to a follower of the Russian mystic Nikolay Roerich, but the letters had used signs and symbols and engaged in Washington gossip and some philosophizing that, if made public, would have made him look foolish. If the correspondence had gotten out it could wreak havoc, perhaps even defeat the national ticket.[16]

But how could they get the president to drop Wallace? The party needed Roosevelt in 1944: he was the champion vote-getter of the century, and the Democrats were up against a formidable Republican candidate, Governor Thomas E. Dewey of New York. Roosevelt wanted to run, and the party leaders, if matters came down to it, would have to take any vice presidential running mate he chose. It was awkward in the extreme to deal with the issue openly, for that would involve relating that the leaders expected the president not to survive a fourth term. The president did not think his health was poor; Admiral McIntire was not telling him that. The International News Service reporter at the White House, Robert G. Nixon, who saw him a great deal, believed Roosevelt thought he would take a fourth term, and after that a fifth. He was completely unaware of his own personal situation. The president was highly intelligent, sensitive to criticism, vindictive, and likely to turn against any messenger who sought to inform him.[17]

The party leaders undertook a veritable conspiracy to persuade him to accept a reliable man as his running mate. The principal figure in this effort was a wealthy oilman from California, Edwin W. Pauley, who became party treasurer in 1943. Pauley later wrote about his actions, which were considerable.[18] A big, tall, confident man, outgoing and capable, he went to work in a way to which he was accustomed, which was to move in a straight line toward his goal. One of his first moves was to "have a huddle," as he put it, with the president's appointments secretary, Pa Watson, who was much like Pauley—a close confederate of Roosevelt, he was straightforward yet politically sensitive. Watson was alarmed by the president's physical condition, and he agreed to give oval office appointments to anti-Wallace delegates to the forthcoming national convention and keep pro-Wallace people out of the office. Pauley enlisted the postmaster general, Frank C. Walker, a balding, inconspicuous man with twinkling eyes. A longtime Roosevelt loyalist, Walker was co-owner of a theater chain based in New York and Scranton. He also brought in the party's secretary, George E. Allen, a roly-poly man-about-Washington. He secured the cooperation of the national chairman, Robert Hannegan, the same who as St. Louis chairman in 1940 had ensured Truman's victory over Governor Stark. Hannegan was a strapping former athlete who had become a lawyer, and he knew all about ward politics and the human relations involved with holding a party together.

The fact that Hannegan was national chairman deserves some explanation, for Truman did not put him there to arrange the vice presidential nomination for himself. For one thing, the Pauley group was essentially anti-Wallace, not pro-Truman; during the spring of 1944 it considered several individuals to replace Wallace and was not closely looking at Truman until other possible candidates for some reason failed to attract the president and the group. For another, Hannegan's rise to the chairmanship had little to do with the vice presidential problem in 1944. After his assistance to Truman in 1940, he had lost out in St. Louis politics—the Democrats were fighting—and Truman obtained for him the local post as collector of internal revenue and in 1943 the commissioner's post in Washington. Late that year Postmaster General Walker, then chairman of the national committee, decided he needed relief from his post and asked Truman to be chairman; the senator refused, as he was busy with his committee, and recommended Hannegan. The two friends consulted about the job, and Truman told Hannegan not to take it unless the president personally asked him. The president called him. Hannegan went back to Truman and asked, "What do I do now, coach?" Truman laughed and told him to take it.[19] Hannegan was a natural candidate for the job and probably received it for that reason.

By the late spring of 1944 the Pauley conspiracy seemed to be working. Roosevelt definitely had turned against Wallace. Then another awkwardness entered; namely, that the president typically did not tell Wallace, thinking that somehow he would get the word. As his wife once said, "This is just like Franklin, he always hopes to get things settled pleasantly and he won't realize that there are times when you have got to do an unpleasant thing directly, and, perhaps, unpleasantly."[20] He hoped that a series of subtle messages would persuade the vice president of the inevitable.

The president may have hoped to do him in by getting him out of the country at an inconvenient time, just when the convention was approaching and the vice president needed to organize his supporters. According to Wallace's diary the vice president suggested a trip to Russia, and Roosevelt opted for China, perhaps because he was disposing of Nelson by sending him to the same place. Wallace was to go on a fact-finding tour. The president instructed him to make a side trip to Siberia.

Having disposed of Wallace—or so he thought—the president sought to dispose of the vice presidential hopes of his assistant president, Byrnes, who had noted the president's declining health and was himself aspiring to the presidency. Here he created another confusion. As he did not want Wallace, he similarly did not want Byrnes. He trusted that Byrnes, who was not altogether tactful, would do himself in and that he, the president, might hasten the process once in a while. Byrnes had antagonized White House staffers by listening to their opinions around the table with Roosevelt and then going in to see the president privately to advance his own. His personality also rubbed against that of the president; he was constantly threatening to resign if the president did not do this or that.[21] To help bring the result he wished, Roosevelt seems to have allowed, perhaps even encouraged, party leaders to spread the word that because Byrnes was from South Carolina and bore the burden of the South's racial attitudes he would lose Negro votes in New York City and other large northern cities.[22]

At this juncture the name of Truman arose. The leaders arranged a dinner conference with Roosevelt on the evening of July 11, 1944, at which Pauley, Hannegan, Walker, and Allen were present, together with Edward J. Flynn (leader of the Bronx), Mayor Edward J. Kelly of Chicago, and the president's son-in-law, the husband of his daughter Anna, John Boettiger. For a day or two after this meeting the group believed it had talked Roosevelt into accepting Truman. At the meeting the attendees told Roosevelt what he already knew, that Wallace and Byrnes were unacceptable. No one mentioned the president's health. They recommended Truman. The president knew of the good work of the Truman committee, and he knew the senator had voted down the line for New Deal measures, even the court proposal; that must have appealed to him. The preceding February the senator had come out for a presidential fourth term, and that would have appealed to him as well. But he hardly knew Truman; relations were not close. He had not seen Truman since March and would not talk with him, except by telephone, until August. He asked Boettiger to go out and get a *Congressional Directory* to find out Truman's age. The son-in-law returned with the book, and Pauley took it and held it in his lap: everyone but the president knew Truman was only two years younger than Roosevelt.

After the group left the study, Walker asked Hannegan to use some excuse, such as that he had left his jacket, and go back and get the agreement in writing—everyone understood that an oral statement by the president might not hold. Roosevelt wrote a note on a piece of scratch paper, and Hannegan went back downstairs and, patting his jacket pocket, said to Walker, "I've got it." The president dated it July 19, the opening day of the Chicago convention.

But even after the meeting and the writing out of a presidential note Truman's nomination was by no means certain. Just before the meeting broke up, the president assigned two difficult tasks: the notifying of Wallace and Byrnes that they were out. He told Hannegan to see Vice President Wallace, and Walker to see Byrnes. These missions, undertaken by their respective missionaries, took place the next morning, Wednesday, July 12. Unfortunately, Wallace refused to believe he was out unless the president himself told him; he would withdraw only if the president advised him to. Like the party leaders he had noticed the president's physical decline and knew renomination meant the presidency. Upon return from China and Siberia he had seen the president, who employed his best on-the-one-hand, on-the-other-hand approach. Roosevelt said the party leaders thought the vice president would harm the ticket. Some people had spoken of Wallace as the person who wanted to give a quart of milk to every Hottentot (Wallace protested he had not said that, and the president expressed surprise). Also, it would be awkward for Wallace's family if the convention refused him. On the other hand, the president said, "I hope it will be the same old team." No one was more American than Wallace, no one more of the American soil. The president could not think of accepting criticism of the vice president. He promised a letter saying that if he, Roosevelt, were a delegate to the convention he would vote for Wallace. He added, disconcertingly, "Even though they do beat you out at Chicago, we will have a job for you in world economic affairs."[23]

Byrnes's visitor, Walker, encountered the same difficulty—Byrnes refused to withdraw unless the president asked him to.[24] Walker tried to negotiate with Byrnes's intimate friend, Leo T. Crowley, head of the Foreign Economic Administration. The next day, Thursday, July 13, Crowley telephoned Walker and then came to see him, insisting that he, Crowley, being on friendly terms with the president, could work matters out. On Friday, Walker and Hannegan had lunch with Crowley and Byrnes at Crowley's suite in the Mayflower Hotel, and Walker told both men, flatly and unequivocally, as he had before, that Byrnes was out—Roosevelt did not want him on the ticket. That day, July 14, after the lunch, Byrnes called the president; Roosevelt told the assistant president that he had not said to the leaders that he was against Byrnes, that the leaders had only expressed their own preference for Truman.

Roosevelt allowed both Wallace and Byrnes to go to the convention, each believing he had presidential support. Each also thought he could force his nomination on the convention, Wallace by exhibiting a presidential letter, Byrnes by citing a presidential conversation. Byrnes had heard Roosevelt tell him that he was the man best qualified to be vice president; he had been a court stenographer in his youth and had made shorthand notes of his telephone conversation with the president.

The party leaders had to forestall these enterprises, and because Wallace was going to receive a letter they dealt with his candidacy first. Saturday, July 15, the president's train stopped in the Chicago rail yards—he was on his way to the West Coast and thence by ship to Hawaii, where he would confer with his Pacific commanders—and Hannegan went aboard. Reporters outside the car timed Hannegan's visit at fifty-two minutes. They later believed he was obtaining a typewritten version of the note handwritten on July 11 after the leaders' conference. He did get a typed version, which he was to use during the convention, but for most of the time he was arguing for a toning down of the Wallace letter. As finally written, that letter said uncertainly that the president, if a delegate, would vote for Wallace, but that he did not want to dictate to the convention. It became known as the "kiss-of-death" letter.

Meanwhile, the Byrnes candidacy had taken an interesting turn. Truman had been in Missouri and on Friday morning was about to pull out of the driveway in his car, en route to Chicago, when a telephone call came from Byrnes. He said that the president had given him "the go sign," and he asked Truman to nominate him. Truman promised to do so. Byrnes already knew from Walker, who had told him point-blank on Wednesday, that he was not Roosevelt's choice, but he nonetheless committed Truman. When Truman learned about this maneuver several years later, he justly thought Byrnes was trying to close off the possibility that Truman might be the nominee ("Byrnes being the slick conniver that I've found him to be thought he was doing himself a favor and putting over a smart maneuver on me").[25]

In the days that followed, the situation became even more exquisitely complicated. What happened on Friday, Saturday, and Sunday, July 14–16, was that Byrnes pushed so hard and so convincingly that Hannegan came to believe the president had changed his mind. When the chairman of the national committee talked with the president in Chicago on Saturday, he heard him say pleasant things about Byrnes—so pleasant that he decided Roosevelt had fixed on Byrnes, exactly as Byrnes had been saying. The next day, Sunday, Hannegan became Byrnes's advocate among the party leaders.

Hannegan was misled by Roosevelt's canny assertion aboard the train that Byrnes was all right but that the chairman must "clear it with Sidney," meaning Sidney Hillman, the vice president of the Congress of Industrial Organizations and head of its political action committee. An emigrant from Lithuania who had gotten his start in the Chicago pants-cutting industry, as well as a longtime labor organizer who had seen the possibility of bringing the CIO's membership into a political alliance on labor-related issues, the small, quick-talking Hillman had marshaled several million dollars for his purposes, which in sum were to ensure the president's reelection. He was an important figure but a malleable one. Roosevelt knew Hillman was for Wallace first but would accept anyone the president wanted. He had talked with him in Washington the preceding Thursday and probably encouraged him not to accept Byrnes, who had lost support of labor leaders by announcing a wartime administration policy of "hold the line" on workers' wages. The president thought he had gotten Wallace out through the kiss-of-death letter, and he translated Hillman's dislike of Byrnes to mean Byrnes was out too— even though he told Hannegan two days later he was for Byrnes.

Until a breakfast meeting with Hillman on Tuesday morning, July 18, Truman could not have known he, the senator, might receive the nomination. He went to Chicago committed to Byrnes, who seemed the president's choice. On Monday opposition duly developed, led by Hillman; when the leaders telephoned the president that evening, en route to San Diego, reporting that labor would not take Byrnes and they did not dare put another conservative candidate into the running unless Byrnes was out—it would split the conservative vote and give Wallace the nomination—the president told them to "go all out for Truman."[26] Hannegan probably told Truman the news that evening. But the senator could not be sure what a presidential endorsement meant, for he knew the president's inconstancy. Byrnes was still in the race and would withdraw only on Wednesday morning. Wallace was continuing to look strong. The next morning the Missouri senator breakfasted with Hillman, whom he asked to support Byrnes; Hillman refused, saying Wallace was labor's first choice, Truman its second. At that point the senator knew not only that Roosevelt was saying he was for Truman, but also that the president perhaps had pushed Hillman. If Roosevelt publicly went to Truman, Wallace could lose.

Consternation seized the man from Missouri. He needed someone to talk to; it was clear that he had not thought everything out. During the spring he had known he was being mentioned for the vice presidency. One must assume he found the possibility attractive, in spite of—or maybe because of—his many claims to the contrary: claiming not to be a candidate has always been a good stance, and he had heard the talk about Roosevelt's health. But he had watched the nomination get into a tangle, with Wallace refusing to withdraw and Byrnes entering the race. In the days before the convention it appeared that Byrnes was the president's choice, and Byrnes had told him so. Now, suddenly, this turnaround.

He put through a call to Tom Evans in Kansas City.[27] "Are you my friend?" was the query.

"I hope so. Why?"

"If you are," said Truman, "I need you up here to help keep me from being vice president. How soon can you get up?"

"I can come right away."

"Well, come on. I need you."

Arriving in Chicago, Evans heard the senator say again he did not want the vice presidency.

"Why, that's ridiculous," said Tom.

"Well, I don't want to drag out a lot of skeletons out of the closet," was the reply.

Tom turned serious. "Now wait a minute," he said. "This is something I don't know anything about. I didn't know you had skeletons. What are they? Maybe I wouldn't want you to run either, but you've got to tell me; what are these skeletons?"

"The worst thing," he heard Truman say, "is that I've had the boss," meaning Bess, "on the payroll in my Senate office and I'm not going to have her name drug over the front pages of the papers and over the radio."

In 1941 Truman had put Bess on the payroll at an annual salary that soon became $4,500, a considerable salary for that time and the highest among his office staff. Though many senators had similar arrangements, it was a most unfortunate thing to have done (he did not take part in another traditional senatorial perk, however—the acceptance of honoraria for speeches). He had succumbed to the family pressures that had been draining his income over the years. He had a high salary—by 1944 he received $10,000 a year—but he was maintaining two residences and supporting relatives on both sides of the family. On his own side were his mother and Mary Jane, who in 1940 moved from the farm to a bungalow in Grandview; on his wife's were her mother and possibly one or more of Bess's brothers—the latter by this time all had jobs, but two of them were alcoholics and may not have kept their paychecks. Bess did not spend much time in the office. In 1943 he put Mary Jane on the payroll at $1,800 a year, and she lived in Grandview.[28]

It may be that another skeleton bothered him, although he did not mention it to Evans. Margaret Truman has ascribed her father's hesitation to accept the vice presidential nomination to a concern on the part of her mother. He must have told her about the encouragement he was getting. The two had few secrets; in her biography of her mother, Margaret has related her mother's fury when the atomic bombs were dropped on Japan—fury not that they were dropped, but that her husband had not told her of them.[29] In the biography Margaret asserts that Bess did not want her husband to be vice president, which meant president, because the publicity that surrounds all occupants of the White House would reveal—of all things!—the suicide of David W. Wallace. Such sensitivity seems overdrawn; just why a suicide in 1903 should have been so sensitive in 1944 defies imagination. But Margaret also has revealed that one of her aunts chose the summer of 1944 to tell her, for the first time, that her grandfather had committed suicide. When she inquired of her father, who was by then the candidate for the vice presidency, he was furious; he warned Margaret never to mention it to her mother, after which he went in search of the aunt.[30]

A third concern must have been what one can only describe as Bess's unreasoning and yet undeniable general dislike of the White House. Bess never forgave President Roosevelt for what he tried to do to her husband in the 1940 primary. She had no patience with the calculations that politics sometimes require, and she saw no reason for Roosevelt's behavior other than callousness, which may have been the case. Beyond that she may have believed that the glare of publicity that surrounded 1600 Pennsylvania Avenue was bad for the inhabitants. Both she and her husband disliked Mrs. Roosevelt's public activities, not understanding that an empty marriage lay behind them. They disliked the divorces of the Roosevelt children, perhaps laying those problems to upbringing in the White House. But while the precise reason for her feeling is hard to know, the feeling itself certainly was present. In the months before the Chicago convention she had managed to keep it under control, believing the vice presidential nomination was too remote to worry about. Now the reality was at hand.

With such concerns Truman needed guidance by the leaders, and on late Wednesday afternoon, July 19, the group gathered in the national chairman's suite in the Blackstone Hotel across the street from the convention hotel, the Stevens, and sent for him. With their man sitting on one twin bed and Hannegan on the other, the chairman put through a telephone call to Roosevelt in San Diego and told the president the senator was a contrary Missouri mule. Roosevelt replied loudly, so everyone in the room could hear: "Well, you tell him if he wants to break up the Democratic Party in the middle of a war that's his responsibility." He banged down the receiver.

Hannegan turned to Truman. "Now what do you say?"

The candidate momentarily did not say a thing. With everyone in the room looking at him, he got up and began walking around the room. "Well," he at last responded, "if that is the situation I'll have to say yes, but why the hell didn't he tell me in the first place."[31]

Early the next evening, Thursday, Hannegan released the note, now in the form of a typed-up letter, that the president had given him at the leaders' meeting ten days before. It said, somewhat ambiguously, that the president would be pleased to run either with Truman or with "Bill Douglas"—William O. Douglas, associate justice of the Supreme Court. Roosevelt was fond of Douglas, and may have included his name for that reason, but had told Douglas nothing of this backhanded recommendation. The inclusion of Douglas also had the virtue of not seeming to dictate to the convention.

That same evening Wallace's supporters, perhaps seeing the way things were going, tried to stampede the convention. Mayor Kelly's arrangements had included tickets that looked like dollar bills. Unfortunately, his assistants printed each day's tickets on the same-color paper, and that Thursday night the Wallace-ites entered the hall in such numbers that ticket takers were unable to read what day's tickets they were accepting. After the president was nominated for a fourth term, a rebellion broke out in the huge auditorium, Chicago Stadium, as Wallace's partisans, packed in the galleries, gained access to the floor. With Senator Samuel D. Jackson of Indiana, a Wallace supporter, as temporary chairman, the situation was dangerous—Wendell Willkie had stampeded the Republican convention in 1940. The organist was playing the Wallace song, "Iowa, Iowa, that's where the tall corn grows!" Signs reading "Frank and Hank" were ready.

The party leaders managed to bring things under control. The convention manager, Pauley, sent an emissary to tell the organist to change his tune or he, the emissary, would cut the organ's cable with a fire ax. As mayor of the host city Kelly used his authority to declare the overcrowded hall a fire hazard. Hannegan turned to the reluctant Jackson with a vengeance: "You get up there right now and I mean now—and recognize Dave Lawrence," he shouted, "or I'll do it for you!"[32] He propelled Jackson to the microphones to recognize Mayor Lawrence of Pittsburgh, a reliable party man, who moved a recess until next day (when Kelly could reissue floor tickets). The leaders then had the organist, now under control, play loudly so that many people in the hall did not know the convention had adjourned.[33]

Harry Truman's political future became certain late Friday afternoon, July 21, 1944, when the delegates voted a second ballot in nomination of a vice presidential candidate. The senator chose Bennett Clark to give his nominating speech, but found Clark that morning, about 6:30, drunk, in a room on the top floor of the Sherman Hotel. Truman managed to get into the room only by following a valet with a suit of clothes. Told of the speech, Clark mumbled something in a thick tongue. Sobered with a pot of coffee, he was put to work. In case he did not make it Truman asked a Missouri friend, Sam Wear, to prepare a speech.

When the roll call commenced for the first ballot the party leaders were in control. On this ballot their tactic was to encourage favorite sons, which subtracted from Wallace's total and avoided warning the Wallace forces of what was to come. As the word was passed, Truman's strength built up, and on the second ballot he became the convention's choice, 1,031 to 105. Even Henry Wallace voted for Truman.

The party's choice made a hasty acceptance speech, basing his remarks on a scrawled set of notes: "Honor. I've never had a job I didn't do with all I have. I shall continue in the new capacity as I have in the U.S. Senate, to help the commander in chief to win the war and save the peace. I have always been a supporter of Franklin D. Roosevelt in domestic and foreign policy and I shall continue to do just that with everything I have as V.P."[34]

3

Despite all the publicity from the investigating committee, his Senate service during his first term, and the fact that *Time* magazine described him as the most prominent member of Congress, Truman was not well known when he received the vice presidential nomination nor, for that matter, when he became president. On the train going out to California, President Roosevelt told his military chief of staff, Admiral William D. Leahy, that his running mate was going to be Truman. Said the admiral, "Who the hell is Truman?" When in April 1945 Truman's later biographer, Robert J. Donovan, then a soldier in Belgium, heard that Roosevelt had died, he was the only individual in his barracks who knew who Roosevelt's vice president was.[35]

In the months after the convention Truman did what was required of him in relative obscurity. On August 18 he lunched with Roosevelt, on the grass behind the White House, under an oak tree that the vice presidential nominee believed Andrew Jackson planted. Photographers swarmed around the two, who were in shirtsleeves. During the lunchtime conversation the president expressed strong support for Truman, who afterward wrote Bess: "He gave me a lot of hooey about what I could do to help the campaign and said he thought I ought to go home for an official notification and then go to Detroit for a labor speech and make no more engagements until we had had another conference." Roosevelt said some other things, one about his own wife: "[T]he president told me that Mrs. R. was a very timid woman and wouldn't go to political meetings or make any speeches when he first ran for governor of N.Y. Then he said, 'Now she talks all the time.'"[36]

He also told his running mate about the atomic bomb.[37]

Back on the subject of the campaign, Roosevelt said, "I'll not be able to do any campaigning, you'll have to do it all, and there's one request I want to make of you."

Truman asked what it was.

"I want you to promise me you'll not do any flying."

The senator said, "Oh! Mr. President, why do you make that request? I like to fly and I could cover so much more ground."

"Harry," was the answer, "I'm not a well man, we cannot be sure of my future."[38]

This was as close as Roosevelt ever came to admitting he was ill.

The president's debility shocked Truman. Afterward he told Harry Vaughan that Roosevelt was very feeble, that when pouring cream in his tea his hands shook so much he put more cream in the saucer than in the cup. The president, he said, spoke with difficulty. "It doesn't seem to be any mental lapse of any kind, but physically he's just going to pieces. I'm very much concerned about him."[39] To reporters Truman said: "He's still the leader he's always been, and don't let anybody kid you about it."

For the senator the campaign began with the notification ceremony, August 31, at Lamar. He invited Senator Tom Connally, who talked so long the nominee had only a few minutes. The ceremony was, however, gratifying for Martha Ellen Truman, who sat on the platform. Already she had displayed pride in her Harry: "Am I proud of him? Say, I knew that boy would amount to something from the time he was nine years old. He could plow the straightest row of corn in the county. He could sow wheat so there wasn't a bare spot in the whole field."[40]

Truman conducted his campaign largely from a railroad car attached to passenger trains. He made fifty-four speeches or talks and shook hands with perhaps a hundred thousand voters. He liked to think half his speeches were quoted in newspapers across the country, but little appeared in the papers, for World War II was demanding attention after the Normandy invasion in June.[41] In the Pacific everything was going well, with General Douglas MacArthur's troops landing in the Philippines and great battles at sea taking the fight out of the Japanese navy. The reporter Robert Nixon remembered Truman saying he drew crowds of two or three dozen people, all over the country. The remark amused the nominee, who chuckled over it.[42] It may have been true. Roosevelt, incidentally, paid no attention to Truman's speeches, nor to those of the Republican presidential contender, Dewey, and he did little campaigning until just before the election.[43]

On the train trips Truman enjoyed the company of Tom and Mamie Lou Evans. One of Tom's tasks was to stand on the rear platform and wave as the train went through small localities at sixty or seventy miles an hour, cinders and dirt flying, onlookers beholding a tall, gray-headed man with glasses who waved at them. The Evanses made Truman feel at home. One night in a hotel suite, after Truman had gone to bed, Tom and Mamie Lou sat up with a few drinking friends and became pretty noisy. They disturbed the nominee, who after a tiny knock emerged from his room, clad in pajamas and an old, faded bathrobe, and said, "Oh, please let me come in and join the party." After a drink and a few minutes of conversation, Mrs. Evans took him by the arm, led him back, and said, "Well, we'll all go to bed; you must get your rest; we've been disturbing you." It was then that she discovered the candidate had washed his socks and hung them up, and that he had been performing this task through the campaign. She "just gave him the dickens," Tom remembered, and said, "After this, I'll wash your socks."[44]

The campaign's sole uneasy moment occurred when Truman and his small party joined Henry Wallace for an evening of speeches at Madison Square Garden in New York. The senator waited and waited until it was virtually time for the meeting, with Wallace nowhere in sight. He began to believe that in this region of Wallace partisans, with a massive audience that was certain to cheer for Wallace and might boo Truman, the then vice president was trying to arrive late so as to receive a personal ovation. It turned out that Wallace had simply decided to walk to the Garden and underestimated the time necessary to get there.[45]

After the election, Truman, on January 20, 1945, was sworn in during a ceremony on the rear portico of the White House. It was a suitable wartime reduction of the usual ceremonial, convenient to the president, who would not have to make a strenuous public appearance. After both men took the oath they were to receive guests in the public rooms. The president, however, retired. His face during the ceremonies struck onlookers as gaunt. Truman's later attorney general, Tom Clark, remembered it for the rest of his life.[46]

Shortly after Truman became vice president, a melancholy event occurred in Kansas City: Tom Pendergast died. He had spent a year and a day in Leavenworth before returning to the city he had ruled to spend his remaining years as an outcast: a convicted felon, he had lost his civil rights; despite a plea to regain them, he did not. One of the parts of his sentence was that although he could live in Kansas City he could not travel outside it. He had not told his wife about his betting, and she left him when she learned of it.

His daughter ignored him. When his death was announced there was speculation as to whether Truman would attend the funeral. Without hesitation he asked for an army bomber and flew out; equally without hesitation he gave the reason—"He was always my friend and I have always been his."

After the funeral the vice president returned to Washington and his duties, which his predecessor during the Coolidge administration, Charles G. Dawes, had defined as two. One was to preside over the Senate, Dawes said, and the other to inquire each morning as to the president's health.

For the most part the presiding was enjoyable, if only because his presence in or near the chamber meant that he had not left the colleagues and life he had known. He received a fine office in the capitol, which he described as "gold-plated." He was also able to retain his former office, with all its familiar furnishings. He had access to the dining room of the Upper House, and the committee rooms were available if he desired to walk into them and see what was going on. He spent his days in the same huge building with the chambers at each end and the wondrous dome in the middle; every day the tourists passed through, and some would notice the serious man with the gray hair and glasses and wonder who he was (unless a capitol policeman was there to identify him).

Beyond question he was not as busy. He had given up the investigating committee shortly after the nomination, and campaigning had taken time. Now time seemed on his hands. "What are you going to do with your spare time?" a reporter inquired. "Study history," was the response. For the rest of it, he told the reporter, he would pay attention to the Senate. He was a bit jagged in his explanation. "Well," he was quoted as saying, "while Garner was vice president there was hardly a day when at least half the members of the Senate did not see him in his office or talk to him somewhere around the capitol. In the past four years I doubt if there are half a dozen senators all told who have been in the vice president's office. You can draw your own conclusions."[47]

Only in one instance did his duties in the Senate become serious, and that was when Roosevelt asked him to ensure that the Senate would agree to the naming of Wallace as secretary of commerce. After the inaugural the president unceremoniously dismissed his commerce secretary, Jesse H. Jones, a crusty Texas banker whom Roosevelt had complained about for years. The president privately described him as "Jesus H. Jones." He was too independent, and his most recent independence had been what seemed a connivance with Texas politicians before and during the Chicago convention: an anti-Roosevelt faction of the Democratic party, of which Jones's nephew was a member, had refused to give half of Texas's votes to Roosevelt. The Senate, however, was in no mood to replace Jones with Wallace, and to get the nomination through it was necessary to detach the Reconstruction Finance Corporation from the commerce department, for the senators claimed not to trust Wallace with money. Even after that separation, Truman had to twist many arms. To embarrass Wallace the senators went to the extreme of arranging a tie vote, forcing Truman to break it.

There remained the problem of the president's health. In the preceding months Truman had watched the president deteriorate. At the outset, after the nomination, he had gone back to Independence and there talked with two close friends. Visiting with Postmaster Edgar Hinde, he took off his big Masonic ring and tapped it on the desk. "Hinie," he said, "what if that old man would die, wouldn't I be in one hell of a shape?" The response was, "Brother, you sure would." He went to city hall to see the mayor. "Sermon," he said, "what in the world would I do if I should become President of the United States?" Sermon responded, "You're asking me?" "Yes," was the reply, "I am." Sermon gave some advice. Returning to Washington the vice president and Eddie McKim attended a White House reception for the cast of the movie *Woodrow Wilson,* a celebration of the World War I president whose ideas concerning a League of Nations, the film said, had been ahead of his time. While the two were in the White House, Eddie watched Roosevelt. He and Eddie walked out the east entrance. After they were outside Eddie said, "Hey bud, turn around and take a look. You're going to be living in that house before long." Truman responded, "Eddie, I'm afraid I am. And it scares the hell out of me."[48]

Shortly after the election he telephoned his friend Harry Easley, the Webb City, Missouri, banker, and asked to meet him in Kansas City. The two spent the night in the penthouse suite at the Muehlebach:

> He told me just lying there in bed after things quieted down that he had been lonesome ever since the day they put the Secret Service on him, and that he had not yet seen the President at all. He told me that the last time he saw him that he had the pallor of death on his face and he knew that if he lived that he would be President before the term was out. . . . I think it frightened him, even the thought of it.[49]

Years later Easley remembered his friend said something more. It showed what sorts of rumors were making the rounds about Roosevelt's health. According to Easley, Truman told him the president had suffered a stroke while returning from the Teheran Conference with Churchill and Stalin in November–December 1943 and that the heavy cruiser *Augusta* had circled around in the mid-Atlantic until his daughter Anna, accompanying him, brought him out of it.

The weeks turned into months. Spring was in the air, and nothing had happened, though the talk of ill health continued. On April 11, after a luncheon in the office of the secretary of the Senate, Leslie Biffle, Senator Wheeler went around to the vice president and advised him not to attend a dinner to which the group present had been invited, a dinner given for labor delegates from Britain, Russia, and several other countries. The delegates were on their way to San Francisco for the conference on formation of the United Nations.

"They're friends of yours and mine," Truman said.

"I am afraid there's a bunch of Communists among them and something might occur that would embarrass you later," Wheeler advised. "You're going to be President."

Truman said he had already accepted the invitation to the dinner, and the senator responded, "Tell them you had forgotten you had another engagement." Just then Hannegan, in whose honor the luncheon had been held, came up, and Wheeler told him what he had said. Hannegan agreed.[50]

The next afternoon seemed at first like every other afternoon in the Senate. Discussion was about water power and irrigation. Senator William Langer of North Dakota was sounding off, with the vice president in the chair. Leverett Saltonstall of Massachusetts was almost the only other senator on the floor, and after a while a page approached with a pink slip in Truman's handwriting: "Governor, will you take this seat for a while? I want to see a soldier boy from home in my office." Saltonstall nodded and went down to sit on the dais. Truman said he would not be gone more than half an hour. Someone had put an apple on his desk, and Saltonstall asked what he would do if he, the senator, ate the apple. The vice president said he would have to fine the senator.[51] About an hour and a half later he returned, recessed the Senate, and slipped over to the other side of the capitol for a drink with Speaker of the House Sam Rayburn and a few friends.

Then lightning struck. When he came into Sam's hideaway office the speaker told him that Stephen Early, who had given Truman some bad times a few years before, had called and asked him to call back immediately. The men in the room watched as he got through and heard Early ask him to come at once to the White House. Memories differ as to what Truman said. He may have said nothing, holding up his hand, or may have told them only that he had to leave. Perhaps it was Rayburn who remembered the words best.[52] "Holy General Jackson!" he blurted. "Steve Early wants me at the White House immediately!" Recovering, he said in a half-whisper, "Boys, this is in the room. Keep this quiet. Something must have happened."

Chapter Nine

A New President

The story of how Harry Truman learned he was president of the United States has been told many times yet continues to hold its fascination. It is a story both of inevitability and of surprise. In the limousine on the way over to the White House, it occurred to him that the funeral of an old friend of Roosevelt, Bishop Julius W. Atwood, had taken place that day, and "maybe the President was in town . . . and wanted to go over some matters with me before returning to Warm Springs." Nonetheless, Steve Early had said he should come straight to the front entrance of the White House and directly up to the family quarters on the second floor, not to the oval office in the west wing. Truman had taken off from Rayburn's hideaway at a run—not stopping to look for his secret service escort, although he did go back to his office to pick up his hat. There he told Vaughan he was going to the White House and would call back in fifteen minutes. Vaughan joked that the vice president could not become president unless he, his assistant, was present. Without comment, the vice president went out to the north side where he found his driver and car and threw himself into the backseat; the limousine moved out into the traffic. When he arrived he was escorted to the elevator and thence to a sitting room, where the first lady was waiting together with Anna, Anna's husband, and Early. Mrs. Roosevelt rose to meet Harry Truman. She put her arm around his shoulder and said gently, "The President is dead."

He asked Mrs. Roosevelt if there was anything he could do for her.

She asked the new president if there was anything they could do for him.[1]

When he heard the news it was 5:30, and already he had been president for two hours. He went to the oval office and called home to Bess. Margaret answered and began to tease her father about not being there for dinner when she had a date that evening. In a tight voice he said, "Let me speak to your mother." Margaret passed over the phone in a huff. Moments later, Bess appeared in the doorway to her daughter's room, tears streaming down her face. Margaret got out of the party dress she planned to wear on the date and dressed for her father's swearing-in.[2] In the course of the next hour or so Bess and Margaret were driven to the White House and visited briefly with Mrs. Roosevelt; Attorney General Francis Biddle called other members of the cabinet; Chief Justice Harlan F. Stone was found and came to the president's office; members of the White House staff searched frantically for a Bible.

By 7:00 the inaugural group had assembled in the cabinet room. The chief justice stood at the end of the long table, and Truman stood under the portrait of Woodrow Wilson. In his hand was a small, red-edged Bible someone found in a bookcase. The chief justice began, "I, Harry Shipp Truman . . . " Truman raised his right hand and responded, "I, Harry S. Truman . . . " When the oath was done, the chief justice added, "So help you God," a phrase not in the official oath. "So help me God," said the president, as he raised the Bible to his lips. The time on the clock beneath the portrait of one of Harry Truman's great figures in American history was 7:09.

1

How would Truman compare with Roosevelt? Americans thinking about presidential responsibilities as Truman took on his new role wondered what would happen to the republic. If they could remember Truman's name, they wondered what they knew about him.

As months and then years passed, they began to think they knew who Truman was, and a reputation gathered about him that for the most part was not very complimentary. Indeed, Truman's popularity with his fellow Americans stood high only until the end of World War II in Europe and Asia; after this it began to go down, and it stayed down until the end of his terms, with two notable ups. One was in 1948, when he fought for his political life and won (although less than half the eligible voters bothered to vote either for him or his opponent, Governor Dewey); the other was at the outset of the Korean War, when national unity gathered behind him and his measures. Mostly people looked at him in boredom, sometimes askance, taking him at his word when he said he was an ordinary man who happened to be president.

People missed the physical appearance of Roosevelt, who looked every inch the president, even in his wheelchair. FDR's face was that of a man accustomed to prominence—according to the historian Eric F. Goldman, he was a "dazzling Hyde Park patrician." For Truman, Goldman could find no better description than "grayish little county judge." Bob Nixon noticed how differently the two presidents dressed. Roosevelt wore handmade shirts that bore his monogram on their cuffs; he liked jackets, and into the breast pocket would carefully crush a handkerchief so it looked just right. Truman dressed "like he had just come off of Main Street in Independence, Missouri." His clothing was "store boughten." He was a neat dresser, but everything was too precise. He had a pressed crease in the sleeves of his coat, and a handkerchief in his outside pocket would have four, even five, peaks, as if he had just received the coat from a dry cleaner. He was addicted to two-colored shoes: some were mesh, some were in two tints of blue, some were in high yellow.[3]

As public speakers the two presidents were completely different. Truman spoke with a twang compared with the elegance of his predecessor, who sounded better over the air than any of his successors, save the actor-president of the 1980s and the Democratic president of the early 1990s. People also missed the patrician headshaking of FDR, for if Truman made any motions while speaking he moved his hands up and down, palms turned inward, a gesture known as "chopping wood."[4] The words and phrases of the speeches were quite different too. Roosevelt's speeches contained humor and asides, planned or otherwise. For the most part they offered presidential thoughts; the orator never forgot that he was the nation's instructor in good government. Although dignified by nature, the new president let his speechwriters repeat the homey phrases and thoughts that did not sound well in speeches. Compared to the speaking of Roosevelt, Truman betrayed a lack of cultivation, of finish.

For a generation and more after 1945, Americans underestimated Truman, and only in the 1970s, after several more presidents, did they recognize his virtues. It had taken that long for a rural Baptist upbringing and a lifelong commitment to the principles of Masonry to be recognized as traits of importance to the nation's highest office. Truman's constant virtues, and the errors and even sins of at least one of his successors, have now made the Missouri president into a folk hero: a plain-speaking, straight-talking, ordinary fellow (people thought) who did what he saw as his duty without turning his obligation into opportunity for personal gain. Today, it seems that his plain ways were a throwback to the Puritan fathers' meaning of the world *plain:* the unadorned life that is stripped of excesses in appearance so that it exists as a testament to the principles beneath.

Ironically, it may have been Truman's humble ways that suited him so well to his task. He had no illusions about the true significance of ceremonial requirements such as twenty-one-gun salutes, which he knew to be for the institution of the presidency and not for himself. He realized that for his own good he must keep himself separate from the presidency, and he was in fact successful in preventing his sense of self from becoming the role he assumed. He knew that when people came to see him, they came to see the president, not Harry Truman. He strove mightily to keep the two people apart. John Hersey, who studied his subject carefully in preparation for his *New Yorker* profile, spent a few days following the president through his daily duties. He remembered how

President Truman seemed to think of himself sometimes in the first person and sometimes in the third—the latter when he had in mind a personage he still seemed to regard, after nearly four years in office, as an astonishing tenant in his own body: the President of the United States. Toward himself, first-personally, he was at times mischievous and disrespectful, but he revered this other man, his tenant, as a noble, history-defined figure.[5]

His capacity to keep himself somewhat separate from his role as president was perhaps the central difference between Truman and Roosevelt in office, but their presidencies differed in a variety of other respects. To begin with, Truman was physically vigorous when he came to be president. Roosevelt was only two years older, but illness had worn him down. When Truman hurried up the walk toward his office on the morning after his swearing-in, which incidentally happened to be Friday the thirteenth, he was the picture of health as a crowd of photographers ran along in front of him. A scene impossible during the Roosevelt administration, it was symbolic of far more than the contrast with the late president's well-known infirmity. Truman undertook a schedule that tripled Roosevelt's, moving visitors in and out of his office with dispatch, signing letters in shifts, meeting groups for short talks, posing in the rose garden for photographers, making excursions to deliver speeches, and often spending evenings at formal events. As he had done since the farm years, he got up at 5:30 every morning; he was at his office within minutes, long before secretaries arrived and the working day formally began.

Unlike Roosevelt, Truman was attentive to his health. During his Senate years he put himself in the hospital several times for complete goings-over because of a persistent stomach problem; the difficulty was traced to fatigue, stress, and some foods. From that time on, he said he was fine as long as he got enough sleep, exercise, and buttermilk. He walked, swam, and sunbathed every day that weather and his schedule permitted, even during the most hectic times. Evidently his brief sessions in the late morning sun served to renew him for many more hours of work each day.

For mental relaxation he played poker with friends whenever he could. Rarely more than a twenty-five-cent bettor, he loved what he called his little "games of probability." Bess gave—or, if in Independence, sent—him pocket money for these. "Thanks for the ten," he would write. "If you need it, I'll send it back." Without money he didn't play, and his letters make frequent references to his winnings—when there were any, they were seldom more than ten dollars. Once Bess passed along forty dollars paid by Mrs. Wallace toward grocery expenses. He gravely responded that he wished her mother would just sit back and let him assume her financial worries; then he added, "Don't tell her, but I'll invest her payment . . . in a game of chance."[6]

In addition to humility, and physical fitness, and his almost childlike penchant for poker, his personality set him apart from Roosevelt in another way: he had a tenacious ability to focus on a problem and make a decision. Roosevelt was quite the opposite. For one thing, FDR knew and must have cherished Ralph W. Emerson's Phi Beta Kappa address of 1839, in which the philosopher noticed that every popgun was not the crack of doom. He knew that many problems went away. Moreover, he was in office so long that he became almost proprietary about the presidency, believing almost that it was his by longevity, and he therefore began to take decisions lightly. Perhaps he held power for so long that he lacked a sense of urgency about the machinery of government; when people around him insisted that a particular matter was of utmost importance, he would listen with half an ear. He had heard it all before. William Hopkins, in charge of White House files during most of the Truman administration, once said:

> Mr. Roosevelt would go away on a trip and he'd come back, and he'd be busy with something else, and then he'd go away again and come back, and I have had papers waiting for President Roosevelt's signature piled on the table behind his desk for six months. They'd stand there for six months waiting for his signature. Even, for example, pardons or paroles, and an individual who was waiting for his pardon spent six months longer in the penitentiary than he would have if the President had signed.[7]

On larger decisions, as on smaller, Roosevelt became almost impossible. In 1941, when mobilization creaked and threatened to stall, he watched with benign indifference, and it was the Missouri senator who created the committee. Similarly, the president ignored the insufficiencies of wartime offices and officers. Of course, in his last year he had problems focusing on all sorts of things.

Truman knew it was his duty as president to make judgments and carry them out. Dean Acheson said, "I acquired the greatest respect and admiration for the president's capacity to understand complex problems and to decide. This is one of the rarest qualities possessed by man. Too frequently the mind vacillates between unpleasant choices and escapes through procrastination."[8] Having served under Roosevelt, Acheson remembered Truman (not FDR, to whom he devoted some contemptuous lines in his memoirs) as "the captain with the mighty heart," and dedicated the book to the Missouri president; he published it in 1969, when Truman was ill and the onetime secretary of state could have said anything he pleased. At the front of Truman's White House desk was the legendary sign, "The Buck Stops Here." His Missouri political handyman, Fred Canfil, had seen such a sign while visiting the federal reformatory at El Reno, Oklahoma, and asked the warden for a duplicate; Truman received it in October 1945. The saying had originated in the old frontier days, when players at poker tables used a marker or counter, often a knife with a buck-horn handle, to indicate the person whose turn it was to deal. If the player did not want to deal, he could pass the responsibility by passing the "buck," as the counter came to be called. Truman's refusal to do so had been a hallmark of his political career from the county level up.

The Harvard political scientist Richard E. Neustadt, a White House staff member who in academe wrote about presidential "decision making," has written that Truman invariably made decisions on almost all subjects that came to his attention. An admiring British biographer, Roy Jenkins, wrote: "If Goering, when he heard the word culture, reached for his gun, Truman, when he heard the word problem, reached for a decision." Truman, however, was no fool, and he did not decide everything at once. He would make a "jump" decision, a snap judgment, but thereafter would hold his final decision as long as possible, mulling it over: "I was always thinking about what was pending and hoping that the final decision would be correct. I thought about them on my walks. I thought about them in the morning and the afternoon and thought about them after I went to bed and then did a lot of reading to see if I could find some background of history which would affect what had to be done."[9]

The new president also knew when the time was ripe for inaction. The Berlin blockade of 1948–1949 was a good example. Some advisers, including top-ranking generals, told him Berlin was indefensible and he should withdraw U.S. forces; other advisers, also including top-ranking generals, said he had only one option—to push through an armed convoy from Helmstedt, the nearest American-held point, into the city. Truman took neither course. Eventually what he considered only a delaying tactic, the airlift, solved the problem.

Part of the new president's refusal to pass the buck came from his essential directness, another trait that set him apart. Roosevelt could be left-handed, Machiavellian. Behind the bonhomie and exuberance that he showed to visitors was a willingness to play both sides. As early in his career as 1913, when he was assistant secretary of the navy, he had intrigued—with anyone who would listen—against his chief, Secretary Josephus Daniels; years later in the White House he was still intriguing. General Marshall found Roosevelt very difficult, and he refused to visit FDR's home at Hyde Park, despite many invitations, for fear the president would use the occasion to maneuver him; the only time he went to Hyde Park was for Roosevelt's funeral. Truman he found a breath of fresh air, hearteningly easy to talk to. Truman, it is safe to say, was never in all his life sly or disloyal. Time was too valuable, life too short, and to have acted unfaithfully would have gone against his Baptist and Masonic principles.

Another critical difference lay in home lives. Although Roosevelt had a family, he was not a family man. His marriage continued only formally after his wife's discovery in 1918 of her husband's liaison with Lucy Mercer. The latter, married and widowed, was present at Warm Springs when he died. Truman's marriage was the core of his life. His first letter to Bess from the White House began, "This is a lonesome place."[10] In some ways the separations, when she was in Independence, caused him the greatest trial of his personal life in the White House years, for the joy he took in his marriage and his fatherhood was interrupted and, as his professional life soared, his domestic life became divided from it to a degree that grieved him terribly. It was only after the White House years, when he was back in Independence—at home with the roses, the cooking of the Trumans' housekeeper, Vietta Garr (Bess did breakfasts, Vietta the rest), and other hometown things he missed so badly—that he felt a whole man once again. The marriage, again, was the point from which he calculated everything. On the Trumans' wedding anniversary in 1957, he sent Bess a year-by-year outline of events in his life keyed to their anniversaries on June 28. Entries ranged along a line that included "broke and in a bad way" (1922), "depression, still going" (1930), "Senate special committee, Margie wants to sing" (1941), and "vice president and president, war's end" (1945). The one constant running through the list was the June date.[11]

The happiness of Truman's family life was clouded with money problems even into the White House years—another way in which his life differed from Roosevelt's. It seems unthinkable to Americans now, after a succession of wealthy first families, that Bess Truman mailed ten-dollar bills to her husband. As late as 1946 there was still not enough excess in the family accounts to afford a new car for Bess. She wrote asking her husband what to do about her old one and he replied: "It seems to me that if you can get a good price for it you may as well sell it and buy a bond, and then when we leave the great white jail [the White House] a new car can be bought." He consoled himself and her by relating that the new postwar cars "won't have the bugs out of them for two or three years anyway."[12]

Compared to Roosevelt and his other predecessors and successors, Harry S. Truman was an anomaly in the most powerful office in the world: a modest, honest, thrifty man who, when teased by his press secretary that he would rather be right than president, replied, "I'd rather be anything than president." It was perhaps inevitable that the same combination of modesty and public decisiveness that made him capable of being president would raise doubts in the public mind. But it was also characteristic of Truman to stand firm. "If you will study the history of our country you'll find that our greatest presidents and congressional leaders have been the ones who have been vilified worst. . . . [H]istory justifies the honorable politician when he works for the welfare of the country," he wrote late in his life.[13]

2

The president's personality gradually came clear to the American people, although it required nearly a generation. In 1945, however, whatever Americans thought or would think of him, Truman's principal problem was something else: to get control of the government of the United States. And here, particularly, he needed to get control of the federal bureaucracy. Sworn in on a Thursday evening, he went back to the Connecticut Avenue apartment for the night; he reappeared in the oval office the next morning and sat down behind the huge desk now cleared of Roosevelt's belongings. An aide looked in and saw him swiveling back and forth, gazing uncertainly through his thick glasses. The aide doubtless thought him confused, uneasy about his inheritance. One suspects he was thinking of how to handle things administratively, especially the bureaucracy. He knew the presidency was the most powerful office in the world if he so managed it: he would have to make the government do his bidding, for otherwise he would be president only in name.

For the moment and, as matters turned out, through his two terms, Congress was not really the problem. If he could not always manage it, at least he knew the reason or reasons. He had spent ten years in the Upper House, and he knew what congressmen were like. It was show horses and workhorses; he knew every personality in the Senate and many in the House. He did not overestimate their resolve or underestimate their frailty. Early in his presidency he told White House staff members, "[Y]ou can't trust a senator when he can get a headline." For example, Congressman J. Buell Snyder of Pennsylvania saw the president and afterward told reporters Truman believed the European war would end in June; the president instructed his assistants to keep Snyder out of the White House except when unavoidable.[14] It was possible, however, to appeal to their better instincts, and during his administration he often did, demonstrating how helpful it was for a president to have had experience in Congress.

Nor was the Supreme Court a problem. According to later critics he made several poor appointments, but that was a matter of judgment—over the years most appointees have not been notable lawyers, only average lawyers possessed of political judgment. His relations with the court were generally good and sometimes excellent. The court turned against him in 1952 with its decision on presidential seizure of the United States Steel Corporation at the height of the Korean War, but no president can gain its support on everything. When in the Senate he often had talked with Justice Louis D. Brandeis, by then retired. Max Lowenthal introduced them, and they had gotten on well, for they both had studied the role of railroads in the national economy. Truman revered the Supreme Court and respected its membership as forming one of the three branches of the government.

His problem was the bureaucracy. Perhaps he remembered the old line about officials in Washington: "A bureaucrat is a man who never writes a letter he signs or signs a letter he writes." The size of the government had increased vastly during Roosevelt's era, and Truman did not object to its enlargement but believed Roosevelt had not managed it well. Roosevelt gave the impression of being a master organizer; someone said he organized a circle, with himself at the hub. In fact, he allowed everything to sprawl and then tried to control and manipulate the jumble—or jungle—in complicated ways. One of his assistants, Corcoran, said the White House was a powerhouse from which there were no transmission lines. He paid little attention to the cabinet, appointing incompetents and sycophants, so Truman thought, and preferred to do the government's work by dealing with undersecretaries and assistant secretaries or through notes to lower officials. Judge Maurice J. Latta, head of White House files at the beginning of the Truman administration, who had been in the White House since the 1890s, said Roosevelt was secretary of every cabinet department, and his cabinet officers really were undersecretaries.[15] He was fond of imposing new layers of bureaucracy or transferring bureaus. He pushed cabinet members or their assistants into public controversies with each other just to see the feathers fly, although the public thought he thereby beheld the competing positions and could better choose his own. As for the White House staff and executive office staff, assistants with vague responsibilities operated at will. Acheson wrote that what looked like chaos was just that.[16]

With the bureaucracy working against itself, Truman had to turn things around. In this regard, he drew on his considerable administrative experience. As a close student of the subject has written, he acted out of a multiplicity of reasons, not just a desire to get hold of the bureaucrats. Dazed by the suddenness of his shift from the Senate into the vice presidency and then the presidency, he naturally chose reorganization as one of his initial responses to his new office. It was a program on which Congress could unite. He could placate Congress, moderate its hostility toward the New Deal and its late leader, and perhaps even unite the Democratic party by reducing conflicts over federal policy. Too, during his experiences in county government and especially in the Senate with the Truman Committee, he had devoted a great deal of time to producing efficiency in government. He believed efficiency was the prime goal, not saving money—which might come from efficiency. He knew, of course, that any attempt to get a reorganization bill through Congress would provoke all sorts of special interests, notably in the time-honored relations between interest groups, career government officials, and congressional committees. He well remembered the rows over passage of the Reorganization Act of 1939, and he was not surprised by the maneuvering that accompanied his own Reorganization Act of 1945, which exempted only a few independent agencies and required both Houses of Congress to veto any presidential proposals of reorganization it did not like within sixty days, as had the act of 1939. Nonetheless, the new president faced up to reorganization with enthusiasm and conviction, if only because of his inheritance from his immediate predecessor.[17]

He began with the cabinet, which even Roosevelt in his last year had admitted was an inadequate group. The late president had been too ill to do much about it, however, even if so inclined. In 1944 FDR had told Ickes that

Secretary of Commerce Jones would have to go, and his departure already had taken place. But he also said that Secretary of Labor Frances Perkins did not add any strength to the administration, that Attorney General Biddle was afraid to do things, and that Secretary of Agriculture Claude Wickard did not amount to much. Truman thoroughly agreed. A few years later, when Jonathan Daniels was finishing what Truman hoped would be a truthful book about his administration, published in 1950 under the attractive title of *The Man of Independence*, he wrote Daniels a letter about the Roosevelt cabinet, which he reconsidered and did not send. In the letter, he described an impossible group of incompetents, prima donnas, and disloyal men more interested in themselves than in the public welfare. Secretary of State Edward R. Stettinius, Jr., was "a fine man, good looking, amiable, cooperative, but never had an idea new or old." Secretary Perkins, he opined, was an estimable woman but "no politician. F.D.R. had removed every bureau and power she had." Secretary of the Treasury Morgenthau, who considered himself expert on foreign relations as well as finance and was author of the Morgenthau Plan to "pastoralize" Germany (that is, denude it of industry), told Truman in the early summer of 1945 that he wanted to attend the Potsdam Conference and would resign if he could not; the president ushered him out of office. Truman said Morgenthau was a "blockhead, nut—I wonder why F.D.R. kept him around." He asked Attorney General Biddle to leave, and he replaced him with Tom Clark. Biddle had favored Justice Douglas for vice president. Secretary Wickard, "a nice man, who never learned how his department was set up," gave way to Clinton P. Anderson. Within three months he retired six of the ten Roosevelt department heads.[18]

In March 1946, and again in September of that year, came the forced resignations of Secretary of the Interior Ickes and Secretary of Commerce Wallace. According to Truman, "'Honest' Harold Ickes . . . was never for anyone but Harold, would have cut F.D.R.'s throat—or mine for his 'high minded' ideas of a headline—and did." As for Wallace, he had "no reason to love me or to be loyal to me. Of course he wasn't loyal."[19] Both resignations were to the credit of the president, although he handled them untidily. But, then, perhaps no one could have handled such messes. They splashed across newspaper front pages as if the president had asked these two illustrious men to do impossible tasks and in all honor they declined and left public office. Actually, both courted dismissal.

The Roosevelt cabinet brought to Truman's mind "the famous story of the Irish Band." The trouble with "the so-called F.D.R. people," he said, was that they all wanted to lead the band. They started at the top and "never polled a precinct or became elected in their lives—a great bunch—at least they're great on ballyhoo."[20]

Other cabinet changes came over the years, including three in the department of state—Stettinius gave way to Byrnes, General Marshall, and Acheson.

Truman replaced Secretary of Defense James V. Forrestal with Louis Johnson, followed by Marshall and Robert A. Lovett. Twenty-four men served as Truman cabinet heads. Of the first half-dozen, four had been congressmen. After Morgenthau's successor, Fred M. Vinson, became chief justice of the Supreme Court in 1946, a St. Louis banker and longtime National Guard friend of the president, John W. Snyder, took his place. Julius A. Krug replaced Ickes, but his faint enthusiasm for the president during the 1948 election caused Truman to give the job to Undersecretary Oscar Chapman. About that time he promoted two career men in other departments: Jesse Donaldson to postmaster general, succeeding Hannegan, who had followed Walker; and Charles F. Brannan to replace Secretary of Agriculture Anderson, who resigned to run for the Senate.

Truman made many good appointments. For state and defense, excepting Johnson, the choices were first-rate. When he made a bad one he moved to correct it, unlike Roosevelt, who kept Secretary of State Cordell Hull around for twelve years. He forced Johnson's resignation with notable lack of tact. "Lou," he said one day to the defense secretary, "I have to ask you to quit."[21]

He saw the cabinet on Friday mornings. It was an intimate group, with never more than one or two visitors. There were no minutes, save for notes the president's appointments secretary took for Truman's personal use. During meetings the president discussed his own memoranda and called on members for their business, one by one. Members left decisions to the president; they did not vote.

For a year or so, Truman sought to make cabinet meetings less official, more offhand and companionable, by instituting luncheons every Tuesday. They seem to have been by invitation and to have included perhaps half the cabinet, usually Attorney General Clark, Secretary of the Navy Forrestal, Postmaster General Hannegan, Secretary of the Treasury Vinson, and Secretary of Agriculture Anderson. When he was in Washington, Secretary of State Byrnes attended. Jocularly, members of the group referred to themselves as the "intellectuals," principally (Anderson afterward wrote) because they were not. Members spoke with each other frankly and amiably, and because there were no minutes they all felt free to say what they thought. But, as time passed, Byrnes tended to inject a note of discord. He felt cheated because of his loss of the vice presidential nomination in 1944 and did not show the president quite the respect that the others did. He also tended to dominate the proceedings. Anderson wrote that he had "a curious way of addressing us, shoving food into his mouth when he talked as if he was taking the time to issue directives but didn't really intend to communicate with us." He had an opinion on everything, foreign or domestic. It was difficult to do business in the Tuesday luncheon sessions when Byrnes was setting everyone straight, and the meetings gradually came to an end.[22]

Of all the individuals who served in the cabinet, the president considered Acheson and Brannan his two best department heads.

The chief executive's second order of business in gaining control of the bureaucracy was to set up an efficient White House staff, which he organized along traditional lines—secretaries for press, correspondence, and appointments, together with a few special assistants. As press secretary he inherited Daniels (who had replaced Early, who at the time of Roosevelt's death was serving temporarily in Pa Watson's place as appointments secretary). By profession and temperament Daniels was a writer, unsuited to the hustle of a White House office, and Truman replaced him with Charlie Ross, his classmate at Independence High. For years Ross had reported for the *St. Louis Post-Dispatch*. Upon Ross's appointment the president and the new press secretary telephoned their old high school teacher Tillie Brown in Independence. In 1901, Miss Tillie had given Charlie a kiss during graduation because he was valedictorian, while the other boys stood around. "Well, don't I get one too?" Harry had asked. Miss Brown replied, "Not until you have done something worthwhile." When the president and Charlie called to tell of the appointment, Harry spoke up. "Hello, Miss Brown, this is the president of the United States," he said. "Do I get that kiss?" "Come and get it," said Miss Tillie.[23]

Ross was a good deal more than a press secretary; if anyone among the staffers acted as principal adviser to the chief executive, he did. Having known the president for fifty years, he could go into his office any time. Ross was not foolish enough to impose himself; he did not often speak out. He was close to the oval office whenever the president needed him.

When Ross died of a heart attack in 1950 his position passed to Joseph H. Short, Jr., who had been the White House reporter for the *Baltimore Sun*. Why the president appointed him is impossible to say; he was a nervous, choleric person. He died suddenly in 1952, and Truman appointed one of the assistant press secretaries, Roger Tubby, who carried on until the administration came to an end.

As secretary for correspondence the president kept Roosevelt's appointee, William D. "Bill" Hassett, a white-haired, courtly New Englander known as "the Bishop." His job was to compose letters for correspondents whose queries were not worth the president's attention; he also handled proclamations for Love Your Dog Week or other occasions for which people solicited the president. Sometimes he got the president out of engagements, as when Helen Rogers Reid invited him to the New York Herald Tribune Forum; Truman asked his correspondence secretary to compose a "Hassett Valentine" of the usual sort, which would have just the right mixture of appreciation and regret.[24] Hassett had a way with words. Sometimes he played with them in other ways, as when he wrote a housing official to "sift out the bottlenecks in this area at every level." But the daily task of letter writing must have been tedious, and Hassett took solace in alcohol and often was away from his desk. After help of one sort or another, including talkings-to by the president's personal physician, Dr. Wallace H. Graham, Hassett would drift back to work, and then there would be another collapse, perhaps when the president was off on a trip. Eventually, the Bishop repaired to a rural parish in his home state of Vermont.

Matt Connelly of the Truman Committee became the third of the principal secretaries, the president's appointments secretary. Tall and handsome, he kept traffic moving in and out of the oval office—not an easy task when every visitor was eager to claim the president's attention. All sorts of people wanted to see the president, and Connelly screened them. Early in the first term the question arose whether William Randolph Hearst could come. "I'm not sending for any of those sons-of-bitches," said the president, "but I'll see them."[25] Later, Connelly's good-hearted nature and the president's desire to see as many people as possible began to pile up visitors, and Truman sent him a memo: "It seems to me that we have seen enough visiting firemen and potential promoters and chiselers. Too many people are talking to me about visits here and there and about jobs and policy." Connelly reduced the list.[26]

Like Hassett, Connelly drank, although unlike Hassett he did not let drinking interfere with his duties. But he carelessly let a St. Louis business-man buy him clothes and make a small stock purchase on his behalf. Years later the businessman got into trouble and drew Connelly into it; a grand jury indicted Connelly for income tax fraud, and he served time in prison. Truman, retired to Independence, arranged a defense fund, flew to Boston to speak at a dinner, and sought a pardon from Attorney General Robert F. Kennedy. When Kennedy dragged his feet, Truman told him—Kennedy had visited the former president in Independence during the 1960 campaign—he had better not come around again and grin at him. He obtained the pardon from Kennedy's successor. It was a sad end for Connelly.

The president appointed John R. Steelman, known as Dr. Steelman because of his Ph.D. in economics and sociology, as *the* assistant to the president, the article showing precedence over the other assistants. Steelman was proud of it and used it on White House stationery and Christmas cards. He handled labor problems, as Byrnes had done for Roosevelt. The president needed the help, for the first part of his presidency saw much labor trouble, and he also had appointed as secretary of labor his friend Schwellenbach, former senator from Washington, who became ill and could not do much.[27] Steelman also handled federal agencies, serving as their channel to the president.

John Steelman's exact role in the administration has never been established—if one may so describe him, he was the administration's mystery man. He appears to have done well in holding off or ending strikes. He carefully managed his relations with Schwellenbach, incurring no ill will. He also dealt with housing, education, surplus property disposal, strategic stockpiling, and manpower. He was supposed to stay out of foreign and defense policy. His forte was to be operations rather than policy. He had an amazing number of responsibilities, but we do not know much about how he handled them. His recently released oral history, made many years ago by archivists at the Truman Library, is carefully general about what could well have been an extraordinary activity.

Among the half-dozen other staff assistants was Donald S. Dawson, coordinator for personnel and patronage, from whose files Truman made appointments save for customhouses and federal courts. During the 1948 election Dawson became the president's advance man as the campaign train moved across the country. He served inconspicuously. Only once did trouble arise, this over his supposed interference with the Reconstruction Finance Corporation. A congressional committee summoned him, but he answered inquiries convincingly and the committee dismissed him back to his White House duties.

Another staffer was a holdover from the Roosevelt administration. David K. Niles was a sad-faced, furtive man, in charge of minorities, including blacks; when the issue of the independence of Palestine loomed, he dealt with Jews. No one understood what Niles did around the White House, and some staffers thought he did nothing. Each weekend he took the train to Boston, where he assisted with the Ford Hall Forum. After the independence of Israel he pushed the case of the new state. At one juncture he composed a fulsome letter from Truman to President Chaim Weizmann that the U.S. president signed without reading, after which Niles put a stamp on it and dropped it in a mailbox—meaning there was no copy of it in the White House record-keeping and mail system. This indiscretion may have hastened his exit from the staff in 1951. He died the next year.

Charles S. Murphy dealt for a while with congressional liaison, and in 1948 he performed yeoman service as coordinator for the Democratic national committee's research bureau, a group of hardworking individuals in a building near Dupont Circle who researched campaign issues and inquiries. Short, often smiling, and unostentatious, Murphy wrote most of the president's major addresses, sending them out to the train by air where they arrived "just in time," to use a description for the industrial procedure of later years. He proved one of the most important staffers in the White House; among other virtues he possessed judgment on political issues, how to anticipate and when best to avoid them.

In 1943 President Roosevelt had created the anomalous office of special counsel for Judge Samuel I. Rosenman, and when the small, retiring Rosenman, who stayed on into the Truman administration, departed in 1946, Roosevelt's successor appointed his then naval aide, the St. Louis lawyer Clark M. Clifford. The latter, tall and handsome like Connelly, even elegant, was a good man to handle legal awkwardnesses in congressional bills and executive orders and give political advice. Clifford returned to private practice in 1950, and during the next generation he became the most influential lawyer in Washington. Secretary of defense under President Lyndon B. Johnson in 1968–1969, he persuaded Johnson to back away from the Vietnam War. His place as special counsel went to Murphy.

Like Connelly, Clifford got into personal trouble years later: in 1991, at the age of eighty-four, he refused to acknowledge his involvement with the Middle Eastern owners of a Washington bank-holding company of which he was chairman. Again, it was a sad end to a remarkable career. During the 1930s he had been a rising lawyer in St. Louis; he came into the White House as assistant naval aide because one of his former clients, James K. Vardaman, Jr., became Truman's naval aide. Clifford made the most of opportunities; while Vardaman was at the Potsdam Conference in July–August 1945, he had little to do, and Rosenman, who had too much, gave him legal work; this eventually took him out of his naval assignments. One has the impression Rosenman regretted the help he gave to Clifford. In the White House both he and Clifford took part in the writing of speeches, and Rosenman was furious when someone—he thought Clifford or Connelly—kept him off the campaign train during the 1948 election.

Clifford cut a swathe at the White House, if maybe not quite as much as he related in his memoirs, *Counsel to the President.* Whether Truman realized that Clifford saw himself as a large figure is hard to say. The president seems to have talked to him about the danger of what he, the president, described as "Potomac fever": a swelling of the head that occurred only in the vicinity of Washington. Clifford's departure from the White House probably was for a different reason, for he may have expected to be attorney general in 1949 when Tom Clark went to the Supreme Court. Unfortunately, Clark, who was a Protestant, took the place of Justice Frank Murphy, who was a Catholic, and the president appointed a Catholic as attorney general.

George M. Elsey, a young Harvard-trained historian who had spent the war as a navy lieutenant assigned to the secret White House communications room, the so-called map room, was Clifford's assistant and afterward one of the president's special assistants. He could draft memoranda, background papers, just about anything. He left the White House in 1951 to assist W. Averell Harriman, administrator of foreign military assistance.

Apart from the staff, but closely associated, were the aides for the military services—Colonel (later major general) Vaughan, Truman's office assistant in 1941–1942, who became military aide; captains Vardaman, Clifford, James H. Foskett (later rear admiral), and Robert L. Dennison (later rear admiral), naval aides; and Colonel (later major general) Robert B. Landry, air aide. Fleet Admiral Leahy was the president's personal chief of staff, an office created by President Roosevelt that allowed Leahy to be an adviser on military subjects, with the latter sometimes crossing into the political.

In initial weeks of the administration, coordination of the secretaries and staff assistants was casual, each bringing problems to the president, and it became apparent that a more expeditious procedure would be to hold morning conferences. Thereafter the three staff secretaries, *the* assistant to the president, the special counsel, the other assistants, and the military aides sat around the president's desk for a half-hour or so beginning at 9:00, and the president parceled out his business and went around the circle for other business. Among those present was Charlie Ross's assistant, Eben A. Ayers, who, unknown to the group, kept a diary that recorded morning conference sessions in detail.

Under Truman the White House staff eventually numbered a dozen secretaries and assistants, and with clerks and typists and other help the group numbered 285 people. By 1972 the staff had grown to 52 secretaries and assistants and a total of 550. In later years it diminished somewhat.

3

In addition to the cabinet and the White House staff Truman had another way to handle the bureaucracy, and this was through the executive office staff. This third group of supervisory officials under immediate control of the president originated from an interesting theoretical framework set out in a report of 1937 by the President's Committee on Administrative Management, an eminent group of political scientists and administrative experts chaired by Louis Brownlow and including Charles E. Merriam and Luther H. Gulick. Its keynote, announced in the report, was "The President needs help." Its solution was what one student described as a plan of salvation by staff: the committee concluded that not only should the White House have an augmentation of six special assistants "possessed of high competence, great vigor, and a passion for anonymity" but also that the president needed an executive office staff. The Reorganization Act of 1939 had allowed Roosevelt to create the Executive Office of the President. Staff totals over the years are difficult to obtain, as people came in temporarily from cabinet departments and independent agencies, but by 1952 the executive office staff numbered 1,166.

The core of the executive office staff became the Budget Bureau, forty people transferred in 1939 from the treasury department. By the time Truman became president the bureau numbered five hundred, and it not merely compiled and supervised the budgets of executive departments and agencies, and brought recommendations for new budgets, but its director also kept the president informed of inefficiencies and recommended changes. The budget always fascinated Truman; people who visited him in the White House found him surprisingly well informed on it. Even in retirement he loved to receive copies and would read them avidly. During his presidency he had several budget directors (Harold D. Smith, James E. Webb, Frank Pace, Jr., Frederick

Lawton), saw them frequently, and seems to have gotten along well with all, even Smith, whom he inherited from Roosevelt and who stayed until June 1946. He later described Smith as an "A-1 conniver."[28] The reason was a bit unfair: Smith resigned because he was having trouble living on his salary, which probably did not please Truman. As matters turned out, he suffered from heart trouble and died not long after going to the International Bank for Reconstruction and Development. After his death the president discovered Smith had kept a diarylike series of memoranda of his weekly conversations in the oval office; his widow gave Truman copies that showed Smith and his assistant moving carefully with the president, as they should have, even maneuvering him a little; such behavior Truman did not like at all.

An addition to the executive office staff in the Truman years was the Council of Economic Advisers, a three-man panel of economists foisted on the executive office by Congress in 1946 in hope the president would use it. Congressmen and economists believed conversion of the economy from war to peace needed guidance, and the possibility of managing the economy, popularized in the 1930s by John Maynard Keynes and his disciples, was attractive. Truman's first CEA chairman, the conservative Edwin A. Nourse, did not work out: "He wanted to see the bankers control the finances of the country, and I didn't. I didn't have anything against the bankers, but the control of the finances, just the same as the control of the rest of the government, ought to be in the hands of the Congress and the President of the United States, nowhere else."[29] Nourse rightly sensed the president preferred his two liberal council members, especially Leon Keyserling, who became Nourse's successor in 1949. Keyserling apparently heard the president describe Nourse as "the old gentleman," probably not a diplomatic description.[30] The younger economist never lacked words and opinions, and he soon was believing his influence was much larger than Nourse's.

During Truman's time no rivalries arose between the Budget Bureau and the CEA. Perhaps this was because staff members moved from one group to the other.

The executive office staff changed because of the creation not merely of the CEA but also of the National Security Council, a result of the National Security Act of 1947 and its 1949 amendments. The NSC became a part of the executive office staff in 1949. Its original membership was the president as chairman, together with the secretaries of state and defense, the three military service secretaries, and other department or agency heads. The 1949 amendments dropped the service secretaries and added the vice president. The primary purpose of the acts of 1947 and 1949 was to unify the military, and the NSC did not seem important. At first it was a purely advisory body for the president, almost moribund. It had a small staff. Truman did not attend, perhaps out of fear the council might interpose itself between him and his cabinet. He excused himself by saying members could speak more freely in his absence. He made the decision to intervene in Korea without consulting the NSC. But that war convinced him he could put the NSC to greater use, and he began to meet with it weekly, turning it into a virtual supercabinet for military and foreign affairs.[31]

Another contribution to organizing the modern American presidency came in 1947 after Congress established the Commission on Organization of the Executive Branch of Government. The Republican Eightieth Congress looked to victory in the 1948 election, and one of the commission's objects was "defining and limiting executive functions." To Congress's surprise Truman greeted this move with enthusiasm, and in a master stroke he appointed an impeccable Republican as chairman of the commission, Roosevelt's predecessor, Hoover.

The way in which Truman invited Hoover to take part in government constituted a heartwarming example of how the Missouri president in all large matters was no partisan. Roosevelt had ignored Hoover, claiming that Hoover had ignored him. This was a half-truth, for Roosevelt had refused to cooperate with his predecessor during the economic crisis that occurred in the months (in those days) between Hoover's defeat in the November 1932 election and his departure from office on March 4, 1933; Hoover tried to get Roosevelt to help with the crisis, and the president-elect chose to believe the president was trying to commit him to a conservative approach. Roosevelt may not have minded an intensification of the banking crisis, so that he, the new president, could resolve it, which he did. In any event Hoover thereafter came to Washington on visits during which he did not call the White House and attempt to pay his respects, and Roosevelt claimed to be hurt by this. On the morning of May 28, 1945, learning that Hoover again was in Washington, Truman, on impulse, nonetheless telephoned him. "Hello, Mr. President," he said.

"Who is this?" asked Hoover.

"Harry Truman," was the response. The president told his predecessor-once-removed that he had already sent a White House limousine to take him to his "old home."

Hoover was beside himself with emotion, one suspects in tears. Upon arrival he bounded up the steps of the front entrance, past Margaret, who was waiting to go to classes at George Washington University. The former president, oblivious to people around him, turned down the hall, along the colonnade, straight for the oval office. One of the older ushers recognized him; otherwise, someone might have stopped him. Margaret asked who the tall man was, and he replied, "Miss Margaret, that's President Hoover."[32]

Truman initially asked Hoover to survey world food supplies. To his astonishment his visitor, without a word, got up and walked out. Secretary of Agriculture Anderson and Secretary of State Byrnes were present, and Truman, offended, turned to them and called Hoover "that son-of-a-bitch." Anderson told the president, "Don't you realize, the man couldn't answer. There were tears in his eyes and he couldn't speak." Twenty minutes later Hoover telephoned, accepting, explaining that he had lost his composure, "Because, Mr. President, since 1932 no one has asked me to do anything for my country. You are the first one."[33]

After Hoover completed this task Truman passed him the work of reorganizing the executive branch, and the Missouri president was as pleased with the result as he had been over the survey of world food supplies. The GOP patriarch unleashed his prodigious energy, served as his own staff director, and put his imprint on all the commission's activities. The first of nineteen reports of the Hoover Commission appeared in 1949. Perhaps to the surprise of the Missouri president, his predecessor handled the commission's work in a nonpartisan way. Truman was accustomed to say privately that Hoover was politically to the right of Louis XIV and had learned nothing since the time of William McKinley, but this did not turn out to be the case. Showing unwonted political judgment, Hoover on November 11, 1948, shortly after Truman's unexpected victory in the presidential election, told a reporter that his task as commission head was not to change the organization of government, presumably making it smaller and more Republican: "Our job is to make every Government activity that now exists work efficiently. . . . It is not our function to say whether it should exist or not."[34] Because of Hoover's sponsorship, and nonpartisanship, the press and Congress quickly took up the commission's detailed proposals, and the president signed them into law.

Truman sought to use not only the abilities of Hoover but also those of the two living Republican candidates for the presidency who had failed of election—Alf Landon of Kansas, and Dewey. He wrote each of them, asking them to call. He brought up no special programs with the others, and nothing came of this bipartisan effort.

Such were the ways in which the presidency developed during Truman's time. He could rightly say, as he did in 1952, that he'd "made more changes and reorganizations in the operation of the Federal Government than all the rest of the Presidents put together."[35] Beginning in 1933 the executive branch of the federal government had grown hugely, from 600,000 civilian employees to 2,600,000 twenty years later, with 4,000 in the judicial branch, 22,500 in the legislative, and 2,570,000 in the executive (500,000 in the post office, 1,300,000 civilian workers in defense). To keep such a huge organization moving in the same direction was a herculean task. By and large he managed it.

To direct such a bureaucracy from the White House the president had begun his tenure in high expectation of reorganizing everything, top to bottom; he sought to accomplish this in part through new reorganization acts, the first of which he obtained from Congress at the end of 1945, good until March 1948—Congress limited it so he would not use it as a platform on which to make fancy, unrealistic proposals designed only to help his election efforts. Long before that time, however, the president had come to see—the leading student of this issue believes his conversion came shortly after he signed the Reorganization Act of 1945, that is, early in 1946—how difficult it was to change the offices and bureaus and lines of authority of the government. Truman's first reorganization act produced so much debate going through Congress that it caused almost more trouble than it was worth. The Hoover Commission, created in 1947, turned out to be a much better solution; over the next years it obtained public and congressional support for reforms the president could not have obtained on his own. Another reorganization bill, passed in 1949, proved much less useful than its predecessor, because of a proviso that a single House of Congress, rather than both Houses, could veto any reorganization measure proposed by the executive.

The reorganization acts and the Hoover Commission gave more power to department heads, creating assistant secretaries and diminishing the authority of quasi-independent bureaus. The president transferred duties and bureaus back to the department of labor, strengthening that weak department; he strengthened the Federal Security Agency under its able and liberal administrator, Oscar Ewing, in preparation for making it a department of health, education, and welfare; and he brought consolidations anticipating the later departments of housing and urban development and of transportation. He created the General Services Administration, improved government in the District of Columbia, reformed the scandal-ridden Reconstruction Finance Corporation and the Bureau of Internal Revenue (renamed the Internal Revenue Service).[36]

In managing the bureaucracy Truman also relied on traditional ways, updated if necessary. His principal organ of direction was the cabinet. The White House and executive office staffs constituted a central secretariat, partly to handle independent agencies, mainly to hold lines of control between the president and departments. The NSC helped out with defense and state. Truman did use staff members as advisers, notably in his morning conferences, leading to suspicion that he was imposing a new layer of management. But he engaged in far less of this activity than did his predecessor. Moreover, he avoided using presidential assistants as special pleaders, as representatives of citizen groups or of projects, although he looked to the future when he allowed Niles to continue dealing with minorities. He would have shuddered to behold what came of that Rooseveltian precedent: turning the White House into a place for pleaders. In a later administration the White House staff contained administrative assistants for the aged, youth, women, blacks, Jews, labor, Hispanic-Americans, the business community, governors and mayors, artists, and citizens of the District of Columbia, and to deal with questions of drug abuse, energy, environment, physical fitness, volunteerism, telecommunications, and—the last seems especially dubious—national goals.

Under his Republican successor, Eisenhower, the White House and executive office staffs remained sensible in size and duties, though Truman did not manage business with the clockwork precision of Eisenhower. When the latter visited White House offices in November 1952, and Truman discussed the use of the White House staff and executive office staff, Ike horrified him by asking who his chief of staff was. The president managed to say without sarcasm that he had none. The notion that someone should stand between him and his staffs bothered him; he considered it a piece of military nonsense, what you could expect from a West Pointer. Even so, Eisenhower's way of handling the presidency was not much different from Truman's. The thirty-fourth president wanted staff duties sharply defined, and staff assistants got together before entering the president's office and decided on common points rather than offering a choice; otherwise, they could see the president whenever they wished, if he was not busy. Governor Sherman Adams of New Hampshire served as his chief of staff until a cloud of suspicion passed over him because he accepted hotel accommodations and a vicuña coat from a Massachusetts mill owner in tax trouble. After Adams's fall, Eisenhower divided his duties.

Presidents after Truman and Eisenhower gave insufficient attention to the cabinet, created elephantine White House and executive office staffs, and, when they lost control of these mechanisms, turned the presidency into an organ of public relations.

Chapter Ten

Ending the War

After the Truman administration had been assembled, its first task was to preside over the end of the war. For Europe the work was fairly easy, although after Germany's surrender another Big Three meeting became necessary, in the tradition of those attended by FDR at Teheran and Yalta. But this did not address the problem of ending the Japanese war. And for both Europe and East Asia the president's task was made vastly more difficult by Roosevelt's appalling failure to tell him anything about foreign affairs. In domestic matters he was well informed; of all twentieth-century presidents he may have been the best prepared. In foreign affairs he knew little more than what he read in the newspapers. "I know nothing of foreign affairs," he told his first postmaster general, Frank Walker, "and I must acquaint myself with them at once."[1]

The new president was a lonely figure as he sought to prepare himself for his high office. Every night he took a briefcase full of documents over to Blair House, to which he and the family had moved temporarily from the Connecticut Avenue apartment. He had hoped to stay in the apartment while Mrs. Roosevelt packed the accumulation of more than twelve years and arranged for movers to transport the trunks and boxes and furniture to Hyde Park, but other people in the apartment house would have been necessarily inconvenienced by the secret service men checking identifications and the general confusion of turning an apartment house into a presidential residence, and so the move to Blair House.

After Mrs. Roosevelt left the White House, Truman and his wife had minor redecorating done; Mrs. Truman and Margaret were surprised to see how shabby the private quarters were, how the Roosevelts had let things run down. Eventually the Trumans moved in, and then the president could carry his briefcase from the west wing to the second-floor private quarters, where he continued to pore over memoranda from officials everywhere in the government, trying to sense the concerns of his predecessor and what to do

about them. He later said he read a stack of papers six feet high, in installments of thirty thousand words, a small book, every night, and very nearly
damaged his eyes permanently—those eyes that were none too strong to
begin with.[2]

1

The end of the European war was a formality: documents were signed in
Rheims, followed by a ceremonial signing by the German military with the
Russians and a simultaneous release of the news in Moscow, London, and
Washington. The Germans fought to the bitter end, in accord with the Rooseveltian pronouncement at Casablanca in 1943 that there could be nought but
unconditional surrender. The pronouncement itself had the partial purpose of
affirming the Western Allies' alliance with the Soviets; it guaranteed no separate peace. Beyond that it held the liability of fighting to a finish. Upon
coming into the presidency Truman might have tried to modify that arrangement, for Germany's plight was hopeless: the quicker the surrender the better. But such an effort would have required herculean diplomatic discussions
with the Soviets, after the Allies, Western and Eastern, had fought the war
largely on separate fronts with little coordination. In Truman's personal papers is no evidence he even thought of a negotiated peace in Europe. Roosevelt, if in good health, might have done so. And so the European war wound
down to its weary end on May 8, 1945.

The first presidential act of importance in foreign relations thereafter
amounted to a fiasco. The president quite simply made an egregious error in
signing his name to an order restricting lend-lease that Undersecretary of
State Joseph C. Grew and Foreign Economic Administrator Leo T. Crowley
handed him on May 11, three days after announcement of the German surrender. The order stopped all lend-lease items not needed for military operations
in the Far East or completion of industrial plants already delivered in part.
The Soviets created an uproar, and it was necessary to turn ships around at
sea once again, reload, and make the best of what looked like disloyalty to
Allies, notably the USSR. Truman later said he had not read the order when
he signed it. He probably had not read every word, but one suspects he knew
more about it than he liked to remember. Grew and Crowley both had warned
him the Soviets would protest. Probably with a sense that he had to make a
decision, and knowing Congress had tired of supporting argumentative Allies, he signed. In retrospect, Grew and Crowley should not merely have
pointed out the consequences but advised him not to sign. They seem to have
gotten themselves only into the middle. Grew, a longtime foreign service
officer, aloof and supercilious, not quick-witted enough for the nimble Truman, thereafter represented to the president all that was bad in the foreign
service; some months later Truman allowed his retirement. Crowley, a politi-

cal operator, whom Roosevelt paradoxically had put in charge of the Federal Deposit Insurance Corporation and more recently of the Foreign Economic Administration, soon turned against the new president politically, and he too departed.[3]

Compared to the end of the European war, creation of the United Nations was a prosaic business. For all his later loyalty to the UN, Truman did not take the birth of the new world organization with great seriousness, if only because he had many other things to do. He was, however, concerned when he learned that the Russian foreign minister, Vyacheslav M. Molotov, was not going to attend the organizing conference in San Francisco. Molotov's absence would have been nothing less than a slap in the face to the president whose country was sponsoring the new organization. Happily the situation turned around. For the foreign minister's presence he could thank Ambassador W. Averell Harriman in Moscow, who when informing Stalin of Roosevelt's death added his personal hope that Molotov, rather than an ambassador or foreign office underling, would head the Russian delegation. Stalin at once consented, either because of momentary emotion—which is difficult to believe—or because he saw the need to display friendship upon a solemn occasion.

Stalin's sending Molotov to the San Francisco Conference led to the now well-known encounter in Washington between the foreign minister and the president. After Molotov made a courtesy call there was a second meeting that turned into a set-to. It did no harm and probably some good. After arranging for an American plane to fly the foreign minister across Siberia to Alaska and thence to the United States, Harriman—at first against Secretary of State Stettinius's objection—took the transatlantic passage, beating his Russian friend to Washington, where he told the president about Russian behavior. At first Harriman was put off by Truman's admissions of ignorance concerning foreign affairs. But Truman was willing to accept coaching, which Harriman undertook; the result was perhaps not exactly what the president in his memoirs said happened but fairly close: "I have never been talked to like that in my life," Molotov reportedly said. "Carry out your agreements and you won't get talked to like that," Truman snapped. Charles E. Bohlen, state department liaison officer with the White House and translator during this exchange, did not remember quite this conversation, only that Truman spoke plainly and Molotov "turned a little ashy" and tried to change the subject. According to Bohlen, Truman cut him off with "That will be all, Mr. Molotov. I would appreciate it if you would transmit my views to Marshal Stalin." Bohlen enjoyed translating these sentences, and he remembered them for the rest of his life. Truman's acting press secretary, Early, afterward asked about pictures, and Molotov was agreeable. Stettinius went into the president's office, but came out and said the president was busy.[4]

It is amusing to note that after this contretemps the president received former ambassador Joseph E. Davies in the oval office. A corporation lawyer, married to the heiress of the Post Toasties fortune, Davies had been a notoriously poor ambassador to the Soviet Union in the later 1930s; he believed everything he heard at the purge trials, and afterward he wrote that a dog would sidle up to Stalin, a child sit on his lap. The president enthusiastically informed Davies that he had told Molotov "where he got off." He said he "gave him the one-two, right to the jaw." Davies was alarmed, and tactfully said so. Truman asked Davies, "Did I do wrong?"[5]

In the developing presidential diplomacy with the USSR there followed two missions that confused observers but probably showed only that Truman was trying to establish the points of view of Stalin and, to a lesser extent, Churchill. The president sent Davies to London, and he sent Harry Hopkins, who long since had left the department of commerce to become Roosevelt's diplomatic troubleshooter, to Moscow.

Of the two missions, that of Hopkins was clearly more important. It was Bohlen's idea, and he suggested it to Harriman. With the war's end, the time seemed right for a new president to try to sort out issues with the Soviets. Harriman consulted Hopkins, who had been ill and spending time at the Mayo Clinic, and Hopkins assented. Harriman propositioned Truman, who was lukewarm, saying Harriman himself could handle any negotiation. The ambassador sensed that Truman felt ill at ease with Hopkins because of the latter's closeness to Roosevelt. In this he was wrong, as the president had gotten along well with Hopkins years earlier when dealing with unemployment problems in Missouri. Truman sent for Hopkins and inquired after his health, and the erstwhile presidential adviser reared up like a fire horse. At that point Truman may have felt that a mission could do no harm, and in any event it would give the appearance of movement in American-Russian relations, allowing the president time to measure the situation.

In Moscow, Hopkins and Harriman held six long sessions with Stalin, in the presence of Molotov and interpreters, and studied the probable issues at the forthcoming Potsdam Conference. A skillful point maker, Hopkins related that American opinion would turn against the Soviet Union if that nation continued to dominate the provisional Polish government, as it was doing. There was never any ill humor, nor any threats. Truman had told Hopkins he could use diplomatic language or a baseball bat if he thought the latter the better approach. The envoy used diplomacy, however, and Stalin followed the procedure he had used at Teheran and Yalta of agreeing outwardly but in fact not yielding. He too was a skilled debater, and Bohlen, who accompanied Hopkins, remembered how he ignored facts that undercut his arguments and twisted others. The meetings did manage to keep negotiations open. Hopkins obtained one concession, on the last day, June 6, over the right of the Soviet Union to veto any agenda item for the proposed UN Security Council. At the San Francisco Conference, Molotov had been sticking for this point. Stalin spoke to the foreign minister in Russian, and Bohlen overheard him saying that it was an insignificant matter and overruling Molotov.

The sending of Davies to Churchill was of lesser importance, and nothing came of it save soon-forgotten irritation. The president may have felt that with such a messenger he could display his independence of British advice. Bohlen, no friend of Davies, suspected that former press secretary Early suggested the Davies mission, because Early was about to take a job with the Pullman Company, of which Davies was a director. Harriman considered the Davies mission "one of the few gauche things Truman did during those first weeks in office." Davies lived up to his reputation. Among other things he told Churchill that all the warnings against communism and Soviet domination of Europe put him in the same camp as Hitler and Goebbels: "I told him frankly that I had been shocked beyond words to find so violent and bitter an attitude, and to find what appeared to me so violent a change in his attitude toward the Soviets. Its significance was appalling. It staggered me." The subject of this tongue-lashing may have realized he was listening to Davies's own opinion, and he seems to have quieted down. After a long evening session at the prime minister's country place, Chequers, at 4:30 A.M. he escorted Davies to his bedroom door and there said he was pleased to converse with someone who was "so familiar with European problems during these years." Davies replied with what he described to his diary as a paean on Churchill's greatness.[6]

Missions accomplished, Truman acted on one matter that was bound to soothe Russian sensibilities: he ordered withdrawal of American troops from the Soviet zone of Germany. The U.S. Army had penetrated the zone on a four-hundred-mile front, to a depth at one point of 120 miles. Beginning on June 21 they moved back. Prior to this action there was an exchange between the president and prime minister that was restrained. "I am unable to delay the withdrawal of American troops from the Soviet zone," Truman advised, "in order to use pressure in the settlement of other problems." "Obviously," Churchill responded, "we are obliged to conform to your decision. I sincerely hope that your action will in the long run make for a lasting peace in Europe."[7]

Much was made of this Truman decision in later years, the contention being that an inexperienced American president gave up a counter with the Soviets, by which he could have extracted something of value, perhaps better Russian behavior in Poland or elsewhere in Eastern Europe. Yet what else could he have done? Bohlen, close to the decision, wrote afterward that a direct benefit was willingness of the Soviets to go along with the Yalta accord on Austria, allowing American and British troops to occupy zones in Germany's former province. Austria otherwise would have become a Soviet satellite. If American troops had not evacuated the Soviet zone, the Russians also could have charged the United States with refusing to live up to an Allied agreement. As one looks back on the American decision, which Truman defended in his memoirs and Churchill opposed "with heavy heart" in his own, it appears thoughtful, the British position theoretical. Any military measures against the Russians, and this might have turned into one, would have had to rest on action by American troops. It was doubtful if the U.S. Army, still at war in the Far East, could have handled a confrontation. Too, the discussions between Stalin and Hopkins, while not encouraging, had shown a continuing Soviet willingness to negotiate, and there was hope for more important concessions than the Russian back-down over the agenda for the Security Council.[8]

Throughout the first weeks of his presidency Truman took mostly positions that revealed his experience in public life, his understanding if not of international affairs then of American domestic politics. There were clear parallels, one of them being that he need not do everything at once, that few developments were irreparable. He was not going to act like Roosevelt—that is, refuse to act, thinking he would get to problems when they arose and if already present they would go away. But he was not going to act for the sake of action, either. Shortly before leaving for Potsdam he received four senators and used the occasion to write privately about their behavior: "They had been overseas, had seen Germany, Italy—and knew *all* the answers. Smart men I'd say." The senators told him ("their song was") France would go communist and so would Germany, Italy, and Scandinavia, and there was grave doubt Britain could survive. "The Pope, they said, was blue as indigo about the situation." Three of them said the European world was at an end, and the president concluded privately that this was hardly true: "Europe has passed out so often in the last 2,000 years—and has come back, better or worse than ever, whichever pleases the fancy, that I'm not impressed with members of the famous 'Cave of the Winds' on Capitol Hill."[9] He was not going to be shoved into solutions that might be unwise.

2

The conference of July 17–August 2, 1945, was from the outset hardly a decisive meeting. The president must have realized he could not hope for much beyond exploration of issues. He was enough of a political observer to know that even an uninterrupted period of negotiation could hardly suffice to resolve great differences.

Still, the conference was necessary for several reasons. Most important, leaders of the three principal allied nations needed to get everything out in the open, to be sure there were no confusions or misestimations. In the past years they had held two conferences; meanwhile, they had sent telegrams, cables, and couriers carrying pouches filled with dispatches. But the end of the European war naturally brought many matters into a different focus, pointing up concerns of the war years. All of this needed utmost clarity, which the Potsdam Conference could provide.

There were other, lesser reasons for conferring. Truman needed a chance to meet his opposite numbers, and so did his assistants, diplomatic and military. His understanding of Europe rested upon the brief acquaintance of 1918–1919, a year in France with an hour or two in northern Italy and part of a day in Monaco. Moreover, he could rest while crossing the Atlantic and sadly needed to do so after his initial weeks in office. He planned to use part of the voyage to study documents, but there would be time for movies and studies of probabilities as well.

The conference also had a dramatic purpose: it gave evidence to the American public that the Truman administration was working for peace. Harriman, a diplomatic sophisticate, already had observed this necessity when, during a respite of the San Francisco Conference, he held a meeting with reporters to inform them of some of his troubles with the Soviet Union. To his amazement Walter Lippmann, who had been writing on American politics for a generation, got up and walked out. In a broadcast the radio commentator Raymond Gram Swing, one of his auditors, related that the only way to obtain trust was to give it. With such feeling in high journalistic places, Truman could never have managed the first months of his presidency without meeting the Russians.

The nation's concern made the trip a subject of large public speculation. Its details fascinated newspaper readers. The president departed Washington by train for Newport News, boarded the heavy cruiser *Augusta*, and set out on his way, in company of another cruiser, the *Philadelphia*, which steamed ahead to smooth the seas. To catch the best weather the cruisers headed straight out into the Atlantic until a few hundred miles off the coast, then turned abruptly to the north toward England and the Channel. From dispatches by pool reporters aboard ship the public learned that the president and his entourage of fifty-three advisers, assistants, and newspapermen ate in the ship's several messes and enjoyed evening movies. What the public did not know was that during the two-week voyage the president gathered a small group of officials and reporter friends to play poker every evening, to the annoyance of Secretary of State Byrnes, who desired to talk over diplomatic matters with his chief.[10]

During the voyage photographers had a field day taking pictures of everything, in particular the drama of two heavy cruisers at sea. Even now, many years later, those photographs of long ago appear as if taken yesterday— prenuclear cruisers with tall silhouettes (no squat superstructures covered with electronic gear) crossing the Atlantic, their wakes stretching out, with long v-shaped waves rolling hundreds of yards, white by day, luminous at night; in the distance stretched the ever-receding, saucerlike horizon. One can sense the occasion and almost hear the heavy breathing of the stacks and wash of the water. The president spent time on the bridge or stood at the prow looking toward the *Philadelphia,* binoculars round his neck, visor cap on his head, a sort of civilian navigator.

Upon passage up from the Azores the weather turned cooler, the sky gray. As the ships moved up the Scheldt the picturesque shoreline emerged, with flocks of fat cattle in the fields. There was no evidence of war until Antwerp, with its broken buildings and other signs of bombing, including scars caused by the "buzz bombs" used in the Battle of the Bulge.

From Antwerp the party drove to Brussels and enplaned for Berlin. The scene there has often been described: convoys passing lines of tattered civilians hauling wood from the country to hovels in the city, using such conveyances as baby carriages, children's wagons, and wheelbarrows; mountains of rubble, shoved aside to allow passage of motor vehicles, lying everywhere; Soviet soldiers in baggy uniforms standing guard; the blue sky of summer and the quietness of the streets, save for the rumble of trucks and a few airplanes, belying the savagery of a few weeks earlier. When the Americans arrived in mid-July, little more than two months had passed since war's end—two months since tanks and artillery had dueled down streets, their flashes and roars competing with the choking smoke, the booms of collapsing buildings, the infantrymen running from one place to another. By the time of the conference the architect of it all, Hitler, had been dead less than three months.

Upon arrival in the unbombed suburb of Babelsberg, the Americans relaxed in their villas, for Stalin came a day late, July 16. He journeyed by train, and there was talk of indisposition. News meanwhile arrived of detonation of a plutonium device at Alamogordo in distant New Mexico, an explosion far beyond estimates of scientists, who expected a TNT equivalent of five hundred to fifteen hundred tons and got twenty thousand.

Just before the conference Truman met Churchill. The prime minister telephoned late on the evening of July 15 and inquired as to when he might see his American opposite. An early riser, Truman mischievously proposed 9:00 A.M. Churchill moved the time back till 11:00. He arrived on the dot; his daughter, however, said he had not been up so early in ten years. The meeting went off pleasantly. "He is a most charming and a very clever person— meaning clever in the English not the Kentucky sense," the president wrote in careful appraisal. "He gave me a lot of hooey about how great my country is and how he loved Roosevelt and how he intended to love me etc. etc. Well. I gave him as cordial a reception as I could—being naturally (I hope) a polite and agreeable person." Churchill tried to "soft soap" him, the president averred. He reminded himself that the basic ingredient of soap was lye.[11]

A private meeting with Stalin the next day proved far more interesting and began what for a short time marked a definite preference of the president for the Russian over the Briton. Set for noon, the appointment opened a bit earlier. Truman was writing at a desk; he looked up and "there stood Stalin in the doorway." Both seem to have been impressed, especially Truman, who begged the Russian to stay for lunch; Stalin insisted he could not, and when Truman countered that he could if he wanted, the premier stayed. The Russian's quietness, brevity, and engaging appearance of modesty struck Truman as a relief from the flattering Churchill. Like FDR, he initially thought that he could deal with Stalin.[12]

On the opening day the conferees assembled in the grand hall of the Cecilienhof, the palace of the last crown prince of Imperial Germany, Henry of Hohenzollern, a huge pile of 176 rooms. The prime minister of Britain and the premier of Soviet Russia insisted that Truman be chairman because in title he was their senior—a head of state, akin to the British king or the president of the USSR—and also because he had journeyed the farthest. This gave the American president opportunity to set out the United States agenda. Part of it was unexceptionable: he desired periodic meetings of the Big Three foreign ministers in which issues could come to discussion if not solution; he wanted similar meetings for allied zonal commanders in Germany. Thereafter the list became controversial—how to carry out the Yalta Declaration on Liberated Europe, the latter a statement of rights and duties of peoples in that area drawn up by the state department and accepted by the Russians during the Yalta Conference. Having raised this question about Soviet behavior in Eastern Europe, he offered to discuss Anglo-American occupation of Italy, the exclusivity of which had nettled the Russians. As the conference wore on he began to press for freedom of Europe's waterways, such as the Kiel Canal and the Rhine, Danube, and other rivers.

The Soviets were much more concrete in their proposals. Stalin wished to discuss a division of Germany's merchant fleet and navy, reparations, trusteeships, relations with former Nazi satellites and the regime of Francisco Franco in Spain, a Soviet position in Tangier and in Syria and Lebanon, and governance and boundaries of Poland. Churchill said he too wanted to discuss Poland.

Agenda topics actually disguised real issues. Approval of such obvious committees as a council of foreign ministers and control councils for occupied countries passed quickly. Carrying out the Yalta Declaration turned into a semantic argument, the Soviets defining what was "democratic": Stalin said that "any freely elected government would be anti-Soviet and that we cannot permit." The Russians wanted immediate recognition of Soviet-dominated regimes in Hungary, Romania, and Bulgaria and refused any serious roles for control councils. On the division of German ships, merchant and naval, Churchill said the Soviets might take their share of merchant vessels but ships of war were horrible weapons and should be sunk. Stalin countered that the Soviet Union would take its share and the prime minister could sink his. On reparations the decision was a nondecision, that each occupying power might take reparations from its own zone. To mollify the Soviets, whose zone was agricultural, the Anglo-Americans promised to give 10 percent of surplus industrial equipment in their zones (whatever "surplus" meant) and set aside another 25 percent to exchange for coal and grain.

Nothing happened with trusteeships and relations with former satellites. The Soviets were attempting toeholds, perhaps footholds, in North Africa and the Middle East, but the Anglo-Americans were in occupation and not about to allow them. As for the Franco regime, neither West nor East cared to topple the dictator who had wobbled from one side to the other; it seemed unwise to take him on when there were other things to do.

Truman made a point about freedom of canals and waterways, and in his memoirs he recalled the brutal manner with which Stalin faced him down, refusing to mention the item in the conference communiqué, which would have been nothing more than an obeisance. Matters did become personal. During the conference's final moments the president looked across the table and said, "Marshal Stalin, I have accepted a number of compromises during this conference to conform with your views, and I make a personal request now that you yield on this point. My request is that the communiqué mention the fact that the waterways proposal has been referred to the Council of Foreign Ministers which we have established to prepare for peace settlements." He explained that this would offer him a chance to discuss the issue with Congress. Before the interpreter could finish translating, Stalin interrupted with "Nyet!" He added, in English, "No. I say no!" Truman turned to his colleagues and said, "I cannot understand that man!" But such was a momentary irritation, after seventeen days with evening sessions that disarranged the work habits of a president accustomed to arising at 5:30 A.M. The American interpreter, Bohlen, beheld no lasting resentment, and the president's memoirs, published after Stalin's death, displayed no vexation.[13]

The conference nominally was conducted according to Truman's agenda, with Soviet and British additions, but discussion circled around the issue of Poland's government and borders. Poland was a sensitive subject because Germany's attack on that country had begun World War II; also, 7 million United States citizens were of Polish origin and tended to vote Democratic. As at Yalta, Poland became the test of Soviet good will. Truman and Churchill— and after the latter received word that the Conservatives had lost the election in Britain, the leader of the Labour party and new prime minister, Clement Attlee—used their best logic, to no avail. Before the conference opened the Anglo-Americans had recognized the government of postwar Poland, after the Soviets included several noncommunist ministers. Meanwhile the Soviets invited sixteen Polish politicians to Moscow and imprisoned fourteen, claiming they had opposed necessary measures of the Red Army. Truman could do nothing about this. As for boundaries, the Western Allies recognized the Curzon Line in the east, a roughly ethnographic line disputed by the Poles, but in the west argued for the line of the Oder and Eastern Neisse, rather than Western Neisse, hoping to exclude Breslau, renamed Wroclaw, from Polish occupation. The Soviets gave control to the Poles.

Such were discussions during a conference that ended in the early morning hours of August 2, after which the principals and their assistants returned home—President Truman flying to Plymouth, England, where he met the *Augusta*. He also met King George VI, aboard a battleship, HMS *Renown*, with the king thereafter visiting the president aboard the *Augusta*.

How well had the president done at his first conference? Admitting that discussion of larger issues could hardly be decisive, was he able to make American positions clear to Soviet and British opposites? One must believe he was. Bohlen thought him a much better negotiator than Roosevelt. The latter improvised, and Truman kept to positions worked out in advance. He was "crisp and to the point," not breezily friendly but "pleasantly distant." There was little room for skill, for subtlety: "Therefore, President Truman's lack of experience in diplomacy was no real handicap." Years later, on the Soviet side, a similar testimony to the president's good behavior at Potsdam appeared in the memoirs of Andrei Gromyko. The then ambassador to the United States remembered particularly the first formal session: "There is Truman. He is nervous but he mobilises all his self-control so as not to show it." Gromyko watched closely and thought the president at times about to smile, but that was a false impression: "I have the feeling that the President is somehow huddled into himself." He was never rude nor discourteous (this was helped, of course, by the fact that his major statements had been prepared so that he only had to read them). The Russian noticed that the president's extempore comments were usually brief and that his advisers and experts were in constant consultation with each other, passing him notes from time to time. Gromyko was to gain a reputation for being unimaginative, but he well caught one later conference scene in which the American president was presented with the opportunity to slip up, to make a perhaps uncharitable remark. A dinner had just concluded, arranged by the president, and after everyone got up from the table Truman sat down at the piano and played— Gromyko did not say what, and probably did not know, but thought the president had practiced carefully (which he could not have). He added that, of course, Truman was well known to be an able amateur pianist. When the president finished, Stalin praised him and said laughingly, "Ah yes, music's an excellent thing—it drives out the beast in man." Young Gromyko at once saw the double meaning; it was not clear, he wrote, whom Stalin had in mind "as the one whose beast had been driven out." Diplomatically, the president chose to be very pleased at these words.[14]

So far as concerned the president's education in foreign affairs, his instruction in what his predecessor had failed to impart, the conference proved helpful, as he knew it would. Two weeks were too short to obtain understanding of European politics, but the president furthered his education nonetheless. He changed his mind about Churchill. For the first days the prime minister insisted on speeches for the record, which bored Truman. Stalin noticed what Churchill was doing and would say sotto voce, "Why don't you agree? The Americans agree, and we agree. You will agree eventually, so why don't you do it now?" But initial dislike lessened, and Truman saw that the Briton, however loquacious, was his friend. "I did like old Churchill," he wrote Margaret. "He was as windy as old Langer [William Langer, senator from North Dakota], but he knew his English language and after he'd talked half an hour there'd be at least one gem of a sentence and two thoughts maybe which could have been expressed in four minutes. But if we ever got him on record, which was seldom, he stayed put. Anyway he is a likeable person." Churchill's electoral defeat later shocked him.[15] At the outset Stalin had impressed him, but by the middle of the conference the admiration had worn off. Stalin's arguments became obnoxious when they consumed time, and Truman's temper flared. The president epitomized this experience by remembering Stalin's supposed retort to a question about the Catholic Church: "How many divisions has the pope?" One of Truman's aides asked Bohlen about it, and the interpreter said he was there every minute of every conversation and never heard it. "It was a hell of a good story anyhow," said the aide. And for the president it typified Potsdam; after leaving, Truman vowed he never wanted to live in Europe and never wanted to go back.[16]

One last concern emerges from the above discussion of Potsdam: might Truman have missed an opportunity to change relations with the Soviet Union in favor of world peace instead of what the world soon received for four decades, namely, a cold war (as Walter Lippmann described postwar foreign relations in a book published in 1947)? Could some herculean effort have had a chance to change history? Certainly the time—the last conference of the war—was historically right for a lessening of tension.

The answer seems clear, from a vantage of nearly half a century—no Western figure at that time could have changed events. The foundational fact of postwar years may well have been the need of the Soviet regime for an enemy in the West, so it could retain its hold on its citizenry. If Western opposition did not exist, the leadership had to invent it. Too, one has here the figure of Stalin, with his sense of human motives and the course of history. The regime understood only equations of power: "Unless Russia is faced with the iron fist and strong language another war is in the making. Only one language do they understand—'How many divisions have you?'"[17] In 1945 the Anglo-American leaders could do nought but negotiate over the status quo defined by the presence of Soviet troops in Eastern Europe, which meant accepting what Churchill in May of that year described (taking a phrase from the late Joseph Goebbels) as an iron curtain. Where Russian armies liberated peoples, there the Soviets determined governments. The date of the invasion of Normandy, 1944, determined the extent of Soviet occupation. Had invasion occurred in 1943 it might have made a difference. But because of the North African invasion in 1942, and its extension into Italy, 1944 was the earliest time the Anglo-Americans could have invaded France. In 1945 men in U.S. divisions also were going home, some for demobilization, others for redeployment to the Far East. They were unprepared, as were people at home, for their government to threaten the Soviet Union militarily; it would have been an incredible course, bringing something close to mutiny in the ranks and impeachment of the president and replacement of his administration.

In this setting Truman's failure at Potsdam to tell the Soviets of American possession of nuclear weapons had little to do with what followed in subsequent years. The Soviets had gone to enormous lengths to spy out the nuclear program and knew what was going on. If they were sensitive to the president's failure to remark the program, their spying displayed a strange lack of trust in the government they expected so much from. What happened displayed only cynicism and no hurt feelings. On July 24 the president walked around the table at Potsdam and told Stalin the United States had developed a new weapon of "unusual destructive force." Stalin's response, "I hope you will use it on the Japanese," masked his own knowledge. As soon as he got back to his quarters, in the company of Marshal Georgy Zhukov and of Molotov, the latter said to him, so Zhukov wrote, "We'll have to talk it over with Kurchatov and get him to speed things up." Igor V. Kurchatov was his nuclear weapons specialist, who had been working on a Soviet bomb since 1943. Years later Harriman remembered a conversation soon afterward with Molotov, who told him smirkingly, "You've given us a great deal of secret information in Potsdam." The foreign minister followed this remark with a resounding, "Ha, ha, ha, ha."[18]

3

The most controversial act of Truman's presidency, beyond all doubt, was the use of nuclear weapons upon Japan during the days following the Potsdam Conference. No single act of his eight years as the nation's chief executive has so concerned historians, political scientists, commentators on public affairs, indeed, the generality of the American people.[19]

The issue, as General Eisenhower said when he first heard of the bombings, is whether it was necessary to "hit them with that awful thing." By the early summer of 1945 the U.S. Army Air Forces and U.S. Navy were having a difficult time finding targets in and off Japan. The air force was flying over the home islands "taking out" city after city. It had all but broken Tokyo in a single napalm raid that created a fire exceeding eighteen hundred degrees Fahrenheit and leveled 15.8 square miles; the numbers of dead reached seventy thousand. In a raid of May, eighty thousand persons perished, this time by asphyxiation between walls of flame that caused rivers to boil, thereby boiling people who had taken refuge in them. With difficulty air force officers identified several cities, including Hiroshima and Nagasaki, sufficiently without bomb damage so that it would be possible to identify destruction wreaked by nuclear weapons. Meanwhile, the navy was conducting a blockade of Japanese waters, and its submarines were so hard put for targets they were sinking ferryboats. Surface ships were bombarding shore installations with impunity. It is tempting to think that if the United States had waited a few weeks or even a few months, Japan might have surrendered without the bombings; then it would have been possible to relate to the world that the American government, despite possession of a terrible new weapon, did not use it.[20]

But could the president have delayed use of nuclear weapons until the war came to an end through conventional bombing and a blockade? He did not think so. Whatever the beliefs of leaders of the U.S. Army Air Forces and the U.S. Navy, the Japanese were obstinately refusing to give up.

The president's decision for nuclear weapons, when it came, was based on two reasons. One was historical: the atrocities with which the Japanese began and thereafter conducted the war. In 1963 a correspondent wrote the retired president about the bomb decision, and the result was a retired-presidential explosion. "You should do your weeping at Pearl Harbor," was the response, "where thousands of American boys are underneath the waves caused by a Japanese sneak attack while we were at peace with Japan."[21] This said nothing about other atrocities, such as Japan's inhuman behavior toward prisoners, notably the Bataan death march, as well as the random shootings and beheadings that continued right up until the end of the war. It might seem today that, in and of itself, the hatred of Japan sown by Pearl Harbor and its aftermaths could not surely have been that important in persuading President Truman and his countrymen to use any weapon on Japan; after all, in the years after World War II relations between the two countries improved miraculously, to a point where hatred disappeared in a mirage, itself almost palpable, of good feelings. But a half-century ago the hatred was there and should not be underestimated.

The other presidential reason for dropping the bombs—and it was much more important than the historical (which might have been described as the emotional)—was the cost of invading the Japanese home islands, the sole remaining conventional military way to force a surrender. It seemed so high as to justify use of any new weapons in the American arsenal.

Initial figures for invasion casualties estimated by the military were highly speculative. Recent benchmarks were the conquest of Iwo Jima, in which 6,200 U.S. soldiers died, and of Okinawa, in which 13,000 soldiers and sailors died. The services' joint war plans committee on June 15, 1945, guessed that invasion of southern Kyushu followed by northwestern Kyushu would cost

25,000 killed, 105,000 wounded, 2,500 missing; a second course, invasion of southern Kyushu followed by invasion of the Tokyo plain (Honshu), would cost 40,000 killed, 150,000 wounded, 3,500 missing; a third, an invasion of southern Kyushu followed by northwestern Kyushu, then the Tokyo plain, would cost 46,000 killed, 170,000 wounded, 14,000 missing. The committee recommended course number two because number one would be a "pure gamble" in persuading Japan to surrender, perhaps necessitating number three with its higher casualties. The military realized their estimates for an invasion of Kyushu (scheduled for November 1) and the Tokyo plain (scheduled for the spring of 1946, with Japan presumably conquered by the autumn of that year) were theoretical. The committee said casualties "are not subject to accurate estimate and any figure cited is admittedly only an educated guess." The next higher planning level, the so-called joint staff planners, excised the committee's figures from the report, and the army's assistant chief of staff, General John E. Hull, wrote a cover memorandum which asserted that "it is considered wrong to give any estimates in numbers."[22]

A White House meeting on June 18 saw an equally inconclusive discussion of possible losses. Truman worriedly said he did not want another bloodbath like Okinawa ("an Okinawa from one end of Japan to the other"). Marshall did not cite the joint war plans committee's estimates (if in fact he knew them) and read only from General Hull's memo. He said he believed casualties on Kyushu would not be more than those on Luzon, which meant not much more than a thousand a day for the first thirty days, or thirty-one thousand. But a thirty-day estimate for Luzon was misleading, for General Tomoyuki Yamashita had divided his forces into three groups and pulled them out of range of naval guns; besides, the heaviest fighting took place after the first month. Admiral Leahy, present at the meeting, said Marshall's calculation was too low, and that a better way to calculate was to take total casualties on Okinawa, which ran 35 percent (46,000), and apply them to the Kyushu operation. He failed to say specifically that if the army went into Kyushu with the force it anticipated, 766,700, that would mean 268,000 casualties, a good deal higher than the joint war plans committee's highest estimate for the invasion not merely of Kyushu but also of Honshu.[23]

Whatever these speculations, in late July and early August came alarming news of a massive Japanese buildup on Kyushu that made all the casualty estimates of June far too low. Allied cryptanalysts discovered the buildup by decoding military traffic in an operation known as ULTRA (not to be confused with the decoding of diplomatic traffic, known as MAGIC). In a remarkable book published in 1992, Edward J. Drea has concluded that the military decodes were "a central factor in the decision to drop the atomic bomb on Japanese cities, one heretofore not fully incorporated into the historical record." By the last days of July and initial days of August it was fully understood in Washington. General Douglas MacArthur, it is true, underestimated it, for he anticipated being the principal military figure in the onslaught on the home islands, the greatest amphibious operation in history—fourteen divisions versus nine at Normandy. But Marshall was paying close attention and was appalled. On June 18 he had estimated 350,000 Japanese on Kyushu. ULTRA now reported 600,000, ready to fight to the death. (This estimate in turn was much too low; after the war it was discovered there were 900,000.) This said nothing of auxiliaries, for on July 2 the Japanese military announced a *levée en masse* of civilians. "In less lofty terms," Drea writes, "these woefully untrained children, old men, and women were beasts of burden who cleaned debris after air raids, portered supplies on their backs, and, armed with bamboo spears, were used as cannon fodder. Americans had witnessed them in all these roles on Okinawa."[24] On Okinawa, Japanese forces had sacrificed the Okinawan people, 200,000 of whom perished.

Everything considered, Truman may not have been wrong when he said after the war that an invasion would have cost 250,000 American casualties and the same number of Japanese; even when speaking or writing he sometimes turned casualties into deaths. Marshall, he later wrote, told him at Potsdam that the invasion of Kyushu and Honshu would cost a minimum of a quarter-million and possibly a million casualties. Stimson, in a widely noticed postwar article, wrote of a million casualties. The president claimed there was a meeting of his military and civil advisers at Potsdam in which they decided to use nuclear weapons, presumably on the basis of Marshall's figures. Postwar critics have deplored these figures. One writer in 1985 explained the calculations of Truman and Stimson as "a subconscious compulsion to persuade themselves and the American public that, horrible as the atomic bombs were, their use was actually humane inasmuch as it saved a huge number of lives." Casualties, he asserted, would have been high but nowhere near the deaths of 120,000 Japanese, many of them noncombatants, caused by the nuclear bombings. Another writer has pointed out that the president's claim of a meeting at Potsdam to discuss dropping the atomic bombs has to be wrong, for four of the participants were keeping diaries and afterward none mentioned the meeting. But whether Marshall did or did not advise Truman of high casualties, whether a meeting occurred or not, the statistics support Truman's later claim. The American preponderance against Japanese defenders on Iwo Jima had been four to one, on Okinawa two and one-half to one. Marshall, on June 18, thought the American attackers on Kyushu would have an advantage of two to one; instead, a month or so later, Japanese forces had the edge against the Americans, six to five, and there would have been more Japanese troops on Kyushu by November 1. For an attacking force to be so outnumbered could have brought tremendous casualties. If one added casualties for Honshu, a million casualties were possible. That could have meant, considering a three-to-one ratio for wounded-to-dead, such as obtained on Iwo Jima, 250,000 U.S. soldiers killed.[25]

For many years Truman has been vilified for using nuclear weapons on Japan, and some of the trouble was his own, for when he defended himself he did it vigorously. For example, in offhand remarks to an enormous 1,200-student "class" at Columbia University in 1959, he said the bombs were "merely another powerful weapon in the arsenal of righteousness." What he had done, he said, was "not any decision that you had to worry about. It was just the same as getting a bigger gun than the other fellow had to win a war and that's what it was used for. Nothing else but an artillery weapon." And again: "All this uproar about what we did and what could have been stopped—should we take these wonderful Monday morning quarterbacks, the experts who are supposed to be right? They don't know what they are talking about. I was there. I did it. I would do it again."[26]

But, of course, he would never forget what happened and why it had had to happen. The "what" and "why" was on his mind for the rest of his life. At a cabinet meeting on August 10 he said—and the point was recorded by Secretary of Commerce Wallace, who had no special reason to defend him—that the thought of wiping out another hundred thousand people was too horrible; he did not like the idea of killing, as he put it, "all those kids," and had given an order that no more such bombs were to be used. As for the "why," during the last days of his life, when he was in Research Hospital in Kansas City, he was visited by his attorney general and later associate justice of the Supreme Court, Tom Clark, who was told to stay for only five minutes, but the retired president wanted to talk about the atomic bomb, and Clark stayed forty-five minutes, listening to Truman defend why he had given the fateful order.[27]

The calculation was complicated, far beyond what contemporary and later observers believed. One must say that now, in the 1990s, when at least much of the debate is over, when, to use the cliché, almost all has been said and done, Truman's decision does not appear as outrageous or stupidly foolish. The president's critics, one suspects, were ready to accuse him because they did not admire other things he did or approved. They were critical because of his well-known decisiveness, which sometimes seemed offhanded. His approach to the presidency differed from that of some of his successors, who did not make decisions but wrapped problems in packages of indecision that involved keeping constituencies, whatever or whoever they are, happy. American politics now appears to consist less of making decisions than of "touching bases," finessing opposition in every quarter, creating happiness, and avoiding irritation. But behind hostile measurements of the president by his detractors, and the difference in ability to decide that marked him off from his successors, one cannot overlook the outlook of his time and the choice he faced. Like almost all of his countrymen, he shared a belief that the Japanese military forces knew nothing of how to wage civilized warfare. With this frame of mind he faced the dreadful choice of ordering the army and navy into an invasion of the home islands, with untold numbers of casualties, or ending the war as soon as possible.

4

Three questions remain about the dropping of nuclear bombs on Hiroshima and Nagasaki. The first is whether Washington really tried to warn Tokyo of what lay in store or merely went through a charade to that effect. The second is whether the bombs or Russian entry brought the great conflict in East Asia to an end. The third is whether the purpose of dropping the bombs was what the Americans said it was or, instead, something they only occasionally seemed to be pointing out—the possibility of postwar use.

In answer to the initial question, one must say that American political and military leaders wanted to end the war without using nuclear weapons but did not know how to do it. It proved impossible to warn the Japanese in a convincing way. There was talk of a demonstration of nuclear power, perhaps over a relatively unpopulated area such as Tokyo Bay, and at night so as to make it more spectacular. Word would have gotten to the highest officials of the Tokyo government and might have brought a surrender. Still, suppose the bomb had not exploded—it required a parachute and timer, and one or both might not have functioned. The Japanese also could have taken American prisoners into the area of the demonstration. Moreover, the United States possessed only two weapons, and to have used one for a demonstration seemed inadvisable.[28]

Truman was unwilling to send an explicit warning that the United States possessed nuclear weapons and would use them. Congress had tolerated an unknown project costing billions, and it might object to an explanation offered an enemy government without informing the legislative body that paid the bill.

Unfortunately, the resultant Potsdam Declaration, which informed the Japanese that if they did not cease fighting they faced "prompt and utter destruction," did not impress the Japanese enough to receive a serious answer. The prime minister chose to ignore it, employing the ambiguous word *mokusatsu*, which means literally "to kill with silence," although it carries a nuance of uncertainty. Tokyo radio used the word, saying the government would *mokusatsu* the declaration and fight on. The English translation became "reject," and the president took it as a rebuff: "When we asked them to surrender at Potsdam, they gave us a very snotty answer. That is what I got. . . . They told me to go to hell, words to that effect."[29] The Japanese leaders did not know that the United States possessed nuclear weapons. They also believed, foolishly, that they could negotiate with the Americans, even though the Japanese were thoroughly aware of the rapine and butchery with which their nation's troops had fought across East Asia. Involved in those deeds was the emperor himself, about whose complicity the West knew little at the time and continued to know little until after the death of Hirohito, when officials of the imperial household revealed a quite different emperor than the world had seen: the emperor supported his military commanders and often gave political advice. As the war was coming to an end the Allies were saying publicly that they would arraign war criminals, and Tokyo officials deluded themselves that it would be possible to bargain to save the skins of people involved; they had in mind an arrangement that would put the matter delicately, in terms of preserving the imperial institution, so that Japanese authorities rather than the Allies would hold any war-crimes trials.

Nothing less than a shock was necessary to jar the regime out of its complacency. A terrible shock it proved to be, involving tens of thousands of people who had nothing to do with the self-serving schemes of Tokyo officialdom.

A second question is whether the bombs or Russian entry brought Japan's surrender. Prior to Hiroshima the civilians and the military divided over continuing the war. The Hiroshima bomb was dropped on August 6, Russian entrance occurred August 8, and Nagasaki was bombed on August 9. Until Nagasaki the cabinet remained deadlocked, civilians against the military. On the evening of August 9–10, the emperor unconstitutionally (under the Meiji constitution he did not have the right to express an opinion, only preside over his councillors) forced a decision for peace. On August 11 Washington offered a condition for what it still described as unconditional surrender, that the emperor must be subject to authority of the Allied supreme commander, which condition the emperor accepted by breaking a second deadlock on August 14.

The truth is that it is impossible to come to a conclusion about this question. In such a welter of events and decisions it is not possible to describe any single factor as a sine qua non.[30] One factor will point in a certain direction, another in the opposite. Soviet entry greatly surprised Japanese officials, even shocked them; Tokyo had counted on using Moscow as a mediator with Washington; the Japanese had no inkling that the Russians were about to enter the war. But, then, against the Soviets' claim that their nation's resort to war persuaded the Tokyo regime to surrender was the date on which the Soviets came in. During preceding months—and they repeated the promise at Potsdam—they had said they would come in three months after the close of the European war. But at Potsdam they gave as the date of their entry August 15. After Hiroshima they clearly jumped the gun, entering six days earlier. Otherwise, with the war about to end on August 14, they would not have had opportunity to share in the spoils.

The final question over the nuclear bombings has been a contention about the very purpose of dropping the bombs. Twenty years after the war a young scholar asserted that the administration used nuclear weapons on the

Japanese to impress the Russians. This was an extraordinary claim, raising doubts about the bona fides of American officials, suggesting they would do anything to confound the Soviet Union. The awkwardness, the sticking point, of such a claim, however, is its lack of proof. Members of the Interim Committee, the advisory group that considered whether to use the bomb, never considered dropping bombs on the Japanese to impress the Russians. Secretary Stimson did write in his diary that when the bomb was ready the Americans could play a master card, whatever that meant—probably ending the war. Byrnes told three nuclear scientists, when they visited him in Spartanburg, South Carolina, that the bomb would impress the Russians. Truman may have said privately to Leahy, "If it explodes as I think it will I'll certainly have a hammer on those boys," perhaps meaning the Russians as well as the Japanese. But the only known public talk about the bomb by an American official was just after the war, between Molotov and Byrnes, during a foreign ministers' conference in London. At a reception in the House of Lords, Byrnes went over to Molotov and jokingly inquired when the Russian foreign minister was going to get his sightseeing completed and "let us get down to business." Molotov, presumably thinking of how Byrnes might force him to cease the sightseeing, asked the secretary of state if he had an atomic bomb in his side pocket. Coming close upon the bombings of Hiroshima and Nagasaki, the remark was tasteless. So was the response of Byrnes: "You don't know Southerners. We carry our artillery in our hip pocket. If you don't cut out all this stalling and let us get down to work, I am going to pull an atomic bomb out of my hip pocket and let you have it." Molotov laughed, as did the interpreter. Some days later Byrnes made a speech and included a plea that the world was looking to the foreign ministers to write a lasting peace. He waxed so eloquent that Molotov paid a tribute to him and said he was more gifted than was he, the Soviet foreign minister, and in addition Byrnes had an atomic bomb.[31]

Although these issues may never be resolved, we do know that on August 14, 1945, reporters thronged the oval office to overflowing, standing so close they could hardly write. It was 7:00 P.M. when the president gave out the news, and reporters rushed for the doors to reach the telephones outside. The president and his wife followed, and went out to the fountain on the north lawn where a vast crowd had assembled beyond the gates. Harry Truman made a "V" sign, and a great cheer went up. He and Bess remained a few minutes, and then they went back into the White House where the president called his mother in Grandview.

Chapter Eleven

To Err Is Truman

*P*residents do not have an easy time after a war. The House of Representatives impeached Abraham Lincoln's successor, and the Senate failed to convict him by a single vote. The Senate defeated Woodrow Wilson over the League of Nations and Treaty of Versailles. At the outset the American people gave Roosevelt's successor an approval rating of 87 percent, but a year and a half later they could not say enough critical things. For the congressional elections in November 1946, the Republican party campaigned on a slogan of "Had enough?" and won majorities in both Houses for the first time since 1928. A freshman Democratic senator, J. William Fulbright of Arkansas, proposed that the nation's chief executive appoint Senator Arthur H. Vandenberg, Republican of Michigan, as secretary of state, and resign; under the then law of succession, this would have brought Vandenberg into the presidency.

1

As soon as the war was over an avalanche of criticism descended. Some of it was of the usual sort after a war; when the president was a war leader it was difficult to say anything about him. Some arose because Roosevelt had held the presidency so long that people had become accustomed to him— they had accepted a notion of what the presidency was like or the type of man who should hold it, and when Truman came along he fractured this notion. People said power had shifted from the Hudson to the Missouri. They saw a Missouri Compromise. They remarked on the new president's rural ways, such as his visit to a county fair in Caruthersville, Missouri, in the autumn of 1945, something Roosevelt never would have done. Everything he did seemed in contrast to Roosevelt, and critically so.

The critics also pounced on the qualifications of Truman's White House assistants, beholding a set of appointees who, they said, never deserved to take up duties at such an address as 1600 Pennsylvania Avenue. Robert S.

Allen and William V. Shannon in *The Truman Merry-Go-Round* described the Truman staff members as a group of stumblebums and weary, faceless hacks: "The mere announcement in April, 1945, that Harry Truman was President flushed them out of every dark cove and thicket." The Truman administration gave fat jobs to fatheads. At first the appointees were funny rather than dangerous: "They were not putting their hands in the till; they were too busy putting their feet in their mouths."[1] Then their qualities emerged. They brought to mind the assistants of President Harding.

Actually the White House staff under Truman was quite a decent group, equal to or better than the Roosevelt staff. The president's principal assistants, such as Ross, Steelman, and the others, performed well. Not that there were no troubles. At the beginning the staff seemed far from perfect, and Robert Nixon, who became a staunch friend of the new president, years later described to an interviewer the people he first saw in April 1945: "Truman brought a bunch of incompetents down to the White House," he said. "They didn't know first base from breakfast." The president himself told him, he said, that coming into office put him in a quandary. "How can I bring *big* people into government when I don't even know who they are, and they don't know me? They know the power of my position, but I've had no broad contacts in life. The only people I knew to bring down to the White House were those that worked in my office on the Hill. All of whom were little small-town people. That's all they were."[2] But there were no real, lasting reasons to believe the staff incompetent. It was only the impression that circulated that made them seem that way. Once in a while, and never in the top tier of assistants, someone would misbehave. The president's first airplane pilot, Lieutenant Colonel Henry T. "Hank" Myers, unbeknownst to the president, was dealing in automobiles, at a time when a new car was hard to get. He resigned in 1948, upon a complaint by the president of the Capitol Cadillac Company; by that date Hank had purchased three Cadillacs, a Packard, a Lincoln, a Chrysler, and was about to accept a Plymouth. His was a case not of incompetence, of course, but of impropriety. A somewhat similar case was that of an erstwhile passenger agent of the Baltimore and Ohio Railroad and native of St. Louis, John Maragon, who aspired to be transportation officer at the White House. He was not a staffer but gave the impression of being one; he kept turning up in inconvenient places with a White House pass that somebody, apparently Harry Vaughan, had given him.

People pointed to the president's friends, and in a few cases Truman admittedly should have extended his friendships in other directions. He did not do himself any favor by bringing George Allen into the White House, for example. Allen had his attractive side, for he was not merely jovial but downright hilarious, and the president needed a little hilarity, especially during the first year and a half after the war; Allen frequently was aboard the presidential yacht. Truman at last exiled him to the Reconstruction Finance Corporation where he stayed for a year as a director and tried to do good by voting against a loan to the Lustron Corporation, a postwar company whose entrepreneur, without putting much of his own money into the enterprise, sought to build prefabricated metal houses to solve the intense postwar housing shortage. Allen's reputation as a White House intimate meanwhile allowed him to obtain directorships in many corporations, and at the time of his death years later he had managed thirty of them.[3]

Another unfortunate friend, in evidence for both presidential terms, was Vaughan, whose maladroitness became a public issue in 1949–1950. The president could not bring himself to dismiss an individual whose loyalty dated back to the confrontation with Brigadier General Berry in 1917. He tried to find a less public place for him but never succeeded.

An episode in Missouri politics in the summer of 1946 hardly helped the president's image. This was his effort to get rid of Representative Roger C. Slaughter, an apparently innocent and worthy sort when he went to Congress promising good behavior to the House Democratic leaders. They put him on the rules committee, and he went over to the Republicans. Truman should have tolerated him as a representative of a subspecies of Missouri political life related to former governor Stark, but he could not take him that way; his very existence in Congress seemed a rebuke to the nation's chief executive, or so Truman came to believe. The president wrote his army friend Jim Pendergast, son of Mike, nephew of Tom, titular head of the remnant of the machine, that "much to my regret" Slaughter was obnoxious. Referring to the onetime Shannon faction of Jackson County Democrats known as rabbits, he said he had not thought he would have to "ask a Pendergast to make a choice between an upstart little rabbit and the president of the United States."[4] To oppose Slaughter he put up a Grandview lawyer of modest attainments, Enos A. Axtell, and mentioned Axtell favorably whenever possible, although on one occasion he could not remember Axtell's first name. The presidential intervention did not work: although Axtell won the Democratic primary, the Republican candidate won the November election.

All this opened the way for another Missouri contretemps, reminiscent of Kansas City politics a decade before, so critics claimed. After the president urged Jim Pendergast to defeat Slaughter, Jim erred on the side of thoroughness, voting many graveyards, including some voters who had died in the cholera epidemic of 1902. A grand jury indicted seventy-one Pendergast supporters. To prove its case it seized the ballot boxes and placed them in a walk-in safe in the basement of the Kansas City courthouse. Thereafter details of the case became murky. Someone placed dynamite against the safe, blew open the door, and took the boxes. This enterprise was handled in an amateurish way that was unexplainable to experts; President Truman's friend Fred Canfil, the U.S. marshal for Kansas City, wrote:

It is my opinion the ballots had all been abstracted from the safe prior to the explosion because it would have been noticeable if any man went out of there carrying a sack containing all of these papers. A bank robber of some long experience, who is in my custody, told me that that type of safe would be opened with a bar or a hammer and it was an insult to men of his profession that explosives were used.[5]

A woman named Mary Bond offered to obtain evidence on the ballot theft if the U.S. district attorney released her husband from jail, and an unidentified person killed her the next night. T. Lamar Caudle, who was in charge of the criminal division of the department of justice in Washington, seemed unenthusiastic about investigating the matter, and he himself afterward went to jail for tax fraud. The justice department official who traveled out to Kansas City to investigate asserted years later that the business manager of the *Kansas City Star* stole the boxes to discredit the remnant of the Pendergast machine.[6] This seemed unlikely; the Pendergast nephew was in no sense as imaginative or hardworking as his father, not to mention his uncle, and it would have been senseless for the *Star* to have taken him so seriously. The case never was solved.

The possible connection of the *Kansas City Star* with the vote fraud scandal over the Slaughter-Axtell primary brings to mind the new president's unfortunate relations with newspaper publishers, who had much to do with spreading the claims that he was a poor inhabitant of the White House. For many years, to be sure, America's newspaper press had been largely in the hands of Republican owners, the notable instance being the chain of papers controlled by William Randolph Hearst, a chain that reached across the country, coast to coast. Hearst himself, yet active when Truman became president, was hostile to Democrats in general, and Truman in particular, but he was less of a source of hostility within his chain than were his editors, by that time all of Hearst's political persuasion. A more prominent source of criticism of the Truman administration was the chain controlled by the prickly publisher of the *Chicago Tribune,* Colonel Robert R. McCormick, and his cousins the Pattersons, who owned leading papers in New York and Washington. All told, "Bertie" McCormick and his cousins published twenty-one politically conservative, anti-Truman newspapers in thirteen cities (Truman called their papers "the McCormick-Patterson axis"). While the president had no real problem dealing with reporters, whom he usually liked, and who liked him, columnists—such as the gossipmonger Walter Winchell and his more influential and somewhat higher-level competitor, Drew Pearson—were chosen by the publishers, and they were a different matter. The columnist Walter Lippmann was typically against government positions, and he did not shy from making criticisms that amounted to hostility; essentially Republican in outlook, he was a hemstitcher who was difficult to endure behind his apparently reasonable periods. Two other columnists, the Alsops, Joseph and Stewart, were more supportive, but they too were trying for points and therefore tended toward criticism; the president privately described them as "the All-slops."[7] But it was the publishers who made life difficult for the Truman administration, and the hostility lasted until the successor of Roosevelt gave way to a president, Eisenhower, whom the publishers appeared to admire.

The newspaper criticism started early in Truman's administration, as soon as the war was over. In September 1945, Budget Director Smith went into the oval office for an appointment and found the president glancing at newspaper editorial clippings. Truman said he was just looking at "the day's poison."[8] From that point, the criticism did not let up: year after year Truman read the newspapers only to see hostile editorials in both the McCormick-Patterson papers and the Hearst papers. The hostility often spilled over from editorial pages into news columns: favorable news was banished to inside pages and unfavorable news highlighted on the front page, right-hand column, while news stories were slanted. The *St. Louis Post-Dispatch* often bothered the president. "I heard a new name for that paper the other day," he wrote a friend. It was "the *St. Louis Post-Disgrace*."[9]

As the president suffered from the slings and arrows of newspaper publishers, he similarly was hurt by his inability as a public speaker. People compared his speeches with those of his predecessor, which meant comparing a Harvard accent to a monotonous Missouri twang. Truman would learn to be effective as a speaker, but the learning came a few years after he assumed the presidency, just before the electoral campaign of 1948, when he learned to speak extempore rather than read potted speeches. Until then he was largely ineffective, and he hated making speeches. He so confessed to Bob Nixon. "Bob," he said, "I can't even make a speech. The newsreel men used to come to me and say, 'Mr. Truman we want you to make a statement about a certain piece of legislation before the newsreel camera!' And I used to say to them, 'Fellows, please get somebody else to do it. Those cameras frighten me, and I just can't do it. I can't make a speech.' I *rarely* ever tried to make one in the Senate."[10]

Claims of incompetence, which emerged from every direction after the war, promoted by a hostile newspaper press and abetted by his admitted incompetence as a speaker, were confirmed in 1946 by two ill-managed cabinet resignations. The first, that of Secretary of the Interior Ickes, arose because of the nomination of Edwin Pauley as undersecretary of the navy. Roosevelt had wanted to designate Pauley for the navy post, but Eleanor Roosevelt appears to have raised objection because of Pauley's stand on the tidelands oil issue—whether oil under the permanently submerged lands beyond the tidal flats (mostly along the coasts of Florida, Louisiana, Texas, and California), estimated to be worth between $40 billion and $100 billion, should be subject to national rather than state jurisdiction. The nomination was languishing at the time Roosevelt died.[11] Truman revived it, for Pauley was the kind of appointee whom the president was seeking—a "big" person. Once legislation passed Congress to unify the armed services, he may have hoped to make him secretary of defense.

Ickes intervened in the Pauley nomination with a heavy hand and in a highly questionable way. At first he told the president he would have to answer questions if called before the pertinent Senate committee, and the president said offhandedly "that of course I [Ickes] must tell the truth but he hoped that I would be as gentle with Pauley as possible."[12] Ickes not merely testified against the nominee but after his, Ickes's, first appearance before the committee sent word via a reporter, Edwin A. Harris of the *St. Louis Post-Dispatch* (who received a Pulitzer Prize for his helpfulness), that hostile senators could make a more convincing case by asking the interior secretary to read from his diary. So requested, he read an extract of September 6, 1944, recording that Pauley had said he could raise $300,000 for the Democratic national committee from oilmen in California who had interest in offshore oil, if the federal government would assure them it would not try to assert title to those oil lands. "This is the rawest proposition that has ever been made to me," Ickes told the committee. The testimony killed Pauley's nomination; the nominee asked the president to withdraw it.

To the American public the Pauley affair, as it became known, seemed only the defeat of a rich oilman, but behind the uproar it was clear that Ickes had acted abominably. He should have told the president he could not support Pauley. Sending Harris to prompt the committee was another below-the-belt tactic. Moreover, if he wanted to "get" Pauley for the rawest proposition anyone ever made to him, why did he wait a year and a half, until February 1946?[13]

Truman took Ickes's resignation and had good reason to do it. Ickes had courted resignation innumerable times during the Roosevelt administration. He did it once with Truman. His behavior reminded George Allen of the epitaph on a tombstone in Oklahoma: "He kept asking for it until he got it."[14]

Nor did Ickes act well after his resignation. Although the secretary suggested he continue in office until the end of March, the president accepted the resignation effective February 15. The innocuous letter the president sent Ickes, composed by Hassett, said, "I also consider that this terminates all of your other governmental activities." In a public reply Ickes snarled, "You will pardon me if I remark that this is in the nature of supererogation. I assure you that I have had no secret design, having resigned as Secretary of the Interior, to hold on to any other office under your jurisdiction." Two years later, March 27, 1948, when the presidential election was stirring public interest, Ickes sent the president an "open letter" advising Truman not to seek the Democratic nomination. "You have the choice of retiring voluntarily and with dignity, or of being driven out of office by a disillusioned and indignant citizenry." He said that many Democrats would vote for Wallace, then an avowed candidate on the Progressive party ticket, that the South would not support the president because southerners considered him weak and unpopular, and that he would drag other Democrats down with him. When Truman did receive the nomination, Ickes supported him, but one must say that the former interior secretary's behavior from 1946 to 1948 marked one of the lesser chapters in his public life.[15]

In September 1946 the president had to take the resignation of the sole Rooseveltian remaining in the cabinet. Again he discovered one of his cabinet members attempting to push him around. As matters turned out, Wallace's departure was much more messy than Ickes's.[16]

It is a well-known, often remarked, story that the secretary of commerce came to see the president on September 10 for an appointment that was for fifteen minutes but probably ran thirty or forty and asked him, among other subjects of discussion, to read a speech that he, Wallace, proposed to give two days later at Madison Square Garden. The president read parts of the speech and assumed everything was all right, even though it dealt with policy toward Russia, a touchy subject as the cold war was then heating up. On the day of the speech, September 12, reporters received advance copies, and Truman had a query in his 4:00 P.M. press conference as to whether he approved of what Wallace was to say; Wallace stated in the text that the president had read the speech and approved it. The president said he approved. Late that afternoon Press Secretary Ross called him. Ross did not have an advance copy but had learned that the state department (which had gotten a copy from the press table) did not like it. As Ross remembered the answer, "The President did not appear alarmed. He said he had given Wallace permission to make the speech for its political effect in New York, and while it might ruffle Byrnes, he did not think it would do any permanent damage."[17]

On that night of September 12 the secretary gave the address before a cheering crowd of twenty thousand people, and the next morning newspapers were full of it. In the words of Clark Clifford, "Wallace spoke and hell broke loose. . . . Oh, boy, it really did!"[18] The speech was a "go slowly" address, dramatically in opposition to what Secretary Byrnes then was advocating in Paris in diplomacy with the Soviets. There was no use getting tough with the Russians: "The tougher we get, the tougher the Russians get." Americans should be careful not to allow national oil rivalries to force them into war (a crisis had erupted over Soviet unwillingness to give up occupation of northern Iran, despite an agreement to leave). They should promise to stay out of political affairs of Eastern Europe (Byrnes was negotiating over those very affairs). "We are still arming to the hilt," Wallace said (in apparent belief that his own country had brought on much of the trouble). The speech was provocative in other ways as well. British machinations, the orator said, were likely to cause international trouble.[19]

Such remarks were out of place for a secretary of commerce; one must consider the probability that Wallace, having lost respect for the president after the Democratic convention in 1944 and believing that Truman was but putty in the hands of a strong secretary of state, was trying to commit him to his own foreign policy views.[20]

The best account of what happened thereafter was set down at the time by Ross in a long dictation made the day Wallace resigned and in an entry the next day in a random diary he was keeping.[21] Because of his closeness to the president he was able to observe everything. After the speech the president had to do something, and he hoped to keep Wallace in the cabinet. The problem was how to keep him quiet. Ross was present during much of a two-hour conversation between Wallace and Truman on Wednesday, September 18, in which Wallace said the country's great issue of the day was foreign policy and he necessarily had to deal with it in his speeches. The president suggested half a dozen other issues—price control, progressive measures in general, and others. Wallace said in effect, "Mr. Roosevelt had his right hand and his left hand and often the left hand did not know what the right hand was doing and vice versa." He wanted to remain in the cabinet as Truman's left hand, as spokesman of the left-wing group among Democrats. He said he represented the "progressive elements" of the party.[22] But this was at a time when Truman was trying to keep issues of foreign policy on a bipartisan basis; the last thing he needed was disunity on such issues within the Democratic party. Wallace said the Republican party was the party of imperialism, the Democratic party the party of peace, and bipartisanship would be dictatorship. He agreed not to make any more speeches until after Byrnes finished his work in Paris, drawing up peace treaties for the former German satellites together with Italy and Finland. Ross thought the arrangement a bad idea, for after the Paris discussions it would be necessary to have the same argument with Wallace all over again. It was a sort of truce.

On the following morning, Thursday, September 19, the president talked with Byrnes by teletype. The secretary of state was obviously unhappy, at one point saying that without agreement on foreign policy within the administration he should resign, as he could not face the Russians. The exchange ended on a note that everything was all right.

Thursday night Clifford called Ross and said he thought the president should call in Wallace the next morning and state the issue: Wallace should make no more speeches without clearing them with the department of state, and otherwise make his speeches outside the cabinet.

Ross and Clifford raised this issue at the Friday morning staff conference, and to their amazement Truman said he had just sent Wallace a longhand letter asking for his resignation. He read the letter, which was brusque, written in anger. It said he no longer had confidence in Wallace.

A phone call came in for the president. It was Wallace. Puzzled, Truman asked Ross if he should talk to Wallace, and Ross said he thought he should. Ross remained during the conversation, which was brief and extremely friendly. Wallace evidently took his dismissal in a decent way. Truman was deeply moved; at one point he remarked, "You are a better man than I am, Henry." Toward the end he said, "I love you still." Wallace evidently responded in kind. Truman told Ross afterward that Wallace said, "I am not going to leave you."

The president told Ross that Wallace was willing either to return or to destroy the dismissal letter, and Truman told him to do the latter. Ross said he trusted Wallace but not the men around him, so the president sent the White House receptionist, William D. Simmons, to the commerce department to retrieve the letter. He called Wallace and apprised him of the fact, and there was a further friendly interchange.[23]

The Wallace resignation hence was a near-perfect mess, in which the president, with an ingenious combination of errors, large and small, arranged his own discomfiture. Earlier that summer Wallace had alerted him to the possibility of confrontation by responding to a presidential inquiry during a cabinet meeting; Truman had told the cabinet he would like memoranda concerning the way American foreign policy should go, and Wallace sent in a huge effusion relating criticisms of American policy that made the cold war appear largely an American enterprise. At the time Truman thought it a manifesto, in the way of former secretary Ickes, by which Wallace soon would manage an exit from the cabinet and entrance into American politics in time to influence the congressional elections, not to mention the presidential election in 1948. He acknowledged it with a noncommittal note of thanks. But he should have considered it a warning, and when Wallace came in with the Madison Square Garden speech, he might well have taken the text from his visitor with suitable thanks, informed Wallace that two days were too short a time to agree to such a speech, and that Wallace should address the Madison Square Garden audience on problems of the department of commerce. Instead, he compounded his errors by telling the press conference on the very day of the speech that he not merely had read it but approved it. When he received the telephone call from Ross, he failed to catch himself up.

Truman felt worse about the Wallace affair than about any presidential action up until that time. After it was all over he decided to spend the weekend aboard the yacht and try to relax, reading and sleeping and maybe taking a little sun on the deck. He told Ross he intended to make a hermit out of himself for a while.

2

After the end of World War II—and quite apart from Slaughter-Axtell, the voting scandal, and the various criticisms, and apart too from the resignations—the new chief executive faced the distressing tasks of demobilization and reconversion. He hoped to make demobilization orderly; months before war's end the services had announced a point system by which the most experienced men could get out first. Along with this arrangement the services wanted to reduce their numbers slowly enough to ensure a proper level of readiness among units designated for the peace time army.

Unfortunately, demobilization became nearly chaotic. In Europe matters proceeded rapidly, according to the army's schedule set out in the point system. But in the Far East, where distances were much longer, the shipping shortage made speed impossible. Servicemen and their wives and girlfriends thereupon put as much pressure on political leaders as they could, which was considerable. The wives organized two hundred Bring Back Daddy clubs, to pursue such activities as sending members of the Senate military affairs committee baby booties inscribed, "I want my daddy back." Thousands of letters in December 1945 bore a stamped legend, "No Boats, No Votes."

Then, on January 4, 1946, the war department announced that the need for overseas troops for the next six months was greater than the number of available replacements, and 1.5 million men eligible for discharge would have to return home over a six-month rather than a three-month period. The result was near insubordination. Twenty thousand men marched to command headquarters in Manila to complain. In Batangas servicemen raised $3,700 to cable protests to the president and pertinent congressional committees and bought full-page advertisements in fifteen leading daily newspapers. A sergeant in Osaka cabled Truman: "Give us our independence or go back to yours."[24]

In Washington an unreported confrontation took place between the president and the columnist Pearson. Pearson had received thousands of petitions, including a cable signed by six thousand men in Guam. After a press conference Pearson went up to Press Secretary Ross and asked to present petitions to the president, signed, he said, by thirty thousand soldiers. Ross told him the press conference was no place to present such items and he would take them himself. Reluctantly, Pearson turned them over and asked if he might speak to the president; Ross said he might. Ross's assistant, Eben A. Ayers, wrote in his diary afterward that he did not hear all the conversation but from what he did hear, and what others heard, Truman told Pearson that he and similar writers and columnists were responsible for the mess over demobilization. The president said it was not demobilization but disintegration, that it was also mutiny. Pearson asked if he might use what the president said, and the president said it was off the record. The president told Pearson, in addition, that the columnist was smart enough—he thought he was—to know better than take part in such an action. Ayers said the president was stirred up and forceful in language, although he did not lose his temper.[25]

About this time the army's chief of staff, General Eisenhower, who replaced Marshall, spoke to a joint session of Congress about demobilization; afterward the president wrote him plaintively, inquiring if it might be possible to restore morale in the army. It was a pathetic inquiry, in regard to a pathetic situation. He wondered if officers at home and overseas had gotten too far removed from their men. "I know what you've been up against in this demobilization. I know you've lost your best and that the untrained and the inefficient are what we have left now. But can't we start over—from the squad up, rebuild that pride and morale which are the backbone of any organization? What can I do to help?"[26]

The army and navy disintegrated in 1945–1946. The president could do almost nothing about it. Many years later the secretary of state in the Kennedy and Johnson administrations, Dean Rusk, who admired Truman, wrote that the president's only error during two terms was doing nothing about demobilization: "I firmly believe the American demobilization tempted Joseph Stalin to embark upon that series of adventures which started the Cold War." Strong presidential leadership, Rusk believes, might have made a difference.[27] Yet the president had little control over the emotionalism that governed demobilization. Almost the only conventional military force the nation possessed was a carrier task force created quietly by Secretary of the Navy James V. Forrestal, who arranged for Admiral Marc A. Mitscher to have the best of everything—men, equipment, supplies—to bring a four-carrier force up to wartime readiness. If trouble with the Soviet Union had escalated into war, the only recourse, other than Mitscher's force, was nuclear weapons, of which just a few, perhaps half a dozen, were available.[28]

Meanwhile, reconversion of the economy was proceeding as best as the president could guide it. Here the problem was that the war had created an enormous fund of personal savings in bank deposits and government bonds, $136 billion; the Roosevelt administration had allowed this buildup because the money raised everyone's morale. Rationing prevented it from getting into the marketplace, and price and wage and rent controls helped. Once the war was over, danger loomed, for to hold down prices was going to be, as the president said, "the toughest domestic job in Washington."[29] The gross national product in 1945 was only $215 billion, and war production took more than half of it; time was necessary, at least a year, probably a year and a half, to return to civilian production. Meanwhile, businessmen were ready for postwar profits and, damn the inflation, wanted to move full speed ahead. Unions wanted to shove up wages and the devil take the hindmost. Union membership in 1945 was higher than at any time before or since—14 million, one-third of the workforce. Because of wartime restrictions union workers had not done as well as they hoped, and postwar reduction of the workweek from forty-eight to forty hours, the reduction being all in overtime (time and a half), meant cutting paychecks by nearly one-third.

The first controversy arose over price and wage controls. During the war the Office of Price Administration had controlled or sought to control 8 million commodities and services, and because of rationing the system worked; but in the postwar era the red, green, and other ration stamps were abandoned, and the government tried to keep prices down through price and wage controls alone. Neither business nor labor wanted these controls, and soon the administration had a fight on its hands.

Businessmen were up in arms; according to a later student of Truman's presidency, their attack on OPA in 1945–1946 was "the most massive and concerted campaign" since their attack on the National Recovery Administration ten years before.[30] The issue turned into a face-off between the president's friend John Snyder, momentarily head of the Office of War Mobilization and Reconversion (later secretary of the treasury), whose instincts were pro-business, and the head of OPA, Chester Bowles. Snyder felt he needed control of OPA, otherwise his control of reconversion would be hopelessly incomplete. Bowles was unwilling to accept Snyder's supervision because he believed Snyder would administer price controls in a conservative way. In meetings on this subject Snyder became emotional, his chin shaking, his eyes misting. In a contest for the president's favor Bowles did not have a chance, for Truman had known Snyder too long. He uncharitably believed Bowles was running for governor of Connecticut.

The arrangement was to get Bowles out of OPA and replace him with Paul A. Porter, who, presumably, would cooperate with Snyder. Truman directed that all individuals involved in price controls assemble in his office on the afternoon of February 14, 1946, and told Matt Connelly to notify them individually, not telling each one the others were coming. All assembled for a conference that lasted two hours, including not only Bowles and Porter and Snyder but also Secretary of State Byrnes, Secretary of the Treasury Vinson, Secretary of Labor Schwellenbach, Attorney General Clark, together with labor mediator Steelman and Press Secretary Ross. Truman told them, "I'm going to be president for the next three . . . years, and by God, I'm going to make it click." He told them to stop talking for the newspapers. He said that if anyone could not go along with his reorganization of authority over price controls, to say so.[31]

By this time it was necessary for Congress to reenact price controls, as the wartime act was expiring. The result was disheartening. Congress voted to continue OPA but mangled the office's authority. Truman came under pressure to sign this bill, but he decided to veto it, and price controls went out the window at midnight, June 30. Prices rose—veal cutlets shot up from fifty cents a pound to ninety-five, milk from sixteen cents a quart to twenty. Consumers rebelled, and Congress enacted a new bill, which Truman signed, but this bill was almost as flimsy as the first, and the hiatus in enforcement destroyed the price-control machinery. In disgust the president sat down at his desk and wrote out a speech he did not give:

[T]hese greedy industrialists and labor leaders who are now crying beef and bacon made no sacrifice, gave up nothing to win the war. These men received time and a half and assured profits and now they have convinced you, the people who are the government, that they should get the profits which we kept them from getting for the blood and sacrifice of the brave men who bared their breasts to the bullets; now [they] have your attention. You've deserted your President for a mess of pottage, a piece of beef—a side of bacon. . . . I can no longer enforce a law you won't support, botched and bungled by an unwilling Congress. You've gone over to the powers of selfishness and greed. Therefore I'm releasing the controls on meat and will proceed to release all other controls in an orderly manner as soon as I can.

To this draft speech he added a sentence of advice for himself: "Tell 'em what will happen and quit."[32]

For the consumer it was *sauve qui peut*. Prices rose 6 percent in July 1946, another 7 by November. On November 9 the president put the remnants of the inflation control program (save for sugar, rice, and rent) out of their misery. OPA became, in Porter's irreverent mind, the Office for Cessation of Rationing and Priorities, or OCRAP.

In the next two years, 1947–1948, prices rose another 25 percent. From June 1946 until they leveled off in December 1948, they rose from 132 (100 equals the 1935–1940 average) to 170.

The president's draft speech had mentioned greedy labor leaders, and this was another disheartening aspect of reconversion—that is, strikes. On New Year's Day 1946, 900,000 workers were out, led by the autoworkers, followed soon by 700,000 steelworkers. The year was to register 116,000,000 days of work lost to strikes, three times higher than ever before.[33] "Big money has too much power," the president wrote his mother and Mary Jane, "and so have big unions—both are riding to a fall because I like neither." He had to confess that it was all a bad business. "The steel people and General Motors I am sure would like to break the unions and the unions would like to break them so they probably will fight a while and then settle so both will lose and in the long run only the man in the street will pay the bill."[34]

The steel strike took a great deal of presidential attention. If steel breached the line of wage and price controls, other industries would follow. Hoping to avoid a strike, the president invited to the White House the leaders of the two sides, Benjamin Fairless, president of U.S. Steel, for management, and Philip Murray for the CIO. The sides were apart over a proposed increase of 4.5 cents an hour. He called each man, separately, into his office and said they must cut out the monkey business. On January 12, 1946, Murray postponed the strike a week. On Wednesday, January 16, Fairless and Murray were still talking, and the president said if there was no agreement the next day, Thursday, he would submit his own proposal, which as it turned out was to split the difference. On the eighteenth, Murray accepted splitting and Fairless did not; the administration released this information to the press, hoping it would put pressure on Fairless. A few days passed, with Fairless holding out. The president said privately it was a question of who was going to run the country, that if he did what he felt like "he'd blow 'em all out." The president of the steel corporation asked the other president to summon the heads of business to Washington for a conference. This was an impossible proposal, and it meant a strike. The other president said, albeit to his staff, that Fairless had given only the appearance of cooperation.[35]

After the steelworkers went out, both sides reduced their demands until only one cent separated them. Someone sent Truman a money order for one cent—to bring the sides together. Not long afterward the strike ended.

As if the president had nothing to do but settle strikes, the twenty railroad brotherhoods announced their workers would go out on May 18. Truman summoned their representatives and talked eighteen of them into an arbitration, but not the leaders of the trainmen and engineers, Alexander Whitney and Alvanley Johnston. Whitney had helped Truman years before in the Senate race of 1940, but he had forgotten all about that.

"If you think I'm going to sit here and let you tie up this whole country, you're crazy as hell," Truman told the two holdout leaders.

"We've got to go through with it, Mr. President," Whitney said. "Our men are demanding it."

"All right," said the president, "I'm going to give you the gun. You've got just forty-eight hours—until Thursday at this time—to reach a settlement. If you don't I'm going to take over the railroads in the name of the government."[36]

The deadline received an extension while the leaders dickered with the president. At one juncture Whitney and Johnston said "no." Steelman told them they could not say "no" to the president of the United States, that just was not done. They said, "No one pays any attention to him." Steelman told them, "You're going to."[37]

On Thursday, May 23, the unions went out, and the nation's railroads closed down. In those days when almost all intercity traffic, passenger and freight, was by rail, this meant economic disaster. Two days later, at 4:00 P.M., the president went before a joint session of Congress and asked authority to draft the strikers. While he was speaking, a slip of paper was handed up to him. "Gentlemen," he said, "the strike has been settled."[38]

While dealing with the railroad unions he was also negotiating with the head of the United Mine Workers, the redoubtable John L. Lewis. In those days coal drove nearly all locomotives and provided half of all industrial energy and two-thirds of all electric power. On May 21 the president signed an order seizing the nation's bituminous mines after a forty-day strike. The government offered concessions and ended the strike on May 29.

In October, just before the congressional elections, and even though the mines were still under government control, Lewis said miners would cancel their contract, meaning "no contract, no work." On October 23 the president told Ross that the night before he had Lewis on his mind and this time would "go to the mat." The miners again went out, albeit after the elections, and the government took an injunction that fined the union $3.5 million and Lewis personally $10,000. The union appealed to the Supreme Court. Truman was obdurate. "I believe everybody in the United States is interested in John L. Lewis and what is going to happen to him," he wrote Vivian's daughter, Martha Ann. "There is not very much that can be done to him but what little there is, we will try to do it." He refused to talk to Lewis, and he referred to him several times before staff members as "that son of a ——." He said that after the Supreme Court chastised the president of the mine workers "he might have Lewis come in and, he said, let him come as far as the door to his office. He said then he might have the two biggest secret service men there and let them boot Lewis out of the place." Lewis tried to get in touch with the president, but Truman was vacationing at the naval base at Key West and refused to take the call. He tried to get in touch with other administration figures. Then, according to Truman, he folded. The reason was "I had a fully loyal team and that team whipped a damned traitor."[39]

The victory over Lewis was too late for the congressional elections, however, and the administration lost badly. In the Lower House, Republican control was secure; it was less so in the Upper House, with three or four moderate GOP senators exercising a swing vote that in the next two years tended to turn in the president's direction. For much of this, to be sure, Truman could thank his woes with reconversion—the dropping of price controls, the brawling between management and labor. By early 1947 public opinion turned against labor. Anti-labor opinion was so widespread that Congress passed the Taft-Hartley Act over a presidential veto, outlawing industry-wide strikes, the closed shop, mass picketing; making unions liable to suits; requiring leaders to file noncommunist affidavits before taking issues to the National Labor Relations Board; setting up cooling-off periods before strikes; prohibiting use of union money for political contributions; giving the president power to obtain injunctions in strikes involving interstate commerce, public utilities, and communications.[40]

3

Foreign policy in the year and a half after Potsdam, down to 1947, did not prove more successful than domestic. This again was hardly the president's fault. War's end necessarily created loose ends in foreign affairs, and no president could have handled them. Truman also was up against the beginning of the cold war, a confusing situation that involved the unexpected irritability and even ferocity of Russian behavior.

Most negotiation in 1945–1946 concerned Eastern Europe—treaties with

Italy and Finland and the former satellites, Hungary, Romania, and Bulgaria. Beginning in 1946, a series of meetings took place in Paris with delegations from those countries, sessions known collectively as the Paris Peace Conference, although they little resembled the Paris Peace Conference of 1919. Secretary of State Byrnes spent much of that year in Paris to ensure that the new governments would be friendly to their neighbor, the Soviet Union, and yet maintain the rights and liberties of their citizens. In the end the Soviets allowed coalition governments of "democratic" parties and gradually subverted them in favor of local communist parties.

A generation afterward a scholarly dispute arose over whether American representatives at the Paris meetings made too much of the desire of American businessmen for an "open door" for commerce in the former German satellites, whether such insistence moved the Soviets to tighter control. Opponents argued that commerce with Eastern Europe never had been large; that President Truman seldom favored the "special interests"; that Henry Wallace himself said, "We cannot permit the door to be closed against our trade in Eastern Europe"; and that the issue was not between capitalism and socialism but between democracy and Stalinism, "between a Europe of independent states and a Europe whose force would be wielded by a single hand."[41]

In Germany hope was that the four allied powers—including France, which had received a zone created out of the American and British zones— would cooperate to carry out the Potsdam agreements. It failed primarily because of French intransigence.[42] In January 1947, the American and British governments created an economic union of their zones, "bizonia," in an effort to make the zones self-sufficient.

On one Soviet-American issue of the time, Russian application for a $6 billion reconstruction loan, made by Molotov in January 1945, the Truman administration, like its predecessor, did nothing, and for understandable reasons. The foreign minister tactfully explained that he was making this request as a favor to save the United States from a postwar depression. The amount of the proposed loan was so large it would have required taking the issue to Congress, which would have opened a debate on Soviet-American relations. Too, after the war Congress was in no mood to dole out money to foreign nations; in July 1946, it barely approved a $3.75 billion loan to Britain. Furthermore, the Soviets did not push the loan issue either at Yalta or at Potsdam. When Stalin raised the subject with Ambassador Harriman in January 1946, on the occasion of Harriman's departure from Moscow, it was almost too late, given the turndown in relations. By that time Soviet heavy-handed actions in Eastern Europe—pushing the weak governments around, letting it be known that Soviet occupation troops were present and might have to protect themselves by ensuring local order, intimating that coalition governments might not suffice for order—were raising large questions in Western capitals, especially in Washington. When Byrnes in April 1946 invited the Russians to discuss a loan, he joined the invitation with inquiries about Soviet policy toward Eastern Europe, and with those inquiries the loan issue lapsed.[43]

The president's part in diplomatic events of late 1945 and throughout 1946 is not easy to discern, and one has the feeling that it was mostly formal. In family letters he stressed busyness with domestic politics. On only a few occasions did he undertake personal contributions to foreign policy, and one of them was to sponsor former prime minister Churchill's "iron curtain" address of March 5, 1946, on the campus of Westminster College in Fulton, Missouri. The speech was an interesting effort on Churchill's part to raise American consciousness of Soviet troublemaking. Westminster was the alma mater of Truman's military aide, General Vaughan, who one day brought the college's president into the oval office; the college president desired to invite Churchill to Fulton to receive an honorary degree. Impulsively, Truman wrote a postscript to the letter: "Dear Winnie. This is a fine old college out in my state. If you'll come out and make them a speech, I'll take you out and introduce you." Churchill at that time was vacationing in Florida. He quickly accepted and came to Washington, where the president prepared to escort him via train to Missouri.[44]

The expedition to Missouri turned out to be an amusing affair. The train had scarcely gotten out of the Washington station before the two leading personalities, joined by Vaughan, the president's personal physician Dr. Graham, Clifford, Ross, and Churchill's Florida host, Colonel Frank Clarke, organized a study of probabilities. According to Dr. Graham, the distinguished guest inquired innocently, "What is this game called po-kah?" The president whispered to Graham, "We've got fresh meat here." Whereupon Churchill proceeded to take his opponents. (There was a variant story; according to Clifford, Churchill suggested the game and said he had been playing it since the Boer War, which caused the company to decide that American honor was at stake; he then played very poorly. At one point he excused himself and went to the men's room, and the Americans decided to be kind and let him win.) Upon arrival in Fulton the guest learned to his consternation that the town, being a college town, was dry. In the nick of time General Vaughan appeared in the guest's suite carrying a bottle, ice, a pitcher of water, and a glass. He was greeted warmly. "General, am I glad to see you," was the response. "I didn't know whether I was in Fulton, Missouri or Fulton, Sahara."

But the address embarrassed the president, who backed away from it. Churchill angered many Americans, who believed he had taken advantage of the president's presence to propose an alliance: "If the population of the English-speaking commonwealth be added to that of the United States, with all that such cooperation implies in the air, on the sea, and in science and industry, there will be no quivering, precarious balance of power to offer its temptation to ambition or adventure." Premier Stalin shortly afterward gave an interview to *Pravda* and excoriated the address:

In this respect, one is reminded remarkably of Hitler and his friends. Hitler began to set war loose by announcing his racial theory, declaring that only people speaking the German language represent a fully valuable nation. Mr. Churchill begins to set war loose also by a racial theory, maintaining that only nations speaking the English language are fully valuable nations, called upon to decide the destinies of the entire world.

The president beat a tactical retreat. Before the presidential party went out to Missouri, Churchill had asked Admiral Leahy to read the speech, and Leahy found nothing wrong with it. Secretary Byrnes visited the British embassy, read the speech, and prepared a summary for the president, who, unperturbed, told former ambassador Davies at a poker party that everything would be all right, that "all Churchill would say was the usual 'hands across the sea' stuff." On the way out Truman evidently saw the text. But when things turned serious he denied he had read the speech, which may have been technically true in that he had not read every word. Simultaneously, he sent word to Stalin that he would be glad to give him a similar opportunity to come and talk to the American people at the University of Missouri at Columbia.

About this time the president may have taken part in a quite different episode in international relations, which involved a decision by the Soviet Union to evacuate troops from the northern part of Iran. At the outset of World War II they had occupied the country along with the United States and Britain to ensure transit of supplies to Russia via the Persian Gulf. The arrangement with the Iranian government was that the powers would leave within six months after the war. When the Russians gave no sign of leaving on the date set for withdrawal by the London conference of foreign ministers, March 2, 1946, the Iranians, upon American prodding, took the issue to the United Nations. In later years Truman claimed that he then gave Stalin an ultimatum to get his troops out; the president said this several times, and he wrote about it in his memoirs ("I told Byrnes to send a blunt message to Premier Stalin"). No record of any such transaction, via cable or phone, has appeared, however, either in the White House files or in those of the state department. It is possible that Churchill's speech at Fulton persuaded the Russians, for if they had remained in Iran they would have become the menace Churchill said they were. In any event Byrnes went to the UN to seek to influence delegations, and one of his assistants wrote, "We fussed and we heckled, applied pressure where we could, and massed an overwhelming majority in the United Nations against the Soviet occupation. I think Joseph Stalin reached a saturation point where keeping his troops in Azerbaijan was not worth the cost in anti-Soviet propaganda."[45]

It was not an easy time, 1945–1946, and as if the troubles with the Russians were not enough for the president to worry about he found himself concerned about the abilities of his two secretaries of state—one of whom he quickly ridded himself of; the second seemed simpatico at the outset, even a welcome addition to the roster of his advisers, but as time passed he turned out to be far less attractive than he had seemed at first.

Truman began his presidency by arranging to get Stettinius out of the department, and this was the right thing to do. Roosevelt had placed Stettinius in the secretaryship so that he, Roosevelt, could run foreign affairs. Moreover, according to the law for succession to the presidency at that time, an Act of 1886, in absence of a vice president the succession devolved upon the heads of executive departments in order of establishment, and Stettinius was next in line. Getting him out was a bit tricky, for the secretary did not especially want to leave; he was concerned that his departure to the United Nations as first permanent U.S. representative would look like, as he told the president, a "kick in the pants." Perhaps with private amusement Truman told him it would not look that way. Whereupon Stettinius had another requirement, that he should have an office and secretary at the White House with White House stationery, and the president said, "Ed, I had already planned on it and thought about it, so why do you bring it up?"[46]

As for Byrnes's appointment, at the beginning it also seemed the right thing to do. Truman appreciated Byrnes's disappointment with the convention in Chicago in 1944—how narrowly Byrnes had missed the presidency— and told the reporter William Helm that this was the reason he appointed Byrnes.[47] To which he might have added other reasons, including Byrnes's prominence in national politics for many years, starting with his appearance in the House of Representatives in 1911. Moreover, Byrnes had been present at the Yalta Conference. He enjoyed power, and Truman did not, and the president needed someone who, unlike the slow-moving Cordell Hull or the incompetent Stettinius, would handle foreign problems, which necessarily involved power. He could get along with people like that, he thought: Byrnes would work under his direction. He of course recalled that after Roosevelt's death Byrnes had fawned over him; Truman's first attorney general, Biddle, acidly hostile, wrote that on the funeral train back from Hyde Park, Byrnes was inseparable from the president, as if he might lose him.[48] He may have enjoyed the fawning, as years earlier when a freshman senator he received none of it. Truman, in April 1945, overlooked all this as part of Byrnes's personality and part of the game of politics. It was necessary to get a successor to Stettinius and Byrnes was available; his nomination would pass the Senate with ease because of senatorial preference.

Over the next months it became clear that Byrnes was not a good replacement. He knew little more about foreign relations than Truman, and he was cocksure, secretive, and a poor administrator of a department that needed organization after twelve years under Hull. He made decisions after consulting a few friends, such as Donald S. Russell, also from South Carolina, who became assistant secretary; Benjamin V. Cohen, one of Roosevelt's brain trusters who became department counselor; James C. "Jimmy" Dunn, who became assistant secretary; and H. Freeman "Doc" Matthews, who headed the division of West European affairs. These were able men, it should be said. But Byrnes and his small group ignored the department, and as Truman discovered by the end of the year ignored him too—the secretary felt that he rather than Truman should have been president, and he looked upon his former fellow senator as an accident of history and not a very good accident at that. As Bob Nixon measured the relationship, "Byrnes' attitude seemed to be that Truman was a nonentity, with no abilities to speak of, no knowledge of how to conduct foreign policy, or much else for that matter."[49]

By early December, Truman could see that Byrnes was undercutting him and tried to bring him up short. His disillusionment with the South Carolinian had been noticeable even before the Potsdam Conference, when an old Missouri friend called at the White House and referred to the secretary by saying, "He's a smart man." The presidential answer was, "Too smart."[50] Relations may have improved when both men went to Potsdam, for on that occasion Byrnes had to keep Truman informed. But in the autumn, beginning with the London conference of foreign ministers, Byrnes's stock fell precipitously, for the secretary was taking no precautions. "God Almighty," he told one of his London assistants, Theodore Achilles, "I may tell the President sometime what happened."[51] By the time of the Moscow conference of foreign ministers in December, relations were close to a showdown. On December 5, Budget Director Smith came in to the oval office for a regular appointment, and the president treated him to an "outburst." Concerned about efficiency of government departments, the director had complained about sloppy administration in the state department, and Truman said he had urged Byrnes to do something about it and added "with some vehemence" that the department was probably worse off than ever.[52] With the conference a few days away Truman talked to former ambassador Davies and said he wanted Davies to talk to Byrnes, that he was fond of the secretary but Byrnes was a "conniver," and that he, the president, had to do some conniving himself "to get the boat steady." He wanted Davies to tell Byrnes about the need to send reports to let the president know what he was doing; he asked Davies to see Byrnes without fail before he went to Moscow. Davies saw Byrnes, and afterward the president, who inquired how the secretary reacted. Davies said he seemed to react favorably.[53]

Whatever Davies told Byrnes did not work because at the Moscow conference the secretary became reckless. Bohlen, who was present, realized that the delegation was not sending back regular reports as at other conferences and asked Byrnes why. In "sharp tones" the secretary said he knew when it was necessary to report and when not. "I was put in my place," Bohlen remembered, "and stayed there."[54] On December 11, Byrnes from Moscow released an explanation of U.S. economic policy toward Germany, supposedly for guidance of occupying authorities, "to make clear the American conception of the meaning of the Potsdam Declaration as it bears on present and impending economic issues in Germany." The president in his morning staff conference was annoyed, saying he did not think he should have to read the newspapers to get U.S. foreign policy—there ought to be some discussion with the man who had to approve it, namely, himself. A bit more than two weeks later occurred a serious Byrnes impropriety: the foreign ministers released a final communique dated December 27 containing a statement on recognition of the former satellite governments, and the president received a copy one hour after release. Visiting in Missouri, he wired Admiral Leahy asking what the admiral knew about it, and Leahy's impish response was the old Will Rogers remark, that all he knew was what he read in the papers.[55]

Byrnes got back from Moscow on Saturday, December 29, and there was a set-to. The president was on his yacht, the *Williamsburg*, on the Potomac below Washington at Quantico. Byrnes sent a message that he was going to make a radio speech the next evening and did not intend to see the president until afterward. Truman invited him down nominally to talk over the speech; they conferred for an hour or more, and the president remembered that Byrnes blamed the state department for not keeping him, the president, informed. Afterward at dinner Leahy needled Byrnes for his independent actions. But there was more to the encounter, for Assistant Press Secretary Ayers in Washington discovered that the original text of Byrnes's message to the president had been quite rude, and that the secret service agent who sent it toned it down. More important, he uncovered maneuvering in regard to the proposed radio broadcast. After Byrnes's hasty visit the president instructed Ross, who was aboard ship, to ask Ayers to see if the Columbia Broadcasting Company would carry the speech. Ross told Ayers that the National Broadcasting Company was going to carry it. Ayers checked with National and found its commitment was for exclusive coverage and that the state department had made the arrangement either immediately after Byrnes's arrival in Washington from Moscow or before. National said that if other networks carried the broadcast it would withdraw. He also learned that the secretary of state was "putting the heat" on the other networks through the Federal Communications Commission, which awarded station licenses; its chairman was calling them, asking them to carry the speech, and saying he was speaking for the president.[56]

After the visit to the yacht Byrnes returned to Washington, came back down to the ship for a New Year's Eve celebration, and then, on January 5, 1946, the president saw the secretary in the oval office. What happened is unclear, although it does seem that the president again rebuked the secretary. Ever afterward Truman claimed to have read him a handwritten letter that criticized Byrnes's position at Moscow and ended with the sentence, "I'm tired babying the Soviets." The text of the letter first appeared in a book published with the president's approval by the radio reporter William Hillman in 1952. Furious, Byrnes—who long since had resigned and returned to South Carolina, broken with the president over domestic policy, and become governor of his state—published an article in *Collier's* declaring that if the president had read such a letter to him he would have resigned.[57] For whatever reason, throughout 1946, until his resignation in January 1947, the secretary was much more careful.

Harry S. Truman taking the oath of office at the White House after the death of President Franklin D. Roosevelt, April 12, 1945. (National Park Service, Abbie Rowe)

Truman in the Rose Garden with General Dwight D. and Mamie Eisenhower, June 1945. (National Park Service, Abbie Rowe)

*Winston Churchill,
Harry S. Truman,.and
Joseph Stalin at the
Potsdam Conference,
July 24, 1945. (U.S.
Army Signal Corps)*

*The president with his
mother and sister in
Grandview, circa 1946.*

The president at the Lincoln Memorial, addressing the thirty-eighth annual conference of the National Association for the Advancement of Colored People, June 29, 1947. (National Park Service, Abbie Rowe)

General George C. Marshall, as secretary of state, leaving for the London conference of foreign ministers, November 20, 1947. (National Park Service, Abbie Rowe)

The beginning and the end of the 1948 campaign for election. (National Park Service, Abbie Rowe [on train])

President Truman greets forty cartoonists at the White House, October 3, 1949. (National Park Service, Abbie Rowe)

Truman with General Douglas MacArthur at the Wake Island Conference, October 15, 1950. At right rear, General Wallace Graham. (Department of State)

With Secretary of State Dean Acheson, December 21, 1950. (National Park Service, Abbie Rowe)

Chapter Twelve

A New Foreign Policy

*T*he principal accomplishment of Harry S. Truman during his nearly eight years in the presidency was to change the foreign policy of the United States, from abstention to participation in the affairs of Europe and the world. To say such a thing after decades of participation seems almost pretentious. As Americans of the present day look back on their country's history, they see not only the nation's incessant moves of policy since Truman's time but also the two world wars of our century. In their minds' eyes they equate the world wars with participation, and in a kind of lapse of thought they are willing to affirm that their government and its citizenry have devoted the entire twentieth century to contemplating and if necessary resolving the confusions and conflicts—what President George Washington in his farewell address described as the combinations and collisions—of powers outside the Western Hemisphere.

Still, the truth is that until 1947, in the midst of Truman's first term, the principal American way with foreign policy was that of Presidents Washington, Jefferson, and Monroe: the old-time view that there was a New World and an Old World; that Almighty God had sifted the choice grain and sent it to the New; and that the interests of humankind—survival of the choice grain—lay in nonintervention in, abstention from, the affairs of the Old. Americans of this earlier time deemed participation in the world wars a temporary proposition. For them, World War I was a matter of "paying the debt to Lafayette." Although President Wilson desired the country to enter the League of Nations, popular support for such an arrangement lasted a very short time, and, as everyone knows, Wilson lost out with the Senate, and his proposed Democratic successor, Governor James M. Cox of Ohio, lost out with the American people. Similarly, after World War II few Americans expected the nation to continue its commitments abroad. President Roosevelt told Stalin at Yalta he did not expect American troops to remain in Europe more than two years.

This outlook came to an end during the Truman administration. The president of that time presided over the change. And more, he guided the change through the toils of political opposition and popular confusion. He did not always do right. In the Truman Doctrine he overstated the need to oppose the Soviet Union to get a large appropriation for Greece and Turkey through Congress, and he persuaded some Americans to consider the USSR a sort of bogey rather than another, if large and important, opponent in the long series of nations that have disliked the United States and sought its discomfiture. Such exaggeration led to the belief that the United States committed itself to oppose communism everywhere. In the Marshall Plan the administration may have thought too much of its assistance to European stability, which for Western Europe was only 10 or 20 percent of aggregate capital formation.[1] The plan's cost was no burden, considering America's economic domination of the world: in the late 1940s the United States possessed half of the world's productive capacity. In the case of the North Atlantic Treaty the administration misestimated the intentions of the Soviet Union, espying a Soviet desire to conquer Western Europe. Still, there were extenuating circumstances for such miscalculation. Taken altogether the achievement from March 1947 to April 1949 was very large.[2]

1

The first move was the Truman Doctrine, a statement of American purpose announced by the president in a speech before Congress on March 12, 1947. A logical procession of moves ensued—the doctrinal statement preceding the economic and military programs—although at the moment the administration did not see matters developing in this clear, careful manner.

The origins of the Truman Doctrine lay in immediate postwar relations with the Soviet Union, in which the current ruler of the USSR chose to reject friendship with the United States and substitute what he had known within Russia since his youth, manipulation and pressure. This course, he must have hoped, would bring the rewards in foreign policy it had produced in domestic affairs. But even while ending coalition governments in Eastern Europe, turning them into communist governments, actions that the Western nations could have considered a legacy of the war, the Soviets began to close off Western influence in Iran, Turkey, and Greece. Simultaneously with refusal to evacuate the northern provinces of Iran had come what both the Turkish and American governments assumed was an attack on Turkish independence: demands to change the Montreux Convention governing the straits into a joint military occupation and for cession of border territories lost after World War I. The Turkish government was vulnerable to this sort of pressure. Turkey had a population of 19 million, an army of five hundred thousand, and a long border with the USSR. The Soviets apparently were attempting to bring the country into the same relationship as they had managed with Poland. All the while the situation in Greece was turning serious. The government that the British army installed in Athens in 1944–1945 went from bad to worse, using its budget for the army and police, inflating the currency, failing to deal with an insurgency on its borders. Despite a pledge to Churchill that the West would have a 90 percent influence in Greece, Stalin encouraged the insurgent leader, General Markos Vafiades, to offer border concessions to Yugoslavia, Albania, and Bulgaria, in return for military assistance ("giving them what they wanted at our expense, so that we might get what we needed to achieve power").[3]

The movement toward a new American policy for Europe gained momentum in the first full year of peace, 1946, with two full-dress analyses of Soviet-American relations. The initial review was George F. Kennan's "long telegram" from Moscow on February 1946, an eight-thousand-word account of Russian policy. The state department had asked for the cable, though doubtless it had no idea Kennan, who was chargé d'affaires, would send such a long explanation. In arousing government officials its importance was undoubted—it came to the attention of Secretary of the Navy Forrestal, who sent copies to friends, and Washington officials began to sense a historical dimension to Soviet behavior. Its influence upon President Truman was less clear. Years later, when Kennan had become well known both as a diplomat and as an author of books and articles, including the "X" article in the journal *Foreign Affairs* in the summer of 1947 that set out the idea of "containment" of the Soviet Union, the diplomat-historian said wistfully that he was not sure Truman had known who he was, even though he briefed the president. "I met with [Truman] once or twice during this period. . . . I suspect he was vaguely aware that there was a young fellow over in the State Department who had written a good piece on the Russians—I doubt whether Truman ever really read anything I wrote, though. Certainly I don't think he grasped my position." The president does not seem to have read the long telegram, nor perhaps ever heard of it.[4]

In September of the same year George Elsey of the White House staff produced a second, somewhat similar, statement of U.S.-Soviet problems, to which after a few emendations the president's special counsel, Clifford, put his own name. Based on information gathered throughout the government, including the long telegram, it was a much more authoritative commentary. Printed and bound in book form, as nicely written as Kennan's essay, it was an impressive seventy-nine pages, offering chapters on agreements with the Soviets, violations, reparations, and Soviet actions affecting American security. The first sentence of its first page established the theme: "The gravest problem facing the United States today is that of American relations with the Soviet Union." Negotiation, it predicted, would not get far: "The general pattern of the Soviet system is too firmly established to be altered suddenly by any individual—even Stalin." That Americans could persuade the Soviets to "change the character of their philosophy and society" appeared highly improbable. The United States needed to stand up to the Soviet Union by assisting friendly governments wherever possible.[5]

Truman's first reaction to the Clifford-Elsey report was to call in all twenty numbered copies and put them under lock and key. The morning after reading it he told Clifford to bring them to him. He may have noticed two indiscreet statements. One was on the Middle East, "an area of great strategic interest to the Soviet Union because of the shift of Soviet industry to southeastern Russia, within range of air attack from much of the Near East." This might have encouraged the U.S. Army Air Forces, about to become independent in the Defense Act of the next year, to open a campaign to station bombers in the Middle East. The other was a flat-out remark that "to maintain our strength at a level which will be effective in restraining the Soviet Union, the United States must be prepared to wage atomic and biological warfare."[6] In any event it was dangerous to put America's Russian policy between two covers, easily available perhaps to some supporter of Henry Wallace, not to mention a Russian spy.

How seriously the president otherwise took the report is difficult to say. He was still unwilling to come out against the Soviet Union. The report was dated September 24; three days earlier he had written former vice president of the United States John Garner that "there is too much loose talk about the Russian situation. We are not going to have any shooting trouble with them but they are tough bargainers and always ask for the whole earth, expecting maybe to get an acre." Some months afterward he wrote his daughter that he had required a year and a half after Potsdam to change his mind about the Soviets. Until the time of the Truman Doctrine he clearly continued to think things over, to see what he could do.[7]

In considering how the president made up his mind about the Soviet Union and prepared himself for his doctrine, evidence other than these two reports lies in two statements he himself drew up, one at the beginning of 1946, the other a year later. The letter to Byrnes of January 5, 1946, related not only how Byrnes should keep the president informed but also what he, Truman, thought about Soviet-American relations. Russian behavior in Iran, he told himself in the letter and perhaps said to Byrnes, was "parallel to the program of Russia in Latvia, Estonia and Lithuania." It was in line with Russia's "highhanded and arbitrary" actions in Poland. At Potsdam the Soviets had faced him down with an accomplished fact in regard to Poland, almost forcing him to agree to Russian occupation of eastern Poland and occupation by the Poles of the area between the Eastern and Western Neisse rivers. At that time the United States had been anxious for Russian entry into the Far Eastern war, and "[o]f course we found later that we didn't need Russia there and the Russians have been a headache to us ever since." The United States, he wrote, should refuse to recognize the governments of Romania and Bulgaria until those regimes complied with the Yalta Declaration on Eastern Europe. The United States should insist on internationalization of Europe's waterways. In the Pacific it should maintain complete control of Japan and the island groups captured in the Pacific war. "We should rehabilitate China and create a strong central government there. We should do the same for Korea." The United States should also force return of lend-lease ships given Russia, and indeed of the entire lend-lease debt. "There isn't a doubt in my mind that Russia intends an invasion of Turkey and the seizure of the Black Sea Straits to the Mediterranean. Unless Russia is faced with an iron fist and strong language another war is in the making. Only one language do they understand—'How many divisions have you?'"[8]

The beginning of the new year, 1947, brought a similar statement. By this time he was writing that he would not allow the Soviet regime to "bulldoze" the United States. He made a list of things to do:

1. Present Russian ambassador to U.S.A. persona non grata, a stable boy who ought to stay in a stable. Does not belong in Washington.
2. Urge Stalin to pay us a visit. We'll send the battleship *Missouri* for him if he'll come, either to Odessa or Leningrad and bring his guard.
3. Settle Korean question on the basis of Moscow agreement [of December 1945] or better, give Koreas a government of their own.
4. Settle the Manchurian question [the Communist Chinese were in occupation, supported by the Soviets] on the basis of the Sino-Russian treaty and support Chiang Kai-shek for a strong China.
5. Agree to a discussion of Russia's lend-lease debt to the United States. Vital.
6. Agree to a commercial air treaty on a reciprocal basis.
7. Make it plain that we have no territorial ambitions. That we only want peace, but we'll fight for it!

The projects varied in importance, but point seven was a good summary. The president thereupon explained himself in a little essay:

The smart boys, columnists, radio commentators etc. wonder why Russia is more amenable to reason now than a year ago. None of them have thought to say either in print or over the air that perhaps someone sent them word that an agreement could be made on a peaceable basis if they wanted it. But if a peaceable basis was not what Russia wanted the U.S.A. would meet them on any other basis. The president stated at the meeting in Berlin in July, 1945, that a free Danube is necessary to Central European peace and Central European economy. That Trieste should be a free port for all Central Europe. That the Dardanelles, Kiel Canal, and the Rhine-Danube waterway should all be free on the same basis to all nations. That Manchuria should be Chinese, that Dairen should be a free port, that Russia should have Kuriles and Sakhalin, that we would control in Japan and the Pacific. That Germany should be occupied as an economic whole by the four powers agreed upon at Yalta; that Austria should not be treated as an enemy country. All agreed to by Russia.

But they'd unlawfully attached part of East Prussia and Germany as far west as the Oder to Poland, and had themselves annexed Latvia, Estonia, Lithuania, and a part of East Prussia to Russia, as well as a large area in eastern Poland.

I told Mr. Byrnes just one year ago that we'd stand for justice and would not be bulldozed. We've pursued that policy and they've caved in just as Lewis did in the coal strike. Because they are the same sort of cattle—bullies and nothing else. We only want justice and a just peace. That we'll have and that we'll get. There is no difference in totalitarian states, call them Nazi, fascist or communist—they are all the same. The present dictatorship in Russia is as terrible as the czar's ever was.[9]

By early 1947 the president was on the verge of making up his mind. The process, however, had been much slower than people then or later believed. It took, in fact, a year and a half after the end of the war before he was willing to move against the USSR.

A public pronouncement was occasioned by the British government's communication to the state department late in February 1947 that it no longer could support the governments of Greece and Turkey. The Truman administration would have to take up the burden, else those countries would pass behind the iron curtain.

There followed a quick series of actions. The cabinet gave immediate approval.[10] The president called a meeting to inform congressional leaders of the need for money, a $400 million appropriation. During the White House session Secretary Marshall made an uncharacteristically muddled presentation—he was usually first-rate when speaking extempore and could summon historical precedents and put matters in perspective. Undersecretary Acheson interrupted his chief and redirected Marshall's statement in more forceful, so Acheson later said, terms. Acheson may have erred here, as he seems to have called up the Russian menace. Allegedly—the point has never had proof—Senator Vandenberg told the president that the best course with Congress was to "scare hell out of the country."[11] The subsequent speech was carefully put together. When the state department speechwriter, Joseph M. Jones, asked Acheson for general guidance on the speech—how far the proposed assistance should go—Acheson gazed out the window of his office, toward the Washington Monument, and said he thought he knew what Roosevelt would have done in such a situation. FDR would have made a pronouncement covering the world, but asked for an appropriation for Greece and Turkey.[12] When Jones's speech went over to the White House, Elsey seized it and chopped its sentences to make it read better and also accord with the president's pithy style.[13] He may have made it a little more scary.

Even so, congressional opposition proved considerable. One of the arguments was that the Greek government was undemocratic and corrupt, which was true, and that Turkey was not a democracy and had been neutral during most of the recent war, also true. Another assertion was that the aid proposal bypassed the United Nations. To such critics, administration spokesmen could only say that while Greece and Turkey were hardly ideal governments, they were capable of improvement. The original bill gave the UN little attention, perhaps because of Acheson's almost violent feelings against the world organization. It was at about this time that he told Dean Rusk the UN was a monkey house.[14] Vandenberg, however, insisted on public obeisances, which the administration made.

Another congressional argument against aid was that the president's request for funds gave no attention to communism outside Western Europe. Representative Walter H. Judd of Wisconsin, a former medical missionary to China, asked why the United States was opposing Soviet machinations in Greece and Turkey and doing little or nothing for China, which was then in civil war. To this point Acheson offered a weak answer, although it made sense. He said that the United States was trying to use its power where it could; to intervene in Greece and Turkey was one thing, but China was something else. Its size and population were in no way comparable to those of Greece and Turkey: "There have been various statements in the press that this was an ideological crusade. That is not what the president is talking about. He is talking about the fact that where a free world is being coerced to give up its free institutions, we are interested. . . . He did not state, and I think no one would state, that that means wherever this situation occurs, one must react to it in exactly the same way."[15]

The bill for aid to Greece and Turkey passed the Senate by vote of 67 to 23 (April 23), the House by 287 to 107 (May 9), and the president signed it on May 15. To a draft of a press release accompanying his signature Truman added a gentle apostrophe: "We are guardians of a great faith. We believe that freedom offers the best chance of peace and prosperity for all, and our desire for peace cannot be separated from our belief in liberty. We hope that in the years ahead more and more nations will come to know the advantages of freedom and liberty. It is to this end that we have enacted the law I have now signed."[16] For some reason the release did not include this statement.

Such was the first, and in some respects the most important, of Truman's moves in foreign policy that took the country away from its isolationist ways. In passing let it be said again, as Acheson told the speechwriter Jones, and later tried to tell Congressman Judd, that the Truman Doctrine, as it came to be called, was not a doctrine that covered the world. In subsequent years critics of the actions of Truman and his successors made many points on this theme. One of their explanations concerned the way in which Acheson had spoken in the meeting with the congressional leaders, perhaps overstating the dangers of Soviet communism. When the Korean War opened, and especially during the Vietnam War, critics blamed involvement on the Truman Doctrine. Without the doctrine, they said, the United States might have minded its own business. They raised up a host of presidential statements about communism, offered in the 1950s and 1960s by Truman's successors, Republican and Democratic alike, and connected them with the doctrine and drew their awkward conclusion. But there was much evidence to the contrary. As John Lewis Gaddis put it later, "Subservience to Moscow made one a target of containment, not adherence to the doctrines of Marx and Lenin."[17] This had become evident after the defection of Yugoslavia from the Soviet bloc in 1948, which brought aid despite that country's communist government. Truman was trying to restore the European balance of power and had neither the intention nor the capability of policing the world.

2

The next move, underway within weeks of announcement of the Truman Doctrine, was the European Recovery Act, to which the president attached the name of his secretary of state.

General Marshall deserved a good deal of the credit for the plan's success, because his personal prestige carried it forward. It is difficult to explain to another generation how the personality of Marshall so impressed leaders of his time. The American military felt that his military leadership had ensured victory—save for the irrepressible MacArthur, American generals revered him. Civil leaders held him in similar high regard. Acheson was accustomed to meeting people who considered themselves great, such as Franklin Roosevelt, whom he heartily disliked ("admiration without affection"), but he held a veneration for Marshall above that for the "great captain with the noble heart," Truman, to whom he dedicated his memoirs; in 1969, when Truman yet was living, Acheson said Marshall was the greatest man he ever knew.[18] Bohlen, who was a sophisticate like Acheson and had also known Roosevelt, made the same judgment; writing his memoirs while dying of cancer, he had no reason to say anything other than what he believed, and his description of how Marshall came into the state department and galvanized the place—how after the preceding secretaries, with their inadequacies, Marshall produced order—was almost emotional.[19] The president on his part told anyone who asked, and many who did not, that Marshall was "the great one" of his years of public office. During World War II he had described the general as the "greatest living American," this when Roosevelt was alive; it was enough to have lost him the vice-presidential nomination.[20] When he became president he soon was mentioning Marshall for every possible office in government, to a point where his assistants thought him slightly touched. It is true that when he sent Marshall to China as ambassador in December 1945 he did it partly to take attention from the resignation of Patrick J. Hurley, a likable conservative who resigned in a huff because, Hurley said, China policy contained glaring inconsistencies and the state department's China desk was full of communists. But the China problem was a difficult one, and the president needed sound judgment: Marshall fit that requirement.

What with the general's prestige it was natural that Truman would appoint him secretary of state. When the general left the country for China, he heard the president say that when the secretaryship became vacant (Truman was out of sorts with Byrnes at precisely that moment) he wanted Marshall for the post. In response Marshall said he would do "any damn thing you want me to do."[21] With embarrassment Acheson became privy to a secret his own then chief, Byrnes, did not know—in Marshall's phrase, during the China mission Acheson was his "rear echelon." In December 1946, when Byrnes submitted his resignation after the Paris Peace Conference, the president told him who his successor would be.

The appointment was a success in every way. For one thing it did not take Marshall long to seize control of the department. He told Acheson to straighten out the "chain of command," a task that Acheson undertook with a vengeance. Then, even more important, Marshall began looking into the primary need of foreign policy at the time (the general had had plenty of experience in getting to the center of things), Europe's economic plight. After the hard, cold winter of 1946–1947, Europe was in straits. The winter wheat had died in the ground. Coal production was so low in Britain that electricity was available in London only a few hours a day, and Europe's industry slowed markedly because of lack of coal. Affairs were especially bad in Germany, where in the Western zones industrial production was 27 percent of prewar levels. In 1936, Germany had produced 85 percent of its food; in 1947 the figure was 25 percent. The United Nations Relief and Rehabilitation Administration was coming to an end on March 31, 1947.

Gradually the possibilities for policy in Western Europe began to appear. Congress was in no mood for more emergency plans; everywhere the idea of long-range planning was in the air. But Marshall wanted action. He had just come back from forty-four sessions of a foreign ministers' conference in Moscow in the spring of 1947, the purpose of which was to consider peace treaties for Germany and Austria, but the conference had accomplished little and gave the impression it was tying up the time of Western foreign ministers while Europe's economy plunged. The secretary kept saying to callers and department officials, "Nobody will believe me." He asked the policy planning staff, a new group under Kennan, to draw up a memorandum, some sort of plan or suggestions. Then the undersecretary for economic affairs, William L. Clayton, who in private life was head of the world's largest cotton merchant firm, Anderson, Clayton and Company, returned from Europe and gave him a memorandum pointing out that Europe did not have the dollars to prime its economic pump. The memorandum became the basis for the Marshall Plan.[22]

It is well known how department officials arranged for Marshall to propose such a plan during a talk at the Harvard commencement on June 5. Truman had little to do with the proposal. Years later Marshall told his biographer, Forrest Pogue, that the arrangements for the speech were so hurried he did not tell the president and later apologized for the failure. After all, though, Truman had approved the whole idea of aid in his speech in March, so nothing was lost.[23] In the talk itself, and subsequent meetings of European leaders, the plan took shape. At the advice of assistants the secretary placed a string in the proposition, that the Europeans must themselves draw up a plan; there could be no more shopping lists. He offered the proposal to all nations "west of the Urals," including the Soviet Union and East European satellites. The British, French, and Russian foreign ministers met in Paris early in June. Molotov refused to take part in a joint proposal, the British and French invited the other nations, the Soviets refused satellite participation, and in September a second Paris conference drew up a plan. Two months later Truman asked Congress for interim aid, telling Leahy privately that his address to a joint session could hurt his administration and party but he was right and could not fail to act. In December the president asked for a first installment of what, when the Marshall Plan ended in 1952, became a $13 billion program. In March 1948 large bipartisan majorities in both Houses appropriated the installment, and Truman on April 3 signed the Recovery Act.

But to relate how the Marshall Plan became reality is hardly to account for the president's part in making the plan possible. He managed it with what a political scientist later ascribed to his successor, Eisenhower, as a "hidden hand."[24] By bringing Marshall into the state department he obtained the reorganization he so wanted. Under Stettinius and Byrnes the department had no chance; its officers were on the outside looking in. Now they took part. Then when the time came to announce a plan Truman credited Marshall— another calculation, for he knew his prestige as president was too fragile to take credit. Clifford had suggested that the president name the program the Truman Concept or the Truman Plan. "No," said the chief executive. "We have a Republican majority in both Houses. Anything going up there bearing my name will quiver a couple of times, turn belly up, and die. Let me think about it a little." A day or two later the president made his decision: "I've decided to give the whole thing to General Marshall. The worst Republican on the Hill can vote for it if we name it after the General."[25]

Last, realizing that any such program needed grassroots support, he did the same thing with it that he had done during the war with his investigating committee; namely, he brought public opinion behind it. He presided over one of the most calculated managements of a program ever to come before Congress. At the outset not everything had been harmonious. Senator Robert A. Taft, Republican of Ohio, said the plan was a Tennessee Valley Authority for Europe, "global New Dealism." Senator Homer Ferguson, Republican of Michigan, beheld a universal Works Progress Administration (Republicans enjoyed comparisons with the New Deal). Former president Hoover favored $4 billion, presumably because the sum was smaller, spread over fifteen months; $3 billion, he said, should be for his favorite foreign program during and after World War I: food. Henry Wallace spoke of a "Martial Plan." Lippmann mildly favored the plan—it was not in opposition to the Soviet Union as was the Truman Doctrine, which he opposed; it avoided globalism; it did not treat nations as "instruments" of American policy but as independent countries; it allowed Europeans to save themselves—but he thought a better course would be for the United States and USSR to leave Europe. Even so, the president knew how to handle such complaints. Henry Stimson, the eighty-year-old, rock-ribbed Republican, chaired the Committee for the Marshall Plan to Aid European Recovery, which enlisted foreign policy associations, church groups, women's clubs, labor unions, chambers of commerce, and the innumerable groups of the knife-and-fork circuit—Rotary, Kiwanis, Lions. In speeches and addresses during the summer, autumn, and early winter of 1947–1948, prior to passage of the first installment of the program, the administration struck a popular chord, with arpeggios of flattery. "Historical records clearly show," Marshall said, "that no people have ever acted more generously and more unselfishly than the American people in tendering assistance to alleviate distress and suffering." And again: "Whether we like it or not, we find ourselves, our nation, in a world position of vast responsibility. We can act for our own good by acting for the world's good."[26]

When the plan came before Congress the Soviet Union helped its passage by conducting a coup in Czechoslovakia, which "sent a shock throughout the civilized world." Everyone thought of Hitler's takeover of Czechoslovakia in 1939. A near crisis atmosphere prevailed when Congress passed the initial appropriation.[27]

It is not easy to assess the result of the plan, save that Europe recovered. During the plan years local resources accounted for most capital formation and the American contribution was marginal—even though the plan's Washington administrator, the Republican industrialist Paul G. Hoffman, said the plan provided the critical margin. Moreover, and despite the infusion of dollars from the plan, there were clear signs that Europe's economy was faltering in 1949, and it may have taken the Korean War, with its offshore orders from the United States, to provide a "takeoff" for the continent's economy, to use the word of Walt W. Rostow. Too, the worst-off economy in Europe was that of the West German zones, and it looked as if the purpose of the plan was to invigorate the former enemy. The late John Gimbel wrote that the real purpose of Marshall and his assistants, which they had to disguise, was to restore German productivity so Germany again could be the powerhouse of Europe; it was necessary to put the German problem in a European context.[28] (That explanation, of course, is too easy. American officials were gingerly about bolstering Germany's economy. Truman told Forrestal that while he did not believe in the plan of former secretary of the treasury Morgenthau to "pastoralize" Germany, neither did he want Germany rebuilt.)[29] But the end result, and one likes to think it was because of the president's program, was beyond question. At the end of two and a half years, industrial output had increased 40 percent above prewar levels and agricultural 20 percent. The plan constituted a second move after the doctrine (the policies, the president later wrote, with resort to Missouri metaphor, were "two halves of the same walnut"). It helped prevent what had seemed the imminent collapse of Western Europe's economy, provided time in which to work for better relations with the Soviet Union, and marked a notable chapter in acceptance by the American people of what would be the nation's new foreign policy for the foreseeable future.

3

The reasoning that took the administration into a multilateral military alliance was more complicated than the origins of the Truman Doctrine and Marshall Plan. It included the continuing troubles in Greece, where despite the Truman Doctrine and its economic and military assistance the insurgents seemed on the verge of winning until 1949. In France and Italy communist parties left the coalition governments, and an election in Italy in April 1948 appeared touch-and-go over whether the Western-backed government would survive. The Italian premier refused an offer of a shipment of arms, for fear the weapons might be turned against the regime that accepted them. In Scandinavia that dismal spring the Soviets were putting pressure on Finland to sign a mutual-assistance pact and pressing the Norwegians for a similar treaty; they did not press the Swedes because the Swedes had an army. To the above prospects was added the coup in Czechoslovakia.

A series of Russian acts in Berlin put fear into Western leaders. On March 5, 1948, the American commander in Germany, General Lucius D. Clay, cabled that for the first time he felt war was possible and that it might come with dramatic suddenness. To a state department memorandum of the same date, on the same subject, the president appended a handwritten note to himself listing trouble spots abroad, beginning with Greece and Turkey, and asking, "Shall we state the case to the Congress, name names and call the turn? Will Russia move first? Who pulls the trigger?"[30] Not long afterward the Soviets cut off land and rail access to the Western sectors in Berlin, and on June 24 they instituted a total land blockade. The next day, June 25, acting on his own, Clay began an airlift. The day afterward the president backed him up.

In the beginning of the Berlin blockade hardly anyone thought an airlift would work, and Truman found himself having to stiffen his advisers, military and civil, most of whom wanted to give up the Western position in the city, deep within the Russian zone. Clay had little faith in the airlift; to a German reporter he said, snapping his fingers, "I wouldn't give you that for our chances." Forrestal, by this time secretary of defense, whose increasingly erratic behavior would bring his resignation and suicide the next year, wanted to abandon Berlin and found support from Secretary of the Army Kenneth C. Royall and Undersecretary William H. Draper, Jr. On July 19 the president had it out in a meeting in the cabinet room:

> Have quite a day. . . . A meeting with General Marshall and Jim Forrestal on Berlin and the Russian situation. Marshall states the facts and the condition with which we are faced. I'd made the decision ten days ago to *stay in Berlin*. Jim wants to hedge—he always does. He's constantly sending me alibi memos which I return with directions and the facts. We'll stay in Berlin—come what may. Royall, Draper and Jim Forrestal come in later. I have to listen to a rehash of what I know already and reiterate my "Stay in Berlin" decision.

Disgustedly he added, "I don't pass the buck, nor do I alibi out of any decision I make." Clay and Ambassador-at-large Robert D. Murphy, summoned to present their views, both wanted the army to push through a convoy from the nearest Western locality, Helmstedt. At the meeting Truman was ready to support a convoy. He said he would sign an order if those present gave it to him. Only Clay and Murphy favored it; the military and Marshall thought U.S. forces too weak.[31]

Having stiffened everyone, it should be added, the president avoided an extreme position. He was not absolutely committed to what he told Forrestal and his other advisers on June 28, that "we were going to stay period." According to a memorandum written later that day by Secretary Royall, he went on to say that his decision was "tentative," that he could make "no black or white decision now," that he would deal with the situation as it developed. The next day he told Leahy he meant to stay "as long as possible," and two days later Leahy informed a Pentagon group a stay would not be until it "would start a war." The president's diary account of the meeting on July 19 seemed clear enough, but it was in fact too clear: at the conference that day he had listened to Harriman, who pushed him hard to "take hold of the crisis," and his diary reaction was more to that point than what he said at the meeting; at the latter he had refused to make a public address, which "might unnecessarily disturb the present delicate international situation." He said to Forrestal the same day, "Our policy would remain fixed . . . until all diplomatic means had been exhausted," after which presumably it might come unfixed. Despite his diary statement, "come what may," he left a way out; staying meant "short of war."[32]

In mid-September occurred another scare. On September 13 the president made a diary entry that has caught the attention of students ever since it appeared in Hillman's book in 1952: "Have a terrific day. Forrestal, Bradley, Vandenberg (the Gen., not the Senator!), Symington brief me on bases, bombs, Moscow, Leningrad, etc. I have a terrible feeling afterward that we are very close to war. I hope not. See Marshall at lunch and feel better although Berlin is a mess." Omar Bradley was army chief of staff, having succeeded Eisenhower; Hoyt S. Vandenberg was chief of staff of the air force; and W. Stuart Symington secretary of the air force. That same day the chairman of the Atomic Energy Commission, David E. Lilienthal, wrote in similar fashion after a conversation with the then director of the Bureau of the Budget, James E. Webb, who evidently had just seen the president:

> Jim Webb came to see me today. The situation in Berlin is bad, he reports. The Russians seem prepared to kick us in the teeth on every issue. Their planes are in the air corridor today, and anything could happen. "Anything—they might walk in tomorrow and shoot Gen. Clay." The President is being pushed hard by Forrestal to decide that atomic bombs will be used, but the National Security Council, Jim has reason to believe, will advise the President that there is no occasion to decide that question right now. "The President has always been optimistic about peace. But he is blue now, mighty blue. It is very hard on him, coming right now particularly."[33]

What could the president do under the circumstances? In the case of the blockade, as weeks passed the air force gathered planes from the Far East and everywhere else, the British sent planes, and the airlift became the way out. Capacity increased and everyone gained confidence. The air force brought in larger planes, increasing loads from two and one-half tons of food and coal to ten; it proved possible to create a new landing field in Berlin; the air force trained pilots in Montana in landing procedures in the city: by October deliveries were averaging close to five thousand tons a day. During one twenty-four-hour period, April 15–16, 1949, Allied planes in 1,398 flights landed a record 12,941 tons. That day planes came in almost every minute, a magnificent show; everyone could see planes coming over—"[T]he roar of the airplanes became the recurring motif of the resistance and the pulsation of the life in the besieged city." Altogether, in 277,804 flights the airlift delivered 2,325,809 tons, more than a ton apiece for 2,250,000 Berliners in the Western zones. Rations of West Berliners actually rose. In disgust the Soviets called off the blockade under a pretext of gaining Western consent for a foreign ministers' meeting in Paris in April 1949.

As for a more general solution to Soviet-American relations, throughout much of 1948 the president cast about for a device or tactic or procedure to keep the Russians under control. When Eleanor Roosevelt wrote wondering what to do, he responded, "We have been blocked at every point by the Russians and to some extent by the French. The Russians have not carried out the agreements entered into at Potsdam." They were waiting for the United States to go into a depression. Though it seemed ridiculous, they thought Wallace was going to win the 1948 election. He told her he was going before Congress the next day to "state the facts," that the Marshall Plan and "the proper strengthening of our military setup" constituted the only hope for peace. At the end of his letter he made a remarkable estimate: "It is the most serious situation we have faced since 1939." He said he would face it with everything he had.[34] In his subsequent address, March 17, 1948, he charged that the world's problems were "chiefly due to the fact that one nation has not only refused to cooperate in the establishment of a just and honorable peace, but—even worse—has actively sought to prevent it." He asked for two measures in addition to the first installment of the Marshall Plan and a supplemental defense appropriation: temporary reenactment of the draft, to bring the services, primarily the army, up to authorized strength; and a long-range military plan of six months of Universal Military Training (UMT) for all American males between the ages of seventeen and twenty-one, upon graduation from high school, otherwise upon reaching the age of eighteen. He planned to abolish the service academies, West Point and Annapolis, and commission officers after not less than one year of service in the ranks and after attendance at special training camps.[35] With UMT it would be possible to bring the military budget down from $13 billion to perhaps $8 billion (though he asked for $4 billion to inaugurate UMT). It would ensure a surplus in the annual budget of that time. He managed to convert General Marshall (perhaps because the general was a graduate of the Virginia Military Institute). He was certain UMT was the right thing to do:

> In November 1945 I asked for universal training and I kept asking for it at intervals up to March 17, 1948. In the early part of 1947 I appointed a commission to get the facts and report it to me on U.M.T. That committee had two leading college presidents on it, two able men of the cloth, two big business men and an able lawyer and a fine woman. They were not for U.M.T. when they started. They assembled the facts and on May 29, 1947, made one of the ablest reports I've ever seen. They were unanimous in their conclusions & recommendations.[36]

UMT never had a chance in Congress. It never came to a vote in either House.

Gradually the president came around to the possibility of a large multilateral treaty of alliance. Here the subtle diplomacy of the British government with the Americans, in the person of the Labour cabinet's foreign secretary, Ernest Bevin, was crucial. Early in 1947 the British had signed an alliance with France, the Treaty of Dunkirk, against any revival of German aggression, and in March 1948 they enlarged it to include the Benelux countries, renaming the alliance the Brussels Pact and changing its purpose into protection against Russian aggression. Even before the latter arrangement Bevin, in December 1947, suggested a larger treaty to Secretary Marshall, albeit talking confusedly of two circles, one being Brussels Pact nations, the other Britain, Canada, and the United States. As months passed, a new instrument emerged including not only the Brussels nations together with the United States and Canada but also the southern nations of Europe, Portugal (not Franco Spain) and Italy, and the northern nations of Norway, Denmark, and Iceland (not Sweden, traditionally neutral), making twelve in all.[37]

Enlargement of the proposed treaty to include more than the Brussels Treaty members raised questions about how much commitment the United States should make. The more signatories the more likely that one of them would drag the United States into war. Congress cherished its constitutional right to declare war. Undersecretary of State Robert A. Lovett (who replaced Acheson in July 1947) negotiated with Senator Vandenberg, seeking to borrow a formula from the Inter-American Treaty of Reciprocal Assistance, the Rio Pact of 1947, whereby "an armed attack against one or more of them in Europe or North America shall be considered an attack against all." This seemed automatic, but in the way of many U.S. engagements with the Latin American nations there was a loophole: "[E]ach of them . . . will assist the party or parties so attacked by taking forthwith . . . such action as it deems necessary." Arranging the casus belli in turn raised a question of connecting the alliance with the UN Charter—how to justify an alliance within an international organization? Again the Rio formula proved useful, for it spoke of the right of individual or collective self-defense recognized by Article 51 of the charter. The North Atlantic Treaty took refuge in Article 51 and did not mention the charter's articles 53 and 54, which required regional organizations to report to the Security Council, of which the Soviet Union was a permanent member. As a stopgap while negotiating these subtleties with the senator, and while the U.S. was not militarily bound to Europe, Lovett suggested a declaration that the president was prepared to negotiate a military alliance with parties to the Brussels Treaty, and in case of Soviet aggression against any parties pending the treaty's conclusion the United States would consider it an unfriendly act. To this Vandenberg uttered a resounding "No" and asked, "Why should Truman get all the credit?" Vandenberg embodied the Rio formula in a resolution the Senate accepted on June 11, 1948, by vote of 64 to 4, thus giving senatorial consent in advance to a satisfactory formula and adorning any future treaty with a resolution named after himself.[38]

As the treaty took shape opposition appeared within the state department, where Bohlen and Kennan opposed it. Bohlen believed the Senate would never consent to a military alliance. He recommended that the administration get Congress to approve a massive military assistance program and let matters go at that; his fallback position was a bilateral treaty of some kind between the United States and Canada on one side, and the Brussels Treaty parties on the other, the groupings separated by the Atlantic, what was known as a "dumbbell" treaty. Kennan saw economic recovery as the proper rationale for policy. He was sure the Russians would not use their military strength against the West.

Truman could not decide what to do. Not only were there the complications of negotiating a multilateral alliance, with the initiatives and counter-initiatives, but there was also the fact that in 1948 he was running for election in the most strenuous contest he had ever engaged in, with exception of the Senate primary fight against Stark in 1940. He was campaigning across the country, making speeches morning to night, from the back of the train and in barnlike auditoriums, with tens of thousands of people hearing him in person, millions over the radio. These were not the best circumstances for thought-fulness. As he cast about for alternatives, much as he had done earlier when thinking of UMT, he succumbed to a suggestion by two speechwriters, David M. Noyes and Albert Z. Carr, respectively a Chicago advertising executive and a journalist. They persuaded him to ask his friend Chief Justice Vinson to fly to Moscow, talk with Stalin, and try to reduce tensions. What Vinson would talk about was up to him.

The suggested Vinson mission was bound to have repercussions. It would have undercut the work of Marshall, then in Paris in delicate talks looking toward the security treaty and a solution to the Berlin blockade. Marshall's credibility rested on the increasing success of the airlift and the firmness the administration showed to the Russians. One wonders why Truman's staff, usually efficient, did not protect the president from this idea of a mission. Instead they urged it on him. The campaign perhaps had worn them out.

The result was a fiasco. The president summoned Vinson to the White House on Sunday, October 3, and proposed the mission; he asked Press Secretary Ross to inform the radio networks of the need for a half-hour of free time to make a speech on the subject. Ross felt required to tell the networks why the president was asking for time, and within a few days the story was out. Meanwhile Truman, on Tuesday, October 5, consulted Mar-shall, who was horrified. According to Bohlen, who was with him, Marshall drafted a reply that began something like this: "Never in the history of diplomatic bungling . . ." When an aide read it back he said, "I cannot send a message like that. I am talking to my President." He dictated a second draft to the effect that he had not kept Truman completely informed and was return-ing to Washington to talk things over. Upon arrival, according to Bohlen, he threatened to resign. But the above may not have been the exact sequence of events. According to Jonathan Daniels, who was with the president, the threat might not have been necessary. The original exchange took place via teletype, after which Truman came back from the communications room at the White House, confronted his advisers, and said "No." They objected. The president listened. "His magnified eyes seemed almost slate gray. Then he said very quietly, 'I have heard enough. We won't do it.'" Daniels said the president got up and went out of the glass-paned door to the terrace by the rose garden and walked back toward the White House alone, "very much alone that day."[39]

As for the two innocents who started it all, Noyes, according to Clifford, had no explanation nor remorse except for, "Well, to hell with it, I quit."[40]

Carr, who had written a presidential speech that was to have gone on the networks, found himself with an extra speech.

In his memoirs Truman spent several pages trying to explain what happened. At one point he said it was not to be a unilateral negotiation, at another that it was. He described the purpose as talking over nuclear issues, in the news because of failure of the Soviets and Americans to agree on a UN plan for international control. He wrote that he canceled the mission after word got out because of informing the networks; in fact word was not out when two days later he talked to Marshall.

The president continued to think over the possibility of a negotiation, in what little time he had to think. In the memoirs of Senator Connally is an account of a visit to the White House at the president's request, in company of Vandenberg, the evening of October 5, the same day the president talked to Marshall by teletype and decided against the Vinson mission. Connally arrived first, and Truman mentioned the mission, which Connally opposed. When Vandenberg came Truman said nothing about the mission but was trying to "work up his courage" to do something and told the senators he was thinking of a person-to-person call to Stalin. Vandenberg and Connally strongly opposed. "You don't know any Russian and he doesn't know any English," Connally said. "Besides there's the question of authenticity. After you finish talking, what will you have? No witnesses or documents. And there's no possible way of telling about commitments agreed upon or promises made regarding the future." Truman looked disappointed, Connally wrote. After the senators left, Vandenberg said to Connally, "[H]e must be feeling desperate about the campaign." Connally, according to himself, said nothing. On his side, Vandenberg, in a book edited by his son and published shortly after his death in 1952, said the White House had telephoned him earlier in the day and asked him to "slip in" through the east entrance at 3:00 P.M. for an off-the-record chat. A few minutes later—obviously after the president talked to Marshall—the White House phoned again and canceled the date. That evening Truman personally called Vandenberg at his apartment in the Wardman Park Hotel and asked if he would come down for a private chat, and there he met Connally. Vandenberg's account otherwise agrees with Connally's.[41]

According to Vandenberg the president continued to consider a telephone call. The senator was keeping a diary and in an entry for October 22 wrote that the *New York Times* reporter James Reston called him in Grand Rapids and said there was a rumor the president had in mind a substitute for the Vinson mission. The senator cryptically wired Matt Connelly, saying he did not approve a call to Stalin; Connelly sent word to the campaign train, and Truman wired back, "Nothing will be done without consultation with you."[42]

Lacking alternatives, the president went back to his plan for a North Atlantic Treaty, which took final form after the election. The Western foreign ministers assembled in Washington early in April 1949, and on April 4 they signed the treaty for their respective governments in a ceremony at the state department. The treaty amounted to a drastic change in policy, the first alliance since abrogation of the French Alliance of 1778 in the year 1800 with the long forgotten Treaty of Mortefontaine. One could have expected an outburst from the many Americans who still thought their country could remain apart from the world; not much was heard about NATO as a departure, for troubles with the Soviets had become so omnipresent that something had to be done.

4

An earlier chapter has attempted to draw Truman's personal qualities at the time he arrived in the presidency, to show what sort of man he was, what kind of leader he might become. Announcement of the great change in American foreign policy in 1947–1949 offered the new president opportunity to put his qualities to the test. There remains the need to ask whether he measured his Russian problem with as much precision, as much care, as his fellow citizens could have hoped—bearing in mind the difference between retrospect and action. For as Truman's secretary of state beginning in 1949, Acheson, so fondly related in the introduction to his memoirs, quoting the historian C. V. Wedgwood, "History is lived forwards but it is written in retrospect. We know the end before we consider the beginning and we can never wholly recapture what it was to know the beginning only."[43]

Here a point needs to be made, namely, that in confronting the Soviet Union the president faced an unprecedented situation. The USSR was sui generis. It was unlike any nation any American leader had ever dealt with.[44]

So little was known about what the country really was like at the time. Generally speaking, Western intelligence of its economic and military strength was poor. There seem to have been few Western operatives inside the USSR. What little the West knew was based on captured German aerial maps and interrogation of German and Japanese prisoners returning from the Soviet Union. At the end of the 1940s, with return of most of the prisoners, this information was drying up. A little information was available from flights by unarmed reconnaissance planes just outside territorial waters taking oblique photographs, otherwise from "accidental" overflights; such procedures covered small parts of the USSR, however, and they were dangerous, for once in a while the Soviets shot down planes. Not until 1956, with the first overflights by U-2 planes, could American leaders be fairly sure Soviet defenses were weaker than those of the United States, and not until satellite reconnaissance commencing in 1961 (unlike U-2s, satellites can photograph through cloud cover) could they be certain.

Nor was the nature of the Soviet regime itself any easier to comprehend.

The Russian government was an enigma, for almost no reliable information was available. Never had a great government been so secretive, so difficult to understand in its workings, its policies, and its purposes. The Soviets did not allow their nationals to talk with foreigners, and newspaper reporters were reduced to attending receptions and reading the Soviet press, which was strictly party-line, almost byzantine in its revelations.

During Truman's time Westerners pinned their hopes on Stalin, believing him a reasonable autocrat. Stalin displayed none of the bombast of his late antagonist in Germany; on the face of things any comparison seemed not merely improbable but impossible. Quiet, soft-spoken, sometimes even humorous, he captivated Truman at Potsdam. The president believed the Soviets could understand U.S. policies if only he, the president, laid them out to Stalin. There were all the stories, apparently true, of atrocities throughout the 1930s. But then Russia, whether under the tsars or commissars, had never been a place for democratic change, and anyway, as Lenin said, one cannot make an omelet without breaking eggs. The emergency of World War II justified a harsh regime, and the collaboration of 1941–1945 washed away rancors.

Stalin was only the latter-day tsar and surely an improvement over the other tsars; in any event, he was held in check by his advisers. The postwar president told his morning conference, "[I]f only Stalin were concerned on the Russian side . . . everything would be all right." He said he liked Stalin— "the old guy." On this occasion Press Secretary Ross said there probably would be questions in a press conference as to whether he and Stalin should meet, and the president said that at Potsdam he asked Stalin to come to the United States and Stalin replied, "God willing." Clifford interjected, "God— and the Politburo." On June 11, 1948, while campaigning in Eugene, Oregon, Truman said, "I got very well acquainted with Joe Stalin, and I like old Joe! He is a decent fellow. But Joe is a prisoner of the Politburo. He can't do what he wants to. He makes agreements, and if he could he would keep them; but the people who run the government are very specific in saying that he can't keep them."[45]

It is easy to say now how these personal appraisals were so wrong. Terror—sheer Stalinist terror—governed the Soviet Union. Stalin's murders numbered far into the millions, in collectivization of the farms, in the purges of the later 1930s, in the virtually leaderless early military actions of World War II (what with the army's officer corps decimated by the purges), in the postwar repressions. All the while the tyrant of the Kremlin kept much information from getting out, relying on the gullibility of his enemies to keep the rest of his secrets. Within the regime he supervised everything without dissent; Hitler had allowed more discussion, even disagreement. Sometimes the dictator would ask assistants why they appeared nervous or shifty-eyed or furtive. In conferences with Westerners he was observed drawing wolves' heads on a pad of paper. His suspicions, which always had been large, affected everything that passed through the Kremlin offices. In his last years his suspicions went to ridiculous lengths; Nikita S. Khrushchev, in the speech to the Twentieth Party Congress in 1956, drew a portrait of a man who was half crazed, perhaps because of arteriosclerosis—he died of a massive stroke. His advisers were lackeys and could do nothing, say nothing, without his consent. Stalin assigned tasks to the Politburo by dividing it into twos or threes, and he so controlled the group that in 1951 he arranged the execution of one of its members. Nor were the foreign ministers, with whom Westerners dealt and whose humors they often analyzed and divined and held up to glasses or placed on diplomatic litmus paper, any more independent. After World War II the prewar foreign minister, Maxim Litvinov, spoke on two occasions to American reporters, telling them the United States should resist Soviet aggression; a few years ago before his death in 1986, Molotov told an interviewer that only a simple oversight had prevented Litvinov's execution. Russia's first postwar foreign minister, Molotov, and second, Andrei Y. Vyshinsky, were completely under Stalin's control. Truman, Byrnes, and Marshall thought this was the case, but they could not be certain. The president rightly considered Molotov a "muttonhead," but he never understood how unimaginative the minister was. According to Andrei Gromyko, who later was foreign minister for twenty-eight years, Molotov was nought but an automaton, admittedly with enormous capacity for work. He worked in an oddly methodical way. One time he had been working on a document for hours and suddenly announced, "I'm going next door to rest for thirteen minutes." He went out, and returned thirteen minutes later "on the dot," looking fresh and ready for more. If he lost his temper it was for well-thought-out reasons; any scenes were contrivances. And behind it all was complete inability to think for himself: "[I]f there was an opportunity to formulate an idea in a fresh way, and if it looked in the least unusual to Molotov, let alone unprecedented, he absolutely refused to allow it." As for Vyshinsky, the prosecutor of the purge trials, Gromyko despised him. Once Vyshinsky received a telephone call from the dreaded chief of the secret police, Lavrenti Beria, and "leapt respectfully out of his chair." After Stalin's death, when Beria was arrested before his execution, Vyshinsky heard the news in a state of shock, his arms on a green baize table, his head resting on them awkwardly, for the moment not uttering a word.[46]

Most intriguing of all, in what we now are beginning to learn, is the likelihood that Stalin, who held the Soviet Union in his hand, was intensely fearful of the United States. Nearly a decade after Truman left office Milovan Djilas published his account of conversations with Stalin at the time of the Greek crisis, of how the dictator told him and his Yugoslav colleague Edward Kardelj, "What do you think, that Great Britain and the United States—the United States, the most powerful state in the world—will permit you to break their line of communication in the Mediterranean Sea? Nonsense. And we have no navy. The uprising in Greece must be stopped, and as quickly as possible."[47] Many years later, with the opening of portions of the Soviet archives, it became evident that at the time of the perhaps defining crisis of the cold war, the Korean War, which convinced the members of the Truman administration that the Soviet Union was bent on extending its control whenever possible, by any means, Stalin may well not have been challenging the United States at all. In fact, it is likely that he had no idea that the United States would intervene and was only giving in to the importunities of his North Korean supporter, Kim Il Sung, fearful that if he did not do so he would lose control of the international communist movement to his East Asian rival, Mao Tse-tung; when, contrary to Kim's almost innumerable assurances, the United States intervened, Stalin immediately drew back, abandoning the North Koreans to the Americans until Chinese intervention forced him to give a modest anti-aircraft and fighter support against American bombing of North Korea. According to the new archival information Stalin had no desire to conquer South Korea and became the victim of his chauvinistic supporter and seeming puppet, Kim, who may also have been playing the Soviets against the Chinese.[48] Stalin may well have feared the United States right down to the time of his death in 1953. Khrushchev's memoirs were published in the West in the 1970s (and in the Soviet Union in 1989–1990) and it was necessary to bring out a supplementary volume of his more indiscreet commentaries in 1990, *Khrushchev Remembers: The Glasnost Tapes.* According to the latter book, "In the days leading up to Stalin's death, we believed that America would invade the Soviet Union and we would go to war. Stalin trembled at this prospect. How he quivered! He was afraid of war. He knew that we were weaker than the United States." Russia's victory in World War II "did not stop him from trembling inside." Stalin, Khrushchev remembered, liked to keep Moscow's anti-aircraft units on twenty-four-hour alert.[49]

But Truman did not know this—he knew only the beginning, not the end. He knew only that he was dealing with a man who, commencing in April 1945, challenged American sensibilities time after time, as if willing to take anything to the limit and beyond. In such a time, whatever the illusions that later years erased, the president of the United States needed to announce a foreign policy that was as logical, as coldly rational, as it could be. This is exactly what he did.

Chapter Thirteen

Whistle-Stop

The election of 1948 marked Truman's greatest personal triumph in the presidency. It was the biggest political upset in American history. Among all the presidential candidates, from 1788 on, no one had come from behind and won in the extraordinary way Truman did.

The president's own party did not want him. In the weeks before delegates were to arrive at the Philadelphia convention, Representative James Roosevelt of California sought support for General Eisenhower, who had just become president of Columbia University. The son of FDR was beginning to look like his father—his face was filling out, the Rooseveltian eyes almost snapped as he gazed over the crowds that came to hear him, and he was developing the famous smile. He was moving toward control of the party in California, gathering a group of disaffected individuals across the country composed of such liberals as Senator Claude Pepper of Florida, as singular in his issues then as later, and several city bosses, including Frank Hague of Jersey City and Jake Arvey of Chicago, the latter now known as Colonel Arvey after his military service. All of them feared defeat if they tried to run on Truman's coattails—in fact, so far as they were concerned he possessed no coat to hang on to. Truman naturally was incensed over this opposition. In preceding years he may have thought a little about Eisenhower's candidacy (no one then knew whether Ike was a Democrat or Republican) and mentioned it to the general more than once. But by 1948 young Roosevelt's support of Eisenhower amounted to defiance. During a "nonpolitical" whistle-stop trip out West in June, nominally to obtain an honorary degree from the University of California at Berkeley, actually for the purpose of stirring the Democracy, he took the opportunity to set Jimmy Roosevelt straight. "Your father asked me to take this job," he said, jabbing his right forefinger into Jimmy's chest. "I didn't want it. I was happy in the Senate. But your father asked me to take it, and I took it. And if your father knew what you are doing to me, he would turn over in his grave. But get this straight: whether you like it or not, I am going to be the next president of the United States." With that he dismissed Jimmy: "That will be all. Good day."[1] He was unable, however, to stop the draft Eisenhower movement until just before the convention. In the previous January the general, who liked the idea of the presidency, had offered a disavowal that was not entirely convincing. For months Ike was unable to improve upon it. At last, early in July, after Truman's White House aides apparently went to the length of getting General Marshall to set Eisenhower straight, the president of Columbia University said what seemed to be a "No." The disgusted Truman told Assistant Press Secretary Ayers that the Kansas general was a "s— a—."[2]

With these preliminaries it did not appear as if Truman had a chance, and his fate seemed confirmed when the Republicans, assembling in Philadelphia in June, chose as his opponent Governor Dewey of New York. Everyone said the governor was a shoo-in, bound to become the thirty-fourth president of the United States. Dewey had enjoyed a near perfect public career. He first came to notice as a prosecutor of gangsters in New York City; the city always had a large supply on hand, and to the surprise of everyone he put them in jail. Ascending into Albany, he gained a reputation as a peerless administrator of the nation's most populous and often most fractious state. He ran for president against Roosevelt in 1944 and failed, but this was hardly his fault, for Roosevelt was a veteran campaigner and the election occurred during the middle of a war; furthermore, he did give Roosevelt a difficult time, as the election yielded the smallest margin of victory FDR received in four campaigns. Against Truman in 1948 he seemed a sure winner. When the Republicans chose as his running mate Governor Earl Warren of California, a popular figure on the West Coast, the by then congresswoman from Connecticut, Clare Luce, announced that Truman was finished. As she put it, he was a gone goose.

The president could not possibly win. His new anti-Russian policy had not yet gained any triumphs. His domestic achievements were a light-year removed from the hopes he announced in a message to Congress in September 1945; they had been negative, against striking railroaders and coal miners. Too, he was still a deplorable public speaker. As late as the spring of 1948 he had not demonstrated he could stir audiences. His Missouri twang appeared out of place on the national scene. His notion of a speech was to get through it as quickly as possible—so he told Leonard Reinsch, who was trying to help him learn to speak better. He made everything worse by continuing his habit of moving one hand, sometimes both, up and down, palms turned inward, as if he were trying to fly. The impression of the electorate was of a well-meaning but small man, not much of a successor to Roosevelt. *Newsweek* asked fifty top newspapermen—David Lawrence, Arthur Krock, Lippmann, and Reston among them—how the election would turn out, and they all elected Dewey. Truman's staff assistants, to a man, saw no hope. Bess Truman herself gave up, asking Tom Evans, "Does he really think he can win?"[3]

1

The campaign of 1948 turned in fair part on personalities, as do most American campaigns—few turn on issues. Here the Democrats found themselves with a good deal more strength than they expected. The great surprise of the next months was the president himself, who displayed an enormous capacity for campaigning. It first became evident in his acceptance speech to the convention. He had taken the train up from Washington to accept, and as luck had it the convention that day locked itself in a series of floor votes and speeches that required hours, this in a hall without air-conditioning. Privately the delegates made the usual jokes about their plight, that everything was so deadly that what they needed was not bourbon but embalming fluid. Evening came and the speakers droned on. The president sat for a while in a small, bare room below the hall's stage and talked to people who came through. After a while he and a few friends went outside on a little balcony to get some fresh air. After his assistants dragged out several overstuffed chairs for the group to sit on, the president occupied himself by watching Pennsylvania Railroad trains. By the time the convention was ready to receive him, at 1:45 A.M., the delegates were sleepy, bone tired, and soaked with perspiration. Undeterred, Truman roused the convention to a frenzy in the first moments of his short speech: "Senator Barkley [his running mate] and I will win this election and make those Republicans like it—don't you forget that!" he shouted. In the course of his marvelous speech—marvelous in the campaign talk that got up Democratic courage ("lifted the delegates out of their doldrums . . . roused admiration for his political course," related *Time* magazine)—he announced a special session of Congress to be held on "Turnip Day," so named after a piece of Missouri wisdom, "On the 25th of July, / Sow your turnips wet or dry."[4] The twenty-fifth was a Sunday, so the president called the session for the twenty-sixth. "They are going to try to dodge this responsibility," he predicted, "but what that 'worst' Eightieth Congress does in this special session will be the test of whether they mean what they say." There were cheers, yells, and the campaign was on.[5]

In the weeks that followed, Truman admittedly was not the complete campaigner. Some of his fighting speeches now read rather badly—gross exaggerations of what was wrong with his opponents; one wishes he had tempered those remarks. It could have been the speechwriters; one of them, Clifford, later confessed he and his colleagues were "really rough" on the Republicans.[6] The president probably encouraged them; when he started to take an opponent apart, he liked to leave nothing but the feathers. And there may have been something deeper than willingness to say more than was necessary. One of the reporters at the White House during the Truman era, Donovan, bureau chief of the *New York Herald Tribune,* naturally of Republican sympathies, has always retained a certain ambivalence about the man he saw so often, "a certain personal narrowness, ineptness, ignorance, impetuosity, and crudeness."[7] These descriptions occasionally fitted the public man. One of them, the crudeness, fitted the private. Perhaps they were the cause of the presidential diatribes against the Republicans.

But Donovan and others who heard Truman's exaggerations in the campaign admitted that the candidate was stouthearted, that adversity brought out his courage. Truman was fighting again, as in 1940, for his political life, and the purposefulness came through. The fighting gave credence to what he said; people went away believing, if only because the president himself believed.

Truman's running mate, Barkley, was his second choice after Justice Douglas. According to some wits Douglas had refused the vice presidential nomination because he disliked taking passage on the *Titanic;* he seems to have told friends he could not be a number-two man to a number-two man. But Douglas was an attractive second-rater—Roosevelt privately called him a Boy Scout—and the party was better off with the Kentucky senator, even if Barkley theoretically did not balance the ticket, Kentucky hardly balancing Missouri.[8] The senator had come up the hard way. His skill at shorthand won him a place in the law office of a Paducah judge, and after admission to the bar he was elected to the House of Representatives in 1912 and to the Senate some years later. He became majority leader in 1937. He was seventy years old in 1948, and the years showed: Truman said it took him five minutes to sign his name. He seemed to be plagued by bad luck: he once lost his glasses during a campaign speech and couldn't see his audience; another time he fell downstairs in the dark and wrenched his knee, and at a fair in Illinois a steer almost ate his straw hat. But he was a speechifier of the old school who could hold audiences, especially southern audiences, a task Truman assigned him. He could find a joke for any occasion. One was about a fellow who had two sons; one went to sea and the other became vice president, and the father never heard of either again. Another was about a fellow who came into a bar to get a drink but couldn't remember the name of it; he told the bartender all he could say was that it was "tall, cold, and full of gin." Whereupon a man leaning on the bar turned to him and snarled, "Sir, you are speaking of the woman I love." Barkley almost never mentioned by name the man running for the presidency on the Republican ticket, but one time he could not resist. In Dover, Delaware, he announced (unbelievably) that he was cutting his speech short. "I don't want you to get wet," he said. "In fact, I don't even want you to get dewey."[9]

On the Republican side the Democrats were almost as fortunate with their antagonists as they were with Truman and Barkley. Dewey had looked extremely good, but beneath appearances were problems that the campaign brought out. Born in Owosso, Michigan, he had attended the University of Michigan, but he took his law degree at Columbia and remained in the East, consorting with rich lawyers in New York City, surrounding himself with ivy leaguers in Albany. He appeared to speak for the sort of upper-crust privilege that World War II had consigned to the dustbin of history. He also showed personal awkwardnesses; Republicans who knew him found him hard to take. He was serious, and seemed to calculate everything; Americans do not want their presidents to be calculators. He was stiff with people, and could be brusque. Donovan, who should have been friendly toward him, could only say he was "an acquired taste," after which he remarked the standoffishness, evidenced by the out-of-style mustache.[10] Dewey could unbend, though, if he just had to: seeking delegates from Oregon, he submitted to such campaign stupidities as wearing, on one occasion, a ten-gallon hat and, on another, an Indian headdress worn by Queen Marie of Romania when she visited the state in the 1920s. He also allowed a group of Coos Bay pirates to capture him, put him on trial, and initiate him into their group by pricking his arm so he could write his name in their guest book with his own blood. At Grants Pass, a nearly naked group of local cavemen ambushed him, and photographers caught him gnawing on a bone given him by the cavemen and loping along in his business suit with them, arm in arm. But afterward he returned to his former ways; the imminence of the presidency reinforced his usual dignity, making him presidential and doing his campaign no good.[11]

His running mate, Governor Warren, appears not to have known why the convention chose him, apart from the honor. He was no political or any other sort of antagonist, and as the Republican candidate for vice president in 1948 he did not try very hard. He traveled across the country in a handsomely furnished special train. Though people liked him, his speeches were a mish-mash of platitudes, and audiences thinned out week after week. Truman liked him a great deal too, and in later years saw much of him. In 1952, when the president went to California to whistle-stop Warren's state for Adlai Stevenson, the California governor got on the train and acted properly. "Mr. President," Warren said, "you're president of the United States, I'm the governor of California, and I'm going out there on that back platform and introduce you."[12] After Warren became chief justice in 1953 he went to Independence annually for sessions of the Truman Library Institute board; the present writer once encountered him inside the door of a local restaurant, where the Institute met for lunch. He was standing there in double-breasted suit, shaking hands with all comers, just like a Methodist minister after church.

Warren was chosen, of course, because he balanced the ticket beautifully: Dewey of New York, he of California. But in the event, he failed to carry his own state.

Henry Wallace headed the Progressive party in 1948, and rank-and-file

Democrats feared that the former vice president and secretary of commerce, dismissed from the cabinet in 1946, would attract all the liberals who detested Truman. The president privately described liberals as crazy; there was no love lost between him and them, although he tried to hide his disdain—he liked some of their ideas but did not think the liberals were practical politicians. But Wallace's candidacy only pushed most liberal Democrats into a new Democratic party organization, Americans for Democratic Action, whose beliefs, apart from the New Deal, were two: no group must divide the Democratic vote, and Wallace's party was a communist front. Wallace sought to make an issue of Democratic foreign policy, which he believed indistinguishable from Republican foreign policy; both major parties were acting in bipartisan cooperation to fight communism in Europe and Asia (with exception of China). Consequently, Wallace found himself occupying positions close to the communist line. He tried to stand away, asking support only from individuals of good will, but the task was impossible.

What hurt Wallace most of all was that the campaign brought out his naïveté. He always had refused to associate with politicians, and thus failed to get the support he needed to go to the top in politics. Truman had said as much in 1945, that during four years of presiding over the Senate, Wallace hardly knew any senators. As Truman liked to say about Herbert Hoover, Wallace never polled a precinct. And his good intentions had a way of turning out badly; for example, his habit of staying in second-class hotels so black supporters could obtain rooms only lent an aura of down-at-the-heels to the candidate and his party. He lacked the imagination to avoid wrong impressions. One thinks of the occasion a few years before when an army colonel was giving him Russian lessons at the Wardman Park Hotel in Washington and the then vice president of the United States challenged his teacher to a footrace back to the Mayflower Hotel on Connecticut Avenue. It was late in the evening and the two men ran through the silent streets. What if a policeman had come along and seen a thief being chased, or worse, two thieves escaping, and arrested them, the story getting into the newspapers? All in all, the campaign only served to bring out the Progressive candidate's essential quality as a loner. As weeks passed, his candidacy virtually disappeared from public view.

Wallace's running mate, Senator Glen H. Taylor of Idaho, did not help things. The senator once had been a country singer, known for performances together with his wife, Dora—they were known as the Glendora Ranch Gang. In 1948 his speeches on domestic policy were thin to the point of invisibility, and on foreign policy they were disastrous: he explained that Progressives welcomed the votes of "pink" communists, who were advocates of nonviolent change, but spurned the votes of red communists. Reporters described him as an Idaho potato. Years later, after leaving the Senate, he removed to California and opened a factory to manufacture Taylor Toppers—that is, toupees.

The States' Rights Democratic party, or Dixiecrats, as a southern editor described them in a word that caught on, a splinter party that promised to take many votes from the Democrats, ran governors J. Strom Thurmond of South Carolina and Fielding Wright of Mississippi. They were no rabble-rousers—they were serious about states' rights and conducted a logical, sensible campaign—but in talking about states' rights they were far behind the times, believing in the federalism of 1787. As the *Greenville [S.C.] News* said, "We stopped talking about states' rights and state sovereignty when we saw the national gravy train headed our way." Ralph McGill of the *Atlanta Constitution*, who suspected tidelands oil interests of supporting Thurmond, similarly remarked the bankruptcy of the term: "Every Kentucky farmer is praying for the United States to invade his rights and hold up the price of tobacco."[13] Moreover, the Dixiecrats were against civil rights for American blacks, and in this respect they were equally behind the times. The Philadelphia convention had seen a savage fight over the civil rights plank sponsored by Mayor Hubert Humphrey of Minneapolis, a plank Truman grudgingly if with secret admiration accepted. When the plank passed, all the Mississippi delegation and half of the Alabama group walked out of the hall. The remaining southerners voted for Senator Richard B. Russell, Jr., for president, against Truman, and Russell received 263 votes to 947.5 for Truman. During the campaign an exchange of letters occurred between Thurmond and Governor William H. Hastie of the Virgin Islands. Thurmond had sent a form letter expressing regret that he and Hastie had never met and remarking, "It is my earnest hope that, during my term of office, you and your family will honor South Carolina with a visit to Columbia and be our guests at the Mansion." Hastie instead invited Thurmond and family to the Virgin Islands to "be our guests at Government House." Only after publication of the letters did Thurmond realize that Governor Hastie was a Negro. His reaction was, "I would not have written him if I knew he was a Negro. Of course, it would have been ridiculous to have invited him." The Dixiecrats believed, with equal foolhardiness, that they could appeal to the South and to some northerners and throw the election into the House of Representatives.[14]

With Wallace on the left, and Thurmond on the right, the Democrats worried themselves nearly to death, for they needed no divisions. But it became evident that the dissenters were attracting few followers. To the liberals and city dwellers whom Wallace was trying to attract, likewise to many southerners, the party was still an emotional matter. In 1948 each splinter party polled 1.1 million votes in a 48-million-vote election.

2

In addition to personalities, the tactics of the Democratic party in 1948 turned out to be far better than those of its opponents. The tactician of the party was James H. Rowe, Jr., a well-known Washington lawyer and Democratic figure who in a long memorandum of September 1947 took the temperature of the moment and prescribed what was necessary for victory. He advised concentrating on the Western vote; pushing for the urban black vote; placing responsibility for congressional inactivity on the Republicans; and undercutting the Wallace-ites whenever possible by advocating New Deal measures and exposing Wallace supporters as communists and fellow travelers. As for the candidate himself, Rowe suggested that Truman sharpen his image overall and be acknowledged as the leader of foreign policy—that he take advantage of the worsening relations with the Soviets.

It is worth pointing out, incidentally, that for many years the authorship of the Rowe memorandum was credited to Clark Clifford. Until Clifford published his memoirs in 1991, Rowe's stellar part in the election was unknown. President Truman disliked Rowe because he was a law partner of the Washington fixer and New Deal figure Tommy Corcoran, and would never have accepted anything Rowe wrote; as a result, Clifford took credit. He changed a few words, eliminated Rowe's complaints about a "Missouri gang," added explanations on labor issues, and put his name on the result.[15]

And so the president, first of all, concentrated on the Western vote, whistle-stopping through the Western states, showing that he not merely was a Middle Westerner but appreciated all those states further west, especially California.

On the rights of black Americans the president was secure and solidly correct.[16] He had sent Congress a message early in 1948 that recommended federal protection of civil rights. During the campaign he went to Texas, and his advance man, his White House staff assistant, Dawson, got out the blacks with no segregation, an unheard-of thing in that part of the world. At Waco the president shook hands with a black woman and the crowd booed. Bess Truman, standing ten feet away, said in a stage whisper, "Don't mind them, Harry! You did the right thing!" As the train was leaving, Mrs. Truman saw a little black girl in a wheelchair and waved to her; the child waved back, and this time the crowd applauded.[17] It is true that in his speeches Truman did not stress civil rights, and he spoke about them only in Harlem during the final days. A later writer remarked quizzically, "It was one of the oddities of the 1948 election that while civil rights significantly affected the outcome, Truman said very little about the issue." The answer, of course, was that he wanted to avoid further southern defections, rely on the record, and allow lesser candidates to rally the black vote.[18]

As for placing responsibility for congressional inaction on the Republicans, the president did so with a vengeance. In fact, he may have engaged in a little exaggeration for the sake of the Democracy. The initials *GOP*, he said, stood for Grand Old Platitudes.[19] As he warmed to the analysis he said they stood for Gluttons of Privilege. The Republicans wanted two families in every garage. He flailed the Hoover administration:

> You remember the Hoover cart . . . the remains of the old tin lizzie being pulled by a mule, because you couldn't afford to buy a new car, you couldn't afford to buy gas for the old one. You remember. First you had the Hoovercrats, and then you had the Hoover carts. One always follows the other. Bear that in mind now, carefully. By the way, I asked the Department of Agriculture at Washington about the Hoover cart. They said it is the only automobile in the world that eats oats.[20]

He attacked the Eightieth Congress, which had Republican majorities in House and Senate, spreading the accusation that it was a great danger to liberty, that it was shaking the pillars of the temple, draining the republic's lifeblood. The Eightieth Congress was in no sense as bad a legislative body; after all, it had approved the Truman Doctrine and Marshall Plan, the Armed Forces Unification Act creating the department of defense, the Selective Service Act; it did not pass New Deal measures, but then neither had its Democratic predecessors, nor would its Democratic successors. Truman doughtily took on the Congress for campaign purposes, and later admitted as much, relating privately that it was not a bad Congress.[21]

The Wallace-ites, he knew, were attempting to say that they, rather than the president, represented the Roosevelt tradition, the principles and ideas of the New Deal; in this regard Truman, who had always voted for the New Deal, had no reason to hesitate. And so he asserted his devotion to what by 1948 might have seemed leftward-leaning programs but were yet attractive to a majority of Americans, thereby stealing the thunder of the Wallace-ites. When Truman accepted Rowe's plan he was in fair part undertaking to reassemble the New Deal coalition that had won four campaigns for FDR. The times were different, the leading personality—a Missouri president—assuredly different. Harry Truman did not admire Roosevelt the man, writing privately that he was "an awful egotist," and he certainly hated Roosevelt's son, James. But he believed in Roosevelt's political ideas; he admired the professionalism of their choice, their ability to win elections.

The sharpest cut he took at the Wallace-ites was to describe them openly, while making a speech in New York City, as communists. The remark was a bit unfair, though not a long way from the truth, for there were communists among the Wallace supporters—Wallace himself had said he would accept voters of all hues. Speaking in what was nothing less than a hotbed of Wallace-ites, he told his New York audience that he would not accept any support from "Henry Wallace and his communists."

Truman made no apologies for his anti-Soviet foreign policy—which, to be sure, he did not describe as anti-Soviet. He presented himself as the leader of the Western nations against the inhuman policies of the Soviet Union.

There could be no mistaking where the buck stopped in foreign policy. As to taking advantage of foreign policy, he did not follow this Rowe recommendation, though he came close in considering the possibility of a mission by Chief Justice Vinson. That latter flirtation one must assume combined both what he considered the national interest—a settlement with the Soviet Union—and his personal interest, but when the two purposes seemed to clash he backed away from the entire enterprise. Had he known that Rowe was the author of the memorandum he certainly would have ascribed to him the advice of taking advantage of foreign policy—Corcoran, he could be sure, would do anything that was unethical as long as it was advantageous.

In standing for the above Rowe recommendations, sans the very last, the president undoubtedly sharpened his image with his fellow countrymen. And with two additional tactics he did even more to make his purposes stand out. One of the additions came from Clifford, and this was that he should court labor. For Truman that was easy to do—he always had had a soft spot in his heart for labor, especially during and after the horrendous primary campaign for reelection to the Senate in 1940, when labor had come out foursquare for him. In the campaign eight years later he stressed his veto of the Taft-Hartley Act, as hard as he could. As it turned out, the act was not the slave-labor act he said it was; the country lived easily with it. The Republican-dominated Congress nonetheless gave him opportunity to predict a labor disaster if Dewey won. The labor leader Jack Kroll described the Dewey program as Uncle Tom's Doghouse for labor; Truman said in Hartford that the GOP favored "labor-baiting, union hurting, yellow-dog open-shop contracts," and in Akron, the Rubber City, he announced that the Republicans had tasted blood when they passed Taft-Hartley.[22] Among national unions only the electricians supported Dewey.

Then there were the farmers. A case can be made that a chance arrangement by the Eightieth Congress, refusal to allow the Commodity Credit Corporation to build more grain storage bins in the summer of 1948, threw the election to Truman. When the president was setting out on one of his whistle-stop trips, Matt Connelly handed him a reminder from Secretary Brannan about the bins. The grain harvest that year was huge, causing market prices to tumble: corn dropped from $2.46 a bushel in January to $1.21 in November, parity support was $1.53, and with no bins farmers could not collect parity payments. In his first major farm speech, a huge rally at Dexter, Iowa, held in September during a plowing contest, Truman lambasted the Republicans for taking money from the farmers. The speech was a triumph. After the president went through his written text he talked to the throng about how he could sow 160 acres of wheat "without leaving a skip"; he had that information from a prejudiced witness, he said: his mother. The farmers went wild. After that speech he sometimes bragged as to how at Dexter he had plowed under a lot of Republicans. The reporter Bob Nixon, who accompanied the president on his trips, was approached by a farmer who knew he was a member of the press and of the presidential party and volunteered the farmers' opinion of the Democratic candidate. "Young fellow," he said, "I want to tell you something. We farmers here in the Midwest like President Truman. What he says and how he says it makes sense to us. We don't care for this smart-aleck fellow from New York, who doesn't know anything about our farm problems."[23] In November the president took Ohio, hitherto rock-ribbed Republican, in large part on the farm issue.

The president thus opted for tactics, for issues and procedures, that were bound to make a difference. The speech at Dexter, Iowa, illustrated another tactic he had been developing—a brand-new ability in oratory. He had gradually come to notice his deficiencies in reading speeches, on one hand, and his capabilities in speaking extempore, on the other. His advisers noticed the difference too: when he spoke off-the-cuff, what he said took on immediate urgency and, especially, partook of the Truman personality, which was direct, interested, concerned, and filled with information—Truman absorbed information easily and often knew more than his speechwriters. He had been using texts only as crutches against memory lapses and his natural hesitation, being president, to take chances, for gaffes could pass instantly into the newspapers and then require weeks, even months, of work to get around or get over. When the campaign began he hence was almost prepared to become more personal in his expression, to make interpolations and ad libs to texts, and even to speak from outlines—as he tended to do with his whistle-stop speeches. The whistle-stops required the orator to mention what each small city, town, or, literally, whistle-stop manufactured or was famous for, after which he could make a few general remarks about the Republicans and about what the nation really needed, instead of what the GOP orators said it needed, and move on. For this reason the whistle-stop speeches tended to be triumphs. On some of the major speeches of the campaign the president also introduced the verve that came from offhand remarks, notably in the St. Louis speech that closed the campaign, in which he took over a huge audience and turned it into a raging Democratic mob.

Vastly helpful in the electoral chemistry was a sort of litany that developed between the president and his audiences. It had happened early in the speechmaking, indeed during the June nonpolitical trip, in Albuquerque, when some man with a big voice shouted from the galleries, "Give 'em hell, Harry!" A great roar went up. As soon as he could be heard the orator shouted back some such remark as, "I'm going to—I'm going to!" or "I never give anybody hell. I just tell the truth on the Republicans, and they think it's hell!" Such comments brought delirium, after which the orator could say anything and draw tumultuous applause.[24]

Against all this hullabaloo—a grand mixture of truth (Truman would have said, firmly and decisively) and, well, perhaps exaggeration, maybe hyperbole, and (whatever one thought of the logic) a wondrous, boisterous, shouting piece of excitement, the sort of thing that would have amused Andrew Jackson, embarrassed John Quincy Adams, brought laughter to Abraham Lincoln, regaled Theodore Roosevelt, perhaps brought a flicker of interest from Woodrow Wilson, and even (though he would have winced at the source of the commotion) produced approval from Franklin Roosevelt—against this sometimes great quadrennial production of American politics the Republicans were nonplussed. Their only response, and one must suppose they thought it wisdom, was to present a front of calm reason and especially—Dewey liked the word—statesmanship. They were going to bring statesmanship to the White House, they said. Dewey wanted to hold both the conservatives and liberals of his party. He thought it was impossible to move in the direction of either; if he went left that would be me-tooism, if he went right it would be another Hoover administration. His Albany speechwriters avoided anything that might make trouble. They went to such lengths that the Democratic national committee collected and published the gems of Deweyan thought. To the farmer he said, "I pledge to you that your next administration will cooperate with the farmers of the country to protect all people from the tragedy of another dust bowl." On oil: "I propose to you that we get an administration that will devote itself seriously to a wise and intelligent use of oil reserves." And again: "Everyone that rides in a car or bus uses gasoline or oil." On forests: "I propose that we develop a national policy that will really save our forests through federal, state, and local cooperation." On the nation's rivers: "Our streams should abound with fish." On the future: "Your future lies ahead of you." At the Alfred E. Smith Memorial Dinner on October 21 he said, "By a simple rediscovery of our devotion to human rights and the protection of others from the abuse of those rights, we can draw a line through every conflict and draw it straight and true. It can be drawn so that both civil liberty and social responsibility complement and fortify each other." In the same speech he drew the world-shaking conclusion that "[t]he highest purpose to which we could dedicate ourself is to rediscover the everlasting variety among us."

In offering these bromides Dewey did not add the sort of rhetorical approach that Truman did; his advisers carefully wrote out his speeches, which he read in his attractive baritone voice, but the speeches lacked the directness and force and convincing eye contact, one might say, the kind of spontaneity that only an address made without notes, or many notes, can give. Dewey's appearances were no political revivals; they lacked the evangelical enthusiasm—slapping the Bible, pounding it, rolling in the aisles—that came to be expected from any great Truman conclave. Believers went to hear Dewey to commune with him, and they went away believing. But no souls were saved.

3

Down to the end, when the president's victory became clear as returns filtered in during the night after the election, the omens favored Dewey. Elmo Roper quit taking samples on September 9, with the comment that only a political convulsion could prevent Dewey from winning. On election eve he said, "I stand by my prediction. Dewey is in." The Crossley poll had 49.9 percent for Dewey, 44.8 for Truman. Gallup was about the same. Newspaper editorials favored Dewey—65 percent of editorial writers, 78 percent of circulation. The Truman campaign chest—as good a barometer as any—was virtually empty. Joseph P. Kennedy and Bernard Baruch, usually angelic in supporting Democrats, made no effort to help; Kennedy would not support a lost cause, and Baruch refused to be a member of the party's finance committee. Radio networks cut off the president in the middle of speeches because the money ran out (although sometimes his managers arranged cut-offs, so as to solicit money). Party officials rushed currency to radio stations, for it came in too late to allow checks to clear. The party barely received enough to keep the presidential train going; eight times the train could not get out of a station without frantic telephoning to secure such amounts as $1,500, $2,000, $5,000.

The candidate refused to give up, putting his faith in the crowds, which admittedly were getting larger. He told his friend Evans they spelled victory. "Yes, I'm going to win," he told Tom.

"I've always said," was the response, "you ought to be the international president of the Optimist Club because you've always been an optimist, but what do you base it upon?"

The president of the United States showed him a chart of electoral votes. "These crowds that have come to the train to see me," he said, "just can't mean anything but victory."[25]

Near the end he went aboard the *Williamsburg* for a little rest. Admiral Dennison asked how he was making out. The answer: "I'm elected."

"How do you know that, Mr. President?"

"Well, I'm a politician, and I understand people and I can tell. I just know that I'm elected."[26]

The closest he came to an admission of defeat was in conversation with the chairman of the national committee, Senator J. Howard McGrath of Rhode Island. "It's been going well, very well," he said. "But it's a strain." He was silent for a moment, then added, "But it's worth it, Howard. Even if we should fail, we're building a better Democratic Party for the future."[27]

Years afterward, the memories for the night of the vote were as bright as yesterday. Cabell Phillips spent election night at the theater in New York City, watching the Lunts in "something or other somewhere on 47th Street." At the second intermission he strolled over to a neighboring bar where a radio commentary was coming in, with jumbled vote totals, precinct numbers, names of states. Then, "with a swallow of Scotch just on its way past the windpipe," he heard a phrase that caused him to gasp and strangle: "Truman's lead now looks almost unassailable. If he can hold his edge in Ohio . . ." Coughing, choking, slapping a dollar on the bar, he headed at a run for his office at the *New York Times*, three blocks away. Halfway he remembered his new topcoat, left in the theater, worth $47.50. "To hell with it," he said.

Returns were not clear until the following morning at 9:30 when the Ohio vote came in; after a sudden chatter of teletypes, radio announcers across the nation grabbed their microphones to proclaim, in near hysteria: "Ohio has gone Democratic! This puts Truman over the top. . . . Ladies and gentlemen, President Truman has won the election!"[28]

The popular vote was not even close, 24.1 million to 21.9. The Democrats won both houses of Congress, 54 to 42 in the Senate, 263 to 171 in the House.

Thereafter came the apologies and explanations, which were as much a part of the election as the result itself, and almost as memorable. The editors of the *Washington Post* sent the famous telegram to the victor:

YOU ARE HEREBY INVITED TO ATTEND A "CROW BANQUET" TO WHICH THIS NEWSPAPER PROPOSES TO INVITE NEWSPAPER EDITORIAL WRITERS, POLITICAL REPORTERS AND EDITORS, INCLUDING OUR OWN ALONG WITH POLLSTERS, RADIO COMMENTATORS AND COLUMNISTS FOR THE PURPOSE OF PROVIDING A REPAST APPROPRIATE TO THE APPETITE CREATED BY THE LATE ELECTIONS. THIS MAIN COURSE WILL CONSIST OF BREAST OF TOUGH OLD CROW EN GLACE. (YOU WILL EAT TURKEY.)[29]

The Alsop brothers, whose election-day column was announcing Dewey's cabinet, opted for crow but asked that theirs be fricasseed. The actress Tallulah Bankhead, a Truman supporter, also sent a telegram: "The people have put you in your place." The radio comedian Fred Allen reported, "This year the polls went to the dogs, rather than the other way around."[30]

For the pollsters themselves, no simple appraisal sufficed. Truman partisans made fun of them, to the tune of the Whiffenpoof song:

Gentleman pollsters, up in a tree,
Doomed from here to eternity,
God, please save us from Tom Dewey,
Baa, baa, baa.

The most solemn of the lot, who liked to be known as Dr. Gallup, had invented a rule by which each poll he took he lumped into those that preceded, drawing conclusions from the whole. Hence the conservatism of his estimates: Truman was behind at the beginning of the campaign, and Gallup's method grossly underestimated the president's gains. Moreover, Gallup stopped polling more than two weeks before the election; a great many voters remained undecided until the end—15 percent of those sampled had not decided, twice as many as in the election of 1944. Pollsters disregarded undecided votes on the theory that they were not likely to vote, or divided them between the parties in the same proportions as decided voters. Over half voted, however, and voted for Truman in a ratio of two to one. The pollsters also did not interview enough people of only grade-school education, of whom in those days there were large numbers. Perhaps they avoided such people out of fear of getting incoherent answers. As Gallup later said, "When you get down to the foreign-born and so on you have one devil of a problem interviewing."[31]

What voter group proved decisive? Truman himself, Professor Truman of the Electoral College, someone described him, believed labor put him over. "Labor did it," were his first words when he walked into the Muehlebach in Kansas City on the morning after the election. Labor certainly supported him—Taft-Hartley, whatever its reality, was bad medicine for the Republicans. Because of the difficulties in 1946 with the railroad brotherhoods, miners, and CIO steelworkers, his standing with labor at first had not been at all good. The brotherhoods had vowed to get him out of the White House, the miners considered him a strikebreaker, and relations with the CIO were no better. In the case of the CIO's president, Murray, there was a special awkwardness—the president seemed unable to forget that at the Chicago convention in 1944 the labor leader had been for Wallace. When Murray occasionally came to the oval office Truman would sit behind his big desk and tap his knee with an envelope opener and say, "I know what you think of me, Phil." Murray also had clashed with the president's close friend John Snyder, and he suspected Snyder told Truman about it. Early in 1948 the head of the CIO's political action committee, Kroll, supported Eisenhower, and Murray was sure the news got back. In early summer the president asked the CIO leader to come by for a visit when he next was in Washington, and Murray found reason not to be in Washington. But gradually things came around. The brotherhoods returned to the fold, the miners forgot their irritation, and the steelworkers and other big CIO unions began to see that they were doing well and could distinctly do less well under a Republican administration with pro-business officials running everything. Truman brought Max Lowenthal into the White House as an adviser primarily on labor issues, and Lowenthal devoted much time to bringing labor leaders into touch with the administration. Murray visited the president and called a truce, and gradually the truce turned into friendship. After the election, at 9:30 A.M., Wednesday, November 3, before Dewey conceded, Murray telephoned Truman in Kansas City and said, "I called to congratulate you on your election, and to convey for our entire staff our admiration for your great conduct of this campaign." The president broke down and wept. "Phil, come in to see me any time," was his response, "the door is always open. I want your advice, and maybe sometime I can help you with advice." He thanked him for his support. Two days later, in the White House, Murray saw the president for a few minutes and said,

"We have sometimes and frequently misunderstood each other. I want to speak to you about myself. . . . I have made my mistakes, and will make more. It may be that sometime you will want to get your boot out to kick me. All I say is if the time comes tell me about it first, the kick in the pants will then be more welcome to me."

"It is manly of you to speak of your mistakes," said the president. "I have made mistakes too."

"It is manly of you to say so," said Murray.

"I want to see a great deal of you," said the president.

Both men were in tears.[32]

Some contemporary writers thought Truman won because of the farmers—because of the storage bins. Here, too, he assuredly obtained support. The manager of the Republican campaign, Herbert Brownell, believed that the GOP lost out mainly because of the "gradual slippage" of the farm vote. Agricultural prices fell nearly 50 percent near the end of the campaign, and farmers had to sell their grain at low prices. Truman charged, of course, that it was the lack of storage bins, which Brownell admits was true—another sign of what was bedeviling the Dewey campaign, namely, lack of support from Republicans in Congress who were devoted to Senator Taft rather than Dewey.[33]

The poll-taker Louis Harris thought Truman won because of the small-town Ohio vote. On October 11 the president whistle-stopped such localities as Lima, Ottawa, Deshler, Fostoria, Willard, and Rittman, despite comment by know-it-alls that it was a waste of time to turn out a few hundred people on the railroad tracks. But Ohio proved crucial to his election, and this single supposedly unsophisticated trip may have given him the victory.[34]

Did the election offer any lessons for the future? People soon were saying it was antediluvian, for several reasons. For one, 1948 was the last time that labor voted as a bloc in a presidential election. With the decline of blue-collar industries and the rise of technology, which used a quite different type of worker, and with the marked increase of service industries, the very idea of a labor vote seems to have disappeared. For another, the rapid increase in the size of American farms because of cost of machinery has made farmers far less important in American politics than they once were. The year 1948 may have been the farmers' last hurrah. Transportation also was changing, and the changes dramatically affected politics, removing national candidates from the train to the plane. Bryan first had used the train for campaigning, and Truman much preferred it, as he was so good at speaking off the rear platform. His running mate, Barkley, asked the national committee for a DC-3 and used it to advantage, becoming the first candidate to fly about the country. In 1952, Eisenhower and Stevenson frequently left their trains to fly to distant places, and thereafter the campaign train passed into history. And last in considering change, there was the largest change of all, the coaxial cable; after its appearance nothing was the same. A few Americans had seen President Roosevelt on television when he opened the World's Fair in New York in 1939. The government then froze construction of stations during the war. For half a dozen years afterward television had no meaning in politics; when Truman delivered his state-of-the-union speech on television in 1947, there were fewer than twenty stations, mostly on the East Coast, and just over a hundred thousand sets. Then occurred the massive change: the campaign of 1952 was thoroughly televised, and by 1972, when the nation watched Truman's funeral, there were nine hundred stations and 60 million sets.

And yet in one single respect the presidential campaign of 1948 offered a lesson that no candidate in subsequent years should have forgotten. This was that a candidate must himself be sincere; he must not merely possess some vision for what the country needs but believe in it and consider himself a— to use a seventeenth-century phrase well understood in Puritan theology— chosen instrument for that grand purpose. In that single respect Truman made a superb candidate. He knew what the United States should do in the postwar era, in domestic and foreign affairs, and by 1948 he had enough experience to take the country through the necessary hoops toward his goals. He was wise enough to know that many other people might also be able to help with that task, that he could not accomplish it by himself. He knew that even in the office of president of the United States he was not irreplaceable, that many other of his fellow citizens could handle the office. But as he so often said to visitors, he was the man whom fate, in the accident of the death of Franklin Roosevelt, had placed in the oval office, and he was going to do his best. He believed he needed more time, and that his opponent was nought but a fast-talking easterner. His countrymen warmed to this message, and they gave him the time.

Chapter Fourteen

Fair Deal

*T*he domestic reform programs of many American presidents are for-gotten almost as soon as announced, but this did not happen in the case of Truman's program. Many Americans, even today, remember Roosevelt's New Deal, and the similarity of the words Truman chose, Fair Deal, helped make his program memorable. But there was something beyond that—probably the way in which he communicated to the American people how deeply he felt about the need for social justice, and how apart from politics he felt that need was or, at the least, should be.

As it happened, the proposals that Truman sent to Congress usually died in their pertinent committees. He tried to see them through, but Congress would not respond. For a while the reason was the disinterest of the Eightieth Congress. But even the Democratic Congress that followed was not much in-terested in reform. Popular attention turned elsewhere: in February 1950, to the first anticommunist pronouncements of Senator Joseph R. McCarthy of Wisconsin; in June, to the Korean War. Even after Truman left office, the heightening of the cold war during the Eisenhower and John F. Kennedy administrations obsessed the country. A dozen years passed before President Lyndon B. Johnson again took up a program of economic and social change.

Under Truman civil rights for black Americans did receive considerable support, and it is possible to say that during his presidency the black revolu-tion, the attainment of rights long denied, really began. Truman announced his program in 1947 with the report entitled "To Secure These Rights." By executive order the president began desegregation of the armed services, to which the Korean War gave much encouragement. The army discovered that it could not afford the inefficiency of segregation. During the Truman era, however, Congress was not very receptive to civil rights. In final analysis the president had to turn to the third branch of government, the judiciary. He instructed Attorney General Tom Clark to prepare amicus curiae briefs in support of crucial cases involving segregation, briefs arguing among other things that *Plessy v. Ferguson* (1896) was unconstitutional. When the court heard this argument, all that remained was to announce the fact a few years later in *Brown v. Board of Education of Topeka.*

Civil liberties, unlike rights, did not fare well during Truman's presidency. It was not that he was insensitive to them, but rather that the times were out of joint as the concern over communism was increasing. Two years after World War II, the president instituted a loyalty program, a saddening innovation for the government of a democratic republic. Senator McCarthy began campaigning for internal security, and the outbreak of war vastly assisted the senator's work. Truman did what he could to stand against the times, but it was impossible, considering the fear of communism. The discovery of spying within the government, which took place during and after World War II and included several serious cases, unnerved everyone. Apart from a few instances of German sabotage before American entry into World War I, and a slight German activity in 1941–1942, this was the first time in American history that such efforts had taken place. For years afterward subversion constituted a major concern of administrations, resulting in expenditure of billions for protection that was difficult to assess.

Last, during his White House years Truman sought to arrange a fair deal for world Jewry, which during World War II had been subject to horrors hitherto unknown in Western civilization. Like his fellow Americans he was outraged by what had happened. In equity, he believed, Jews deserved a refuge, and he beheld British-mandated Palestine (Britain had received the mandate a generation earlier, under the League of Nations) as the best place for them to go. He did not advance his program for the Jews because he thought it would help him in the election of 1948. "We have the Zionist Jews in the office every day," the publicity director of the Democratic national committee, Jack Redding, told the president, "and the pressure is building up a terrific head of steam." To Redding's surprise the answer was: "It's no use putting pressure on the committee. The Palestine issue will be handled here, and there'll be no politics involved."[1] Truman recognized the new Jewish state, Israel, immediately after its creation because, he thought, it promised a fair solution to the world Jewish problem.

1

The Fair Deal program had its origins in the Rooseveltian New Deal, modified by the experience and insights of FDR's Missouri successor. Truman acutely understood the enormous problems and difficulties that afflicted most Americans during the Great Depression. During his work in the 1930s as presiding judge for Jackson County and then as senator, he tried to support any program that would make life easier for his constituents. The government, he became convinced, could never go back to the smallness and especially the narrowness of view of earlier years. It was all right for the Republicans to lament the passage of the American way, the dangers the New Deal presented to capitalism, the need to preserve the initiative of Americans by not giving them government handouts; all those commentaries, he said, were interesting, and bore up under the experiences of the distant past, but they had little connection with what happened beginning in 1929.

As a county executive and then as senator, Truman was grateful for what Roosevelt did, but he easily saw that the New Deal had come to an end after 1937 and something needed to be done to revive it. As soon as World War II ended he was ready. Economically, he needed to take measures to prevent the country from falling into another Great Depression. The Soviets were counting on that chance. (No one in 1945 could know that for the next half-century and more there would be no Great Depression, only a series of recessions, none serious.) As for social issues, it was equally clear that the New Deal had only touched many of them, in particular the issue of civil rights. Much more needed to be accomplished.

The Fair Deal really had two incarnations, one in September 1945, the other in January 1949, after the election. The war ended with the formal Japanese surrender on September 2, 1945, and four days later the president sent to Congress a massive message, sixteen thousand words, the longest up to that time, save for a massive message by Theodore Roosevelt of twenty-one thousand words in 1901. The president set out twenty-one points of possible legislation—a number perhaps related to the guns fired off for a presidential salute, or the age at which Americans once considered themselves legally certifiable adults. Certainly the points were impossible to remember in detail. Briefly put, they asked for an increase in the minimum wage, full employment, a better chance for labor to bargain collectively, more security for farmers, a tax reduction, and public works. The president spoke of decent housing, medical care, and education, in addition to help for small business and development of river valleys and facilities for air transport. These niceties, some possible in the immediate future, others in years to come, he grouped with concern for nuclear regulation and military unification and other programs not allied to the way Americans lived day to day, year to year.

Looking back on this initial program with all its points, one wonders about the wisdom of dumping such a cornucopia on Congress. There was just too much. Maybe the president saw advantage in, so to speak, getting it off his chest. In which case he might have chosen a better presenter of the program than the assistant he inherited from Roosevelt, Judge Rosenman; FDR's speechwriter lacked the magic that the playwright Robert E. Sherwood injected into presidential speeches. Sherwood might have dolled up the message of September 6, but Rosenman seems merely to have inquired of all the executive departments and agencies what they wanted and put the wish list into rough order, which was no magic formula.

Almost needless to add, Congress received the message with the same lack of enthusiasm with which Rosenman compiled it. Nothing happened to most of the proposals for enlarging the New Deal. The others Congress dealt with piecemeal over the following months and years. The Fair Deal awaited reconversion of the economy, which then was in course, and after that the measures of Truman's foreign policy, beginning in 1947. The crisis with the Soviet Union swept away all possibility of pursuing a domestic program until those measures had been followed through and until, of course, the president won the 1948 election.

After winning in 1948 the president was ready to try again, and he wrote into his state-of-the-union message of January 4, 1949, just before his inauguration, the phrase *fair deal*, giving a name to the program.[2] Other commentaries he drafted for that address did not remain. He thought also of telling Congress that he had gone through three and a half years of trouble beginning in September 1945 when he first proposed his domestic program; that the people now had elected him and it was up to Congress to support him. He thought also of adding what his predecessor described as "the God-stuff": "I pray God constantly for guidance. I hope you'll do that too. Then this great country which God has chosen to lead the world to peace and prosperity will succeed in that undertaking."[3] Putting these additions aside he settled for the ringing phrase likening his program to that of Roosevelt. He did not go into detail.

After the inaugural, a great occasion, he sent up an economic message that contained much of what he wanted. Later he sent a medical message. The economic message looked to enlargement of social security, the principal enactment of the "second New Deal" in the mid-1930s. It mentioned enlargement of the minimum wage, amendment of the Clayton Antitrust Act of 1914, and measures recommended by the commission headed by former president Hoover for more efficient running of the federal government. It also sought novel farm legislation, federal aid to education, low-cost public housing, higher taxes on corporations and better-off individual Americans, and repeal of the Taft-Hartley Act.

The economic program was large, and the president enthusiastic, and Congress enacted some parts of the program. Social security legislation turned out fairly well—10 million people were added to the rolls, old-age and survivors' benefits were doubled, and provisions for children and the disabled were improved. It was enough of a difference for some observers to claim that the Social Security Act of 1950 constituted a major overhaul of the system. The minimum wage rose from forty to seventy-five cents, employees covered by it increased, and there were safeguards against child labor. The Celler-Kefauver Act of 1950 forbade companies to buy assets of competitors, plugging a loophole in the Clayton Act; like the new Social Security Act, it was a major move.[4] The Hoover reforms passed—several economy and efficiency measures, especially the Reorganization Act, which provided that the House or Senate upon receiving a plan from the president for reorganizing part of the executive branch would have to reject it in sixty days, else it would stand approved.

On the minus side, Truman came to see that his victory in 1948 had given him little leverage with Congress, and the result was defeat of his proposed farm legislation. He championed a remarkable plan of his secretary of agriculture, Charles Brannan, who long before had observed that New Deal farm programs only helped the 2 percent of the nation's farmers who produced one-fourth of agricultural output—the big farmers. For the rest the acts restricted acreage, encouraging farmers to use science and ingenuity to increase yields. Brannan wanted to ration production by opening all produce—grains, tobacco, cotton, animal husbandry—to support, albeit with an interesting restriction: support could only be for eighteen hundred "units" (each unit was defined as an equivalent, such as thirty-two dozen eggs or ten bushels of corn). This meant two things. For one, the large farmer would have no more support units than the small, and hence would be on his own after he received his units; his lower costs would be of value to the national farm economy as a whole but not allow him to cash in on the support program. Second, the Brannan plan, as it was called, encouraged each farmer obtaining support to produce at the lowest possible cost, for the cheaper he produced the more he made. The advantage of the proposed system was that it removed the disguise from government-inspired attempts to restrict production, making restriction open, tied to the support units. An aspect of openness was that support payments were to be direct to farmers, in the form of subsidies, not roundabout for reduction of acreage.[5]

For a short while the Brannan plan looked like it could be adopted, but then the Farm Bureau Federation, always conservative, refused to go along. So did former secretary of agriculture Clinton Anderson, by this time senator from New Mexico. Businessmen wanted no support program at all, and if that was impossible then the least program necessary to keep farmers quiet. They were against the Brannan plan because of subsidies. They liked to forget the not-so-open protection they enjoyed through the tariff. The plan failed of passage, with a substitute arranged that amounted to a patchwork favoring producers of cotton, tobacco, and wheat. The Korean War then brought prosperity to farmers and made the plan unattractive.

The remaining parts of the economic program fared no better. Federal aid to primary and secondary education came up against arguments for equal allotment of money to black and white schools and money to parochial schools, and civil rights leaders and Catholics rose up. Eleanor Roosevelt sought to help the president by raising questions about public support for parochial schools, but Francis Cardinal Spellman of New York pronounced her anti-Catholic.

In housing, the administration's modest goal was "a decent house in a good environment for every American family." Truman signed the Housing and Rent Control Act (1949) allowing for low-cost public housing. It started with 156,000 units by 1952, an altogether inadequate figure. The program originally had much support from all groups, but as housing for most people became available—this after the intense wartime and postwar shortage—there was less support for public housing.[6] As for taxes for corporations and higher-income Americans, that proved difficult because of a recession in 1949, with unemployment up to 7.6 percent in February 1950, before dropping to 5.2 percent in June. Meanwhile, in May 1949, the House of Representatives voted down an administration-sponsored attempt to repeal the Taft-Hartley Act, and thereafter a series of industrial disputes, which caught public attention and engendered much disapproval, killed repeal.

Better medical care—insurance, expansion of medical, dental, and nursing schools, facilities, research—lost to claims of "socialized medicine" by the American Medical Association, although Congress did increase support for hospital construction. The president argued with one congressional committee for forty-five minutes in favor of federal support to medical education, to no avail. Dr. Sam E. Roberts of Kansas City spent a summer in England and wrote the president of the fearful destruction of incentive when people "guarantee everything from birth to the grave." The president wrote back, "[W]hen we find thirty-four per cent of our young men and women unfit for military service because of physical and mental defects, there is something wrong with the health of the country and I am trying to find a remedy for it." He concluded, rather jaggedly, "I'd suggest you doctors had better be hunting for a remedy yourselves unless you want a drastic one." But it was hard work reforming doctors. "Most doctors in the country are interested in what I am trying to do, and the vast majority of them would like to see it done," he wrote another Missouri friend, "but there is a clique in control of the American Medical Association which is like the old guard clique that controlled the Republican Party out of power." The late 1940s and early 1950s were a wonderful time to have instituted socialized medicine, that is, health care for all Americans, for it was long before medical costs climbed into the stratosphere— long before American physicians had accustomed themselves to high incomes and good living, before patients came to think that the unseen hand of insurance would pay everything, with the devil taking the hindmost through free if interminably slow care in the emergency room. As late as 1954, medical costs were incredibly cheap, though Truman, by that time in retirement, thought them high: "Most people can't pay $12.00 to $25.00 a day for a hospital room and $500.00 for a minor operation." But nothing was done, the system of free enterprise got out of control, and forty years later costs were rising toward 20 percent of the gross national product, leaving, as another president named after Thomas Jefferson sought to tell his fellow Americans, a third of them without any insurance, economic basket cases in event of illness.[7]

One must ask why after the election the president found it so difficult to enact his domestic program. Part of the reason was that he came up against the perennial factionalism of Congress, where despite division into Democrats and Republicans, and despite the administration's wide margin in the Eighty-first Congress—Democratic by 263 to 171 in the House, 54 to 42 in the Senate—votes for programs were along narrow lines of interest rather than by party. Too many members spoke for special interests. Truman once characterized Senator Russell as "the great Georgia Senator, representative of the National Chamber of Commerce, the Coca-Cola Company, etc."[8] By 1949–1950 congressmen also had been voting along a line of conservatives versus liberals for a decade, since the conservative coalition of the late 1930s overwhelmed the New Deal. Divisions also could occur between urban and agricultural congressmen, or along regional lines, or among congressmen representing interests too numerous to mention or calculate. Put differently, members of the president's party took interest in the Fair Deal only for the election, after which they went their separate ways.

The president's inability to control Congress, so far as concerned voting for the Fair Deal, derived in part from his own actions. He did not punish the Dixiecrats, and he should have; they kept their posts in the congressional hierarchy, and many were in control of committees. Another problem was that Truman, as a former senator, resented the way the Roosevelt administration twisted arms and pushed members—he did not want anything to do with such crudities. He preferred to deal with congressional leaders, the big four, or call a few individuals. Calling tended to work. It did not take much time, for one thing; when the president calls an individual, he gets through immediately. And Truman was effective in such conversations. But he did not call enough members. Another reason relations with Congress deteriorated, one that also marked a revulsion against Roosevelt's procedure, was his way of dealing with departments and agencies. Rather than pulling strings from the oval office, he preferred for department and agency heads to make their own presentations to Congress.[9]

In remarking Truman's failures it is important not to overlook his grudges against members, some of which he bore far too long, whatever the provocation. He disliked Senator Fulbright of Arkansas for the suggestion of 1946 that he, Truman, resign in favor of a Republican administration. Paul H. Douglas of Illinois seemed half-baked and theoretical, and he treated Douglas, a proud man, that way. Estes Kefauver of Tennessee similarly bothered him. Several members of the Lower House got on his nerves, and he showed it openly, as when he told F. Edward Hebert of Louisiana, who wanted a day of prayer against communism, to read the president's recent Thanksgiving proclamation (the president quite simply had asked his countrymen to pray for peace). He thought representatives were tyros compared to senators because their districts were so small, and he probably assumed that small districts meant small minds. By keeping these truths to himself and buttering up people he disliked, he might have done a good deal better with Congress.

Another factor inhibiting him with Congress, albeit a factor difficult to be sure of, may have been his fatigue. The campaign had been a virtuoso performance. To anyone who watched, it was obvious he was tireless, emotionally subject to no worries, and a better campaigner than the worldlings who surrounded him. But it had been a herculean task and he needed rest. He told his assistant press secretary, Eben Ayers, in April 1950, a year and more later, "I just can't take it any more."[10] The remark was about seeing so many White House visitors. It had a larger meaning, however, namely, that he needed to rest.

Also, by the second term the country was becoming more conservative, and this mood militated against the Fair Deal. For twenty years, since 1929, Americans had been through upheavals—the depression, the New Deal, war, reconversion, a new foreign policy. If conservatism means, in its largest sense, a feeling against change, keeping things as they are, the country was conservative.[11]

2

The man who reached the presidency in 1945 was an unlikely supporter of civil rights, and what followed during Truman's nearly eight years must have astonished friends and foes. From all appearance he was "safe" on civil rights. He came from a border state, from a rural background unaffected by residence in Independence. Early in the 1920s, running for eastern judge, he was careless in filling out a questionnaire about civil rights, and the Kansas City chapter of the National Association for the Advancement of Colored People refused to endorse him. It is true that in 1926 when he ran for presiding judge—which meant he ran at large throughout the county, including all the Kansas City wards—he paid more attention. But then during this race and his subsequent eight years in office he was only following the policy laid down by Boss Pendergast, who courted black support.[12]

As senator in 1935–1944, Truman showed no major signs of racial consciousness. He wrote Margaret in 1937 about attending a White House dinner where everything was served and "[a]ll these things were in courses, deftly placed and removed by an army of coons." He added: "I suggested to Mrs. Minton that these Negroes were evidently the top of the black social set in Washington."[13] The Indiana senator's wife, he knew, was from negrophobic southern Indiana. For this same period there is other, similar testimony. Years later, when Truman was president, one of his southern friends chose to embarrass him by relating what he said in 1938 when the Wagner-Van Nuys antilynch-ing bill was before the Senate. "You know I am against this bill," he had told this friend, "but if it comes to a vote, I'll have to vote for it. All my sympathies are with you but the Negro vote in Kansas City and St. Louis is too impor-tant."[14] A decade later, and reflecting his outlook for the 1930s, his sister, Mary Jane, told Jonathan Daniels, "Harry isn't any more in favor of nigger equality than I am." Speaking for herself in later years, her brother in earlier, she said there was not one black in Grandview and no one wanted them.[15]

As late as October 1945, Truman was capable of racial remarks, if in private. When the jazz pianist Hazel Scott, wife of Congressman Adam Clay-ton Powell of New York, was denied use of Constitution Hall, which was owned by the Daughters of the American Revolution, a potentially ugly situation arose. Bess Truman was scheduled to attend a DAR tea at the Sul-grave Club, and Powell sent a telegram asking her not to go. Bess, privately, bristled. She wrote Mary Paxton, "I was plenty burned up with the wire I had from that ———— in NY."[16] The president too was incensed, and told George Allen, who was going to New York, to look up that "damn nigger preacher" who said things about "the madam" and kick him around.[17] Powell did not assist matters by remarking that Mrs. Truman, who went to the tea, was the Last Lady of the Land. Publicly, the president must have instructed Hassett to prepare a suitable effusion; the presidential letter said the right things, that artistic talent was not the exclusive property of any one race or group and that one of the marks of a democracy was willingness to respect and reward talent without regard to race or origin. Privately, Truman blacklisted Powell from all social activities at the White House.

What then happened was the conversion of Harry Truman. Just how this occurred is not clear. It may have come from the realization that, as he liked to say, once he moved into 1600 Pennsylvania Avenue he was president of all the people. More likely it took place when, in September 1946, a group of blacks met in the oval office and calmly and frankly told him of racial actions in the South during the last year. Probably the visitors told how two black couples, driven in a car by a white farmer, were taken out and shot near Monroe, Georgia, because one of the men had stabbed a white who made advances to his wife. Another incident undoubtedly shocked the president, this about a black veteran, Isaac Woodard, yet wearing his uniform, who was taken off a bus in Batesburg, South Carolina, and blinded by policemen who jabbed their nightsticks into his eyes. Truman was visibly shaken and exclaimed, "My God! I had no idea it was as terrible as that! We've got to do something."[18] In December he appointed a group to see to the black cause; its chairman was Charles E. Wilson, president of General Electric, and its mixed membership was impressive.

Students of the Truman administration, almost without exception, have been certain about the president's conversion, and with much new evidence available the change of mind seems irrefutable. The author of a scholarly book on Truman and civil rights, published in 1970, was convinced the president never did a thing for black Americans unless he had a personal or political reason. The writer so disliked what he saw as Truman's racism that he awarded the president a few grudging words of praise only to subtract them in following pages, telling how time after time Truman said the right words and followed with nothing. The president set up his phrases only to let public or congressional inaction knock them down. But against this judgment are many others.[19] The president's White House assistants knew something had changed. Elsey, who saw a lot of Truman, said years later, "I think he probably had a much broader outlook on these matters after he became president. . . . I certainly think he meant absolutely everything he said. . . . I don't think there was anything phony about that at all. It wasn't a sham, it wasn't a pretense, it wasn't a lot of hot air *just* for political purposes. I believe that he believed what he was advocating there." When Charles Murphy was asked about civil rights—"[T]here are some historians who say that Mr. Truman's pronouncements on civil rights were taken from the standpoint of political expediency. What would you say about that?"—he answered: "I would say that is just as wrong as it can be." Tom Clark, attorney general and later Supreme Court justice, remembered, "He would just—sometimes we'd get to talking and he would tell me about, how when he was growing up—about the discrimination against the blacks, and how they couldn't get to first base, and everybody used them and things of that kind, you know. He was going to try to do something about it, that's what he told me."[20] Similarly he talked to Jonathan Daniels:

> I got to thinking about the Negro problem in the Senate. We had no real problem at home. But in railroad cases came upon situation where in Louisiana [and] Arkansas in the old days coal shovelers were Negroes but when [railroads] turned to oil burners white men wanted the jobs and shot men off the engines—and cases like that boy that got his eye knocked out in South Carolina.[21]

Max Lowenthal, who served in the White House as a special presidential assistant during several months in 1948, heard a story along the same lines from Truman's administrative assistant for minority affairs, David Niles. According to Niles, he and the president had been talking with a black visitor, perhaps two visitors, and

> there had just been some incident, I think a lynching. Dave said we needed another Wickersham Commission [such as President Hoover had appointed to examine into the working of Prohibition] (I remember that some months ago the president said, before the report of the Civil Rights Commission, when I was with him, that Dave was in effect acting as the secretary of "our Wickersham Commission"). The president said: let's set one up. Dave had to go, as he

almost always does the latter half of the week, to New York and Boston. When he returned on Monday there was a memo on his desk from the president, which said in effect: I was very serious about creating that commission, go to it, give it all you've got. Later, when some good names were disinclined to serve on the commission, Dave would go to the president who personally phoned them to serve.[22]

The result was appointment of the committee and issuance of its report, "To Secure These Rights," in October 1947. A frank document, it amounted to a ten-point civil rights message that went to Congress on February 2, 1948. The president asked for a law against lynching, revival of the Fair Employment Practices Committee that had disbanded after World War II, an end to discrimination in interstate transportation, and protection of voting rights. He did not confer with congressional leaders before sending it.

Reactions were quick in coming—reactions in which the president stood his ground. At a White House luncheon a national committeewoman from Alabama, Mrs. Leonard Thomas, told him, "I want to take a message back to the South. Can I tell them you're not ramming miscegenation down our throats? That you're for all the people, not just the North?" He read her the Bill of Rights, a copy of which he was carrying in his coat pocket. Then he said, "I'm everybody's president. I take back nothing of what I propose and make no excuse for it." Listening to the argument, a White House waiter became so excited he accidentally knocked a cup of coffee out of the president's hand.[23]

Vivian Truman went after his brother. "It looks to me as though there was only one thing left now that you could do—that would be to have old Franklin [Roosevelt] up to the White House for dinner. I am sure," he wrote, "the coons would shout your praises from then on." The response was unwavering: "I know there are some people who are decidedly disgruntled with the proposals made in the Bill of Rights Message but that Message is strictly in line with the Democratic Platform and presented nothing new to the Congress. It's never been stated all at once in one Message however, and I thought it was about time to do something about it."[24]

The immediate effect of the president's civil rights program was on the election of 1948, and it almost goes without saying that if Truman did not really care about civil rights he never would have gone in that direction. A dozen years later, when all was over, he could joke about what he did. He told two interviewers in 1959 that his committee's report "almost gave the Southerners hydrophobia."[25] Just at the moment when the Wallace-ites were trying to remove the liberal left wing of the Democratic party, the South went into rebellion on the right. Why did he do it? Possibly to reach black voters, who held swing votes in half a dozen northern states. But he really needed to temporize, to offer some sort of medicine to save the South from hydrophobia. Caution dictated silence or, at most, ambiguity.

The Democratic convention in the summer of 1948 was seized by the civil rights advocates. The president, watching from the wings as his own moderate proposal for a civil rights plank went down to defeat in the face of a rebellion led by the mayor of Minneapolis, Hubert H. Humphrey, and by former representative Andrew J. Biemiller, together with the black congressman from Chicago, William L. Dawson, was privately proud of the way the rebels carried out their proposal. "A Negro alternate from St. Louis makes a minority report suggesting the unseating of Mississippi delegation," he wrote. "Vaughn is his name. He's overruled. Then Congressman Dawson of Chicago, another Negro, makes an excellent talk on civil rights."[26]

The ensuing campaign did not stress civil rights, Truman doubtless staying away from the topic because he knew it was divisive. During his brief excursions into the South he stressed economic questions, continuing the New Deal and easing into the Fair Deal program he would announce again the next year.[27] The South had gained immensely from the New Deal, and it was a good subject. Only once did he get into civil rights, and that was in the speech of October 29 in Harlem. The speech was a historical first for a president and gave substance to his position. It was no major effort, and consisted of a brief tribute to his committee. He reaffirmed the civil rights message of February 2, his "determination to attain the goal of equal rights and equal opportunity." The speech was written by Philleo Nash, who worked in the office of David Niles.

In considering the Truman effort to bring fairness into the lives of black Americans, to give them the benefits of the Bill of Rights, it is necessary to relate that he obtained very little from Congress, just as in his Fair Deal program. After considerable pressure he usually could get measures through the House, but the Senate was impossible. The sticking point was Rule 22 of Senate procedure, in effect since 1917, which provided for everyone, including southern senators, to have a say. The rule gave southerners the right to filibuster civil rights issues. Allegedly, the rule allowed for cloture, but it was set up in such a way that it did the opposite by obfuscating the issue. Members went back and forth on procedure regarding cloture, what properly was necessary to shut off debate—whether two-thirds of the membership, two-thirds of those present, two-thirds of those present and voting, a majority, or something else altogether—or whether cloture might be invoked only for a pending measure, not a motion regarding a pending measure. It was impossible for outsiders to know whether proposals for cloture were serious, for the technicalities were so obscure. Northern senators with large black constituencies had to be careful, and Rule 22 was just what they needed. All the while their southern colleagues put on the pressure, intimating a need for compromise, for a senator's vote for cloture would bring a southern vote against that senator over some other issue. Occasionally southerners let important legislation stack up while they argued the subtleties of Rule 22.

With such obscurities the anti–civil rights senators defeated all the proposed Truman legislation.

To the president's chagrin, civil rights debates in the Senate circled around revival of the wartime Fair Employment Practices Committee (FEPC), something that should have been obviously fair and appropriate. The revived committee would give black Americans an economic chance, not present them with barriers and double standards, but Congress, principally the Senate, denied the president such a forum. In the decade between 1942 and 1952 seventy bills were introduced in both Houses. He faced defiance in the South, and in the Senate an alliance developed between southern Democrats and midwestern Republicans. Proposals like an FEPC gave a platform to such rabble-rousers as Senator James Eastland of Mississippi, who said the president's program was "to secure political favor from Red mongrels in the slums of the great cities of the East and Middle West" who planned to defile "the pure blood of the South." He railed against Truman's spokesmen in the Upper House: "This much is certain," he said. "If the present Democratic leadership is right, then Calhoun and Jefferson Davis were wrong. If the present Democratic leadership is right, then Thaddeus Stevens and Charles Sumner were right, and Lee, Forrest, and Wade Hampton were wrong. If the President's civil-rights program is right, then reconstruction was right. If this program is right, the carpetbaggers were right." He deplored the "organized mongrel minorities" that controlled the government. "I am going to fight it to the last ditch. They are not going to harlemize the country."[28] Truman had to wait until 1964 to see a statutory FEPC enacted in the Civil Rights Act of that year.

Lacking support in the Senate, the president nonetheless managed to move his program forward by two executive orders, one much more important than the other. The less important was Executive Order No. 9980, which created a Fair Employment Board within the Civil Service Commission. Its record was mixed, mainly because discrimination in government agencies, save for facilities in the South, was difficult to uncover and especially to prove. As the board pointed out, "Actual discrimination may be so subtly disguised under ostensibly correct procedure that it is difficult to identify or clearly establish."[29] Perhaps the board's membership was part of the difficulty; its members were not as active as they might have been. But then they had to move against customs and procedures that had been sanctified for decades, since the beginning of federal government, and the task was large. Slowly the board moved ahead and obtained some satisfaction within the state department and the bureau of printing and engraving, but other areas that had been filled with prejudicial personnel arrangements proved almost impervious to change.

Much more important was Executive Order No. 8981, which looked to desegregation of the armed forces. The racial scene in the services was scandalous, if viewed from any perspective of fairness. As Truman's committee report remarked, as late as 1947 the services commissioned few blacks. The navy was worst, with two black officers—and none in the marines. Personnel assignments were antediluvian; blacks could not enlist in any branch of the marines other than the steward's branch. The army had a 10 percent ceiling for black personnel, and fewer than one black in seventy was commissioned. On July 26, 1948, the same day as he issued the executive order for fair employment within the government, and the day before the special "Turnip Day" congressional session, the president issued Executive Order No. 8981, providing for an end to segregation in the services; as chief executive this was within his competence—Congress could not stop him.[30] Under the executive order for the military Truman appointed the Committee on Equality of Treatment and Opportunity in the Armed Services; eventually, with assistance from the manpower crisis during the Korean War, everything worked out. He chose former solicitor general Charles H. Fahy as committee chairman. A lawyer from Louisiana, Fahy said to Truman, "Mr. President, do you want to see the armed services integrated or do you want a report?" The president answered, "This is not an attempt to give a report. I want the armed services integrated." Fahy then came up against the army, where General Bradley, from the president's own state, Missouri, made trouble. The day after the executive order Bradley declared at Fort Knox, "[T]he Army is not out to make any social reforms. The Army will put men of different races in different companies. It will change that policy when the Nation as a whole changes it."[31] But by the time of the Korean War the president had persuaded the army to commit itself to integration in a gradualistic manner—in March 1950, he signed a secret agreement to reinstitute the quota if the new policy brought "disproportionate balance of racial strength."[32] Then the opening of the war brought the need for men, placed in effective units. Bradley's successor, General Collins, ordered integration. His assistant, General Anthony McAuliffe, said afterward, "We didn't do it to improve the social situation," but because of efficiency.[33] By the time of the armistice in Korea, in the early summer of 1953, according to General Mark W. Clark, the average squad was composed of "four white Americans, one Negro American, two and a half Koreans and the remainder Puerto Ricans, Mexicans, Hawaiians, and American Indians."[34] The war similarly forced integration of the other services.

The other effective way—apart from executive order—that Truman promoted civil rights was through working with the Supreme Court. Here he first saw to it that Attorney General Clark got the message. In talks at the poker table the president told him about his own Missouri experience; Clark amusedly remembered, years later, that he thought Truman was poking him up because, knowing Clark was from Texas, the president was unsure of his bona fides. The result was that the justice department under Clark brought amicus curiae briefs in Supreme Court cases that challenged the separate-but-equal decision of 1896 and prepared the way for striking it down in 1954.

The first important case involving civil rights was *Shelley v. Kraemer* (1948), in which Chief Justice Vinson, speaking for five other justices (the remaining three disqualified themselves), declared that housing covenants directed toward a group of people "defined wholly in terms of race and color" were in violation of the Fourteenth Amendment and hence no court could enforce them. This was perhaps a small move and produced only some integrated private housing. Still, it did provide alternatives to the ghettos.

Far more important were three cases decided in 1950: *Henderson v. U.S.*, declaring segregation of railroad dining cars illegal under the Interstate Commerce Act; *McLaurin v. Oklahoma State Regents*, forbidding separation of a black student from other students at the University of Oklahoma, this under the Fourteenth Amendment; and *Sweatt v. Painter*, also under the amendment, forbidding a separate black law school in Texas. All these decisions were decided by votes of 8 to 0. Thurgood Marshall, later a justice of the Supreme Court, who as a lawyer had fought for favorable consideration of these cases, said after the decisions, "The complete destruction of all enforced segregation is now in sight."

All in all, considering the times, Truman did remarkably well with civil rights—through making brave and decent statements, raising issues when he had little personally to gain, and urging their adoption publicly and privately because it was the right thing to do. Given the intransigence of the Senate, the execution of his program had to be by executive order and in cooperation with the High Court. The results were touchingly appreciated by black leaders. An almost emotional letter from Roy Wilkins, dated January 12, 1953, when the president was about to leave office, has often been quoted:

> Mr. President, I want to thank you and to convey to you my admiration for your efforts in the civil rights field, for your pronouncements and definitions of policy on racial discrimination and segregation. . . . [N]o Chief Executive in our history has spoken so plainly on this matter as yourself and acted so forthrightly. . . . Yours was sheer personal courage, so foreign in the usual conduct of political office, high or low. . . . As you leave the White House you carry with you the gratitude and affection of millions of your Negro fellow citizens who under your leadership have seen the old order change right before their eyes.[35]

3

Civil liberties, unlike civil rights, lacked the beacon of presidential leadership, and the Truman administration was the worse therefor. The president gave occasional guidance, but that was hardly enough. There were so many other lights shining that the American people were bewildered.

Let it be said that for civil liberties the period was most difficult, comparable only to the 1790s, when many frenzied people thought the Reign of

Terror in France might transfer itself to the United States, or to 1919–1920, when bolshevism in Russia raised similar fear.

Unlike its analogues, the reputation of the era after World War II, which lasted well into the 1950s, beyond the Truman administration, by some account until collapse of the Soviet Union, had some basis in fact. Even now, the Soviet threat gone, the full story is not available. Enough is known, however, to say that subversion was a very real problem, no figment of imagination.

The worst trouble lay not with Russian-born but with recruited agents, and most of it in the machinations of three British spies, H. A. R. "Kim" Philby, Donald Maclean, and Klaus Fuchs, respectively representing British intelligence, the diplomatic service, and the nuclear establishment. They penetrated the CIA, state department, Manhattan Project, and its successor, the Atomic Energy Commission. By the end of the Truman era Philby was under a cloud and separated from anything of a classified nature, Maclean had escaped to the Soviet Union, and Fuchs had confessed and was in jail. But much had been lost.[36]

On the American side the guilty were less able. The most important were members of the ring run by Julius Rosenberg, probably with the knowledge and perhaps cooperation of his wife, Ethel, which included David Greenglass and Harry Gold. Smaller figures were the confessed couriers Whittaker Chambers and Elizabeth T. Bentley. Suspects turned up over the years, such as Judith Coplon in the justice department, William W. Remington in the commerce department, and Nathan G. Silvermaster in the Farm Security Administration; the damage they could have done would not have been large. Not the slightest evidence ever appeared incriminating members of the foreign service stationed in China, who raised the ire of Ambassador Hurley in 1945, most of whom he drove to other positions, whence they passed into forced retirement. Still an enigma in the calculation of American spying is the case of Alger Hiss, who was convicted only of perjury.[37]

Underneath popular fear of subversion was a foundation of fact. But one must add hastily that most of the accusations heard during this parlous time came to nothing. Now and then a minor spy would appear, likely as not a well-meaning fellow traveler of the 1930s, a former spy because of disenchantment with the Nazi-Soviet Pact of 1939. But it takes professionals to catch professionals, and the effort to round up such people (and, in the case of Hiss, try them for perjury) was not worth the time and attention lavished upon it.

And what should the president have done about all this? With the end of World War II the security issue came to public attention and acquired the proportions that made it so intractable.[38] The Igor Gouzenko case, discovered in October 1945, was proof the Russians had infiltrated the Manhattan Project in a ring run out of the Soviet embassy in Ottawa. In the congressional elections of 1946 the Republicans took advantage, pledging to "clean the communists and fellow travelers out of government." They wanted a statutory definition of loyalty, which the president rightly saw as a possible witch-hunt.

After election of the Eightieth Congress he decided he would have to do something. Late in November he set up the Temporary Commission on Employee Loyalty, and on March 22, 1947, he adopted its recommendations in Executive Order No. 9835, the Federal Employee Loyalty Program.

The loyalty program did not produce much in the way of disloyal employees, and in fact was its own proof that the need was for counterintelligence by the FBI and the CIA, established that same year for international measures. The Truman program resulted in a "name check" of each employee. Whenever derogatory information came up there was to be a probe, then the case was to go to a tiered loyalty board, the final group being housed in Washington. One of the points of investigation was membership in or association with organizations designated by the attorney general as subversive. Intellectual curiosity and reform could become identified with communism. Still, by mid-1952, when more than 4 million people, actual or prospective employees, had gone through the check, boards had charged only 9,077, brought 2,961 to hearings, and dismissed or denied employment to 378—.002 percent of the total. None of the discharged cases led to discovery of espionage.

It is a good question whether Truman sized up the situation correctly, and in retrospect one wishes he had tried to avoid his executive order. The order's lack of results was not the problem so much as the witch-hunting it encouraged, the very thing he did not want. The standard by which government officials dismissed people was "reasonable grounds . . . for belief that the person involved is disloyal." That was bad enough. Early in 1951 the administration made the standard worse by allowing the review board to adjudge "reasonable doubt."[39] Almost anything could justify dismissal. Clark Clifford has written of his regret that the administration did this, regret also that Truman never took back what he thought was the need for an administration program, never felt instituting one was a mistake.[40] To this it is only possible to guess that the president knew more about subversion—Prime Minister W. L. Mackenzie King of Canada made a special trip to Washington to inform him of the Gouzenko case—and had better understanding of the political pressure for a program.

In asking whether Truman might have avoided a program there is another factor worth consideration, namely, pressure from the powerful head of the FBI, J. Edgar Hoover. It is now possible to see that Hoover was a malign influence on American government, a most unfortunate official. The FBI managed many of its duties well, but the coterie of top officials within the agency whom Hoover controlled and bent to his personal and political purposes made the place a satrapy rather than a government agency. Hoover was constantly pushing for more rules about loyalty, and in his many contacts with congressmen he was quite willing to insinuate that the Truman administration was soft on communism.

The president's relations with Hoover were not good, and for the most part he managed to keep Hoover at arm's length. Some years ago a top Hoover aide told an interesting story in this regard.[41] When Truman became president, Hoover sent word throughout the ranks of the FBI that he wanted any agent or other bureau employee who knew Truman personally to advise the director of that fact. After much pondering, an agent who was the son of a longtime Truman friend reluctantly decided to identify himself. Hoover was delighted, and instructed the agent to renew his acquaintance with the new president and carry a message for Mr. Hoover. The message, relayed by the old friend's son to the new president, was that Hoover and his organization stood ready, without resort to the attorney general, to comply with any request the chief executive might make. No thanks, Truman told his friend's son, and added: tell Mr. Hoover that any request I have I'll pass on—through my attorney general. Truman never made a request of Hoover, directly or through the attorney general. The chilliness in the relationship between Truman and the FBI director that followed the president's rebuff never thawed.

Hoover's attempt to get close to Truman may have provoked the president to agree with his first budget director, Harold Smith, who on May 11, 1945, told Truman the FBI should not be spending federal money merely to satisfy curiosity concerning the sex life of Washington bureaucrats and members of Congress. The next day Truman wrote a note to himself saying, "We want no Gestapo or Secret Police. F.B.I. is tending in that direction."[42]

It must have been with the president's knowledge that at the outset of the administration Attorney General Clark refused Hoover the right to undertake wiretaps. Here there had been a saddening situation. Although the Federal Communications Act of 1934 had made tapping unlawful, President Roosevelt in 1940 issued a secret directive to Attorney General Robert H. Jackson, later associate justice of the Supreme Court, to tap "persons suspected of subversive activities." Jackson decided that if information from a tap was not divulged outside the government it would be legal. This sophistry lasted into the 1960s, when the Supreme Court ruled that the Fourth Amendment forbade warrantless wiretapping. But in 1945, under Clark, Hoover could get no taps. In a remarkable oral history Clark's executive assistant, H. Graham Morison, has related how for two years, 1946–1947, while in Clark's office, he held off the director. Morison accumulated Hoover's wiretapping requests, "those damn things," in his desk drawer until he had about fifty. Whereupon "Edgar" called Clark and said, "I want to know why some fifty requests for wiretap were not acted upon."[43]

"Well," was the attorney general's answer, "I guess Graham Morison has them. It is his job to first review them."

Clark called Morison, who said, "Tom, you revere our Constitution; I know you do, I've talked to you about it."

Clark told Hoover there would be no wiretaps. The astonished attorney general told Morison, "My God, I thought I would never see the day when somebody would 'buck' Edgar! He has walked over every Attorney General since Attorney General Stone [attorney general in the Coolidge administration and later chief justice of the Supreme Court]. You know he has a political line to the Congress."

Morison's reply was, "Well, blame it on me."

Clark's response was, "That's what I intend to do."

Remembering this exchange, Morison recalled his relations with Hoover afterward, which were remarkably good. When former Senator A. B. "Happy" Chandler stepped down as baseball commissioner, Hoover recommended Morison for the job; Morison did not want it but was pleased at the gesture. After Clark's assistant left the justice department, Hoover and his deputy, Clyde Tolson, used to invite him to lunch every two weeks at the old Harvey's Restaurant. When Hoover died, Morison was invited by the family to attend the funeral.

Supporting Clark against Hoover, as he presumably did, Truman looked good on wiretapping. Unfortunately at the same time he either asked for or allowed a wiretap on the former New Deal brain truster Thomas Corcoran, who during World War II had developed a lucrative law practice based on his Washington connections; among other clients, he represented the Chinese Nationalist government and defense contractors.[44] Transcripts went to the president's military aide, General Vaughan. Corcoran, though, suspected his phone was tapped, and to the amusement of his friends did most of his intimate phone calling from a booth in a Connecticut Avenue drugstore, deducting the nickels from his income tax as a business expense. After his death, five thousand pages of transcripts in the Truman Library were opened to researchers.

The president's civil liberties record is thus mixed. His Federal Employee Loyalty Program was no achievement. His wiretapping record was marred by the Corcoran case. Then it was his ill luck to be afflicted by the House Un-American Activities Committee (HUAC), by the McCarran Internal Security Act of 1950, by the McCarran-Walter Immigration Act of 1952, and, beginning in 1950, by the errant Senator McCarthy. He tried to fight these four phenomena, but it was a losing battle from the start, given the popular climate of opinion.

With the HUAC, headed in 1948 by Representative J. Parnell Thomas of New Jersey, who soon was convicted of taking salary kickbacks from his congressional staff, there was little the president could do other than decry its existence. If the House wanted such a special committee he could not prevent it, especially during the Eightieth Congress. Years later he offered his opinion of HUAC publicly: "I've said many a time that I think the Un-American Activities Committee in the House of Representatives was the most un-American thing in America."[45]

When Congress passed the McCarran Internal Security Act the president vetoed it, only to see it pass over his veto by an overwhelming margin: only forty-eight members of the House and ten senators voted to sustain the president. The act was a legal and administrative monstrosity, so wrote the Truman biographer Cabell Phillips, "destined to be fought over in the courts for more than a decade and adding little to the net security of the nation."[46]

The McCarran-Walter Immigration Act of 1952 was another monstrosity, its purpose being to restrict immigration, meanwhile making certain that no communists got into the United States. Again it passed over Truman's veto, with the president lacking just two votes to sustain the veto in the Senate. The president privately annotated a copy of the veto message, with scathing comments on the bill's unfairness:

> This is nothing short of outrageous!
> What a friendly piece of legislation! What a contribution to world peace and understanding!
> If this is equalization I do not know the definition of discrimination!
> This is a totalitarian approach.
> When a premise is wrong it cannot be corrected by written gobbledegook!
> This is a dinger!
> This is a violation of the Bill of Rights. In my opinion it is Justinian law.
> An agreement to ex post facto!

Section 340(a) provided that citizenship of a naturalized citizen could be revoked if within ten years he was convicted of contempt for refusing to testify as a witness in any proceeding before a congressional committee concerning "his subversive activities." To this the president added in hand, "This one section is ample reason for a veto!" The president's distress is saddening to read: "A citizen of this great country is a person with a very great privilege. Every citizen of the United States is the equal of every other citizen under the Constitution and the law regardless of his race creed or point of origin. . . . There are no second-class citizens in this Republic."[47]

Last there was McCarthy, whom Truman underestimated when he appeared on the scene in February 1950 claiming, "I have here in my hand a list"—a supposed list of communists in the state department, never produced, that purportedly had 205 names but in subsequent public remarks diminished to 81 and finally 57 names. The president wrote Secretary of Commerce Charles Sawyer that he, Truman, was en route to Grand Coulee to discuss power development, and "I think by the time I arrive at Grand Coulee evidence will have been presented which will put Mr. McCarthy in the 'doghouse' for good and we won't have to mention him any more even politically."[48] But then a Senate committee under Millard E. Tydings of Maryland investigated McCarthy's charges and brought in a critical report that produced a fiasco because voting was by party line, even including Senator Margaret Chase Smith, Republican of Maine, who together with other anti-McCarthy senators had announced a "Declaration of Conscience." The vote came out forty-five Democrats against McCarthy, thirty-seven Republicans for. In the autumn elections McCarthy campaigned against Tydings, who was defeated.

Truman did what he could against the man from Wisconsin. He made scathing comments at his press conferences, declaring there was "not a word of truth" in McCarthy's allegations and telling reporters McCarthy and his supporters were "the greatest asset the Kremlin had." When Senator Taft accused the president of libeling McCarthy, Truman asked a reporter, "Do you think that is possible?" McCarthy said General Marshall was incompetent; Truman told a press conference the charge was not worth commenting on.[49]

The president composed a letter in which he told McCarthy off:

> I read your telegram of February eleventh from Reno, Nevada, with a great deal of interest and this is the first time in my experience, and I was ten years in the Senate, that I ever heard of a Senator trying to discredit his own Government before the world. You know that isn't done by honest public officials. Your telegram is not only not true and an insolent approach to a situation that should have been worked out between man and man but it shows conclusively that you are not even fit to have a hand in the operation of the Government of the United States.
>
> I am very sure that the people of Wisconsin are extremely sorry that they are represented by a person who has as little sense of responsibility as you have.[50]

But then he did not send it, and time passed—busyness intervened, and civil liberties slipped into a trough such as it had fallen into only twice before. The security issue seemed hopeless. Truman's record would have looked better if he had said more, but he chose to stand back from this dismal fray.

4

For Truman the fourth and last of his efforts to achieve fairness in the lives of others concerned creation of a refuge for Jews in Palestine. In this regard it is worth setting out his position, which was hardly what people thought it was. All he wanted to do was ensure a fair deal for Jews around the world and especially in Western Europe, where the Nazis had turned their lives into chaos. He was not really a Zionist. Even after he took measures that made him seem one, he never felt that way. In later years, as he grew old, he could break into tears whenever people praised him for creating the Jewish state. The sentiment touched him; he felt that in his presidency, which people often maligned during the 1950s and 1960s, he had done his best, his damnedest he liked to say, and he appreciated a little praise. To outsiders it seemed that he was carrying the torch for Zionism and always had, but in reality he beheld a great wrong and tried to right it. To use another of his favorite phrases during his retirement, "that was all there was to it."

In a general way he had thought about the Middle East for many years. He grew up in the era of the suffering Armenians; everyone knew about them. As a young man, he had also read the family's large-print Bible, if only because it was easier to read than the few other books in the Truman household. As he looked at illustrations in the Bible, the rounded houses and hills, the hanging gardens of Babylon, he must have wondered why there could not be peace in the region. When he became president he soon was believing that if peoples of the Middle East would cease quarreling, they could turn the place into what it once had been, "a revival of the Garden of Eden that would take care of thirty million people and feed all the Near East."[51] Point 4, the fourth point in his inaugural address of 1949 that took on a life of its own, pledging technical aid to developing nations around the world, attracted him for this reason; it came to his attention just after the independence of Israel, when war had broken out with the Arab states. It offered the prospect of organizing the place according to one of his favorite models, the Tennessee Valley Authority. Within the United States he had dreamed of a Missouri Valley Authority. Likewise his dream of a TVA in the Middle East.

The Middle East issue arose at one point during the Potsdam Conference. Churchill had a quick response: he told the president that he, the prime minister, would not welcome a four-power conference over it. Of course, he said, if the United States wanted to take Britain's place as the principal power in the area, that would be different. Truman's answer was, "No, thanks."[52]

One must inquire whether subsequently the president received instruction on Zionism from his haberdashery friend Eddie Jacobson. The truth is that it is hard to know. Eddie had an open entrée to the White House, and during Truman's presidency he saw the president at least two dozen times, in addition to meeting him other places, such as New York, Key West, and Kansas City. During the 1948 campaign he traveled with the president. But how much conversation during visits turned on Palestine, on what would become the State of Israel, is unclear. Eddie's lawyer, A. J. Granoff, accompanied Eddie between five and eight times, so Granoff estimated. A dedicated Zionist, Granoff remembered that he spoke up about the subject several times. He also remembered that until late in 1947, when the issue came to a vote in the United Nations General Assembly, Eddie never thought much about Zionism. Eddie, he said, was a "card-carrying Reformed Jew" who never gave world Jewry a thought. Granoff never remembered talking with Eddie about Palestine, Jewish history, the annihilation of six million Jews, or its historic effect on the world. "It would be just like having discussed Greece or Babylonia with him. It never occurred to me, or it never occurred to him. We never discussed such things."[53]

If Eddie Jacobson and his lawyer advanced Zionism with the president, there also was a counterforce. The Zionists went after Truman so hard in the first year or two after the war that he quickly tired of their representations. In October 1945 he wrote Virginia C. Gildersleeve, who had been one of the American delegates to the San Francisco Conference, "The Jewish and Arab situation in the Near East is a most difficult one and has caused us more difficulty than most any other problem in the European Theater. I am hopeful that we will get it worked out on a satisfactory basis." The next month he drafted, but did not send, a sharp letter to Senator Joseph H. Ball of Minnesota opposing creation of a Jewish homeland. A year later in a letter to Ed Pauley he pronounced a curse on the whole problem:

> That situation is insoluble in my opinion. I have spent a year and a month trying to get some concrete action on it. Not only are the British highly successful in muddling the situation as completely as it could possibly be muddled, but the Jews themselves are making it almost impossible to do anything for them. They seem to have the same attitude toward the "underdog" when they are on top as they have been treated as "underdogs" themselves. I suppose that is human frailty.

He wrote Pauley during the time when the American nation was enduring more industrial strikes—both capital and labor trying for more of the national pie—than at any earlier time in history, and he likened the Palestine problem to labor problems. At one time business in America, he explained, was top dog, labor the underdog. Conditions had reversed and labor was misbehaving: "The only fellow who suffers is the innocent bystander who tries to help."[54]

As regards Zionist pressure, Rabbi Abba Hillel Silver of Cleveland made a special contribution to presidential ill humor. Head of the American Zionist Emergency Council, he seemed an influential Jewish leader. He boasted of four hundred local chapters of his council, spread across the country. That may have been so, but it was beyond dispute that he did not possess a scintilla of tact. Even to Zionists he was insufferable. During a meeting in New York, Rabbi Stephen S. Wise, a gentle man, pleaded with him that he, Wise, was an old man and there was plenty of time, and room, for Silver to be in the limelight of Zionism. Silver turned on his heel and strode off. On July 2, 1946, calling at the White House, he literally pounded on the president's desk, an opportunity he did not receive again. Truman never forgave him. He linked him with the terrorism of Jewish extremist groups in Palestine. "Terror and Silver," he once wrote an assistant, "are the contributing causes of *some*, not all of our troubles."[55]

Such efforts to push the president around confirmed him in his belief that whatever drama was about to unfold in the Middle East it should be in charge of the British government, not the American. After all, the British needed to do something in the postwar world other than, as a later prime minister reportedly said, play Greece to America's Rome, and they could put their talents to use in the Middle East. He considered his role to be only advisory, seeking some practical solution.

The British, he believed, for all their finesse, were slow at whatever they undertook and needed American suggestions. In the autumn of 1945, perhaps when not yet fully irritated by the Zionists, he advised the British publicly that they should issue 100,000 more certificates (the mandate's equivalent of visas) for immigration of Jewish displaced persons from Western Europe; he reiterated that advice a year later prior to the 1946 congressional elections. Between the two pronouncements committees investigated the Palestine problem, an Anglo-American committee appointed late in 1945, which reported after a few months, and a cabinet committee. The former proposed continuation of the mandate and an eventual UN trusteeship; the latter committee, organization of two communities, Jewish and Arab, with joint economic and diplomatic representation. Neither proposition proved satisfactory to the Jews and to the Arabs.

The scene then shifted to a series of events in 1947–1948 that brought the independence of the State of Israel, events that in retrospect seemed foreordained. In truth this was hardly the case. The administration did not want leadership in Palestine, hoping the British would do something, but one thing led to another.

It has often been related how creation of Israel occurred in three stages, all affected and in the second stage sponsored by the government of the United States. First came the vote on the UN resolution for partition, on November 29, 1947, then the sudden move of the U.S. representative in the UN, Senator Warren Austin, on March 19, 1948, in favor of great-power (United States, Britain, France) trusteeship, and last the arrangement of American recognition of the new state on May 14, 1948. The first stage began when the British, early in 1947, gave the Palestine problem to the UN. The world body appointed a committee that arrived at the same judgment as President Truman's cabinet committee. The report went to the General Assembly, and the president found himself under intense pressure: it became evident that if local forces decided who should govern Palestine, the well-armed Jewish militia would win. The solution proposed by the UN was for two communities under joint governance. The proposal favored, indeed would result in, a Jewish state, because Jewish forces would dominate. A vote for two communities was a vote for one.

Truman personally supported the first stage, that is, the UN proposal for partition, but for a long while the outcome was unclear. There was opposition in the department of defense led by Secretary Forrestal, who seized every occasion, and sometimes spoke when there was none, to announce his hostility to a Jewish state in Palestine. The prospect offended him. He declared it against the national interest, for in any future war the United States would need Middle East oil. The head of the Near East division of the state department, Loy W. Henderson, agreed and was almost as vociferous as Forrestal. Too, Zionists overplayed their hand in bringing pressure on the small nations of the UN. Such tactics appalled Truman. Granoff later said the Zionists were unsure the president would support partition until two weeks before the vote, when Jake Arvey of Chicago called the president to say that the state department was undercutting American policy. This angered Truman, according to Arvey, and he summoned his department people and passed the word to support his policy. Jacobson, who was keeping a diary, recorded that Truman said he swung the votes of several delegations. The General Assembly voted for partition by three votes beyond the necessary two-thirds majority.[56]

After the vote, Jacobson called Granoff and said, "I got a brainstorm." Granoff asked what was on his mind, and Jacobson said that the two of them should go to Washington and thank the president for supporting partition, saying only, "Mr. President, thank you and God bless you." Granoff told Eddie, "Do you call that a brainstorm? That's an inspiration." They went and received a welcome, with the president remarking, "Sit down, you bastards, sit down." The subject turned to other matters. It was Eddie's twenty-eighth wedding anniversary, and Truman at first confused the occasion when Eddie asked him what it was, and said, "Twenty-eight, 1919, why, you and I were on Twelfth and Baltimore Streets losing our . . . in that store." He then remembered he had taken Eddie and Bluma to Independence to escape the wedding send-off, and from there they had gone to St. Louis for the wedding trip.[57]

Similarly, in the second of the three stages leading to Israeli independence, the Zionists nearly lost. Trusteeship, proposed by Austin at the UN, could have ruined everything. That would have meant supervision of Palestine by the powers. Truman actually had agreed to trusteeship, perhaps absent-mindedly, while on a trip to Bermuda aboard the *Williamsburg*, but it was now necessary for the president to back away from trusteeship, no easy thing to do. On the day before Austin's move the president had met with Chaim Weizmann, then visiting New York, who shortly would be president of the State of Israel, and assured him that there would be no change in policy from partition—a green light to Weizmann's Jewish Agency, the principal Zionist group in Palestine—and this meant that there would be no military intervention by the United States, the only nation that could have put troops in Palestine. Truman thought he would be told of any decisions to the contrary before announcements were made, but the state department had forgotten to tell him about the Austin proposal. The morning after the Austin speech of March 19, the astonished president, reading about his policy in the newspapers, called his counsel, Clifford. "Can you come down right away?" he asked Clifford. "There's a story in the papers on Palestine and I don't know what's happened. I don't understand this. How could this have happened? I assured Chaim Weizmann. . . . He must think I am a . . ." He was in "the most embarrassing position of his presidential career—not excepting the position he was put in by the Wallace episode." So judged Charlie Ross, who ought to have known. The truth of the matter could not come out. "Telling it would have made out the P as vacillating, or ignorant of something of the most vital importance, or both; and the truth, moreover, could only have been accompanied with a wholesale repudiation of the state department. What a dilemma!" At a meeting to try to find out what had happened, Truman said, "They have made me out a liar and a double-crosser! We are *sunk*." Still, Austin gradually muddled the American proposal, which was largely forgotten.[58]

Matters moved to the third stage, independence, and again the position of the administration was not altogether sure. Support for independence came only after a meeting involving Clifford, Truman, and Secretary Marshall. This White House meeting of May 11, 1948, in which the president asked Clifford to present the case for recognition, was a fiery affair. When Clifford talked the next year with Jonathan Daniels, he was still warm about what Marshall had said to him, which was that he, Clifford, had no business being at the meeting. Marshall also warned Truman that if the president were to follow Clifford's advice and if in the election he, the secretary, were to vote, he would vote against the president. Truman ended the appalling session by saying he would look "very carefully at the matter of recognition."[59] Thereafter Clifford dealt with Undersecretary Lovett, who managed to gain Marshall's unenthusiastic assent to recognition.

Let it be said, in passing, that Clifford pushed hard for recognition, according to his own accounts ventured forty years and more after the fact. It was an audacity for him to have put himself up against the distinguished secretary of state in such an important matter; even if the president allowed him to make the case, it was not wise of Clifford to have taken the assignment, and if he simply had to take it (one suspects from his memoirs that he did not hesitate) he did not have to push the issue as if he were in court. Moreover, afterward he played fast and loose with Lovett. By Clifford's own testimony the president had said to him, "[B]e careful. I can't afford to lose General Marshall." Notwithstanding, he told the undersecretary of state, "Bob, there is no chance whatsoever that the President will change his mind on the basic issue. . . . [I]f anyone is going to give, it is going to have to be General Marshall, because—I can tell you now—the President is not going to give an inch." When three days later Lovett suggested waiting a few hours until after the UN General Assembly, then in session, adjourned around ten that night, Clifford pulled another fast one. He told Lovett he would check with the president, waited approximately three minutes, called back, and said delay was out of the question.[60]

The new state declared its independence at midnight on May 14–15, 1948, Tel Aviv time, which was 6:00 P.M., May 14, Washington time. U.S. recognition came at 6:11 P.M., Washington time.

The aftermath of recognition was as awkward for the administration as the moves leading to it. A few minutes after the deed was done, Marshall called Dean Rusk, in charge of UN affairs in the department, and told him to "get up to New York right away to keep our U.N. delegation from resigning en masse." Knowing nothing of what had taken place in Washington, the UN delegation was still proposing trusteeship. After a hasty trip Rusk told them, "[Y]ou just have to bite your tongue at the back end."[61]

The president designated James G. McDonald, head of the Foreign Policy Association and an ardent Zionist, as his special representative (recognition was de facto, not de jure, and he could not formally appoint an ambassador) to the new state, and announced the appointment without consulting Secretary Marshall. Upon receiving the envoy at the state department, the secretary brusquely told McDonald he did not like the president's procedure. En route to Israel, McDonald passed through London, where Foreign Secretary Bevin received him. Bevin had charged on the floor of the House of Commons that Truman wanted the refugee Jews to go to Israel because he did not want them in New York. For this Truman privately described him not merely as a boor but as a "son-of-a-bitch." When McDonald appeared at the foreign office the foreign secretary growled and glowered and talked about President Truman, pounding the table, almost shouting, charging that the Jews were ungrateful for what Britain had done for them in Palestine, that they had shot British police and soldiers, hanged several of them, and now were alienating British opinion by their attitude toward Arab refugees. Ambassador Lewis Douglas, who accompanied the American envoy, sought to calm the secretary, who only snarled in reply that what with the Berlin crisis and Britain's economic troubles it was just too bad he and his colleagues had to bother with Palestine.[62]

The president, one might conclude, had stepped into a diplomatic minefield when he tried to help the Jews find a refuge in Palestine. He had begun with the idea, taken out of the Armenian tribulations of the 1890s and youthful reading of the Bible, vastly reinforced by what happened under Hitler, that the Jews "deserved a home." From there matters passed almost out of control. A few days after recognition he tried to set out his thoughts in a letter to the leader of the Liberal party in New York, Dean Alfange. "The main difficulty with our friends, the Jews in this country," he wrote, "is that they are very emotional—they, the Irish and the Latin Americans have something in common along that line. The President of the United States has to be very careful not to be emotional."[63] His first purpose was to work for 145 million people, he said. Of those people, as became evident in subsequent years, few wished to go to Israel; instead, half a million Israelis came to the United States. Nonetheless, Jewish-Americans in large numbers supported Israel. The president's second objective, he had added, was peace in the world. He believed that a refuge in Palestine, in 1948 to become the State of Israel, was part of his secondary task.

Chapter Fifteen

The Korean War

*I*n a closed system like the Soviet Union, where everything depends on the judgment of a dictator, it is likely to be only a matter of time before such an individual, in his relations with other countries, makes a massive miscalculation; such we now can see is probably what happened with the Korean War. Stalin seems to have had no idea that when the North Koreans attacked the South Koreans the United States would intervene. With the opening of the Soviet archives after the collapse of the USSR, an American researcher has obtained a document that shows the communist head of North Korea, Kim Il Sung, almost bombarding Stalin with pleas to allow an attack on South Korea—he sent Stalin no less than forty-eight telegrams. Kim wanted to unify Korea; he argued that all Koreans, north and south, desired a single country, and in this respect he was a nationalist representing the hope of his countrymen. According to the researcher, Stalin at last gave in, upon Kim's repeated assurances that the Americans would not intervene. The date was set for June 25—the invasion took place, and the Americans intervened. Fearful of the power of the United States, Stalin then drew back; prior to the Chinese intervention, he would have allowed the roll-up of Kim's government and troops, which very nearly took place.

Chinese intervention naturally made a difference. The Soviets had signed a mutual defense pact with Communist China in February 1950, and Stalin could not treat relations with the Chinese lightly. He therefore was a bit more supportive, sending a few pilots and antiaircraft batteries to guard the Yalu bridges in November 1950, and more in the spring of 1951. The American researcher believes that Stalin's uneasy relations with Chairman Mao, his fear that the Chinese would dispute his leadership of the international communist movement, may have led him initially to approve Kim's plan to attack South Korea.[1]

The Americans, on their part, may be forgiven for refusing to believe that an attack by a puppet state using Soviet equipment could have occurred without Stalin's consent. Nor did they believe that the unification of Korea by

Kim would be the end of matters—that the war could be only a Korean, not a large international, affair. The Truman administration saw the war as a probe and Kim as a stalking-horse: the Soviets were trying to see how far they could go, and after Korea would come an attack on Iran or, if the Soviet Union were sufficiently emboldened, West Germany, and there might follow the communization of all Western Europe. Hence it was necessary to intervene with the full force of American power and prevent this naked aggression.

1

For the United States the background of the Korean catastrophe lay in several developments of preceding years, in most of which President Truman was only modestly involved. One was the success of the occupation of Japan. The occupation tended to make the Truman administration feel that everything in East Asia was under control, that whatever loose ends there were could be handled by MacArthur and his assistants, that it was possible to give attention in foreign affairs to the rivalry with the Soviet Union—the cold war—which focused on events in Europe.

In Japan, MacArthur was the man on the scene and gave every evidence he was in charge. His public persona proved a remarkable substitute for the imperial authority of preceding years. Every day he carried out a routine in which he was driven in the mornings from his residence in the former American embassy to his headquarters in the Dai Ichi Building in Tokyo and in the evenings back to his residence; each day a respectful crowd of Japanese, and a few Americans and foreigners visiting Tokyo, gathered at the front of the building and watched the spectacle of arrival and departure. In policy he pursued a series of liberal measures. The new "MacArthur constitution" (its opening words were, "We the people of Japan . . ."), nominally the work of the Diet, forbade military forces. The general sponsored such economic reforms as breakup of the *zaibatsu*, or family-owned industrial enterprises, and breakup of landed estates, dividing the latter into plots and selling them on favorable terms to the peasants who farmed them. He supported labor unions and even "the right to work," which was at issue in the United States. In politics he sponsored woman suffrage and generally introduced advanced Western ideas. In 1948–1949 the government in faraway Washington instructed its proconsul to relax some of the more rigorous economic and political reforms; the *zaibatsu* received a new lease on life, and politically it became possible for former officials of the wartime Japanese government to become active again. Economically, the Detroit banker Joseph M. Dodge arranged an arduous currency reform and straitened the rights of workers, to the advantage of industrialists and export prices, and his measures, together with the push to the economy provided later by offshore purchases during the Korean War, laid the basis for Japan's economic "miracle," at the same time that Western Europeans were making arrangements for their own miracle. Politically Japan retained many of the MacArthur reforms, and in 1951 the country would obtain a peace treaty with its former enemies.

Then there were the simultaneous post–World War II developments in China, which unlike those in Japan were hardly to the taste of the Truman administration—and about which essentially it proved impossible to make changes. Unlike policy in Japan, policy toward China failed. The failure was another part of the background of what was to become the Korean catastrophe.

It was the unfortunate fate of the United States during World War II that it supported an incompetent government on the Asian mainland, the Nationalist government in China. Its leader managed everything, and that itself was incompetence; as General Joseph W. Stilwell, commander of the China-Burma-India theater, wrote his wife, a one-man dog was a great institution, a one-man government was not.[2] Beyond that, Chiang surrounded himself with sycophants and relatives, trusting that the Allies, principally the United States, would get him through the war with Japan. After that he intended to even the score with his communist rival, Mao. The Chinese Nationalists based their power on money and "pull"—commodities that failed to hold the allegiance of their troops, even when the United States lavishly equipped them. The Chinese Communists based theirs on the hopes of the Chinese people, however cruelly they were to disappoint them.

Truman knew the situation in general, as it was no secret by the time he came into the White House, but the experience of General Marshall in China in 1946 was—so far as the president was concerned—the clinching point. When Marshall came home from China in January 1947 to become secretary of state, he filled the president's ears with Chiang's incompetence.

Marshall had gone out to China as a representative of the president because his predecessor, Ambassador Hurley, had "blown up" over America's China policy, resigning his position in a six-page jeremiad to the president. Hurley was a conservative Republican, an oilman from Oklahoma who served as secretary of war during the Hoover administration and proceeded to ingratiate himself with President Roosevelt. How he managed to get in the graces of FDR, who disliked Republicans, is difficult to know, but he did. Roosevelt sent him on fact-finding missions and eventually to China as ambassador, where he was totally unsuited. He believed the last word in Chiang Kai-shek's name was his last name—that is, he was Mr. Shek—and so described him in dispatches. He described the communist leaders Mao Tse-tung and Chou En-lai—thinking the description funny—as Mousey Dung and Joe N. Lie. His assistants, many of whom spoke Chinese, loathed him. He believed them communist dupes. When he was back on a leave in the United States, he lost his temper and quit. "The astonishing feature of our foreign policy is the wide discrepancy between our announced policies and our conduct of international relations," he began his letter to the president.

"Look what this son-of-a-bitch has done to me," said the president at a cabinet luncheon as he passed around the letter of resignation. For the six-page letter Hurley received the president's thanks in a letter of six lines.[3]

It was Secretary of Agriculture Clinton Anderson who suggested that Truman appoint Marshall to take the headlines from Hurley. The president said he was reluctant to put additional tasks on the general, who had just resigned after six years as army chief of staff. He had in mind to appoint Marshall president of the Red Cross. But that afternoon he telephoned the general; Marshall accepted and hung up. He later explained that he was just moving into what he thought was to be his retirement house in Leesburg when the phone rang; Mrs. Marshall was upstairs, and he was concerned she would hear him, for he wanted to break the news himself. As matters turned out, before he could perform that task she heard the news over the radio.

Marshall had success the following year in bringing together the two sides, supporters of Chiang and supporters of Mao. He attended hundreds of conferences. But by midyear there was evidence he was failing; each side thought it could win.

When he returned he told Truman of the situation, and from that point the United States had no China policy other than "let the dust settle." Each time the subject of China came up in cabinet, or Truman discussed it with Marshall and his successor Acheson, the conclusion was the same. Administration officials tended to blame the Nationalists. Lieutenant General Albert C. Wedemeyer went to China on a fact-finding mission in 1947 in hope of succeeding where Marshall failed. He drew up a report that excoriated the Nationalists. In a staff meeting the president said he could not release the report because it would pull the rug out from under the Nationalist government. Clifford interjected that the Nationalists had pulled it out from under themselves. In 1949 the president told David Lilienthal that "grafters and crooks" in the Chiang regime had no interest in the millions upon millions of Chinese who did not have enough to eat; that $2.5 billion had gone into China in recent years and "I'll bet you that a billion dollars of it is in New York banks today. . . . It's all for those grafters and crooks; rest of the people in China don't matter. General Marshall went over there and studied it for a year. He came up with a plan for two-thirds representation by the Nationalists and one-third by the so-called communists and they turned that down. Well, nothing can be done about China until things kind of settle down." Truman, Marshall, and Acheson believed that both sides misinterpreted everything the United States did or said. As Marshall related in 1949, "One of our generals said 'good morning' to somebody and that was reflected in all the papers as a hideous example of our duplicity." Perhaps the problem was antiforeignism: Truman wrote Senator Vandenberg, "The Chinese, as you know, are fundamentally antiforeign, and we must be exceedingly careful to see that this antiforeign sentiment is not turned in our direction."[4]

And so China policy went on hold, despite criticism from the Republicans in Congress, who were willing to be bipartisan about European matters but not those in the Far East. Wags described the Atlantic as the Democratic ocean, the Pacific as the Republican. How much Republican feeling really stood in favor of serious economic and military support for China is difficult to say, for the GOP was in a position where it did not need to deliver. Representative Judd announced the illogicality of aiding Greece and Turkey economically and not aiding China, conveniently forgetting that China was a much larger country. Surely the Republicans did not mean military support; at one moment of truth two of the leading Senate Republicans agreed that none of them advocated sending American troops.[5]

That China policy could have come to dead center early in 1947 was saddening in the extreme, and yet it is difficult to see what else the Truman administration could have done; the basic error—supporting the Nationalists—had been made during the war. To use the expression of the first wartime American ambassador, Clarence E. Gauss, it would have been better to have "pulled the plug" on the Nationalists and supported the Chinese Communists. But that was difficult in the middle of a war. At the end the Truman administration flew Nationalist troops to the coastal cities to displace the Japanese, which was a mistake; John Carter Vincent, in charge of the China desk in the state department, told his superiors it would give the impression of support for the Nationalists. The Chinese Communists chose to believe that the Americans had given massive wartime aid to the Nationalists, which was true, and that they were continuing it to defeat the communists, which was not true. After the war the new American president hoped for peace in China, an amalgamation of the two regimes, Nationalist and Communist, and General Marshall tried his best to obtain it, but neither side wanted to compromise.

If after the war the United States had stood farther away from Chiang, would matters have gone any better? Perhaps the People's Republic of China in 1949–1950 would not have assaulted and imprisoned the American consul general in Mukden, Angus Ward, and mistreated other foreign service officers. But, then, if support for the Nationalists brought this result, it was also true that when the British government recognized the new regime the Chinese Communists virtually placed the British ambassador under house arrest; friendliness received the same reward as supposed enmity.[6]

Acheson in 1949–1950, until the Korean War, hoped it might be possible to adjust relations between Peking and Washington, and Truman went along with him in this hope. When the Chinese Communists took over, the Truman administration, with any sort of encouragement, would have arranged a modus vivendi, trusting that over the long future the traditional special relationship of America and China would triumph. Instead, Chairman Mao had no desire to improve relations with the United States; chose to "lean to one side," as he put it, that of the Soviet Union; intervened in the Korean War; and made recognition impossible for more than twenty years.

Meanwhile three calculations persuaded the Truman administration to avoid any commitment to the independence of South Korea and unwittingly encouraged Kim's ambition to unify Korea. First, there was the example of one large, costly failure on the mainland of East Asia—the collapse of the Nationalists. Second, the U.S. Army needed all the troops it could obtain for keeping a garrison in Western Europe and in posts around the world, including a reserve in the United States; it wanted out of South Korea. Third, there was danger that any support for South Korea would draw the administration into another debacle involving the footloose Nationalists who had transferred their government to Taiwan. GOP partisans sided with the Taiwan Nationalists. Support for South Korea would bring calls for support for Taiwan. The latter course seemed imprudent even to consider, not to mention sponsor, for the administration anticipated the conquest of Taiwan by the Communist Chinese late in 1950.

The result was an early write-off of South Korea. Truman, as president, doubtless should have watched both theaters of foreign relations, East Asia as well as Europe; but the task was not easy, especially because of the political nature of much talk about East Asian affairs, and he allowed planning to drift under the control of the military. In September 1947, the joint chiefs reported to the secretary of defense, who sent their report to the secretary of state: "[F]rom a standpoint of military security, the United States has little strategic interest in maintaining the present troops and bases in Korea." In a memorandum of February 1948, the joint chiefs concluded: "[E]ventual domination of Korea by the USSR will have to be accepted as a probability if U.S. troops are withdrawn." In April 1948, the president signed a policy statement: "The United States should not become so irrevocably involved in the Korea situation that an action taken by any faction in Korea or by any other power in Korea could be considered a casus belli for the United States." On March 1, 1949, MacArthur told a British journalist: "[O]ur line of defense runs through the chain of islands fringing the coast of Asia. It starts in the Philippines and continues through the Ryukyu Archipelago, which includes its main bastion, Okinawa. Then it bends back through Japan and the Aleutian Island chain to Alaska." This definition neatly left out Korea. The last U.S. troops left South Korea in June 1949. In November of that year, perilously close to the Korean War, an outline of East Asian policy prepared for review by the president offered an interesting commentary: "The United States will deal with any direct aggression against an Asian state through the machinery of the UN, except in the case of states under US occupation or to which the US has special treaty obligations." There was no treaty obligation to support the government in Seoul, grandly known—after a UN-supervised election in which the government in North Korea refused to take part—as the Republic of Korea. As the American ambassador to Seoul, John J. Muccio, related the situation years later, "Putting it bluntly, the plan was to turn the problem over to the U.N. and to get out of the way in case of trouble."[7]

In January 1950, Secretary Acheson gave his later famous speech to the National Press Club in Washington excluding Taiwan and South Korea from the U.S. defense perimeter. In April an interviewer asked the chairman of the foreign relations committee, Senator Connally, if he thought the United States should abandon South Korea. The answer: "I'm afraid it's going to happen, whether we want it or not." After this confession Acheson and Muccio issued statements weakly declaring that the United States valued the independence of South Korea.[8]

From public statements the Soviet Union could know the Truman administration was not going to support South Korea. As for the military advice behind them, it probably went to Moscow through the agency of the British diplomat Maclean, then in Washington as first secretary of the embassy. He had access to top-secret NATO documents as well as all exchanges between Washington and London.[9]

During all this statement making and sending, public and private, President Truman himself did not say anything publicly or privately. Years later Acheson said no one expected an attack, but supposed instead that South Korea would slide under the iron curtain because of guerrilla activity or psychological warfare, perhaps political pressure. For this reason, probably, CIA reports throughout the spring of 1950 that "the North Koreans might at any time decide to change from isolated raids to a full-scale attack" (as Truman described the reports in his memoirs) did not make much of an impression upon the president and his advisers.[10]

In the last months before the opening of the Korean War officials in Washington were considering a paper that became known as NSC—National Security Council—68; after the war began the paper seemed to take on meaning. Could it be that in a larger sense, beyond the possibility of hostilities in Western Europe, the administration really was alert to the worldwide dangers? That critics at the time and later did not appreciate how it was involved in global calculation of a position well beyond the Truman Doctrine, the Marshall Plan, and NATO—calculation necessary to preserve the American republic and indeed democracy throughout the world?

NSC-68 looked forward to a dangerous new world, but the president did not share its forebodings and gave it little attention. It was a long document, sixty pages, and required close reading. It beheld a dark future in foreign affairs, a large and formidable fight against worldwide communism. Among other recommendations it looked to (but did not specifically mention) a tripling of the military budget. Truman was at Key West when it arrived, and—perhaps mystified by its prognosis and certainly concerned about its cost—he asked for an ad hoc committee to advise on how to do what the document asked. He gave no advice on how the committee should act, only stipulating the presence on the committee of the acting chairman of the Council of Economic Advisers, Keyserling. Charles Murphy, who had become presidential counsel after Clifford's resignation the preceding year, worked with the committee, the first and perhaps only time he met the senior staff of the NSC (unlike his predecessor he chose not to deal with national security affairs). He wondered to himself how the president was going to explain to the American people such a turnaround about money for the defense establishment. When the committee began its deliberations everyone looked to Keyserling to say where the money would come from, and he provided little wisdom. "Well, I don't know how much we can afford," he would answer, "but you haven't gotten there yet." These delphic utterances, Murphy said, went on all spring, until the Korean War intervened and made possible what NSC-68 announced as necessary. The president did not get around to signing the paper until late September, and then he gave it an uncertain future by characterizing it as "a statement of policy to be followed over the next four or five years."[11]

What was in the presidential mind in 1949–1950 when the Korean War was imminent? Let it be said that Truman was concerned about economics, not politics, as two virtual economic crises confronted the administration in Japan and in Western Europe. In Japan at the time of the Marshall Plan the United States had instituted the Dodge Plan, which was duly conservative: it envisioned the economic rise of Japan out of the doldrums, "off the American taxpayer's back," through allowing more freedom to the *zaibatsu*. The plan did not involve any transfusion of American funds, as in Western Europe, but rather holding down wages and salaries in hope that Japan's products could again go forth to East Asian countries as in prewar times. Unfortunately the expected markets did not immediately appear, and in 1949–1950 there was concern in Washington that the plan would only impoverish rather than revive Japan. Similarly in Western Europe the Marshall Plan was reviving production but not markets, and the hoped-for economic rise seemed to depend on the United States' indefinite filling of the dollar gap—this with the Marshall Plan due to end in 1951. For the Far East the administration did not know what to do. For Western Europe the president appointed a committee headed by the president of the University of North Carolina, Gordon Gray, and hoped that its members would discover that their wisdom was greater collectively than individually.[12]

The president took his outlook from the above realities and fears, but he adjusted it to his own instinctive ideas. He knew, of course, of the economic impasses in Japan and Europe, and the talk that economies might turn downward and take the American economy with them, as the Russians were hoping. Doubtless the economic talk, muffled as it was, easily caught his attention, for it could affect that cherished Truman economic barometer, the national budget, especially if a huge military program were imposed upon the budget as the authors of NSC-68 wanted to do. But what seems to have happened is that the president's inveterate buoyancy, so evident during the 1948 election and on many other occasions in his public and private life, again entered into his outlook. The result was a belief that in spite of signs of trouble it was necessary to look beyond them, to take the large view. Incredible as it may seem, in the very days prior to the Korean War the president announced not merely the end of his foreign policy of bolstering Western Europe and East Asia (by which he meant Japan and perhaps South Korea) but the beginning of a new era. Early in 1950 he had come to believe that the United States, through great good fortune, at last had climbed to a wonderful new plateau. Greek-Turkish aid and its successive economic and military measures had arranged the country's foreign policy. Point 4 was a small if notable capstone. It seems difficult to imagine that in the very imminence of the greatest crisis of his presidency Truman could be so obtuse, but such was the case. In a letter to Bess of June 11, 1950, he told what he had just done in two speeches: "The speech at Columbia [Missouri] and the one in St. Louis make a complete résumé of the foreign policy of the United States. No one can misunderstand it or garble it. Acheson will make six speeches in the next month, and I am sure there will be no misunderstanding our position. It has taken five years to get to this point." He reviewed for his wife the leading recent figures in Western history, including Russian leaders, and remarked that they had "brought us to this point." He hoped that "all of us who are left may take us to the right conclusion."[13]

The speeches at Columbia and St. Louis told what he had in mind. At the commencement of the University of Missouri, June 9, he spoke of economic measures: "It is about these economic measures in our program for peace and freedom that I speak particularly today." He spoke of Point 4: "The world into which this college class is graduating today," he said, "needs that sort of constructive, creative leadership in foreign economic affairs." He wished, he said, that he could see the next half-century, the greatest age in history, in which some of the graduates of the university would see a world of untold, unimagined wonders. To those young Missourians he was pouring out his heart. "Read Alfred Tennyson's *Locksley Hall*," he told them, affirming that Tennyson had seen the future a century earlier. The next day at the Jefferson Memorial in St. Louis he said virtually the same, although he was not speaking of *Locksley Hall* as when he had looked down (so he wrote Bess) "on those 2,000 young people in the rain on Friday."[14]

2

Years later, in retirement, Truman met groups of high school students in the auditorium at the library. After he spoke about the functioning of American government, including the presidency, the students would ask questions.

Frequently they asked about his most difficult decision as president, and invariably the answer was, "The decision to enter the Korean War."[15]

Little did the students know what that decision meant, or how intensely difficult it was; when the North Koreans struck South Korea with such massive military force, the attack seemed no simple North Korean enterprise but one backed by the Soviet Union. This was no sliding of South Korea under the iron curtain because of guerrilla activity, psychological warfare, or political pressure. This was a crude takeover. At stake was the authority of the United Nations, which had announced the formation of the Republic of Korea in 1948. At stake was the credibility of the United States; with forces close at hand in Japan the United States had to respond, otherwise its credibility would disappear. At stake might be the safety of Japan, for less than a hundred miles separated Pusan from Shimonoseki across the strait of Tsushima. At stake was the American position in Iran and West Germany. And for Truman personally it was the collapse of his private dream, epitomized by *Locksley Hall*, which he had just made public but not affixed in the minds of his fellow Americans before the North Koreans and their Russian sponsors dashed it. As Undersecretary of State Webb recalled, "he thought he'd done so much to prevent that, so much to make it a better world than to have continuing war. This really was a very hard blow for him to have to go into a fight."[16]

The way in which the news came to the president and how he then moved into action is well known. It often has been told how Acheson called the nation's chief executive at Independence on a Saturday night, June 24, 1950, American time, fourteen hours earlier than in Seoul and Tokyo, to relate the opening details of the invasion. When the secretary called again around noon the next day, Truman packed, headed for the Kansas City airport, and was aloft within minutes of arrival, leaving several members of his staff behind.

As for what he had in mind, there was no doubt. The president's daughter helped him pack, and she wrote in her diary, "Northern or Communist Korea is marching in on Southern Korea and we are going to fight." General Graham told two reporters at the airport, "The boss is going to hit those fellows hard."[17]

Reaching Washington, the president met Acheson, Undersecretary Webb, and Secretary of Defense Johnson, and the four rode into the city. "By God, I'm going to let them have it," he said. Secretary Johnson, sitting in a jump seat, turned to face the president, put out his hand, and said, "I'm with you, Mr. President." Because of the tension that had developed between Johnson and Acheson over China policy, foreign policy in general, and military policy (Johnson was a big, blustering bully of a man with presidential ambitions who undercut Acheson over China policy by leaking information to the Nationalists, sending one of his assistant secretaries regularly to New York to talk with the Nationalist ambassador, the wily Wellington Koo), Webb thought he had better intervene, so he said, "Mr. President, we have done a great deal of work with all concerned during the last two days. We have distilled our recommendations into three specific ones, and I think you should hear these carefully worked out recommendations before making up your mind as to any action to be taken." The president in effect said, "Well, O.K., of course, but you know how I feel."

After the car reached Blair House, Johnson and Acheson entered and turned to the left, into a room in which the joint chiefs and other officials were waiting. Truman turned to the right into a cloakroom. Webb walked in after him, closed the door, and outlined the three steps he and Acheson thought necessary—the use first of the air force, second of the navy, and third of ground forces, and the latter only after a day or two in view of the fact the UN Security Council was meeting in New York. The president and Webb then walked out together.

The group first had dinner. After the servants cleared the dishes and left the room, it got down to business. The feeling of the attendees was that the Russians were testing their limits. Secretary of the Army Pace recalled the mood over two decades later: "The feeling was very unanimous there." The president himself recorded this conclusion in a diary entry of June 30: "Russia is figuring on an attack in the Black Sea and toward the Persian Gulf." Webb remembered Truman "incensed about Russians; he thought that they were going to try to really take over the world at that point."[18]

The UN's future was high on the presidential list of calculations, indeed, highest if one could have disposed of the Russian challenge—and that challenge itself he saw as directed not so much to the United States as to the UN. Ambassador-at-large Philip C. Jessup remembered him sitting in a window seat in the room at Blair House, repeating half to himself, "We can't let the U.N. down! We can't let the U.N. down!" After the decision to intervene, Jack Hickerson of the state department was having a drink with the president. "I have hoped and prayed," Truman said,

> that I would never have to make a decision like the one I have just made today. But I saw nothing else that was possible for me to do except that. Now, with this drink, that's out of my mind. Jack, there's something I want you to know. In the final analysis I *did this* for the United Nations. I believed in the League of Nations. It failed. Lots of people thought that it failed because we weren't in it to back it up. Okay, now we started the United Nations. It was our idea, and in this first big test we just couldn't let them down. If a collective system under the UN can work, it must be made to work, and *now* is the time to call their bluff.[19]

From the decision came the Security Council resolution of June 25 branding North Korea an aggressor, and on June 27 the resolve recommending assistance by UN members to South Korea in restoring peace. By that time the air force and navy had been at work nearly twenty-four hours. On June 30 the president authorized army troops to fight in Korea. On July 7 the UN gave command of UN troops to the United States.

All this was possible because the Russian member of the Security Council had absented himself since January in protest against Nationalist China's representative sitting at council meetings in place of a representative from Communist China. Absence of the Russian member of the Security Council showed the complete surprise of the Soviets over such a U.S. action. Some months later an American sat next to the Soviet diplomat Vyshinsky at a dinner and asked why the Russians constantly pretended to think the United States was going to attack the Soviet Union. Vyshinsky said they did not know how to take the United States: "Look at Korea. You did everything you could to tell us you were not interested in Korea, but when the North Koreans went in, you put your troops there. We just can't trust you Americans."[20]

In passing it is worthwhile remarking the way in which the president and the administration twisted the mechanism of the UN to make it work for their purpose, which was to get UN support for an essentially American intervention. All this was remarked at the time and has bedeviled any analysis of the opening days of the Korean War ever since, and there is no point in disguising it.[21] The absence of the representative of the Soviet Union from the Security Council was doubtless the Russians' fault, but a construction of the Charter allowing a vote on so important a matter as intervention in Korea, without obtaining consent of the Soviet Union, was surely a twist. Article 27, paragraph 2, of the Charter relates, "Decisions of the Security Council on procedural matters shall be made by an affirmative vote of seven members including the concurrent votes of the permanent members." The intent of the Charter is easy to see; it is also easy to see the American opportunity, which probably violated at least the spirit of the Charter. When the UN approved military action on June 27, as mentioned, the United States already had taken military action. A further problem was inclusion of Nationalist China among the permanent members of the Security Council; when Nationalist Chinese officials departed the mainland for Taiwan in 1949, the seat probably should have gone immediately to the Communist Chinese government.

After the decision to intervene, three presidential failures followed, each large in its implications. The first was failure to take a declaration of war. Secretary Pace asked the president about a declaration and the response was, "Frank, it's not necessary. They are all with me." This was in reference to overwhelming popular approval of intervention.[22] It is possible Truman took his lead from advice offered by Senator Connally, to whom he inquired, "Do you think I'll have to ask Congress for a declaration of war?" Connally resorted to analogy: "If a burglar breaks into your house, you can shoot at him without going down to the police station and getting permission. You might run into a long debate by Congress, which would tie your hands completely. You have the right to do it as commander-in-chief and under the UN Charter."[23] Much more likely the rationale for this decision can be attributed to Acheson, to whom Truman looked for legal and particularly constitutional advice. Acheson had been the law clerk of Justice Brandeis, and he customarily walked from his house down to the state department every day with Justice Felix Frankfurter. On July 3 the secretary advised the president against going to Congress; that same day the department sent over a list of eighty-five instances when presidents sent American forces into combat without congressional permission. Charitably one might say that what Truman described to a reporter as a "police action" may have looked like that at the beginning and only gradually appeared larger. Still, from the outset the proportion of the war was fairly evident; this was no overland expedition to Tripoli, no landing of Marines in Panama, no putting down of revolutionaries in Haiti or the Dominican Republic or Nicaragua.

A second failure was on the home front, so to speak, a failure to ask for price controls; if the president had asked for controls he could have had them, and this might have stopped the inflation that followed the outbreak of the war—inflation that resulted from expectation of a rise in military spending, most of it preceding the actual increase in spending. At the first meeting in Blair House, Sunday night, June 25, Webb wanted to consider administrative bottlenecks, really economic bottlenecks. Truman said everyone was tired and the group should attend to such matters the next day. Speaker Rayburn afterward advised the president that he, Rayburn, could get priority and allocation controls if Truman did not ask for price controls; knowing how unpopular the latter were during World War II, Truman went along with Rayburn. The president did not freeze prices until January 1951.

In the litany of failures the worst in its consequences was the permission given to MacArthur on September 27, 1950, to cross the thirty-eighth parallel. This was the decision that precipitated massive Chinese intervention, what MacArthur described as an entirely new war. At the beginning of the war Truman had placed the Seventh Fleet between Communist China and Taiwan; that act may have been more provocative than people thought, as Peking had been talking of an invasion of Taiwan and considered the island its own territory. But the move across the parallel surely persuaded the Chinese Communists that the time had come to attack UN forces. MacArthur's tactics after crossing the parallel also must have encouraged the Chinese; according to his successor, General Matthew B. Ridgway, he flung troops into North Korea with abandon; of the UN force of 377,000, only a hundred thousand were at the front, far too few for invading the huge fanlike area of North Korea—the troops were a tempting target when so spread out. In his memoir of the war Ridgway referred to the tactics of General George A. Custer. Still, the attempted rolling up of a neighboring communist state, after Stalin had agreed to an invasion (and Mao too; Kim had inquired of him), must have been the primary reason for the Chinese attack.

Some of the sangfroid of the decision to send UN forces north related to the quickness with which the possibility of going north appeared. MacArthur's immensely successful Inchon landing, close to Seoul, on September 15, had caught the North Korean army in a pincers and collapsed it as a viable force, leaving forty thousand men behind the new UN line for mopping up. Euphoria settled upon the joint chiefs in Washington and, more important, upon their civilian leaders; the UN, dreaming of unification through intervention, gave its blessing to the enterprise on October 7.

For this the president again was responsible, even if in fact he only presided over the error of virtually all his advisers. The state department's two Soviet experts, Bohlen and Kennan, advised against crossing the parallel, but Rusk favored the crossing. In 1945 he had helped choose the parallel as the dividing line between the occupying American and Russian forces; he felt rightly that it was an artificial line, but wrongly that the Chinese would not go to war. MacArthur loved the idea of crossing the parallel; after Inchon his prestige was high and he doubtless was banking on it. His Republican allies in Congress were all behind the possibility of crossing the parallel; they would have interpreted any halt as willingness of the president to appease communism. And the Democrats needed a scent of victory for the upcoming congressional elections.

In these miscalculations, the last approaching a blunder (Acheson afterward described it as the principal error of his secretaryship), the Wake Island Conference of October 14 was merely a sideshow. The White House staff thought it good public relations. This probably was the reason it was distasteful to the president.[24] The trip was exceedingly rigorous, and the perhaps two hours in which Truman and his accompanying assistants talked with MacArthur were ludicrously inadequate for judgments about anything. Robert Nixon, the INS White House reporter, flew in an accompanying plane and remembered the dull hours in the air. The planes were the most advanced of their time, powered by four engines, propeller- rather than jet-driven, and capable of 220 miles an hour. But the 14,404–mile round-trip was a long way, and the flight out required all day and all night. Then there was the landing on Wake, a small strip of sand with virtually no vegetation. The place boasted one automobile, a two-door sedan belonging to the airline manager, in which the president and MacArthur rode, with the other conferees taking a bus. MacArthur gave one of his famous monologues, and the president's special counsel, Murphy, who was normally a levelheaded observer, was vastly impressed: "He spoke very persuasively, very plainly, very understandably. He just laid it out cold. And when he explained why and how we had won the war and why it was *impossible* for the other side to do anything about it, why, I understood precisely what he was saying, and I was convinced completely."[25] The main topic was whether to accept Chiang Kai-shek's offer of thirty-three thousand of his best troops, and the group turned down the offer. It was a tired topic—it had come up before, in discussions at the outset of the war, and one has the feeling it was the main topic at Wake because there were no worthwhile topics discussed at Wake. Rusk discovered afterward that the Nationalists made the offer only on "categorical assurance that it would be turned down by the Americans."[26] The one thing that stood out in discussion was MacArthur's statement that the Chinese would not come in and the troops would be out of Korea perhaps by Christmas. When the war turned serious with the Chinese intervention, this remark disturbed Truman the most.[27]

On October 25 the Chinese first engaged South Korean forces approaching the Yalu, but they broke off contact on November 7. On November 23, MacArthur announced his "end the war" offensive. Two days later the Chinese attacked in huge force, not the fifty to sixty thousand that MacArthur spoke of at Wake but three hundred thousand (plus a reconstituted North Korean army of sixty-five thousand).

By that time a series of calamities, personal as well as public, had begun to afflict the president, and they are worth recording to show how he managed with great effort to draw the right conclusion from the concatenation of events: the conclusion being that the United States must not widen the war. It was impossible to redeem the errors of the past, but it was possible to make a right decision for the future, which Truman and Acheson and the joint chiefs thereupon made.

The president's initial tribulation was the attempt of two Puerto Rican nationalists to assassinate him on November 1, an attempt that came far closer to success than the attackers realized. They themselves were pitifully deluded and had not the slightest idea if the president was present in Blair House when they attacked the guards at the entrance. Oscar Collazo, released from prison twenty-nine years later, said, "[T]he only thing we knew was that any incident that took place before his residence would be of international consequence. And it would bring world attention to Puerto Rico. That was the main idea." The U.S. imperialists, he said, had forced him from his farm during the 1930s, and he had moved to New York. By 1950 he was a churchgoer and family man, with a wife and three daughters, earning $71 a week as a metal polisher for a company that manufactured women's purses. He met Griselio Torresola, and they anticipated the imperialists massacring their Puerto Rican brothers on the streets in Puerto Rico. He told his wife, "Goodbye, darling. We must be free. We can no longer be slaves of the United States." The two men came up to Blair House together, one behind the other.[28]

In the resultant shootout Torresola was killed, Collazo wounded, and a guard, Leslie Coffelt, killed. The president was upstairs on the third floor taking a nap, and he put his head out a window to see what was happening. According to Truman one of the guards yelled, "Get back!" According to another account the guard shouted, "Get back, you dumb bastard!"[29] It was a near thing. If the nationalists had waited fifteen or twenty minutes more they could have caught the president as he came down the front steps to his automobile; he was planning to go to Arlington to lay a wreath.

Afterward Truman wrote Ethel Noland, "I was the only calm one in the house. You see I've been shot at by experts and unless your name's on the bullet you needn't be afraid—and that of course you can't find out, so why worry."[30] But precautions for the president thereafter doubled and tripled, and never again during his presidency was Truman able to walk or travel with the lightheartedness and light-guardedness that preceded the attempted assassination. When he went from Blair House across Pennsylvania Avenue to the White House he rode in a limousine with seven inches of steel on the floor and thick bullet-proof glass. No longer could he go to the annual re-unions of the 35th Division and lead the parade by walking through city streets lined with bystanders.[31]

The death of Coffelt shocked the president and his wife, and although they did what they could, attending the funeral and attempting to comfort his widow, they never forgot his sacrifice. Truman had a bronze plaque put up outside Blair House. Then someone moved it to an inconspicuous place. One day in 1958 the former president was taking a walk in Washington past Blair House and scrutinized the building, as if searching for something, then sud-denly stopped. "Where is it?" he said heatedly. "Where the hell has it gone to?" He was furious.[32]

At the very end of the month, November 30, 1950, Truman got himself into a confusion over public policy that proved highly embarrassing. During a news conference that day he read a statement about the atomic bomb and its possible use in the Korean War. According to John Hersey, "Unfortunately, the statement contained nothing that a hard-boiled city-desk man would con-sider news, so when the President . . . told the reporters to ask questions, they got ready to do some news manufacturing." A reporter for the *New York Daily News*, John Doherty, asked about the weapons that might have use in Korea: "Will that include the atomic bomb?" The president flat-footedly answered, "That includes every weapon that we have." Doherty's question and Tru-man's answer went out in indirect discourse, but it was obvious that the president had said he might use the bomb.[33] Answering questions before a clamorous House of Commons, uncertain if General MacArthur might have his finger on a nuclear trigger, Prime Minister Attlee took alarm and invited himself for a visit to Washington. At the very time that Truman was attempt-ing to deal with the Chinese intervention, he had to spend hours talking with Attlee and his party.

While Attlee was visiting, late in the afternoon of December 5, Charlie Ross slumped over at his desk next to the oval office and died instantly. The president had known him since the early 1890s and had attended a function with him that morning; Ross had helped with the Attlee meeting that afternoon.

The next morning the president read a review of Margaret's Constitution

Hall concert the night before by the *Washington Post* music critic Paul Hume, a devastating and very personal review; as General Marshall told the president, the only thing he did not criticize was the varnish on the piano of the accompanist. Truman lost his temper, wrote an intemperate handwritten letter, and had a White House messenger mail it. A newspaper friend of Hume's, who saw the letter, managed to memorize it and without Hume's knowledge published most of it. Margaret at first said her father could not have used language like that, and then said she appreciated his "insistence on being a human being first, and the devil take the hindmost."[34]

All the while, as he put affairs in a diary entry of December 9, "in addition to personal matters I've had conference after conference on the jittery situation facing the country. Attlee, Formosa, Communist China, Chiang Kai-shek, Japan, Germany, France, India etc. I've worked for peace for five years and six months and it looks like World War III is here."[35] During this worst time of his presidency Truman summoned powers of courage that passed far beyond what ordinary men and women apply to their own troubles. This was a test of all the stamina he could bring to bear. He had to be so very careful that his other concerns would not unbalance his judgment. Attlee's merciless decision to take the president's time would have been enough in itself, if only out of tiredness from running an international negotiation at the same time as deciding national policy. The British, too, proposed that UN forces in Korea cut and run. Truman had to hold them to better behavior.[36]

At this juncture MacArthur lost his nerve and was sending such gloomy reports that a committee consisting of Rusk, Kennan, and "Doc" Matthews called on Marshall and asked that less attention be paid to MacArthur's reports and more to recovering the army's combat capability. General Marshall, usually a tower of strength, was passing MacArthur's appraisals to the White House without attempting to judge them.

The great issue was not any uncertainty over what the Chinese had done or might do—Chinese troops were attempting to drive UN forces out of Korea. It was, rather, what this effort, if successful, might mean for U.S. prestige everywhere in the world.

There were two parts to the resulting decision. One was that the United States would not cut and run—no matter how bad the prospects, there would be no just getting out. Fighting had the virtue, too, of taking time, and that might give more opportunity to size up the situation. The other part was that everything, including Chinese and Russian policy, would be limited: there would be no unlimited war, despite suggestions from Tokyo. Late in November former vice president John Garner offered some advice. It was in the form of a short, handwritten note with a PS: "In re Russia, if it is to be, why not now?" The president must have smiled wryly, knowing his friend to be an expert on domestic politics, an innocent on foreign. Perhaps it placed a light touch on what otherwise was a very heavy-handed series of events.[37]

As the days passed, moving toward the Christmas that MacArthur had spoken of, Korean affairs came back into focus. The death of Lieutenant General Walton Walker in a jeep accident brought his replacement by Ridgway—perhaps no better a soldier, but resolute appearing, hand grenade hanging from the right shoulder strap, first-aid kit from the left. Ridgway went right up to the front, ate GI food, slept in a tent during freezing weather, and told Washington that corps and division commanders were not doing their duty and needed replacement. He appeared everywhere up and down the line. Shortly after the new year, and following a retirement of the Eighth Army behind the Han River and a second evacuation of Seoul, he stabilized the front. His troops then massed artillery, zeroed in on the insanely bunched Chinese troops, cut them to pieces, and began an offensive that took UN forces back up toward the thirty-eighth parallel.

3

The dismissal of MacArthur from his Far Eastern commands—as a five-star general he held his rank for life and it was impossible to retire him—focused a vast wrath on the president; yet when compared with the disappointment in having to intervene in Korea, and with the decisions that followed, it was an event that was not on the same scale.[38]

Truman's antipathy to MacArthur traced back to 1942 when the general, then in the Philippines, went by PT boat and submarine to Australia, leaving his second-in-command, Lieutenant General Jonathan M. Wainwright, to surrender to the Japanese. Truman had known Wainwright in the 1930s; they had met in Reserve camp. "I'm not very fond of MacArthur," he wrote Margaret. "If he'd been a real hero he'd have gone down with the ship."[39]

The animus had continued, year after year. On May 13, 1944, he wrote Margaret, "No good soldier is a speechmaker or a showman. That's why we don't like Dugout Douglas from Australia."[40] The speechmaking or showmanship referred to was the general's announcement after walking through the surf at Leyte—after infantrymen had gone ashore—that "I have returned." The "Dugout Doug" reference was to the nickname assigned him by the men on Bataan before that bastion fell; MacArthur visited them once or twice and spent most of his time in the Malinta tunnel on Corregidor.

The most critical Truman commentary, private like those above, came shortly before the end of the Pacific war, on June 17, 1945. By this time Senator Truman had become president of the United States:

> Mr. Prima Donna, Brass Hat, Five Star MacArthur. He's worse than the Cabots and the Lodges—they at least talked with one another before they told God what to do. Mac tells God right off. It is a very great pity we have to have stuffed shirts like that in key positions. I don't see why in hell Roosevelt didn't order Wainwright home and let MacArthur be a martyr. . . . We'd have had a real

general and a fighting man if we had Wainwright and not a play actor and a bunco man as we have now. Don't see how a country can produce such men as Robert E. Lee, John J. Pershing, Eisenhower, and Bradley and at the same time produce Custers, Pattons, and MacArthurs.[41]

By September of that year, with World War II over both in Europe and in the Far East, the president was tiring rapidly of MacArthur. Just what the general had done at that moment to incur the presidential wrath is not clear, but Truman was of a mind to relieve him. He told his staff conference he was "going to do something with that fellow," who had been "balling things up." He said he was tired of "fooling around."[42]

It was a pity Truman did not do the job right then. MacArthur was preening himself on his independence, telling Paul H. Nitze, "I have absolutely no use for the people in Washington, including the President. Nobody in my command is going to have any relationships with anybody in Washington."[43]

But the president had too much to do at the moment. There were many other decisions to make. He had already replaced most of his cabinet members, with Ickes and Wallace yet to go. His relations with Secretary Byrnes were increasingly awkward. He did invite MacArthur to come home for a visit, twice (the general had not visited the United States since 1937). MacArthur refused both invitations. On January 22, 1948, Truman wrote the onetime ambassador to Germany, James W. Gerard, "I think he is expecting to make a grand march across the country about a month before the Republican convention." Years later, in 1959, he reminisced that if the general had come back when he had first invited him, "I think, in all probability, I would have relieved him then."[44] Perhaps MacArthur sensed the possibility.

The Wake Island conference allowed the protagonists to meet. At the outset Truman privately reiterated his ancient prejudices, writing Nellie Noland, "Have to talk to God's righthand man tomorrow . . . Too much for a farm boy." Nor were first impressions better, for MacArthur tried to put down the president, just as he had done Truman's predecessor—in Honolulu in 1944, he arrived at President Roosevelt's ship after the other greeters had come aboard. Truman was not about to have any more of that: when his plane landed at Wake he looked out from a window on a small group of reporters and officials and saw MacArthur sitting in a jeep behind the crowd; the president sat in his plane until the general, who had flown in the night before, got out of the jeep and joined the group. When the president descended from his plane, the officers present saluted the nation's chief executive and commander-in-chief. Robert Donovan, present at Wake, noticed that MacArthur did not salute, although Truman may not have seen that small sign of lèse-majesté. He did notice MacArthur's appearance, though, and a month and more later it still rankled: "his shirt unbuttoned, wearing a greasy ham and eggs cap that evidently had been in use for twenty years." After these brushes the president and general greeted each other cordially, and Truman returned from Wake in belief that "Mac" was a good soldier and loyal.[45]

Disillusion was not long in coming, however, and the reasons—three willful actions on the part of the general in 1950–1951—have been recited many times. MacArthur had sent a statement to the national encampment of the Veterans of Foreign Wars, to be read on August 28, 1950, and the president learned of it two days earlier when a news magazine jumped the gun and published it. The statement was incendiary: "Nothing could be more fallacious than the threadbare argument by those who advocate appeasement and defeatism in the Pacific that if we defend Formosa [Taiwan] we alienate continental Asia." He added: "Those who speak thus do not understand the Orient." Truman forced the general to withdraw the statement. Then, because of Ridgway's military successes and because the Soviet representative at the UN had suggested a truce, authorities in Washington drew up a draft presidential statement that looked to a cease-fire and negotiation, and on March 20, 1951, notification of its imminent release went by radio to MacArthur. Four days later he made his own offer to negotiate, threatening otherwise to extend the war to China. "The thing that really cost him his job was, I sent him a telegram on the 20th of March with a program to consult our allies—all 16, or how many there were [13]—on the sending of an ultimatum to the Chinese for withdrawal. He made that statement himself and deleted two paragraphs about the consultations. I never was so put out in my life."[46] On April 5 came the final act, when the Republican minority leader of the House, Joseph W. Martin, stood up and read to his colleagues a private letter received from the general containing more remarks: "It seems strangely difficult for some to realize that here in Asia is where the Communist conspirators have elected to make their play for global conquest, and that we have joined the issue thus raised on the battlefield, that here we fight Europe's war with arms while the diplomats there still fight it with words; that if we lose the war to Communism in Asia the fall of Europe is inevitable, win it and Europe most probably would avoid war and yet preserve freedom." There followed the unbending conclusion: "[W]e must win. There is no substitute for victory."

Why MacArthur did all this is difficult to say. It could have been just a few "bad days" where he lost all perspective, for it was curious that his letter to Martin was dated March 20, meaning that because of the international dateline he signed it the day before, Washington time, March 19. The next day the message arrived from Washington that the president was drafting a peace proposal, and only a few days later he announced his own. In five days in March he cast the die. Or it could have been a gradual failure of understanding, a slow loss in perspective, because of the years of foreign residence? Or he might have underestimated Truman at Wake—the conference was too obviously a public relations affair. Army Secretary Pace thought it was the possibility of a political career: "I felt that the crowds around the Dai-Ichi Building were getting to be very small; I felt that his period of glory there had passed; he was a great student of history; I felt he felt Mr. Truman could be easily defeated and that if he [the general] could be fired under dramatic circumstances he could return and get the Republican nomination for President and run for President against Mr. Truman." This was possible, although the general told the president at Wake he was sorry about the VFW message, "that he was not in politics at the time and that the politicians had made a 'chump' (his word) of him in 1948 and that it would not happen again." In 1948 he had allowed supporters to enter his name in the Wisconsin primary, where he received a small vote. Secretary of State Acheson offered still another explanation, years later, that may have been closest to the mark. MacArthur, he opined, was "a jackass."[47]

Fortunately, with the time at hand to dismiss the general, the president possessed an open-and-shut case. To anyone who was not emotional, Truman's position was unexceptionable. He did not have to base it on a series of willful actions, however convincing. He did not need to cite his authority as commander-in-chief under the Constitution, however pertinent; MacArthur had a way with words and would have talked his way around the Constitution anyway. A directive from the White House, dated December 5, 1950, at the height of the crisis over Chinese intervention, had put the Far Eastern general in a box: he directly violated it. The directive was the work of Edward W. Barrett, assistant secretary of state for public affairs, and the presidential staffer Elsey. Both had been concerned about how during the Chinese crisis so many officials, principally military, were "shooting off their mouths" about strategy and policy. In a matter of an hour or so they drafted and gained approval for two directives that required clearances on all statements dealing with military and foreign policy. The intention was to shut up the military, but to avoid that appearance they double-barreled the statement. Military people could not talk about foreign-policy matters without state department clearance, nor diplomatic and state department people about military matters without Pentagon clearance. Months later, when MacArthur's behavior needed measurement, the directive to the military became the yardstick.[48]

The day following the Martin reading, that is, Friday, April 6, the president knew what he had to do: "MacArthur shoots another political bomb through Joe Martin, leader of the Republican minority in the House," he wrote in his diary. "This looks like the last straw. Rank insubordination." Again he referred to "our Big General in the Far East." That morning he consulted Marshall, Bradley, Harriman, and Acheson. Marshall temporized. Not until Monday, April 9, having secured unanimous consent of the joint chiefs, did he agree to MacArthur's relief.[49] Bradley prepared an order dated Tuesday, April 10, and the president signed it Monday afternoon.

There followed a confusion that the general's advocates claimed was intentional. Marshall wanted Army Secretary Pace to tell MacArthur of his dismissal, as Pace was then in Japan. The problem was that any communication to Japan would have to pass through MacArthur's headquarters, where MacArthur's intelligence chief, Major General Charles A. Willoughby, would have intercepted it. Marshall peremptorily sent Pace to Korea, without explaining why; the message could go to Korea through diplomatic channels. But a power failure at Pusan prevented Pace from receiving it. Meanwhile, a *Chicago Tribune* reporter scared the president's press secretary, Joe Short, into believing the *Tribune* had the story and would break it the next day. General Bradley and Assistant Secretary Rusk concluded that because of the *Tribune*'s right-wing sympathies, MacArthur knew what was afoot and would steal a march on the president and resign. At 10:00 that night, April 9, they went to Blair House to see Truman and talked with him for two hours. When the president heard the news he said, sitting there in his dressing gown, "That son-of-a-bitch isn't going to resign on me! I want him fired." The issue was partly personal, as MacArthur had treated him shabbily, but in the main it was constitutional. As he explained to his visitors,

> I am just an ordinary American citizen but I am also the President of the United States; there is no office in the world which carries so much responsibility. There may be a million other Americans who could hold this office as well as I, but I am holding it and I intend to fill it to the best of my capacity. I'll be darned [he may have said something else] if I will turn this office over to my successor with its prerogatives impaired by an American general.

For the benefit of doubters, and in addition to MacArthur's actions against the president, and the constitutional issue, the nation's chief executive could cite the directive of December 5. Rusk and Bradley drafted a statement for the press and released it at 1:00 A.M. on Tuesday, April 10. Meanwhile the news went by usual army radio channels to the Dai Ichi Building in Tokyo.[50]

From outward evidence MacArthur took his dismissal quietly. Army channels were slow, and he learned of it from an aide who heard it on a radio broadcast. He ordered preparation for a quick departure. Privately, though, he was furious; he remarked to his successor, Ridgway, that the president was crazy, lacking "mental stability," that an "eminent medical man" in touch with Truman's personal physician, Dr. Graham, told him "that the President was suffering from malignant hypertension; that his affliction was characterized by bewilderment and confusion of thought," that the malignancy had caused him to threaten the music critic. The medical man said the president "wouldn't live six months." MacArthur told Ridgway he would move to New York and make speeches and "raise hell."[51]

Truman's ability to take the heat was now sorely tested. According to Rusk, the last thing the president said to him and Bradley the night of the dismissal was a generous remark about MacArthur's return: "General Mac-

Arthur has not been home since World War II. He has not received the hero's welcome to which he is entitled and which the American people will want to give him."[52] Not only did the general come home to the adulation of millions; within the first two days the White House received two hundred and fifty thousand telegrams protesting MacArthur's dismissal. In a private meeting of Republican members of Congress, Senator Taft suggested that Congress impeach the president. William E. Jenner, Republican of Indiana, said so openly on the Senate floor.

The president held straight to his course. Roger Tubby, by this time assistant press secretary, brought in a stack of telegrams and indicated there were bushel baskets more, many of them attacking the president ("It's too bad the Puerto Ricans didn't get him," "The President ought to be impeached"). Truman said in effect, "See that fireplace over there? Go put them in the fireplace and set a match to them. The American people will come to understand that what I did had to be done. Now what's next on your agenda?"[53]

Years later Cabell Phillips interviewed the retired chief executive in advance of his seventy-fifth birthday and asked routinely that he recall the half-dozen most difficult decisions during the presidency. When Truman finished reciting them Phillips said he had failed to mention the dismissal of Mac-Arthur. "That must have taken a bit of courage," he said. "Courage had nothing to do with it," Truman snapped, his eyes flashing. "He was insubordinate and I fired him, and that's all there was to it. Sure, I knew there would be a lot of stink about it. But it was the right thing to do and I did it, and I've never lost any sleep over it since."[54] A cartoon drawn during the MacArthur controversy said it all. It showed a senator saying, "Who does Truman think he is? President of the United States?"

On MacArthur's side the rest was anticlimax. The general closed his address to Congress with the lines, "Old soldiers never die, they just fade away." It was an authentic British Tommy story, but what it really meant was that an old soldier never dies at the front but lives to collect his pension—the young soldiers die. The general and administration officials gave much testimony during joint hearings of the Senate foreign relations and military affairs committees, and here a chance remark by General Bradley took the headlines. "So long," Bradley said, "as we regarded the Soviet Union as the main antagonist and Western Europe as the main prize," MacArthur's strategy "would involve us in the wrong war at the wrong place at the wrong time and with the wrong enemy." Senator Brien McMahon, Democrat of Connecticut, raised questions about Europe and the need for troops, and what the joint chiefs decided, and MacArthur again lost out, having to say, "Well, senator, I am a theater commander and I don't know all of the details that you refer to." McMahon afterward whispered to an assistant, "Now I've got him. I've really got him. He is a theater commander, he doesn't know anything really about what's happening in the rest of the world."[55] The hearings began early in

May and ended late in June—they comprised two million words, eight thousand pages, too much for most Americans to think about. The general made trips to receive welcomes in cities across the country, but as time passed the crowds thinned. He spent the rest of his time in New York in the Waldorf Towers, into which he had moved, with a long, long wait, thirteen years, until his death in 1964.

The might-have-beens of history are always worth looking at, and it is curious how badly MacArthur played his hand once he decided to challenge the Truman administration. If he had acted with more circumspection, been more of a statesman, not stirred up so much isolationist sentiment, avoided talking about East Asia versus Western Europe, trusted to patriotism rather than clarity—he could have become president of the United States. The story is complicated but the possibility clear. In 1951, President Truman sent Eisenhower to Europe to organize NATO forces. The question was how long the general would stay there: he was considering running for the presidency on the Republican ticket. His principal rival was Senator Taft. He was taken aback by Taft's reputation for isolationism and deeply concerned about the senator's increasing importance within the party. Taft had begun to deal with international affairs when Senator Vandenberg took ill with cancer; Vandenberg died just at the time MacArthur returned to the United States. Without Vandenberg to guide the Republicans in bipartisanship, cooperating with the Truman administration, the task had fallen to Taft, who was obviously reluctant to take it up. During a brief trip home to the United States, Eisenhower arranged a meeting with Taft at the Pentagon, where without ado he made the senator a virtual proposition. He asked Taft to support NATO; he had decided, although he did not tell Taft this, to stay out of politics, not try for the GOP nomination, if Taft would agree. For Taft it was a great opportunity. But the senator could not make up his mind—he probably was trying to find a formula by which he could keep Eisenhower out of politics and still pursue his increasingly isolationist views. The popular adulation of MacArthur was so overwhelming, the general's reception in the United States so boisterously enthusiastic, that Taft must have thought MacArthur's position on foreign affairs was about to triumph. At this point MacArthur, indirectly, hurt himself very badly. The intriguing possibility, in which MacArthur might have entered the White House, was that Taft in 1951–1952 was promising that if chosen as the Republican nominee he would take MacArthur as his vice presidential running mate. With Eisenhower not a candidate, Taft would have received the nomination and probably won the election, for 1952 was a Republican year. The senator was to die of cancer in 1953—in which case MacArthur would have become president.[56]

Chapter Sixteen

A New Military Force

In the business of running the federal government Truman faced no more vexing problem than that of organizing a new military force suitable for the postwar years. The easy part of the task—though it was in no sense a task he could accomplish in a few moments, for it took intense negotiations with the generals and admirals and their civilian superiors—was to set up the formal organization. At the end of two years, in the Defense Act of 1947, that work was essentially accomplished. To the traditional services, the U.S. Army and U.S. Navy, the act added a third service, the U.S. Air Force. The third service had become necessary because during World War II the U.S. Army Air Forces had been autonomous, and it was perfectly clear that air power would play a large role in any future war. The Defense Act placed over the three services the National Military Establishment (NME), the name of which was changed to department of defense in 1949. Presiding over the new department was a secretary of defense, whose importance was visible through removal of service secretaries from cabinet meetings.

After the formal changes the president expected great results, and here he was to be sadly disappointed. He expected the services to present unified budget requests that took account of possible duplication of missions. He was much concerned that the services save money by avoiding unessential expenditures. A balanced national budget including a surplus seemed necessary to keep the postwar economy on an even keel, to prevent inflation, and to avoid depressions or recessions, and reasonable defense expenditures would have helped very much to accomplish that important purpose. Instead he found the services fighting over the budget, fighting each other and, of course, the president himself, not caring a whit for unification, each doing what seemed right in its own eyes.

He also had to consider the place of nuclear weapons in any future war. He had to decide whether to share knowledge of how to make nuclear weapons with the British government and, more important, with the Soviets; in any event, he had to try to obtain an agreement with the USSR to limit or even abolish these weapons. He had to decide whether the American military should have custody of U.S. weapons. In 1949–1950 it fell to him to make the decision to go ahead with the H-bomb.

All the while the services busied themselves with plans for using nuclear weapons, which disturbed Truman, for it was a dangerous albeit momentarily pointless exercise. The plans were several years ahead of their time. It is a curious fact that in 1945–1950—with all the talk about presidential decisions on sharing nuclear weapons, limitation, abolition, custody, and the H-bomb—the actual weapons available to the military were few; indeed, there were none in 1947 because the new Atomic Energy Commission (AEC) had no technician teams to assemble bomb components. Moreover, until the Korean War the Strategic Air Command was incapable of dropping nuclear weapons anywhere near targets in the Soviet Union.

After June 1950, the president and the military services turned to more conventional calculations, such as putting ground forces into Western Europe to protect NATO against Soviet attack. The Korean War called attention to NATO's vulnerability. Moreover, because of that war three times as much money was available as had been in 1945–1950, and that made the assignment of expensive army divisions to the continent, with all of their supporting troops, much easier.

1

The president had counted on the NME to help him reduce the national debt. Compared to the $26 billion debt after World War I, the government's debt after World War II was mountainous: over ten times as much, $280 billion. The president wrote a friend in New York, with whom he enjoyed corresponding about budget problems, that the debt was his "principal worry." He knew the federal budget intimately. The comptroller of the defense department, Wilfred J. McNeil, once related that Truman was "familiar with it, particularly up until the Korean war started. He was quite familiar, even with some of the details in major programs. He had done his homework."[1] His several budget directors saw him in regular, standing appointments. Webb, with whom he established a considerable rapport, saw him almost every day. With the result, one might add, that Truman was one of the least spendthrifty of twentieth-century presidents. As mentioned in a previous chapter, of the eight budgets he prepared, four were in surplus. Three of the deficit years reflected defense buildup during the Korean War. All in all, surplus exceeded deficits $22.5 billion to $12.1 billion, a ratio of two to one.

Unfortunately for the president's hopes to make large reductions in the debt, the new U.S. Air Force's leaders were full of plans to spend money.

Before the Korean War its two principal civilian advocates were Thomas K. Finletter and Stuart Symington, able men whom the president liked. It was difficult to hold them down. Finletter was controlled, introverted, dispassionate, unemotional; Symington was flashy, flamboyant, political, fond of publicity.[2] Finletter was an establishment easterner, Symington from St. Louis. The two capitalized on the belief of many Americans that air power was the key to the future, that former ways of war were obsolete. Because of the cost of planes the air force already was taking the lion's share of the military budget. But it wanted more, and for that purpose used a numbers game with the public. During the war the air force had 243 combat groups; at the end of the war General Carl Spaatz tentatively suggested 105 groups, asked for 70, and settled for 55. As soon as the air force's leaders could, they asked for 15 more, a total of 70. The latter became a magic figure—necessary, the air force said—and accounted in large part for the failure of Truman's substitute for the draft, Universal Military Training, as air force enthusiasts could show that an additional 15 groups would cost only a fraction of the $4 billion start-up cost of UMT. "All this controversy over the number of groups is beside the question," Truman wrote in exasperation. "If the Congress succeeds in running from U.M.T. with a slight air force increase then our defense budget can never come down. Never is a long time too."[3] The air force, with its rapidly promoted generals, men who had been lieutenants and captains half a dozen years earlier, cared nothing for the national debt, Truman believed. Having obtained a divorce from the army, it preened itself by establishing an Air Force Academy and designing its own blue uniforms.

When it came to money, the navy was as uncooperative as, maybe worse than, the air force. The navy desired expensive aircraft carriers, even though the Budget Bureau saw them as a duplication of air force bombers. What was more, the navy included the marines, an organization that wanted to be a fourth service. In an undated memo in a file that Truman's private secretary, Rose Conway, perhaps inadvertently labeled "Navy, Secy. of Marines," the president wrote to himself, not the addressee: "To the Congress: I've been looking over this Marine Bill which places a ceiling of 400,000 men on the Marines. This is rank discrimination. If the Army has 3,500,000 so should the Marines have 3,500,000."[4]

The navy's admirals openly opposed the president's budget program. On an occasion at the British embassy no less a personage than Admiral Nimitz announced he would fight any reduction of the navy's prerogatives to the last ditch. He held forth about UMT and said it was of no value. Word of these opinions got to Truman, who thought of dismissing the five-star admiral. "Nimitz does not know that I know he said it," the president confided to his budget director, Smith, "but I think it is pretty bad business for an Admiral in his position." A month later, when Smith and an assistant went in to see the president, Truman held up an article in Collier's entitled "Truman's Unhappy

Year." He said the navy's behavior was the worst he had encountered, worse than the Ickes-Pauley affair.[5]

The worst of all the fighting among the services over the budget, by far, came in 1949 and took the form of a veritable "revolt of the admirals"—it was entirely a navy affair. The nominal issue was effectiveness of air force bombers versus capabilities of navy bombers aboard carriers. Behind the statement-making lay the budget, and surrounding it the question of unification. The navy thought it improper for one service to let another service cut its budget. In September of that year a disgruntled navy captain with an illustrious record as a flier in World War II, John G. Crommelin, Jr., who was in line for promotion to rear admiral, leaked documents criticizing the air force's new bomber, the eight-engined B-36, by far the largest plane the air force ever adopted. The documents claimed the B-36 was nought but a challenge to the navy's budget, the air force trying to sink the navy by championing behemoths of the sky. As soon as his identity became known, Crommelin was put up for court-martial. During an investigation by the House Armed Services Committee, in which the chairman, the navy advocate Carl Vinson, a Democrat from Georgia, rashly promised immunity to any serving officer who wanted to speak his mind, most of the navy's high officers, active or retired, including the chief of naval operations, Admiral Louis E. Denfeld, came to Crommelin's defense. They used every contention they could think of to demonstrate that the B-36 was an improper carrier of nuclear bombs to the Soviet Union and asserted that all three services should share in an attack, indeed, would have to share if the United States were to win against this implacable enemy.

During some of the most rambunctious hearings ever held on Capitol Hill, filled with rhetorical smoke, sixteen-inch guns flashing and booming, battleships crossing the *T,* the navy had its day. A few air force advocates, including Secretary Symington, remarked unctuously that the hearings were undercutting the administration. That was putting the case mildly. The revolt threatened the entire movement toward budgetary control; it challenged the authority of the new secretary of defense at that time, Johnson, the admirals saying they had no confidence in him. It embarrassed the then secretary of the navy, Francis P. Matthews, who foolishly confessed to congressmen that as a Nebraska native he had never been afloat except for managing a rowboat on one of the lakes in his state. It embarrassed the secretary of state, Acheson. Discussions by the admirals as to which service should have the honor of attacking the Soviet Union hardly constituted the sort of talk that required ventilation in public; the president told Acheson the department needed to do something to offset such commentaries.

After everything was over, the president relieved Denfeld, whom he had just reappointed to a second term, replacing him with an intelligent flying admiral, Forrest P. Sherman, who had taken no part in the revolt. Privately he wrote Harold Ickes, with whom he again had become friendly, "There is only one way to handle insubordination and that is to put a stop to it."[6] Ickes knew whereof he spoke.

Each year the services got into the same budget arguments. Consider budget discussions during 1948–1949, looking to the fiscal year 1950 (which in those days meant July 1, 1949, through June 30, 1950). The military leaders initially estimated that carrying out Halfmoon, one of the plans of defense discussed below, would require $30 billion. They came down to $23.6. By October 1948, the chiefs had not agreed to a lower figure, and Forrestal submitted two plans to the president, one totaling $16.9 billion, the other $14.4, the figure Truman wanted. The services argued to the president that $14.4 billion would allow hostile operations to be carried out only from Britain, the larger sum from the Mediterranean. How they drew this conclusion was a mystery. Forrestal urged the larger budget. The president called in Eisenhower, then president of Columbia University. The Defense Act of 1947 provided no chairman of the joint chiefs, and he wanted Eisenhower as an unofficial "presiding officer" to keep the navy and air force from taking their cases to Congress. Eisenhower obtained an agreement that promptly came apart, and the general might have had something to do with collapse of his own agreement. He wrote in his diary, "I personally and very earnestly believe that $15 billion to $16 billion per year is all that this country need spend for security forces, if it is done every year (with some additional amounts to cover past deficits)."[7] It is clear he wanted Forrestal's $16.9. He persuaded his service colleagues to agree, at least in public, on $14.4, but may have encouraged them to try, however they might, for $16.9. Truman would have none of it and requested $14.4, the division being $5 billion for the air force, $4.8 for the army, and $4.6 for the navy. Congress appropriated $13.9.

That spring of 1949, trying to get what he could for the military services but barely keeping them under control, and believing Truman had placed him in this no-win position to hurt his chances in the 1952 presidential election, the president of Columbia became so upset he perhaps suffered a heart attack; his personal physician, Major General Howard McC. Snyder, diagnosed his ailment publicly as a case of food poisoning occasioned from a dinner of Mexican food. Under Snyder's care the general took several weeks off in recuperation.[8]

The NME might have helped Truman bring fiscal sanity to the services if he had had better help from his first secretary of defense, Forrestal, whose presence in the NME was an administrative disaster. A rugged-looking man with a flattened, fighter's nose, Forrestal was his second choice; he had intended to appoint Secretary of War Robert Patterson, who instead wanted to return to his New York law firm and recoup his personal finances. This left the secretary of the navy, who, it became evident, was a psychiatric case. Forrestal was correct in one of his administrative beliefs, in that he thought people problems were 90 percent of organization problems. Still, in working out people problems he went beyond his responsibilities as secretary of defense, taking interest in problems that involved far more people than he could handle; he produced memoranda, made telephone calls, and scheduled lunches involving talk and speculation, the paper results from which he placed in filing cabinets. After a few years and much editing, the result became *The Forrestal Diaries*.[9] All the while he compromised issues to a point that there was little left of them. He passed any decisions to the president, calling him on the telephone, sending him memos. One day Truman's naval aide, Admiral Dennison, was in the oval office, and the president asked mischievously, "Do you know who the secretary of defense is?"

Dennison played along with the query and said, "Yes sir, Jim Forrestal."

"You're wrong," said the president. "*I'm* the secretary of defense. Jim calls me up several times a day asking me to make a decision on matters that are completely within his competence, but he passes them on to me."[10]

Forrestal had several ways of avoiding decisions. One was to present a budget that excluded such needs as oil. Then he could go to Congress for a supplementary appropriation. Another was to make empty promises. When he was secretary of the navy he proved expert at this. One day Truman told the budget director, Webb, "I want to finance them for another year at 15 percent below the present level of expenditures." This meant a loss of $700 million. Webb gave Forrestal a direct order to cut the money from the forthcoming estimate. Forrestal said, "All right. I'll do that." Weeks later, during a lunch with Webb, the secretary said the department was working on the estimate. At the end of the lunch, the then comptroller of the navy, McNeil, came in. When Forrestal went out of the room to answer a telephone call, Webb discovered Forrestal had not even told McNeil to make the estimate. The next day Webb put fifty people on the project and himself drew up the navy budget.[11]

Truman endured Forrestal through the election year of 1948, when his dismissal might have caused an uproar. The president forced his resignation after the new year.

During all these contentions, let it be added, the services were hardly in fighting trim. Anyone could see that, especially the 15 million veterans—most of them chose to remove themselves, as far as possible, from anything military and looked down their noses at the men and a few women who stayed in or joined up. As far as the veterans could observe, the services were full of incompetents and misfits. It was amusing to watch the postwar displays of service ribbons, including the omnipresent good conduct medal, a piece of cardboard and red cloth signifying nothing. Leaders of the services agreed with the veterans about the saddening state of the forces. General Bradley, taking over as army chief of staff from his friend General Eisenhower in 1948, was appalled by what he inherited: nothing more than an administrative army. In Germany and Japan the army was half clerks, half policemen. In the United States he had only one division remotely describable as combat-ready, the Eighty-second Airborne at Fort Bragg, North Carolina. "The Army was thus in no position whatsoever to backstop a get-tough policy of containment vis-à-vis the Soviets," Clay Blair has written with Bradley. "Actually, the Army of 1948 could not fight its way out of a paper bag."[12]

The budget battle went on until the Korean War threw everything to the winds. The military budget submitted for fiscal 1951 totaled $55.5 billion, and Congress appropriated more. The air force obtained 110 groups. The admirals secured all the big carriers they wanted. (By a twist of fate, the new and very expensive Polaris submarines joined the fleet not long afterward, giving the navy an enormous piece of the military budget, a major, even the principal, role in nuclear warfare, and the privilege of being first to take on the Soviet Union.)

Beginning in June 1950, critics accused Truman of having so held down the military as to have invited a debacle. To this the president could say little in public. To have been in any way effective he would have had to reply with complex figures and get into such issues as to whether land-based planes were more effective than carrier planes. He would have had to discuss the self-serving testimony of air force generals, the emotional testimony of admirals, the zeal of civilian supporters. He would have had to reveal the tragic incapacity of his first secretary of defense.

2

In a thoughtful and, more than that, a brilliant, book about American nuclear policy, McGeorge Bundy has set out the second aspect of military calculations for President Truman during the half decade after World War II. As an erstwhile Harvard dean and national security adviser to two presidents, he offers an arresting interpretation. He clearly does not admire Truman's handling of nuclear issues. The thirty-third president, he writes, was a good man, and well-meaning, but unwilling to see the sides of issues. He believes Truman liked safe solutions, was mechanical in making decisions, only took ways out that appeared in oval office presentations, and tended to support the military. His great predecessor, had he lived, might have done better. Franklin Roosevelt would have thought over problems; he would have turned them over in his mind; he would have contemplated them.[13]

This is an arresting interpretation, but in Truman's case Bundy, it does appear, is not altogether fair. Truman's openness—sometimes his voluble openness—tended to make him seem less contemplative than he was. After all, it was Truman who shortly before the Japanese surrender said he did not want to order nuclear bombings again because of what that might mean "for all those kids." Not long afterward he was speaking with Budget Director

Smith and worried out loud that the army was demobilizing too rapidly. "There are some people in the world," he said, "who do not seem to understand anything except the number of divisions you have." Smith remarked, "Mr. President, you have an atomic bomb up your sleeve." The president replied, "Yes, but I am not sure it can ever be used." Three years later, speaking this time to a group of military and civil advisers, he said, "I don't think we ought to use this thing unless we absolutely have to. It is a terrible thing to order the use of something that is so terribly destructive, destructive beyond anything we have ever had. You have got to understand that this isn't a military weapon." He went on, in the vein of what he said about the time of Hiroshima and Nagasaki: "It is used to wipe out women and children and unarmed people, and not for military uses. So we have got to treat this differently from rifles and cannon and ordinary things like that." Some months later he repeated himself: "[I]t's important for everybody in the world and for our children and their children. It not only will affect the security of the country and is tied in with our military things, but it will affect health, and the industrial setup of the whole doggoned world." When, that same day, Lilienthal read him the figures of bombs ready and numbers planned for the next two years, his face was a picture, Lilienthal wrote, and his eyes, enlarged by his glasses, as bright as the head of the AEC had ever seen them. "Boy," he said, "we could blow a hole clean through the earth!" Then he added, "Wouldn't it be wonderful when January 1, 1951, comes around, if we could take the whole business and dump it into the sea?"[14]

During the Korean War the president was discussing military plans with the joint chiefs. One of the chiefs, Hoyt Vandenberg, remarked, "If the Chinese enter the war, this will mean the use of atomic weapons."

Harry Truman came out of his chair, turned to Vandenberg, and said, "Who told you that?"

The general said, "That's part of our strategic doctrine."

Truman said, "You are not going to put me in that position. You'd better go back and get yourself some more strategic doctrine!"[15]

Truman's acquaintance with nuclear weapons divided, in the postwar years, into several moments or periods when the nuclear issue came clearly to his attention and demanded his decision. In each case he dealt with his problem in what does seem to have been a remarkably clearheaded way. The initial instance was the cabinet meeting of September 21, 1945, often remarked by students of the period. In deference to Secretary of War Stimson—who was leaving the government that day, full of years and honors—the session that day considered the question of sharing nuclear secrets with the British and particularly the Soviet governments. Stimson had spent his last months watching over the nuclear program, which he had made his particular interest, and favored an approach to the Soviets. The subject was congenial to him, a fine point of debate after which he could leave such issues to other hands.

But as matters turned out, and to use the comment of Acheson, "The discussion was unworthy of the subject." Stimson desired only a diplomatic approach, not an openhanded passing of whatever the U.S. scientists knew. The presumption would be that the Soviets would offer a quid pro quo for the money the nuclear project had cost. Instead, some cabinet members misconstrued the debate to be whether to give away the secrets. They were totally unprepared on this complicated subject, and hardly knew what was a nuclear secret and what common scientific knowledge. They responded by sketching their opinions in airy detail. Moreover, the president, although asking each individual to make further comments in writing, as he probably should have done in advance of the discussion, told the members he was not asking a decision, but only opinions, and that he would make the decision if necessary; that was simply his way with cabinet sessions. He did not say it, but the members should have known that he could hardly make an independent decision and would have to involve Congress.[16]

After the discussion, and reception of papers, Truman released an ambiguous public statement on October 3 promising discussion with Britain and Canada and thereafter talks with "other nations." He meanwhile had made an approach to Vandenberg and Connally, to see if there might be a Senate committee to investigate his recommendations; they misinterpreted his approach into thinking in terms of a committee to investigate the diplomatic and military meaning of the new weapons.[17] In November the president held a perhaps unfortunate conference with Prime Minister Mackenzie King and his British opposite, Attlee, for which he made almost no preparation, and almost nothing came from it. Congress, stirred up, gradually turned to other problems.

This first essay over nuclear issues, in this case over sharing, seemed inconclusive, which it was, but Truman discovered there was little he could do about offering nuclear information to Britain and the Soviet Union. The nuclear program had been in large part American, and his fellow citizens were in no mood to share it. This he could find out only after the above-mentioned explorations. Each could be considered a failure, but on so important a matter as nuclear sharing it was necessary to move tentatively, which he did; at the end he found out how far he could go, which was nowhere.

The next presidential effort over the new weapons concerned limitation, perhaps even abolition, which he attempted first through the Acheson-Lilienthal report drawn up by the then undersecretary of state and the chairman of the Tennessee Valley Authority, assisted by the wartime head of the Los Alamos laboratory for constructing nuclear weapons, J. Robert Oppenheimer. To present an American plan to the United Nations the president chose the World War I economic mobilizer, Bernard M. Baruch.

Truman's handling of the limitation or abolition of nuclear arms was to create not merely disappointment but criticism, contemporary and later, and it is possible that he could have done better. Critics contended that he never wanted limitation, not to mention abolition, and only went through the motions. This was not true.[18] As in sharing, he was up against the feeling of most Americans that nuclear energy presumed some kind of secret that the United States must not release, especially to the Russians, until it received a quid pro quo, diplomatic or military or both. The president and all informed observers knew better, especially with publication of the Smyth Report, named after the Princeton University physicist, Henry D. Smyth, who put it together. The report revealed many of the wartime procedures and left little to the imagination save technology. Still, the public and through it Congress was intractable on sharing without an equivalent. By some contemporary measurements the effort to obtain Russian acquiescence to limitation or disarmament came to grief on this single public misapprehension. And there were other misunderstandings. Acheson, Lilienthal, and Oppenheimer all believed the new weapon needed a scientific solution, and they proposed one in their report, which surprisingly, especially in the case of Acheson, was almost devoid of political content. Last, the president chose Baruch for presentation of the plan, and Baruch antagonized its authors, partly by renaming it the Baruch plan, partly by inserting a proviso for "swift and sure" punishment of violators not subject to Security Council veto. He meant that if any nation, presumably the Soviet Union, failed to fulfill its promises under the plan, it was subject to UN military action. The proviso was meaningless because only the United States was strong enough to chastise the USSR.

Swift and sure punishment might have been enough to defeat the Baruch plan, but the Soviet Union had no intention of subscribing to it anyway. The Soviets presented their own plan that demanded destruction of all weapons (that is, U.S. weapons). Only then—the simplicity of their plan was breathtaking—would the Russians consider participation in an international authority.

The president's part in the American plan was to support the Acheson-Lilienthal report and allow Baruch to change it slightly, hoping that Baruch's conservative reputation would rebuff American critics. Truman seems to have believed that the plan might work, and as late as the summer of 1948 he refused to allow the joint chiefs of staff to advance a military plan that depended on nuclear weapons; he related to them that it might not merely prove unacceptable to the American people but a disarmament agreement would make it impossible. Only in 1949, after the Berlin blockade raised so many questions, did he give up hope for an agreement. On July 14, 1949, he told a secret meeting on policy: "I am of the opinion we'll never obtain international control. Since we can't obtain international control we must be strongest in atomic weapons."[19]

The custody issue was the next to obtain consideration, this in the summer of 1948 after the Czech coup sounded the alarm over European security, when the first appropriation for the Marshall Plan had passed, and the Berlin issue had turned into crisis. As mentioned in an earlier chapter, the military wanted custody of the country's nuclear arsenal, and Truman at the outset refused. "As long as I am in the White House," he told Clifford, who relayed the point to Lilienthal, "I will be opposed to taking atomic weapons away from the hands they are now in, and they will only be delivered to the military by particular order of the President issued at a time when they are needed."[20]

At a meeting with Forrestal and the service secretaries and the military shortly afterward, the president heard the counterarguments. At the outset the military spokesman prejudiced the services' side by reading a long document and then starting to read the annexes. Truman reached for the documents and said, curtly and unpleasantly, "I can read." Lilienthal followed with the case for presidential custody, which he did not read.

During the meeting Air Force Secretary Symington made comments that almost spoiled the occasion. "Our fellas at Sandia think they ought to have the bomb. They feel they might get them when they need them and they might not work."

The president looked at him hard and said, "Have they ever failed to work?"

"No, but . . ." was the reply.

After similar comments from Secretary of the Army Royall and from Forrestal the president closed the session by saying he could not make up his mind at the moment but would let the group know. "You have got to understand," he added, "that I have got to think about the effect of such a thing on international relations. This is no time to be juggling an atom bomb around."[21] Not long afterward, Truman told Forrestal that he was going to "keep in his hands the decision as to the use of the bomb, and did not propose to have some dashing lieutenant colonel decide when would be the proper time to drop one."[22]

A year later the matter came up again. Lilienthal and his fellow commissioners were in the president's office, and the arrangement was for Commissioner Lewis Strauss to raise the civilian-military issue. Strauss did not see an opening, and so Lilienthal raised it. "Mr. President," he said, "we are determined to carry out your policy of an entirely civilian administration of atomic energy in all of its aspects. You have shown every sign of intending that that is the way it should be. I want to be frank to say that there are elements in the military establishment—not the whole of it at all, but strong elements—that don't agree with you and are pretty outspoken about it and are causing some difficulties."

The president drew himself up and "practically sticking his chin into my face" said, impressively, "Well, I'm the Commander in Chief."

Lilienthal said Truman had shown that clearly the previous summer on the custody issue, and the commissioners did not want to come "running to Papa" with their troubles.

"Well," was the reply, "Papa won't hesitate to use the strap if that's what it takes." The president had been grinning, and "his grin spread into a full-scale laugh."[23]

The custody issue took a different turn two years later, April 6, 1951, when a crisis arose in Korea akin to the two crises that had so worried Truman in 1948 in regard to Berlin. Lilienthal's successor as chairman of the AEC, Gordon Dean, saw the president that day and according to his office diary "was told by him that the situation in the Far East is extremely serious." There was a heavy concentration of troops just above the Yalu in the part of Manchuria across from the northwestern corner of Korea, a very heavy concentration of planes parked on airfields tip-to-tip, and seventy Russian submarines at Vladivostok, with others off southern Sakhalin. The president believed the Chinese and Russians were ready to push the UN out of Korea and might attempt to take Japan, with the submarines cutting supply lines to Korea and Japan. (The day Dean saw the president was the day after Representative Martin read General MacArthur's incendiary letter to the House, the same day Truman decided, though he did not relate the point, to dismiss MacArthur, signing the general's relief orders the following Monday, effective Tuesday—all this evidence of how shockingly inconvenient was MacArthur's insubordination.) The joint chiefs had asked for custody of nuclear weapons and in Dean's presence Truman signed a release for nine bombs, which in the next days passed under control of General Vandenberg. He said no decision had been taken on using them, and would not until after a committee of the National Security Council explored the matter, and that in no event would the U.S. Air Force use such weapons in North Korea, not because of any issue of diplomacy or humanity but because the mountainous terrain would make them ineffective.[24] It is unclear whether the nine bombs later passed back under control of the AEC.

During the Truman administration a quite different issue was whether to allow bombs outside the United States. In the spring of 1948, Truman refused to allow out of the country any B-29 bombers modified to carry nuclear bombs. Bomb groups that went to England were conventional. Not until July 1950, after the opening of the Korean War, would he allow even the non-nuclear components of nuclear bombs to go overseas. But then the war, like its distant cousin the Vietnam War fifteen years later, gradually broke down resistance to what now seems to have been errant policy. At the outset the nonnuclear components went to storage bins on Guam, where they could be close but not too close to Korea. Because most of them were to be used against the Soviet Union, they were loaded aboard aircraft carriers in the Atlantic or Mediterranean, and then later stored at facilities in Newfoundland and Britain. In January 1953, just before going out of office, the president gave up his position set forth so sharply in 1948 and approved overseas shipment of completed weapons assemblies.

The principal nuclear decision during Truman's presidency was the go-ahead for the hydrogen bomb in January 1950. Actually, in September 1949 the president had signed an order transferring $300 million to the AEC, and the order amounted, Truman said months later, to a decision.[25] That was arguable, for the money was to increase the commission's production of fissionable material, not to go ahead with the hydrogen bomb. Still, increased availability of bomb stuff did point in the direction of the large bomb, for it showed what might be described as expansive thinking. It was a straw in the wind for the decision to come on January 31.

Before the decision of January there was a marked division of opinion within the administration, although the consensus was in favor. The five-member AEC at first divided three to two against the H-bomb, the majority led by Chairman Lilienthal; then two commissioners switched, making the vote four to one in favor. The AEC's general advisory committee of distinguished scientists all opposed. Two members, however, Enrico Fermi and I. I. Rabi, wobbled, favoring only a moratorium on development, "bilateral if possible, unilateral if necessary"; they felt that any commitment not to build should depend on similar Soviet restraint, which they believed could be checked out by analysis of air samples, without on-the-spot inspection. The joint chiefs of staff were in favor, even though the United States was more vulnerable to bombing of large metropolitan areas than was the Soviet Union; they saw such a bomb as a deterrent force, and also believed there was danger in the Soviets' getting it first. Congress's joint committee on atomic energy was in favor. In the state department the then deputy undersecretary, Rusk, contended that the Soviets would develop the new weapon regardless of what the United States did, and hence it was better to go ahead. Acheson agreed, and on this issue he almost lost his temper with the head of the policy planning staff, Kennan. He had asked for a report from the staff and instructed them that he wanted "as much fact and analysis as possible" and admonished them not to spend time on "the ultimate moral question." Kennan vigorously opposed the big bomb, and in a memorandum to Acheson that he later said was the most important he ever wrote he argued that development of the hydrogen bomb would take the United States and the Soviet Union into an arms race and end diplomacy, that if the United States stayed out the USSR might likewise. Acheson was furious with his subordinate, reportedly telling him that "he ought to resign from the Foreign Service and go out and preach his Quaker gospel but not push it within the Department."[26]

The president made the decision in a meeting that lasted seven minutes. He had designated a committee of Lilienthal, Acheson, and Secretary of Defense Johnson, and the committee advised going ahead, two to one. This may have been the only time that Acheson ever agreed with Johnson on anything. Lilienthal made a statement of his position: "I thought the decision the president would make, however carefully worded, however casually issued, would be construed throughout the country as confirming our present course in respect to how the country could best be defended; that it magnified some of the weaknesses that were growing greater every month, namely, our chief reliance upon atomic weapons in the defense of this country and Europe." The president interrupted, relating that discussion might have gone differently if Senator Edwin C. Johnson of Colorado, a member of the joint committee on atomic energy, had not raised the H-bomb issue publicly. There had been so much talk in Congress, and everywhere, and people were so excited, he did not have any alternative but to go ahead. "Can the Russians do it?" he asked. Everyone agreed they could. "In that case," he said, "we have no choice. We'll go ahead." He adjourned the meeting and issued an announcement that afternoon.[27]

It may have been the shortness of this meeting that concerned Bundy and brought him to say that Truman lacked the quality of contemplation. To take into another level of competition what already was a race, what with the Soviets exploding a nuclear test device late in August 1949, was a serious matter, whether made in January 1950 or the preceding September. If only for the record, the president might have lengthened the January session—although no one was making notes and there is no reason to believe he knew Lilienthal was keeping a diary.[28]

It is barely possible that the quickness of the H-bomb decision owed a good deal to the Fuchs case, news of which became public a few days afterward. Fuchs must have helped the Soviets substantially with their nuclear explosion of August 1949; the test device was of an implosion, Nagasaki-type bomb, more efficient than the Hiroshima bomb and one that Fuchs had known all about. Moreover, during and after World War II there had been speculations and theoretical studies on constructing an H-bomb, and Fuchs had taken part in them. Actually the American theories then favored were headed in a wrong direction, and it was possible to argue that he could not have betrayed anything important in that regard and that he might even have been helpful, as he would have passed on erroneous information. Nonetheless, the discussions about a large American bomb had gotten into public print and Fuchs's confirmation of them was enough in itself to urge the Soviets into the new competition. Indeed, it was learned some years later, from an official Soviet biography of the nuclear expert Kurchatov, that the Soviet A-bomb team was at work on an H-bomb before the American program got under way, and it later became evident that Andrei Sakharov had begun study of the theory of the hydrogen bomb before 1949.

Fuchs had come under suspicion through a chance wartime operation of the FBI, which in 1944 obtained so-called one-time pads (a system of five-digit random groups of numbers added to five-digit groups of codes, used once and then destroyed) from the Soviet purchasing office in New York City.

Already agents possessed the remnants of a charred Soviet code book found on a battlefield in Finland. With the pads and the book a possibility arose, and when the cold war heated up an American cryptanalyst gave his attention to the problem and broke the code. One of the first documents pointed toward the Rosenbergs. After the analyst produced a top-secret report written by Fuchs while in the Manhattan Project at Los Alamos, the FBI in August 1949 asked AEC security to investigate Fuchs. One of the AEC commissioners close to J. Edgar Hoover, Strauss, probably learned about Fuchs as early as October 13; the FBI request was made known at a commission meeting on November 2. Surely the FBI would have briefed the president sometime between August and October. If Truman had not learned from Director Hoover he could have learned from Strauss, who, aroused over what he considered a need not to take the nuclear competition to a new level but to catch up with the Soviets, probably went to his friend Sidney W. Souers, secretary of the National Security Council, like Strauss a banker by profession, also like Strauss a wartime rear admiral, who saw Truman regularly. Thus, Truman must have known about Fuchs's espionage well before the meeting with Lilienthal, Acheson, and Johnson on January 31. This knowledge, combined with what Truman and his assistants surmised, could well explain why he needed only seven minutes to make the H-bomb decision.[29]

3

Some account is necessary of the several plans for defense of the United States against the Soviet Union during the years 1945–1950, plans that involved use of nuclear weapons—and along with those plans, which bore the names Pincher, Makefast, Broiler, Halfmoon, and Offtackle, the complete unreadiness of the military to carry them out. It was a strange situation, essential to analyze in any appraisal of the Truman administration.

The American nuclear plans were startlingly imaginative.[30] The plan named Pincher, generated by the air force in June 1946, assumed that at the beginning of hostilities American occupation troops in Europe and Asia would either withdraw to unspecified "tenable areas" or go home. Britain would hold, but Korea and possibly Italy and the Mediterranean would come under Soviet occupation. Then, because the United States and its allies would "enjoy a definite superiority in naval forces" and "a qualitative superiority in air and ground forces," in addition to nuclear bombs, the Western Allies would roll back their adversary. Another air force plan, Makefast, anticipated six B-29 groups operating from Britain and Egypt within four months of opening of hostilities, and hypothesized that such a force could destroy three-fourths of the Soviet Union's petroleum-producing capacity in nine months and severely limit mobility of Soviet ground and air forces in one year.

In August 1947 the joint chiefs revised and updated Pincher, under the name Broiler. Like its predecessor it anticipated withdrawal of Allied ground forces in Europe and Asia. Simultaneously U.S. strategic air forces would conduct an air-atomic offensive against the Soviets. That offensive would offer a "tremendous strategic advantage" because of the sole possession of nuclear weapons by the United States. The air-atomic campaign would stabilize the Soviet ground offensive in the war's first six months, and in the next six would assist Allied forces in recapturing territory—all this because it would disrupt Russian war production.

In May 1948, just before the Berlin blockade, the joint chiefs came up with a "short-range emergency war plan," Halfmoon, which like its predecessors called for evacuation of Western Europe. As for bombing the Soviet Union, the Strategic Bombing Survey after World War II had shown that certain industries were vital to an enemy; destruction of these key industries could finish off war-making capacity. The theory behind Halfmoon was that the Soviet transportation system was too widespread to be vulnerable, and bombing such industries as steel, aircraft, and electric power plants would take too long. But seventeen cities contained two-thirds of the Soviet Union's petroleum industry; they were likely targets. Upon being briefed on May 5, President Truman ordered an alternate plan based on conventional forces. As the Berlin crisis deepened, with the Western airlift at first chancy, he assured Secretary Forrestal that "if it became necessary" he might allow nuclear weapons and endorsed NSC-30, a National Security Council document that looked in that direction. He "prayed that he would never have to make such a decision," but if it became necessary he would do so.[31] Halfmoon envisioned bombers deploying to bases in Britain, Khartoum-Cairo-Suez, and Okinawa.

In December 1949 a plan named Offtackle replaced Halfmoon. It similarly assumed loss of the Continent, for "while the countries which have signed the Atlantic Pact will have improved economically and militarily, they will be unable, with the exception of the United Kingdom, to effectively resist being overrun and occupied by Soviet forces." It proposed holding a substantial bridgehead, or if that proved infeasible then the earliest practicable return so as to prevent exploitation and communization. In the course of withdrawal and eventual reoccupation the U.S. Air Force would bestow a terrible nuclear retribution upon the USSR. The plan's full details were classified, but contemporary air force planning was "to deliver the entire stock pile of atomic bombs, if made available, in a single massive attack," and to strike seventy Soviet urban areas with 133 nuclear bombs in thirty days.

As for the realities, the actual nuclear forces the American military could have mustered behind their plans, a mere statement of the small numbers of bombs available in the early postwar years makes clear that the contingency plans were unrealistic in the extreme. According to government figures now available, by the end of June 1946 the United States nuclear stockpile consisted of nine weapons. A year later the number had risen to thirteen. By mid-1948 the figure was fifty. Thereafter numbers rose dramatically, to perhaps (and these figures are not official) three hundred by the opening of the Korean War, four hundred by January 1, 1951, and slightly less than a thousand by the time Truman left office.[32]

A further problem was that available weapons were directly affected by several important technicalities. One was the need for teams of technicians to put bomb components together so as to ready weapons for use; it took twenty-four men and nearly two days to ready a single bomb. In January 1947 the military's teams departed with the changeover from military to civil control; the AEC had no teams, and it is an open question as to how long it took to secure them. Then, because of the need to recharge a weapon's batteries, the bomb could not remain in a plane ready for dropping for more than forty-eight hours. Moreover, a vital part of the bomb, the polonium initiators, necessary to ready a critical mass, had a half-life of 138 days and were in short supply in 1947. Lilienthal told Gregg Herken of his shock when he took over from the army and went to Los Alamos to the weapons laboratory: "Actually we had one [bomb] that was probably operable when I first went off to Los Alamos; one that had a good chance of being operable."[33] This in the year when the nation was embarking on a provocative policy toward the Soviet Union.

Nor was the Strategic Air Command (SAC) capable of dropping bombs with accuracy until the time of the Korean War. The demobilization of 1945–1946 gravely affected the readiness of SAC crews. For the next two years the command was under the nominal guidance of General George C. Kenney, a well-known figure during World War II, but the effective commander was Major General Clements McMullen. He reduced SAC's readiness to a shambles through a program known as cross-training, which required pilots to be competent in nonflying duties and crew members in other aircrew positions. McMullen trained his crews on targets that were too easy when compared to what would occur under combat conditions, and at low altitudes, ten or fifteen thousand feet. In January 1949 General LeMay, who had taken command of SAC from Kenney the preceding October (when it became clear that SAC might have to protect the Allied position in Western Europe), sent all his bomb groups over Dayton, Ohio, near Wright Field, in a simulated bombing. He gave the crews 1938 maps of Dayton, required them to make passes at high altitude, and sent them in at night. By chance the weather was poor, with thunderstorms. The result was a fiasco. Not a single plane fulfilled its mission. LeMay was so shaken by the bomb runs that he described that night as the darkest in air force history.[34]

It was a thoroughly inadequate situation, and no one below the president seems to have had all the information concerning it. Officers who made up nuclear plans did not know how many bombs were available, and General Groves was reluctant to release bomb numbers. In February 1947 Forrestal and

Nimitz had to provide recommendations on production rates. Neither knew the size of the stockpile nor the current rate of production, but each assumed the other did. (They agreed to continue the current rate.)[35] Spaatz and Kenney appear not to have known much about the readiness of SAC, leaving the problem to McMullen. Whether LeMay, once he found out, told Vandenberg, or the latter then told the secretary of the air force, is difficult to say.

And what did President Truman think of all this? He obviously disliked the nuclear plans, considering them inhuman and also dangerous to talk about. Like most politicians, he had little use for theoretical exercises and may have considered them such. He knew bomb figures, getting them probably at first from Eisenhower and then from Lilienthal. When the latter briefed him he noticed the president had them firmly in mind—Truman could recite them. Indeed, on two occasions he actually did recite them in massive breaches of security; in 1946 he told a White House staff meeting the nation had seven bombs, and the next year he told his World War I Battery D lieutenant, Vic H. Housholder, that the country had thirteen bombs.[36] He seems to have had little idea of the technicalities that bore on the readiness of bombs. He understood some of SAC's weakness. In a meeting with NATO foreign ministers on the evening before they signed the treaty, April 3, 1949, he told them, "To be sure, we have the atomic bomb; but we must recognize the present limitations of our strategic methods for delivering it."[37] Like the rest of the American people he seems to have taken refuge in the mere existence of American bombs, whatever the problems of readying them or carrying them to their targets. In February 1949 he admitted to Lilienthal that "the atomic bomb was the mainstay and all he had; that the Russians would have probably taken over Europe a long time ago if it were not for that."[38]

By mid-1950 matters were in better shape. Bomb production was rising rapidly. An arrangement with Britain and Canada, concluded in January 1948, gave the United States the entire production of uranium mines in the Belgian Congo. Fat Boy plutonium bombs, known as Mark III weapons, were being replaced by Mark IV bombs, which used only half the plutonium and weapons-grade uranium. Mark III weapons required artisans; they were tailor-made. Mark IV bombs meant assembly lines. All the while SAC was learning how to drop bombs on targets. The air force was mastering aerial refueling, changing from a hose-and-reel system to a flying boom, which greatly extended the range of its fleet of B-29s and B-50s and thus made bases in Europe, Africa, and the Far East—unsafe because of political instability, political sensitivity, or proximity to the Soviet Union—no longer necessary. B-36s were about to become available in quantity, possessing a range of eight thousand miles. But the B-36s were prop planes and therefore slow, and they were plagued by design and maintenance problems, and in 1953–1954 they began to be replaced by the B-52 jets that became venerables of the air; the air force kept them in the air, albeit with modifications, for the next forty years.

The nation's passage from 1945 to 1950 was an uneasy affair as one looks back at it. The gradual bringing together of plans and the capacity to carry them out was far too slow for comfort. It was a dangerous half-decade when national security depended on something the United States did not possess. Because of the work of the Soviet agent Maclean, whose high position in the British embassy in Washington gave him access to everything that passed between the state department and the foreign office, the Russians must have received copies of some if not all of the nuclear contingency plans. In 1945–1948 they probably knew about the United States' small stock of weapons, for Maclean sat on the British-Canadian-American committee that distributed production from the Congo mines and possessed a pass to the AEC's Washington offices that he used many times.[39] They probably did not know of the near-total lack of weapons because of the unavailability of technicians and plutonium initiators, nor how inefficient SAC was. Fuchs's spying, however, may have revealed something more important, namely, the working of the radar fusing mechanism of the Mark III weapons; until AEC scientists could replace the Mark IIIs, or design and procure other fusing devices, the Soviets might have been able to nullify that part of the nuclear arsenal. If the Mark IV bombs had the same fusing mechanism, they could have nullified the entire nuclear arsenal.[40]

4

A solution to one of the marked inadequacies of the new postwar military forces, the extraordinary weakness of the U.S. Army, came into view beginning with the Korean War, when it proved necessary for the next three years, until the Korean truce of 1953, to put six U.S. divisions into South Korea to protect that nation against the North Koreans and Chinese. Simultaneously the Truman administration moved to reinforce the garrison in West Germany, raising its strength from two to six divisions, all the while furnishing massive military aid to NATO allies. Prior to that time Bradley and his literary collaborator Blair described the army as unable to fight. General Marshall said it did not have enough troops to defend Ladd Field near Fairbanks in Alaska, the best possible SAC base against Russia, closest to the USSR, the approaches all being under U.S. control. During these years the Soviet Union possessed huge conventional forces; their numbers were subject to speculation, but their size was undoubted.[41]

The present pages are not the place to describe the way in which NATO became a counter against Soviet ground strength. President Truman left the task largely to Secretary Acheson and to the two secretaries of defense, Marshall and Lovett, who followed Johnson beginning in the summer of 1950. Occasionally he advised them, but for the most part he took their advice. Suffice it to relate how the effort to put force behind the North Atlantic Treaty began the same day as the president ratified it, July 6, 1949, when the administration sent to Congress the bill for the allies' requests for military aid. The hope was that Western Europeans would use their own manpower to create the new ground force, as had happened in Greece. There was economic slack in Europe—young men could be spared—whereas the United States had full employment. But the bill ran into trouble and began to move only after the president on September 23 announced the Soviet nuclear test of August 29. On October 6 he signed the bill appropriating $1.3 billion for allies around the world, of which $900 million was for NATO. Congress required proof of how the nations would use aid, and this meant negotiation of bilateral agreements with each beneficiary. By the Korean War the allies had received little military aid from the appropriation, $49 million worth, although they had obligated almost all of it. Beginning in June 1950 matters moved with more dispatch. Congress opened the treasury for unprecedented defense assistance in peacetime, $5 billion for fiscal 1951. In January 1951 the president sent General Eisenhower to Europe to organize allied forces, and the general remained for more than a year, until he returned to accept the Republican nomination for the presidency. His appearance galvanized Europeans. It also galvanized Americans, who proved willing to go ahead with what was an awkward enterprise—return of the U.S. Army to Western Europe a half-dozen years after almost all divisions had gone home. The GOP produced a "great debate" over sending the four additional divisions to Europe. Some of the debate was over granting authority to a Democratic president who had the nerve to announce the Truman Doctrine, take credit for the Marshall Plan, win another term in the presidency in 1948, arrange the North Atlantic Treaty, conduct the Korean War without express authority from Congress, and dismiss MacArthur. Eisenhower's appointment—the administration had not planned things that way (the general was a natural choice to head NATO)—blunted the oratory of the great debate.

Scholarly interpretation of the reasoning behind the decision to reinforce NATO has varied over the years. In his memoirs Charles Bohlen asserted that Korea was the cause: "It was the Korean War and not World War II that made us a world military power." The leading student of the United States and NATO, Lawrence S. Kaplan, has stressed Korea and fear of a Russian feint in the Far East and major war in Western Europe. Walter LaFeber has sought to show that a movement to raise European force levels was underway prior to June 1950, and the Korean War only led to political rather than military concern—it produced the great debate. "NSC-68, the initial commitment to French Indochina, the growing attractiveness of the Pentagon's plan for rearming and integrating West Germany, Acheson's and Bevin's anger over the Schuman Plan being created without sufficient consultation with London and Washington—all these events had helped decide where the heart, and thus the treasure, of U.S. policy would be located."[42]

What to make of LaFeber's reasons for NATO? It is difficult to support his contention about NSC-68, a document that did not go anywhere until the Korean War made it seem prophetic. The first American commitment in March 1950 for support of French troops in Indochina may not have been a matter of enthusiasm on the part of Acheson, who asserted years later that the French "blackmailed" the United States by demanding commitment in order to participate in NATO. As for the German problem, whatever the Pentagon's desire to rearm and integrate Germany, perhaps for the purpose of getting its clerks and policemen back to the United States and forming them into fighting divisions, such a course did not gain support from the Truman administration until June 1950, when it became clear that the Soviets might be able to field an attacking army from East Germany just as they had done from North Korea. Like all Americans—not to mention the French, to whom the idea was anathema—Truman had hesitated to allow a new German army. Just before the Korean War he sent a memorandum asking Acheson to call home High Commissioner John J. McCloy, who was looking into force levels among the NATO allies, so that McCloy, Johnson, Acheson, and the president might sit down and discuss the proper approach to a police force for Germany that "will maintain order locally and yet not be allowed to develop into a training ground for a military machine that can combine with Russia and ruin the rest of the world." Reading two defense department reports, one urging German rearmament, the other cooperation with Franco Spain, Truman wrote that both were "decidedly militaristic and in my opinion not realistic with present conditions." Across the top of the page he wrote in longhand, "Both as wrong as can be."[43] To be sure, much of the history of NATO over the next years would be a search for a formula for German participation. The French were about to produce the Pleven plan for inclusion of German troops at battalion strength, followed by a European Defense Community (EDC) that went through a series of drafts until meeting defeat in 1954 at the hands of the nation that proposed it. By that time the other allies were willing to include the Germans. In 1954 the Senate, by vote of 88 to 0, passed a resolution to give the West German government full sovereignty if France did not ratify EDC. For all these things Korea was responsible. As for the Schuman plan of 1950, sponsored by the French foreign minister, Robert Schuman, which made possible the integration of the French and West German iron and steel complexes under a supranational authority, the European Coal and Steel Community, its negotiation does not appear to have aroused Acheson to bolster NATO, which implied, sooner or later, German rearmament, to get back at the French.

More important than the reason or reasons for the NATO buildup, however, was the fact that by the end of the Truman administration a new military force, a combination of conventional and nuclear armaments, at last sufficed to support the nation's diplomacy.[44]

Chapter Seventeen

Nadir

After a year or so of the Korean War, it is sad to relate, Harry Truman came close to losing control of the government of the United States. A Gallup poll in November 1951 found that his countrymen, when asked whether they approved or disapproved of his presidency, awarded him less than one-fourth approval; his rating was 23 percent, one point lower than President Nixon received just before being forced out of office in 1974. A good bit of the critical judgment came because the Korean War had failed to come to an end. It went on month after month, sometimes (when the Chinese wanted to make a point) turning into hard fighting along the entrenched positions across the middle of the peninsula. Half of the American deaths during the war (the total number of deaths was 54,246, with 33,629 killed in battle) occurred during this time. MacArthur's dismissal added to the criticism. But beyond these matters the president permitted trouble with his military aide, General Vaughan, together with contentions over the Reconstruction Finance Corporation, and several poor appointments in the always sensitive Bureau of Internal Revenue, to get out of hand. Things came to such a pass that he dismissed his attorney general, Howard McGrath, as a scapegoat, although McGrath, a charming Irishman, a little bibulous and lazy, was incapable of carrying presidential sins into the wilderness. Nor was that all; in the spring of 1952 the threat of a steel strike over a few cents an hour for union workers persuaded him to seize the mills under the "inherent powers" of the president as commander-in-chief. He failed to anticipate the judgment of the Supreme Court, which was against inherent powers. Everything came down to the presidential election that year, and the president's enemies turned it into a referendum on the administration. With the Republicans' nomination of a national monument, Eisenhower, the outcome was not in doubt. The defeat of the Democratic candidate, Governor Adlai E. Stevenson of Illinois, became the defeat of the administration.

Perhaps the basic problem, the cause of it all, was that Truman was getting tired. He had too much on his mind—too many duties, foreign and domestic, not to mention ceremonial duties. John Hersey followed him around for a short time in 1951, the same year as the low rating, in preparation for a profile in the *New Yorker,* and described how he was "making his diurnal way through the thickets of power—the rank, trackless, strangely beautiful tangles of dreadful responsibilities and pompous trivialities through which he was obliged to move."[1] In 1951–1952 he was getting on in years, near the end of his sixties. When the nation entered the Korean War and the Chinese intervened he had shown a steely willingness to carry things through, far more resolution than most Americans who were willing, so they told the poll takers, to pull the troops out of Korea. In European affairs he challenged the Soviets by sending four more divisions to NATO. But he had been "taking it," to use one of his favorite phrases, too long, and a series of misestimates in domestic affairs brought an inglorious end to his presidency.

1

The "mess in Washington," as Stevenson witlessly described several domestic contentions in the Truman administration's second term, was the sort of political mess that contained too many errors of judgment to dismiss and yet was basically about minor or irrelevant matters. Stevenson used the phrase when answering a questioner who had asked about the situation. "As for the mess in Washington," the candidate began. With that he placed his foot neatly where it should not have been. By popular wisdom, the phrase referred to the so-called five percenters, individuals in Washington who arranged government contracts for businessmen and charged five percent plus a downpayment and monthly retainer; it referred to the Reconstruction Finance Corporation (RFC), particularly its chief examiner, E. Merl Young, who after leaving the agency gave his wife a mink coat that cost $9,540, paid for by a lawyer for a firm seeking an RFC loan; it referred to the Bureau of Internal Revenue, where several collectors, including an appointee in St. Louis, used their offices to enrich themselves; it referred to the culmination of all this when the president had to dismiss an attorney general whose career had assisted his own, who had served as chairman of the Democratic national committee when the president was running for election in 1948.

The first of several congressional inquiries into the Washington mess had begun in the summer of 1949, in regard to the five percenters, and turned into an investigation of the affairs of a man very close to the president, his military aide. Whatever the concern of the Senate subcommittee, the focus constantly shifted back to Vaughan. The investigation escaped control of an aging Democrat from North Carolina, Clyde R. Hoey, who affected the old-time dress of a senator, even to a string tie; Hoey was no match for two stalwart Republicans, Karl Mundt of South Dakota and Joseph McCarthy of Wisconsin.

The Hoey Committee began work after a tip from a Boston furniture manufacturer, a former reporter, who told a newsman about a Washington influence peddler, a retired army colonel named James V. Hunt. The colonel claimed to know the army's quartermaster general, the former war assets administrator, and especially one of his "closest and dearest" friends, General Vaughan. Hunt worked for 5 percent of any contract he obtained, together with a downpayment of one thousand dollars and five hundred dollars a month for expenses. He distributed matches that bore the legend, "Swiped from Harry S. Truman."

Under prompting by Mundt and McCarthy, the investigation moved from Hunt, an uninteresting exhibit, to his friend. A reserve officer, hardly a major general in a real sense, Vaughan was an easy target. He possessed little military bearing; fat and balding, he poured himself into his uniform. Someone said he looked like an unmade bed.[2] His rows of bright ribbons infuriated the regulars. Nonetheless, they had to deal with him as his office was the official army channel to the oval office. His other task, as he himself described it, was to provide scenery for the president on formal occasions. It turned out that he provided scenery for other people—during the 1948 campaign he asked Hunt to obtain the matches from a St. Louis supplier when the president's supply ran low. In other ways he obliged the Hoey Committee. Reporters accosted him in Union Station and asked about the five percenters; Vaughan said Washington contained three hundred of them, which may have been true but was no proper admission from a White House aide. His own record as a fixer emerged, wherein he displayed a willingness to help anyone who came along. When he had been secretary to Senator Truman in 1940–1942, he made it his business to do favors for constituents, and he continued this work as military aide, not realizing that a call from the White House was far more impressive than a call from a senatorial assistant.

Among Vaughan's improprieties was the affair of the freezers. He had taken interest in the predicament of Bess Truman, who, staying in Independence for months at a time, was receiving all sorts of gifts of food from townspeople and through the mail; because she had no place to keep it, the food invariably spoiled. At this time, 1945, refrigerators and freezers were almost impossible to obtain, and a chance visitor heard Vaughan talking with Mrs. Truman and arranged to have a friend send a freezer to 219 North Delaware, as well as to the addresses of several administration officials. These freezers were primitive mechanisms, and after Mrs. Truman's went off and spoiled the contents she had a truck take it away. The other freezers enjoyed checkered histories. But the fact that the addressees accepted them, allowing a perfume manufacturer, whose representative needed a European flight on a government-owned plane so as to procure scents for his business, to pay for them (they did not know that), scored the transaction as the peddling of influence. The recipients would have done well to remember a saying of Sam

Rayburn: "You just don't take it unless you can eat it, drink it, or smoke it in twenty-four hours."[3]

When Vaughan began to testify, it turned out he also had befriended the quondam agent of the Baltimore and Ohio, Maragon, the same who desired to be White House traffic officer. Vaughan seems to have given him the White House pass, and Maragon kept it, despite the president's instruction to the secret service to lift it. Maragon went on a trip to Greece with an American mission, and word of his presence and talk of White House "pull" got into the newspapers.

Then there was the affair in the Washington suburb of Arlington, on February 22, 1949, at which the Reserve Officers Association gave an award to Vaughan. At this private ceremony, which the president supposed was off-the-record, Truman made a short talk. Vaughan (as well as many other Washington-based officers) had accepted a medal from the Argentine government, then under the dictatorship of Juan D. Perón, known for anti-American behavior and for providing refuge to escaped Nazis. The columnist Walter Winchell had attacked Vaughan for accepting the medal. "I am just as fond of and just as loyal to my military aide as I am to the high brass," the president said at the Arlington meeting, "and want you to distinctly understand that any s.o.b. who thinks he can cause any one of these people to be discharged by me by some smart-aleck statement over the air or in the paper, has got another think coming." The statement got into the newspapers.

Though he was not a drinker, Vaughan had a reputation for being a boozer. He was also a devout churchgoer, but even in this respect he got into trouble, as when he told a church class: "You have to give the Roman Church credit. When the War Department requests a bishop to supply 20 priests for chaplains, he looks over his diocese and picks out the 20 best men. But it is different in the Protestant Church. Frequently a Protestant does not have a church at the moment or is willing to go on vacation for three years."[4]

Comedians took advantage of the president's attachment to Vaughan. The humorist-pianist Victor Borge was wont to remark, during concerts, "My next number will be a classic by Beethoven—the Deep-Freeze Concerto, by Harry S. Beethoven." He would pause a moment and say, "You will recognize the beat—Vaughan-two, Vaughan-two." Borge said it broke up audiences.

Throughout the Hoey investigation the president supported Vaughan. Their friendship went back a long time; in World War I and the reserves they had traversed the ranks of the field artillery, from lieutenant to full colonel. Vaughan had been in Truman's Senate office, and during World War II he had gone to Australia, where he was in a bad plane crash and almost became a cripple. He was a marvelous teller of jokes impossible to use in his defense. He was a first-rate poker companion. He undoubtedly advised the president many times, as his critics contended, but the president paid no attention to the advice and accepted only the jokes and camaraderie. Just before Vaughan left the White House to testify before the Hoey Committee on August 30, 1949, he received the following reassurance: "Harry, this investigation is entirely political, trying to embarrass me by discrediting you. You have nothing to hide. Go up there and tell the committee anything they want to know. You have been conducting your office in the way I want you to conduct it. When I want it conducted differently, I'll tell you so."[5] To make his ordeal easier Truman, in a White House ceremony, presented him with a medal fashioned from a Truman campaign button and a 1949 inaugural badge. It was inscribed:

Harry Vaughan
Whipping Boy First Class

The general thought the inscription so touching that when he wrote his memoirs he entitled them "Whipping Boy First Class."

Truman might have survived the problems over Vaughan had it not been for other problems. In addition to the five-percenter inquiry there was a senatorial investigation of the Reconstruction Finance Corporation. Another good Senate Democrat, Fulbright of Arkansas, chairman of the banking and currency committee, happened into this investigation. The RFC had done great things during the 1930s, lending to banks and industrial corporations. It had done some good things during the war. But it should have passed off the scene at war's end. It continued, however, and went downhill in personnel and quality of loans. The Lustron Corporation received millions in government loans to produce prefabricated houses of enameled steel, dramatically needed because of the housing shortage. Unfortunately, it could not begin to produce them rapidly enough, lost money regularly, and failed. Merl Young, whose wife acquired the coat, went to work at Lustron at two and one-half times his RFC salary. Mrs. Young, it turned out, was a White House secretary who worked closely with Mrs. Truman. Young and his wife were from Missouri.

As happened with the Hoey committee, so with the Fulbright committee: the investigation turned toward criticism of the president, specifically for tolerating corruption, generally for displaying bad judgment. The former charge was without foundation, the latter arguable. There was talk of the influence upon the president of his assistant, Donald Dawson, who before going to the White House in charge of personnel matters—Dawson's task was to "vet" nominees before their appointments—worked several years at the RFC. Presumably Dawson, also from Missouri, installed his own cronies in the loan agency. A split within the RFC's board of directors made the situation doubly awkward, as Dawson advised the president to side with one faction against the other. Eventually he went before the Fulbright Committee and showed he not merely had done nothing wrong but had behaved in his sensitive post in the White House with utmost good judgment. He made no secret of his opinions about the division in the board, and that he advised the president, but showed it would have been foolish of him not to. Dawson, who had seemed an éminence grise, emerged from his ordeal unscathed. Part of the reason was that, unlike Vaughan, he had remained inaccessible to news-papermen until the time came to testify.

Where the president erred in the RFC investigation was neither in the Young nor in the Dawson affair, which for different reasons did not touch him, but in treatment of the committee's chairman, whom he disliked because of the latter's suggestion after the congressional elections of 1946 that he, the president, should resign. After the committee discovered Young's misbehavior, Fulbright and two other committee members went to the White House and asked the president to reform the RFC. Fulbright knew party unity required keeping the investigation under control. Instead the president called Senator Charles W. Tobey of New Hampshire out of a committee executive session and told him, "The real crooks and influence peddlers were members of this committee, as we might soon find out." He charged that "a great many mem-bers of Congress had accepted fees for their influence in getting R.F.C. loans for constituents." He waspishly arranged to have all letters from congressmen asking intervention in RFC loans sent to the White House, and he found two letters showing that Fulbright, who had said that agency loans to hotels were improper, supported a loan for a Hot Springs, Arkansas, resort hotel. All the while he talked privately about Fulbright, whom he described as an overedu-cated Oxford s.o.b. and referred to as Senator Halfbright. The descriptions must have gotten back. Seeing that the president had no intention of reform-ing the RFC, Fulbright on February 2, 1951, released a preliminary committee report entitled "Favoritism and Influence."[6]

The third contretemps that arose about the same time was in regard to the Bureau of Internal Revenue (BIR). Fault lay again with the president, this time not for inept handling of trouble once it appeared but for failing to take preventive action.

Charles Murphy was usually a presidential defender, and years after-ward in regard to the BIR scandals said the appointees in question had all come in during the Roosevelt administration and hence were not Truman's fault—but in this Murphy was wrong.[7] The individual who unwittingly did a considerable damage was Truman's friend Hannegan, who after yeoman service during the 1940 senatorial primary had become collector of internal revenue in St. Louis at Truman's recommendation. Hannegan was a model collector and gave not the slightest problem; he was efficient and able. In-deed, he was so good that he became commissioner—his appointment was no piece of political backslapping by Truman, for Hannegan deserved it. But at that juncture Hannegan probably unconsciously erred; he had been a politician for most of his adult life, loved politics, thought politics without even thinking politics—and Hannegan simply saw the BIR as a place full of possible appointments and, therefore, saw nothing wrong with installing worthy Democrats in them. Alas, a worthy Democrat in St. Louis—an attractive, deeply religious, well-meaning, but financially uninspired Democrat—caught his attention, a political hack named Joseph P. Finnegan. Finnegan took Hannegan's place in St. Louis. After Hannegan became commissioner he similarly, inadvertently, politicized collectorships in all the BIR's sixty-four districts. This may have had something to do with the most unfortunate appointment, as his successor as commissioner of internal revenue, of another hack, Joseph V. Nunan. Nunan unavoidably appointed hacks, and eventually was himself indicted and convicted of evading $91,086 in income taxes and sent to prison.

What happened with the BIR was what one might have suspected—word of illegal activity by the collectors got to Congress, and the Senate investigated, requiring dismissal not merely of Finnegan but of collectors in Boston, Brooklyn, and San Francisco as well. Every one of the miscreants was a product of an urban political machine. Finnegan, it turned out, after appointment as collector in sensitive St. Louis, had continued his law practice, and he sought to sell insurance to St. Louis companies with delinquent taxes. Worse, he reportedly fixed tax cases and was delinquent on his own taxes to a sum of $2,444. In association with the lawyer William M. Boyle, Jr., he helped procure an RFC loan for the American Lithofold Corporation, from which he and Boyle took retainers. Boyle's connection with Finnegan deeply embarrassed the president. A native of Kansas City, Boyle had been a staff member of the Senate investigating committee, and then went to work for the Democratic national committee, becoming its chairman in 1949. While with the national committee he continued his law practice, like Finnegan, and took the Lithofold Corporation retainer. He may not, incidentally, have been much of a lawyer. When he went before a Senate committee and a member asked, "Mr. Boyle, what kind of law do you practice?," he sputtered for a bit and said, "Well, well, legal law, of course."[8] Not too long afterward he resigned the national committee chairmanship. The president gave him an enormous testimonial dinner in the Auditorium in Kansas City, catered from the Muehlebach Hotel.

Attempting to clean up the BIR the president dismissed the agency's chief counsel, Charles Oliphant, son of the distinguished law professor and treasury general counsel Herman Oliphant. The junior Oliphant had traveled to world series baseball games and other events in the plane of a friend under investigation for tax fraud; he had also accepted loans and gifts from a high-powered Washington lobbyist, Henry W. "the Dutchman" Grunewald, and given BIR jobs to applicants backed by Grunewald. In 1952 the president sent to Congress a proposal, which became law, establishing twenty-five BIR district offices, each headed by a civil service appointee. He proposed an independent inspection service. He recommended civil service status for postmasters, customs officials, and U.S. marshals, but none of these latter proposals passed.

Senate committees thus brought accusations or aired evidence of misbehavior. In each case the initiative came from the Hill. The president's handling of these cases was hardly admirable; he stonewalled one, became defensive on the second, and waited too long to take action with the third.

2

The department of justice should have protected the president against the five percenters, trouble in the RFC, and crooks in the BIR—failure to do so led to the resignation of Attorney General McGrath in April 1952. By that time Truman needed a scapegoat, and McGrath was at hand and seemed a good candidate, but he really was not the type. Why the president failed to handle the justice department until that late date is difficult to say. Roswell Gilpatric, wise observer of governmental bureaucracies, once said Truman did not really understand the legal profession and gave too little attention to his cabinet department dealing with the subject.[9] That may have been the problem. He was also busy. And he was tired out.

During the president's first term everything at justice had run fairly well as soon as Roosevelt's last attorney general, Francis Biddle, departed and Tom Clark took over. Truman arranged Biddle's exit without ceremony: he told Steve Early to call him and take his resignation. A Philadelphia socialite, accustomed to circulating in exclusive places, as well as a Roosevelt loyalist and supporter of Douglas in 1944, Biddle resented Truman's accession to the presidency. His replacement was an intelligent, sensible, modest man, who had been helpful to Truman when the latter was chairman of the investigating committee and Clark headed justice's war frauds unit.[10]

The justice department under Clark was especially effective in its antitrust division headed by J. Edgar Hoover's friendly opponent, Graham Morison. Under Biddle antitrust suits had been few, and dossiers piled up. Morison gathered and pressed them. An ex-marine, he was honest as he could be and had had extensive legal experience in New York City. Clark supported Morison's antitrust prosecutions, and so did the president, who after his own investigating-committee experience was much interested in them.[11]

Then, in 1949, Justice Frank Murphy of the Supreme Court died, and the president decided to name Clark to the vacancy. This virtually dictated that McGrath would become the new head of the justice department. Murphy had been "the Catholic justice" on the court. Clark was a Protestant, and it was necessary, it seemed, to appoint a Catholic to the justice department.[12] McGrath also had been close to the president, serving selflessly as chairman of the national committee during the 1948 election, a post other Democrats avoided. He deserved a reward. His appointment, incidentally, may have led to the decision of the president's then counsel, Clifford, who perhaps had hoped for the justice appointment, to leave the White House staff and go into private practice.

It gradually became evident that McGrath's appointment to justice was a mistake. Like Clark he was intelligent, sensible, and modest. He supported the antitrust prosecutions, signing anything Morison brought in. But he lacked Clark's drive. As Morison related, Bernard Baruch may have told him to "get out into the high grass and keep his tail down." Morison thought he was waiting for another vacancy on the High Court. McGrath's do-nothing approach eventually got Truman into difficulty, for if the department had been watching its business it could have prevented or at least handled the investigation of the "mess in Washington," deflecting criticism from the president.

Truman at last began to lose patience with McGrath. He learned through the press that one of the attorney general's principal assistants, Lamar Caudle, the same who in 1946 was slow to investigate the Kansas City ballot theft, was accepting favors from individuals or people close to individuals who were in tax trouble. Caudle's wife had purchased a mink coat for fifteen hundred dollars, assisted by a lawyer who dealt with her husband on tax cases. There was a question whether she paid all the cost—and it turned out that the lawyer had written off another nine hundred dollars as a business expense. Caudle sold an airplane, hardly a task for an assistant attorney general, for thirty thousand dollars, to a man close to two tax delinquents, and took five thousand dollars for the work. The president fired him, going right over the head of McGrath. By the end of 1951 he was looking for a replacement for McGrath, whom he had in mind as ambassador to Spain. He offered the justice job to former presidential counsel Judge Rosenman, who demurred, believing himself too obviously unneutral to be convincing as attorney general. He went to Senator Wayne Morse of Oregon, a Republican about to turn Democrat. Truman told Morse: "Howard McGrath is a fine fellow but he can't do the job. You can write your own ticket. It isn't often that a President gives anyone an offer like this. I'm satisfied that 99.9 per cent of our people are fine public servants. Apparently I've got a few rotten apples in the barrel. I want you to clean them out." Morse told him he was a Republican and this was a job for a Democrat. Truman said the senator was an independent, just what he wanted. Morse said he would have to appoint a lot of people and this would cause "every Democrat on the Hill to be on my neck." Morse had five years to go on his second Senate term; Truman had one year in his second presidential term. Not quite sure he should "flip" to the Democrats, Morse thought Eisenhower might get the Republican nomination instead of Taft. He consulted three Oregon friends, and two told him to refuse.[13] The president then asked a former appeals judge who had been dean of Charlie Murphy's law school at Duke, R. Justin Miller. Someone discovered Miller had said in a speech that the FBI was a law enforcement agency, a policeman; this offended Hoover, and Truman withdrew the offer. The president delegated Murphy to break the news. It was the only time the loyal Murphy thought of resigning.[14]

The president called a meeting of McGrath, Hoover, and the chairman of the Civil Service Commission, Robert Ramspeck, and suggested they form a commission and clean up the mess in Washington. As he wrote afterward, "There were loud outcries against the suggestion by all three of the gentlemen."[15]

He sought to place the problem in a three-man independent commission composed of Judge Thomas F. Murphy of New York, a handlebar-mustachioed jurist with a reputation as the government attorney who obtained the conviction of Alger Hiss; Dr. Daniel Poling, the prominent Baptist clergyman of Philadelphia; and David E. Bell of the American Trust Company. Murphy accepted and reneged, Poling accepted, and Bell refused, claiming busyness with his bank work. Truman asked Arthur Flemming, a former member of the Civil Service Commission and prominent Republican, and Flemming did not answer the president's letter.

The president thereupon resorted to a single outside investigator, Newbold Morris of New York City, a wealthy lawyer and the son-in-law of Judge Learned Hand, who recommended him to McGrath. Neither Truman nor McGrath really knew Morris, who had been active in Republican politics and twice sought the mayoralty of his city on a reform ticket.

Morris's appointment to clean up the mess only added to the mess. He came down to Washington in a reforming mood and followed one error with another. He challenged a Senate committee, telling its members they had diseased minds. He concocted a huge questionnaire for federal officials, including cabinet officers, in which he asked detailed questions about their incomes. The president earlier had told Charlie Murphy, in regard to a questionnaire a congressional committee wished to distribute to BIR personnel, "If one was sent to me for answer, I'd tell the sender to go to hell."[16] He thought better of this sentiment and decided to go along with Morris, and then seems to have changed his mind, deciding Morris was impossible.

In what became a thick situation Attorney General McGrath thought Morris should go but was confused as to who should handle the dismissal. Truman gave the impression to McGrath that Morris should leave. McGrath proposed to do the job, but as he remembered the sequence of events, Murphy called not long after and said he, Murphy, should handle the resignation. That afternoon, April 2, 1952, Queen Juliana of the Netherlands arrived at the Washington airport, and McGrath was present. Catching the president alone he pressed for a decision. Joe Short, press secretary, was nearby, and McGrath called him over to join the discussion. "He came over," McGrath remembered, and my God, no sooner were the words out of my mouth than the son-of-a-bitch exploded, "What has the President got to do with this? You brought Morris down here." Well, I was dumbfounded. I said, "I brought him here with the President's approval and consent, and you took him over. You gave him his independence. Are you mad?" With this the President is smart; he walks away. The press gets the story that a disagreement is going on in a public place, and I said, "Look, Joe, let's not argue it here. I'll meet you at the White House."[17]

There may have been a bit more to the airport scene than McGrath described. Robert J. Donovan has written that Short not only blamed McGrath for Morris's inadequacies but also suggested that McGrath resign. Short told his assistant, Roger Tubby, that McGrath then said, "If I go, I'll really blow the lid off!" Donovan did not know what was bothering McGrath. "What explosive exposé McGrath may have had in mind, if any, is a mystery." In 1986 a group of McGrath's papers came up for sale in Rhode Island. One of the items in those papers was a twenty-five-page FBI memorandum outlining Morris's supposed communist activities. Possibly McGrath had in mind to release it.[18]

At the White House that evening McGrath had it out with Murphy and Short: "It was about six o'clock. Murphy and Joe are there. They are violent . . . blaming me for Morris. The whole thing was bitched up. They said the President was being made the victim. 'You brought him down,' Short is saying. . . . I said, 'Well you sons of bitches, I'll get rid of him. Don't think you can pull this . . . on me. I know what you're up to. I can handle this myself.' And I left." The next morning the president told McGrath, concerning the firing of Morris, "Howard, you always come up with the right answer." As the closest student of this contretemps, Andrew J. Dunar, has written, "That sealed Morris's fate."[19]

Then it was McGrath's turn to go. Just before an afternoon press conference that same day, Truman talked with his staff, and the group advised him to fire McGrath because the latter was so slow-moving. Perhaps the president recalled the FBI report; Short must have told him about it. In a low voice Truman said he thought he would have to dismiss McGrath. He picked up the telephone and did it, on the spot, in front of the staff. "I have a press conference in a little while," he said to the attorney general, "and I think I ought to announce your resignation." Stunned, McGrath could only acquiesce.[20]

The president told the press conference he had not talked to McGrath about firing Morris, and said rather that he had learned of the firing from the press service ticker, which was probably true. After firing McGrath he sent him a handwritten letter that may have been close to what he was thinking. If McGrath had threatened the president with the FBI report the letter would have mollified him. Among other things the president said, "The happenings in the Newbold Morris case were very disturbing to me. I want you to know that my fondness for you has not changed one bit. Political situations sometimes cause one much pain."[21]

The administration was almost over, having little more than nine months until January 20, 1953, but the aftermath of McGrath's dismissal was disquieting in a way quite removed from the former attorney general's effort, if such it was, to blackmail the president. The disquieting aspect of it, if one can believe Graham Morison, whose account has the ring of truth, is that the president was looking for anyone, just anyone, for attorney general, and asked Connelly, who suggested a drinking friend, Judge James P. McGranery, formerly in the justice department. According to Morison, Clark had wanted McGranery out of justice, and Morison arranged an appointment to the circuit court in Philadelphia. But McGranery's wife, Rowena, had plans for him, and every weekend McGranery and Rowena went to Washington and sat outside Truman's office waiting to go in and say hello. The president had a habit of making snap decisions when angry, according to Morison, and said to Connelly, in effect, "Who in hell will I appoint?" Matt should have said, "Ask Graham Morison," but instead said, perhaps remembering a drink or two, that, well, McGranery was the man.[22]

Morison claimed the Pennsylvania delegation in Congress bitterly opposed McGranery; that he, Morison, arranged the judgeship partly to get him off their backs; and that out of twenty-seven opinions McGranery wrote that were reviewed by the higher court, three-fourths were reversed. According to Morison, after his nomination as attorney general McGranery sold out to Senator McCarran, who, in exchange for getting him through the judiciary committee, demanded dismissal of several antitrust cases and a settlement of the Dollar Steamship case, the latter a suit against the government that Morison believed totally without merit. Morison found out about McCarran's demands from one of the chief staff members of the committee who had been in the marine corps and with whose help Morison had run through many nominees. This individual called Morison, and they went out to lunch and he told him.[23] Fortunately for the president, McGranery served the remaining months with no notice of what the head of the antitrust division asserted as truth. One month after McGranery took office, on a weekend when Truman was out of the city, Morison resigned.

In management of "the mess in Washington," one must conclude, Truman acted out of several impulses, all unhelpful. One was ordinarily admirable—his unwillingness to believe every popgun was the crack of doom. During his many years of public office he often measured the need for action and discovered he did not have to act. Once during a reception the journalist Vermont Royster met him and out of politeness—it was a low point in the president's fortunes—said he hoped Mr. Truman felt well. The president replied with a grin, "I never trouble trouble until trouble troubles me." He knew it was impossible to run a large operation such as the federal government without having scandals around—every president had scandals. "I don't think there were a greater number in the administration in which I was head that there had been in previous administrations," he said in 1959, "and that there have been in this administration which followed me." In all this he was correct. And yet, perhaps out of tiredness, as the passage of years brought weariness, he let scandals go too long.[24]

He was also an essential controversialist; he saw politics as controversy. In his days during the harsh goat-rabbit rivalries of Jackson County, he learned politics as a struggle, attended with exaggeration but also serious infighting, together with meanness (he hoped the latter would be on the other side), bringing out the worst in the human spirit if allied with the chance to gain money or power. His historical reading reinforced experience. He beheld himself as the heir of Presidents Jefferson and Jackson. He hoped for a Claude Bowers or Marquis James to attack his enemies. Meanwhile, he would lead the attack.[25]

Last, there was affection for friends. Dunar has related his "remarkable inability to separate himself from inconvenient people." The president's friend Tom Evans thought this his greatest weakness. Tom was uncertain it was weakness, but the quality bothered him. Tom, the Kansas City tycoon of drugstores and radio station KCMO, could not act that way with his own businesses. Edgar Hinde, postmaster of Independence, wrote, "Anybody who's ever been a friend of his, you better not say anything against, because they've got to hit him right in the face before he'll drop them. And I think that's one of Harry's big faults. He stays with some of these boys who are throwing him some curves, and he should have let them go." According to the Kansas City reporter Helm, "Truman regarded every man as a gentleman until he showed up as another package. This trait cost him dearly."[26]

Usually he was a canny fighter with a wonderful sense of when to back off and compromise, provided compromise was honorable. In the second term, in domestic politics, he lost this ability.

3

While the troubles with the department of justice turned into confusion, the possibility arose of a steel strike. The president's decision to seize the mills under his inherent constitutional powers as commander-in-chief of the armed forces led to a notable defeat for executive authority in the landmark Supreme Court decision of *Youngstown Sheet and Tube Company v. Sawyer*.[27]

The facts of the steel case are easy to set out. At the end of 1951 a crisis was at hand, with the United Steelworkers of America lacking a contract and the companies refusing to give the steelworkers the raises they demanded. If steel wages and prices went up drastically, other industries would follow the steel formula and across-the-board price controls, which had gone into effect in January 1951, would collapse and inflation surge to new heights—in the first months of the war, between June 1950 and March 1951, the consumer price index had risen 8 percent, for an annual rate of 12 percent. Even though prices for the rest of 1951 rose only 2.5 percent, the worry of another surge was there. Moreover, the president was receiving stentorian advice from his cabinet, including Secretary of Defense Lovett, that steel was essential to the war, that a work stoppage would be a national disaster, that it was necessary to avoid a strike at all costs. Acting on this advice, he seized the mills on April 8, 1952. As he explained to a correspondent shortly thereafter, "The main difficulty with the situation is the fact the owners simply refused to negotiate—they wanted to make a condition precedent [a higher price per ton for steel before they granted a wage increase] and I won't agree to conditions precedent." He told his correspondent that industrial managers were better off at that moment than ever before: "There never was a time when there was a more balanced economy as it affects farmers, laborers and industry than there is now in this United States of ours." He said he had to represent the 155 million people of the nation against the demands both of labor and of Wall Street.[28]

After seizing the mills he did nothing more than ask the owners to keep two sets of books—one for Secretary of Commerce Charles Sawyer and one for themselves—and go on running the mills their own way, albeit with steel prices and workers' wages the same. The owners thought the president would use the seizure to raise wages, but he did not. He asked them to send representatives to Washington to meet with union officials and arrive at a new wage scale. The owners did so, but added their condition precedent. At the same time they decided to take their case to court. Judge David A. Pine of the District of Columbia decided in favor of return of the mills. The government appealed, and the circuit court stayed Judge Pine's ruling and passed the case to the Supreme Court.

At this juncture, Truman maintained thereafter, the High Court wrecked what could have been an agreement between the union and the owners by announcing it would hear the case promptly. This was all the owners needed. They withdrew from the Washington negotiations.

The president was confident the High Court would uphold his seizure. He was even truculent: "This is your fight! This is the people's fight!" he told the Americans for Democratic Action. He excoriated the companies: "The purpose is to preserve high profits for the steel companies and prevent wage increases for the steelworkers. That shows exactly where the Old Guard stands. It shows that their hearts lie with the corporations and not with the working people. It proves that the old Republican leopard hasn't changed a single spot." In a press conference he stated the constitutional issue, rather injudiciously. A reporter asked what kind of seizure law he would like Congress to enact—would he prefer statutory power? Truman responded, "The President *has* the power, and they can't take it away from him." He was arguing for inherent powers, his powers as commander-in-chief. Questioned as to whom he was referring by "they," who could not take the power away from him, he identified Congress and the courts.[29]

When the Supreme Court's ruling came down on June 2, it astonished the president. The decision was six to three, in favor of sustaining Pine. Truman's supporters were Chief Justice Vinson and justices Minton and Stanley F. Reed. Former attorney general Clark, who in 1949 had written a memorandum supporting Truman's inherent powers, voted the other way.

The immediate result was a strike that shut down the steel industry for fifty-three days. Having shown their muscle as well as the purity of their constitutional principles, the owners thereupon concluded an agreement with the union that was close to what they could have accepted months before. It was a nearly useless strike except, Truman might have said, to make the owners' points and demonstrate their defiance of the president.

To his chagrin, the president had made a serious miscalculation. Indeed, he had made several. For one thing, his handling of economic controls, the root cause of his predicament, had been in error. Sam Rayburn had thought across-the-board controls, including price controls, were politically dangerous, in view of the resistance to them during World War II. Truman's new chairman of the Council of Economic Advisers, Keyserling, who was quite unlike his conservative predecessor, Nourse, reinforced Rayburn's opinion, if for a different reason; Keyserling believed the way to handle Korean War production was to expand the economy rather than to restrict domestic consumption. He told a Senate committee, "We'll never be able to out-control the Russians, but we can outproduce them." He told an economic conference that people who desired stronger controls were confusing the Korean War with World War II, "engaging merely in hackneyed slogans out of the past."[30] It turned out that he was right—the economy would not overheat, in fact was capable of enormous expansion: the standard of living had gone down a little from 1945 to 1950, but with the war it began moving up; it doubled without substantial inflation from 1950 to 1965; it doubled again, with inflation, from 1965 to 1980. But controls nonetheless should have been placed on the economy earlier than January 1951. People needed the reassurance of across-the-board controls, including price controls. Lacking that, they panicked. They remembered World War II, when in 1941–1942 the economy possessed a great deal of slack, having barely recovered from the depression. Everyone knew that in 1950 production was at peak levels, with little slack, which was a scary situation, and at the beginning of the Korean War popular fear produced scare buying, running up the consumer price index.

A second miscalculation, and it became apparent after the case was before the Supreme Court, was that the president to his chagrin discovered that there was no steel crisis and never had been. To seize the mills had been unnecessary. "The President," Truman had snapped, "has the power to keep the nation from going to hell." But the nation was not going to hell, and it would not have gone to hell, even if he had done nothing to prevent a strike. The nation passed through the strike with almost no harm to national security. Steel stocks in the hands of finishers were enough to allow them to continue production with hardly any difficulties. The president apparently had received pat answers from such cabinet members as Lovett, who recalled that in the past any steel strike was bound to have national repercussions. Secretary Sawyer, an able man, was probably too busy in his role of imminent or actual manager, however nominal, of the nation's huge steel industry, eighty-six companies, with vast mills and six hundred thousand workers, to inquire within his own department concerning stocks of steel held by manufacturing concerns. For all of the federal government's statistical gathering, at a crucial juncture it failed.

A third miscalculation by the president was that he used inherent powers to seize the mills, rather than a statutory enactment already at hand: he could have used the Taft-Hartley Act. Prior to World War II, presidents had invoked their inherent powers only three times to justify seizure of property during labor disputes, and the courts had never ruled on the legality of such seizures. The Korean War also was not popular enough to allow use of inherent powers. During World War II the companies had announced a price rise, the Office of Price Administration had rolled it back, and steel profits fell during the war. The companies knew that during the Korean War they were dealing with a much different, a much weaker, political situation. The mill owners said the president deprived them of their property without due process, violating their civil rights. They produced a mighty propaganda, going on the radio and taking newspaper advertisements. The American people believed them. They saw no emergency. It was ridiculous, they contended, to let the president pose as commander-in-chief when he had not even asked Congress for a declaration of war. Members of the House of Representatives filed fourteen resolutions of impeachment. The United States Chamber of Commerce and the American Association of Newspaper Publishers censured the president. Newspapers attacked him as a Caesar, Hitler, bully, and lawbreaker. It was necessary, people said, to reduce him to size, to make him realize he was one citizen among 155 million.

During this melee the department of justice gave no advice at all. McGrath resigned five days before the seizure. McGranery's confirmation took weeks, as the Senate looked at him with care, as it should have; McGrath's successor did not take the oath until May 27, much too late to obtain a reasoned department opinion. To be sure, he could not have offered a sensible one himself.

It is possible that Truman obtained some poor advice from Chief Justice Vinson. The court contained five Roosevelt and four Truman appointees, and it must have seemed that they would support the president. Robert J. Donovan, in the second volume of his presidential biography, published in 1982, has related that the president received a confidential opinion from Chief Justice Vinson that to seize the mills was constitutional. Donovan at first refused to divulge his source: "It's a man that I have known and used as a news source for thirty years and he's absolutely trustworthy." Reporters guessed that the source was former secretary of the treasury Snyder, but when they sought him out by telephone—Snyder was then living in South Carolina—he refused to say whether he had been Donovan's source or to discuss what, if anything, Truman said to him in confidence about Vinson. After Snyder's death some years later, Donovan admitted his source was Snyder. Moreover, Margaret Truman in her biography of her mother, published in 1986, wrote that before seizing the mills her father conferred with Vinson, who assured him the move was legal and the court would support him. Margaret ventured a personal detail, that the chief justice and his wife often flattered the Trumans, raising the possibility that Vinson flattered the president once too often.[31]

If indeed Vinson gave Truman an unofficial opinion, it would explain the president's sangfroid over his assertion of inherent powers. It also would have been a gross breach of judicial ethics as well as of the separation of powers, as the *New York Times* affirmed upon publication of Donovan's book, in an editorial citing two eminent legal authorities.[32]

Still, it is troublesome to credit Truman as having received a private opinion. In favor of the Donovan and Margaret Truman stories, as the *Times* pointed out, is the fact that Vinson easily could have given an opinion. He and Truman were close. The *Times* obituary for the chief justice, who died in 1953, related, "Both the President and the Chief Justice had telephones by their beds and regularly held long talks late at night, in which the President received Mr. Vinson's advice and counsel on many problems." Against the possibility of a private opinion is the fact that the president for two years in the mid-1920s attended lectures at the Kansas City School of Law and knew he could not properly receive information on the steel case from the chief justice. In the midst of the court's deliberations he wrote his new attorney general, McGranery:

> I was as sorry as I could be that I couldn't get to your ceremony yesterday but you understand perfectly the reason why I didn't come. I want no implication that I have in any way lobbied with the High Court in the Steel Case. The night before last, when I went to the meeting held by the Jewish National Fund, I found two Judges of the High Court there. If I had known they were going to be there I would not have gone but I didn't know it until I arrived.[33]

Whatever the truth of the matter, the president clearly had miscalculated in choosing to take his stand on inherent powers, suffering a terrible rebuff at the hands of a court that should have been friendly. He hardly needed this critical judgment about his powers in the midst of an unpopular war and, to be sure, in the midst of a presidential electoral contest in which Truman's candidate, Stevenson, was up against the most attractive candidate the Republican party had nominated in years, since the era when Truman saw Theodore Roosevelt make a speech in Kansas City.

4

For Truman the election was anticlimactic, as he was not running, but he rightly felt that his policies, his stewardship during nearly eight years, his administration, were before the American people. He believed that the Democratic candidate, who turned out to be Stevenson, should go down the line for what he, Truman, had done for the country. He had good reason to feel that way, for he had taken the country through perilous times, with foreign policy at last, by 1952, on an even keel. In domestic affairs he had had less success, but no one could have said he had not tried, and the times were against him. Nonetheless, he had managed reconversion during his first term, and the country had not tumbled into another Great Depression; by 1952 the economy was rolling along, with the American people unsure it was their president who had assisted matters (they credited themselves with the improvement) but still happy in their new prosperity. Truman rightly felt that the country should vote Democratic, in thankfulness, and people who disagreed could believe otherwise if they wished. It seemed to him that Stevenson, taking the nomination, should run on a platform supporting the Truman administration. It also seemed to him that the party could win. He knew that he had maintained the Roosevelt coalition of big-city voters and farmers and, despite the cries of the Dixiecrats, the Solid South. In these hopeful conclusions, however, the president was to be sorely disappointed.

Stevenson was difficult to persuade to accept the nomination. It is not clear whether Truman again toyed with the candidacy of Eisenhower on the Democratic ticket, as he may have done for the election of 1948. Possibly he did.[34] If so, Stevenson may have heard of it. Eventually, when Eisenhower's Republican instincts became unmistakable, Truman went over to Stevenson. And in this regard, as if he had not had enough trouble in his second term, he got into more. Stevenson looked like a winner. His grandfather had been vice president under Cleveland in 1893–1897. He had attended Choate and Princeton. He was governor of a large state and a generation removed from the Truman people—the president, Barkley, Vinson. He made excellent speeches and was Lincolnesque in his sensitivities and apparent sensibleness. But along with these recommendations he possessed, as time would tell, a notable, indeed fatal, flaw: he could not make up his mind. Truman talked with the governor early in 1952, and Stevenson seemed to think he had promised the people of Illinois another gubernatorial term—as if a presidential nomination could not supersede the promise. Weeks passed and nothing happened.

For a short time in March, Truman considered running again, for he was exempt from the Twenty-second Amendment, passed in 1951, which forbade any president to run more than twice or more than once after having served more than two years of some other person's term. The president's renomination was not as ridiculous as it sounded, even considering his low ratings in the polls. In a time when primaries were not decisive, he could have ensured his nomination through the control all sitting presidents usually exert over conventions. He did not want to do it. Ever since his election the president had been against another term. The third term, he believed, nearly killed Roosevelt, and the fourth became little more than an occasion for his death. After the 1948 election, General Vaughan was in the oval office one day and asked the president whether he would run in 1952. "Have you lost your mind?" was the response. Truman explained that only if the country was in a war would he consider it.[35] But in March 1952, driven to distraction by Stevenson, he did consider it, and assembled a small dinner party at Blair House and sounded the group. Whereupon his guests all firmly said no. "That was the frankest meeting I ever heard in my life," said Vinson, who was present. Murphy thought the group unanimous, and there were a dozen or more people.[36] To show his appreciation the president gave each member a silver dollar minted in 1884. Not long afterward, on March 29, he made a public announcement.

Only after the convention opened did Stevenson give in. He telephoned the president and said his friends wanted to nominate him and asked if Truman would object. "Well, I blew up," the president remembered, "and talked to him in a language I think he'd never heard before, told him that since January 28, 1952, I had tried . . ."[37]

After the convention the Illinois governor treated the campaign as something quite apart from the Truman administration; he sought to keep a wide distance from the president. He put campaign headquarters in Springfield, not Washington or New York, and displaced the chairman of the national committee, Frank E. McKinney of Indianapolis, in favor of a relative unknown, a Chicago lawyer, Stephen A. Mitchell. He asked Truman nothing about how to campaign, and he refused the president's offer to go out on the hustings.

By early August, Truman was bristling. He composed a letter to Stevenson, which he did not send, in which he related how he could not stand snub after snub: "It seems to me that the Democratic Candidate is above associating with the lowly President of the United States." He said he would go out to Montana to dedicate the Hungry Horse Dam, and make a public power speech, and "get in a plane and come back to Washington and stay there."[38] Not long afterward Stevenson allowed the *Oregon Journal* to mousetrap him into answering the "oft-heard question" of "Can Stevenson really clean up the mess in Washington?" "As to whether I can clean up the mess in Washington," was the answer, foolishly prepared by an assistant, but over Stevenson's signature, "I would bespeak the careful scrutiny of what I inherited in Illinois and what has been accomplished in three years." The letter doubled this error by remarking, "As you well know, I did not want the nomination and received it without commitments to anyone about anything—including President Truman." The president retorted, fortunately in private, with another unsent letter that detailed various advice and ended with "I'm telling you to take your crackpots, your high socialites with their noses in the air, run your campaign and win if you can. . . . Best of luck to you from a bystander who has become disinterested."[39]

As the campaign heated up, Eisenhower got into trouble on two counts. Initially the general had moved around the country making speeches from the back of an observation car, "crossing the thirty-eighth platitude." Then he made up with his rival Taft, and his advisers persuaded him to campaign against the Democrats both on domestic and on foreign issues—that is, criticize Truman policy. Senator Mundt, cochairman of the GOP speakers bureau, invented the formula K_1C_2: Korea, communism, and corruption. Shortly afterward came Eisenhower's difficulties. Campaigning in Wisconsin he was persuaded to delete from a speech in Milwaukee a fulsome reference to General Marshall, deferring to Marshall's critic, Senator McCarthy. He did not know his assistants already had distributed the text to reporters, who noticed the deletion and made the most of it. The other difficulty was discovery that seventy-six individuals for two years had been giving his vice presidential running mate, Senator Nixon, an eighteen-thousand-dollar "financial comfort" to combat communism and corruption.

Eisenhower managed to stand away from these awkwardnesses. He said nothing about the Marshall deletion and allowed Nixon to obfuscate the financial comfort by the "Checkers" speech, in which he related that someone had given him the dog Checkers and he would not give it back, and that Pat, his wife, possessed a simple cloth coat, not a fur coat. Truman, however, was furious about the Marshall deletion. "I think this made President Truman as mad as anything that I know of *ever*," Murphy said, years afterward. "And I think the more he thought of that the madder he got and the less he thought of General Eisenhower."[40]

The campaign wore on, and Stevenson relented about letting Truman help with speeches; the president wanted to do it for the party if not the candidate. In October he went out on another whistle-stop trip, making 211 speeches and covering 19,000 miles, during which he "shook hands with a quarter of a million people, gained five pounds and put all of my staff to bed." He flailed the general, whom he had admired in uniform but could not stand in mufti: "The Republicans have General Motors and General Electric and General Foods and General MacArthur and General Martin and General Wedemeyer. And they have their own five-star general running for President. . . . I want to say to you that every general I know is on this list except general welfare, and general welfare is in with the corporals and privates in the Democratic Party." Once again the whoops and shouts, the urgings to "Give 'em hell, Harry!" and "Pour it on!" For Eisenhower's refusal to endorse General Marshall, the orator reserved some of his choicest invective. Years later he remembered he "took the hide off" Eisenhower, "skinned him from the crown of his head to the heel of his foot."[41]

As for what gave the election to the Republicans, it mainly was the attractiveness of their candidate, Eisenhower; he was almost unbeatable. Apart from him, it was an amalgam of the issues in Mundt's formula. And though the strength of each is difficult to discern, surely Korea was foremost. The war had bogged down into brutal fighting for worthless hills. It cost as many American casualties, dead and wounded, as defense of South Korea in the summer and autumn of 1950. When the Soviets asked for a truce early in 1951, the Americans obliged by negotiations that went on and on. The North Koreans insisted on repatriation of prisoners, and the Americans refused, having had experience with Russian prisoners after World War II who went to their deaths or Siberia. "We will not buy an armistice by turning over human beings for slaughter or slavery," the president said. His words should have enlisted every patriot, but the country was booming economically, tired of a war it did not understand, and gave the president no support.

Truman did his best to "get" Eisenhower on Korea. Near the end of the campaign Eisenhower, at behest of his advisers, declared that if elected he would "go to Korea." It was sheer opportunism; there was not a thing he could do in Korea. Moreover, in the litany of military and civilian statements by administration officials, made publicly or privately in 1947–1950, about how Korea was no place to defend with American arms, Eisenhower had signed the primeval document, that of September 1947, that Forrestal then sent to Marshall. The Eisenhower speech came on Friday evening. The next morning Senator Morse called the president. "Mr. President," he said, "are you aware of the fact that Eisenhower misrepresented the facts time and time again in his Detroit speech last night?"

Truman said he knew it and his staff was at work preparing an answer.

"I called you to make a suggestion," Morse said. "You will find down in the Pentagon Building a document, I don't know the date, it was late in 1947, in which the Joint Chiefs of Staff, acting through the Secretary of Defense, recommended that the troops be taken out of South Korea as a matter of military policy and military strategy. Eisenhower was chief of staff of the Army at the time. The military felt that Korea was no place to have our troops. In fact, the document used the language to the effect that the troops should be taken out as a matter of 'military policy and strategy.'"

The president said, "Yes, I recall it very well."

Morse said that if Truman got him the document he would use it in a speech the following Monday.

Truman said, "I'll have it up to you in an hour." In the event he had it up in less than forty-five minutes.[42]

But one Eisenhower speech in Detroit was worth a thousand documents revealed by a senator in Minneapolis, and the president could do little other than, after the election, offer his personal plane to the president-elect. Eisenhower went to Korea and months later obtained a truce after threatening, through Secretary of State Dulles, to extend the war to China and presumably use nuclear weapons, the tactic Truman had denied MacArthur.

The election passed both the presidency and the two Houses of Congress to the Republicans; it was the first time the party won the executive and legislative branches since 1928. Eisenhower took 55 percent of the popular vote. It was a personal victory for the general and seemed a repudiation of the Truman administration. But it was a classic "surge" election, in which all short-term forces operated in favor of one party, a shift in virtually all interest groups. It was also a "deviating" election, because the normal Democratic majority in the country remained intact.

Over the next weeks Truman was a lame duck. He arranged for his successor to come to the White House and see the executive offices and talk with the cabinet and staff, hoping to avoid the acrimony that attended the transition from Hoover to Roosevelt in 1932–1933. The meeting passed with a minimum of ill will, although photographers caught Eisenhower, who possessed an interestingly mobile face, looking at Truman in a quizzical way. It was a chance expression among many photographs, but newspaper editors printed it. Afterward the president told a staff member that Eisenhower would hardly understand the presidency. "He'll sit here, and he'll say, 'Do this! Do that!' *And nothing will happen.* Poor Ike! It won't be a bit like the Army. He'll find it very frustrating."[43] The incoming staff members, who began to come around to the East and West Wings and the executive office building, did not get along well with the outgoing staff. Governor Sherman Adams of New Hampshire made a nuisance of himself with his bustling around, and Truman remembered that he, still president, told Adams it was not time for the takeover and that Adams could go out in the middle of Pennsylvania Avenue and sit down.[44]

On inaugural day Eisenhower refused to do the traditional thing and come into the White House to greet the outgoing president; he simply drove up in his car and sent word he was ready to go to the capitol. During the ride Truman tangled with him. According to the man of Independence, Eisenhower observed the crowds and said he had refused to come to Truman's inauguration in 1949 because he was sure more than half the people would be applauding him instead of Truman.

I turned around to him and said, "Ike, you'd have come if I'd ordered you, don't worry about that," and that ended the conversation until we got to the

Capitol Building and then we were in the room waiting to go out onto the platform in the capitol when he said that somebody had caused his son to come to the inauguration. He thought it was just a way to embarrass him. I said, "If it is, I embarrassed you because I ordered your son to come and he ought to be here."[45]

In actual fact Eisenhower had attended the 1949 inaugural. Four years later Major John S. D. Eisenhower had been in Korea, and the president had ordered him home as a courtesy to his father.

Not long after that, in one brief moment in front of the reviewing stand, the majesty and power of the presidency came to an end. As Harry S. Truman left the scene of so much of his life since he had arrived in Washington as a freshman senator in January 1935, Margaret Truman reminded her father that he was now "Mr. Citizen." She smiled as she said it, and he smiled back. All had not gone well during the second term—the five percenters, RFC, BIR, department of justice, the misestimates that brought the humiliation of giving back the steel mills to their owners, and then the election. It had not been the best of times. But now, the former president might have said, it was all history.

Around the side of the Delaware Street house, 1953. (St. Louis Post-Dispatch)

The former president and Mrs. Truman in Key West, Florida, March 1968, visiting Margaret and her family.

With Detective Mike Westwood, August 1969. (Kansas City Star)

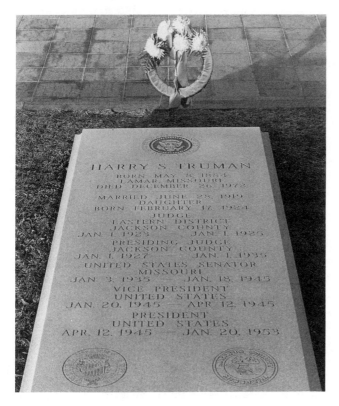

HARRY S. TRUMAN
BORN MAY 8, 1884
LAMAR, MISSOURI
DIED DECEMBER 26, 1972
MARRIED JUNE 28, 1919
DAUGHTER
BORN FEBRUARY 17, 1924
JUDGE
EASTERN DISTRICT
JACKSON COUNTY
JAN. 1, 1923 — JAN. 1, 1925
PRESIDING JUDGE
JACKSON COUNTY
JAN. 1, 1927 — JAN. 1, 1935
UNITED STATES SENATOR
MISSOURI
JAN. 3, 1935 — JAN. 18, 1945
VICE PRESIDENT
UNITED STATES
JAN. 20, 1945 — APR. 12, 1945
PRESIDENT
UNITED STATES
APR. 12, 1945 — JAN. 20, 1953

The president's grave site.

Chapter Eighteen

Retirement

1

Coming back to Independence offered the first reward of retirement. Truman vastly enjoyed the small town, where he could take morning walks and see people, tipping his hat to ladies, replying in kind to gentlemen, or look upon the houses with their well-kept front yards—grass mowed in summer, leaves raked during leaf time, yards kept free of swirling trash year-round. The town's history reached into the past, but, unlike Kansas City, Independence had not developed: its population approached 20,000, not much larger than when he was presiding judge.

Another attraction of coming home was that he and his wife at last could own the house. In the spring of 1953 they bought out the three Wallace sons; Mrs. Wallace had died intestate, and the family agreed to fix the house's worth at $25,000. The Trumans already had made a few changes, such as painting it white, with green trim, and replacing rotted millwork and broken roof slates. In 1950 a carpenter extended the back porch six feet so the president could read the morning papers in privacy or Bess hold sessions of the bridge club in summers—the house had no air-conditioning. Curiously, after the Trumans bought the house they put very little money into it. They spent so little on it that, when they passed on, someone said that only the paint held it together. The National Park Service, which took it over, had to spend several hundred thousand dollars shoring it up.

Return to the house after the presidency also meant that the secret service was gone. In 1945 the service had moved into a booth at the rear of the "summer White House." Neither the president nor his wife admired the booth, especially its proximity to the kitchen and back porch; they soon relegated its inhabitants to the barn that had become a garage. In 1947 the secret service put up an iron fence. Former president Hoover had urged Truman to put up the fence because of the tourists. "If you don't," he advised, "they'll tear the place down." The decision to do so may have come after Bess, as she sat one day in one of the side rooms of the house, heard people talking in the vestibule; when she went to investigate she found two women who had walked in the front door. But in January 1953 it was possible to think that any need to separate the Trumans from the American people had come to an end, for the American people would pay no attention to an ex-president. According to the law at the time, the agents had to go. The agents departed.

After the Kennedy assassination in 1963, the secret service came back. The Trumans welcomed them with distaste. This time the "guards" unostentatiously established their headquarters not in a booth or in the barn but in a bungalow across the street on the corner of Truman Road and Delaware. They placed a television camera on top of the RLDS building at the end of the block to the south. Another of their measures was what became known as the talking gate, whereby tourists could come up to the front gate and ask something, such as if the house was open, and the gate would tell them it was not. Gradually the convenience of protection—and the helpfulness of the agents, who did small chores around the house—endeared the secret service to the occupants.[1]

In the years when the secret service was absent the retired president relied on Detective Mike Westwood as a bodyguard and occasional driver. When the service returned, the agents were unhappy with Mike, who was one of the world's worst drivers, but Truman would not allow his dismissal. The service and the president arrived at a modus vivendi whereby Mike acted mainly as a bodyguard.

After settling into the house and arranging an office in the Federal Reserve Building in Kansas City, Truman set about writing his memoirs, which took much of his time until 1955. Published in two volumes, they had several purposes, all easily understandable. The most important was to record the author's life. He had set down some of his experiences during the leisure of the vice presidency—as presiding officer of the Senate in early 1945 he produced several dozen handwritten pages of description, twelve thousand words. A second purpose was to prevent other writers from imposing their judgments. Partisanship had surrounded his presidency, and as a reader of presidential biographies he knew what had happened to some of his predecessors. "I have been reading a book about me. . . . It contains more misstatements and false quotations than it contains facts and true statements from people purported to have been interviewed."[2] A third reason for the memoirs was to educate young people. During his years in office he had encountered so much ignorance that he wanted to share his reverence for the presidency. Young people could read his memoirs or, as he liked to put it, "my history," and understand what the presidency of the United States was about.

For all the former president's experience with books, it was a pity that the assistants he chose to help with the memoirs served him so poorly.[3] He needed the best—ideally a writer or two who had produced books and could work rapidly and write well—so as to place his ideas and actions in the best possible light. Unfortunately, he began by asking advice from William Hillman, who in 1952 had produced the book about the president that published the letter to Secretary Byrnes. Hillman was an editor of *Collier's*, but he was mostly a radio reporter, not a writer. He consulted his friend David Noyes, responsible in part for the proposed Vinson mission to Russia. The result was recommendation of two memoir assistants who were so incompetent they nearly brought the project to a halt.

Noyes secured the first of these individuals by recommending a professor of journalism at the University of Southern California, Robert E. G. Harris. After some months the professor managed a hundred and fifty thousand words that Truman believed made up a series of pleasant tales suitable for the *Saturday Evening Post*, "My Life and Happy Times in the White House, by Harry S. Truman as told to Robert E. G. Harris." He wanted history, he said, not stories. He put them on a shelf in the office of Rose Conway, who returned to Independence with him as his personal secretary. On top of the stack he placed a memo sheet on which he wrote, "Good God, what cr—!"

He asked Hillman and Noyes to get someone else, and Hillman made the choice this time: an adjunct professor of history at Georgetown University, Morton Royce, who had published his dissertation and was then at work on a multivolume history of the world. Royce, by March 1954, produced a narrative that took the Truman presidency from April to July 1945. The due date for the manuscript, set by its publisher, Doubleday, was June 30, 1955.

At this juncture Truman took charge. He wrote to the president of the University of Missouri and the chancellor of the University of Kansas for recommendations. He thereupon received another temporary assistant, who was followed by one who lasted. The temporary one left for an appointment as director of the journalism program at a Big Ten university; the one who lasted was a young political scientist at Lawrence, Francis H. Heller, already the author of three books, who brought the memoirs project to completion.

Heller pushed the memoirs into order, but he could not change everything; the result was a book that was a mishmash, with virtues and defects. The first volume dealt with the president's initial year, which its subtitle improperly pronounced *Year of Decisions*. The second covered the remaining seven years, an impossible grouping, and bore the subtitle *Years of Trial and Hope*. Beneath these signboards the president mustered his thoughts. The first volume began with April 12, 1945, and soon turned to an excruciatingly long description of the Potsdam Conference, issue after issue, many of which even by the time of publication had become of minor importance. After this recital the writers wedged in a sixty-odd-page rundown of Truman's life, from birth to 1945. Here the prose tightened and the narrative came alive, for the author of record was the author in fact; he knew his past and told it straightforwardly and frequently with humor. As one would expect, his assistants fooled with these pages, trying to make Truman's prose sound like theirs, but for the most part clarity prevailed. The narrative then resumed the footslogging through the presidency, chapter after chapter. The president read each chapter as it came out of the shop, watching for factual lapses but believing that if he had Ph.D.'s doing the work it had to be good. Because he was the centerpiece of the narrative, he probably found it interesting in ways readers would not. Before cutting, the manuscript totaled 2 million words, but the final version was six hundred and fifty thousand.

Doubleday did its best to promote the memoirs, which *Life* magazine excerpted and the *New York Times* serialized. Someone, perhaps the publisher of *Life,* Henry Luce, gave General MacArthur an advance copy; the general obliged with a vitriolic attack on his former commander-in-chief, which Truman wisely chose not to answer. The book received reviews in all the newspapers and magazines. A British publisher brought out a cut-down version, and hundreds of copies of the Doubleday edition poured into Truman's office in Kansas City with requests that he autograph them. During a marathon session in Kansas City he autographed four thousand copies, whipping off his signature for several hours at a rate of nine or ten to the minute. In an article entitled "Good of you to do this for us, Mr. Truman," the writer for the *New Yorker,* Philip Hamburger, described the scene.[4]

The retired president enjoyed the activity of producing the memoirs, and he felt that he had gotten his point of view before the country and probably forestalled some critical historians, perhaps from New England. This was his reward for the enterprise. He made very little money from the book. He received no royalties, merely a flat payment of $670,000, and had to pay two-thirds of the royalties in tax; he calculated he netted $37,000 after he had provided for his assistants.[5]

While the memoirs were coming out he was arranging for construction of a library building to house his memorabilia and papers, similar to the library building constructed on President Roosevelt's estate at Hyde Park. In this regard the first question was where to put the building, and two suggestions quickly came to nought. During the presidency he had thought of putting it on the Grandview farm, and he sent out his staff assistant, Elsey, who encountered a problem that neither the president nor he had anticipated. Elsey tramped over the farm in the company of an architect and Vivian Truman, and Vivian pointed out where he thought the library ought to be. It was, Elsey remembered, a depressed area, swampy in one corner, with a railroad track right behind it. The architect and Elsey kept pointing to an attractive site across the road, on a rise with a view in all directions, and asked why the library could not go there. "Ain't no use wastin' good farmland on any dang library," was the response.[6] After Harry Truman left the presidency his friend Ed Pauley proposed the campus of the University of California at Los Angeles and offered a nearby house in which the retired president might live while the building went up. Truman did not give much attention to that suggestion. Privately, although he never told Pauley, he detested California in general, and Los Angeles in particular. He considered California a mecca for all the cranks in the country, many of whom, so he said, came off the farms of Iowa and Kansas.

It gradually became apparent that the ex-president wanted the library in Independence, near the house, and when the town's mayor proposed using part of Slover Park, at the north end of Delaware where the latter crossed U.S. Route 24, the matter was settled. The location delighted Truman, who could either walk from his house to the library or point his green Chrysler in the right direction and be there in three minutes.

The design of the building was less of a problem than the location. The former chief executive may have hoped that the library, like the Independence courthouse, would be Georgian style, or art deco, like the skyscraper courthouse in Kansas City. Instead, the architects—there were three, including two local men—brought in a plan for an Egyptian temple, like that of Queen Hatshepsut across the Nile from Luxor. Actually, the plan suited the building's purpose, with columns in front to give éclat to ceremonies and practical rows of rooms inside in the fashion of a large C. It could handle all the library's wants: there were galleries for the museum, a stack area and search room for the books and files, and administrative offices at the rear with an office for Truman. The construction firm of William Massman in Kansas City broke ground in 1955, and Truman arranged a dedication in the summer of 1957. The cost was $1.75 million, paid by private donations.

As long as he was able, which meant from 1957 until 1964, Truman used the library office almost every day. His routine was unvaried. He arose between 5:00 and 5:30 A.M., took a brisk walk with Mike, and then came back to the house to work on newspapers until 7:00 or 7:15, when Mrs. Truman would come downstairs and prepare a simple breakfast of coffee, juice, an egg, and a piece of ham or bacon. About 7:45 he got into the car and headed down to the library to sort the mail. Visitors would appear, sometimes for most of the morning; when he was not occupied with visitors, he dictated letters, often as many as forty or fifty a day. Then it was home for lunch at 11:30, back in an hour and a half, and home for a nap before dinner. "When I go back home, we have dinner at night, usually, and hardly ever go out anywhere. I spend up until bedtime catching up on my reading that I have neglected."7

He was proud of the library, even though he knew he was its principal exhibit. He loved to take visitors through, making wry remarks. Going into the search room he would wave at the portrait of himself in Masonic regalia and say, "And there's the Pope." He would go to the exhibit containing photographs of all the World War II five-star admirals and generals and name them, omitting MacArthur. When auditors gasped and looked expectantly, he paused as long as the occasion allowed, then waved airily at the photo and said, "And there's the right hand of God." The tour included the room of the 35th Division, complete with one of the few surviving French seventy-fives. The tour guide might pause in the foyer before Thomas Hart Benton's huge mural *Independence and the Opening of the West* and point out daubs in the upper right-hand corner that he himself had painted, under supervision of the artist. Then it was to the large rug hung on a nearby wall, gift of that young man, the Shah of Iran, from his grateful people for presidential assistance in 1946. The other rooms held domestic memorabilia and a mixed bag of Oriental scrolls and vases. Downstairs were the political buttons, from the beginning of their use in U.S. political campaigning, and the coin collections. In the far southeast corner near a freight elevator sat the family car of the 1930s, refurbished in the Chrysler factory, to make old-timers remember when windshields were small and headlights looked like lamps and cars had real bumpers and running boards, real metal, and paint jobs in a few classic colors, including the Truman green.

He hoped the library would become a regional center for the study of the presidency:

> I always thought that a fellow who had started on a farm and had gone through all the political setup that there is, from precinct to President, when he came to that point where it was time to quit, he ought to quit and then go back and see if he couldn't give people information on what caused the greatest government in the history of the world to run, and I'm a nut on the subject, I guess.

He envisioned his library attracting scholars from Missouri and surrounding states, which contained eight state universities and as many agricultural colleges, and forty-three small colleges and city universities. Indeed, as he thought about the possibilities, they became larger: "This will be a Cultural Center for that part of the country between Pittsburgh and Denver and the Canadian border and the Gulf of Mexico." Here in the library scholars could come and read documents to their hearts' content—3.5 million items, filling fifteen hundred file drawers. As soon as archivists finished arranging the general files, he permitted their opening. The more private files would open later; when two biographers pressed him about the "private papers," he said he would open them when he was "good and ready."[8]

During his lifetime he refused to allow paintings of himself or postcards with his likeness in the public part of the library. He did not want the library turned into what some correspondents described as the Truman Memorial Library.

The library contained a small auditorium, which seated perhaps two hundred people, and it was not long before the former president put it to use: he began talking to groups of high school students, as many as he could get into the auditorium, two or three groups, sometimes four or five, each day.

The procedure may have reminded him of how the Pope met pilgrims, but he gave lectures on the presidency and, unlike the Pope, answered questions. The queries often were the same, such as, "What did you have for breakfast?" More thoughtful—but he could have done without the thought—was the question, "Mr. President, why did you drop the atomic bomb on the Japanese?" To all questions he answered measuredly and occasionally with humor, although he never employed humor with the atom-bomb question. When someone asked him why he talked to high school students instead of college students, he replied that college students thought they knew everything already; he was attempting to be a teacher. He estimated he talked to more than two hundred thousand high school students.

2

Long before retirement Truman had become a politician, to employ the word he admired, and it was impossible to get politics out of his system. Once he returned to North Delaware and adjusted to the office in the Federal Reserve Building and then the far more convenient one in the library, he resumed his study of politics, the study that had fascinated him since the early 1920s.

Because of his experience as president, he naturally took interest in presidential politics—candidates particularly, but issues too. As for the candidates, in the first years he could do little other than regret Stevenson's losses in 1952 and 1956 and the reason—in the main, he believed, Stevenson's unwillingness to take advice. As in 1952, so four years later, Stevenson charmed the convention but did not charm Truman. Indeed, in 1956, for a day or two at the convention, and against the odds, the former president came out for Harriman, a hopeless candidate. Tom Evans, for the only time in his life, saw Bess Truman upset. In tears she pleaded with him, "Tom, can't you do something to stop Harry, he's making a fool of himself." Tom could do nothing ("Well," he remembered, "I say you don't change the man very often"). After several years Truman had not relented, and he explained himself in roundabout fashion: "I wanted to get myself in a position where I would not be a handicap to Stevenson, because I knew he was going to be nominated"; or, in a retort to people who said he was an albatross around Stevenson's neck: "If I was an albatross, I wanted to take it off his neck."[9]

He made pronouncements about his successor in the White House, whom he despised. He believed the general a captive of Republican businessmen and bosses.[10] Once, when Eisenhower came to Kansas City, Truman called the hotel and told whoever responded that he would like to come and pay his respects. No one called back, and Truman was certain the slight was intentional. At the inaugural of President John F. Kennedy in 1961, Truman sat near Eisenhower but managed not to speak to him.

Eisenhower, incidentally, was not fond of Truman either, although he did manage to avoid talking about him in public. In private the thirty-fourth president of the United States was caustic. In the first year of his presidency he told an administration official who, unbeknownst to him, was keeping a diary, that "Truman didn't know any more about government than a dog knows about religion."[11]

Truman and Eisenhower made up at the time of Kennedy's funeral in 1963. The retired Democratic president was staying at Blair House when someone received a message supposed to have come from the retired Republican president: Eisenhower wanted to know if he could pick up Truman to go to the funeral. Truman's former naval aide, Admiral Dennison, could not remember who answered the telephone, a butler or secret service man or someone. "I called the Statler and got through to General Eisenhower," he recalled.[12]

"Thank God, I've got you on the phone," said Ike. "I don't seem to be able to get through to anybody."

"What can I do for you?" asked the admiral.

"All I want to know is whether Mamie and I could stop by to pick up President Truman and Margaret to go to the cathedral," was the response. "I don't intend to go to the graveside and I don't suppose President Truman does either."

"Well, General," Dennison said, "I'll call you back."

"Well," said Ike, "that's no problem. I'll hold the phone."

"Well, the President is right here," Dennison replied. He asked Truman, who said, "Certainly."

The Eisenhowers called for Truman and daughter, and after the funeral they brought them back to Blair House. Truman asked the Eisenhowers to come in for a drink or coffee and they accepted. Soon everyone was talking animatedly, and when the Eisenhowers really had to go, Truman—to the horror of the secret service—went out to the curb and talked while the car waited to take them away.

With Eisenhower's vice president, Truman was less forgiving, and with reason—Nixon, during the vice presidential race in 1952, had come close to calling the president a traitor. In Texarkana, Texas, on October 27, Nixon said that real Democrats were "outraged by the Truman-Acheson-Stevenson gang's toleration and defense of communism in high places." The retired president demanded a retraction. In 1956 he designated a charity to which Nixon, running for reelection to the vice presidency, might contribute and ensure his personal absolution ("May I suggest that this contribution be made to the Red Cross of Korea, a country in which the Republicans have professed such a deep interest during the past few years"), but Nixon did not contribute.[13] When Truman visited Washington late in 1953 and went to the capitol, where senators thronged around him in enthusiasm and extended privileges of the floor, he would not go on the floor, much as he wanted to, until someone got the vice president out of the chair. In 1960, with Nixon running for the presidency, antagonism came into the open again. In debates with his Democratic opponent Nixon vowed that if he got into the White House the schoolchildren of America would never hear him use the kind of language Truman employed. The former president went to California to get even, and in Oakland he announced, "There is only one product of this state that does not measure up to its high standards—and that is Richard Nixon, Trickie Dickie, the political opportunist."[14] He graded Nixon's experience as vice president with a minus, that of the Democratic candidate for the presidency with an A plus. "You don't set a fox to watching the chickens just because he has a lot of experience in the hen house."[15] After Eisenhower and Nixon left office, with Nixon defeated for the presidency, Truman watched while his enemy obtained nomination for the governorship of California. He went out again and, to a yelling, stomping crowd at the Fairmont in San Francisco, he made a speech from notes scrawled on a scrap of paper: "The people shut the *front* door on him. Watch out that they don't sneak him in through the *back* door." And on an envelope: "Fine man [Governor Edmund G. "Pat" Brown]. Clean fight. Character ass'n and dirty name calling. Choice between Brown good Gov. and a kindly man and the opposite in a mean, nasty fellow." And on another envelope:

> That fellow couldn't get into the front door of the White House. Now he's trying to sneak in over the transom. Russian visit [of Nixon]. The Russian people wanted to learn something from him but Khrushchev taught him something. Khrushchev has been threatening to bury the free world and now that fellow [Nixon] boasts that he will bury the Democratic Party and its leaders here in California. Didn't come here to tell California what to do—but what not to do to the detriment of the great state. But the situation that has developed in Calif. has importance outside your borders. It affects the whole nation. An effort is underway to revive the man's political future. I am here to help prevent it.[16]

Truman was in Washington in 1964 and attended a Gridiron Dinner where, before he could turn his back, he encountered Nixon asking if he, Nixon, could get him a drink. Needing the drink, Truman said yes, and afterward the two spoke in friendly fashion. During the subsequent speeches Nixon related how he had gotten Truman a drink "and he didn't even have someone taste it before he drank it." When Nixon became president in 1969 he went to Independence, called at Delaware Street, met the retired president afterward in the library, and played the "Missouri Waltz" on the grand piano in the administrative offices' foyer.

The retired president's concern for presidential personalities lessened in the 1960s with the nation's choice of two Democrats, Kennedy and Johnson. The Kennedy candidacy at first irritated Truman a great deal, for the Massachusetts senator had been inattentive to his duties in the Upper House, absenting himself from roll calls and taking little interest in issues. He was a show horse, not a workhorse. Truman considered him a playboy, a callow youth. And behind him stood his imperious father. Kennedy's Catholicism meant nothing to the man of Independence; many of his friends were Catholics, including so many of his men in Battery D, those wonderful soldiers from Rockhurst College. As Truman said in several letters while Kennedy was picking up delegates and moving toward the nomination, it was "not the Pope but the pop." But after the convention made its choice, the former president lined up as a good Democrat beyond the choice and said nice things about Kennedy. The new president then invited him to the White House during the winter of 1961–1962, and the Trumans accepted with alacrity and went to Washington, where they greatly enjoyed themselves. During the occasion a photographer snapped the Trumans and Kennedys dressed formally, apparently ready for a social affair, and the Trumans obviously were very pleased. It was the first time they had been in the mansion since January 1953. During this same occasion Jacqueline Kennedy charmed the retired president, and one of Truman's letters offers some evidence that he kissed her in the rose garden. The young president's assassination in 1963 shocked Truman—made him physically ill, in fact. He took to his bed, unable to issue a statement.

Relations between Truman and Kennedy's successor also were cordial, although they had a momentary downturn in 1960. In the beginning, just after World War II, when the Texan was a member of the Lower House and Truman was president of the United States, Johnson had cultivated Truman. Then Johnson squeaked into the Senate in 1948 by virtue of the stuffed ballot box in the town of Alice. During Truman's second term Johnson was thoughtfully cooperative. After the Missouri president left Washington, "LBJ" kept in touch. Truman needed influential men in Congress to whom he could make suggestions. Sam Rayburn was his man in the House, and Johnson became his agent in the Senate. Johnson was addicted to telephone calls, and there must have been many of them. There also were letters. The correspondence was one-sided, considering that Truman wrote his own letters to Johnson and Johnson's office staff wrote his to Truman; it was an audacious arrangement, not to give personal attention to letters to the former president, but Johnson got away with it.

In preparation for the 1960 Democratic national convention in San Francisco, Johnson nearly overreached himself. Truman had planned to attend, and had even chosen his suite. Then Rayburn came out to Independence on a Friday and stayed overnight and told him what was going to happen. The Kennedys were going to offer the vice presidency to Johnson, who had announced publicly he would not take it; but Johnson was going to fool them and take it. For Truman this information amounted to a double blow. He had been supporting Symington for the presidential nomination, and about this time the Kennedys were talking to Symington about the vice presidency. Rayburn recommended that Truman not go to San Francisco and find himself, as in 1956, an outsider. After Rayburn left the next day, Truman announced he would not go.[17]

During the campaign the Democratic candidates did everything in their power to make Truman feel better. The Kennedys fussed over him. Johnson went to Independence immediately after the convention, and Tom Evans took him to the library, where he and Truman closeted themselves for a long time. During the campaign Johnson returned on numerous occasions. By 1964, Truman was back in the fold, and he publicly described the Republican presidential candidate, Senator Barry M. Goldwater, as a "damn fool"; privately, he referred to him as a horse's ass.[18]

In regard to issues, on domestic politics during the 1950s and 1960s Truman was quick to raise good Democratic points, but the issues of this period did not really concern him much. He saw, to be sure, that Eisenhower was a moderate Republican, and that whatever the strength of the conservative opposition in the GOP there was little that either wing could do to the Roosevelt-Truman programs that had begun because of the depression and become permanent during the better economic times that came out of the war and the postwar years. Eisenhower himself—despite occasional bluster such as the so-called Dixon-Yates affair, which concerned the attempt to bring private power into the Tennessee Valley—could not make many changes in the New Deal–Fair Deal. During the 1960s the Democrats, back in control, announced even more measures that accorded with the foundational policies of the foundational presidencies.

On foreign policy, a subject that during Truman's years of retirement loomed larger than domestic politics, the former president often found himself hesitating to pick up political cudgels because of the need for national unity. Much as he disliked Eisenhower, he knew the choices were hardly numerous and usually neither Democratic nor Republican. He noticed the way his successor, a professional army man, moved against the defense department; the military leaders were jostling Eisenhower for larger budgets, and the Republican president was none too cooperative. If Eisenhower's predecessor had any complaint against foreign policy in the 1950s, it was not the military side but pronouncements in favor of the Nationalist Chinese on Taiwan, a regime that Truman considered impossible of reformation.

He found the Latin American situation, in particular Cuban developments, disquieting. He refused to take Fidel Castro seriously. At an American Legion convention in 1961 he described him as a good-for-nothing: "I always said that if that fellow had a shave and a haircut and a new suit of clothes, he might be a little different kind of guy."[19]

During the 1960s the times were out of joint; forceful solutions to problems, national as well as international, were on the horizon. Some of the former president's Missouri heritage returned in domestic politics, as when reporters shouted at him during one of his morning walks in New York City, where he was visiting Margaret, "What do you think of Martin Luther King receiving the Nobel Prize?" His answer, sadly off-the-cuff, was, "I didn't give it to him." Although he generally approved of the Kennedy-Johnson domestic policies, he heartily disliked demonstrations of any sort, including civil rights demonstrations; he did not think they were the proper way to obtain a hearing in a democracy. In foreign affairs during that second decade of retirement, Vietnam was the principal issue. The old statesman's health began to fail just before that issue heated up, however, and he said very little about Vietnam.

3

In such ways the years passed. As long as he was able, Truman signed copies of the memoirs, raised money for the library through speeches, and traveled about the country on political missions. For the rest of his time he sought to show the American public how a retired president could grow old gracefully.

On three occasions he went abroad. In 1956, just after Margaret married *New York Times* reporter Clifton Daniel at the Episcopal church in Independence, the former president and his wife took an extended trip to England, France, and Italy. They went with Mr. and Mrs. Stanley Woodward; Stanley had been chief of White House protocol. The group took along a personal secretary and thirty pieces of luggage. They called upon former prime minister Churchill, who had stepped down the year before after a second ministry. The two former world leaders enjoyed visiting and spending a day together at Chequers; Churchill showed Truman a few of his paintings, selected from the hundreds he had done, which he housed in a nearby barn. In 1958, the Trumans took a second trip, with Mr. and Mrs. Sam Rosenman. They gave no interviews, spending time quietly in Italy and southern France, where they stayed in a small château. The third trip was in 1964 when the king of Greece died; President Johnson asked Truman to represent him at the obsequies. The former president flew to Athens in a jet, accompanied by his son-in-law, who watched him stay up virtually the whole flight, playing poker. After fulfilling his duties, he and the party took the long plane trip home.

The highlight of the European trips was the ceremony in 1956 at Oxford University when Truman received an honorary degree. For this occasion he attired himself in a red robe and Henry VIII hat and stood in a group of dons. At the beginning he may have considered it just another honorary degree, with more than the usual pretentiousness, but the ceremony became memorable in several ways. The university held it in a theater designed by Christopher Wren. Officials conducted much of it in Latin and described him as *Harricum Truman*. The public orator recited his success in foreign policy and broke the solemnity of the occasion when he spoke of the electoral victory in 1948, invoking the lines of Virgil to describe Dewey's plight: "The seers saw not your defeat, poor souls! Vain prayers, vain promises, vain Gallup Poll!" But when admission came to the ancient fellowship of Oxford, with salutation of "Truest of allies, direct in your speech and your writings, and ever a pattern in simple courage," the former president burst into tears.[20]

He continued to leaven American life with his remarks. The stories that circulated were not just the usual tales surrounding a public figure; they showed a personality far more attractive than his fellow citizens were accustomed to. Consider one of his own stories, which he used to illustrate the difference between Republicans and Democrats. After his return to Independence in January 1953, he had taken the train to San Francisco to sail for the Hawaiian Islands, where he and his wife spent a month on the private island of their friend Ed Pauley. In San Francisco he called at the house of the head of the steamship company whose liner he was to take, to have dinner. The chauffeur got him to the right neighborhood but chose the wrong house. Truman rang the bell and "an unmistakable Republican-looking gentleman opened the door."

"Does Mr. Killion live here?" Truman asked.

"No," the man said, and drew back to study his visitor. "By the way," he added, "I hope your feelings won't be hurt—but you look exactly like Harry Truman."

"I hope yours won't either," was the response, "but I *am* Harry Truman."

Telling the story he explained: "As I say, travel can be broadening. I still treasure the memory of the expression on that gentleman's face. Incidentally, he lived only a block away from Killion's house, but couldn't tell us where Killion lived!"[21]

One morning, Truman pulled up in the parking lot of his Kansas City office to find Randall Jessee of the local television station rigging up his camera. The papers had been carrying news of a Republican suggestion to rename the Democratic party the Democrat party, and Jessee asked the former president what he thought of the idea.

"I think that's just fine, Randall," he replied. "Providing, of course, they let us change the name of their party to the Publican Party. You know, in the Bible those publicans and big-money boys didn't come off too well!"[22]

Truman and the comedian Jack Benny became fond friends, for they appreciated each other's quickness. The comedian came out to Independence in 1959 to spend a week filming a show with the former president. Benny was concerned that the show be dignified. "This has got to be a dignified show, or I'll kill myself," he told Truman.

"Listen, Jack," said Truman, "I've got this undertaker friend . . ."[23]

Along with the wit was a sense of the ridiculous. The porter at Frank Spina's Kansas City barbershop, Bob Brown, remembered a time after the presidency when a big fellow from Texas sat in the front chair loudly telling a Texas joke about Truman, unaware that the former president was in the back chair. The barber whispered and pointed, letting the Texan know Truman was behind him. The fellow leaped out, sheet and all, to shake Truman's hand, telling everyone how he admired Truman. The ex-president had a good laugh. Then the Texas man got his little boy to meet Truman.

"Son," he said, "I want you to meet Mr. Truman, he used to be president."

Truman reached out to shake hands, but the boy would not shake. He looked up at his father and said, "So what?" Truman had another laugh.[24]

Then there was the modesty. Senator Edmund S. Muskie, a candidate for the vice presidency in 1968, came to Independence for advice. "Tell the truth," said the old man. When the senator said his way of telling the truth was not that of Truman's, the retired president said, "Be yourself."[25]

Sol Stolowy of Kansas City made suits for Truman, and the two often talked. One day Sol said, "You know, Mr. President, I come from Poland, and never could this happen for a Jewish boy to be making clothes for a president. Only in America." The response was: "In the U.S. anything can happen. I was a farm boy, and I became president."[26]

Truman also was thoughtful. One time when he was talking to an audience of high school students in Los Angeles, a youngster stood up and said, "What do you think of our local yokel?" He meant Governor Pat Brown. Incensed, Truman told the young man it was disgraceful to describe the state's governor in such a way. The audience broke into applause. But as the meeting continued the speaker began to sense what he had done: he had crushed his inquirer. Afterward, he had the youth brought to him and the two talked at length; Truman asked him about his school grades and his hopes and invited the boy to correspond with him.[27]

Two *Fort Worth Star-Telegram* reporters once arrived to interview Truman at the library, at a time when a distinguished foreign visitor was expected. Initially, public relations people sent by downtown Kansas City businessmen chased them out of the library parking lot. Then a car drove into the lot—it was Truman. One of the reporters explained their plight. Truman told them to come with him, inside the library, where he sent the public relations people packing. He gave the men a tour of the library, talked with them for two hours, and invited them to a luncheon for the ex-president of Mexico. As lunchtime approached, someone noticed faces peering in a window, and Bess Truman went to investigate. The faces belonged to tourists from North Carolina, who had come to find the library closed. She invited them in. "All in all," the two very pleased reporters wrote in an article that appeared after the former president's death, "being on the inside looking out for a change made for a most memorable morning. But then Harry Truman was a most memorable man."[28]

As the years passed, the president's crotchets, of which he possessed a few, began to come out, sometimes in humor, sometimes with more ridicule than he intended. One inspiration was the playing of the "Missouri Waltz," which had become the official state song in 1949. Truman hated the piece and sometimes said so. Once he was in a private dining room in Washington and had to go to the men's room. While he was en route, the band leader in the ballroom spotted him and began playing the "Missouri Waltz." To a friend he remarked, "It's getting so you can't go to the men's room any more without them playing that song." Another time, on the Ed Murrow show, he described the waltz's provenance, which was not much—an Iowan had composed it and originally called it "Hushaby my baby." Then he said, "I don't give a damn about it. . . . It's as bad as 'The Star Spangled Banner' so far as music is concerned." For the remark he received dozens of letters.[29]

As he indulged his preference for good music, so he did not hesitate to set out his perhaps less instructed wisdom for painting. He hated modern art, which he described as "ham-and-egg" art (meaning it looked like the artist had thrown an egg at the canvas and smeared it with ham). During the European tour in 1956 he had a two-hour conversation with Pablo Picasso. It must not have gone well. Afterward he received a letter from an inquirer at Roosevelt University in Chicago, asking about the availability of Picasso to accept a commission from the university. The answer was snappy: "It seems to me that a University named Roosevelt would try to obtain one of our able American painters for your purpose rather than a French Communist caricaturist."[30]

Such thoughts about painting showed themselves again when a publicist for the Missouri artist Benton sought Truman's approval: he did not obtain it. Truman had been insulted by Benton's statehouse mural in Jefferson City. "In the first place I know nothing about Art with a capital A, particularly the frustrated brand known as Modern. I don't like Mr. Benton's Kentuckian. . . . Both of my grandfathers were from Kentucky . . . They did not look like that long necked monstrosity of Mr. Thomas Hart Benton's."[31] (But then, later, the retired president relented, after seeing that Benton was only celebrating, not caricaturing, the people of Missouri's early settlement.)

He wrote Senator Kefauver, a politician he hardly admired, who had been investigating juvenile delinquency: "If you want my opinion—which you did not request but which I gladly volunteer—the best cure is for the mamas and papas to stay at home and raise their families. The responsibility of bringing up the next generation rests squarely on their shoulders. I do not believe in baby-sitters . . . just because the parents are too lazy to look after them."[32]

When he lectured at Columbia University in 1959, someone asked what he thought of the chances of a woman becoming president. "I've said for a long time," was the response, "that women have everything else, they might as well have the presidency."[33]

Truman was not a profane man, but he dispensed a little more than the normal quota of cuss words. At a ceremony in Springfield, the dedication of an armory to his cousin Ralph—with amplifiers, radio microphones, and television cameras on—the orator suddenly could not recall the name of Lieutenant General Ben Lear, who had relieved his cousin "Snapper" from command of the 35th Division in 1941 just before Pearl Harbor. He stopped dead in the middle of the speech, leaned over, and asked Louis Truman, Ralph's son and a three-star general, "Louis, what was that son-of-a-bitch's name that cashiered Snapper?"[34]

By this time physical problems had begun to drag him down. Early in his retirement years, in 1954, while attending an outdoor showing at the Starlight Theater in Kansas City of the Broadway musical *Call Me Madam*—a celebration of Truman's minister to Luxembourg, the Oklahoma heiress and party-giver Perle Mesta—he suffered a gall-bladder attack that confined him to Research Hospital for two weeks. In 1963 he went to the hospital for repair of a hernia. But the real blow came on October 13, 1964, when he slipped on a mat in the second-floor bathroom and fell forward on his right side, striking his chest against the tub, fracturing two ribs, and incurring multiple contusions on his right eyebrow and forehead. A maid discovered him on the floor, unconscious, and called the police and an ambulance. From this shock he never really recovered; he appeared desultorily at the library, keeping no regular hours, until he went to the hospital again in the summer of 1966 for an attack of colitis. Thereafter he visited the library twice, once during Nixon's appearance there on March 21, 1969, and finally in 1971 to look over a new wing on the building's east side that closed the space in the C.

He also suffered from an arthritic hip, for which he took old-time measures, resorting to a nearby chiropractor, Dr. John F. Meise. Between 1966 and 1969 Dr. Meise treated him at least two hundred and fifty times. Mike Westwood brought him in. Sometimes Bess came, and when he was in the adjusting room the doctor left the door open so she could be with them.[35]

Because of his health problems it was difficult for him to take walks, and he gave up the army pace of 120 steps per minute, going along as well as he could, accompanied by Mike, who carried a walkie-talkie in case of trouble. Almost never did he go out by himself. Once he slipped out the back door and through the alley to Maple Street and across to the barbershop of George Miller, who had cut his hair since Frank Spina retired and moved to Florida. Miller's wife, who did Bess's hair, called the house, and Bess sent the secret service after him. On another visit to the Miller shop, this time accompanied by Mike, he got in the chair and then noticed he had left his false teeth at home. A photographer came along and snapped a picture of Miller, Mike, and the president in the chair grinning. For years Miller kept the photograph on the wall.[36]

Mary Jane Truman noticed the decline, visible in his face. "He doesn't look a thing like he used to," she told a reporter.[37] "He always had a full face and always looked so well. He takes a miserable picture now, he's so thin.

And he's always taken such a nice picture." His eyes, always weak, looked starry behind the thick lenses. He heard badly, and his speech was slurred. He was pitifully frail.

In 1971, Benton did a painting entitled *The Old President*, in which he portrayed a white-haired old man, shirt collar and suit loose, hawk-nosed. "He's a skull now," Benton said. "You can see the man without the jowls and the fat." Contrary to Mary Jane, he liked what he saw. "The old man looks better as an old man than he did as a young man. You get that fat off of him and you see that chicken-hawk face and also his sensitivity. . . . You didn't ever see the real man, you saw only the mask." The artist showed the portrait to Bess, who said, "That's him." The remark pleased Benton. "What the hell more do you want?"

Randall Jessee took photographs of Benton working on the portrait, the last photographs of Harry Truman. They were as honest as the portrait. The old president was sitting in a chair behind the small desk in the study, a pile of books under one arm, holding a book in his arthritic hands, engrossed in it.

Books occupied his last years. Shelves filled the study, from floor to ceiling on three sides and over the window on the fourth—there were books about history and the presidency and especially presidents Jefferson and Jackson. When he ran out of books he went to the public library. The Chrysler pulled out of the back driveway, with Mike driving, Truman in front clasping a cane between his knees, and Bess in back. With a secret service car discreetly behind, they drove the few blocks to the library, where Mrs. Truman went in and gathered an armload.

As the end approached, he was in and out of Research Hospital three times, for colitis and other problems. He complained of "a little hot wire here," pointing to his head. His eyes were "changing around." He held Card No. 1 of Medicare, given him by President Johnson during a ceremony at the library, and during his last hospital visit, which began early in December 1972, his room cost $59.50 a day, part of which Medicare paid. He was there twenty-two days, and his personal physician, Dr. Graham, issued eighty bulletins.

Finally, his kidneys failed and his heart was unable to pump enough blood. Everything collapsed. Dr. Graham on December 26 announced "a complexity of organic failures causing collapse of the cardiovascular system."

The funeral was a mixture of pomp and circumstance—the pomp being what any U.S. Army–conducted funeral must be, the circumstance that of a small town with the Truman Library on its grassy knoll to the north of U.S. Route 24. The center of attraction had personally approved elaborate military plans for a five-day state funeral. "A damn fine show," he had said. "I just hate that I'm not going to be around to see it."[38] Bess modified the plans, but they remained elaborate. For several years the army contemplated what it needed to do in order to carry out Operation Plan Missouri (for a while, until 1969 when the event took place, it also contemplated Operation Plan Kansas, for former president Eisenhower). The Missouri Plan required attention because of the lay of the land: the army arranged small feeder roads that went up from Delaware Street on both sides of the Route 24 viaduct; the rises were long and gentle so that horses pulling a caisson would have no difficulty.

The circumstance of the funeral, Independence, offset the pomp. From the Truman Library attendees could espy the Catholic church's brick spire to the southeast, and over the houses due south rose the courthouse of which Truman had been so proud. The library was a suitable public place; outside, it was nondescript, while in the foyer before the Benton mural lay the coffin upon a catafalque covered by the flag. Nearby was the room honoring the 35th Division, with its prize exhibit the French seventy-five. The room and gun were a proper testimony to the work, now done, of a battery captain.

After the funeral the army fired howitzers in a twenty-one-gun salute. An observer noted that the sun had been shining, but as the salute rang out, echoing over the town, the sun went under, the sky turned gray, the wind blew, and the temperature dropped fifteen degrees in ten minutes.

Harry S. Truman was buried in the library courtyard. The slab of Barre, Vermont, granite bore the following description, chosen by the grave's occupant:

Harry S. Truman
Born May 8, 1884
Lamar, Missouri
Died December 26, 1972

Married June 28, 1919
    Daughter
Born February 17, 1924
    Judge
    Eastern District
    Jackson County
January 1, 1923–January 1, 1925
    Presiding Judge
    Jackson County
January 1, 1927–January 1, 1935
    U.S. Senator
    Missouri
January 3, 1935–January 18, 1945
    Vice President
    United States
January 20, 1945–April 12, 1945
    President
    United States
April 12, 1945–January 20, 1953

Notes

Chapter One. Early Years

1. Mary Ethel Noland, "Nancy Tyler Holmes' Motto Fitting," *Jackson County Historical Society Journal* 10 (fall 1967): 8–9.

2. William Hillman, *Mr. President*, 39; Harry S. Truman, *Memoirs: Year of Decisions*, 53.

3. Truman always believed his grandfather purchased this land in the vicinity of Sacramento. During his presidency California officials made a check of records but could not find anything. His biographer Jonathan Daniels doubted the story and so informed the president (Daniels to Truman, January 16, 1950, president's secretary's files, box 298, "Daniels, Jonathan"; unless indicated, all manuscripts are from the Harry S. Truman Library, Independence, Missouri). Sacramento was in the vast estate of John A. Sutter, who obtained his first grant in 1841 and another in 1845. The gold rush brought his ruin and the dispersal of his estate—his workers left and squatters came. Sacramento was laid out in 1848. Solomon Young did not arrive until 1854—according to *The History of Jackson County Missouri: Containing a History of the County, Its Cities, Towns, Etc.* (Kansas City, 1881), 987. Young doubtless approved the account in the latter volume.

4. Truman interview, November 12, 1949, by Jonathan Daniels, 72. These notes, in the Daniels papers in the Truman Library, were for Daniels's 1950 biography, *The Man of Independence*. The president told another story of a man who went to Lawrence, Kansas, for a Masonic ceremony and while visiting in a house saw that the owners had acquired a Bible belonging to the Lipscomb family. When he returned he told one of the younger Lipscombs, who wrote asking for it. He received no answer and wrote again, and in response to the second letter the Kansans took a razor, cut out the family pages, sent them, and kept the Bible.

5. Margaret Truman, *Harry S. Truman*, 50.

6. Ibid., 48. "In her later years, Aunt Mary handled the stove work. Neither she nor anyone else in the family let me in on this secret all during my girlhood years. . . . For a while I was convinced that I was a female dropout, because I loathed the idea of cooking from a very early age, and still do it under protest" (ibid.).

7. June 28, 1884, quoted in *Truman-Prairie Country Visitor*, spring–summer 1986, vertical file, Truman Library.

8. The average size of a Missouri farm in 1880–1890 was 129 acres (*Historical Statistics of the United States: Colonial Times to 1970* [Washington: Government Printing Office, 1975], 1:461).

9. To Philip B. Perlman, December 22, 1951, vertical file.

10. Robert H. Ferrell, ed., *The Autobiography of Harry S. Truman*, 6. Hereafter cited as *Autobiography*.

11. "Independence, Missouri: Its Schools, Churches, Residences, Improvements, Etc." (n.p., 1902).

12. Edward R. Schauffler, *Harry Truman: Son of the Soil*, 11.

13. Daniels, *Man of Independence*, 47.

14. For the Paxtons' memories of Delaware Street, see Mary Gentry Paxton [Keeley], *Mary Gentry and John Gallatin Paxton;* see also "In Memory of Mary Slover," *Jackson County Historical Society Journal* 6 (July 1965): 10. Mary Paxton Keeley oral history, by J. R. Fuchs, 46–48. Elizabeth Paxton Forsling, "Remembering Delaware Street," *Jackson County Historical Society Journal* 3 (May 1962): 7–12. See also Julia Twyman Fite, "Six Twyman Doctors," ibid. 6 (March 1965): 4–6. Elizabeth Forsling wrote that visiting Delaware Street at the turn of the century was like reaching up to the top shelf of a library, taking down an old leather volume, blowing off the dust, and turning the pages.

15. Keeley oral history, 23–24, 27–28.

16. Bela Kornitzer, "Harry Truman, Musician and Critic," *Pathfinder*, January 9, 1952, p. 26.

17. "The Music Critic and the President: The Second Time Around," *Whistle Stop* 16, no. 2 (1988), reprinted from Brian Lingham, *Harry Truman: The Man—His Music. Whistle Stop* is the newsletter of the Harry S. Truman Library Institute, which is composed of friends of the library.

18. Leroy V. Brant, "Music's Significant Place in Modern Life," *The Etude*, October 1946, 545.

19. *Public Papers of the Presidents: Harry S. Truman, 1948*, 265.

20. Mary Paxton Keeley, *Back in Independence*, 212.

21. For Clinton's Drugstore, see the brochure "Independence, Missouri" cited in note 11 above; Truman, *Year of Decisions*, 141–42; Richard Lawrence Miller, *Truman: The Rise to Power*, 36–37; Harry S. Truman to Margaret Truman, June 23, 1941, family correspondence file, box 10.

22. Address from rear platform of a train, Galesburg, Ill., May 8, 1950, *Public Papers, 1950*, 296.

23. Charles Robbins and Bradley Smith, *Last of His Kind: An Informal Portrait of Harry S. Truman*, 40.

24. Robert H. Ferrell, ed., "Harry Truman's Advice to Teachers," *Phi Delta Kappan* 62 (1980): 262. Truman wrote out this August 30, 1957, address to the Independence teachers, and the original is in postpresidential files, speech files, box 16, "Teachers Meeting, Independence, Missouri."

25. The volumes of *Great Men and Famous Women* were as follows: vol. 1, *Soldiers and Sailors;* vol. 2, *Statesmen and Sages;* vol. 3, *Workmen and Heroes;* and vol. 4, *Artists and Authors.*

26. "Independence," *Encyclopedia of the History of Missouri*, 6 vols. (New York: Southern History, 1901), 3:350.

27. Jonathan Daniels oral history, by J. R. Fuchs, 105: "Roosevelt's mind, intellectually, was far less stereotyped than Truman's, and maybe that explains why Roosevelt was not as simple and direct as Truman."

28. Merle Miller tapes, tape 4, Truman Library.

29. Dinner for members of Congress given by the Civil Air Patrol, May 14, 1952, *Public Papers, 1952–1953*, 330.

30. John Hersey, *Aspects of the Presidency*, 43. Hersey's book is a reprinting of two *New Yorker* profiles, one of Truman and one of President Gerald R. Ford.

Chapter Two. The Bank

1. "Two Years in the Army," general file, pertaining to family, business, and personal affairs, box 21, "Military Service, Longhand notes by H. S. Truman regarding."

2. Letter of December 14, 1918, in Robert H. Ferrell, ed., *Dear Bess: The Letters from Harry to Bess Truman, 1910–1959*, 286.

3. John K. Hulston to author, August 16, 1983. In his later years Ralph Truman lived in Springfield, Missouri, and often stopped at Hulston's law office. In a letter to Ralph, now in the Truman Library, Harry Truman referred to the Texas trip. The Independence cousin referred to the fact that on a Texas trip, presumably this one, he (Harry) proved a sissy.

4. "Spalding's Commercial College," *Encyclopedia of the History of Missouri*, 6:31. For a more recent account of the metropolis see Andrew Theodore Brown and Lyle W. Dorsett, *K.C.: A History of Kansas City, Missouri*.

5. The typewritten letter is in the papers of Mary Jane Truman, oversize file, item 10. "My Aunt Laura lived at Third and Campbell [in Kansas City]. She was voted the most beautiful girl in Jackson County and awarded the prize, but as is usual in such cases there was a protest. She gave the prize back to the judges and she was again given it unanimously. Her married name was Mrs. W. B. Everhart. Two of her daughters are still living, and will confirm what I'm saying" (*Autobiography*, 21).

6. Quoted in Daniels, *Man of Independence*, 59.

7. Annotations by Truman to Frank McNaughton and Walter Hehmeyer, *This Man Truman*.

8. Memorandum by J. R. Fuchs, May 31, 1963, vertical file; annotations to McNaughton and Hehmeyer, *This Man Truman*. Ethel Noland said that, according to her cousin, when he worked for L. J. Smith he could not even keep red ink, because "the hobos," the workers, would drink it when they were sobering up (oral history, by J. R. Fuchs, 92).

9. Schauffler, *Son of the Soil*, 21–22. Schauffler talked with Green, then in Kansas City and employed by the U.S. Army Air Forces as an auditor in a Ford Motor Company assembly plant.

10. Commerce Bank files, copies in miscellaneous historical documents file, box 10, document 308.

11. Miller, *Rise to Power*, 49–50.

12. *Autobiography*, 20.

13. Commerce Bank files, miscellaneous historical documents file, box 10, document 308.

14. Carrie Westlake Whitney, *Kansas City, Missouri: Its History and Its People, 1808–1908*, 2 vols. (Chicago: S. J. Clarke, 1908), 2:681, 683.

15. Commerce Bank files, miscellaneous historical documents file, box 10, document 308.

16. Ibid., document 309.

17. *Autobiography*, 20.

18. Walter Williams, ed., *The State of Missouri: An Autobiography* (Columbia, Mo., 1904), 265, 270–71.

19. Whitney, *Kansas City, Missouri* 2:682.

20. *Autobiography*, 21.

21. Vertical file.

22. News conference, September 8, 1949, *Public Papers, 1949*, 472.

23. Harry S. Truman to Jacob Billikopf, August 5, 1949, president's secretary's files, box 113, "Bi-Bl."

24. *Autobiography*, 22.

25. January 10, 1911, *Dear Bess*, 20.

26. Schauffler, *Son of the Soil*, 26–29. The story is corroborated in Mary Ethel Noland oral history, by J. R. Fuchs, 94ff.

27. Harry S. Truman to Margaret Truman, May 13, 1944, in Margaret Truman, ed., *Letters from Father: The Truman Family's Personal Correspondence*, 52.

28. Truman interview, November 12, 1949, by Daniels, 72.

29. Merle Miller tapes, tape 4. Roosevelt was one inch taller than Truman—five feet, eleven. Harold F. Gosnell, *Truman's Crises: A Political Biography of Harry S. Truman*, 24.

30. His parents would not give permission because they were "unreconstructed Southerners" (Harry S. Truman, *Mr. Citizen*, 204). For the farm visit see *Autobiography*, 28.

31. Harry S. Truman to Edwin C. White, April 26, 1952, president's secretary's files, box 327, "W"; Harry S. Truman to John L. Blue, December 26, vertical file.

Chapter Three. The Farm

1. September 2, 1911, *Dear Bess*, 44. For the subject of the present chapter see Robert H. Ferrell, *Harry S. Truman: His Life on the Family Farms*.

2. Bill Renshaw, "President Truman: His Missouri Neighbors Tell of His Farm Years," *Prairie Farmer*, May 12, 1945, p. 5, vertical file.

3. Speech of February 17, 1959, postpresidential files, invitations file, box 81, "Invitations Massman-Rockhurst"; see also *Autobiography*, 30–32.

4. *Autobiography*, 30.

5. July 1, 1912, *Dear Bess*, 88.

6. Annotation by Truman to McNaughton and Hehmeyer, *This Man Truman*, 26ff.

7. July 22, 1912, *Dear Bess*, 90.

8. October 1, 1911, and September 2, 1913, ibid., 50, 136.

9. January 30, 1912, ibid., 70.

10. June 24, 1912, ibid., 87.

11. Truman interview, October 21, 1959, "Mr. Citizen" file, box 2, folder 2.

12. November 28, 1911, *Dear Bess*, 61.

13. March 23 and June 24, 1912, ibid., 79, 87.

14. December 30, 1913, and May 9, 1911, ibid., 32, 151.

15. "April Fool's Day," 1915, ibid., 80.

16. December 9, 1913, ibid., 149.

17. September 17 and 30, 1912, ibid., 97, 99.

18. September 9, 1912, ibid., 96.

19. Schauffler, *Son of the Soil*, 37.

20. May 3 and 9, 1914, *Dear Bess*, 31–33.

21. December 31, 1910, ibid., 18.

22. Gaylon Babcock oral history, by J. R. Fuchs, 21.

23. Letter to Bess, March 17, 1914, general file, pertaining to family, business, and personal affairs, box 2.

24. Margaret Truman, *Bess W. Truman*, 30.

25. June 22, 1911, *Dear Bess*, 39.

26. July 12, 1911, ibid., 40.

27. May 12, 1914, ibid., 168.

28. January 23, 1917, ibid., 213.

29. Noland oral history, 49.

Chapter Four. The Army

1. *Autobiography*, 41.

2. Harry S. Truman to Fred Truman, September 21, 1943, senatorial file, box 168, "Truman, Fred."

3. Daniels, *Man of Independence*, 90.

4. July 14, 1917, *Dear Bess*, 225.

5. October 21, 1917, ibid., 232.

6. January 10, 1918, ibid., 239–40.

7. March 5, 1918, ibid., 247.

8. March 3, 1918, ibid., 246–47.

9. January 27, 1918, ibid., 241.

10. October 15 and 28 and November 11, 1917, ibid., 231, 233, 235.

11. The Stafford automobile was produced by Terry Stafford in Topeka and then in Kansas City, and its manufacturer finished 314 of them. Truman's car was about number 200, a good place in the series. An open touring car with a top that buckled down, it boasted Prestolight lamps and seated five passengers. It served its purpose mightily when he was on the farm, allowing him to bypass the unwieldy public transportation of the time—railroads with trains that did not keep schedules, together with streetcars from Kansas City or Sheffield to Independence. He bought the car used for six hundred dollars. When he went overseas he sold it, by that time a virtual wreck, for two hundred, and told Jacobson that he, Eddie, had something to learn in salesmanship.

12. Harry H. Vaughan oral history, by Charles T. Morrissey, 3–5. "Mister" was the army's customary address of that time for a second lieutenant.

13. Memorandum, May 14, 1934, in Monte M. Poen, ed., *Letters Home by Harry Truman*, 39–40.

14. March 10, 1918, *Dear Bess*, 248.

15. March 21, 1918, ibid., 252; Truman, *Year of Decisions*, 149.

16. March 26 and 27, 1918, *Dear Bess*, 253–54.

17. April 1918 (undated), ibid., 256.

18. May 19, 1918, ibid., 262.

19. Letter to Bess, June 19, 1918, *Letters Home*, 49–50.

20. April 23, 1918, *Dear Bess*, 260.

21. Vere C. Leigh oral history, by J. R. Fuchs, 10–11.

22. McKinley Wooden oral history, by Niel M. Johnson, 42, 47–48, 50. At the present writing, 1994, one member of Battery D survives—Wooden, age ninety-nine.

23. Miller, *Rise to Power*, 138.

24. Wooden oral history, 53–54.

25. Meisburger in *Peoria Journal Star*, May 6, 1970.

26. Truman, *Year of Decisions*, 152.

27. November 29, 1918, *Dear Bess*, 283; Harry S. Truman to Ethel Noland, December 18, 1918, *Letters Home*, 63.

28. Wooden oral history, 70–71.

29. January 21, 1919, *Dear Bess*, 293.

30. Sermon interview, September 26, 1949, by Jonathan Daniels, 24.

31. April 24, 1919, *Dear Bess*, 298.

32. Wooden oral history, 87–88.

33. Vertical file.

34. *Harry S Truman, Late a President of the United States: Memorial Tributes Delivered in Congress*, 68.

Chapter Five. Boom and Bust

1. Years later he visited Walter Slagel of Skaneateles, New York, who had been a first lieutenant in the regiment. Both men had bought wedding rings for their wives at the same time (*Skaneateles Press*, April 29, 1960).

2. Lenore K. Bradley, "Memories of Bess Truman, Part II," *Whistle Stop* 11, no. 3 (1983).

3. The story appeared in the *Examiner* the same day. Vertical file.

4. "You have your dad's tenacity and your ma's contrariness, and together they should make you" (Harry S. Truman to Margaret Truman, November 14, 1946, *Letters from Father*, 82).

5. December 28, 1945, *Dear Bess*, 523–24.

6. Remarks at National Plowing Match, Dexter, Iowa, September 18, 1948, *Public Papers, 1948*, 498.

7. Truman, *Bess W. Truman*, 103–4.

8. "My father, however, was not quite as tolerant of his opinionated mother-in-law. Perhaps he and Grandmother Wallace were never destined to get along under the same roof because she was from a town family and he from a country one. For whatever reason, while they never argued in public, there was much that they disagreed upon in private" (*Letters from Father*, 220).

9. Truman, *Bess W. Truman*, 70–85.

10. Conversation of August 12, 1983.

11. Tom Leathers, "A Look Back," *Kansas City Town Squire*, July 1975, vertical file.

12. Ted Marks oral history, by J. R. Fuchs, 27–28.

13. "I want [to] follow a mule down a corn row all the rest of my days or be a congressman or something where I can cuss colonels and generals to my heart's content" (Letter to Ethel Noland, December 18, 1918, *Letters Home*, 64).

14. According to Miller, *Rise to Power*, 153, all the money went to Truman. Truman

himself said the money from the hogs went into the haberdashery ("My Impressions of the Senate, the House, Washington, etc.," undated, senatorial file, box 168, "Biographical Material").

15. November 28, 1919, general file, pertaining to family, business, and personal affairs, box 11, "Correspondence, general 1919."

16. Miller, *Rise to Power*, 156.

17. William M. Reddig, *Tom's Town*, 163–64.

18. Miller, *Rise to Power*, 158–59.

19. Eben A. Ayers diary, September 4, 1948, Robert H. Ferrell, ed., *Truman in the White House: The Diary of Eben A. Ayers*, 267–68.

20. General file, pertaining to family, business, and personal affairs, box 12, "Battery 'D' Banquet 1920."

21. Ibid., box 16, "Programs 1914–1925."

22. Edward D. McKim oral history, by J. R. Fuchs, 33–34. According to McKim, Truman had to pay "important money"—a couple of hundred dollars—for the row at this reunion.

23. Harry S. Truman to Edward H. Prell, January 21, 1922, general file, pertaining to family, business, and personal affairs, box 11, "Correspondence, General, January–July 1922."

24. Miller, *Rise to Power*, 205.

25. For the tangled history of the bank loans the best published source is ibid., 259–60, 335–37. During Truman's presidency the editor of the *American Mercury*, William Bradford Huie, published a blistering account of the haberdashery's finances, "In the *Mercury*'s Opinion," in his magazine's issue of May 1951, 544–51. In anticipation of a published response, which he never made, Truman assigned his White House assistant, Eben A. Ayers, to go to Kansas City and obtain what information he could from Jacobson and other individuals. Ayers's materials are in his papers, box 23. In an article of a year later, the issue of May 1952, concerning publication of William Hillman's *Mr. President*, entitled "Truman's Embarrassing Book," 121–26, Huie repeated his allegation that the president failed to repay the debts.

26. Harry S. Truman to Dickson Jay Hartwell, May 16, 1949, vertical file.

27. Hillman, *Mr. President*, 173.

28. In 1951, Truman told Ayers he thought he had accounts in Independence and at Fairmount nearby. See conversation of August 3, Ayers papers, box 23, "Personal-Ayers, E.-trip to Kansas City (June 19–30, 1951)."

29. Omar Robinson, attorney for the bank, in *St. Louis Star-Times*, July 24, 1934. "They took the farm but gave me no credit," Truman wrote years later in "My Impressions of the Senate."

30. Fred A. Boxley to Truman, January 8, 1935, Ayers papers, box 23, "Personal-Ayers, E.-trip."

31. There is no way to get behind the above testimony. Ayers excerpted the above account from Boxley's papers in 1951; a few of the papers later came to the Truman Library, but not this correspondence. Truman had stored his Senate papers for the first term, apparently in the basement of the treasury building next to the White House, and they were either lost or by error destroyed.

Chapter Six. County Judge

1. Cabell Phillips, *The Truman Presidency: The History of a Triumphant Succession*, 20.

2. Maurice M. Milligan, *Missouri Waltz: The Inside Story of the Pendergast Machine by the Man Who Smashed It*, 101–2. The best account of the Pendergast organization is Lyle W. Dorsett, *The Pendergast Machine*.

3. Reddig, *Tom's Town*, 132.

4. Dorsett, *Pendergast Machine*, 16.

5. Ibid., 42–43.

6. Darrell Garwood, *Crossroads of America: The Story of Kansas City*, 181.

7. A silver-tongued scamp, Reed went to the U.S. Senate and made a national and international reputation as the nemesis of President Wilson during his fight for the League of Nations. The senator had asked Wilson to appoint his friend R. Emmet O'Malley postmaster of Kansas City, and the president, with reason, was opposed (for O'Malley see below); this was the beginning of Reed's opposition, which eventually focused on the League. Truman hated Reed, whom he knew in later years. It always struck him as poetic justice that Reed died by falling down a flight of stairs; he presumed Reed was drunk (Truman interview, November 12, 1949, by Daniels, 70).

8. Milligan, *Missouri Waltz*, 57.

9. *Kansas City Star*, quoted in ibid., 87.

10. Truman's Republican road engineer, N. T. Veatch, Sr., believed the paving of the creek was a good idea. The initial reason for paving, of course, was to sell concrete, but it also helped keep the water away from Nichols's shopping mall, which was in a low area (N. T. Veatch oral history, by J. R. Fuchs, 82–84). Years later, in 1977, Brush Creek nonetheless overflowed, filling the mall with several feet of water and ruining several millions of dollars' worth of merchandise in the stores.

11. For the pages that follow see Miller, *Rise to Power*, 164–204, 217–61.

12. Reddig, *Tom's Town*, 105.

13. Harold M. Slater, "The Ku Klux Klan," *St. Joseph (Mo.) News-Press*, September [?], 1977, vertical file; see also Edgar G. Hinde oral history, by J. R. Fuchs, 50–52.

14. John Woodhouse interview, November 19, 1986, by Niel M. Johnson, miscellaneous historical documents file, box 24, document 648.

15. McKim oral history, 43.

16. *Independence Examiner*, March 10, 1922.

17. Brown Harris to Truman, January 7, 1947, president's secretary's files, box 298, "Correspondence relating to Harry S. Truman—biographical." "It was a hot fight but the soldier stuff and the soldier boys watching the ballot boxes won for me" ("My Impressions of the Senate").

18. Truman interview, October 21, 1959, "Mr. Citizen" file, box 2, folder 2.

19. Ibid.

20. Harry S. Truman, *Truman Speaks*, 7.

21. Letter of February 23, 1937, general file, pertaining to family, business, and personal affairs, box 10.

22. Harry S. Truman to John H. Twyman, July 9, 1922, general file, box 11, "Correspondence general, January–July 1922."

23. *Independence Examiner*, June 1, 1923, vertical file; for another version of Jarboe's remark see Miller, *Rise to Power*, 184–85.

24. Miller, *Rise to Power*, 182–83.

25. A copy of this undated speech is in Spencer Salisbury papers, box 1, Jackson County Historical Society, copies in the Truman Library.

26. General file, box 13, "Jackson County Court, Election 1924." For reasons never clear, Pendergast Democrats were called Goats, Shannon supporters Rabbits.

27. Truman and McElroy also took measures against petting on county roads, and the *Kansas City Star* reported "dog days for the 'snuggle puppy'" (Miller, *Rise to Power*, 189–90).

28. Henry A. Bundschu, *Harry S. Truman: The Missourian*, 10.

29. "The President's Savings and Loan Background," *Savings and Loans* (June 1945): 5, 29, vertical file.

30. Salisbury papers, box 1. The advertisements are in Truman's hand.

31. Quotation from Daniels cited in Noland oral history, 138. McKim oral history, 48–49.

32. Miller, *Rise to Power*, 213, 215–16. Miller has looked closely at this affair and believes Truman blameworthy for selling to an incompetent group and issuing no warning to depositors who could have suffered along with Houchens. Truman stayed on as a director. At this time, to be sure, there was no such thing as federal depositors insurance.

33. *Kansas City Star*, March 13, 1974, vertical file; Truman, *Bess W. Truman*, 112.

34. July 25, 1923, and July 9, 1925, *Dear Bess*, 314, 319. She told Ethel Noland: "A woman's place in public is to sit beside her husband, be silent and be sure her hat is on straight." Jhan Robbins, *Bess and Harry: An American Love Story*, 38.

35. *New York Times*, April 22, 1984.

36. July 7, 1925, *Dear Bess*, 317.

37. July 11, 1927, ibid., 329.

38. Truman ill-naturedly assumed that Kemper and his candidate split the fees.

39. Hinde oral history, 69.

40. Andrew J. Dunar, *The Truman Scandals and the Politics of Morality*, 10.

41. Undated speech, apparently 1924, general file, pertaining to family, business, and personal affairs, box 17.

42. Lenore K. Bradley, "Building Jackson County," *Whistle Stop* 13, no. 2 (1985).

43. Account on White House stationery, vertical file.

44. Speech of October 7, 1929, vertical file.

45. Franklin D. Mitchell, "Who is Judge Truman?: The Truman-for-Governor Movement of 1931," *Midcontinent American Studies Journal* 7 (1966): 3–15; James E. Ruffin to Truman, June 19, 1931, Ruffin papers, miscellaneous historical documents file, box 18, document 498.

46. April 14, 1933, *Dear Bess*, 348.

47. April 23 and May 7, ibid., 350, 353.

48. "My Impressions of the Senate."

Chapter Seven. Senator from Pendergast

1. Daniels, *Man of Independence*, 172, 174–75; Miller, *Rise to Power*, 301.

2. Senator Bennett C. Clark was anti-Pendergast until Truman's nomination for the Senate, after which he caved in and supported the boss; he needed Pendergast for reelection in 1938.

3. Dorsett, *Pendergast Machine*, 103, 106–7.

4. Vina L. Montgomery of Jacksonville, Illinois, wrote Governor Park that she was doing a theme on the Pendergast machine. Could he tell her what it was? "The so-called Pendergast machine," the governor responded, "is an organization of fighting Democrats built up on service and achievement. It has its captains and lieutenants running down to every block in Kansas City. Between elections these workers spend much time and money looking after the welfare of the unfortunate people of the community, caring for them in case of illness or when they are out of work. And naturally, when election day comes, these people are loyal to those who have helped them in time of need" (Letter of November 25, 1936, Park papers, folder 1678, Western Historical Manuscript Collection, University of Missouri–Columbia).

5. James Aylward, Jr., *Kansas City Times*, July 23, 1982, vertical file. See also Aylward's oral history, by J. R. Fuchs.

6. Aylward oral history, 63–64.

7. Years later some evidence appeared that Pendergast put Cochran into the race as a stalking-horse for Truman, to keep the St. Louis vote from going to Milligan. Cochran had been secretary to William L. Igoe when the latter was congressman, and Igoe and Bernard L. Dickmann controlled a St. Louis faction friendly to Pendergast. When the interviewer Fuchs asked Aylward whether this could have been true, the former county chairman vehemently denied the possibility. "Why, that is so untrue it is unbelievable. Now, how could you practically enter into a conspiracy with a group of political leaders in the city of St. Louis to run one of their favorite sons for office and expect them to agree with you to get so many votes for him so that we could nominate Truman for the United States Senate. Why, you know that's foolish—it's unbelievable. Way out! Crazy! They couldn't control it even if it was undertaken. How could that be done?" (Aylward oral history, 88–89). Cochran probably was an independent candidate, no stalking-horse. Still, one wonders. Pendergast was a wily operator, who may not have told his county chairman everything he, the boss, was doing; in the oral history Aylward believed Pendergast was for Reed in 1932. On the question of whether Pendergast put Truman into the race so he would lose, see Jonathan Daniels's interview with Colonel Southern, September 26, 1949, 21; Hinde oral history, 89–90, 93.

8. Mildred Lee (Latimer) Dryden oral history, by J. R. Fuchs, 2–3.

9. Vertical file.

10. "My Impressions of the Senate."

11. Hulston to the author, July 11, 1991; see also the Missourian's *An Ozarks Lawyer's Story, 1946–1976*, 171.

12. Daniels, *Man of Independence*, 170.

13. Truman to Park, June 6, 1934, Park papers, folder 2199; Buford to Park, July 21, folder 2200.

14. Park papers, folder 2200.

15. In the history of vote fraud it is worth noting that if Pendergast nominated Truman in 1934 and sent him on his way to the presidency, so Jim Smith of Jersey City elevated Woodrow Wilson to the governorship of New Jersey in 1910; in 1948, Congressman Lyndon B. Johnson went to the Senate because in the town of Alice, Texas, after the polls closed, someone added ballot box 13 containing 203 ballots, all but one of which were for Johnson (Johnson won the state by 87 votes); in 1960, John F. Kennedy achieved the presidency by 110,000 votes in an election marked by fraud in the close states of Illinois, Texas, and Missouri (Kennedy carried Illinois by 8,000). On the

Republican side, there was the election of Benjamin Harrison in 1888, achieved in his home state of Indiana, where reliable members of the GOP each arranged, with assistance of five-dollar gold pieces, for four cooperative citizens to vote in what contemporaries described as "blocks of five."

16. Harry S. Truman to George Collins, October 2, 1939, miscellaneous historical documents file, box 14, document 403.

17. *Kansas City Times*, December 18, 1934, vertical file.

18. Alfred Steinberg, *The Man from Missouri: The Life and Times of Harry S. Truman*, 124.

19. Truman interview, September 10, 1959, "Mr. Citizen" file, box 2, folder 2.

20. Steinberg, *Man from Missouri*, 130.

21. Truman interview, November 12, 1949, by Daniels, 63.

22. Wheeler was a conservative Democrat, but Truman never forgot him. "His viewpoint is almost opposite to mine but you must understand that sixteen years ago Burt Wheeler was one of the few Senators in the Senate who was in any way decent to the junior Senator from Missouri and I can't forget that. That doesn't necessarily mean that he has any influence with me as to policy but I shall continue to like him as long as I live" (Harry S. Truman to James E. Murray, February 10, 1951, president's secretary's files, box 328, "Wheeler, Burton K").

23. Remarks to a group of new Democratic senators and representatives, April 6, 1949, *Public Papers, 1949*, 199–200.

24. During the 1930s, Truman evidently had to borrow occasionally from the Hamilton National Bank. Years later, in 1951, he attended and spoke at a retirement dinner for Joshua Evans, Jr., and thanked the latter: "Mr. Evans used to be willing to float a little slow paper once in a while, and I never forgot it." He then quoted Billings (*Public Papers, 1951*, 121). See Henry W. Shaw, *Josh Billings Trump Kards* (1877).

25. June 17, 1935, November 24, 1937, October 9, 29, 1939, general file, pertaining to family, business, and personal affairs, box 10.

26. "Record," August 3, 1937, senatorial file, box 168, "HST, Personal Correspondence, 1937."

27. Senatorial file, box 168, "Correspondence for 1938."

28. Miller, *Rise to Power*, 268–69.

29. Ibid., 276.

30. Tom L. Evans oral history, by J. R. Fuchs, 767–68.

31. December 11, 1935, *Dear Bess*, 382.

32. Miller, *Rise to Power*, 280.

33. For the act see Eugene F. Schmidtlein, "Truman the Senator." Schmidtlein was the first researcher in the Truman Library and is thoroughly conversant with national and Missouri politics of the Senate era.

34. November 10, 1937, general file, pertaining to family, business, and personal affairs, box 10.

35. Miller, *Rise to Power*, 288.

36. Max Lowenthal interview, August 31, 1949, by Jonathan Daniels, 11; Miller, *Rise to Power*, 286.

37. October 29, 1937, *Dear Bess*, 40.

38. Schmidtlein, "Truman the Senator," 161–63.

39. Roswell L. Gilpatric oral history, by Jerry N. Hess, 1–3.

40. Steinberg, *Man from Missouri*, 149.

41. Evans oral history, 205.

42. Milligan, *Missouri Waltz*, 165.

43. Reddig, *Tom's Town*, 280.

44. Truman interview, November 12, 1949, by Daniels, 58; Miller, *Rise to Power*, 272.

45. Truman to Stark, January 20, and Stark to Canfil, March 16, 1936, miscellaneous historical documents file, box 18, document 497. Stark put a note in a letter to Truman of March 11, 1937: "On anything you are vitally and personally interested in, please pin a little note to the sheet of paper; otherwise, I will assume that you wrote it as a matter of politics. L.C.S." (Stark papers, folder 7226, Western Historical Manuscript Collection, University of Missouri–Columbia).

46. Martha H. Swain, *Pat Harrison: The New Deal Years*, 158–59, 285–86.

47. Years later Truman described Milligan as "a dumb cluck who never won a case" (annotation by Truman to McNaughton and Hehmeyer, *This Man Truman*, 82). "He didn't convict anybody. He played Gestapo on T. J. and told him he'd prosecute his family and T. J. confessed to a legal crime not a wrong per se" (ibid., 83). Truman believed the Kansas City police chief, Otto Higgins, a "real crook" and O'Malley "the real villain in the piece" (ibid., 84).

48. 75th Cong., 3d sess., *Congressional Record* 83, pt. 2, 1962.

49. Ibid., 1962–63.

50. Harry S. Truman to Joseph H. Leib, February 21, 1938, published in *Kansas City Star*, September 15, 1978, vertical file.

51. For Anna Roosevelt Boettiger's comment about her father, see Henry A. Wallace diary, August 16, 1944, Wallace papers, University of Iowa Library, Iowa City; she told this to a friend, Norman Littell, who informed the diarist.

52. Miller, *Rise to Power*, 311–12.

53. Ibid., 314.

54. Burton K. Wheeler, *Yankee from the West*, 373.

55. Stark papers, folder 7331.

56. Harry Easley oral history, by J. R. Fuchs, 44–45.

57. Evans oral history, 250–51.

58. Ibid., 262–65. John K. Hulston later interviewed Olive Truman, widow of Senator Truman's cousin Ralph, who had a different story about how Milligan entered the senatorial race. According to her, Senator Clark enticed him in a St. Louis hotel, and Ralph was present during the conversation (letter of July 11, 1991).

59. Edward Jacobson interview, September 27–28, 1949, by Jonathan Daniels, 25. Jacobson exhibited the card under glass in his Kansas City menswear store.

60. Schmidtlein, "Truman the Senator," 233. Schmidtlein checked all outstate papers.

61. Watson papers, box 14, "President's Memos (Original), April 6, 1940," Alderman Library, University of Virginia, Charlottesville. B. Marvin Casteel, former superintendent of the state highway patrol, was director of Missouri's WPA.

62. Hinde oral history, 85–87.

63. *St. Louis Post-Dispatch*, July 6, 1940, vertical file.

64. Clark's statement was typical stump Missouri: "It is one of poor Lloyd's unfortunate delusions that he is the only honest man in Missouri—indeed in the world—and that anyone who happens to differ with him, particularly anyone who doubts that he is temperamentally and mentally suitable for service in the United States Senate, is controlled by the powers of darkness and evil." When Stark was

running for governor he "licked Pendergast's boots until he obtained his support." Stark talked about the 1934 election, in which he claimed Truman was "fraudulently elected" with sixty thousand Kansas City ghost votes, but no one ever proved they were fraudulent. And in the 1936 election, Stark himself certainly received fraudulent votes. See Clark papers, folder 365, Western Historical Manuscript Collection, University of Missouri–Columbia.

65. Truman carried St. Louis by 8,411. I am indebted to William Hannegan, son of the St. Louis chairman, for pointing out how Sermon and Harper probably influenced his father, as well as for calling attention to Harper's oral history, by J. R. Fuchs, 10, 13–16, 23, and to an article by Alfred Fleishman, "Truman—How He Really Made It," *St. Louis Business Journal,* August 24–30, 1992. Bill's father held the wards' votes until the last moment, and the son remembers the surprise of his aunt, a ward worker, to see Truman's name on the party slips instead of Stark's. As for management of delivery wards, Bill once met one William Kunz, who, he thought, lived in the Hannegan apartment house and voted therefrom. Kunz said he had been in military service and was not voting (William Hannegan to the author, September 1, 1992).

66. Harry S. Truman to Margaret Truman, August 12, 1940, general file, pertaining to family, business, and personal affairs, box 10.

Chapter Eight. Wartime Washington

1. It never occurred to Roosevelt that Truman would replace him, the retired president told his son-in-law, Clifton Daniel. See E. Clifton Daniel oral history, by J. R. Fuchs, 50.

2. *Public Papers, 1950,* 307–8. "After events moved around, through no arrangement on my part, I became President of the United States, and General Marshall was Chief of Staff. He was out in my office one day, and my Secretary, Mr. Connelly, said, 'General, if the man in the other room'—which happened to be me—'were to ask the same question now that he did in 1940, what would you say?' And the General said, 'Well, I would tell him the same thing, only I would be a little more diplomatic about it.'"

3. Interview with Reathel Odum, May 8, 1989.

4. Letter of June 19, 1941, general file, pertaining to family, business, and personal affairs, box 10.

5. See Roger Edward Willson, "The Truman Committee"; Schmidtlein, "Truman the Senator"; Wilbur D. Sparks oral history, by Jerry N. Hess (Sparks was a committee staff member); Robert F. Maddox, *The Senatorial Career of Harley Martin Kilgore,* 111–39.

6. Vaughan oral history, 54.

7. Schmidtlein, "Truman the Senator," 291–99; Willson, "The Truman Committee," 26, 29–30.

8. William P. Helm, *Harry Truman: A Political Biography,* 151–52; Truman interview, November 12, 1949, by Daniels, 64. According to Maddox, *Senatorial Career,* 111–12, Kilgore believed the committee arose from a conversation with Truman on a Washington-bound train from West Virginia, where the senators had been attending the inauguration of Governor Matthew M. Neely; they were talking about the Civil War's "committee on the conduct of the war."

9. In August, Truman managed an increase to $50,000. During his chairmanship

into 1944, the committee received a total of $360,000, this to investigate hundreds of billions of expenditures; the committee, so Truman later told Jonathan Daniels (interview of November 12, 1949, 64), perhaps a bit appreciatively, saved taxpayers $15 billion.

10. Schmidtlein, "Truman the Senator," 259–65; Willson, "The Truman Committee," 97–98, 101. Kilgore was chairman of a subcommittee that went to Alaska and there had an encounter with the imperious Somervell. The general arrived for a hearing flanked by four brigadier generals and several majors. At one point Somervell needed a refill of a glass of water, and he handed his empty glass to a brigadier general who handed it to a major.

11. Maddox, *Senatorial Career*, 122–27.

12. Willson, "The Truman Committee," 345, 352–53, 421–22; Walter Hehmeyer oral history, by J. R. Fuchs, 28ff. (Hehmeyer was in charge of press relations for the committee.)

13. Sparks oral history, 25–26.

14. For the following pages, see Robert H. Ferrell, *Choosing Truman: The Democratic Convention of 1944*. Also Brenda L. Heaster, "Who's On Second?"; David McCullough, *Truman*, 292–320.

15. Robert H. Ferrell, *Ill-Advised: Presidential Health and Public Trust*, 28–48.

16. For the letters see Ayers diary, April 23, 1947, *Truman in the White House*, 177; J. Samuel Walker, *Henry A. Wallace and American Foreign Policy*, 50–60.

17. Robert G. Nixon oral history, by Jerry N. Hess, 128. "He's the only president in our history that saved the country twice. There was a structure built about him that made people take for granted that he was going to live forever. I'm sure he thought so too. I don't think it ever crossed his mind—the shadow of death. Now this may be a key to it in a sense. Rosenman . . . said something to the effect that it really didn't matter who was the choice for the vice presidency" (ibid., 66–67). Samuel I. Rosenman was the president's speechwriter, known officially as his special counsel.

18. Pauley wrote a remarkable memorandum for Jonathan Daniels about his advocacy of Truman for the vice presidency. He did not date it but must have written it in 1948 or 1949. The original is in the White House central files, confidential files, box 30, "The President." With assistance of the writer Richard English he prepared another account, "Why Truman Is President"; never published, it too is in the above-mentioned file.

19. Vaughan oral history, 71.

20. Jonathan Daniels, *White House Witness, 1942–1945*, 257.

21. Samuel I. Rosenman oral history, by Jerry N. Hess, 26; Daniels, *White House Witness*, 257.

22. Ferrell, *Choosing Truman*, 12–13, 28–30.

23. John M. Blum, ed., *The Price of Vision: The Diary of Henry A. Wallace, 1942–1946*, 361–63, 365–67, 371 (entry undated).

24. Walker, "Assisting Roosevelt," 213–16. The Frank C. Walker papers in the archives of the University of Notre Dame, South Bend, Indiana, contain drafts of an autobiography composed by Walker in the early 1950s, which the present writer has brought together in an unpublished manuscript, "Assisting Roosevelt: An Autobiography."

25. Harry S. Truman to Charles G. Ross, January 22, 1950, president's secretary's files, box 321, "Political—Vice Presidential Nomination—1944."

26. Walker, "Assisting Roosevelt," 236.

27. The following is from the Evans oral history, 322, 335–37.

28. Bess went on the Senate payroll on July 1, 1941, at $2,280 per year, which increased to $4,500 in June 1942. She continued this salary in the vice president's office through March 1945. Mary Jane went on the payroll September 1, 1943, at $1,800 per year, and her salary remained the same through March 1945. In April 1945, the sergeant at arms of the Senate was making $8,000, the majority and minority secretaries, $4,800. In the vice president's office Mildred Dryden, clerk, made $2,520, and Reathel Odum, assistant clerk, $2,340. Messengers and laborers made respectively $1,400 and $1,740. The wives of Vic Messall and Harry Vaughan both had worked in the office. On April 30, 1942, Senator Truman wrote Bess: "I'm sure glad you went to the office. It's much better for you to go there a few days a week and see what goes on. . . . You don't have to say a word only just drop in and do some signing. It helps all concerned" (*Dear Bess*, 474). After the vice presidential nomination the newspapers mentioned Bess's being on the payroll, and one of the secretaries in the office, Mrs. Dryden, arranged the following release: "Mrs. Truman handles all the Senator's personal mail and works on the editing of the Committee Reports. She comes into the office two or three times a week and takes the material home with her. She works with the Senator on it at night, since he has no time for it during office hours" (Vertical file, "HST—Senator"). The senator himself explained as follows: "She is my chief adviser. I never write a speech without going over it with her. I have to do that because I have so much to do and I never make any decisions unless she is in on them. She also takes care of my personal mail" (*New York Herald Tribune* bureau release, unidentified newspaper, July 27, 1944, vertical file). The senator was emotional about Bess's involvement, as he admitted to the reporter Edwin A. Harris of the *St. Louis Post-Dispatch*: "I well remember a late afternoon in his office (in the Senate Office Building), when we were alone. I had asked him, for publication, whether he carried Bess on his payroll and why. He said she earned every cent there as a secretary and assistant, and that their expenses in Washington were so high he had to do it that way. Then he choked up for a moment, pulled a letter from his drawer, and read a part of it. It was, he said, from the wife of a Republican governor, and it called his wife a vicious name (bitch, I believe) because she was on his payroll. To get the sequence straight, I had published the story about Bess being on the payroll, and the vicious letter came to him later, commenting on the story, which was carried nationally. Anyway, Truman came as near to crying as I had ever seen him. I stood at the window, feeling foolish and helpless, wanting very much to walk over and put my hand on his shoulder, but I did not. After a few moments he recovered and put the letter away" (Harris to Richard H. Rovere, Richard H. Rovere papers, box 15, folder 1, State Historical Society of Wisconsin; courtesy of Brenda L. Heaster).

By this time Truman was buying bonds with perhaps 10 percent of his salary; he had paid off the campaign debt for 1940. The best analysis of this problem may well be by Miller, *Rise to Power*, 338: "If Truman felt poor, and his private writings show that he did, it was only a relative measurement against the far wealthier people he dealt with every day."

29. Truman, *Bess W. Truman*, 270–71.

30. Ibid., 233–35.

31. *Autobiography*, 90.

32. J. Leonard Reinsch, *Getting Elected: From Radio and Roosevelt to Television and Reagan*, 5–11. Reinsch was an assistant in managing the convention.

33. J. Leonard Reinsch oral history, by J. R. Fuchs, 28–29.

34. Miscellaneous historical documents file, box 1, document 7. The speech notes translated as follows: "You don't know how very much I appreciate the very great honor which has come to the state of Missouri. It is also a great responsibility which I am perfectly willing to assume. Nine years and five months ago I came to the Senate. I expect to continue the efforts I have made there to help shorten the war and to win the peace under the great leader, Franklin D. Roosevelt. I don't know what else I can say, except that I accept this great honor with all humility. I thank you" (*New York Times*, July 22, 1944).

35. Leahy interview, August 31, 1949, by Jonathan Daniels, 13; Robert J. Donovan, *Conflict and Crisis: The Presidency of Harry S. Truman, 1945–1948*, 7.

36. August 18, 1944, *Dear Bess*, 509–10.

37. Evans oral history, 450–54. According to Admiral Leahy, "Truman told me that FDR had told him much about situation though not details" (Leahy interview, August 31, 1949, by Daniels, 13). There has been a good deal of comment that Truman knew nothing about the nuclear program until Secretary of War Henry L. Stimson told him briefly, immediately after his swearing-in, and then gave him the details on April 25. This misinformation doubtless began with Truman's statement to that effect in his memoirs. Clark Clifford, in *Counsel to the President*, 57–58, relates that Truman told him "on many occasions" that he knew nothing about the bomb until Stimson told him. But the weight of testimony, as Clifford might put it, does seem on the other side, that Truman knew of the bomb project in general even before talking with Roosevelt. According to Byrnes, who told him of the bomb on the way back from Roosevelt's funeral, "he knew of the project generally through his Senate Committee work" (*All in One Lifetime*, 282). Truman himself said that the first word he had about a nuclear bomb came when his assistant on the investigating committee, his old friend Canfil, got into Oak Ridge and Hanford (interview, November 12, 1949, by Daniels, 67). It was after Canfil's inquiries that Stimson telephoned the senator to ask that he cease such probings.

38. Robert H. Ferrell, ed., "A Visit to the White House, 1947: The Diary of Vic H. Housholder," 326. "In July [August], 1944, in White House garden, soon after convention, Roosevelt said: 'Harry, don't fly! You can't tell when you will have to take over this job'" (Charles G. Ross diary, April 19, 1946, Ross papers). In the memoirs Truman did not touch the health problem, relating that when Roosevelt asked him how he was going to travel, he said he would use a plane, and the president advised, "Don't do that, please. Go by train. It is necessary that you take care of yourself" (*Year of Decisions*, 5).

39. Vaughan oral history, 77.

40. In his memoirs, *My Name is Tom Connally*, 275, the senator said only, "I made a brief speech." For Mrs. Truman's remarks see *Life* magazine, August 21, 1944, vertical file.

41. Harry S. Truman to Thomas Van Sant, November 28, 1944, Van Sant papers.

42. Nixon oral history, 218–19.

43. Robert E. Sherwood and Judge Rosenman, writing Roosevelt's speeches, did not pay any attention to what either Truman or Dewey was saying (Rosenman oral history, by Jerry N. Hess, 30–33).

44. Evans oral history, 407–8, 411.

45. Reinsch oral history, 29–31.

46. Tom Clark oral history, by Jerry N. Hess, 35.

47. Luther Huston, "The Vice President Talks of His New Job," *New York Times Magazine*, January 21, 1945, vertical file.

48. Hinde oral history, 124–25; Schauffler, *Son of the Soil*, 15; Edward D. McKim interview, September 29, 1949, by Jonathan Daniels, 32; McKim oral history, 106.

49. Easley oral history, 98–99.

50. Wheeler, *Yankee from the West*, 375.

51. Leverett Saltonstall, *Salty: Recollections of a Yankee in Politics*, 115.

52. McNaughton and Hehmeyer, *This Man Truman*, 208.

Chapter Nine. A New President

1. Diary entry of April 12, 1945, in Robert H. Ferrell, ed., *Off the Record: The Private Papers of Harry S. Truman*, 15. The president seems to have composed this portion of his diary notes within two or three days of events.

2. *Souvenir: Margaret Truman's Own Story*, 83–85.

3. Eric F. Goldman, *Rendezvous with Destiny* (New York: Knopf, 1952), 406; Nixon oral history, 154. Truman told John Hersey he wore double-breasted suits because he didn't happen, like some single-breasted fellows he knew, to own "a watch chain with a Phi Beta Kappa key on one end and no watch on the other" (*Aspects of the Presidency*, 6).

4. Reinsch oral history, 144.

5. Hersey, *Aspects of the Presidency*, 9.

6. Robert H. Ferrell, *Truman: A Centenary Remembrance*, 136.

7. Vaughan oral history, 87. Compare Hopkins's assessment of the Truman administration's expediency: "Unless we're waiting for an action of some other department, nothing stays in the White House over 48 hours."

8. Phillips, *Truman Presidency*, 131.

9. "Actually, every major decision of his presidency—Hiroshima and Nagasaki, the Truman Doctrine and the Marshall Plan, NATO, the H-bomb, the Korean intervention, the dismissal of MacArthur—was the product of careful political or diplomatic planning and group consensus, not individual whim" (Alonzo L. Hamby, "An American Democrat: A Reevaluation of the Personality of Harry S. Truman," 52). The Jenkins quotation is from the Hamby article. For "jump decisions" see Truman interview, September 10, 1959, "Mr. Citizen" file, box 2, folder 1.

10. Ferrell, *A Centenary Remembrance*, 139.

11. June 28, 1957, *Dear Bess*, 568.

12. Ferrell, *A Centenary Remembrance*, 139.

13. *Autobiography*, 116.

14. Ayers diary, April 26 and June 5, 1945, *Truman in the White House*, 15, 41.

15. Vaughan oral history, 85–86.

16. "One often reads of Franklin Roosevelt that he liked organizational confusion which permitted him to keep power in his hands by playing off his colleagues one against the other. This, I think, is nonsense. Such is a policy of weakness, and Roosevelt was not a weak man. Furthermore, it did not keep power in his own hands; it merely hindered the creation of effective power by anyone. Roosevelt had no trouble in commanding Colonel Stimson, General Marshall, and Admiral King, far stronger men than Wallace, Jones, Lehman [Herbert Lehman, former governor of New York], or Hull. He understood military organization. On the other hand, he was tone deaf to the subtler nuances of civil government organization. This was messed up in his adminis-

tration for the simplest of reasons: he did not know any better" (Dean Acheson, *Present at the Creation: My Years in the State Department,* 47).

17. William E. Pemberton, *Bureaucratic Politics: Executive Reorganization during the Truman Administration,* 6–7, 15–16, 31. See also Stephen Hess, *Organizing the Presidency* (Washington: Brookings Institution, 1976).

18. Harold L. Ickes diary, July 9, 1944, Manuscript Division, Library of Congress, Washington, D.C.; Harry S. Truman to Jonathan Daniels, February 26, 1950, *Off the Record,* 174. Truman said privately that he did not want a woman in the cabinet (Ayers diary, September 14, 1945, *Truman in the White House,* 78); Matthew J. Connelly oral history, by Jerry N. Hess, 376–77. Morgenthau's diary for the summer of 1945 does not of course support Truman's recollection; the secretary of the treasury believed the new president liked him, sensed he and the president were like brothers, had arranged to go to France but was willing to stay in the United States while the president attended the Potsdam Conference, desired assurance that he could remain in the cabinet until the Japanese surrender, and then when Truman proved ambivalent about his remaining offered his resignation (Morgenthau diary [microfilm], Franklin D. Roosevelt Library). Word came that Biddle was "sore" and had talked to Ickes and advised the latter not to resign but get fired first and then cause all the trouble he could, and the president said, "I don't give a damn what he says" (Ayers diary, May 28, 1945, *Truman in the White House,* 33). Biddle's memoir, *In Brief Authority,* is glowingly appreciative of Roosevelt, modestly so of Truman.

19. Harry S. Truman to Jonathan Daniels, February 26, 1950, *Off the Record,* 174.

20. Letter to Maury Maverick, May 12, 1948, president's secretary's files, box 61, "Texas."

21. Memorandum by Charles G. Ross, September 12, 1950, Ayers papers, box 7; Truman diary, September 14, 1950, *Off the Record,* 191–93.

22. At the beginning of the administration the president suggested lunches twice a week at the White House, perhaps Tuesdays and Thursdays. "I am very anxious to get things set up as soon as we possibly can, so that the Executive Branch of the Government can be operated through the Cabinet" (president's secretary's files, box 154, "cabinet—general, 1945–51"). For the result see Clinton P. Anderson, *Outsider in the Senate: Senator Clinton P. Anderson's Memoirs,* 76–78.

23. Schauffler, *Son of the Soil,* 90.

24. Ayers diary, September 27, 1945, *Truman in the White House,* 84.

25. Ayers diary, June 4, 1945, ibid., 23.

26. September 30, 1945, president's secretary's files, box 117, "Connelly, Matthew J."

27. Schwellenbach told Truman, "I am a complete failure as Secretary of Labor, and I have let you down" (Harold D. Smith diary, May 29, 1946). Truman kept him until his death in 1948.

28. Harry S. Truman to Jonathan Daniels, February 26, 1950, *Off the Record,* 174.

29. Truman interview, September 10, 1959, "Mr. Citizen" file, box 2, folder 1.

30. Francis H. Heller, ed., *The Truman White House: The Administration of the Presidency, 1945–1953,* 184.

31. Truman did not want anyone other than himself, the secretary of state, or the undersecretary to preside over the NSC; he did not want the secretary of defense or the vice president to do so (James E. Webb to Alfred D. Sander, February 3, 1971, Webb papers. Webb was undersecretary of state from 1949 to 1952).

32. Truman interview, October 21, 1959, "Mr. Citizen" file, box 2, folder 2; Truman,

Mr. Citizen, 118–20. Richard Norton Smith, in an introduction to Timothy Walch and Dwight M. Miller, eds., *Herbert Hoover and Harry S. Truman: A Documentary History*, 4–5, is unsure of Truman's recollection.

33. *Chicago Sun-Times*, December 27, 1972, vertical file. The account is by U.S. Tax Court Judge William M. Fay, confirmed by Anderson.

34. Pemberton, *Bureaucratic Politics*, 89–90.

35. Harry S. Truman to Fred I. Kent, April 5, 1952, president's secretary's files, box 125, "Kent, Fred I. (folder 2)."

36. Pemberton, *Bureaucratic Politics*, 52, 61, 97, 107–9, 123–24, 153, 158, 173.

Chapter Ten. Ending the War

1. Frank C. Walker diary, April 15, 1945, Walker papers.

2. Harry S. Truman to Carl A. Hatch, December 1, 1952, president's secretary's files, box 121, "Ha-He"; Smith diary, February 28, 1946.

3. The blunder was not failure to inform the president of the possible consequences, George C. Herring, Jr., has written, but disagreement among Truman's advisers on what measures to take and especially the rigid interpretation given the order by Crowley and the government committee overlooking Soviet lend-lease (Herring, *Aid to Russia, 1941–1946: Strategy, Diplomacy, the Origins of the Cold War*, 203–6). The author points out that the administration already had tightened requirements for lend-lease to Britain.

4. W. Averell Harriman and Elie Abel, *Special Envoy to Churchill and Stalin, 1941–1946*, 453–54; Truman, *Year of Decisions*, 82; Charles E. Bohlen, *Witness to History, 1929–1969*, 213; Ayers diary, April 23, 24, 1945, *Truman in the White House*, 13–14.

5. Joseph E. Davies diary, April 30, 1945, Davies papers, Library of Congress.

6. For the Hopkins and Davies missions see Bohlen, *Witness to History*, 215; Harriman and Abel, *Special Envoy*, 463; Henry H. Adams, *Harry Hopkins*, 389–94; George McJimsey, *Harry Hopkins: Ally of the Poor and Defender of Democracy*, 380–92; conversation of May 26–27, 1945, in *Foreign Relations of the United States: 1945, Conference of Berlin (The Potsdam Conference)*, 1:64–78; Davies diary, May 26, 1945.

7. Harriman and Abel, *Special Envoy*, 478. See David Herschler, "Retreat in Germany: The Decision to Withdraw Anglo-American Forces from the Soviet Occupational Zone, 1945."

8. Bohlen, *Witness to History*, 216; Harriman and Abel, *Special Envoy*, 478–79. Four years later the president had changed his mind: "[I]f I had known then what I know now, I would have gone to the eastern [*sic*] boundaries of Russia" (interview, August 30, 1949, by Daniels, 4). And again: "If I had been in touch with the whole situation at that time, I don't think I would have withdrawn the American Army from the eastern boundary in Germany, and then we wouldn't have serious trouble, but I labored under the feeling, as did a great many other people, that the Russians would keep their agreements" (interview, September 9, 1959, "Mr. Citizen" file, box 2, folder 1). But, surely, easy as it sounded, Truman's retrospective course would have been most unwise.

9. Truman diary, July 7, 1945, *Off the Record*, 48.

10. "I remember at one point, this nervous Jimmy Byrnes, who was pretty full of himself, just having been made Secretary of State, came to me very much perturbed,

not in a smiling, jocular fashion at all, but quite perturbed, and said, 'Mr. Nixon, will you boys (as he called us) please leave the President alone?'

"I said, 'Mr. Secretary, what are you talking about?'

"And he said, 'I mean leave him alone in the evening. Stop occupying all of his hours. I've got to tell him what's supposed to go on at this conference.'

"And I smiled and said, 'Well, Mr. Byrnes, I will have to apologize, but,' I said, 'I have no control over this.' I said, 'Why don't you go to the President and ask him to leave *us* alone?'" (Nixon oral history, 270–71).

11. Truman diary, July 16, 1945, *Off the Record*, 51–52.

12. Truman diary, July 17, 1945, ibid., 53.

13. M. Truman, *Harry S. Truman*, 279; Bohlen, *Witness to History*, 235.

14. Bohlen, *Witness to History*, 228, 239; Andrei Gromyko, *Memories*, 113.

15. Truman, *Year of Decisions*, 363; Harry S. Truman to Margaret Truman, July 29, 1945, general file, pertaining to family, business, and personal affairs, box 10; Nixon oral history, 79.

16. Robert L. Dennison oral history, by Jerry N. Hess, 82–83; Ayers diary, August 7, 1945, *Truman in the White House*, 60.

17. Harry S. Truman to Byrnes, January 5, 1946, *Off the Record*, 80.

18. Georgii K. Zhukov, *Memoirs of Marshal Zhukov* (New York: Delacorte, 1971), 674–75; interview, May 31, 1967, Harriman papers, box 869, Chadwin file, Manuscript Division, Library of Congress.

19. J. Samuel Walker, "The Decision to Use the Bomb: A Historiographical Update."

20. The latest discussion of these issues is in Leon V. Sigal, *Fighting to a Finish: The Politics of War Termination in the United States and Japan, 1945*.

21. Harry S. Truman to George A. Warmer, September 23, 1963, vertical file.

22. For the joint war plans committee report see Barton J. Bernstein, "A Postwar Myth: 500,000 U.S. Lives Saved," *Bulletin of the Atomic Scientists* 42.6 (June–July 1986): 38–40. Hull's comment is in minutes of June 18, 1945, meeting at White House, *Foreign Relations of the United States: 1945, Conference of Berlin*, 1:905.

23. *Foreign Relations of the United States: 1945, Conference of Berlin*, 1:909; William D. Leahy diary, June 18, 1945, Leahy papers, Library of Congress.

24. Edward J. Drea, *MacArthur's ULTRA: Codebreaking and the War against Japan, 1942–1945*, 204, 213, 222. For twenty years after the war, ULTRA was classified, its work unknown. MAGIC became known immediately because of the Pearl Harbor investigation. ULTRA showed how formidable were Japanese defenses. MAGIC, which historians and political scientists and journalists measured closely, stressed how Japanese officials and diplomats were attempting to end the war.

25. For a summary of Truman's several estimates of lives saved by the nuclear bombings see Bernstein, "A Postwar Myth," 38. Stimson made his assertion of one million casualties in an article in *Harper's* in 1947. The critic mentioned above is Rufus E. Miles, Jr., "Hiroshima: The Strange Myth of Half a Million American Lives Saved," *International Security* 10.2 (fall 1985): 138. Bernstein, in "A Postwar Myth," is equally critical: "Perhaps in the aftermath of Hiroshima and Nagasaki, Truman developed a need to exaggerate the number of U.S. lives that the bombs might have saved by possibly helping render the invasions unnecessary. It is probably true, as he contended repeatedly, that he never lost any sleep over his decision. Believing ultimately in the myth of 500,000 lives saved may have been a way of concealing ambivalence, even from himself. The myth also helped deter Americans from asking troubling questions

about the use of the atomic bombs" (40). For the question of whether the Potsdam meeting could have occurred see Bernstein's review of Richard Rhodes's *The Making of the Atomic Bomb* in *Physics Today* 41.12 (December 1988): 118–21.

26. Harry S. Truman, *Truman Speaks*, 67, 73, 93.

27. Blum, ed., *Price of Vision*, 474; Clark oral history, 88–89.

28. McGeorge Bundy, *Danger and Survival*, 72–73, suggested the possibility of neutral observers at Alamogordo. But if the test had failed?

29. John K. Emmerson, *The Japanese Thread: A Life in the U.S. Foreign Service*, 236–37; Sigal, *Fighting to a Finish*, 151–53; Truman, *Truman Speaks*, 74.

30. See Bundy, *Danger and Survival*, 82, 85–86, 89–90, 93–94. Bundy regrets the dropping of the Nagasaki bomb, which may not have been necessary; little would have been lost by delay. He also regrets that the three principal reagents in the chemistry of surrender—the decision to drop the bomb, the imminence of Soviet entry, and the decision to allow the Japanese to keep the emperor—did not have careful analysis by a group of officials meeting in the weeks prior to Potsdam.

31. Gar Alperovitz, *Atomic Diplomacy: Hiroshima and Potsdam*, 226–42 (the author published a revised edition in 1985 and repeated his assertions); Truman interview, November 12, 1949, by Daniels, 67; the Interim Committee's failure to discuss any connection between dropping the bombs and impressing the Russians is in Fredrick J. Dobney, ed., *Selected Papers of Will Clayton*, 128; the Molotov remarks are in Walter J. Brown, *James F. Byrnes of South Carolina: A Remembrance*, 313, 316–17; for criticism of Alperovitz see Robert J. Maddox, *The New Left and the Origins of the Cold War*, and Thomas T. Hammond, "'Atomic Diplomacy' Revisited," *Orbis* 19 (1975–1976): 1403–28. "The idea of using the bomb as a form of pressure on the Russians never entered the discussions at Potsdam" (Harriman and Abel, *Special Envoy*, 490); "[N]ever did I hear President Truman or any of his colleagues discuss the use of the bomb against Japan in terms of American-Soviet relations" (Clifford, *Counsel to the President*, 59). Bundy, *Danger and Survival*, 650–51, describes the Alperovitz book as "both sloppy and tendentious," asserting that the author "reached the conclusion he wanted, but his own evidence repeatedly failed to sustain it."

Chapter Eleven. To Err Is Truman

1. Robert S. Allen and William V. Shannon, *The Truman Merry-Go-Round*, 48–50.

2. Nixon oral history, 176.

3. During the Truman years Allen cultivated Eisenhower, whom he had met during the war, and one week drove the Eisenhowers from New York to Gettysburg and showed them the farm they eventually bought. Friendship with the Eisenhowers doubtless assisted him with the collecting of directorships.

4. Harry S. Truman to Jim Pendergast, May 21, 1946, *Off the Record*, 88–89.

5. Fred A. Canfil to Harry S. Truman, undated letter (ca. July 1947), president's secretary's files, box 306, "Canfil, Fred A."

6. H. Graham Morison oral history, by Jerry N. Hess, 47–54. Morison's account is lurid. Attempting to find a man who might have become an informer, he discovered that this individual had left Missouri. "Four days later an item appeared in the press that there had been a serious automobile crash and a 'shoot-out' in rural Indiana and this guy who had called me had been killed. I also learned that the *first* news person on

the scene from outside the state was the Business Manager of the *Kansas City Star* who took a private plane to the site to make sure he was dead and could not talk!" (54)

7. "Proper name is Allslop!" Annotation by Truman to Steinberg's *Man from Missouri*, in the Truman Library.

8. Harry S. Truman to Dr. W. L. Brandon, November 22, 1951, president's secretary's files, box 113, "Br–Bz."

9. Smith diary, September 13, 1945.

10. Nixon oral history, 159–60.

11. During the fight over the nomination Mrs. Roosevelt said her husband never would have nominated a man like Pauley, but after the death of Secretary of Defense James V. Forrestal in 1949, Truman's naval aide, Admiral Dennison, went out to Forrestal's Georgetown house and in a drawer of the table beside his bed (and this was all that was in the drawer that Dennison could remember) found a memorandum from Truman's predecessor supporting Pauley (Dennison oral history, 60–61).

12. Ickes diary, February 3, 1946.

13. As early as April 29, 1945, Ickes had written in his diary that he would ruin Pauley if the latter pressed him hard enough—at this time rumor said that Pauley wanted the secretaryship of the interior (Graham White and John Maze, *Harold Ickes of the New Deal: His Private Life and Public Career*, 230). One can only assume that Ickes considered Pauley's "rawest proposition" far more of a political and personal danger than an illegality. Ickes's two biographers set out the secretary's tangled personal life and extraordinary delusions and suspicions.

14. George E. Allen, *Presidents Who Have Known Me*, 176.

15. President's secretary's files, box 158, "Interior—Secy. of the—Harold L. Ickes." In 1949, Ickes wrote Raymond Robins that he still considered Truman a small man and it was too late for the president to grow (White and Maze, *Harold Ickes of the New Deal*, 236).

16. For Wallace see Edward L. Schapsmeier and Frederick H. Schapsmeier, *Prophet in Politics: Henry A. Wallace and the War Years, 1940–1965;* Blum, ed., *Price of Vision;* Walker, *Henry A. Wallace and American Foreign Policy;* and Richard J. Walton, *Henry Wallace, Harry Truman, and the Cold War.* For Wallace's resignation see John L. Kelley, "An Insurgent in the Truman Cabinet: Henry A. Wallace's Effort to Redirect Foreign Policy."

17. Ross diary, September 21, 1946, Ross papers, box 21, "Personal diary 1946—typed draft."

18. Truman diary, September 17, 1946, *Off the Record*, 94; Dennison oral history, 59; Herbert Agar, *The Price of Power: America since 1945*, 63.

19. Wallace made changes in the speech after the president looked it over, and the deletions and additions favored the Soviets: of the deletions, two were neutral and one pro-U.S.; of the additions, one was neutral, one pro-U.S., two pro-Russian.

20. Wallace had written Justice Hugo L. Black of the Supreme Court that he "felt warranted in going to almost any lengths if I could use the current situation to help prevent war" (Kelley, "Insurgent in the Truman Cabinet," 87).

21. Memorandum, September 20, 1946, president's secretary's files, box 156, "Commerce, Secretary of—Henry A. Wallace"; Ross diary, September 21.

22. During the course of the resignation no statement Wallace made hurt him more with the president than the remark that he should be the president's left hand. Truman interpreted it as the end justifying the means. He so wrote Bess on September 20, 1946 (*Dear Bess*, 539) and added, "I believe he's a real Commie and a dangerous

man." He said the same to the reporter William Helm (*A Political Biography*, 234) and to Jonathan Daniels (interview of November 12, 1949, 68).

23. The letter has disappeared and Clark Clifford (*Counsel to the President*, 121) relates that the president destroyed it (including presumably any copies, of which there was at least one). This is the only instance the present writer knows of something that was identified but did not survive in the president's papers; his private secretary, Rose Conway, invariably filed everything she received, including unsent letters, hand-written or dictated. Wallace himself could not recall its contents other than that they were "of a low level" and contained no profanity (Blum, ed., *Price of Vision*, 629, quoting a Wallace oral history). As Press Secretary Ross remembered the letter, it said Truman had no confidence in Wallace and wanted his resignation. It referred to a statement by the columnist Drew Pearson that Wallace had made six copies of a memorandum to the president of the preceding summer and showed one to an Associated Press correspondent, and stated further that the commerce department had given out full details of the conversation with the president of Wednesday, September 18, 1946 (Ross diary, September 20).

24. R. Alton Lee, "The Army 'Mutiny' of 1946."

25. Ayers diary, January 8, 1946, *Truman in the White House*, 113–14.

26. Harry S. Truman to Dwight D. Eisenhower, letter of January 16, 1946, *Off the Record*, 81.

27. Dean Rusk, *As I Saw It: As Told to Richard Rusk*, 156.

28. Wilfred J. McNeil oral history, by Jerry N. Hess, 179–80; David Alan Rosenberg, "U.S. Nuclear Stockpile 1945 to 1950." The figure of a half-dozen was the president's estimate; see Ayers diary, October 14, 1946, *Truman in the White House*, 161. Years afterward Harriman was speaking with Arthur M. Schlesinger, Jr., and making points about the point system of demobilization in 1945–1946. "No one," he avowed, "has ever destroyed their own military strength as rapidly as we did and nobody can question that. That was done. It was brought home to me very clearly, Arthur, because of this —— —— point system." Schlesinger, a World War II veteran, said he had a different view of the point system. Unperturbed, Harriman continued: "I early suspected that the Communists had something to do with the point system" (Harriman interview, May 31, 1967, Chadwin file, box 869, Harriman papers).

29. So Truman told the head of the Office of Price Administration, Chester Bowles (*Promises to Keep: My Years in Public Life, 1941–1969*, 126).

30. Phillips, *Truman Presidency*, 107.

31. Ayers diary, February 14, 1946, *Truman in the White House*, 132–33.

32. For this draft speech composed sometime during October 1946, see *Off the Record*, 100–102.

33. It was not such a tremendous number of days, considering there were more than 60 million workers—equal to two days each, not more than a couple of holidays. R. Alton Lee, *Truman and Taft-Hartley: A Question of Mandate*, 15, compares the percentage of workers on strike in relation to the total labor force for the years following the end of both World Wars; the percentage in 1919 was 20.8 and in 1946, 14.5.

34. Letter of January 23, 1946, *Off the Record*, 83.

35. Ayers diary, January 12, 16, 18, 24, 1946, *Truman in the White House*, 118–20, 122–23.

36. Phillips, *Truman Presidency*, 114–15.

37. Ayers diary, May 23, 1946, *Truman in the White House*, 148.

38. Phillips, *Truman Presidency*, 117–18.

39. Ross diary, October 23, 1946; Harry S. Truman to Martha Ann Truman, November 27, 1946, president's secretary's files, box 332, "Truman, J. Vivian"; Ayers diary, December 7, 1946, *Truman in the White House*, 163–65; Truman diary, December 11, 1946, *Off the Record*, 104. The Supreme Court in 1947 lowered the UMW's fine to $700,000.

40. Lee, *Truman and Taft-Hartley*, 49–79.

41. Arthur M. Schlesinger, Jr., "Introduction," in Robert Dallek, ed., *Dynamics of World Power: Documentary History of U.S. Foreign Policy, 1945–1973* (New York: Chelsea House, 1973), 1:xxxi–xxxii. Lynn Etheridge Davis, *The Cold War Begins: Soviet-American Conflict over Eastern Europe*, believes conflict arose over American commitment to the Atlantic Charter.

42. John Gimbel, "On the Implementation of the Potsdam Agreement: An Essay on U.S. Postwar German Policy," *Political Science Quarterly* 87 (1972): 242–69, also Gimbel's *The American Occupation of Germany*. This author was the leading scholar of postwar German policy and wrote that a speech Secretary Byrnes gave in Stuttgart in September 1946 was not really a blast against the Soviet Union but a full statement of policy on Germany. It contained anti-French references, claiming that France had been the stumbling block to organizing the German economy on a four-power basis (France was not a signatory of the Potsdam protocol). The French wanted German territory; their zone also was largely agricultural, and unlike the Anglo-Americans they were making a modest profit on exports. With resignation of Secretary of Commerce Wallace, the congressional elections, and the Truman Doctrine and Marshall Plan of 1947, memory of French intransigence faded, replaced by belief that the Soviet Union had prevented four-power cooperation in 1945–1946.

43. Thomas G. Paterson, "The Abortive American Loan to Russia and the Origins of the Cold War, 1943–1945," *Journal of American History* 56 (1969–1970): 70–92. Clark Clifford wrote that Truman favored a loan as late as September 18, 1946, but after reading a report that Clifford's assistant, Elsey, wrote on Soviet-American relations he never mentioned a loan again (Clifford, *Counsel to the President*, 129).

44. For the following account of the Westminster College trip see Jeremy K. Ward, "Winston Churchill and the 'Iron Curtain' Speech," *History Teacher* 1 (1968): 5ff.; E. F. Van Zandt, "Missouri Remembers the 'Iron Curtain,'" *This Week*, September 3, 1967, vertical file; William E. Parrish, "Winston Churchill Visits an American Westminster," vertical file; Ross diary, March 7, 9, 1946; Vaughan oral history, 138–39, 141–42; Dr. Graham to author; Clark Clifford, *If I Should Write a Book* (John McGovern lecture to the Cosmos Club of Washington, October 16, 1986, privately printed), 12–14, vertical file; *New York Times*, March 14, 1946; Leahy diary, March 3, 1946; Davies diary, February 11, 1946; draft presidential speech, April 17 (?), 1948, *Off the Record*, 132.

45. Truman, *Years of Trial and Hope*, 95; *Off the Record*, 80; conversation with Dr. Graham. The Truman Library has the president's telephone logs, and they show no calls to the Kremlin during 1946. The president first voiced the business of a virtual ultimatum to the Soviets over Iran during a press conference. Assistant Press Secretary Roger Tubby told Alfred Steinberg, "I went over to the State Department and found the letter in question. It was certainly a strong letter telling Stalin to keep his hands off Azerbaijan Province in Iran, but it was not an ultimatum. We had to issue a correction" (Steinberg, *Man from Missouri*, 352). See also Tubby's oral history, by Jerry N. Hess, 28–31. But Truman repeated it in *Truman Speaks*, the lectures at Columbia, and added that Ambassador Harriman delivered the message. Harriman denied he was the messenger (*New York Times*, April 25, 1960). In 1962 the former president told Herbert Druks

(*Harry S. Truman and the Russians, 1945–1953*) that he gave the Russians a week to begin withdrawal and six to complete it, and he threatened to send the U.S. Navy as far as the Persian Gulf and send American troops back to Iran. Compiling historical documents for the period, the department of state could find nothing; see *Foreign Relations of the United States: 1946*, vol. 7, *The Near East and Africa* (Washington: Department of State, 1969), 348–49. Loy W. Henderson of the department's Near Eastern and African division told Herbert Feis (*From Trust to Terror: The Onset of the Cold War, 1945–1950*, 84) that, so far as he knew, Truman never sent an admonitory message. For the comment about Byrnes and the UN see Rusk, *As I Saw It*, 126. A remarkable account of relations with the erstwhile Persia appears in James F. Goode, *The United States and Iran, 1946–1951: The Diplomacy of Neglect;* also Mark H. Lytle, *The Origins of the Iran-American Alliance, 1941–1953;* for its more general subject, see Bruce R. Kuniholm's excellent *The Origins of the Cold War in the Near East: Great Power Conflict and Diplomacy in Iran, Turkey, and Greece.*

46. In his memoirs Acheson described Stettinius as a man who "had gone far with comparatively modest equipment" (*Present at the Creation*, 88). Upon his appointment the reporter Walter Trohan went down to the University of Virginia and looked up his grades as an undergraduate. "They were so bad I didn't have the heart to do a story on them and point out that the American Secretary of State had been given grades far below passing in politics, economics and history" (*Political Animals: Memoirs of a Sentimental Cynic*, 208). Stettinius was not an elected official, and for this reason alone Truman believed he should not succeed to the presidency. The president also believed that he, himself, should not have the right to appoint his own successor. In 1947 new legislation provided that upon the death of a president and succession of a vice president, the next successor would be the president pro tem of the Senate and thereafter the heads of executive departments. Shortly after Truman became president Stettinius went to San Francisco to attend the conference drawing up the UN Charter; Truman asked George Allen to go out and sound him on his resignation, and Allen put the case awkwardly, irritating the secretary (Allen, *Presidents Who Have Known Me*, 172–73. See also Thomas M. Campbell and George C. Herring, eds., *The Diaries of Edward R. Stettinius, Jr., 1943–1946*, 398–401). Stettinius should have been irritated, considering the messenger. In any event the president arranged for him to be the first permanent U.S. representative to the UN. For this post the secretary had his two requirements, for which see the Stettinius diary, June 25, 1945, Stettinius papers, box 245, "calendar notes June 1–26, 1945," University of Virginia library, Charlottesville. That summer Budget Director Smith presented a letter to the president for signature asking several hundred thousand dollars for Stettinius as ambassador to the UN, and said he thought it took care of the former secretary and his retinue rather well. Truman laughed and said, "Retinue is the right word" (Smith diary, July 6, 1945).

47. Helm, *A Political Biography*, 233. Without quoting the president Jonathan Daniels wrote that "as a man who had received what Byrnes thought was to be his, he felt oddly in Byrnes's debt" (*Man of Independence*, 308). Truman admitted as much in *Year of Decisions*, 23.

48. Biddle, *In Brief Authority*, 364.

49. Nixon oral history, 246.

50. The visitor was Alex Sachs, Jackson County's road engineer when Truman was presiding judge. Reminiscence by his son Howard, 1978, miscellaneous historical documents file, box 10, document 312.

51. Theodore Achilles oral history, by Richard D. McKinzie, 5. He added, "but I'm never going to tell those little . . . at the State Department anything about it."

52. Smith diary, December 5, 1945.

53. Davies diary, December 8, 19, 1945.

54. Bohlen, *Witness to History*, 250–51.

55. Ayers diary, December 12, 1945, *Truman in the White House*, 101–2; Truman interview, August 30, 1949, by Daniels, 4; Leahy interview, August 31, by Daniels, 13. Upon return to Washington on December 28 the president told Leahy that "he was not consulted by Secretary Byrnes in the agreements made at the Moscow Conference of Foreign Ministers" (Leahy diary, December 28). See also Truman memorandum, January 10, 1946, president's secretary's files, box 159, "State, Secy. of—James F. Byrnes."

56. Leahy diary, December 29, 1945; Ayers diary, December 29, 1945, January 1, 2, 1946, *Truman in the White House*, 107–9, 111–12; Truman interview, August 30, 1949, by Daniels, 4; Clark Clifford interview, October 26, 1949, by Daniels, 44. Robert L. Messer, *The End of an Alliance: James F. Byrnes, Roosevelt, Truman, and the Origins of the Cold War*, 160–61, says that Byrnes, while in Moscow, sent the state department no less than twenty-seven messages, some of which went to Truman, and one of which the president marked. He admits they were routine messages, not addressed to the president, but adds that it was impossible to send personal messages safely from Moscow, that the secretary had not sent personal messages before, and that Truman at no time sought to find out more of what was going on. (Messer does not raise the possibility of sending a courier to one of the Western European capitals, whence messages could have been safely transmitted to Washington.) "While Byrnes spent his Christmas arguing with Molotov about the Balkans and Iran, Truman was at home with his family in Independence. While Byrnes flew halfway around the world through blinding snowstorms in a C-54 transport plane, Truman cruised down the Potomac on his new yacht playing poker with his friends."

57. For the Byrnes letter see *Off the Record*, 79–80. The president had given Hillman access to his private papers, and the result was a tasteless volume, *Mr. President*, celebrating the president as a statesman; Truman liked Hillman, and he spent much time with him after retirement; he may have felt that the book would provide the reporter with income. Its single newsworthy item was the Byrnes letter. In the summer of the previous year Eben Ayers was helping bring together the president's personal papers, and "The President said that 'I read that letter to Byrnes, right here in this office with him sitting right there where you are. I told him I was not going to give him the letter but I wanted to read it to him.' The President said Byrnes' face was fiery red after the President finished" (Ayers diary, July 26, 1951, Ayers papers, Truman Library). A few years later Francis H. Heller, assisting the retired president with his memoirs, asked about the *Collier's* article; the answer was, "Jimmy Byrnes is entitled to his memory and I am entitled to mine—it's that simple" ("Harry S. Truman: The Writing of His Memoirs"). Robert Messer believes the letter of January 5 "was not just meant for Byrnes alone. The evidence strongly suggests that it was not meant for Byrnes at all. . . . Writing it may have served as a catharsis for Truman's growing dissatisfaction with Byrnes as secretary but his immediate inability to get rid of him" (*End of an Alliance*, 163–64).

Chapter Twelve. A New Foreign Policy

1. Michael J. Hogan, *The Marshall Plan: America, Britain, and the Reconstruction of Western Europe, 1947–1952,* 431–32.

2. John Lewis Gaddis, "Was the Truman Doctrine a Real Turning Point?," argues that the Korean War was the turning point, not the measures of 1947–1949; that the war looked to the future, whereas 1947–1949 looked to the past. Insofar as concerns the military industrial complex and the Vietnam War, Gaddis is correct, but surely the Truman Doctrine, Marshall Plan, and NATO, while taking their origins out of the immediate past, Russian intransigence in 1945–1947, constituted a break. The past did not allow permanent intervention in Europe. One could contend that the military industrial complex and Vietnam War were perversions of what Truman had in mind.

3. Howard Jones, *"A New Kind of War": America's Global Strategy and the Truman Doctrine in Greece,* 17–31. For another appraisal see Lawrence S. Wittner, *American Intervention in Greece, 1943–1949.*

4. Kennan interview, October 31, 1974, in John Lewis Gaddis, *Strategies of Containment: A Critical Appraisal of Postwar American National Security Policy,* 54. Admiral Dennison did not think Kennan had any influence at the White House, "certainly not with President Truman" (Dennison oral history, 125–27). Clifford similarly recalled that Kennan had little influence (Clifford oral history, 86, 89). Elsey thought there was nothing new in the "X" article: "[W]hat he said there were the views that he was known to have had and indeed were largely shared by the administration. It wasn't as though he was proposing something brand new, a new course. As I recall it, my reaction was, 'Fine, this is exactly what our foreign policy is, the way we're going.' This is just simply expressing publicly what, in a somewhat blunter fashion than was normal, what the . . ." Q: "You did not see it as anything new?" A: "No" (George M. Elsey oral history, by Jerry N. Hess, 375–76). The present author has seen no reference to Kennan among all the presidential papers in the Truman Library. A recent exploration of the question of novelty is Joseph M. Siracusa, "Will the Real Author of Containment Please Stand Up: The Strange Case of George Kennan and Frank Roberts," *Newsletter of the Society for Historians of American Foreign Relations* 22 (September 1991): 1–27. Roberts was Kennan's British counterpart in Moscow, and in dispatches of March 17 and 18, 1946, he reported almost identically what Kennan reported in the long telegram. Months later, on September 27, the Soviet ambassador in Washington, Nikolai V. Novikov, sent a long dispatch analyzing American foreign policy, and this dispatch was released by the Soviets in July 1990. See Kenneth M. Jensen, ed., *Origins of the Cold War: The Novikov, Kennan, and Roberts "Long Telegrams" of 1946;* see also John Lewis Gaddis, ed., "The Soviet Side of the Cold War: A Symposium," *Diplomatic History* 15 (1991): 523–63.

5. For the report see Arthur Krock, *Memoirs: Sixty Years on the Firing Line,* 419–82.

6. Quotations from 1, 77, original copy of Clifford-Elsey report in the Truman Library.

7. Truman to John N. Garner, September 21, 1946, president's secretary's files, box 187, "Russia 1945–46"; to Margaret Truman, in *Bess W. Truman,* 304.

8. *Off the Record,* 79–80.

9. Undated, president's secretary's files, box 60, "Campaign Strategy Speech Data."

10. "This is the first Cabinet meeting that I have attended where a definite decision was reached and clearly announced" (Leahy diary, March 7, 1947).

11. Charles E. Bohlen, *The Transformation of American Foreign Policy*, 86–87.

12. Joseph M. Jones, *The Fifteen Weeks (February 21–June 5, 1947)*, 159.

13. Jones was quite proud of the speech as he produced it (*Fifteen Weeks*, 148–70). For White House changes see Elsey oral history, by Hess, 297–98.

14. Thomas J. Schoenbaum, *Waging Peace and War: Dean Rusk in the Truman, Kennedy, and Johnson Years*, 149. Kennan thought any reference to the UN would only complicate matters. Acheson systematically excised many references to the UN from early drafts (Bruce R. Kuniholm, "Loy Henderson, Dean Acheson, and the Origins of the Truman Doctrine," in Douglas Brinkley, ed., *Dean Acheson and the Making of U.S. Foreign Policy*, 75).

15. Jones, *Fifteen Weeks*, 192–93.

16. Undated, Clifford papers.

17. Gaddis, "Was the Truman Doctrine a Real Turning Point?" 392.

18. Acheson, *Present at the Creation*, p. xvii.

19. Bohlen, *Witness to History*, 259.

20. Years later, on May 21, 1952, the president wrote the principal of Wheeler High School, in Wheeler, Indiana, who had asked him what people—Stalin, Churchill, Queen Elizabeth II—impressed him most: "I have met a great many distinguished people of this age since I have been President. I have been closely associated with General George C. Marshall, whom I consider one of the great men of this age." In the next sentence he mentioned President Roosevelt (president's personal files, box 608).

21. Truman interview, August 30, 1949, by Daniels, 8.

22. Robert H. Ferrell, *George C. Marshall*, 107–8; Dobney, ed., *Selected Papers of Will Clayton*, 198, 201–4, 208–9, 213–14.

23. Forrest Pogue, "Marshall and Acheson: The State Department Years, 1945–1949," in Brinkley, ed., *Dean Acheson*, 225. Acheson told Pogue the same thing.

24. Fred I. Greenstein, *The Hidden-Hand Presidency: Eisenhower as Leader* (New York: Basic Books, 1982).

25. Clifford, *Counsel to the President*, 144.

26. Ferrell, *George C. Marshall*, 128–29.

27. Richard M. Freeland, *The Truman Doctrine and the Origins of McCarthyism: Foreign Policy, Domestic Politics, and International Security, 1946–1948*, 276–87, contends that the administration used the war scare of early 1948 to get the initial Marshall Plan appropriation through Congress. The author of this well-written and in many ways thoughtful book says: "There is no reason to believe that the President was fearful of war in March 1948." Also: "It seems impossible to avoid the conclusion that the war scare of 1948 was yet another exercise in crisis politics by the Truman administration" (both quotations, 286). But Freeland took this conclusion from the Truman memoirs, not being able to use presidential commentaries that came to light in recent years, for which see below. For the same theme see Frank Kofsky, *Harry S. Truman and the War Scare of 1948: A Successful Campaign to Deceive the Nation*.

28. John Gimbel, *The Origins of the Marshall Plan*, 4.

29. Walter Millis, ed., *The Forrestal Diaries*, 379.

30. President's secretary's files, box 154, "Cabinet-meetings, 1946–1950." Two days before the Clay cable the president wrote his daughter, Margaret, "a long, hair-raising letter" in which he said there might be war with the Soviet Union in thirty days. *Bess W. Truman*, 315–16. Kofsky, *Harry S. Truman and the War Scare of 1948*, 233–68, asserts that the administration invented the scare, partly to assist the aircraft industry, which

without government orders would have passed into bankruptcy, but mainly to get the first Marshall Plan appropriations through Congress so as to influence the Italian elections. He cites a comment by Clay to the general's biographer, Jean Edward Smith, *Lucius D. Clay: An American Life*, 466–68, that the often-quoted cable of March 5 to the director of army intelligence in Washington, Lieutenant General Stephen J. Chamberlin, in which Clay said war might come "with dramatic suddenness," was only an effort to gain congressional support for a draft: Clay did not believe war was imminent. He remarks how Forrestal seized upon the cable and made the most of it, even leaking it to the *Saturday Evening Post,* and that Clay was moved to protest to General Bradley. But the war scare clearly existed. Moreover, Clay's assistant for intelligence, who sent the cable, has disputed his former chief's remark to Smith, and related that the cable was no ploy.

31. *Off the Record,* 145; Robert D. Murphy, *Diplomat among Warriors,* 316.

32. Daniel F. Harrington, "The Indecisive Mr. Truman: The President and the Berlin Blockade" (paper presented at the Northern Great Plains History Conference, Duluth, Minnesota, 1980, courtesy of the author), 3–4. For the blockade there is an enormous literature but see the same author's "American Policy in the Berlin Crisis of 1948–1949."

33. *Off the Record,* 148–49; *The Journals of David E. Lilienthal: The Atomic Energy Years, 1945–1950,* 406.

34. Truman to Eleanor Roosevelt, March 16, 1948, *Off the Record,* 125–26.

35. Truman planned for four months of service the first year, two the second, followed by membership in the reserves, with thirty days each year for three years in summers, or the National Guard for a similar period, and after that a furlough to the regular reserve for three more years. He would have required attendance of individuals with minor physical defects (Memorandum dictated while at Olympia, Washington, June 23, 1945, president's secretary's files, box 146, "Agencies-Military Training").

36. Draft speech, undelivered, April 17 (?), 1948, *Off the Record,* 132.

37. A man of great strength of purpose, Bevin was the leading European statesman in inviting the United States to take part in Europe's problem of security. He first had talked to Marshall and then made a statement in the House of Commons. For his signal contribution see Alan Bullock, *Ernest Bevin: Foreign Secretary, 1945–1951;* Richard A. Best, Jr., *"Co-operation with Like-Minded Peoples": British Influences on American Security Policy, 1945–1949.* The literature on how Britain led the United States into NATO is extensive, for which see Terry H. Anderson, *The United States, Great Britain, and the Cold War, 1944–1947,* a foundational volume; together with Robert M. Hathaway, *Ambiguous Partnership: Britain and America, 1944–1947;* Elisabeth Barker, *The British between the Superpowers, 1945–1950* (Toronto: University of Toronto Press, 1983); Donald Cameron Watt, *Succeeding John Bull: America in Britain's Place, 1900–1975* (Cambridge: Cambridge University Press, 1984); Henry Butterfield Ryan, *The Vision of Anglo-America: The US-UK Alliance and the Emerging Cold War, 1943–1946;* David Dimbleby and David Reynolds, *An Ocean Apart* (New York: Random House, 1988); and Robert H. Ferrell, "The Formation of the Alliance, 1948–1949," in Lawrence S. Kaplan, ed., *American Historians and the Atlantic Alliance,* 11–32.

38. For the treaty's awkwardnesses with the UN Charter see Lawrence S. Kaplan, *The United States and NATO: The Formative Years,* 3, 44, 48, 116–17; Achilles oral history, 20–21.

39. Bohlen, *Witness to History,* 269; Truman, *Years of Trial and Hope,* 212–17; Daniels,

Man of Independence, 28–29. Memory differed over what the president said to his staff when he listened to their objections to canceling the mission. Carr recalled he merely said in a pleasant voice, "Well, maybe it isn't that bad," and left the room (Albert Z. Carr, *Truman, Stalin, and Peace,* 119–20).

40. Clifford interview, October 26, 1949, by Daniels, 49.

41. *My Name Is Tom Connally,* 331; Vandenberg diary, undated, together with entries of October 5, 8, 1948, in Arthur H. Vandenberg, Jr., and Joe Alex Morris, eds., *The Private Papers of Senator Vandenberg,* 456–59.

42. Vandenberg diary, October 22, 23, in Vandenberg and Morris, eds., *Private Papers of Senator Vandenberg,* 459–60.

43. C. V. Wedgwood, *William the Silent* (London: Jonathan Cape, 1967), 35, quoted in Acheson, *Present at the Creation,* xvii.

44. John Lewis Gaddis, "The Tragedy of Cold War History."

45. Ayers diary, October 18, 1947, *Truman in the White House,* 203–4; Donovan, *Conflict and Crisis,* 400; *Public Papers, 1948,* 329.

46. For Stalin see Robert C. Tucker, *Stalin in Power: The Revolution from Above, 1928–1941,* the distinguished second volume of a proposed three-volume biography by the leading American scholar; Dimitri Volkogonov, *Stalin: Triumph and Tragedy,* by a Russian colonel general responsible for the army's political education, whose father was shot in the purges; and Alan Bullock, *Hitler and Stalin: Parallel Lives,* by the leading British scholar. Truman's remark about Molotov is in a memorandum of June 2, 1954, *Off the Record,* 305. For Soviet foreign ministers see Arkady Vaksberg, *Stalin's Prosecutor: The Life of Andrei Vyshinsky;* Gromyko, *Memories,* 314–18, 322.

47. Milovan Djilas, *Conversations with Stalin,* 182.

48. Kathryn Weathersby, "New Findings on the Korean War," *Bulletin of the Cold War International History Project,* Woodrow Wilson Center (fall 1993): 1, 14–18; see also the same author's "Soviet Aims in Korea and the Origins of the Korean War, 1945–1950: New Evidence from Russian Archives" and "The Soviet Role in the Early Phase of the Korean War: New Documentary Evidence."

49. *Khrushchev Remembers: The Glasnost Tapes,* 100–101.

Chapter Thirteen. Whistle-Stop

1. Donovan, *Conflict and Crisis,* 401. Donovan's source was Henry Nicholson of the secret service, who was present. Truman's memory was that "I got him into a corner and told him, 'You're one hell of a fellow. Here I am trying to do everything I can to carry out your father's policies. You've got no business trying to pull the rug out from under me'" (interview, November 12, 1949, by Jonathan Daniels, 69). Years later Truman remembered: "And I took him in the back room and told him that he ought to have his head punched because if his father hadn't had the support of the people whom he was trying to malign right then and there, he'd never have been president in the first place; and that if he felt like taking it to the conclusion, that's just what he'd get, and he went out with the others so he wouldn't get punched" (Truman interview, October 21, 1959, "Mr. Citizen" file, box 2, folder 2).

2. Ayers diary, July 6, 1948, *Truman in the White House,* 264. Eisenhower wanted a nomination by both parties and asked Chester Bowles if it would be possible. See Bowles's autobiography, *Promises to Keep,* 173. Bowles thought him naive, but one

wonders, for he possessed enormous appeal. He might have stampeded both conventions if he had made just a little more effort. Truman took him seriously and had Clifford and Secretary of the Army Royall draft an unambiguous statement for Eisenhower to send to Pepper, the senator most actively opposing Truman's nomination (*Counsel to the President*, 214). See also Senator Pepper's autobiography, *Eyewitness to a Century*, chap. 5, "Dump Truman," 126–68, together with Krock, *Memoirs*, 242–44. Dewey, too, took Eisenhower seriously, and at one point he went to see the general with a lawyer-like assessment of reasons he should not permit anyone to drag his name through the mud of politics (Richard Norton Smith, *Thomas E. Dewey and His Times*, 481).

    3. Evans oral history. Mrs. Truman asked Clark Clifford the same question: "Do you think that Harry really believes he is going to win?" (*Counsel to the President*, 189). Early in October the president entertained a small group of writers employed by the national committee to help with campaign speeches. "The most vivid memory I have is, I would say it was probably nearly nine thirty when we said good night to the President, when he was ready to go upstairs, and he went around and shook the hand of everybody and said, if he said it once he said it three or four times, 'On election day we'll all celebrate together.' And he said it with the firmest of convictions. This was a small group. It was not the usual talk for public consumption. This was his firm belief. I remember catching the expression on Mrs. Truman's face at that moment, which was quite clear, that she herself didn't think this would happen. And on Margaret's face there was the same thing" (Johannes Hoeber oral history, by Jerry N. Hess, 42). "Mother was pessimistic about his chances. Not once throughout the spring or summer of 1948, or even in the fall when the campaign was picking up steam, did I hear her express any confidence in Harry Truman's election. When I or anyone else among the tiny band of true believers told Dad he was going to win in spite of the polls or the newspapers or the empty campaign chest, Mother remained silent" (M. Truman, *Bess W. Truman*, 318).

    4. The rest of the verse was, "Harvest the turnips the 25th of October, drunk or sober."

    5. Some years later two researchers asked the former president what was his most successful speech. Answer: "I believe it was my acceptance address at the Democratic National Convention. That speech was something of a personal spiritual milestone. From that time on, I never doubted that we would win" (interview, May 23, 1953, in Eugene E. White and Clair R. Henderlider, "What Harry S. Truman Told Us about His Speaking," *Quarterly Journal of Speech* 60 [1960]: 39).

    6. Clifford oral history, 281.

    7. Donovan, *Conflict and Crisis*, 436.

    8. For William O. Douglas's reasons for refusing Truman see his *The Court Years, 1939–1975*, 289–90. Generally his memoirs are hostile to Truman.

    9. Irwin Ross, *The Loneliest Campaign: The Truman Victory of 1948*, 209–10.

    10. Donovan, *Conflict and Crisis*, 412.

    11. For parades Truman often sat up on the top of the backseat of a convertible, but Dewey refused to do that sort of thing, despite pleas from cameramen. Truman waved his hat, but not Dewey. In Barstow, California, a photographer for the *Washington Star* arranged for a cowboy to ride up to the rear platform of Dewey's train and present the candidate with a hat. "Do you think anyone had to arrange such a stunt with Truman? Not on your life" (Ollie Atkins, *Washington Star*, November [?], 1948, vertical file). Atkins said the only problem in photographing Truman was his glasses, which bounced light,

and that Dewey did not photograph well with a wide grin—indeed, he was very bad on close-ups—because his teeth were too widely spaced (he had lost some front teeth in a high school football scrimmage and refused to have remedial dental work).

12. Truman interview, September 9, 1959, "Mr. Citizen" file, box 2, folder 1.

13. Jules Abels, *Out of the Jaws of Victory*, 223; Harold Lew Wallace, "The Campaign of 1948," 322.

14. Russell was not about to leave the Democratic party; shortly before the election he announced he would vote for Truman (Gilbert C. Fite, *Richard B. Russell, Jr.: Senator from Georgia*, 239–41). For the Hastie affair see Ross, *Loneliest Campaign*, 232.

15. See Gary A. Donaldson, "Who Wrote the Clifford Memo? The Origins of Campaign Strategy in the Truman Administration."

16. See chap. 14, 293–95.

17. Robbins, *Bess and Harry*, 125.

18. Ross, *Loneliest Campaign*, 238. The best study of Truman and civil rights is Donald R. McCoy and Richard T. Ruetten, *Quest and Response: Minority Rights and the Truman Administration*.

19. Rear platform remarks at Bridgeport, Conn., October 28, 1948, *Public Papers, 1948*, 898.

20. Address at the state fairgrounds, Raleigh, N.C., October 19, 1948, *Public Papers, 1949*, 823–24.

21. For a fair account see Susan M. Hartmann, *Truman and the 80th Congress*.

22. Truman quoted in Abels, *Out of the Jaws of Victory*, 226.

23. Nixon oral history, 624.

24. "Give 'em hell," vertical file. In *Mr. Citizen*, 160, the president remembered that this litany started in Seattle.

25. Evans oral history, 523–24.

26. Dennison oral history, 55.

27. Jack [John M.] Redding, *Inside the Democratic Party*, 276–77.

28. Phillips, *Truman Presidency*, 246–47.

29. The telegram continued: "THE DEMOCRATIC NATIONAL COMMITTEE HAS AGREED TO FURNISH THE TOOTHPICKS TO BE USED BY THE GUESTS WHO (IT IS FEARED) WILL REQUIRE MONTHS TO GET THE LAST OF THE CROW OUT OF THEIR TEETH. WE HOPE YOU WILL CONSENT TO DELIVER THE ADDRESS OF THE EVENING. AS THE DEAN OF AMERICAN ELECTION FORECASTERS (AND THE ONLY ACCURATE ONE) IT IS MUCH DESIRED THAT YOU SHARE WITH YOUR COLLEAGUES THE SECRET OF YOUR ANALYTICAL SUCCESS. DRESS FOR GUEST OF HONOR, WHITE TIE; FOR OTHERS—SACK CLOTH. THE WASHINGTON POST WILL BE HAPPY TO ARRANGE THIS DINNER FOR ANY DATE THAT SUITS YOUR CONVENIENCE AND PLEASURE" (Telegram of November 3).

30. Joseph C. Goulden, *The Best Years, 1945–1950*, 421.

31. Ross, *Loneliest Campaign*, 251–52, 315; Rensis Likert, "The Polls: Straw Votes or Scientific Instruments," *American Psychologist* 3 (1948): 556–57.

32. Max Lowenthal diary, November 5, 1948, Lowenthal papers, box C–27–2, archives of the University of Minnesota, Minneapolis. Lowenthal that day talked with Murray, who told him of the above conversations.

33. Herbert Brownell and John Burke, *Advising Ike: The Memoirs of Attorney General Herbert Brownell* (Lawrence: University Press of Kansas, 1993), 83–84.

34. Richard O. Davies, "Whistle-Stopping through Ohio."

Chapter Fourteen. Fair Deal

1. Redding, *Inside the Democratic Party*, 149.
2. Clifford oral history, 347–49.
3. Ayers papers, box 24, "Personal, Truman, Harry S."
4. Donald R. McCoy describes the Celler-Kefauver Act as possibly the most important antitrust legislation enacted during all the years since passage of the Clayton Antitrust Act (*The Presidency of Harry S. Truman*, 181).
5. "I propose no controls over American farmers or their farms which are not now in the law. . . . As a matter of fact, my program works against controls by disposing of the surpluses which give rise to the need for control" (Charles F. Brannan on the radio program *On Trial*, February 24, 1950, vertical file). See also Allen J. Matusow, *Farm Policies and Politics in the Truman Years.*
6. See Richard O. Davies, *Housing Reform during the Truman Administration*, 136–37, 142.
7. Letter of September 8, 1949, *Off the Record*, 165–66; Truman to Sam Wear, October 25, 1950, vertical file; Truman diary, January 9, 1954, *Off the Record*, 303. See Monte M. Poen, *Harry S. Truman versus the Medical Lobby: The Genesis of Medicare.*
8. McCoy, *Presidency of Harry S. Truman*, 186. For the object of Truman's scorn see Fite, *Richard B. Russell, Jr.*
9. Charles S. Murphy oral history, by Jerry N. Hess, 253ff.
10. Ayers diary, April 28, *Truman in the White House*, 347.
11. Alonzo L. Hamby, *Beyond the New Deal: Harry S. Truman and American Liberalism*, 512, offers an interesting reason for the Fair Deal's failure. The founding fathers, he argues, envisioned the president as directing foreign policy but not so for domestic. "Their design for domestic problems . . . was very different; it was based on a diffusion of power and responsibility designed to give important interests a veto over legislation which might affect them adversely. Throughout the history of the Republic, the system has functioned about as planned."
12. Larry Grothaus, "Kansas City Blacks, Harry Truman and the Pendergast Machine," *Missouri Historical Review* 69 (1974–1975): 65–82.
13. Truman to Margaret Truman, April 7, 1937, general file, pertaining to family, business, and personal affairs, box 10.
14. William C. Berman, *The Politics of Civil Rights in the Truman Administration*, 10, quoting from Samuel Lubell, *The Future of American Politics*, 2d. ed. rev. (Garden City, N.Y.: Doubleday, 1956).
15. Mary Jane Truman interview, by Jonathan Daniels, 35.
16. Undated, Mary Paxton Keeley papers, box 1. The blank is in the original.
17. Ayers diary, October 13, 1945, *Truman in the White House*, 89.
18. Walter White, *A Man Called White: The Autobiography of Walter White*, 330–31.
19. Truman moved "only because he had no choice: Negro votes and the demands of the cold war, not simple humanitarianism—though there may have been some of that—produced whatever token gains Negroes were to make in the years Truman inhabited the White House" (Berman, *Politics of Civil Rights*, 240). But see Richard S. Kirkendall's memorial address at the University of Missouri, 1973, in *Harry S Truman, Late a President of the United States*, 107, which asserts that Truman "did more on behalf of the civil rights of black Americans than any of his predecessors in the twentieth century." Barton J. Bernstein in Alonzo L. Hamby, ed., *Harry S. Truman and the Fair Deal*

(Lexington, Mass.: D. C. Heath, 1974), 60, remarks that "his advocacy of rights for Negroes was unmatched by any twentieth-century president." McCoy and Ruetten, *Quest and Response*, 349, conclude, "The upshot was not a revolution in the lives of America's minority peoples, but by the end of the Truman administration substantial progress had been made." For a recent appraisal supporting these judgments see William E. Leuchtenburg, "The Conversion of Harry Truman."

20. Elsey oral history, by Hess, 449–50; Murphy oral history, by Hess, 226–27; Clark oral history, 140. Clark may have remembered the drafting of the president's message to Congress just after the calling of the special session in the summer of 1948. During one of the speech sessions the attorney general sent in a message concerning the civil rights passages: he wanted to soften them, so as not to excite congressmen from the South. Where the draft introduced the president's comments on civil rights with the words, "I urge," Clark wanted to say, "call attention of the Congress to." As soon as this was read to the president the answer was "No" (Lowenthal diary, July 26, 1948).

21. Truman interview, August 30, 1949, by Daniels.

22. Lowenthal diary, May 18, 1948. Alonzo Fields was chief White House steward during Truman's presidency, and served under Hoover, Roosevelt, and for a short time Eisenhower; he had no doubt of Truman's good will. Hoover hardly noticed the White House help, Roosevelt likewise (he eliminated separate white and colored dining rooms by making the help all black, but when black helpers went to Hyde Park they ate in the kitchen). But after Truman left the White House and Fields removed to Boston, whenever the former president came to the city Fields would find out what hotel Truman was staying in and then place himself in a position "where he might see me, and he always does. He will call out to me amidst all the people he is with, 'Hello there, Fields,' and make his way to me and shake hands. Then he will say, 'Come on up. I want to talk to you.' . . . I would not have dared to assume that President Roosevelt would expect to see me anywhere and recognize me in public. Of course it has been so long since I have seen President Hoover that I doubt that he would even remember my name" (*My 21 Years in the White House*, 186).

23. Steinberg, *Man from Missouri*, 303–4.

24. Vivian Truman to Truman, February 6, Truman to Vivian Truman, February 9, president's secretary's files, box 332, "Truman, J. Vivian," folder 2.

25. Interview with William Hillman and David Noyes, September 10, 1959, "Mr. Citizen" file, box 2, folder 2.

26. Truman diary, July 13, 1948, *Off the Record*, 142. For the floor fight over the Humphrey-Biemiller proposal see McCoy and Ruetten, *Quest and Response*, 123–27.

27. Richard S. Kirkendall in Allen Weinstein and Moshe Ma'oz, eds., *Truman and the American Commitment to Israel*, 34.

28. Leuchtenburg, "Conversion of Harry Truman," 62; Berman, *Politics of Civil Rights*, 88.

29. McCoy and Ruetten, *Quest and Response*, 251–52; for Executive Order No. 10308 (December 3, 1951) establishing a Committee on Government Contract Compliance, see 275–81.

30. On this general subject see Richard M Dalfiume, *Desegregation of the U.S. Armed Forces: Fighting on Two Fronts, 1939–1953;* also McCoy and Ruetten, *Quest and Response*, 221–50.

31. Berman, *Politics of Civil Rights*, 119–20. At a pre–press conference briefing with

the president, Max Lowenthal heard General Vaughan bring up the question of Bradley's statement. The president said he would have to talk to Bradley, and meanwhile said he had not seen Bradley's statement (Lowenthal diary, July 29, 1948).

32. Hamby, *Beyond the New Deal*, 343.

33. Eric F. Goldman, *The Crucial Decade* (New York: Knopf, 1956), 184.

34. Mark W. Clark, *From the Danube to the Yalu* (New York: Harper, 1954), 197–98, quoted in McCoy and Ruetten, *Quest and Response*, 241.

35. Vertical file.

36. For the British spies see below.

37. Allen Weinstein, *Perjury: The Hiss-Chambers Case*, is the best book.

38. The two clearly are related, for which see Earl Latham, *The Communist Controversy in Washington: From the New Deal to McCarthy*; Alan D. Harper, *The Politics of Loyalty: The White House and the Communist Issue, 1946–1952*; Robert Griffith, *The Politics of Fear: Joseph R. McCarthy and the Senate*; Athan G. Theoharis, *Seeds of Repression: Harry S. Truman and the Origins of McCarthyism*.

39. Hamby, *Beyond the New Deal*, 468.

40. Clifford, *Counsel to the President*, 175–78, 182.

41. See *Seattle Times*, December 26, 1972, vertical file.

42. Smith diary, May 11, 1945; *Off the Record*, 22.

43. For the above and following, see Morison oral history, 30, 36, 54–55.

44. For Corcoran see Donovan, *Conflict and Crisis*, 30; Kai Bird and Max Holland, "The Tapping of 'Tommy the Cork,'" *The Nation*, February 8, 1986, vertical file; Allan J. Lichtman, "Tommy the Cork: The Secret World of Washington's First Modern Lobbyist," *Washington Monthly*, February 1987, 41–49, vertical file.

45. *Truman Speaks*, 111.

46. Phillips, *Truman Presidency*, 377.

47. The annotated copy is filed with a letter from the president to Senator Estes Kefauver, June 30, 1952, president's secretary's files, box 128, "McCarran-Walter bill."

48. Truman to Charles Sawyer, April 20, 1950, president's secretary's files, box 155, "Commerce, Secy. of—Charles Sawyer."

49. Hamby, *Beyond the New Deal*, 396.

50. Truman to Joseph McCarthy, February 11 (?), 1950, *Off the Record*, 172.

51. Truman, *Years of Trial and Hope*, 233–34.

52. Truman, *Year of Decisions*, 379.

53. A. J. Granoff oral history, by J. R. Fuchs, 49, 56–58. Toward the end of his life Jacobson pointed out that he did not regard himself as a political Zionist and had never joined any Zionist organization (Frank J. Adler, *Roots in a Moving Stream: The Centennial History of Congregation B'nai Jehudah of Kansas City, 1870–1970*, 201).

54. Truman to Virginia Gildersleeve, October 15, 1945, official file, box 204; Truman to Joseph H. Ball, November 24, 1945, in Monte M. Poen, ed., *Strictly Personal and Confidential: The Letters Harry S. Truman Never Mailed*, 43; Truman to Edwin W. Pauley, October 22, 1946, president's secretary's files, box 184, "Palestine—Jewish Immigration."

55. Peter Grose, *Israel in the Mind of America* (New York: Knopf, 1982), 229; Adler, *Roots in a Moving Stream*, 209n; presidential comment on a memorandum for the president by David K. Niles, May 12, 1947, president's secretary's files, box 184, "Foreign-Palestine."

56. Granoff oral history, 65; for the Arvey telephone call see *Oregonian*, November 23, 1972, vertical file; Millis, ed., *Forrestal Diaries*, 346; memorandum to Truman by

Matthew J. Connelly, November 25, 1949, White House central files, confidential file, box 30, "The President." Loy Henderson remembered a telephone conversation with the deputy head of the delegation to the UN, Herschel Johnson. When Henderson asked if American representatives had done any "arm-twisting," Johnson burst into tears: "Loy, forgive me for breaking down like this, but Dave Niles called us here a couple of days ago and said that the President had instructed him to tell us that, by God, he wanted us to get busy and get all the votes that we possibly could; that there would be hell if the voting went the wrong way" (Michael J. Cohen, *Truman and Israel*, 168).

57. Granoff oral history, 37–40.

58. In an interview with Jonathan Daniels, October 26, 1949, 45, Clark Clifford blamed Marshall for the confusion: "Marshall didn't know his . . . from a hole in the ground. Marshall left every one of those who had done this thing to the President in power, not a hair singed." See also Ross diary, March 29, 1948; *Off the Record*, 126–27; Schoenbaum, *Waging Peace and War*, 171–72. A recent article by Bruce J. Evensen, "A Story of 'Ineptness': The Truman Administration's Struggle to Shape Conventional Wisdom on Palestine at the Beginning of the Cold War," *Diplomatic History* 15 (1991): 353–58, contends that public opinion moved the president away from trusteeship. See also by the same author, *Truman, Palestine, and the Press: Shaping Conventional Wisdom at the Beginning of the Cold War*, 151–75. This is possible, but Truman's testimony at the time was all to the fact of surprise. What seems evident is that during the Bermuda trip he agreed to trusteeship, believing the department would tell him before going over to it, also that time might solve everything. He evidently did not remember signing off on the new policy and may have signed inadvertently.

59. Clifford told Jonathan Daniels, "I picked up my books and papers. I had lost cases before. I felt, however, that I had really presented the case, and I was outraged by the terrible . . . the Boss had gotten in April [March]" (interview of October 26, 1949, 46). When he spoke before a joint session of Congress on the centenary of Truman's birth he still recalled the occasion: "Then the President said 'Clifford will make his presentation' and I made it. And as I made it, General Marshall's face got redder and redder and redder, and finally at the end he exploded. He said, 'I don't understand what is going on here.' He said, 'We didn't come over to have an emotional experience of these various elements; we came over to consider a complicated foreign policy problem and to consider certain international laws that are applicable to this issue'" (98th Cong., 2d sess., *Congressional Record* 130, no. 58, 3451). See also Clifford, *Counsel to the President*, 9–15, 24. Marshall never spoke to Clifford again. Some of Marshall's friends told him he ought to resign. "No, gentlemen," he said. "You do not take a post of this sort and then resign when the man who has the constitutional responsibility for making a decision makes one. You can resign at any other time for any other reason, or for no reason at all, but not that one" (Rusk, *As I Saw It*, 151).

60. Clifford, *Counsel to the President*, 17.

61. Schoenbaum, *Waging Peace and War*, 177.

62. Dealing with Bevin on Palestine, Douglas often found himself in the middle of shouting matches. See Robert P. Browder and Thomas G. Smith, *Independent: A Biography of Lewis W. Douglas*, 303–17. See also James G. McDonald's *My Mission in Israel, 1948–1951* (New York: Simon and Schuster, 1951), 24–26; Ayers diary, January 22, March 21, 1949, *Truman in the White House*, 291, 300.

63. Truman to Dean Alfange, May 18, 1948, president's secretary's files, box 184, "Palestine 1948–1952."

Chapter Fifteen. The Korean War

1. See the articles and working paper cited above, chap. 12, n. 48, by Kathryn Weathersby, who gained access to a foreign ministry background report, "On the Korean War, 1950–1953, and the Armistice Negotiations," dated August 9, 1966, citing pertinent telegrams showing Kim's persistence. It seems unlikely that the foreign ministry would deceive itself. A different interpretation of Stalin's and Kim's responsibility is offered by General Dimitri Volkogonov, military adviser to President Boris Yeltsin, and Gavril Korotkov, senior fellow at the Russian defense ministry's Institute for Military History, for which see "Secrets of the Korean War: Forty Years Later, Evidence Points to Stalin's Deep Involvement," *U.S. News and World Report*, August 9, 1993, 45–47. Korotkov has said he has seen still-classified documents in the Russian defense ministry indicating that Stalin and Kim talked in March 1949. He believes Stalin pushed Kim into attacking and promises publication of a manuscript entitled "The Generalissimo's Last War."

2. Jonathan Spence, *To Change China: Western Advisers in China, 1620–1960* (Boston: Little, Brown, 1969), 248.

3. Russell D. Buhite, *Patrick J. Hurley and American Foreign Policy*, 253–81; Hurley to Truman, November 26, 1945, Truman to Hurley, November 27, official files, box 292.

4. Ayers diary, May 15, 1949, *Truman in the White House*, 310; conversation of May 11, 1949, *Journals of David E. Lilienthal*, 2:525; comment by General Marshall at a round-table discussion in the department of state, October 8, 1949, in 82d Cong, 1st sess., U.S. Senate, *Hearings of the Committee on the Judiciary on the Institute of Pacific Relations*, 15 parts (Washington: Government Printing Office, 1951–1952), 5:1655; Truman to Senator Vandenberg, March 27, 1950, official files, box 184.

5. In debate leading to the China Aid Act of 1948, Representative Judd said in the House, "Not for one moment has anyone contemplated sending a single combat soldier in. . . . So it is important to make clear when we speak of military aid . . . it is supplies, training and advice, nothing further" (Tang Tsou, *America's Failure in China, 1941–1950*, 363). In a Senate debate in June 1949, Senator Connally asked Senator Owen Brewster whether he and other senators would have sent an army into China. Brewster responded, "I never proposed to send an army into China." On the same occasion Senator William F. Knowland stated without contradiction that "there has never been a proposal on the part of those who are critical of the policy we have pursued in the Far East to send an army to China" (ibid., 363–64).

6. See Gary May, *China Scapegoat: The Diplomatic Ordeal of John Carter Vincent*. For the recognition issue see Nancy Bernkopf Tucker, *Patterns in the Dust: Chinese-American Relations and the Recognition Controversy, 1949–1950;* the same author's "China's Place in the Cold War: The Acheson Plan," in Brinkley, ed., *Dean Acheson*, 109–32; and Edwin W. Martin, *Divided Counsel: The Anglo-American Response to Communist Victory in China*. In 1951 Truman told William Hillman, "The red government in China are just a bunch of bandits. They have murdered our citizens over there, confiscated the property of the United States in all the great cities and I can't deal with a bunch of thugs and murderers, and don't intend to deal with them as long as I am President" (interview of December 14, president's secretary's files, box 209, "Mr. President").

7. Ronald J. Caridi, *The Korean War and American Politics: The Republican Party as a Case Study;* John Edward Wilz, "The Making of Mr. Truman's War," in *The Historical Reillumination on the Korean War* (Seoul: War Memorial Service, 1990), 106 (the book is

the proceedings of an international conference, June 24–27, 1990, commemorating the fortieth anniversary of the opening of the war); Matthew B. Ridgway, *The Korean War*, 7; Omar N. Bradley and Clay Blair, *A General's Life*, 528; the paper dated November 14, 1949, is in president's secretary's files, box 170, "PSF Subject"; John J. Muccio oral history, by Richard D. McKinzie, 14.

8. Wilz, "Making of Mr. Truman's War," 112.

9. For the activities of Maclean see Verne W. Newton, *The Cambridge Spies: The Untold Story of Maclean, Philby, and Burgess in America*. Guy Burgess was a fellow diplomat.

10. Wilz, "Making of Mr. Truman's War," 114.

11. Charles S. Murphy oral history, by Hugh Heclo and Anna Nelson, 53–54. The literature on NSC-68 has increased to sizable proportions ever since the document itself was published in the *Naval War College Review* 33 (1980): 34–57. An early account was by Samuel F. Wells, Jr., "Sounding the Tocsin: NSC 68 and the Soviet Threat," *International Security* 4 (1979): 116–58. More recently has been Steven W. Guerrier, "NSC-68 and the Truman Rearmament, 1950–1953"; Paul H. Nitze, *From Hiroshima to Glasnost: At the Center of Decision*; Ernest R. May, ed., *American Cold War Strategy: Interpreting NSC 68*; and the excellent short accounts in Samuel R. Williamson, Jr., and Steven L. Rearden, *The Origins of U.S. Nuclear Strategy, 1945–1953*, 133–38, and Rearden's "Frustrating the Kremlin Design: Acheson and NSC 68," in Brinkley, ed., *Dean Acheson*, 159–75. It is clear that at the outset little happened with NSC-68. Keyserling and his fellow member of the Council of Economic Advisers, John Bates Clark (Nourse had resigned and there was no new third member), saw no harm in raising the defense budget a billion or two (Keyserling oral history, by Jerry N. Hess, 113–15). Truman was willing to support an extra half-billion for the $13 billion budget for the fiscal year 1951 (July 1, 1950–June 30, 1951). He told a press conference on May 4, 1950, that one could expect a smaller military budget (tentatively $12.1 billion) for fiscal 1952 because of the effect of foreign aid.

12. Thomas J. McCormick, *America's Half-Century: United States Foreign Policy in the Cold War*, 72–98. This shrewd analysis surely errs in its overestimate of the importance of NSC-68 and also in saying that as the Truman administration confronted the question of what to do it had a choice (negotiate with the Soviets, concentrate on the dollar gap and lower the U.S. tariff, undergo massive militarization). That the militarization during the Korean War assisted the Western European and Japanese markets seems indisputable. But it was no choice—it was happenstance.

13. *Dear Bess*, 561–62.

14. For the speeches see *Public Papers, 1950*, 464–68, 473–77.

15. Philip D. Lagerquist, "Mr. Truman and His Library," *Whistle Stop* 11.4 (1983).

16. Webb to John W. Snyder, April 25, 1975, Webb papers, box 456, "General Correspondence-S, 1973–75," folder 2. The literature of the origins of the Korean War is huge, and the best recourse is the review article by Rosemary Foot, "Making Known the Unknown War: Policy Analysis of the Korean Conflict in the Last Decade." Notable in the literature is Bruce Cumings's two-volume *The Origins of the Korean War* (vol. 1, *Liberation and the Emergence of Separate Regimes, 1945–1947*, and vol. 2, *The Roaring of the Cataract, 1947–1950*). Cumings gives primacy to the civil aspects of the conflict and undertakes to demonstrate that the North Koreans managed the attack with slight external involvement and initially had widespread support from South Koreans. He believes that Korea was a part of a worldwide conflict between socialism

and capitalism, manifested within the United States as a struggle between nationalists and internationalists. Secretary of State Acheson, he says, threw the victory to a coalition of capitalists and internationalists. But see William Whitney Stueck, Jr., *The Road to Confrontation: American Policy toward China and Korea, 1947–1950* and "The Korean War as International History," *Diplomatic History* 10 (1986): 291–309, in which Stueck wrote that Kim was hardly independent: "Mao provided him with experienced manpower, and Stalin supplied the airplanes and heavy equipment that gave Korea its margin of superiority over the South. North Korea may have been an assertive pawn in an international chess game, but it was a pawn nonetheless" (294). The 1993 revelations from the Russian archives support Stueck. See also the excellent book by Charles M. Dobbs, *The Unwanted Symbol: American Foreign Policy, the Cold War, and Korea, 1945–1950;* James I. Matray, *The Reluctant Crusade: American Foreign Policy in Korea, 1941–1950;* Rosemary Foot, *The Wrong War: American Policy and the Dimensions of the Korean Conflict, 1950–1953;* Burton I. Kaufman, *The Korean War: Challenges in Crisis, Credibility, and Command;* Peter Lowe, *The Origins of the Korean War.*

17. Robert J. Donovan, *Tumultuous Years: The Presidency of Harry S Truman, 1949–1953,* 195–96. The following account is from the above-mentioned letter from Webb to Snyder.

18. Frank Pace, Jr., oral history, by Jerry N. Hess, 70; Truman diary, *Off the Record,* 185; Murphy oral history, by Heclo and Nelson, 71.

19. Donovan, *Tumultuous Years,* 197; John D. Hickerson oral history, by Richard D. McKinzie, 108–9.

20. Schoenbaum, *Waging Peace and War,* 208.

21. For what follows see the letter by Ephraim Schulman to the editor of the *Newsletter of the Society for Historians of American Foreign Relations* 24 (March 1993): 47–48.

22. Pace oral history, 79. Pace's answer was, "Yes, Mr. President, but we can't be sure that they'll be with you over any period of time."

23. *My Name Is Tom Connally,* 346. The senator later changed his mind: "[T]he Republicans reiterated that Congress should have declared war instead of permitting the President to take action. I believed a declaration of war unnecessary because we were fighting to preserve the status quo of South Korea. However, when this attack became blatant later on, I wished that Congress had declared war against North Korea. As a matter of political strategy it would have been a wise move, despite the delay and hell-raising it might have caused" (351).

24. Charles S. Murphy oral history, by Charles T. Morrissey, 191–92. Almost whimsically, Murphy credited the idea of the conference to George Elsey, who went out as the advance man to Hawaii. "George had been a lieutenant in the Navy in World War II and when he went out to Hawaii he was dealing with naval people from Admiral Radford on down and he would tell them what they had to do. I think he got quite a kick out of it."

25. Ibid., 196–97.

26. Schoenbaum, *Waging Peace and War,* 213.

27. Dennison oral history, 149; Pace oral history, 93.

28. *Kansas City Times,* September 11 (?), 1979, vertical file.

29. Truman wrote the attenuated version to Ethel Noland, November 17, 1950, *Off the Record,* 199; Harry F. Rosenthal in *Kansas City Times,* September 7, 1979, published the other (vertical file).

30. Truman to Ethel Noland, November 17, 1950, *Off the Record,* 199.

31. Nor could he take his morning walks with perhaps, as happened in 1945, a single secret service man. "When I take my morning walk at 7 A.M. a guard walks beside me and he's always a fine man and a congenial conversationalist. Behind me are three more good men, athletes and *good shots,* across the street is another good man and a half block behind me is a car with maybe five or six well equipped guards. It is a hell of a way to live" (Truman diary, February 20, 1952, *Off the Record,* 239–40).

32. *Washington Post,* March 3, 1958, vertical file.

33. Hersey, *Aspects of the Presidency,* 56–57, 60.

34. Edward T. Folliard oral history, by Jerry N. Hess, 21. In 1951, Hume sold the letter to Bridgeport industrialist David Starring for $3,500. He had sponsored a concert by the soprano Lotte Lehmann and needed the money. Starring sold the letter to New Haven businessman Leonard J. Horowitz who allowed *Variety* to print the entire text:

> I've just read your lousy review of Margaret's concert. I've come to the conclusion that you are an "eight ulcer man on four ulcer pay."
>
> It seems to me that you are a frustrated old man who wishes he could have been successful. When you write such poppycock as that in the back section of the paper you work for it shows conclusively that you're off the beam and at least four of your ulcers are at work.
>
> Some day I hope to meet you. When that happens you'll need a new nose, a lot of beef steak for black eyes, and perhaps a supporter below!
>
> Pegler [Westbrook Pegler, the columnist], a guttersnipe, is a gentleman alongside you. I hope you'll accept that statement as a worse insult than a reflection on your ancestry. H.S.T.
>
> (*Independence Examiner,* August 18, 1966, vertical file)

The last sale of the letter was to Malcolm Forbes, Sr., whose son, Malcolm Forbes, Jr., gave the letter to President William J. Clinton for what eventually will be the Clinton Library.

In 1958, Hume appeared at the library in Independence and told Sergeant Story at the reception desk to tell Truman, then in his office, that he was "the music critic from the *Washington Post.*" Story went in, and a few seconds later Hume could hear Truman laughing. Story escorted Hume to the office, and the president and the critic spent maybe an hour, including a tour of the library. When Hume was about to leave, Truman jabbed him in the ribs and said, "I've had a lot of fun out of you and General MacArthur over the years. I hope you don't mind?" Hume gave assurance that he had never minded and was pleased to be in such "high-ranking company" (memorandum of a telephone conversation with Hume, December 21, 1979, by Elizabeth Safly, vertical file). Truman much enjoyed writing letters and, generally speaking, putting his ideas on paper; it was often his habit to write letters that he or his staff did not send. See Monte M. Poen, "'Rose, File it': What Harry Truman's Unmailed Letters Tell Us about the Thirty-third President," in William F. Levantrosser, ed., *Harry S. Truman: The Man from Independence,* 371–78, also Poen's edited *Strictly Personal and Confidential.* Jonathan Daniels remembered President Wilson's letter about knocking Bryan into a cocked hat and the letter during the first Cleveland administration by the British minister, Lionel Sackville-West, about the best way to help Britain being to vote for the Democrats. See his "How Truman Writes Those Letters," *Collier's,* February 24, 1951.

35. Truman diary, December 9, 1950, *Off the Record,* 204.

36. The Truman-Attlee talks must have been known almost immediately to Stalin and Mao, as Maclean in London received a written report each day, encoded in a one-time pad, and the uncensored transcript, together with a copy of the report Attlee made to his cabinet upon return. See Newton, *Cambridge Spies*, 297, 300.

37. John Garner to Truman, November 23, 1950, president's secretary's files, box 311, "Garner, John Nance." The army did not want to use nuclear weapons in Korea for three reasons: they would not be productive, for North Korea was mountainous and the terrain would limit the extent of explosions; there was a moral problem in using such weapons against a small country; if they proved ineffective their function as a shield for Europe would be lessened or lost (Pace oral history, 137). Moreover, the air force was just beginning to solve its problems with delivering nuclear weapons, for which see below.

38. The leading accounts of the Truman-MacArthur troubles are John W. Spanier, *The Truman-MacArthur Controversy and the Korean War*; D. Clayton James, *The Years of MacArthur: Triumph and Disaster, 1945–1964*; and Michael Schaller, *Douglas MacArthur: The Far Eastern General*. Schaller's book recently has caught attention of readers such as the present writer, who have found MacArthur's egoism unbearable; it is a highly critical biography. But see the gentle criticism of Sodei Rinjiro, "Janus-Faced Mac-Arthur," *Diplomatic History* 15 (1991): 621–29, who takes not only Schaller to task but also Howard B. Schonberger (*Aftermath of War: Americans and the Remaking of Japan, 1945–1952*): "Douglas MacArthur was a man of contradiction, not a simple opportunist. Just as he was a man of both war and peace, so also was his character Janus-faced. One side—vainglorious, pompous, arrogant, narcissistic—could very well be as self-serving as Schaller's devastating portrait. But MacArthur also had another side, magnanimous and inspirational, that could drive people toward higher purposes" (627–28).

39. Letter of June 30, 1942, in M. Truman, ed., *Letters from Father*, 44.

40. Ibid., 51.

41. *Off the Record*, 47.

42. Ayers diary, September 18, 1945, *Truman in the White House*, 81. At the staff conference that morning the president passed around a cartoon showing someone reading a newspaper with headlines crediting MacArthur with everything in Japan and a caption noting that Eisenhower had to have an army in Germany.

43. Nitze, *From Hiroshima to Glasnost*, 39.

44. For the Gerard letter see president's secretary's files, box 60, "Presidential Candidates"; Truman interview, October 21, 1959, "Mr. Citizen" file, box 2, folder 2.

45. Truman to Nellie Noland, October 13, 1950, *Off the Record*, 196; Donovan, *Tumultuous Years*, 283–84; Truman memorandum, "Wake Island," November 25, 1950, *Off the Record*, 200. Ambassador Muccio flew out to Wake with MacArthur, and during the flight the general sat down beside him and spoke of his disgust of "being summoned for political reasons." As Muccio put it, he was "mad as hell" (John J. Muccio oral history, by Jerry N. Hess, 79–80). For Truman's generally positive feeling about MacArthur after returning from Wake, see Ayers diary, October 19, 1950, *Truman in the White House*, 377.

46. Interview with William Hillman, January 9, 1952.

47. Pace oral history, 108; Truman memorandum, "Wake Island," November 25, 1950; Acheson interview, 1970, by Alden Whitman, *New York Times*, October 13, 1971.

48. Elsey oral history, by Hess, 305–6.

49. *Off the Record*, 210–11. Truman told Robert Nixon that Marshall said, "Mr. Presi-

dent, you should have fired that s.o.b. two years ago" (Nixon oral history, 828–29). The president placed a similar remark in his memoirs, expletive deleted. But see Doris M. Condit, *History of the Office of the Secretary of Defense: The Test of War, 1950–1953*, 103–5.

50. Pace oral history, 106; Donovan, *Tumultuous Years*, 356; Schoenbaum, *Waging Peace and War*, 221; Dean Rusk to Harold Stein, October 14, 1957, Stein papers, box 9, "Walter Millis." Schoenbaum has Bradley and Rusk going over to the White House (this had to be Blair House) late in the evening. Donovan relates that Harriman, Short, and Connelly accompanied them. Rusk, *As I Saw It*, 172, has the Truman quotation slightly differently: "There are a million Americans that could be president as well as I can, but goddammit, I am the president. And I am not going to turn this office over to my successor with its prerogatives impaired by an American general!"

51. Bradley and Blair, *A General's Life*, 637.

52. Dean Rusk to Harold Stein, October 14, 1957, Stein papers, box 9, "Walter Millis."

53. Roger W. Tubby in Heller, ed., *The Truman White House*, 87.

54. *New York Times*, December 31, 1972, quoted in *Harry S Truman, Late a President of the United States*, 59.

55. Francis O. Wilcox oral history, by Donald A. Ritchie, 118–19, Senate historical office, copy in Harry S. Truman Library. Senator J. William Fulbright released the full transcript of the hearings in 1973, for which see John Edward Wiltz, "The MacArthur Hearings of 1951: The Secret Testimony," 169–76.

56. Diary entry of November 28, 1959, in Robert H. Ferrell, ed., *The Eisenhower Diaries*, 373. For this interesting speculation see Bradley and Blair, *A General's Life*, 645.

Chapter Sixteen. A New Military Force

1. Truman to Fred I. Kent, April 14, 1949, president's secretary's files, box 125, "Kent, Fred I. (folder 1)"; McNeil oral history, 199.

2. Gilpatric oral history, 23. David H. Stowe recalled, "Stu Symington in those days was really one of the biggest hawks we had, and I can recall on at least two occasions the President asked Admiral Souers [executive secretary of the National Security Council, 1947–1950] and myself to visit with him and as he said 'tie a can to this rocket'" (Stowe oral history, by Morrissey, 76–77).

3. Draft speech (undelivered), April 17 (?), 1948, *Off the Record*, 133.

4. Undated memorandum in president's secretary's files, box 158, "Navy, Secy. of Marines."

5. Smith diary, February 28, March 20, 1946.

6. Quoted in Donovan, *Tumultuous Years*, 113.

7. Diary entry of February 19, 1949, Ferrell, ed., *The Eisenhower Diaries*, 157.

8. Ferrell, *Ill-Advised*, 63–70.

9. *The Forrestal Diaries* was a hastily declassified corpus of diary entries and miscellaneous materials.

10. Dennison oral history, 22.

11. Forrestal went to the president and said, "You've got to fire this fellow Webb. My God, he's a terrible operator." Truman said, "You had your chance" (Murphy oral history, by Morrissey, 81–83). For Forrestal see Arnold A. Rogow, *James Forrestal: A*

Study of Personality, Politics, and Policy; Townsend Hoopes and Douglas Brinkley, *Driven Patriot: The Life and Times of James V. Forrestal.*

12. Bradley and Blair, *A General's Life,* 474.

13. Bundy, *Danger and Survival,* 174, 186–87.

14. Smith diary, October 5, 1945; entries of July 21, 1948, February 14, 1949; *Journals of David E. Lilienthal,* 2:391–471.

15. Rusk, *As I Saw It,* 126.

16. For a detailed memorandum of the discussion by Forrestal see president's secretary's files, box 157, "Defense, Secy. of—James Forrestal—special letters"; see also Gregg Herken, *The Winning Weapon: The Atomic Bomb in the Cold War, 1945–1950,* 30–31; Bundy, *Danger and Survival,* 139.

17. Smith diary, October 5, 1945.

18. Considering Truman's closeness to Acheson it is impossible to believe. "In reference to the argument that the atomic energy proposals of 1946 were a ploy, I can say that on Mr. Acheson's part they certainly were anything but. I well remember his jubilant (for a time at least) conviction there was a way to deal with international control of atomic energy and can remember and see him coming into the outer office at the State Department aglow with enthusiasm for the Acheson-Lilienthal staff proposals. I also know his really deep disappointment that the proposals were (probably) mishandled and that they came to naught, realizing ultimately that they would have, regardless of any correct handling" (Barbara Evans to the author, June 30, 1972; Evans was Acheson's longtime personal assistant).

19. David Alan Rosenberg, "American Atomic Strategy and the Hydrogen Bomb Decision," 76.

20. Entry of June 30, 1948, *Journals of David E. Lilienthal,* 2:377.

21. Ibid., 390–91.

22. Millis, ed., *Forrestal Diaries,* 458.

23. Entry of May 11, 1949, *Journals of David E. Lilienthal,* 2:527–28.

24. Roger M. Anders, ed., *Forging the Atomic Shield: Excerpts from the Office Diary of Gordon E. Dean,* 107–9, 137–43.

25. Ayers diary, February 4, 1950, *Truman in the White House,* 340–41.

26. Acheson, *Present at the Creation,* 346.

27. Entry of January 31, 1950, *Journals of David E. Lilienthal,* 2:632; Steven L. Rearden, *History of the Office of the Secretary of Defense: The Formative Years, 1947–1950,* 453.

28. A few days later he told the morning conference that the United States had to make the H-bomb, although no one wanted to use it. He said the country needed it for bargaining purposes with the Russians (Ayers diary, February 4, 1950, *Truman in the White House,* 340–41).

29. For the Fuchs case see Robert Chadwell Williams, *Klaus Fuchs: Atomic Spy;* the one-time pads are in Robert J. Lamphere and Tom Schachtman, *The FBI-KGB War: A Special Agent's Story,* chap. 6, "The Break," 78–98; for the briefing of the AEC see Richard Pfau, *No Sacrifice Too Great: The Life of Lewis L. Strauss,* 114–18.

30. An account of the plans is in Rosenberg, "American Atomic Strategy"; Herken, *Winning Weapon;* Harry R. Borowski, *A Hollow Threat: Strategic Air Power and Containment before Korea.* Texts are in Steven T. Ross and David Alan Rosenberg, eds., *America's Plans for War against the Soviet Union, 1945–1950.*

31. Borowski, *Hollow Threat,* 130.

32. David A. Rosenberg, "U.S. Nuclear Stockpile 1945 to 1950," 26; Rearden, *Formative Years*, 439; Williamson and Rearden, *Origins of U.S. Nuclear Strategy*, 153.

33. Rosenberg, "U.S. Nuclear Stockpile," 27–29; Herken, *Winning Weapon*, 196–97.

34. Borowski, *Hollow Threat*, 167.

35. Rosenberg, "U.S. Nuclear Stockpile," 28.

36. Ayers diary, October 14, 1946, *Truman in the White House*, 161; Ferrell, ed., "A Visit to the White House," 329.

37. Miscellaneous historical documents, box 23, document 626.

38. Entry of February 9, 1949, *Journals of David E. Lilienthal*, 2:464.

39. Newton, *Cambridge Spies*, 148–49, 157ff., 178–79.

40. Williamson and Rearden, *Origins of U.S. Nuclear Strategy*, 125. Radar jamming was one of the Soviets' highest priority research-and-development programs during the 1950s. It could have been to jam the fusing mechanism on U.S. bombs, or to confuse SAC's targeting, which was based on synthetic radar images (Rearden to the author, September 27, 1993).

41. The strength of the Soviet army during these years is difficult to calculate, and the best recourse is by numbers of troops. Khrushchev claimed in 1960 that Soviet armed forces decreased from 11,365,000 in 1945 to 2,874,000 in 1948. Most Western estimates of the time were around 4,000,000. Divisional counts were much less accurate. In 1949 Truman said the Soviets had 500 divisions. In 1950 Marshall put the number at "over 260." The usual estimate was 175, with the satellites furnishing 75 more. But Soviet divisions were not up to strength: about two-thirds were at partial strength or were cadres, and satellite divisions were unreliable. Moreover, these divisions were small, 9,000 to 12,000 men, and a slice (including supporting units) came to 13,000 to 15,000. Western divisions averaged 11,000 to 18,000, and a slice brought the figure to 40,000. The Soviets may have had the Western equivalent of 43 divisions. Considering that USSR forces needed to defend two frontiers, east and west, the Western Allies could meet Soviet strength if, as indeed they eventually did, they could marshal 25 divisions in their own territory. See Matthew A. Evangelista, "Stalin's Postwar Army Reappraised."

42. The Bohlen quotation is in Kaplan, *The United States and NATO*, 146; Walter LaFeber, "NATO and the Korean War: A Context," in Kaplan, ed., *American Historians and the Atlantic Alliance*, 47–48.

43. Thomas Alan Schwartz, *America's Germany: John J. McCloy and the Federal Republic of Germany*, 122. "The Korean War shifted opinions decisively toward rearmament. Political and psychological pressure from Bonn interacted with congressional pressure in Washington to produce a powerful momentum for action" (126).

44. In *Origins of U.S. Nuclear Strategy*, Williamson and Rearden argue that Truman's fiscal conservatism, his desire to hold down the military budget, a desire he displayed until June 1950 and reasserted after the Korean War stabilized in 1951–1952, quixotically created the very reliance on nuclear strategy he sought to avoid. Budget constraints limited conventional forces. The era of nuclear plenty that opened with the design breakthrough in 1948 made nuclear forces cheaper (until appearance of the enormously costly nuclear carriers of the 1960s and thereafter); by 1952 the explosive power of one ton of TNT costing seventeen hundred dollars could be obtained in nuclear form for twenty-three dollars. A whole "family" of nuclear weapons became possible—meaning smaller battlefield weapons—and for a while the idea of smaller weapons attracted political leaders, scientists, and military men, who feared a world-

wide nuclear holocaust, clouds of radiation drifting everywhere, if SAC went to the Soviet Union. The costly rearmament of Western Europe made battlefield weapons attractive. And what to think of this interpretation? It seems essentially correct—there was a terrible result here, in which fiscal conservatism (perhaps it went back to failure of the haberdashery in 1922) produced what Truman wanted to avoid. But given the unprecedented political and military issues that he had to deal with in 1945–1953—demobilization and reconversion at home, reconstruction in Western Europe, forestalling political defeat in 1948, the Korean War, all the while attempting to divine the Soviet Union's purposes in Europe and Asia—it does appear that he did well. Whatever the later imbalance, his administration brought conventional and nuclear forces to an impressive level.

Chapter Seventeen. Nadir

1. Reprinted in Hersey, *Aspects of the Presidency*, 110.
2. Dennison oral history, 176.
3. Nixon oral history, 178.
4. Vertical file.
5. Dunar, *Truman Scandals*, 64.
6. Ibid., 88–89. In the effort to avoid public controversy, Senator Paul H. Douglas accompanied Fulbright to the White House, and he remembered how the president listened and then followed with a momentary silence as he looked out the window at the slanting rain. "I guess you are right," he murmured. He rose and vigorously shook hands and the interview was over (*In the Fullness of Time: The Memoirs of Paul H. Douglas*, 224).
7. Murphy oral history, by Hess, 407–8.
8. Ibid., 407–8.
9. Gilpatric oral history, 47.
10. When Early called and asked for the resignation of Biddle, the latter went to see Truman, and the president admitted he did not feel like facing him. Biddle walked over, touched his shoulder, and said, "You see, it's not so hard." In his memoirs Truman said Biddle had recommended Clark, which Biddle denied (Biddle, *In Brief Authority*, 365–66).
11. Morison's oral history is full of stories, but for some reason is one of the least read histories in the Truman library.
12. The business about a Catholic appointment, either to the court or to justice, encouraged Clare Boothe Luce, herself a convert, to tell a then-current joke about Clark, who allegedly wanted the Catholic seat on the court; according to her, he asked someone how long it took to qualify (Wilfrid Sheed, *Clare Boothe Luce* [New York: Dutton, 1982], 7).
13. A. Robert Smith, *The Tiger in the Senate: The Biography of Wayne Morse*, 132–34. During the 1952 campaign Morse soured on Eisenhower, registered as a Democrat, and while showing his prize cattle at a fair, he used an absentee ballot and called in reporters as he filled it out.
14. Murphy oral history, by Hess, 418ff.
15. Memorandum of December 26, 1951, *Off the Record*, 221.
16. Hamby, *Beyond the New Deal*, 464–65.

17. Dunar, *Truman Scandals*, 117.

18. Donovan, *Tumultuous Years*, 380. The present writer saw the papers, then in possession of Robert Bennett of East Greenwich, Rhode Island.

19. Dunar, *Truman Scandals*, 118.

20. Ibid.

21. Truman to J. Howard McGrath, April 17, 1952, president's secretary's files, box 115, "Attorney General—J. Howard McGrath." McGrath does not seem to have understood what happened to him, despite his explanations, cited above. About this time he talked with Arthur Krock, presumably giving the inside story of his dismissal. Krock innocently took it as that, but McGrath said nothing beyond relating Truman's increasing lack of confidence in him (Krock, *Memoirs*, 257–60).

22. Morison oral history, 198–99, 201–3, 343, 347, 350–51, 356–66. According to Morison, McGranery and his wife were in Truman's outer office when McGrath was dismissed. "Bring him in," said the president. But this was wrong, as Donovan relates; using the Tubby diary he shows that Truman called McGranery in Philadelphia during the same staff meeting at which he dismissed the attorney general (*Tumultuous Years*, 381). Tubby allowed Donovan to see the diary, now in the Yale University archives. Tubby died in 1993; the diary is closed until the year 2050.

23. Morison oral history, 203–4, 368–69.

24. Royster in *Wall Street Journal*, September 22, 1982, vertical file; Truman interview, October 21, 1959, "Mr. Citizen" file, box 2, folder 2.

25. His device would be his memoirs, an honest record of the administration. "The lies are beginning to be solidified and made into historical 'facts.' Let's head them off now while we can. The truth is all I want for history. If I appear in a bad light when we have the truth that's just too bad. We must take it. But I don't want a pack of lying so-called historians to do to Roosevelt and to me what the New Englanders did to Jefferson and Jackson" (memorandum to Elsey, February 15, 1950, Elsey papers, box 68, "Historical programs—President's Historical queries").

26. Dunar, *Truman Scandals*, 158–59; Evans oral history, 749; Hinde oral history, 82; Helm, *A Political Biography*, 6.

27. The principal accounts of the steel strike are Charles Sawyer and Eugene P. Trani, *Concerns of a Conservative Democrat*, 255–57, and Maeva Marcus, *Truman and the Steel Seizure Case: The Limits of Presidential Power*.

28. Truman to Fred I. Kent, May 31, 1952, president's secretary's files, box 125, "Kent, Fred I. (folder 2)."

29. Marcus, *Truman and the Steel Seizure Case*, 99–100, 196.

30. Hamby, *Beyond the New Deal*, 447–48.

31. Donovan, *Tumultuous Years*, 386; *New York Times*, August 24, 1982; "Truman Seizes Steel," 53; Truman, *Bess W. Truman*, 385.

32. *New York Times*, August 28, 1982.

33. Ibid., August 24, 1982; Truman to McGranery, May 28, 1952, president's secretary's files, box 316, "McGranery, James." Years later Justice Clark was asked if Truman ever sought advice from him or, so far as he knew, from Vinson. "No," was the answer, "he never asked me any questions after I was on the Court. I think he thought that that would be inappropriate. There is some rumor that he did talk to Fred, but I rather doubt it" (Heller, ed., *The Truman White House*, 33).

34. Krock, *Memoirs*, 267–69, claims that on November 5, 1951, Truman talked with Eisenhower and said his offer of the Democratic nomination, as made earlier, still held.

Eisenhower replied that his differences with the Democrats, such as over labor issues, were too large to be bridged. That same afternoon the president received the Supreme Court and told several of its members of his conversation. Krock's source was Justice Douglas. The latter, to be sure, disliked Truman, if only because of the Roosevelt letter to Hannegan in 1944.

35. Vaughan oral history, 111–12.

36. Murphy oral history, by Hess.

37. Truman interview, September 9, 1959, "Mr. Citizen" file, box 2, folder 1. For a while the president pushed Barkley for the nomination, and Barkley was willing, even though seventy-one. See Sawyer and Trani, *Concerns of a Conservative Democrat*, 278–83. Sawyer was the president's representative at the convention.

38. Undated letter, *Off the Record*, 266–67.

39. Undated letter, ibid., 268–69.

40. Murphy oral history, by Hess, 425.

41. Truman to Daniel R. Fitzpatrick, November 21, 1952, president's secretary's files, box 311, "F"; *Harry S Truman, Late a President of the United States*, 125; Truman interview, October 21, 1959, "Mr. Citizen" file, box 2, folder 2.

42. Smith, *Tiger in the Senate*, 150–52.

43. Hersey, *Aspects of the Presidency*, xvi.

44. Truman interview, November 11, 1960, postpresidential files, box 2, tape 78.

45. Truman interview, October 22, 1959, "Mr. Citizen" file, box 2, folder 2.

Chapter Eighteen. Retirement

1. The expenses for the Trumans' security were $1,200 for the guardhouse, $5,400 for the wrought-iron fence, and $22,000 for alarms and the closed-circuit television security system, according to Comptroller General Elmer B. Staats of the General Accounting Office (*Kansas City Times*, October 12, 1973). The little house on the corner of North Delaware rented at $4,200 a year. The salaries of the agents totaled $182,000 (Ron Cockrell, *The Trumans of Independence: Historic Resource Study*, 389).

2. Memorandum by Truman, January 16, 1954, *Autobiography*, v.

3. For the following account I am indebted to much conversation with Francis H. Heller and to his "The Writing of the Truman Memoirs" and "Harry S. Truman: The Writing of His Memoirs."

4. *New Yorker*, November 19, 1955, 120–39.

5. Truman to John W. McCormack, January 10, 1957, *Off the Record*, 346–47.

6. Elsey oral history, by Charles T. Morrissey, 44–45.

7. Interview, September 10, 1959, "Mr. Citizen" file, box 2, folder 1.

8. Ibid.; to W. Francis English, May 22, 1952, president's secretary's files, box 310, "E." By 1984 the library boasted 12.6 million pages of manuscript material, 5 million of which were White House files, as well as 76,000 still pictures, 2,630 recordings, 650 motion pictures, and 44,000 books (*Independence Examiner*, January 19, 1984, vertical file). The president's private papers began to open in 1977; the "Dear Bess" letters opened in 1983.

9. Evans oral history, 687; interview, September 9, 1959, "Mr. Citizen" file, box 2, folder 1.

10. "Eisenhower will win," he said privately in 1956. "A decent man, but a bad

president. He is the captive of the Republican bosses and big business and doesn't know it" (Joseph C. Jahn in *Birmingham [Alabama] News*, December 26, 1972, vertical file). In mid-July 1956, Jahn spent four hours on the train with Truman, passing through Pennsylvania, with the injunction that he could not publish until Truman died. During his campaign appearances for Stevenson in 1952 and 1956, the former president received disrespectful receptions—youngsters booing and waving "I Like Ike" signs—and was sure that GOP leaders arranged them, getting students out of school and paying them fifty cents apiece to go down to the train and be disrespectful. One time in Ohio he met a Catholic priest who ran the fifty-cent kids off the platform. The priest was for Eisenhower but knew decent behavior (interview, September 9, 1959, "Mr. Citizen" file, box 2, folder 1).

11. Clarence B. Randall diary, October 2, 1953, Randall journals, box 1, Dwight D. Eisenhower Library.

12. The following is from Dennison's oral history, 207ff.

13. Truman to Leonard W. Hall, September 11, 1954, *Off the Record*, 340.

14. Advance copy of speech of October 28, 1960, vertical file.

15. *Independence Examiner*, October 21, 1960, vertical file.

16. Notes for speech of September 11, 1962, *Off the Record*, 405–6.

17. Randall S. Jessee oral history, by William D. Stilley, 35–38.

18. The former comment got into print; the latter he related to his next-door neighbor, the Reverend Thomas Melton (interview with Mr. Melton). Goldwater's 1964 retort was that in 1948 the Democrats nominated a damn fool at their convention and he turned out to be a pretty good president (*Kansas City Star*, August 2, 1964, vertical file).

19. Address at the annual convention, August 5, 1961, vertical file.

20. Lenore K. Bradley, "A Yank at Oxford," *Whistle Stop* 14, no. 4 (1986).

21. *Mr. Citizen*, 63.

22. *Missouri Life*, January–February 1976.

23. *Independence Examiner*, December 27, 1974, vertical file.

24. Edward Meisburger, *The [Kansas City] Call*, November 4, 1966. Meisburger, Truman's sergeant in Battery D, had another story about Brown, who had told the former president a few years before, in the midst of the civil rights struggle in the South, that he was going down to Mississippi to visit a sister and admitted he hoped there would not be any trouble down there for him. "Mr. Truman wrote down his office and his home telephone numbers and told me to keep them handy, and if anybody gave me any trouble to get on that phone and call him collect night or day and he would take care of things. I never had no trouble, but I felt awful good knowing where I could get help if I needed it."

25. *Harry S Truman, Late a President of the United States*, 172.

26. *Kansas City Times*, October 15, 1983, vertical file.

27. Ibid., April 9, 1959.

28. *Fort Worth Star-Telegram*, December 26, 1972, vertical file.

29. For the men's room anecdote see clipping of March 30, 1962, unidentified newspaper, vertical file; for the "Star Spangled Banner" episode, see *Kansas City Times*, February 3, 1958, vertical file. The daughter-in-law of the composer of the "Missouri Waltz" visited the library in 1963 and said the composer originally wrote the song around 1914, as a piano piece (vertical file).

30. Ayers diary, February 21, 26, 1946, *Truman in the White House*, 134, 136; Truman

to Dale Pontius, June 15, 1958, miscellaneous historical documents file, box 10, document 327.

31. Vertical file.

32. *Kansas City Star,* August 22, 1955, vertical file. "Besides, children nowadays have too many gadgets to fool with and not enough chores."

33. *Harry S Truman, Late a President of the United States,* 43.

34. John K. Hulston, *An Ozarks Lawyer's Story, 1946–1976,* 333.

35. *Kansas Chiropractic Association Journal* 22 (March–April 1986): 44–45, vertical file.

36. Conversations with Mr. and Mrs. George Miller.

37. The following, including the next paragraph, is from Harry F. Rosenthal, *Wabash [Indiana] Plain Dealer,* May 8, 1972.

38. *Harry S Truman, Late a President of the United States,* 117.

Bibliography

Manuscripts

Anderson, Clinton P. Papers. Manuscript Division, Library of Congress, Washington, D.C.

Ayers, Eben A. Papers and diary. Harry S. Truman Library, Independence, Mo.

Barkley, Alben W. Papers. University of Kentucky Library, Lexington.

Barnard, Ellsworth. Papers. Lilly Library, Indiana University, Bloomington.

Bell, C. Jasper. Papers. Western Historical Manuscript Collection, University of Missouri–Columbia.

Boettiger, John R. Papers. Franklin D. Roosevelt Library, Hyde Park, N.Y.

Brandt, Raymond P. Papers. Western Historical Manuscript Collection, University of Missouri–Columbia.

Bundschu, Henry A. Papers. Harry S. Truman Library.

Byrnes, James F. Papers. Special Collections, Clemson University Library, Clemson, S.C.

Canfil, Fred. Papers. Harry S. Truman Library.

Clark, Bennett Champ. Papers. Western Historical Manuscript Collection, University of Missouri–Columbia.

Clifford, Clark. Papers. Harry S. Truman Library.

Connelly, Matthew J. Papers. Harry S. Truman Library.

Dancy, Keith W. Diary. Archives, Liberty Memorial, Kansas City, Mo.

Daniel, Clifton and Margaret. Papers. Harry S. Truman Library.

Daniels, Jonathan. Diary. Southern Historical Collection, Wilson Library, University of North Carolina, Chapel Hill.

———. Papers. Harry S. Truman Library.

Davies, Joseph E. Papers and diary. Manuscript Division, Library of Congress.

Decker, Clarence R. Papers. Harry S. Truman Library.

Dickmann, Bernard F. Papers. Western Historical Manuscript Collection. University of Missouri–Columbia.

Donnell, Forrest C. Papers. Western Historical Manuscript Collection, University of Missouri–Columbia.

Early, Stephen T. Papers. Franklin D. Roosevelt Library.

Elsey, George M. Papers. Harry S. Truman Library.

Evans, Tom L. Papers. Harry S. Truman Library.

Farley, James A. Diary. Manuscript Division, Library of Congress.

Flynn, Edward J. Papers. Franklin D. Roosevelt Library.

Grady, Henry F. Papers. Harry S. Truman Library.

Halsted, Anna Roosevelt. Papers. Franklin D. Roosevelt Library.

Hannegan, Robert E. Papers. Harry S. Truman Library.

Harriman, W. Averell. Papers. Manuscript Division, Library of Congress.

Hassett, William D. Papers. Harry S. Truman Library.

Hickok, Lorena. Papers. Franklin D. Roosevelt Library.

Hillman, Sidney. Papers. Labor-Management Documentation Center, Martin
    P. Catherwood Library, Cornell University, Ithaca, N.Y.

Holland, Lou E. Papers. Harry S. Truman Library.

Housholder, Vic H. Papers. Harry S. Truman Library.

Ickes, Harold L. Diary. Manuscript Division, Library of Congress.

Jacobson, Edward. Papers. Harry S. Truman Library.

Johnson, Louis A. Papers. Alderman Library, University of Virginia, Char-
    lottesville.

Keeley, Mary Paxton. Papers. Harry S. Truman Library.

————. Papers. Western Historical Manuscript Collection, University of Mis-
    souri–Columbia.

Leahy, William D. Papers and diary. Manuscript Division, Library of Congress.

Lowenthal, Max. Papers and diary. Archives, University of Minnesota, Min-
    neapolis.

Mag, Arthur. Papers. Harry S. Truman Library.

Marquis, George C. Papers. Harry S. Truman Library.

Messall, Victor R. Papers. Harry S. Truman Library.

Mitchell, Stephen A. Papers. Harry S. Truman Library.

Morgenthau, Henry, Jr. Diary (microfilm). Franklin D. Roosevelt Library.

Morison, H. Graham. Papers. Harry S. Truman Library.

Murphy, Charles S. Papers. Harry S. Truman Library.

Murray, Philip. Papers. Archives, Mullen Library, Catholic University of Amer-
    ica, Washington, D.C.

Nash, Philleo. Papers. Harry S. Truman Library.

Niles, David K. Papers. Harry S. Truman Library.

Noland, Mary Ethel. Papers. Harry S. Truman Library.

Odum, Reathel. Papers. Harry S. Truman Library.

Park, Guy B. Papers. Western Historical Manuscript Collection, University of
    Missouri–Columbia.

Randall, Clarence B. Diary. Dwight D. Eisenhower Library, Abilene, Kans.

Roosevelt, Franklin D. Papers. Franklin D. Roosevelt Library.

Rosenman, Samuel I. Papers. Franklin D. Roosevelt Library.

Ross, Charles G. Papers and diary. Harry S. Truman Library.

Rovere, Richard H. Papers. State Historical Society of Wisconsin, Madison.
Salisbury, Spencer. Papers. Harry S. Truman Library.
Sanders, Ted J. Papers. Harry S. Truman Library.
Sawyer, Charles. Papers and diary. Harry S. Truman Library.
Short, Beth Campbell. Papers. Western Historical Manuscript Collection, University of Missouri–Columbia.
Slater, Harold M. Papers. Harry S. Truman Library.
Smith, Harold D. Papers and diary. Harry S. Truman Library.
Snyder, John W. Papers. Harry S. Truman Library.
Souers, Sidney W. Papers. Harry S. Truman Library
Stark, Lloyd C. Papers. Western Historical Manuscript Collection, University of Missouri–Columbia.
Stayton, E. L. Papers. Jackson County Historical Society, Independence, Mo.
Stein, Harold. Papers. Harry S. Truman Library.
Stettinius, Edward R., Jr. Papers and diary. Alderman Library, University of Virginia.
Tiernan, L. Curtis. Papers. Harry S. Truman Library.
Truman, Harry S. Papers. Harry S. Truman Library.
Truman, Ralph E. Papers. Harry S. Truman Library.
Van Sant, Thomas. Papers. Harry S. Truman Library.
Vinson, Fred. Papers. University of Kentucky Library, Lexington.
Walker, Frank C. Papers and diary. Archives, Hesburgh Library, University of Notre Dame, South Bend, Ind.
Wallace, Henry A. Papers and diary (microfilm). University of Iowa Library, Iowa City.
———. Papers. Franklin D. Roosevelt Library.
Wallgren, Monrad C. Papers. Harry S. Truman Library.
Walsh, Jerome K. Papers. Harry S. Truman Library.
Watson, Edwin M. Papers. Alderman Library, University of Virginia.
Webb, James E. Papers. Harry S. Truman Library.
Wiggins, A. L. M. Papers. Harry S. Truman Library.
Wilcox, Francis. Papers and diary. Harry S. Truman Library.
Willkie, Wendell L. Papers. Lilly Library, Indiana University, Bloomington.
Woodward, Stanley. Papers. Harry S. Truman Library.

Oral Histories

Unless otherwise indicated all oral histories are deposited
in the Harry S. Truman Library.

Achilles, Theodore, by Richard D. McKinzie. 1972.
Allen, George E., by Jerry N. Hess. 1969.
Ayers, Eben A., by Jerry N. Hess. 1967–1970.
Aylward, James P., by J. R. Fuchs. 1968.

Babcock, Gaylon, by J. R. Fuchs. 1964.

Barringer, Lewis T., by J. R. Fuchs. 1969.

Barrows, Roberta, by Niel M. Johnson. 1987.

Battle, Lucius D., by Richard D. McKinzie and Theodore A. Wilson. 1971.

Benton, Thomas Hart, by Milton F. Perry. 1964.

Bolling, Richard, by Niel M. Johnson. 1988–1989.

Bowman, Welbern, by Niel M. Johnson. 1981.

Brandt, Raymond P., by Jerry N. Hess. 1970.

Bunker, Lawrence E., by Benedict K. Zobrist. 1976.

Burrus, Rufus B., by Niel M. Johnson. 1985.

Chiles, Henry P., by J. R. Fuchs. 1961–1962.

Clark, Tom, by Jerry N. Hess. 1972–1973.

Clifford, Clark, by Jerry N. Hess. 1971–1973.

Connelly, Matthew J., by Jerry N. Hess. 1967–1968.

Daniel, E. Clifton, by J. R. Fuchs. 1972.

Daniels, Jonathan, by J. R. Fuchs. 1963.

Dawson, Donald S., by J. R. Fuchs. 1977.

———, by William D. Stilley and Jerald L. Hill. 1976.

Dennison, Robert L., by Jerry N. Hess. 1971.

Dryden, Mildred Lee, by J. R. Fuchs. 1963.

Easley, Harry, by J. R. Fuchs. 1967.

Elsey, George M., by Jerry N. Hess. 1969.

———, by Charles T. Morrissey. 1964, 1969–1970.

———, by William D. Stilley and Jerald L. Hill. 1976.

Evans, Tom L., by J. R. Fuchs. 1962–1963.

Faris, Edgar C., Jr., by J. R. Fuchs. 1971.

Feinberg, Abraham, by Richard D. McKinzie. 1973.

Folliard, Edward T., by Jerry N. Hess. 1970.

Gilmore, Durward W., by Niel M. Johnson. 1989.

Gilpatric, Roswell L., by Jerry N. Hess. 1972.

Goddard, Sterling E., by Niel M. Johnson. 1980.

Granoff, A. J., by J. R. Fuchs. 1968.

Grube, Esther M., by Niel M. Johnson. 1981.

Hall, Ruby Jane, by Niel M. Johnson. 1980.

Halvorson, H. H., by J. R. Fuchs. 1967.

Harper, Roy W., by J. R. Fuchs. 1978.

Hehmeyer, Walter, by J. R. Fuchs. 1969.

Henderson, Loy W., by Richard D. McKinzie. 1973.

Hickerson, John D., by Richard D. McKinzie. 1972–1973.

Hinde, Edgar G., by J. R. Fuchs. 1962.

Hoeber, Johannes, by Jerry N. Hess. 1966.

Holt, Mr. and Mrs. George T., by Niel M. Johnson. 1981.

Jessee, Mr. and Mrs. Randall S., by Philip C. Brooks. 1964.

Jessee, Randall S., by William D. Stilley. 1975.

Judd, Walter H., by Jerry N. Hess. 1970.

Keeley, Mary Paxton, by J. R. Fuchs. 1966.

Keyserling, Leon H., by Jerry N. Hess. 1971.

Lawton, Frederick J., by Charles T. Morrissey. 1963.

Leigh, Vere C., by J. R. Fuchs. 1970.

Lowenthal, Max, by Jerry N. Hess. 1967, 1969.

McGrath, Harold I., by J. R. Fuchs. 1970.

McKim, Edward D., by J. R. Fuchs. 1964.

McNeil, Wilfred J., by Jerry N. Hess. 1972.

Marks, Ted, by J. R. Fuchs. 1962.

Meador, John, by Niel M. Johnson. 1980.

Montgomery, Hannah Clements, by Niel M. Johnson. 1980.

Morison, H. Graham, by Jerry N. Hess. 1972.

Muccio, John J., by Jerry N. Hess. 1971.

———, by Richard D. McKinzie. 1973.

Murphy, Charles S., by Jerry N. Hess. 1969–1970.

———, by Hugh Heclo and Anna Nelson. 1980.

———, by Charles T. Morrissey. 1963.

Neustadt, Richard E., by Hugh Heclo and Anna Nelson. 1980.

Nixon, Robert G., by Jerry N. Hess. 1970.

Noland, Mary Ethel, by J. R. Fuchs. 1965.

Osborn, Frederick, by Richard D. McKinzie. 1974.

Pace, Frank, Jr., by Jerry N. Hess. 1972.

Perkins, Frances, by Dean Albertson. Oral History Collection, Oral History Research Office, Butler Library, Columbia University, New York, N.Y. 1955.

Perkins, Pansy, by Niel M. Johnson. 1981.

Peters, Mize, by J. R. Fuchs. 1963–1964.

Reinsch, J. Leonard, by J. R. Fuchs. 1967.

Roach, Neale, by Jerry N. Hess. 1969.

Roosevelt, Eleanor, by Joseph Wall. Oral History Collection, Oral History Research Office, Butler Library. 1957.

Rosenman, Samuel I., by Jerry N. Hess. 1968–1969.

———, by Joseph Wall. Oral History Collection, Oral History Research Office, Butler Library. 1957.

Sanders, Ted J., by Niel M. Johnson. 1982.

Sandifer, Durward V., by Richard D. McKinzie. 1973.

Sims, Pauline, by Niel M. Johnson. 1981.

Slaughter, Stephen S., by Niel M. Johnson. 1984.

Sparks, Wilbur D., by Jerry N. Hess. 1968.

Steelman, John R., by Charles T. Morrissey. 1963.

Stowe, David H., by Hugh Heclo and Anna Nelson. 1980.

————, by Charles T. Morrissey. 1963.

————, by William D. Stilley and Jerald L. Hill. 1976.

Strode, John J., by Niel M. Johnson. 1980.

Swoyer, Martha Ann, by Niel M. Johnson. 1983.

Truman, Fred L., by Niel M. Johnson. 1983.

Truman, Mary Jane, by Jerald L. Hill and William D. Stilley. 1976.

————, by Stephen and Cathy Doyal and Fred and Audrey Truman. 1975.

Tubby, Roger, by Jerry N. Hess. 1970.

Vanatta, Regna, by Niel M. Johnson. 1980.

Vaughan, Harry H., by Charles T. Morrissey. 1963.

Veatch, Nathan Thomas, Jr., by J. R. Fuchs. 1961.

Wallace, Henry A., by Dean Albertson. Oral History Collection, Oral History Research Office, Butler Library. 1951.

Webb, James E., by Hugh Heclo and Anna Nelson. 1980.

Weddle, Margaret, by Niel M. Johnson. 1981.

Wilcox, Francis O., by Donald A. Ritchie. U.S. Senate Historical Office, copy in Harry S. Truman Library. 1984.

Williams, Maxine, by Niel M. Johnson. 1983.

Wooden, McKinley, by Niel M. Johnson. 1986.

Wyatt, Robert, by Niel M. Johnson. 1980.

Books, Articles, Dissertations, Theses

Abell, Tyler, ed. *Drew Pearson Diaries, 1949–1959.* New York: Holt, Rinehart and Winston, 1974.

Abels, Jules. *Out of the Jaws of Victory.* New York: Holt, 1959.

————. *The Truman Scandals.* Chicago: Regnery, 1956.

Abramson, Rudy. *Spanning the Century: The Life of W. Averell Harriman, 1891–1986.* New York: Morrow, 1992.

Acheson, Dean. *Present at the Creation: My Years in the State Department.* New York: Norton, 1969.

Adams, Henry H. *Harry Hopkins.* New York: Putnam, 1977.

————. *Witness to Power: The Life of Fleet Admiral William D. Leahy.* Annapolis: Naval Institute, 1985.

Adler, Frank J. *Roots in a Moving Stream: The Centennial History of Congregation B'nai Jehudah of Kansas City, 1870–1970.* Kansas City: The Congregation, 1972.

Agar, Herbert. *The Price of Power: America since 1945.* Chicago: University of Chicago Press, 1957.

Albion, Robert Greenhalgh, and Robert Howe Connery, with Jennie Barnes Pope. *Forrestal and the Navy.* New York: Columbia University Press, 1962.

Allen, George E. *Presidents Who Have Known Me.* New York: Simon and Schuster, 1950.

Allen, Robert S., and William V. Shannon. *The Truman Merry-Go-Round.* New York: Vanguard, 1950.

Allison, John M. *Ambassador from the Prairie or Allison Wonderland.* Boston: Houghton Mifflin, 1973.

Alperovitz, Gar. *Atomic Diplomacy: Hiroshima and Potsdam.* New York: Simon and Schuster, 1965.

———. *Cold War Essays.* New York: Anchor, 1970.

Anders, Roger M., ed. *Forging the Atomic Shield: Excerpts from the Office Diary of Gordon E. Dean.* Chapel Hill: University of North Carolina Press, 1987.

Anderson, Clinton P. *Outsider in the Senate: Senator Clinton P. Anderson's Memoirs.* Cleveland: World, 1970.

Anderson, Terry H. *The United States, Great Britain, and the Cold War, 1944–1947.* Columbia: University of Missouri Press, 1981.

Appleman, Roy E. *Disaster in Korea: The Chinese Confront MacArthur.* College Station: Texas A & M University Press, 1989.

———. *Escaping the Trap: The US Army X Corps in Northeast Korea, 1950.* College Station: Texas A & M University Press, 1990.

———. *Ridgway Duels for Korea.* College Station: Texas A and M University Press, 1990.

———. *The United States Army in the Korean War.* Vol. 1, *South to the Naktong, North to the Yalu.* Washington: Government Printing Office, 1961.

Backer, John H. *The Decision to Divide Germany: American Foreign Policy in Transition.* Durham: Duke University Press, 1978.

———. *Priming the German Economy: American Occupation Policies, 1945–1948.* Durham: Duke University Press, 1971.

———. *Winds of History: The German Years of Lucius DuBignon Clay.* New York: Van Nostrand Reinhold, 1983.

Barker, John T. *Missouri Lawyer.* Philadelphia: Lippincott, 1949.

Barkley, Alben W. *That Reminds Me.* Garden City, N.Y.: Doubleday, 1954.

Baruch, Bernard M. *Baruch: The Public Years.* New York: Holt, Rinehart and Winston, 1960.

Bell, C. Jasper. *The Story of a Missourian.* Kansas City: Privately printed, 1971.

Belmonte, Laura Ann. "Anglo-American Relations and the Dismissal of MacArthur." Master's thesis, University of Virginia, 1991.

Berman, William C. *The Politics of Civil Rights in the Truman Administration.* Columbus: Ohio State University Press, 1970.

Bernstein, Barton J. "Clash of Interests: The Postwar Battle between the Office of Price Administration and the Department of Agriculture." *Agricultural History* 41 (1967): 45–57.

———. "The Postwar Famine and Price Controls, 1946." *Agricultural History* 38 (1964): 235–41.

———. "The Removal of War Production Board Controls on Business, 1944–1946." *Business History Review* 39 (1965): 243–60.

————. "Seizing the Contested Terrain of Early Nuclear History: Stimson, Conant, and Their Allies Explain the Decision to Use the Atomic Bomb." *Diplomatic History* 17 (1993): 35–72.

————. "The Struggle over the Korean Armistice: Prisoners of Repatriation?" In *Child of Conflict: The Korean-American Relationship, 1943–1953*, edited by Bruce Cumings, 261–307. Seattle: University of Washington Press, 1983.

————. "The Truman Administration and Its Reconversion Wage Policy." *Labor History* 6 (1965): 214–31.

————. "The Truman Administration and the Steel Strike of 1946." *Journal of American History* 52 (1966): 791–803.

————, ed. *Politics and Policies of the Truman Administration.* Chicago: Quadrangle, 1970.

————, ed. *Towards a New Past: Dissenting Essays in American History.* New York: Pantheon, 1968.

Bernstein, Barton J., and Allen J. Matusow, eds. *The Truman Administration: A Documentary History.* New York: Harper and Row, 1966.

Best, Richard A., Jr. *"Co-operation with Like-Minded Peoples": British Influences on American Security Policy, 1945–1949.* Westport, Conn.: Greenwood, 1986.

Biddle, Francis. *In Brief Authority.* Garden City, N.Y.: Doubleday, 1962.

Biles, Roger. *Big City Boss in Depression and War: Mayor Edward J. Kelly of Chicago.* DeKalb: Northern Illinois University Press, 1984.

Bird, Kai. *The Chairman: John J. McCloy and the Making of the American Establishment.* New York: Simon and Schuster, 1992.

Blair, Clay. *The Forgotten War: America in Korea, 1950–53.* New York: Times Books, 1987.

Bland, Larry I., ed. *George C. Marshall Interviews and Reminiscences for Forrest C. Pogue.* Lexington, Va.: G. C. Marshall Research Foundation, 1991.

Blum, John M., ed. *The Price of Vision: The Diary of Henry A. Wallace, 1942–1946.* Boston: Houghton Mifflin, 1973.

Bohlen, Charles E. *The Transformation of American Foreign Policy.* New York: Norton, 1969.

————. *Witness to History, 1929–1969.* New York: Norton, 1973.

Borg, Dorothy, and Waldo Heinrichs, eds. *Uncertain Years: Chinese-American Relations, 1947–1950.* New York: Columbia University Press, 1980.

Borowsky, Harry R. *A Hollow Threat: Strategic Air Power and Containment before Korea.* Westport, Conn.: Greenwood, 1982.

Bowles, Chester. *Promises to Keep: My Years in Public Life, 1941–1969.* New York: Harper and Row, 1971.

Boylan, James. *The New Deal Coalition and the Election of 1946.* New York: Garland, 1981.

Bradley, Omar N., and Clay Blair. *A General's Life.* New York: Simon and Schuster, 1983.

Brands, H. W. *Inside the Cold War: Loy Henderson and the Rise of the American Empire, 1918–1961.* New York: Oxford University Press, 1991.

Bray, Robert T. *Archaeological Survey and Testing at the Truman Farm Home and Grounds, Grandview, Missouri.* Kansas City, 1983.

Briggs, Ellis. *Farewell to Foggy Bottom: The Recollections of a Career Diplomat.* New York: McKay, 1964.

Brinkley, Douglas, ed. *Dean Acheson and the Making of U.S. Foreign Policy.* London: Macmillan, 1993.

Browder, Robert P., and Thomas G. Smith. *Independent: A Biography of Lewis W. Douglas.* New York: Knopf, 1986.

Brown, Andrew Theodore. *The Politics of Reform: Kansas City's Municipal Government, 1925–1950.* Kansas City: Community Studies, 1958.

Brown, Andrew Theodore, and Lyle W. Dorsett. *K.C.: A History of Kansas City, Missouri.* Boulder, Colo.: Pruett, 1978.

Brown, Walter J. *James F. Byrnes of South Carolina: A Remembrance.* Macon, Ga.: Mercer University Press, 1992.

Bruenn, Howard G. "Clinical Notes on the Illness and Death of President Franklin D. Roosevelt." *Annals of Internal Medicine* 72 (1970): 579–91.

Buckley, Roger. *Occupation Diplomacy: Britain, the United States and Japan, 1945–1952.* New York: Cambridge University Press, 1982.

Buhite, Russell D. *Patrick J. Hurley and American Foreign Policy.* Ithaca: Cornell University Press, 1973.

———. "Soviet-American Relations and the Repatriation of Prisoners of War, 1945." *The Historian* 35 (1973): 384–97.

———. *Soviet-American Relations in Asia, 1945–1954.* Norman: University of Oklahoma Press, 1981.

Bullock, Alan. *Ernest Bevin: Foreign Secretary, 1945–1951.* New York: Norton, 1983.

———. *Hitler and Stalin: Parallel Lives.* New York: Knopf, 1992.

Bundschu, Henry A. *Harry S. Truman: The Missourian.* Kansas City: *Kansas City Star,* 1949.

Bundy, McGeorge. *Danger and Survival.* New York: Random House, 1988.

Burns, Richard Dean, comp. *Harry S. Truman: A Bibliography of His Times and Presidency.* Wilmington, Del.: Scholarly Resources, 1984.

Byrnes, James F. *All in One Lifetime.* New York: Harper, 1958.

Campbell, Thomas M., and George C. Herring, eds. *The Diaries of Edward R. Stettinius, Jr., 1943–1946.* New York: New Viewpoints, 1975.

Caraley, Demetrios. *The Politics of Military Unification: A Study of Conflict and the Policy Process.* New York: Columbia University Press, 1966.

Caridi, Ronald J. *The Korean War and American Politics: The Republican Party as a Case Study.* Philadelphia: University of Pennsylvania Press, 1968.

Carr, Albert Z. *Truman, Stalin, and Peace.* Garden City, N.Y.: Doubleday, 1950.

Catledge, Turner. *My Life and the Times.* New York: Harper and Row, 1971.

Chen Jian. "The Sino-Soviet Alliance and China's Entry into the Korean War."

Working paper no. 1, Cold War International History Project, Woodrow Wilson International Center for Scholars, June 1992.

Childs, Marquis W. *Witness to Power.* New York: McGraw-Hill, 1975.

Chrisman, James R. "The Rhetoric of the Presidential Campaign of 1948: A Content Analysis of Selected Addresses of Harry S. Truman and Thomas E. Dewey." Ph.D. diss., Oklahoma State University, 1974.

Clay, Lucius D. *Decision in Germany.* Garden City, N.Y.: Doubleday, 1950.

Clements, Kendrick A., ed. *James F. Byrnes and the Origins of the Cold War.* Durham: Carolina Academic Press, 1982.

Clifford, Clark. *Counsel to the President.* New York: Random House, 1991.

Clifford, J. Garry. "President Truman and Peter the Great's Will." *Diplomatic History* 4 (1980): 371–85.

Cochran, Bert. *Harry Truman and the Crisis Presidency.* New York: Funk and Wagnalls, 1973.

Cockrell, Ron. *The Trumans of Independence: Historic Resource Study.* Omaha: National Park Service, 1985.

Coffin, Tris. *Missouri Compromise.* Boston: Little, Brown, 1947.

Cohen, Michael J. *Truman and Israel.* Berkeley and Los Angeles: University of California Press, 1990.

Coiner, Miles W., Jr. "The Grand Opera House and the Golden Age of the Legitimate Theatre in Kansas City." *Missouri Historical Review* 67 (1972–1973): 407–23.

Coit, Margaret L. *Mr. Baruch.* Boston: Houghton Mifflin, 1957.

Coles, Harry L., and Albert K. Weinberg. *Civil Affairs: Soldiers Become Governors.* Washington: Government Printing Office, 1964.

Coletta, Paolo E. *The United States Navy and Defense Unification.* Newark: University of Delaware Press, 1979.

Collins, J. Lawton. *Lightning Joe: An Autobiography.* Baton Rouge: Louisiana State University Press, 1979.

———. *War in Peacetime: The History and Lessons of Korea.* Boston: Houghton Mifflin, 1969.

Colman, Elizabeth Wheeler. *Mrs. Wheeler Goes to Washington.* Helena, Mon.: Falcon Press, 1989.

Colville, John R. *The Fringes of Power: 10 Downing Street Diaries, 1939–1955.* New York: Norton, 1985.

Combs, Jerald A. "The Compromise that Never Was: George Kennan, Paul Nitze, and the Issue of Conventional Deterrence in Europe, 1949–1952." *Diplomatic History* 15 (1991): 361–86.

Conant, James B. *My Several Lives: Memoirs of a Social Inventor.* New York: Harper and Row, 1970.

Condit, Doris M. *History of the Office of the Secretary of Defense.* Vol. 2, *The Test of War, 1950–1953.* Washington: U.S. Department of Defense, 1988.

Condit, Kenneth W. *The History of the Joint Chiefs of Staff: The Joint Chiefs of Staff and National Policy.* Vol. 2, *1947–1949.* Wilmington, Del.: Glazier, 1979.

Connally, Tom. *My Name Is Tom Connally.* New York: Crowell, 1954.

Conquest, Robert. *The Great Terror: A Reassessment.* New York: Oxford University Press, 1990.

Cook, Laura F. "Dean Acheson: United States Policy toward China, 1949." Senior honors thesis, Williams College, 1987.

Cornell, Cecilia Stiles. "James V. Forrestal and American National Security Policy, 1940–1949." Ph.D. diss., Vanderbilt University, 1987.

Costello, John. *Mask of Treachery.* New York: Morrow, 1988.

Cotton, James. *Asian Frontier Nationalism: Owen Lattimore and the American Policy Debate.* Atlantic Highlands, N.J.: Humanities Press, 1989.

Cray, Ed. *General of the Army: George C. Marshall, Soldier and Statesman.* New York: Norton, 1990.

Cumings, Bruce. *The Origins of the Korean War.* Vol. 1, *Liberation and the Emergence of Separate Regimes, 1945–1947.* Vol. 2, *The Roaring of the Cataract, 1947–1950.* Princeton: Princeton University Press, 1981, 1990.

Dalfiume, Richard M. *Desegregation of the U.S. Armed Forces: Fighting on Two Fronts, 1939–1953.* Columbia: University of Missouri Press, 1969.

Danchev, Alex. *Oliver Franks: Founding Father.* New York: Oxford University Press, 1993.

Daniel, Clifton. *Lords, Ladies and Gentlemen: A Memoir.* New York: Arbor House, 1984.

Daniels, Jonathan. *The Man of Independence.* Philadelphia: Lippincott, 1950.

———. *White House Witness, 1942–1945.* Garden City, N.Y.: Doubleday, 1975.

Davidson, Eugene. *The Death and Life of Germany: An Account of the American Occupation.* New York: Knopf, 1959.

———. *The Nuremberg Fallacy: Wars and War Crimes since World War II.* New York: Macmillan, 1973.

———. *The Trial of the Germans: An Account of the Twenty-two Defendants before the International Military Tribunal at Nuremberg.* New York: Macmillan, 1966.

Davies, Richard O. *Defender of the Old Guard: John Bricker and American Politics.* Columbus: Ohio State University Press, 1993.

———. *Housing Reform during the Truman Administration.* Columbia: University of Missouri Press, 1966.

———. "Whistle-Stopping through Ohio." *Ohio History* 71 (1962): 113–23.

Davis, Kenneth S. *The Politics of Honor: A Biography of Adlai E. Stevenson.* New York: Putnam, 1967.

Davis, Lynn Etheridge. *The Cold War Begins: Soviet-American Conflict over Eastern Europe.* Princeton: Princeton University Press, 1974.

Davis, Polly Ann. *Alben W. Barkley: Senate Majority Leader and Vice President.* New York: Garland, 1979.

Davis, Vincent. *The Admirals Lobby.* Chapel Hill: University of North Carolina Press, 1962.

———. *Postwar Defense Policy and the U.S. Navy, 1943–1946.* Chapel Hill: University of North Carolina Press, 1966.

Deibel, Terry L., and John Lewis Gaddis, eds. *Containing the Soviet Union: A Critique of US Policy.* Oxford, Eng.: Pergamon, Brassey's, 1987.

Diebold, William, Jr. "The Marshall Plan in Retrospect: A Review of Recent Scholarship." *Journal of International Affairs* 41 (1988): 421–45.

Dierenfield, Bruce J. *Keeper of the Rules: Congressman Howard W. Smith of Virginia.* Charlottesville: University of Virginia Press, 1987.

Dingman, Roger. "Atomic Diplomacy during the Korean War." *International Security* 13 (1988–1989): 50–91.

Divine, Robert A. *Second Chance: The Triumph of Internationalism in America during World War II.* New York: Atheneum, 1967.

Djilas, Milovan. *Conversations with Stalin.* New York: Harcourt, Brace and World, 1962.

Dobbs, Charles M. *The Unwanted Symbol: American Foreign Policy, the Cold War, and Korea, 1945–1950.* Kent, Ohio: Kent State University Press, 1981.

Dobney, Fredrick J., ed. *Selected Papers of Will Clayton.* Baltimore: Johns Hopkins University Press, 1971.

Doenecke, Justus D. *Not to the Swift: The Old Isolationists in the Cold War Era.* Lewisburg, Pa.: Bucknell University Press, 1979.

Donaldson, Gary A. "Who Wrote the Clifford Memo? The Origins of Campaign Strategy in the Truman Administration." *Presidential Studies Quarterly* 23 (1993): 747–54.

Donovan, Robert J. *Conflict and Crisis: The Presidency of Harry S Truman, 1945–1948.* New York: Norton, 1977.

———. *Nemesis: Truman and Johnson in the Coils of War in Asia.* New York: St. Martin's–Marek, 1989.

———. "Truman Seizes Steel." *Constitution* 2 (fall 1990): 48–57.

———. *Tumultuous Years: The Presidency of Harry S Truman, 1949–1953.* New York: Norton, 1982.

Dorough, C. Dwight. *Mr. Sam.* New York: Random House, 1962.

Dorsett, Lyle W. *The Pendergast Machine.* New York: Oxford University Press, 1968.

Douglas, Helen Gahagan. *A Full Life.* Garden City, N.Y.: Doubleday, 1982.

Douglas, Paul H. *In the Fullness of Time: The Memoirs of Paul H. Douglas.* New York: Harcourt Brace Jovanovich, 1971.

Douglas, William O. *The Court Years, 1939–1975.* New York: Random House, 1980.

Drea, Edward J. *MacArthur's ULTRA: Codebreaking and the War against Japan, 1942–1945.* Lawrence: University Press of Kansas, 1992.

Druks, Herbert. *Harry S. Truman and the Russians, 1945–1953.* New York: Speller, 1966.

Dunar, Andrew J. *The Truman Scandals and the Politics of Morality*. Columbia: University of Missouri Press, 1984.

Eckes, Alfred E., Jr. *The Search for Solvency: Bretton Woods and the International Monetary System, 1941–1971*. Austin: University of Texas Press, 1975.

Edmonds, Robin. *Setting the Mould: The United States and Britain, 1945–1950*. New York: Oxford University Press, 1986.

Edwards, India. *Pulling No Punches: Memoirs of a Woman in Politics*. New York: Putnam, 1977.

Edwards, Lee. *Missionary for Freedom: The Life and Times of Walter Judd*. New York: Paragon House, 1990.

Elliott, Mark. "The United States and Forced Repatriation of Soviet Citizens, 1944–47." *Political Science Quarterly* 88 (1973): 253–75.

Emmerson, John K. *The Japanese Thread: A Life in the U.S. Foreign Service*. New York: Holt, Rinehart and Winston, 1978.

Etzold, Thomas H., and John Lewis Gaddis, eds. *Containment: Documents on American Policy and Strategy, 1945–1950*. New York: Columbia University Press, 1976.

Evangelista, Matthew A. "Stalin's Postwar Army Reappraised." *International Security* 7 (1982–1983): 110–38.

Evensen, Bruce J. *Truman, Palestine, and the Press: Shaping Conventional Wisdom at the Beginning of the Cold War*. Westport, Conn.: Greenwood, 1992.

Farnsworth, Beatrice. *Aleksandra Kollontai: Socialism, Feminism, and the Bolshevik Revolution*. Stanford: Stanford University Press, 1980.

———. *William C. Bullitt and the Soviet Union*. Bloomington: Indiana University Press, 1967.

Farrar, Ronald T. *Reluctant Servant: The Story of Charles G. Ross*. Columbia: University of Missouri Press, 1969.

Feis, Herbert. *The Atomic Bomb and the End of World War II*. Rev. ed. Princeton: Princeton University Press, 1966.

———. *Between War and Peace: The Potsdam Conference*. Princeton: Princeton University Press, 1960.

———. *The China Tangle*. Princeton: Princeton University Press, 1953.

———. *From Trust to Terror: The Onset of the Cold War, 1945–1950*. New York: Norton, 1970.

Ferrell, Robert H., *Choosing Truman: The Democratic Convention of 1944*. Columbia: University of Missouri Press, 1994.

———. *George C. Marshall*. New York: Cooper Square, 1965.

———. *Harry S. Truman: His Life on the Family Farms*. Worland, Wyo.: High Plains, 1991.

———. *Harry S. Truman and the Modern American Presidency*. Boston: Little, Brown, 1983.

———. *Ill-Advised: Presidential Health and Public Trust*. Columbia: University of Missouri Press, 1992.

————. *Truman: A Centenary Remembrance.* New York: Viking, 1984.

————, ed. *America in a Divided World, 1945–1972.* New York: Harper and Row, 1975.

————, ed. *The Autobiography of Harry S. Truman.* Boulder: Colorado Associated University Press, 1980.

————, ed. *Dear Bess: The Letters from Harry to Bess Truman, 1910–1959.* New York: Norton, 1983.

————, ed. *The Eisenhower Diaries.* New York: Norton, 1981.

————, ed. *Off the Record: The Private Papers of Harry S. Truman.* New York: Harper and Row, 1980.

————, ed. *Truman in the White House: The Diary of Eben A. Ayers.* Columbia: University of Missouri Press, 1991.

————. ed. "A Visit to the White House, 1947: The Diary of Vic H. Housholder." *Missouri Historical Review* 78 (1983–1984): 311–36.

Fields, Alonzo. *My 21 Years in the White House.* New York: Coward-McCann, 1961.

Fink, Gary M., and James W. Hilty. "Prologue: The Senate Voting Record of Harry S. Truman." *Journal of Interdisciplinary History* 4 (1973): 207–35.

Finn, Richard B. *Winners in Peace: MacArthur, Yoshida, and Postwar Japan.* Berkeley and Los Angeles: University of California Press, 1992.

Fite, Gilbert C. *Richard B. Russell, Jr.: Senator from Georgia.* Chapel Hill: University of North Carolina Press, 1991.

Flynn, Edward J. *You're the Boss.* New York: Viking, 1947.

Foot, Peter. "The American Origins of NATO: A Study in Domestic Inhibitions and Western European Constraints." Ph.D. diss., University of Edinburgh, 1984.

Foot, Rosemary. "Making Known the Unknown War: Policy Analysis of the Korean Conflict in the Last Decade." *Diplomatic History* 15 (1991): 411–31.

————. *A Substitute for Victory: The Politics of Peacemaking at the Korean Armistice Talks.* Ithaca: Cornell University Press, 1990.

————. *The Wrong War: American Policy and the Dimensions of the Korean Conflict, 1950–1953.* Ithaca: Cornell University Press, 1985.

Foreign Relations of the United States: 1945, Conference of Berlin (The Potsdam Conference). 2 vols. Washington: Department of State, 1960.

Fossedal, Gregory A. *Will Clayton, the Marshall Plan, and the Triumph of Democracy.* Stanford: Hoover Institution Press, 1993.

Foster, James C. *The Union Politic: The CIO Political Action Committee.* Columbia: University of Missouri Press, 1975.

Fraser, Steven. *Labor Will Rule: Sidney Hillman and the Rise of American Labor.* New York: Free Press, 1991.

Freeland, Richard M. *The Truman Doctrine and the Origins of McCarthyism:*

Foreign Policy, Domestic Politics, and International Security, 1946–1948. Rev. ed. New York: New York University Press, 1985.

Freidel, Frank. *Franklin D. Roosevelt: A Rendezvous with Destiny*. Boston: Little, Brown, 1990.

Fried, Richard M. *Men against McCarthy*. New York: Columbia University Press, 1976.

———. *Nightmare in Red: The McCarthy Era in Perspective*. New York: Oxford University Press, 1990.

Friedman, Leon. "Election of 1944." In *History of American Presidential Elections*, edited by Arthur M. Schlesinger, Jr., Fred L. Israel, and William P. Hansen, 4:3009–96. New York: Chelsea House, 1971.

Gaddis, John Lewis. "The Emerging Post-Revisionist Synthesis on the Origins of the Cold War." *Diplomatic History* 7 (1983): 171–90.

———. "Intelligence, Espionage, and Cold War Origins." *Diplomatic History* 13 (1989): 191–212.

———. *The Long Peace: Inquiries into the History of the Cold War*. New York: Oxford University Press, 1987.

———. *Strategies of Containment: A Critical Appraisal of Postwar American National Security Policy*. New York: Oxford University Press, 1982.

———. "The Tragedy of Cold War History." *Diplomatic History* 17 (1993): 1–16.

———. *The United States and the Origins of the Cold War, 1941–1947*. New York: Columbia University Press, 1972.

———. "Was the Truman Doctrine a Real Turning Point?" *Foreign Affairs* 52 (1973–1974): 386–402.

Gallicchio, Marc S. *The Cold War Begins in Asia: American East Asian Policy and the Fall of the Japanese Empire*. New York: Columbia University Press, 1988.

Ganin, Zvi. *Truman, American Jewry, and Israel, 1945–1948*. New York: Holmes and Meier, 1979.

Gardner, Lloyd C. *Architects of Illusion: Men and Ideas in American Foreign Policy, 1941–1949*. Chicago: Quadrangle, 1970.

Garwood, Darrell. *Crossroads of America: The Story of Kansas City*. New York: Norton, 1945.

Gerson, Louis L. *John Foster Dulles*. New York: Cooper Square, 1968.

Giacalone, Rita A. "From Bad Neighbors to Reluctant Partners: Argentina and the United States, 1946–1950." Ph.D. diss., Indiana University, 1977.

Giglio, James N., and Greg G. Thielen. *Truman: In Cartoon and Caricature*. Ames: Iowa State University Press, 1984.

Gilbert, Martin. *Winston Churchill*. Vol. 8, *Never Despair, 1945–1965*. Boston: Houghton Mifflin, 1988.

Gillingham, John. *Coal, Steel, and the Rebirth of Europe, 1945–1955: The Germans and French from Ruhr Conflict to Economic Community*. New York: Cambridge University Press, 1991.

Gimbel, John. *The American Occupation of Germany.* Stanford: Stanford University Press, 1968.

———. *The Origins of the Marshall Plan.* Stanford: Stanford University Press, 1976.

———. *Science, Technology, and Reparations: Exploitation and Plunder in Postwar Germany.* Stanford: Stanford University Press, 1990.

Giovannitti, Len, and Fred Freed. *The Decision to Drop the Bomb.* New York: Coward-McCann, 1965.

Goncharov, Sergei, John Lewis, and Zue Litai. *Uncertain Partners: Stalin, Mao and the Korean War.* Stanford: Stanford University Press, 1993.

Goode, James F. *The United States and Iran, 1946–1951: The Diplomacy of Neglect.* New York: St. Martin's, 1989.

Goodwin, Craufurd D. W., and R. Stanley Herren. "The Truman Administration: Problems and Policies Unfold." In *Exhortation and Controls: The Search for a Wage-Price Policy, 1945–1971,* edited by Craufurd D. W. Goodwin, 9–93. Washington: Brookings Institution, 1975.

Gorman, Joseph B. *Kefauver: A Political Biography.* New York: Oxford University Press, 1971.

Gormly, James L. *The Collapse of the Grand Alliance, 1945–1948.* Baton Rouge: Louisiana State University Press, 1987.

———. *From Potsdam to the Cold War: Big Three Diplomacy, 1945–1947.* Wilmington, Del.: Scholarly Resources, 1990.

Gosnell, Harold F. *Truman's Crises: A Political Biography of Harry S Truman.* Westport, Conn.: Greenwood, 1980.

Goulden, Joseph C. *The Best Years, 1945–1950.* New York: Atheneum, 1976.

Graebner, Norman A. *The New Isolationism: A Study in Politics and Foreign Policy since 1950.* New York: Ronald, 1956.

Grant, James. *Bernard M. Baruch: The Adventures of a Wall Street Legend.* New York: Simon and Schuster, 1983.

Griffith, Robert. *The Politics of Fear: Joseph R. McCarthy and the Senate.* Lexington: University of Kentucky Press, 1970.

Gromyko, Andrei. *Memories.* London: Hutchinson, 1989.

Grothaus, Larry H. "The Negro in Missouri Politics, 1890–1941." Ph.D. diss., University of Missouri, 1970.

Guerrier, Steven W. "NSC-68 and the Truman Rearmament, 1950–1953." Ph.D. diss., University of Michigan, 1988.

Hahn, Peter L. *The United States, Great Britain, and Egypt, 1945–1956: Strategy and Diplomacy in the Early Cold War.* Chapel Hill: University of North Carolina Press, 1991.

Hamburger, Philip. "Good of You to Do This for Us, Mr. Truman." *New Yorker,* November 19, 1955, 120–39.

Hamby, Alonzo L. "An American Democrat: A Reevaluation of the Personality of Harry S. Truman." *American Political Science Review* 106 (1991): 33–53.

———. *Beyond the New Deal: Harry S. Truman and American Liberalism.* New York: Columbia University Press, 1973.

———. "Harry S. Truman: Insecurity and Responsibility." In *Leadership in the Modern Presidency,* edited by Fred T. Greenstein, 41–75. Cambridge: Harvard University Press, 1988.

Hand, Samuel B. *Counsel and Advise: A Political Biography of Samuel I. Rosenman.* New York: Garland, 1979.

Harbutt, Fraser J. *The Iron Curtain: Churchill, America, and the Origins of the Cold War.* New York: Oxford University Press, 1986.

Harper, Alan D. *The Politics of Loyalty: The White House and the Communist Issue, 1946–1952.* Westport, Conn.: Greenwood, 1969.

Harriman, W. Averell, and Elie Abel. *Special Envoy to Churchill and Stalin, 1941–1946.* New York: Random House, 1975.

Harrington, Daniel F. "American Policy in the Berlin Crisis of 1948–1949." Ph.D. diss., Indiana University, 1979.

———. "Kennan, Bohlen, and the Riga Axioms." *Diplomatic History* 2 (1978): 423–37.

Harris, Edward A. "Harry S. Truman: 'I Don't Want to Be President.'" In *Public Men: In and Out of Office,* edited by J. T. Salter, 3–21. Chapel Hill: University of North Carolina Press, 1946.

Harry S Truman, Late a President of the United States: Memorial Tributes Delivered in Congress. Washington: Government Printing Office, 1973.

Hartmann, Susan M. *Truman and the 80th Congress.* Columbia: University of Missouri Press, 1971.

Hathaway, Robert M. *Ambiguous Partnership: Britain and America, 1944–1947.* New York: Columbia University Press, 1981.

Haynes, Richard F. *The Awesome Power: Harry S. Truman as Commander in Chief.* Baton Rouge: Louisiana State University Press, 1973.

Heaster, Brenda L. "Who's on Second?" *Missouri Historical Review* 80 (1986): 156–75.

Hechler, Ken. *Working with Truman: A Personal Memoir of the White House Years.* New York: Putnam, 1982.

Heed, Thomas J. "Prelude to Whistle Stop: Harry S. Truman, the Apprentice Campaigner." Ph.D. diss., Teachers College, Columbia University, 1975.

Heller, Francis H. "Harry S. Truman: The Writing of His Memoirs." In *Political Memoir: Essays on the Politics of Memory,* edited by George Egerton, 257–73. London: Frank Cass, 1994.

———. "Truman." In *The History Makers,* edited by Lord Longford and Sir John Wheeler Bennett, 32–35. New York: St. Martin's, 1973.

———. "The Writing of the Truman Memoirs." *Presidential Studies Quarterly* 13.1 (1983): 81–84.

———, ed. *Economics and the Truman Administration.* Lawrence: Regents Press of Kansas, 1981.

————, ed. *The Korean War: A 25-Year Perspective.* Lawrence: Regents Press of Kansas, 1977.

————, ed. *The Truman White House: The Administration of the Presidency, 1945–1953.* Lawrence: Regents Press of Kansas, 1980.

Heller, Francis H., and John R. Gillingham, eds. *NATO: The Founding of the Atlantic Alliance and the Integration of Europe.* New York: St. Martin's, 1992.

Helm, William P. *Harry Truman: A Political Biography.* New York: Duell, Sloan and Pearce, 1947.

Henderson, Richard B. *Maury Maverick: A Political Biography.* Austin: University of Texas Press, 1970.

Herken, Gregg. *Counsels of War.* New York: Knopf, 1985.

————. *The Winning Weapon: The Atomic Bomb in the Cold War, 1945–1950.* New York: Knopf, 1980.

Herman, Jan Kenneth. "The President's Cardiologist." *Navy Medicine* 81 (March–April 1990): 6–13.

Herring, George C., Jr. *Aid to Russia, 1941–1946: Strategy, Diplomacy, the Origins of the Cold War.* New York: Columbia University Press, 1973.

Herschler, David. "Retreat in Germany: The Decision to Withdraw Anglo-American Forces from the Soviet Occupational Zone, 1945." Ph.D. diss., Indiana University, 1977.

Hersey, John. *Aspects of the Presidency.* New Haven and New York: Ticknor and Fields, 1980.

Hess, Gary R. *The United States' Emergence as a Southeast Asian Power, 1940–1950.* New York: Columbia University Press, 1987.

Hewlett, Richard G., and Oscar E. Anderson, Jr. *A History of the United States Atomic Energy Commission.* Vol. 1, *The New World, 1939–1946.* University Park: Pennsylvania State University Press, 1962.

Hewlett, Richard G., and Francis Duncan. *A History of the United States Atomic Energy Commission.* Vol. 2, *Atomic Shield, 1947–1952.* University Park: Pennsylvania State University Press, 1969.

Hillman, William. *Mr. President.* New York: Farrar, Straus and Young, 1952.

Hixson, Walter L. *George F. Kennan: Cold War Iconoclast.* New York: Columbia University Press, 1989.

Hogan, Michael J. *The Marshall Plan: America, Britain, and the Reconstruction of Western Europe, 1947–1952.* New York: Cambridge University Press, 1987.

Holloway, David. *The Soviet Union and the Arms Race.* Rev. ed. New Haven: Yale University Press, 1984.

Hoopes, Townsend, and Douglas Brinkley. *Driven Patriot: The Life and Times of James V. Forrestal.* New York: Knopf, 1992.

Hua, Gingzhao. *From Yalta to Panmunjom: Truman's Diplomacy and the Four Powers, 1945–1953.* Ithaca: East Asia Program, Cornell University, 1992.

Hulston, John K. *An Ozarks Lawyer's Story, 1946–1976.* Republic, Mo.: Privately printed, 1976.

Huthmacher, J. Joseph. *Senator Robert F. Wagner and the Rise of Urban Liberalism.* New York: Atheneum, 1968.

Isaacson, Walter, and Evan Thomas. *The Wise Men: Six Friends and the World They Made.* New York: Simon and Schuster, 1986.

Jacobson, Edward. "Two Presidents and a Haberdasher—1948." *American Jewish Archives* 20 (April 1968): 3–15.

James, D. Clayton. *Command Crisis: MacArthur and the Korean War.* Colorado Springs: U.S. Air Force Academy, 1982.

———. *The Years of MacArthur: Triumph and Disaster, 1945–1964.* Boston: Houghton Mifflin, 1985.

James, D. Clayton, with Anne Sharp Wells. *Refighting the Last War: Command and Crisis in Korea, 1950–1953.* New York: Free Press, 1993.

Jenkins, Roy. *Truman.* New York: Harper and Row, 1986.

Jensen, Kenneth M., ed. *Origins of the Cold War: The Novikov, Kennan, and Roberts "Long Telegrams" of 1946.* Washington: U.S. Institute of Peace, 1991.

Johnson, U. Alexis, with Jef Olivarius. *The Right Hand of Power.* Englewood Cliffs, N.J.: Prentice, Hall, 1984.

Jones, Howard. *"A New Kind of War": America's Global Strategy and the Truman Doctrine in Greece.* New York: Oxford University Press, 1989.

Jones, Howard, and Randall B. Woods. "The Origins of the Cold War: A Symposium." *Diplomatic History* 17 (1993): 251–76.

Jones, Joseph M. *The Fifteen Weeks (February 21–June 5, 1947).* New York: Viking, 1955.

Jones, Robert H. *The Roads to Russia: United States Lend-Lease to the Soviet Union.* Norman: University of Oklahoma Press, 1969.

Josephson, Matthew. *Sidney Hillman: Statesman of American Labor.* Garden City, N.Y.: Doubleday, 1952.

Kaplan, Lawrence S. *A Community of Interests: NATO and the Military Assistance Program, 1948–1951.* Washington: U.S. Department of Defense, 1980.

———. *NATO and the United States: The Enduring Alliance.* Updated ed. New York: Twayne, 1994.

———. *The United States and NATO: The Formative Years.* Lexington: University Press of Kentucky, 1984.

———, ed. *American Historians and the Atlantic Alliance.* Kent, Ohio: Kent State University Press, 1991.

Kardelj, Edvard. *Reminiscences: The Struggle for Recognition and Independence. The New Yugoslavia, 1944–1957.* London: Blond and Briggs, 1982.

Kaufman, Burton I. *The Korean War: Challenges in Crisis, Credibility, and Command.* Philadelphia: Temple University Press, 1986.

Keeley, Mary Paxton. *Back in Independence.* Chillicothe, Mo.: Privately printed, 1992.

[Keeley], Mary Gentry Paxton. *Mary Gentry and John Gallatin Paxton.* Chillicothe, Mo.: Privately printed, 1967.

Kelley, John L. "An Insurgent in the Truman Cabinet: Henry A. Wallace's Effort to Redirect Foreign Policy." *Missouri Historical Review* 77 (1982–1983): 64–93.

Kemper, Donald J. *Decade of Fear: Senator Hennings and Civil Liberties.* Columbia: University of Missouri Press, 1965.

Kennan, George F. "The Failure in Our Success." *New York Times,* March 14, 1994.

———. *Memoirs, 1925–1950.* Boston: Little, Brown, 1967.

———. "The Sources of Soviet Conduct." *Foreign Affairs* 25 (1946–1947): 566–82.

Kepley, David R. *The Collapse of the Middle Way: Senate Republicans and the Bipartisan Foreign Policy, 1948–1952.* Westport, Conn.: Greenwood, 1988.

Kertesz, Stephen D. *Between Russia and the West: Hungary and the Illusion of Peacemaking, 1945–1947.* Notre Dame: University of Notre Dame Press, 1984.

———. *Diplomacy in a Whirlpool.* Notre Dame: University of Notre Dame Press, 1953.

———, ed. *The Fate of East Central Europe.* Notre Dame: University of Notre Dame Press, 1956.

Khrushchev, Nikita Sergeyevich. *Khrushchev Remembers.* Vol. 3, *The Glasnost Tapes.* Boston: Little, Brown, 1990.

Király, Béla K. "The Aborted Soviet Military Plans against Tito's Yugoslavia." In *At the Brink of War and Peace: The Tito-Stalin Split in a Historic Perspective,* edited by Wayne S. Vucinich, 273–88. New York: Columbia University Press, 1982.

Kirk, Elise K. *Music at the White House: A History of the American Spirit.* Urbana: University of Illinois Press, 1986.

Kirkendall, Richard S. "Election of 1948." In *History of American Presidential Elections,* edited by Arthur M. Schlesinger, Jr., Fred L. Israel, and William P. Hansen, 4:3099–3211. New York: Chelsea House, 1971.

———. "ER and the Issue of FDR's Successor." In *Without Precedent: The Life and Career of Eleanor Roosevelt,* edited by Joan Hoff-Wilson and Marjorie Lightman, 176–97. Bloomington: Indiana University Press, 1984.

———. *A History of Missouri, 1919 to 1953.* Columbia: University of Missouri Press, 1986.

———, ed. *The Harry S. Truman Encyclopedia.* Boston: G. K. Hall, 1989.

———, ed. *The Truman Period as a Research Field.* Rev. ed. Columbia: University of Missouri Press, 1974.

Knappen, Marshall. *And Call It Peace.* Chicago: University of Chicago Press, 1947.

Koenig, Louis W. *The Truman Administration.* New York: New York University Press, 1956.

Kofsky, Frank. *Harry S. Truman and the War Scare of 1948: A Successful Campaign to Deceive the Nation.* New York: St. Martin's, 1993.

Kolko, Joyce, and Gabriel Kolko. *The Limits of Power: The World and United States Foreign Policy, 1945–54.* New York: Harper and Row, 1972.

Krock, Arthur. *Memoirs: Sixty Years on the Firing Line.* New York: Funk and Wagnalls, 1968.

Kuklick, Bruce. *American Policy and the Division of Germany: The Clash with Russia over Reparations.* Ithaca: Cornell University Press, 1972.

Kuniholm, Bruce R. *The Origins of the Cold War in the Near East: Great Power Conflict and Diplomacy in Iran, Turkey, and Greece.* Princeton: Princeton University Press, 1979.

Lacey, Michael J., ed. *The Truman Presidency.* New York: Cambridge University Press, 1989.

Lamphere, Robert J., and Tom Schachtman. *The FBI-KGB War: A Special Agent's Story.* New York: Random House, 1986.

Larson, Deborah W. *Origins of Containment: A Psychological Explanation.* Princeton: Princeton University Press, 1985.

Lasby, Clarence G. *Project Paperclip: German Scientists and the Cold War.* New York: Atheneum, 1971.

Lash, Joseph P. *A World of Love: Eleanor Roosevelt and Her Friends, 1943–1962.* Garden City, N.Y.: Doubleday, 1984.

Latham, Earl. *The Communist Controversy in Washington: From the New Deal to McCarthy.* Cambridge: Harvard University Press, 1966.

Launius, Roger D., and Coy F. Cross II. *MAC and the Legacy of the Berlin Airlift.* Scott Air Force Base, Ill.: Military Airlift Command, 1989.

Leahy, William D. *I Was There.* New York: Whittlesey House, 1950.

Lee, R. Alton. "The Army 'Mutiny' of 1946." *Journal of American History* 53 (1966–1967): 555–71.

———. *Harry S. Truman: Where Did the Buck Stop?* New York: Lang, 1991.

———. *Truman and Taft-Hartley: A Question of Mandate.* Lexington: University Press of Kentucky, 1966.

Leffler, Melvyn P. "The American Conception of National Security and the Beginnings of the Cold War, 1945–1948." *American Historical Review* 89 (1984): 346–81.

———. *A Preponderance of Power: National Security, the Truman Administration, and the Cold War.* Stanford: Stanford University Press, 1992.

Leuchtenburg, William E. "The Conversion of Harry Truman." *American Heritage* 42 (November 1991): 55–68.

———. *In the Shadow of FDR: From Harry Truman to Bill Clinton.* 2d ed. Ithaca: Cornell University Press, 1993.

Levantrosser, William F., ed. *Harry S. Truman: The Man from Independence.* Westport, Conn.: Greenwood, 1986.

Libbey, James K. *Dear Alben: Mr. Barkley of Kentucky.* Lexington: University Press of Kentucky, 1979.

Lieberman, Joseph I. *The Scorpion and the Tarantula: The Struggle to Control Atomic Weapons, 1945–1949.* Boston: Houghton Mifflin, 1970.

Lilienthal, David E. *The Journals of David E. Lilienthal.* Vol. 2, *The Atomic Energy Years, 1945–1950.* New York: Harper and Row, 1964.

Lindert, Peter H. "Long-Run Trends in American Farmland Values." *Agricultural History* 62 (summer 1988): 45–85.

Lingham, Brian. *Harry Truman: The Man—His Music.* Kansas City: Lowell, 1985.

Lord, Russell. *The Wallaces of Iowa.* Boston: Houghton Mifflin, 1947.

Lowe, Peter. *The Origins of the Korean War.* London: Longman, 1986.

———. "The Settlement of the Korean War." In *The Foreign Policy of Churchill's Peacetime Administration, 1951–55,* edited by J. W. Young, 207–31. Leicester, Eng.: Leicester University Press, 1988.

Lukacs, John. *The End of the Twentieth Century and the End of the Modern Age.* New York: Ticknor and Fields, 1993.

———. *A New History of the Cold War.* Garden City, N.Y.: Doubleday, 1966.

———. *Year Zero.* Garden City, N.Y.: Doubleday, 1978.

Lukas, Richard C. *Bitter Legacy: Polish-American Relations in the Wake of World War II.* Lexington: University Press of Kentucky, 1982.

Lundestad, Geir. *America, Scandinavia, and the Cold War, 1945–1949.* New York: Columbia University Press, 1980.

———. *The American Non-Policy toward Eastern Europe, 1943–1947: Universalism in an Area Not of Essential Interest to the United States.* Tromsö, Norway: Universitetsforlaget, 1978.

Lytle, Mark H. *The Origins of the Iran-American Alliance, 1941–1953.* New York: Holmes and Meier, 1987.

MacArthur, Douglas. *Reminiscences.* New York: McGraw-Hill, 1964.

McAuliffe, Mary. *Crisis on the Left: Cold War Politics and American Liberals, 1947–1954.* Amherst: University of Massachusetts Press, 1978.

McCagg, William O., Jr. *Stalin Embattled, 1943–1948.* Detroit: Wayne State University Press, 1978.

McClellan, Woodford. "Molotov Remembers." Review of *Sto sorok besed s Molotovym* (One Hundred Forty Conversations with Molotov) by Felix Chuyev. *Cold War International History Project Bulletin* 1 (spring 1992): 17–21.

McClure, Arthur F. *The Truman Administration and the Problems of Postwar Labor, 1945–1946.* Rutherford, N.J.: Fairleigh Dickinson University Press, 1969.

McCormick, Thomas J. *America's Half-Century: United States Foreign Policy in the Cold War.* Baltimore: Johns Hopkins University Press, 1989.

McCoy, Donald R. *The Presidency of Harry S. Truman.* Lawrence: University Press of Kansas, 1984.

McCoy, Donald R., and Richard T. Ruetten. *Quest and Response: Minority Rights and the Truman Administration.* Lawrence: University Press of Kansas, 1973.

McCullough, David. *Truman*. New York: Simon and Schuster, 1992.

McGhee, George. *Envoy to the Middle World: Adventures in Diplomacy*. New York: Harper and Row, 1983.

McGuire, Jack B. "Andrew Higgins Plays Presidential Politics." *Louisiana History* 15 (1974): 273–84.

McJimsey, George. *Harry Hopkins: Ally of the Poor and Defender of Democracy*. Cambridge: Harvard University Press, 1987.

McLellan, David S. *Dean Acheson: The State Department Years*. New York: Dodd, Mead, 1976.

McLellan, David S., and David C. Acheson, eds. *Among Friends: Personal Letters of Dean Acheson*. New York: Dodd, Mead, 1980.

Macmillan, Harold. *Tides of Fortune, 1945–1955*. New York: Harper and Row, 1969.

McNaughton, Frank, and Walter Hehmeyer. *Harry Truman: President*. New York: Whittlesey House, 1948.

———. *This Man Truman*. New York: McGraw-Hill, 1945.

Maddox, Robert F. *The Senatorial Career of Harley Martin Kilgore*. New York: Garland, 1981.

Maddox, Robert James. *From War to Cold War: The Education of Harry S. Truman*. Boulder, Colo.: Westview, 1988.

———. *The New Left and the Origins of the Cold War*. Princeton: Princeton University Press, 1973.

Maney, Patrick J. *The Roosevelt Presence: A Biography of Franklin Delano Roosevelt*. New York: Twayne, 1992.

———. *"Young Bob" La Follette: A Biography of Robert M. La Follette, Jr., 1895–1953*. Columbia: University of Missouri Press, 1978.

Marcus, Maeva. *Truman and the Steel Seizure Case: The Limits of Presidential Power*. New York: Columbia University Press, 1977.

Markowitz, Norman D. *The Rise and Fall of the People's Century: Henry A. Wallace and American Liberalism, 1941–1948*. New York: Free Press, 1973.

Martin, Edwin W. *Divided Counsel: The Anglo-American Response to Communist Victory in China*. Lexington: University Press of Kentucky, 1986.

Martin, George. *Madam Secretary: Frances Perkins*. Boston: Houghton Mifflin, 1976.

Martin, Joe. *My First Fifty Years in Politics*. New York: McGraw-Hill, 1960.

Martin, John Bartlow. *Adlai Stevenson of Illinois*. Garden City, N.Y.: Doubleday, 1976.

Mastny, Vojtech. *Russia's Road to the Cold War: Diplomacy, Warfare, and the Politics of Communism, 1941–1945*. New York: Columbia University Press, 1979.

Matray, James I. *The Reluctant Crusade: American Foreign Policy in Korea, 1941–1950*. Honolulu: University of Hawaii Press, 1985.

Matusow, Allen J. *Farm Policies and Politics in the Truman Years*. Cambridge: Harvard University Press, 1967.

May, Ernest R. *"Lessons of the Past": The Use and Misuse of History in American Foreign Policy*. New York: Oxford University Press, 1973.

————. *The Truman Administration and China, 1945–1949.* Philadelphia: Lippincott, 1975.

————, ed. *American Cold War Strategy: Interpreting NSC 68.* New York: St. Martin's, 1993.

May, Gary. *China Scapegoat: The Diplomatic Ordeal of John Carter Vincent.* Washington: New Republic Books, 1979.

————. *Un-American Activities: The Trials of William Remington.* New York: Oxford University Press, 1994.

Mayers, David. *George Kennan and the Dilemmas of US Foreign Policy.* New York: Oxford University Press, 1988.

Mazuzan, George T. *Warren R. Austin at the U.N., 1946–1953.* Kent, Ohio: Kent State University Press, 1977.

Mee, Charles L., Jr. *Meeting at Potsdam.* New York: Evans, 1975.

Messer, Robert L. *The End of an Alliance: James F. Byrnes, Roosevelt, Truman, and the Origins of the Cold War.* Chapel Hill: University of North Carolina Press, 1982.

Miller, James Edward. *The United States and Italy, 1940–1950: The Politics and Diplomacy of Stabilization.* Chapel Hill: University of North Carolina Press, 1986.

Miller, Richard Lawrence. *Truman: The Rise to Power.* New York: McGraw-Hill, 1986.

Milligan, Maurice M. *Missouri Waltz: The Inside Story of the Pendergast Machine by the Man Who Smashed It.* New York: Scribner's, 1948.

Millis, Walter, ed. *The Forrestal Diaries.* New York: Viking, 1951.

Milward, Alan S. *The Reconstruction of Western Europe, 1945–1951.* Berkeley and Los Angeles: University of California Press, 1984.

Minear, Richard H. *Victors' Justice: The Tokyo War Crimes Trial.* Princeton: Princeton University Press, 1971.

Miscamble, Wilson D., C.S.C. *George F. Kennan and the Making of American Foreign Policy, 1947–1950.* Princeton: Princeton University Press, 1992.

Mitchell, Franklin. *Embattled Democracy: Missouri Democratic Politics, 1919–1932.* Columbia: University of Missouri Press, 1968.

Moran, Lord [Charles McM. W.]. *Churchill: The Struggle for Survival, 1940–1965. Taken from the Diaries of Lord Moran.* Boston: Houghton Mifflin, 1966.

Morgan, Anne Hodges. *Robert S. Kerr: The Senate Years.* Norman: University of Oklahoma Press, 1977.

Munro, John A., and Alex T. Inglis, eds. *Mike: The Memoirs of the Right Honourable Lester B. Pearson, 1948–1957.* New York: Quadrangle, 1972.

Murphy, Robert D. *Diplomat among Warriors.* Garden City, N.Y.: Doubleday, 1964.

Nagai, Yonosuke, and Akira Iriye, eds. *The Origins of the Cold War in Asia.* New York: Columbia University Press, 1977.

Neal, Steve. "Our Best and Worst Presidents." *Chicago Tribune Magazine,* January 10, 1982.

Nelson, Anna Kasten. "President Truman and the Evolution of the National Security Council." *Journal of American History* 72 (1984–1985): 360–78.

Nesbitt, Henrietta. *White House Diary.* Garden City, N.Y.: Doubleday, 1948.

Newton, Verne W. *The Cambridge Spies: The Untold Story of Maclean, Philby, and Burgess in America.* Lanham, Md.: Madison, 1991.

Nitze, Paul H. *From Hiroshima to Glasnost: At the Center of Decision.* New York: Grove, Weidenfeld, 1989.

Olson, Sarah M. *Historic Furnishings Report: Harry S. Truman Home, Harry S. Truman National Historic Site.* Harpers Ferry, Va., 1986.

Pach, Chester J., Jr. *Arming the Free World: The Origins of the United States Military Assistance Program, 1945–1950.* Chapel Hill: University of North Carolina Press, 1991.

Paige, Glenn D. *The Korean Decision, June 24–30, 1950.* New York: Free Press, 1968.

Parks, Lillian Rogers, and Frances Spatz Leighton. *My Thirty Years Backstairs at the White House.* New York: Fleet, 1961.

Parrish, Scott. "A Diplomat Reports." Review of *Vospominaniya Diplomata: Zapiski 1938–1947* (Recollections of a Diplomat: Notes, 1938–1947) by Nikolai V. Novikov. *Cold War International History Project Bulletin* 1 (spring 1992): 16, 21–22.

Paterson, Thomas G. *On Every Front: The Making and Unmaking of the Cold War.* Rev. ed. New York: Norton, 1992.

———. *Soviet-American Confrontation: Postwar Reconstruction and the Origins of the Cold War.* Baltimore: Johns Hopkins University Press, 1973.

Patterson, James T. *Mr. Republican: A Biography of Robert A. Taft.* Boston: Houghton Mifflin, 1972.

Pearson, Nathan W., Jr. *Goin' to Kansas City.* Urbana: University of Illinois Press, 1987.

Pemberton, William E. *Bureaucratic Politics: Executive Reorganization during the Truman Administration.* Columbia: University of Missouri Press, 1979.

———. *Harry S. Truman: Fair Dealer and Cold Warrior.* Boston: Twayne, 1989.

Pepper, Claude D., and Hays Gorey. *Pepper: Eyewitness to a Century.* New York: Harcourt Brace Jovanovich, 1987.

Peterson, F. Ross. *Prophet without Honor: Glen H. Taylor and the Fight for American Liberalism.* Lexington: University of Kentucky Press, 1974.

Peterson, Gale E. *President Harry S. Truman and the Independent Regulatory Commissions, 1945–1952.* New York: Garland, 1985.

Pfau, Richard. *No Sacrifice Too Great: The Life of Lewis L. Strauss.* Charlottesville: University Press of Virginia, 1984.

Phillips, Cabell. *The Truman Presidency: The History of a Triumphant Succession.* New York: Macmillan, 1966.

Pickersgill, J. W., and D. F. Forster, eds. *The Mackenzie King Record.* Vol. 2., *1944–1945.* Toronto: University of Toronto Press, 1972.

Pisani, Sallie. *The CIA and the Marshall Plan.* Lawrence: University Press of Kansas, 1991.

Poen, Monte M. *Harry S. Truman versus the Medical Lobby: The Genesis of Medicare.* Columbia: University of Missouri Press, 1979.

———, ed. *Letters Home by Harry Truman.* New York: Putnam, 1984.

———, ed. *Strictly Personal and Confidential: The Letters Harry Truman Never Mailed.* Boston: Little, Brown, 1982.

Pogue, Forrest C. *George C. Marshall.* Vol. 4, *Statesman.* New York: Viking, 1987.

Pollard, Robert A. *Economic Security and the Origins of the Cold War, 1945–1950.* New York: Columbia University Press, 1985.

Poole, Walter S. *The History of the Joint Chiefs of Staff: The Joint Chiefs of Staff and National Policy.* Vol. 4, *1950–1952.* Wilmington, Del.: Glazier, 1979.

Powers, Richard Gid. *Secrecy and Power: The Life of J. Edgar Hoover.* New York: Free Press, 1987.

Pruden, Edward Hughes. *A Window on Washington.* New York: Vantage, 1976.

Pruessen, Ronald W. *John Foster Dulles: The Road to Power.* New York: Free Press, 1982.

Public Papers of the Presidents: Harry S. Truman, 1945–1953. 8 vols. Washington: Government Printing Office, 1961–1966.

Purifoy, Lewis McC. *Harry Truman's China Policy: McCarthyism and the Diplomacy of Hysteria, 1947–1951.* New York: New Viewpoints, 1976.

Rearden, Steven L. *The Evolution of American Strategic Doctrine: Paul H. Nitze and the Soviet Challenge.* Boulder, Colo.: Westview, 1984.

———. *History of the Office of the Secretary of Defense.* Vol. 1, *The Formative Years, 1947–1950.* Washington: U.S. Department of Defense, 1984.

Reddig, William M. *Tom's Town.* Philadelphia: Lippincott, 1947.

Redding, Jack [John M.]. *Inside the Democratic Party.* Indianapolis: Bobbs-Merrill, 1958.

Reinhard, David W. *The Republican Right since 1945.* Lexington: University Press of Kentucky, 1983.

Reinsch, J. Leonard. *Getting Elected: From Radio and Roosevelt to Television and Reagan.* New York: Hippocrene, 1988.

Resis, Albert. *Stalin, the Politburo, and the Onset of the Cold War, 1945–1946.* Pittsburgh: University of Pittsburgh Press, 1988.

Reston, James. *Deadline: A Memoir.* New York: Random House, 1991.

Rhodes, Richard. *The Making of the Atomic Bomb.* New York: Simon and Schuster, 1986.

Riddle, Donald H. *The Truman Committee: A Study in Congressional Responsibility.* New Brunswick, N.J.: Rutgers University Press, 1964.

Ridgway, Matthew B. *The Korean War.* Garden City, N.Y.: Doubleday, 1967.

Rigdon, William M. *White House Sailor.* Garden City, N.Y.: Doubleday, 1962.

Riste, Olav, ed. *Western Security: The Formative Years. European and Atlantic Defence, 1947–1953.* New York: Columbia University Press, 1985.

Robbins, Charles, and Bradley Smith. *Last of His Kind: An Informal Portrait of Harry S. Truman*. New York: Morrow, 1979.

Robbins, Jhan. *Bess and Harry: An American Love Story*. New York: Putnam, 1980.

Rogow, Arnold A. *James Forrestal: A Study of Personality, Politics, and Policy*. New York: Macmillan, 1963.

Rose, Lisle A. *After Yalta*. New York: Scribner's, 1973.

—————. *Dubious Victory: The United States and the End of World War II*. Kent, Ohio: Kent State University Press, 1973.

—————. *Roots of Tragedy: The United States and the Struggle for Asia, 1945–1953*. Westport, Conn.: Greenwood, 1976.

Rosenberg, David Alan. "American Atomic Strategy and the Hydrogen Bomb Decision." *Journal of American History* 66 (1978–1979): 62–87.

—————. "The Origins of Overkill: Nuclear Weapons and American Strategy, 1945–1960." *International Security* 7 (spring 1983): 3–71.

—————. "U.S. Nuclear Stockpile 1945 to 1950." *Bulletin of the Atomic Scientists* 35 (May 1982): 25–31.

Rosenman, Samuel I. *Working with Roosevelt*. New York: Harper, 1952.

Rosenman, Samuel I., and Dorothy Rosenman. *Presidential Style: Some Giants and a Pygmy in the White House*. New York: Harper and Row, 1976.

Ross, Irwin. *The Loneliest Campaign: The Truman Victory of 1948*. New York: New American Library, 1968.

Ross, Steven T., and David Alan Rosenberg, eds. *America's Plans for War against the Soviet Union, 1945–1950*. 15 vols. New York: Garland, 1990.

Rovere, Richard H. *Senator Joe McCarthy*. New York: Harcourt, Brace, 1959.

Rovere, Richard H., and Arthur M. Schlesinger, Jr. *General MacArthur and President Truman: The Struggle for Control of American Foreign Policy*. 3d ed. New Brunswick, N.J.: Transaction, 1992.

Ruddy, T. Michael. *The Cautious Diplomat: Charles E. Bohlen and the Soviet Union, 1929–1969*. Kent, Ohio: Kent State University Press, 1986.

Rusk, Dean. *As I Saw It: As Told to Richard Rusk*. New York: Norton, 1990.

Ryan, Henry Butterfield. *The Vision of Anglo-America: The US-UK Alliance and the Emerging Cold War, 1943–1946*. Cambridge: Cambridge University Press, 1987.

Salmond, John. *A Southern Rebel: The Life and Times of Aubrey Willis Williams, 1890–1965*. Chapel Hill: University of North Carolina Press, 1983.

Saltonstall, Leverett. *Salty: Recollections of a Yankee in Politics*. Boston: Boston Globe, 1976.

Sand, G. W. *Truman in Retirement: A Former President Views the Nation and the World*. South Bend, Ind.: Justice, 1993.

Sawyer, Charles, with Eugene P. Trani. *Concerns of a Conservative Democrat*. Carbondale: Southern Illinois University Press, 1968.

Schaller, Michael. *The American Occupation of Japan: The Origins of the Cold War in Asia*. New York: Oxford University Press, 1985.

——. *Douglas MacArthur: The Far Eastern General*. New York: Oxford University Press, 1989.

Schapsmeier, Edward L., and Frederick H. Schapsmeier. *Prophet in Politics: Henry A. Wallace and the War Years, 1940–1965*. Ames: Iowa State University Press, 1970.

Schauffler, Edward R. *Harry Truman: Son of the Soil*. Kansas City: Privately printed, 1945.

Schlesinger, Arthur M., Jr. *Harry S. Truman: The Unexpected Champion of Racial Justice*. Independence, Mo.: Harry S. Truman Library Institute, 1992.

——. "Origins of the Cold War." *Foreign Affairs* 46 (1967–1968): 22–52.

——. *The Vital Center: The Politics of Freedom*. 2d ed. Boston: Houghton Mifflin, 1962.

Schmidt, Karl M. *Henry A. Wallace: Quixotic Crusade, 1948*. Syracuse, N.Y.: Syracuse University Press, 1960.

Schmidtlein, Eugene F. "Truman the Senator." Ph.D. diss., University of Missouri, 1962.

Schoenbaum, Thomas J. *Waging Peace and War: Dean Rusk in the Truman, Kennedy, and Johnson Years*. New York: Simon and Schuster, 1988.

Schonberger, Howard B. *Aftermath of War: Americans and the Remaking of Japan, 1945–1952*. Kent, Ohio: Kent State University Press, 1989.

Schwartz, Thomas Alan. *America's Germany: John J. McCloy and the Federal Republic of Germany*. Cambridge: Harvard University Press, 1991.

Schwarz, Jordan A. *Liberal: Adolf A. Berle and the Vision of an American Era*. New York: Free Press, 1987.

——. *The Speculator: Bernard M. Baruch in Washington, 1917–1965*. Chapel Hill: University of North Carolina Press, 1981.

Scobie, Ingrid Winther. *Center Stage: Helen Gahagan Douglas, a Life*. New York: Oxford University Press, 1992.

Sebald, William J. *With MacArthur in Japan: A Personal History of the Occupation*. New York: Norton, 1965.

Sherwin, Martin J. *A World Destroyed: The Atomic Bomb and the Grand Alliance*. New York: Knopf, 1975.

Sherwood, Robert E. *Roosevelt and Hopkins: An Intimate History*. Rev. ed. New York: Harper, 1950.

Shlaim, Avi. *The United States and the Berlin Blockade, 1948–1949: A Study in Crisis Decision-Making*. Berkeley and Los Angeles: University of California Press, 1983.

Sigal, Leon V. *Fighting to a Finish: The Politics of War Termination in the United States and Japan, 1945*. Ithaca: Cornell University Press, 1988.

Simmons, Robert R. *The Strained Alliance: Peking, Pyongyang, Moscow, and the Politics of the Korean Civil War*. New York: Free Press, 1975.

Siracusa, Joseph M. *New Left Diplomatic Histories and Historians: The American Revisionists*. Rev. ed. Claremont, Calif.: Regina, 1993.

Sirevag, Torbjorn. *The Eclipse of the New Deal: And the Fall of Vice President Wallace, 1944.* New York: Garland, 1985.

Skates, John Ray. *The Invasion of Japan: Alternative to the Bomb.* Columbia: University of South Carolina Press, 1994.

Slaughter, Stephen S. *History of a Missouri Farm Family: The O. V. Slaughters, 1700–1944.* Harrison, N.Y.: Harbor Hill, 1978.

Smith, A. Robert. *The Tiger in the Senate: The Biography of Wayne Morse.* Garden City, N.Y.: Doubleday, 1962.

Smith, Alice Kimball. *A Peril and a Hope: The Scientists' Movement in America, 1945–47.* Chicago: University of Chicago Press, 1965.

Smith, E. Timothy. *The United States, Italy, and NATO, 1947–52.* New York: St. Martin's, 1991.

Smith, Gaddis. *Dean Acheson.* New York: Cooper Square, 1972.

Smith, Jean Edward. *Lucius D. Clay: An American Life.* New York: Holt, 1990.

———, ed. *The Papers of General Lucius D. Clay: Germany, 1945–1949.* 2 vols. Bloomington: Indiana University Press, 1974.

Smith, Richard Norton. *Thomas E. Dewey and His Times.* New York: Simon and Schuster, 1982.

Smith, W. Bedell. *My Three Years in Moscow.* Philadelphia: Lippincott, 1950.

Snetsinger, John. *Truman, the Jewish Vote, and the Creation of Israel.* Stanford: Hoover Institution Press, 1974.

Spanier, John W. *The Truman-MacArthur Controversy and the Korean War.* Cambridge: Harvard University Press, 1959.

Spritzer, Donald E. *Senator James E. Murray and the Limits of Post–New Deal Liberalism.* New York: Garland, 1985.

Stavrakis, Peter J. *Moscow and Greek Communism, 1944–1949.* Ithaca: Cornell University Press, 1989.

Steinberg, Alfred. *The Man from Missouri: The Life and Times of Harry S. Truman.* New York: Putnam, 1962.

Steininger, Rolf. *The German Question: The Stalin Note of 1952 and the Problem of Unification.* New York: Columbia University Press, 1990.

Stephanson, Anders. *Kennan and the Art of Foreign Policy.* Cambridge: Harvard University Press, 1989.

Sternsher, Bernard. "Harry Truman." In *Popular Images of American Presidents,* edited by William C. Spragens, 387–409. Westport, Conn.: Greenwood, 1988.

Stiller, Jesse H. *George S. Messersmith: Diplomat of Democracy.* Chapel Hill: University of North Carolina Press, 1987.

Stromer, Marvin E. *The Making of a Political Leader: Kenneth S. Wherry and the United States Senate.* Lincoln: University of Nebraska Press, 1969.

Stueck, William Whitney, Jr. *The Road to Confrontation: American Policy toward China and Korea, 1947–1950.* Chapel Hill: University of North Carolina Press, 1981.

————. *The Wedemeyer Mission: American Politics and Foreign Policy during the Cold War.* Athens: University of Georgia Press, 1984.

Swain, Martha H. *Pat Harrison: The New Deal Years.* Jackson: University Press of Mississippi, 1978.

Taubman, William. *Stalin's American Policy: From Entente to Detente to Cold War.* New York: Norton, 1982.

Taylor, Glen H. *The Way It Was with Me.* Secaucus, N.J.: Lyle Stuart, 1979.

Theoharis, Athan G. *From the Secret Files of J. Edgar Hoover.* Chicago: Dee, 1991.

————. *Seeds of Repression: Harry S. Truman and the Origins of McCarthyism.* Chicago: Quadrangle, 1971.

————. *The Yalta Myths: An Issue in U.S. Politics, 1945–1955.* Columbia: University of Missouri Press, 1970.

————, ed. *The Truman Presidency: The Origins of the Imperial Presidency and the National Security State.* Stanfordville, N.Y.: Earl M. Coleman, 1979.

Theoharis, Athan, and John Stuart Cox. *The Boss: J. Edgar Hoover and the Great American Inquisition.* Philadelphia: Temple University Press, 1988.

Thompson, Kenneth W., ed. *Portraits of American Presidents: The Truman Presidency.* Lanham, Md.: University Press of America, 1984.

Toulmin, Harry A., Jr. *Diary of Democracy: The Senate War Investigating Committee.* New York: R. R. Smith, 1947.

Traubel, Helen. *St. Louis Woman.* New York: Duell, Sloan and Pearce, 1959.

Trohan, Walter. *Political Animals: Memoirs of a Sentimental Cynic.* Garden City, N.Y.: Doubleday, 1975.

Truman, Harry S. *Memoirs.* Vol. 1, *Year of Decisions.* Vol. 2, *Years of Trial and Hope.* Garden City, N.Y.: Doubleday, 1955, 1956.

————. *Mr. Citizen.* New York: Geis, 1960.

————. *Truman Speaks.* New York: Columbia University Press, 1960.

Truman, Margaret. *Bess W. Truman.* New York: Macmillan, 1986.

————. *Harry S. Truman.* New York: Morrow, 1973.

————. *Souvenir: Margaret Truman's Own Story.* New York: McGraw-Hill, 1956.

————, ed. *Letters from Father: The Truman Family's Personal Correspondence.* New York: Arbor House, 1981.

————, ed. *Where the Buck Stops: The Personal and Private Writings of Harry S. Truman.* New York: Warner, 1989.

Tsou, Tang. *America's Failure in China, 1941–1950.* Chicago: University of Chicago Press, 1963.

Tucker, Nancy Bernkopf. *Patterns in the Dust: Chinese-American Relations and the Recognition Controversy, 1949–1950.* New York: Columbia University Press, 1983.

Tucker, Robert C. *Stalin in Power: The Revolution from Above, 1928–1941.* New York: Norton, 1990.

Tucker, Robert W. *The Radical Left and American Foreign Policy.* Baltimore: Johns Hopkins University Press, 1971.

Ulam, Adam B. *The Communists: The Story of Power and Lost Illusions, 1948–1991.* New York: Scribner's, 1992.

——. *The Rivals: America and Russia since World War II.* New York: Viking, 1971.

Underhill, Robert. *The Truman Persuasions.* Ames: Iowa State University Press, 1981.

Vaksberg, Arkady. *Stalin's Prosecutor: The Life of Andrei Vyshinsky.* New York: Grove Weidenfeld, 1990.

Vandenberg, Arthur H., Jr., and Joe Alex Morris, eds. *The Private Papers of Senator Vandenberg.* Boston: Houghton Mifflin, 1952.

Volkogonov, Dimitri. *Stalin: Triumph and Tragedy.* New York: Grove, Weidenfeld, 1991.

Walch, Timothy, and Dwight M. Miller, eds. *Herbert Hoover and Harry S. Truman: A Documentary History.* Worland, Wyo.: High Plains, 1992.

Walker, J. Samuel. "The Decision to Use the Bomb: A Historiographical Update." *Diplomatic History* 14 (1990): 97–114.

——. *Henry A. Wallace and American Foreign Policy.* Westport, Conn.: Greenwood, 1976.

Walker, Richard L., and George Curry. *Edward R. Stettinius, Jr.–James F. Byrnes.* New York: Cooper Square, 1965.

Wall, Irwin M. *The United States and the Making of Postwar France, 1945–1954.* New York: Cambridge University Press, 1991.

Wallace, Harold Lew. "The Campaign of 1948." Ph.D. diss., Indiana University, 1970.

Walton, Richard J. *Henry Wallace, Harry Truman, and the Cold War.* New York: Viking, 1976.

Ward, Patricia Dawson. *The Threat of Peace: James F. Byrnes and the Council of Foreign Ministers, 1945–1946.* Kent, Ohio: Kent State University Press, 1979.

Watkins, T. H. *Righteous Pilgrim: The Life and Times of Harold L. Ickes.* New York: Holt, 1990.

Watt, Donald Cameron. "Britain and the Historiography of the Yalta Conference and the Cold War." *Diplomatic History* 13 (1989): 67–98.

Weathersby, Kathryn. "Soviet Aims in Korea and the Origins of the Korean War, 1945–1950: New Evidence from Russian Archives." Working paper no. 8, Cold War International History Project, Woodrow Wilson International Center for Scholars, November 1993.

——. "The Soviet Role in the Early Phase of the Korean War: New Documentary Evidence." *Journal of American–East Asian Relations* 2 (1993): 425–58.

Weinstein, Allen. *Perjury: The Hiss-Chambers Case.* New York: Knopf, 1978.

Weinstein, Allen, and Moshe Ma'oz, eds. *Truman and the American Commitment to Israel.* Jerusalem: Magnes Press, Hebrew University, 1981.

West, J. B. *Upstairs at the White House.* New York: Coward, McCann and Geoghegan, 1973.

Wheeler, Burton K. *Yankee from the West*. Garden City, N.Y.: Doubleday, 1962.

White, Graham, and John Maze. *Harold Ickes of the New Deal: His Private Life and Public Career*. Cambridge: Harvard University Press, 1985.

White, Walter. *A Man Called White: The Autobiography of Walter White*. New York: Viking, 1948.

Williams, Francis, ed. *Twilight of Empire: Memoirs of Prime Minister Clement Attlee*. New York: Barnes, 1962.

Williams, Robert Chadwell. *Klaus Fuchs: Atomic Spy*. Cambridge: Harvard University Press, 1987.

Williams, William J., ed. *A Revolutionary War: Korea and the Transformation of the Postwar World*. Chicago: Imprint Publications, 1993.

Williamson, Hugh P. *South of the Middle Border*. Philadelphia: Lippincott, 1946.

Williamson, Samuel R., Jr., and Steven L. Rearden. *The Origins of U.S. Nuclear Strategy, 1945–1953*. New York: St. Martin's, 1993.

Willson, Roger Edward. "The Truman Committee." Ph.D. diss., Harvard University, 1966.

Wiltz, John Edward. "The MacArthur Hearings of 1951: The Secret Testimony." *Military Affairs* 39 (1975): 167–73.

———. "Truman and MacArthur: The Wake Island Meeting." *Military Affairs* 42 (December 1978): 169–76.

Wittner, Lawrence S. *American Intervention in Greece, 1943–1949*. New York: Columbia University Press, 1982.

Woods, Randall B. *A Changing of the Guard: Anglo-American Relations, 1941–1946*. Chapel Hill: University of North Carolina Press, 1990.

Woods, Randall B., and Howard Jones. *Dawning of the Cold War: The United States' Quest for Order*. Athens: University of Georgia Press, 1991.

Wright, Peter, with Paul Greengrass. *Spy Catcher: The Candid Autobiography of a Senior Intelligence Officer*. Boston: G. K. Hall, 1988.

Wyatt, Wilson W., Sr. *Whistle Stops: Adventures in Public Life*. Lexington: University Press of Kentucky, 1985.

Wyden, Peter. *Day One: Before Hiroshima and After*. New York: Simon and Schuster, 1984.

Yang Kui-song. "The Soviet Factor and the CCP's Policy toward the United States in the 1940s." *Chinese Historians* 5 (1992): 17–34.

Yarnell, Allen. *Democrats and Progressives: The 1948 Presidential Election as a Test of Postwar Liberalism*. Berkeley and Los Angeles: University of California Press, 1974.

Yergin, Daniel. *Shattered Peace: The Origins of the Cold War and the National Security State*. Boston: Houghton Mifflin, 1977.

Index